HANDBOOK OF METHODOLOGICAL APPROACHES TO COMMUNITY-BASED RESEARCH

HANDBOOK OF METHODOLOGICAL APPROACHES TO COMMUNITY-BASED RESEARCH

Qualitative, Quantitative, and Mixed Methods

EDITED BY

LEONARD A. JASON

AND

DAVID S. GLENWICK

OXFORD
UNIVERSITY PRESS

OXFORD
UNIVERSITY PRESS

Oxford University Press is a department of the University of Oxford. It furthers the University's objective of excellence in research, scholarship, and education by publishing worldwide.

Oxford New York
Auckland Cape Town Dar es Salaam Hong Kong Karachi
Kuala Lumpur Madrid Melbourne Mexico City Nairobi
New Delhi Shanghai Taipei Toronto

With offices in
Argentina Austria Brazil Chile Czech Republic France Greece
Guatemala Hungary Italy Japan Poland Portugal Singapore
South Korea Switzerland Thailand Turkey Ukraine Vietnam

Oxford is a registered trademark of Oxford University Press in the UK and certain other countries.

Published in the United States of America by
Oxford University Press
198 Madison Avenue, New York, NY 10016

A copy of this book's Catalog-in-Publication Data is on file with the Library of Congress
ISBN 978-0-19-024365-4

3 5 7 9 8 6 4 2
Printed in the United States of America
on acid-free paper

CONTENTS

Foreword by Raymond P. Lorion *vii*
Acknowledgments *xi*
About the Editors *xiii*
Contributors *xv*

1. Introduction to Community-Based Methodological Approaches *1*
LEONARD A. JASON AND DAVID S. GLENWICK

SECTION ONE: *Qualitative Approaches*

2. Introduction to Qualitative Approaches *13*
ANNE E. BRODSKY, SARA L. BUCKINGHAM, JILL E. SCHEIBLER, AND TERRI MANNARINI
3. Grounded Theory *23*
ANDREW RASMUSSEN, ADEYINKA M. AKINSULURE-SMITH, AND TRACY CHU
4. Thematic Analysis *33*
STEPHANIE RIGER AND RANNVEIG SIGURVINSDOTTIR
5. Community Narratives *43*
BRADLEY D. OLSON, DANIEL G. COOPER, JUDAH J. VIOLA, AND BRIAN CLARK
6. Appreciative Inquiry *53*
NEIL M. BOYD
7. The Delphi Method *61*
SHANE R. BRADY
8. Ethnographic Approaches *69*
URMITAPA DUTTA
9. Photovoice and House Meetings as Tools Within Participatory Action Research *81*
REGINA DAY LANGHOUT, JESICA SIHAM FERNÁNDEZ, DENISE WYLDBORE, AND JORGE SAVALA
10. Geographic Information Systems *93*
ANDREW LOHMANN
11. Causal Layered Analysis *103*
LAUREN J. BREEN, PETA L. DZIDIC, AND BRIAN J. BISHOP
12. Emotional Textual Analysis *111*
RENZO CARLI, ROSA MARIA PANICCIA, FIAMMETTA GIOVAGNOLI, AGOSTINO CARBONE, AND FIORELLA BUCCI

SECTION TWO: *Quantitative Approaches*

13. Introduction to Quantitative Methods *121*
CHRISTIAN M. CONNELL
14. Latent Growth Curves *133*
MEGAN R. GREESON
15. Latent Class Analysis and Latent Profile Analysis *143*
GLENN A. WILLIAMS AND FRAENZE KIBOWSKI
16. Multilevel Structural Equation Modeling *153*
JOHN P. BARILE

17. Cluster-Randomized Trials *165*
NATHAN R. TODD AND PATRICK J. FOWLER

18. Behavioral and Time-Series Approaches *177*
MARK A. MATTAINI, LEONARD A. JASON, AND DAVID S. GLENWICK

19. Data Mining *187*
JACOB FURST, DANIELA STAN RAICU, AND LEONARD A. JASON

20. Agent-Based Models *197*
ZACHARY P. NEAL AND JENNIFER A. LAWLOR

21. Social Network Analysis *207*
MARIAH KORNBLUH AND JENNIFER WATLING NEAL

22. Dynamic Social Networks *219*
LEONARD A. JASON, JOHN LIGHT, AND SARAH CALLAHAN

SECTION THREE: *Mixed Methods Approaches*

23. Introduction to Mixed Methods Approaches *233*
VALERIE R. ANDERSON

24. Action Research *243*
BRIAN D. CHRISTENS, VICTORIA FAUST, JENNIFER GADDIS, PAULA TRAN INZEO, CAROLINA S. SARMIENTO, AND SHANNON M. SPARKS

25. Community-Based Participatory Action Research *253*
MICHAEL J. KRAL AND JAMES ALLEN

26. Youth-Led Participatory Action Research *263*
EMILY J. OZER

27. Participatory Mixed Methods Research Across Cultures *273*
REBECCA VOLINO ROBINSON, E. J. R. DAVID, AND MARA HILL

28. Photoethnography in Community-Based Participatory Research *283*
KATHERINE CLOUTIER

29. Data Visualization *293*
GINA CARDAZONE AND RYAN TOLMAN

30. Concept Mapping *305*
LISA M. VAUGHN AND DANIEL MCLINDEN

31. Functional Analysis of Community Concerns in Participatory Action Research *315*
YOLANDA SUAREZ-BALCAZAR AND FABRICIO BALCAZAR

32. Network Analysis and Stakeholder Analysis in Mixed Methods Research *325*
ISIDRO MAYA-JARIEGO, DAVID FLORIDO DEL CORRAL, DANIEL HOLGADO, AND JAVIER HERNÁNDEZ-RAMÍREZ

33. Mixed Methodology in Multilevel, Multisetting Inquiry *335*
NICOLE E. ALLEN, ANGELA L. WALDEN, EMILY R. DWORKIN, AND SHABNAM JAVDANI

34. Mixed Methods and Dialectical Pluralism *345*
TRES STEFURAK, R. BURKE JOHNSON, AND ERYNNE SHATTO

35. Community Profiling in Participatory Action Research *355*
CATERINA ARCIDIACONO, TERESA TUOZZI, AND FORTUNA PROCENTESE

Afterword by G. Anne Bogat *365*
Index *369*

FOREWORD

It seems like only yesterday that I prepared a foreword for the first edited volume on community-based research methods by Leonard Jason and David Glenwick (2012). At the time, I explained that my words would attempt to prepare readers for what lay ahead, that is, a *groundbreaking* presentation of widely diverse and, I assumed for many readers, unfamiliar methods that could be applied to the study of community-based issues. Since one is asked to prepare forewords later in one's career, I had no reservation about acknowledging my own lack of familiarity with a number of the methods presented. I could also readily acknowledge that I learned much in reading the volume. In that foreword, I encouraged readers to proceed deliberately through the volume because:

> As noted, readers should proceed with caution—but they should also be buoyed by scholarly curiosity and professional enthusiasm—for I would predict that, if read carefully, the contents of this volume are very likely to change the questions that readers ask and the solutions that they seek. As a consequence, the discipline's rigor will be enhanced, along with its heuristic contributions to our understanding of human behavior within real-life settings and under real-life circumstances. The methods described in this volume add substantially to the tools we will have available to understand, predict, and ultimately influence the healthy development of individuals, groups, and communities. Readers will complete the volume with a broadened sense of community psychology's impact on and relationships with multiple other disciplines. With methodological pluralism will come disciplinary pluralism! (Lorion, 2012, p. xvi)

In the brief short years between publication of that volume with its "mere" 13 chapters and the finalization of this 35-chapter volume, the array of methods available for community-based studies appears to be expanding exponentially! Consider that the 2012 volume distributed the 12 substantive chapters across four groupings:

- Pluralism and Mixed Methods in Community Research (3 chapters)
- Methods Involving Grouping of Data (3 chapters)
- Methods Involving Change Over Time (2 chapters)
- Methods Involving Contextual Factors (4 chapters)

By contrast, the current volume's 34 substantive offerings address three groupings:

- Qualitative Approaches (11 chapters)
- Quantitative Approaches (10 chapters)
- Mixed Methods Approaches (13 chapters)

Each grouping's contents is nearly as large as the original volume's substantive offerings. How can that be? The breadth of topics in each category seemingly reflects both an increase in, and the differentiation within, methods. But more than that, however, I would propose that the first volume's publication legitimized the utilization, and consequently the innovative expansion, of methods by community psychologists. Jason and Glenwick (2012) may have planted seeds that have blossomed into new approaches. Likely they also opened awareness among community psychologists of the opportunity to find and apply information-gathering and analytic methods from disciplines near and far from community-based inquiries. Whatever the case, the tools available to us have expanded dramatically! I can report evidence to that effect based on my experiences as the editor of the *Journal of Community Psychology*. In that capacity, I can attest to the seemingly unending adoption of methods from other disciplines, as well as the creation of entirely new approaches to gather and analyze information. Since the 2012 volume appeared, I have seen increasing numbers of submissions applying the very methods described in the current volume. For several years now, I have regularly been receiving manuscripts whose conclusions were derived through the application of (a) highly sophisticated statistical procedures on quantitative findings; (b) systematically applied analytic methods on qualitative findings; (c) findings based on entirely innovative methods, including photographic images, narrated experiences, and public art (e.g., graffiti); and (d) conceptualizations of community-based processes based on conversations with key informants. The breadth of qualitative, quantitative, and especially mixed methods reports crossing my virtual desk appears to increase monthly.

It goes without saying that community psychology has come a long way from its founders who 50 or so years ago struggled with selecting among a limited number of nonparametric or parametric statistics. As I and many of my generation were punching data on computer cards to cautiously deliver to a computer center that covered an entire floor of a university building, we marveled at the potential of factor analyses (with and without rotation) for uncovering interconnections among seemingly disparate variables. We dismissed the potential value of qualitative reports as unscientific and strove for "hard" findings that would align with our preparation as "scientist-practitioners" and pass muster with colleagues engaged in basic research.

Jason, Glenwick, and I shared much in common as graduates of the University of Rochester's doctoral program in clinical-community psychology. Central to that experience was the opportunity to be mentored by Emory Cowen, a founding member of our discipline and originally a stickler for quantitative analyses. Just as many of us were completing our studies or entering initial positions, something changed. Cowen (1980) publicly distinguished research relating to the generation of hypotheses from that focused on their confirmation. The former acknowledged all that could be learned through systematic observation, qualitative interviewing, focus groups, and other qualitative avenues to gathering information. These new pathways to knowledge were to deepen our understanding of the phenomena before us and thereby enrich our appreciation of the complexity of community processes.

At the time, few tools were either available to us or acceptable to psychology's broader discipline wherein we had to establish our academic bona fides. Those who chose to apply these new methods were also responsible for determining how best to analyze the information they acquired and how to justify its value to journal editors, funding sources, and, as noted, tenure-determining colleagues. Fortunately, that era has generally passed, and the diversity of methods presented in this volume provides a quiver full of arrows to apply to targets of inquiry.

What the present volume does not, however, address is the nature of the targets or even of the hunt. From the outset, community psychology has reflected tension between its pursuit of recognition as a science within clinical psychology's tradition of the scientist-practitioner and its desire to effect change in the lives of those who are underserved, underrecognized, and disempowered. Community psychology began as an ally of the community mental health movement, whose defining purpose was to serve the needs of those with limited access to and acceptance of the reigning intervention strategies. The lack of access was to be addressed by relocating services to the communities in which the underserved lived. The lack of acceptance was to be addressed by creating new forms of intervention tailored to the lives and needs of intended recipients. The lack of effectiveness for those in need was to be addressed in part by broadening the range of options in terms of (a) length (e.g., time-limited therapies), (b) service provider (e.g., paraprofessional and natural caregiver agents), and especially (c) point of intervention (e.g., primary and secondary prevention) along the etiological pathway. Our originating intent was to serve through both innovative services and the gathering of information that would enable our clinical colleagues to enter the communities and lives of those who to that point had been ill-served or underserved.

I raise this point because that same tension lies just beneath the surface of many of this volume's chapters. Focused on explaining the rationale and procedures of their methods, the authors provide the technical details that introduce readers to the potential applications and informational benefits of their procedures. Woven through their recipes and especially their case examples are the variously stated but present themes of gathering new and deeper insights into the lives of the disenfranchised, the disempowered, and the underserved. At times subtly stated and at times explicit, the agenda for applying these innovative quantitative, qualitative, and mixed methods can be found, that is, to create, enable, and accomplish *change*! Albeit variously stated, understanding the status quo is precedent to designing its alteration in a nonrandom intentional direction.

Tempted though I might be to present the evidentiary base for such an assertion, I believe that the authors and readers will be better served by conducting their own investigations to determine whether my conclusion is sustainable. Much is said about the value of the methods for theory-building or confirmation without exactly identifying the theoretical base being referenced. Now and again we see references to paradigm without exactly knowing what is paradigmatic about the work or feeling confident that the nature of a paradigm and the breadth of its scientific implications are applicable (Kuhn, 1962). Both "theory" and "paradigm" appear to be stated more as evidence that the work described is truly scientific rather than being presented as the foundation on which the accumulation of information is gathered and its contribution to the "work of normal science" demonstrated.

Assigning the aforementioned underlying tension to community psychology may, admittedly, reflect projection on my part. My career can be perceived as blindly subservient to the principles of positivism or as focused on seeking and applying practical solutions to real problems. Throughout much of that career, I could call upon colleagues such as Seymour Sarason and Robert Newbrough for reassurance that it need not be either-or but rather both-and. Most convincing, however, was Dokecki's (1992) contribution to a special issue (edited by Newbrough, 1992) of the *Journal of Community Psychology* focused on the future of the discipline in a postmodern world. In his paper, Dokecki explained how Schon's (1983) concept of the "reflective practitioner" offers our discipline a valid alternative to clinical psychology's scientist-practitioner model. The latter gathers knowledge to inform and shape practice. The former model, by contrast, has a different purpose, for it "intends to improve the human situation through the close interplay of knowledge use and knowledge generation" (Dokecki, 1992, p. 27).

Note that for the reflective practitioner knowledge is gathered to serve needs, not to build theory! In support of the legitimacy of that purpose, Dokecki (1992) introduced Macmurray's (1957, 1961) analysis of the person-in-community. My reading of this work reframed the gathering of information through investigation from responding to the question of "What do we want to know?" to "What do we want to do?" In this foreword, I am arguing that the latter question is more applicable to the methods and their intent than is the former. I would further contend that such a defining rationale is entirely consistent with the aforementioned underlying theme perceived by me in reading across this volume's content.

Accepting the possibility that community psychology's purpose is to impact the quality of life and effectiveness of communities for their residents does not lessen its worth but rather focuses its efforts. Participatory action research can be acknowledged as an essential element of community-based interventions both because it assures localization of the work but more importantly engages those to be impacted in both acknowledging need and acting to mitigate that need and thereby alter the status quo to a locally preferred condition. Participatory action research allows those receiving services to define both their nature and the limits of their application. "Better" is determined by participants rather than by provider.

Acknowledging that we engage with communities to "do something" together does not mean we abandon the accumulation of information that has theoretical or paradigmatic import. It does mean, however, that doing takes priority over knowing and that our work and our responsibility are not completed with the acquisition of knowledge or the advancement of science. Those accomplishments add value to our efforts and, admittedly, may lead to tenure, external funding, or disciplinary recognition. They do not, however, lessen our professional responsibility to remain engaged, to continue *our* participation, and to continue the work until released by our partners. To truly enact a participatory action effort requires genuine empowerment of partners over *us*! If we initiate the effort and commit members of a community to engage in assessing their needs, analyzing their resources, and committing to collaboratively moving toward sustainable change, we necessarily commit ourselves (and in many cases our institutions) to remain engaged, however long it takes.

I applaud Jason and Glenwick for their unparalleled success in recruiting the breadth of methodologists gathered for this volume. I further applaud the methodologists for their acknowledgment (intended or not) that community psychology's need for this diversity of methods lies not simply with its evolution as an applied science but most of all with its founding commitment to understanding human needs that would otherwise go unrecognized, underserved, disrespected, and devalued. Our discipline is unlike psychological, social, public health, or public policy sciences, and that difference lies in our defining commitment to become part of the community, wherein we can collaborate with the community as it defines and activates sustainable responses to its needs.

Raymond P. Lorion
Towson University
June 2015

REFERENCES

Cowen, E. L. (1980). The wooing of primary prevention. *American Journal of community Psychology, 8*, 258–284.

Dokecki, P. R. (1992). On knowing the community of caring persons: A methodological basis for the reflective-generative practice of community psychology. *Journal of Community Psychology, 20*, 26–235.

Jason, L. A., & Glenwick, D. S. (2012). (Eds.), *Methodological approaches to community-based research*. Washington, DC: American Psychological Association.

Kuhn, T. S. (1970). *The structure of scientific revolutions* (2nd ed.). Chicago, IL: University of Chicago Press.

Lorion, R. P. (2012). Foreword. In L. A. Jason & D. S. Glenwick (Eds.), *Methodological approaches to community-basedresearch* (pp.xv–xviii). Washington, DC: American Psychological Association.

Macmurray, J. (1957). *The self as agent*. London, England: Faber.

Macmurray, J. (1961). *Persons in relation*. New York, NY: Harper & Row.

Newbrough, J. R. (1992). Community psychology in the postmodern world. *Journal of Community Psychology, 20*, 10–25.

Schon, D. (1983). *The reflective practitioner*. New York, NY: Basic Books.

ACKNOWLEDGMENTS

We are deeply appreciative of our chapter authors, who, on tight time schedules, produced stimulating, integrative, and readable contributions and who graciously worked to comply with our length and style requests. We also are indebted to Raymond Lorion and Anne Bogat for their thoughtful Foreword and Afterword commentaries. In addition, we thank Edward Stevens, Steven A. Miller, Christopher Beasley, Ronald Harvey, Daphna Ram, Doreen Salina, John Moritsugu, and Ariel Stone for their helpful comments and suggestions.

Finally, we greatly appreciate the unflagging support and encouragement of Oxford University Press's editorial staff, particularly Sarah Harrington and Andrea Zekus.

ABOUT THE EDITORS

Leonard A. Jason is a professor of psychology at DePaul University, where he is the director of the Center for Community Research. Dr. Jason received his doctorate in clinical and community psychology from the University of Rochester. He has published over 600 articles and 75 book chapters on such social and health topics as the prevention of, and recovery from, substance abuse; preventive school-based interventions; multimedia interventions; the diagnosis and treatment of myalgic encephalomyelitis/chronic fatigue syndrome; and program evaluation. Dr. Jason has been on the editorial boards of seven peer-reviewed journals and has edited or written 23 books. Additionally, he has served on review committees of the National Institute of Drug Abuse and the National Institute of Mental Health and received more than $34 million in federal research grants. He is a former president of the Division of Community Psychology of the American Psychological Association and a past editor of *The Community Psychologist.*

David S. Glenwick is a professor of psychology at Fordham University. He has been the director of its graduate program in clinical psychology and is currently the co-coordinator of its specialization in clinical child and family psychology. Dr. Glenwick received his doctorate in clinical and community psychology from the University of Rochester. He has edited six books and authored more than 120 articles and book chapters, primarily in the areas of community-based interventions, clinical child psychology, and developmental disabilities, and has been on the editorial boards of four peer-reviewed journals. Dr. Glenwick is a fellow of seven divisions of the American Psychological Association (APA) and has been a member of the APA Continuing Education Committee. He is a past president of the International Association for Correctional and Forensic Psychology and a former editor of the journal *Criminal Justice and Behavior.*

CONTRIBUTORS

Caterina Arcidiacono
University Federico II, Naples

Adeyinka M. Akinsulure-Smith
City College, City University of New York

James Allen
University of Minnesota, Minneapolis

Nicole E. Allen
University of Illinois, Urbana-Champaign

Valerie R. Anderson
Michigan State University, Michigan

Fabricio Balcazar
University of Illinois, Chicago

John P. Barile
University of Hawaii, Manoa

Brian J. Bishop
Curtin University, Bentley

G. Anne Bogat
Michigan State University, Michigan

Neil M. Boyd
Bucknell University, Lewisburg

Shane R. Brady
University of Oklahoma, Oklahoma

Lauren J. Breen
Curtin University, Bentley

Anne E. Brodsky
University of Maryland, Baltimore County

Fiorella Bucci
Ghent University, Ghent

Sara L. Buckingham
University of Maryland, Baltimore County

Sarah Callahan
DePaul University, Chicago

Agostino Carbone
University Federico II, Naples

Gina Cardazone
JBS International

Renzo Carli
University of Rome, Sapienza

Brian D. Christens
University of Wisconsin, Madison

Tracy Chu
Brooklyn College, City University of New York

Brian Clark
Habitat for Humanity, Roanoke Valley

Katherine Cloutier
Michigan State University, Michigan

Christian M. Connell
Yale University, Connecticut

Daniel Cooper
Adler School, Illinois

E. J. R. David
University of Alaska, Anchorage

Urmitapa Dutta
University of Massachusetts, Lowell

Emily R. Dworkin
University of Illinois, Urbana-Champaign

Peta L. Dzidic
Curtin University, Bentley

Victoria Faust
University of Wisconsin, Madison

Jesica Siham Fernández
University of California, Santa Cruz

David Florido del Corral
University of Seville

Patrick J. Fowler
Washington University, St. Louis

Jacob Furst
DePaul University, Chicago

Jennifer Gaddis
University of Wisconsin, Madison

Fiammetta Giovagnoli
University of Rome, Sapienza

David S. Glenwick
Fordham University, New York

Megan R. Greeson
DePaul University, Chicago

Javier Hernández-Ramírez
University of Seville

Mara Hill
University of Alaska, Anchorage

Daniel Holgado
University of Seville

Paula Tran Inzeo
University of Wisconsin, Madison

Leonard A. Jason
DePaul University, Chicago

Shabnam Javdani
University of Illinois, Urbana-Champaign

R. Burke Johnson
University of South Alabama, Alabama

Fraenze Kibowski
Nottingham Trent University, UK

Mariah Kornbluh
Michigan State University, Michigan

Michael J. Kral
Wayne State University, Detroit

Regina Day Langhout
University of California, Santa Cruz

Jennifer A. Lawlor
Michigan State University, Michigan

John Light
Oregon Research Institute, Eugene

Andrew Lohmann
California State University, Long Beach

Raymond P. Lorion
Towson University, Towson

Terri Mannarini
University of Salento, Italy

Mark A. Mattaini
University of Illinois, Chicago

Isidro Maya-Jariego
University of Seville

Daniel McLinden
Cincinnati Children's Hospital Medical Center, Cincinnati

Jennifer Watling Neal
Michigan State University, Michigan

Zachary P. Neal
Michigan State University, Michigan

Bradley Olson
National Louis University, Chicago

Emily J. Ozer
University of California, Berkeley

Rosa Maria Paniccia
University of Rome, Sapienza

Fortuna Procentese
University Federico II, Naples

Daniela Stan Raicu
DePaul University, Chicago

Andrew Rasmussen
Fordham University, New York

Stephanie Riger
University of Illinois, Chicago

Rebecca Volino Robinson
University of Alaska, Anchorage

Carolina S. Sarmiento
University of Wisconsin, Madison

Jorge Savala
University of California, Santa Cruz

Jill E. Scheibler
University of Maryland, Baltimore County

Erynne Shatto
University of South Alabama, Alabama

Rannveig Sigurvinsdottir
University of Illinois, Chicago

Shannon M. Sparks
University of Wisconsin, Madison

Tres Stefurak
University of South Alabama, Alabama

Yolanda Suarez-Balcazar
University of Illinois, Chicago

Nathan R. Todd
University of Illinois, Urbana-Champaign

Ryan Tolman
University of Hawaii, Manoa

Teresa Tuozzi
University Federico II, Naples

Lisa M. Vaughn
Cincinnati Children's Hospital Medical Center, Cincinnati

Judah J. Viola
National Louis University, Chicago

Angela L. Walden
University of Illinois, Urbana-Champaign

Glenn A. Williams
Leeds Beckett University, UK

Denise Wyldbore
University of California, Santa Cruz

HANDBOOK OF METHODOLOGICAL APPROACHES TO COMMUNITY-BASED RESEARCH

1

Introduction to Community-Based Methodological Approaches

LEONARD A. JASON AND DAVID S. GLENWICK

Over the past few decades, community-based applications of the newest research methodologies have not kept pace with the development of dynamic theory and multilevel data collection techniques. To address this gap, the present handbook focuses specifically on aiding community-oriented researchers in learning about relevant cutting-edge methodologies. With this end in mind, it presents a number of innovative methodologies relevant to community-based research, illustrating their applicability to specific social problems and projects. Besides representing a comprehensive statement of the state of the science and art with respect to methodology in the area, the volume is intended to point the way to new directions and hopefully further advances in the field in the coming decades.

BACKGROUND, PURPOSE, AND ORGANIZATION

The methodologies presented in this book adopt a social change perspective that is wider than more typical, person-centered health and clinical interventions (Tolan, Keys, Chertok, & Jason, 1990). Community psychology, as an exemplar of community science, emerged about 50 years ago. As the field evolved, certain recurring themes emerged: prevention (versus treatment), competencies (versus weaknesses), collaboration across disciplines, ecological understanding of people within their environments, diversity, and community building as a mode of intervention. These concepts provided a focus on new ways of thinking about contextual factors and how participants could be more involved in applied research efforts, as well as considering more public health–based, systems-oriented, and preventive approaches (Kloos et al., 2012; Moritsugu, Vera, Wong, & Duffy, 2013). At an influential community methods conference, Tolan et al. (1990) responded to a multitude of issues facing the field, including tensions between achieving scientific rigor through the use of traditional reductionistic research designs and accurately capturing processes involved in real-world interventions with persons in the context of community settings. That conference introduced a dialogue regarding criteria necessary to define research of merit and methodological considerations in implementing ecologically driven research. At a later conference (Jason et al., 2004), leaders in the field further explored the gap between scientific knowledge and practice in community-based research methodologies, with an emphasis on consumer participation (i.e., participatory research).

Complementing methodology and practice in community science is a third realm, that of theory. Heuristically useful theories allow us to describe, explain, and predict phenomena. Additionally, the operationalization of a particular theory through our research aids us in uncovering and specifying the theory's limits with regard to its boundary conditions and ability to generate valid predictions. The methodology that is used in community science research may naturally flow from theory, but this is most possible within the context of a clearly articulated theory. Thus, both clear articulation of theoretical community-related constructs and valid measurement of such constructs are necessary in refining theory and explicating real-world phenomena.

We do not advocate for one predominant theory for community science. Many topics in community science will never coalesce around one theory because they are complex systems comprising multiple mechanisms of operation and change. At a descriptive level, theories in community science, we would argue, should specify what specific aspects of context influence what specific aspects of individuals. Furthermore, the specific mechanisms by which this occurs should be articulated. Ideally, such theoretical positing should lead to relatively unambiguous predictions concerning community-based phenomena (Jason, Stevens, Ram, Miller, & Beasley, 2015). Methods provide the means to test the predictions generated from theories. Given the desirability of theoretical pluralism, we also do not argue for a single method, believing, rather, that there should be a matching between method (or methods, in the case of mixed methods research), on the one hand, and the theoretical underpinnings of a particular research question, on the other hand.

With respect to one salient construct in community science, namely *community*, Heller (2014) recently noted that there is often a lack of a clear theoretical statement about how communities should be conceptualized. Part of the problem stems from the definition of the closely related concept of *neighborhood*, which can vary from a block in a residential community to an online network. In addition, there are a number of mediators of neighborhood effects, including the quality of resources (e.g., libraries, schools, parks), level of community integration (e.g., how well members know each other), and the quality of social ties and interactions. Additional considerations are that not all families respond to community issues in the same way and that neighborhoods change over time. Heller (2014) indicated that impediments that communities confront, such as inadequate resources or insufficient technical knowledge, may require a variety of different strategies. Heller's (2014) ideas have implications for methodology, particularly with respect to the need for community-based researchers to (a) investigate mediators and moderators of phenomena, both within a level and between levels, and (b) conceptualize and operationalize the diverse ways that we can think about community and communities.

Ecological analysis—the overarching framework of the present volume—seeks to understand behavior in the context of individual, family, peer, and community influences (Kelly, 1985, 1990, 2006). As noted by Revenson and Seidman (2002), the field of community psychology (as a discipline within the larger arena of community-based research) has perennially had as its focus the transactions between persons and community-based structures, or, in other words, individuals' and groups' behavior in bidirectional interaction with their social contexts, with an emphasis on prevention and early intervention. Consonant with this perspective, the methodological approaches in this book explore such transactions and provide examples of how to implement and evaluate interventions conducted at the community level. A decade or so ago, Jason et al. (2004) and Revenson et al. (2002) highlighted methodological developments that supported the goals of empirically examining complex individual–environment interactions. A more recent work, by Jason and Glenwick (2012), also described some of the more promising community-level methods but focused just on quantitative methods, to the exclusion of qualitative and mixed methods approaches.

In this chapter we provide an overview of the volume's goals, organizational framework, and individual chapters, with attention to qualitative, quantitative, and (the more recent and burgeoning area of) pluralistic, mixed methods approaches in conceptualizing and addressing community-based problems. The handbook describes how the methodological approaches presented can facilitate the application of the ecological paradigm to the amelioration of social ills. Each chapter discusses how its particular methodology can be used to help analyze data dealing with community-based issues. Furthermore, it illustrates the benefits that occur when community theorists, interventionists, and methodologists work together to better understand complicated person-environment systems and the change processes within communities.

This handbook is intended to reach three critical audiences. The first involves scholars desiring a summary of existing contemporary methods for analyzing data addressing a variety of health and mental health issues. The second involves graduate students in psychology, public policy, urban studies, education, and other social science/human services disciplines designed to prepare students for careers in applied research, public administration, and the helping professions. The third involves practitioners in these fields who conduct program evaluation and consultation activities and who are interested in learning more about and applying these community-based methods.

The volume consists of three sections. Section I focuses on qualitative approaches; Section II on quantitative approaches; and Section III on mixed methods approaches, which combine qualitative and quantitative methods within the same study or project. Qualitative approaches are characterized by (a) an emphasis on understanding the meaning of the phenomenon under consideration to those who are experiencing it; (b) data which typically consist of words, providing "thick description" of the participants' experiences; and (c) active collaboration between the researchers and the participants throughout the research/intervention process (Gergen, Josselson, & Freeman, 2015; Kloos et al., 2012). Examples of qualitative methods are participant observation, qualitative interviews, focus groups, and case studies. Quantitative approaches, in contrast, have the following hallmarks: (a) an emphasis on trying to establish cause-and-effect relationships; (b) data that typically consist of numbers, obtained by the use of standardized measures; and (c) an attempt to produce generalizable findings, as opposed to a qualitative approaches focus on specific contexts (Kloos et al., 2012; Moritsugu et al., 2013). Illustrative of quantitative methods are quantitative description, randomized field experiments, nonequivalent comparison group designs, and interrupted time-series designs.

To promote consistency in format, each chapter is composed of two parts. The first is a critical review of the methodological approach that is the focus of that chapter. Included is the theory underlying the approach, a summary of the steps involved in the use of the approach, and consideration of the approach's benefits and drawbacks. This is followed by a second part presenting either (a) the explication of a social problem or (b) the evaluation of a community-based intervention, thereby demonstrating for the reader how to apply the approach in real-world settings, including analyzing and interpreting the data so obtained.

OVERVIEW OF THE CHAPTERS

Qualitative Approaches

Section I, on qualitative methods, is introduced by Anne E. Brodsky, Sara L. Buckingham, Jill E. Scheibler, and Terri Mannarini (Chapter 2). Their discussion includes the general elements and precepts of the methodology, as well as its utility and applicability to the study, practice, and values of community-oriented research. Brodsky et al. discuss how community psychology, which arose from other movements of the 1960s to question and rethink the dominant paradigms in wellness promotion and illness prevention at the individual and community levels, shares its roots with qualitative methods, which themselves arose from alternative scientific paradigms. The authors mention that this connection goes further, in that the methods that we use are dependent on the paradigms and worldviews that we hold. Thus, Brodsky et al. emphasize that community psychology and qualitative methods are natural partners. The chapter concludes with an example of qualitative community-based work done by the chapter's first author in Afghanistan to explore risk and resilience processes in women's communities.

In Chapter 3, Andrew Rasmussen, Adeyinka M. Akinsulure-Smith, and Tracy Chu discuss grounded theory. Consistent with community psychologists' aim of empowering participants, grounded theory emphasizes developing theoretical frameworks from a close, ground-level examination of data, as opposed to interpreting data by testing a set of a priori hypotheses. This is done through iterative examination of (usually, but not limited to) qualitative data, building from molecular to molar analyses. After a brief history of the basic tenets, the chapter's primary focus is on the specific methods most often currently used and the steps involved in textual analyses (e.g., analyzing transcripts of interviews), leading to the derivation of themes and, ultimately, theory. Several dimensions are presented, from how heavily grounding is emphasized, the role of sensitizing concepts and literature reviews (i.e., a priori knowledge), defining codes, interrater reliability, and the role of research collaborators. Demonstration of the method highlights the authors' involvement in a project involving individual interviews and focus groups with West African immigrant parents and children in New York City, providing stakeholder feedback (i.e., community members' voices) to social service providers.

In Chapter 4, Stephanie Riger and Rannveig Sigurvinsdottir consider thematic analysis, a technique for analyzing qualitative data that involves looking for patterns of meaning that go beyond counting words or phrases. Underlying themes or issues in data are identified and form the basis for theory. Data are analyzed in a several-step process: (a) data familiarization, (b) initial code generation, (c) searching for themes, (d) reviewing themes, (e) defining and naming themes, and (f) reporting the analysis. The authors begin the chapter by placing thematic analysis within the context of qualitative methods in general. They then describe the process of conducting a thematic analysis and illustrate this process with a study of barriers to addressing substance abuse among perpetrators and victims of intimate partner violence in domestic violence court.

Bradley Olson, Daniel Cooper, Judah Viola, and Brian Clark contribute Chapter 5 on community narrative evaluation, a method derived from the personal narrative approach. Personal narratives are structured around individuals' stories, while community narratives, analogously, consist of personal stories collectively forming the foundation of a group's or community's identity. Thus, the two levels are intimately intertwined. Each community has a unique set of narratives that is a potential source of growth and a way for that community to creatively find its alternative narratives as a means of contrasting itself with other, competing, and dominant narratives in society. One primary approach to gathering personal stories and community narratives is through a life story methodology, in which participants describe key episodes in their lives or within the historical life of their community (such as high, low, or transition points). The case example in this chapter focuses on the use of community narratives in the evaluation of a housing and broader community coalition effort to increase the quality of life in a neighborhood in Roanoke, Virginia.

In Chapter 6, Neil Boyd discusses appreciative inquiry (AI). This change methodology focuses on elevating and expanding communities' strengths. Many participatory action research methodologies tend to start with a focus on fixing community problems. In contrast, AI begins with the premise that a community is a center of relatedness and that extending its strengths invokes a reserve of capacity, which, in turn, reshapes its images such that previously viewed challenges can be confronted in radically different ways. The four-stage AI process involves (a) discovering what is good within the system, (b) envisioning positive images of the future, (c) creating actionable designs, and (d) reaching design and goal outcomes. The example of AI presented involved helping injured workers and their representatives achieve their goals over an 18-month period following an AI change intervention.

In Chapter 7, Shane R. Brady discusses the Delphi method, which emphasizes the insights and perspectives of community participants in order to make informed decisions within a direct practice, social planning, and policy context. Grounded in pragmatism, the Delphi method can promote empowerment by giving voice to historically vulnerable groups. It provides a means for dealing with "difference" through providing community participants the opportunity to engage and participate as equals with professional experts and decision makers in generating decisions about a specific issue. The method creates a circle of dialogue among participants on a specific issue of interest, in which they provide direct responses/nominations (and comments on these) until a consensus is reached. The author provides an example of how the Delphi method has been utilized with members of several neighborhoods within a large urban city in decision making about the community's needs and priorities within the context of community development.

Urmitapa Dutta addresses critical ethnography in Chapter 8. This is an approach that connects detailed cultural analysis to wider social structures and systems of power by simultaneously examining dimensions of race, class, culture, gender, and history. The author first discusses the evolution of ethnography in the social sciences; the philosophical assumptions underlying ethnographic approaches; the critical role of the ethnographer in the research process; and key ethical and validation issues in ethnographic research, data collection, analysis, and dissemination. Next, she considers the influence of feminist, critical, indigenous, and postmodern approaches on ethnographic research. The steps involved in conducting collaborative, participatory, and activist ethnographic research are outlined. In the second part of the chapter, research on youth and protracted ethnic conflict in northeast India illustrates how critical ethnographic approaches can reframe existing social problem definitions in ways that underscore marginalized perspectives and create avenues for community-based interventions.

In Chapter 9, Regina Day Langhout, Jesica Siham Fernández, Denise Wyldbore, and Jorge

Savala present participatory action research (PAR) methodology. PAR is an epistemological approach rooted in a critical theory research paradigm. To create social change, researchers and community members collaborate through a systematic process, in which they develop an agreed-upon problem definition to determine what to study, decide on the method(s) to collect and analyze data, arrive at and implement actions to address the problem, and evaluate these actions and their outcomes. The authors describe the underlying theory of PAR and elucidate the steps involved in the process, with attention to the approach's benefits and drawbacks. They then demonstrate how multiple qualitative methods (in this case, photovoice and house meetings) can be combined to collect data within the PAR approach. This case study shows how PAR enabled the authors and the community members to better understand how people in a heterogeneous unincorporated area thought about their neighborhoods, with the goal of developing better strategies for community-based organizing.

Andrew Lohmann's chapter on geographic information systems (GIS) (Chapter 10) reviews several methodologies (e.g., resident-defined, behavioral approaches, experiencing sample method, and grid approaches) actually or potentially incorporating GIS to understand and operationally define neighborhoods. These methodologies fall on various interconnected spectra: (a) from being completely phenomenological (e.g., resident defined) to almost exclusively administrative (e.g., census units), (b) being emically (i.e., within a group) or etically (i.e., between groups) defined, (c) having stability or variability with respect to neighborhood spatial areas, and (d) the availability of the data. The implications of these dimensions are discussed. As an example of how GIS has been used to define and study neighborhoods in spatial terms, the author describes the utilization of the approach as a way of measuring resident-defined neighborhoods in order to investigate manifestations of localized bonding social capital.

In Chapter 11, Lauren J. Breen, Peta L. Dzidic, and Brian J. Bishop consider causal layered analysis (CLA), a methodology that enables the assessment of worldviews and cultural factors, as well as social, economic, and political structural issues, to be considered in understanding the present and in formulating alternative future projections. CLA utilizes a range of textual, visual, and experiential data sources, such as interview transcripts, photos, videos, and field notes. The analysis is structured according to four conceptual layers, progressing from a topical interpretation of the issue, at the topmost layer, to underlying mythologies and metaphors that underpin the issue, at the deepest layer. By identifying these qualities of the issue being investigated, it is argued that there is a greater propensity for the root of the issue to be identified and therefore the opportunity for meaningful, second-order change to occur. An illustration of CLA is provided involving a relational women's sports community, specifically women's participation in roller derby. In this example, CLA facilitated the uncovering of broad social and cultural understandings of the women's roles and expectations.

In Chapter 12, Renzo Carli, Rosa Maria Paniccia, Fiammetta Giovagnoli, Agostino Carbone, and Fiorella Bucci's discuss emotional textual analysis (ETA), a method used in contextual research. As we are aware, words can convey emotional components of a text (e.g., an interview transcript). ETA analyzes the symbolic level of texts as a part of applied research and interventions. In this approach, language is thought of as an organizer of the relationship between the individual contributor of the text and his or her context, rather than as a detector of the individual's emotions. Tracks of these written representations are viewed within the complexity of this relationship. A case example is presented showing the use of ETA in analyzing the interviews of the inhabitants of an urban area regarding their degree of satisfaction and fulfillment with respect to their employment situations.

Quantitative Approaches

Section II focuses on quantitative analytic approaches. In the introduction to this section (Chapter 13), Christian M. Connell provides an overview of these approaches, emphasizing salient considerations that should be taken into account when selecting a quantitative method. He notes both traditional and more sophisticated statistical methods that are relevant in addressing the aims of various types of research questions. The chapter concludes with an analysis of the quantitative methods used in empirical papers within the *American Journal of Community Psychology* from 2012 through 2014, highlighting the growth in the utilization of more contexualized, complex methods.

In Chapter 14, Megan R. Greeson discusses latent growth curves and how they are particularly fruitful for analyzing complex, changing community phenomena over time. Latent growth curves are a subset of structural equation modeling that can be used to examine within-case change across repeated measures. One of its key strengths is its ability to capture nonlinear change, which is often characteristic of both naturally occurring phenomena (e.g., phenomena that oscillate in up-and-down patterns) and intervention responses (e.g., lagged intervention effects). Another key strength is the ability to examine variability in change trajectories, which facilitates investigation of group differences over time. The author presents a case study examining nonlinear change over time with respect to the impact of adolescent dating violence on women's annual earned income.

Chapter 15 by Glenn Williams and Fraenze Kibowski on latent class analysis (LCA) and latent profile analysis (LPA) complements Chapter 14. The main aim of LCA is to split seemingly heterogeneous data into subclasses of two or more homogeneous groups or classes. In contrast, LPA is a method that is conducted with continuously scaled data, the focus being on generating profiles of participants instead of testing a theoretical model in terms of a measurement model, path analytic model, or full structural model (as is the case, for example, with structural equation modeling). As an example of LCA and LPA, the authors present findings on sustainable and active travel behaviors among commuters, separating the respondents into classes based on the facilitators of, and hindrances to, certain modes of travel.

In Chapter 16, John P. Barile writes about multilevel structural equation modeling (MSEM), which offers many advantages over traditional regression approaches in understanding community-based data. MSEM techniques enable researchers to assess individual- and higher level data simultaneously, while minimalizing individualistic and ecological fallacies commonly present in evaluation and intervention research. An advanced statistical methodology such as MSEM is often required to understand the diverse web of ecological determinants of individual and community well-being. The chapter presents the basic tenets of MSEM and identifies circumstances in which this approach is most appropriate. It concludes with a case example of the use of MSEM in an evaluation of community coalitions, in which data from multiple sources at both the individual and collaborative levels were utilized to better comprehend the processes and outcomes associated with successful collaboration.

In Chapter 17, Nathan R. Todd and Patrick Fowler present (a) cluster-randomized trials (CRTs) as a useful research design for evaluating community-level interventions and (b) multilevel modeling (MLM) as an appropriate way to analyze such data. A CRT design is characterized by assigning intact social groups (e.g., schools or neighborhoods) to intervention and control conditions. This design enables studying naturally occurring groups where individual randomization is not possible or where spillover effects within a setting are of concern. Moreover, the design is useful when the intervention target involves changing something about the environment or setting rather than intervening directly with individuals. This is a strong experimental design and can be used to show how intervention at the group level shapes individual outcomes. The authors then discuss the use of MLM as an analytic strategy for determining and interpreting the magnitude and significance of intervention success. Finally, as an example of the design, they highlight preventive school-based interventions aimed at decreasing suicide.

Mark Mattaini, Leonard A. Jason, and David S. Glenwick in Chapter 18 discuss the use of behavioral methods for implementing and analyzing change over time. There is a long tradition of operant designs that have been employed to effect and evaluate change in individual behavior, but these same types of designs also have been utilized to evaluate community-level data. The authors demonstrate how this orientation, including the utilization of time-series data (i.e., data on a particular behavior/phenomenon that are collected and analyzed on several occasions over a period of time), can be invaluable in providing evidence for the impact of ecological domains on community-based phenomena. The chapter concludes with an example of the application of this methodology to document change in urban littering behavior, with discussion of the intervention's policy implications resulting in legislative change.

In Chapter 19, Jacob Furst, Daniela Stan Raicu, and Leonard A. Jason describe data mining (also known as artificial intelligence), which can uncover patterns and relationships within large samples of people, organizations, or communities that would not otherwise be evident because of the size and complexity of the data. Data mining often uses decision trees, which attempt to predict a classification (e.g., high-risk neighborhoods in a community), based on successive binary choices. At each branch point of the decision tree, a characteristic is examined (e.g., gang activity within a community), and the decision tree determines whether a characteristic is important in the outcome or classification. In data mining, multiple characteristics are reviewed, and an algorithm is ultimately developed that best predicts class membership (e.g., high- versus low-risk status). The authors illustrate the application of this method to a chronic health condition, showing how computer-generated algorithms helped guide community organizations and government bodies in arriving at more valid and less stigmatizing ways of characterizing patients.

Zachary P. Neal and Jennifer Lawlor present the use of agent-based simulations to model community-level phenomena in Chapter 20 . This is a methodology in which agents (which can represent, for example, individual people, households, or community organizations) interact with one another by following simple rules within a context specified by the researcher. The goal of these models is to understand how different behavioral rules and contextual factors interact and lead to different outcomes. Such models are able to capture the complexity of community dynamics, which are often nonlinear and unpredictable. The authors provide an example of the model, exploring how spatial patterns of residential segregation impact social networks and the likelihood of relationships between different groups.

In Chapter 21, Mariah Kornbluh and Jennifer Watling Neal describe social network analysis (SNA), which focuses on identifying patterns of relationships among sets of actors in a particular system (e.g., friendships among children in a classroom or collaboration among organizations in a coalition). In this chapter, they describe how to collect network data and how to apply network measures to examine phenomena at multiple levels of analysis, including the (a) setting (i.e., characteristics of the whole network), (b) individual (i.e., an actor's position within the network), and (c) dyad (i.e., network characteristics of pairs of actors). In their case example, the authors illustrate how SNA was used to understand how the structure of teacher-advice networks could facilitate or hinder the spread of classroom intervention practices.

Dynamic social network models are the subject of Chapter 22 by Leonard A. Jason, John Light, and Sarah Callahan. This paradigm is distinguished from other approaches by its emphasis on the mutual interdependence between relationships and behavior change over time. As such, it provides a framework for conceptualizing and empirically describing two-way transactional dynamics. Network studies in community-based research have typically been based on "personal" network data, whereby one person rates all of the other people in his or her network, but the linkages among those individuals are usually not known. This chapter, instead, focuses on the more informative models that can be developed from "complete" network data (i.e., where all possible dyadic relationships among individuals or other entities, such as organizations, are measured, providing a structural map of an entire social ecosystem). The authors provide an example showing how the dimensions of trust, friendship, and mentoring changed over time in the relationships among persons living in substance abuse recovery residences.

Mixed Methods Approaches

Section III of the volume contains chapters featuring mixed methods, illustrating the use and integration of both qualitative and quantitative approaches within a single study or project. In Chapter 23, Valerie R. Anderson provides an introduction to mixed methods approaches in community-based research. The chapter begins with a definition of mixed methods research, an overview of key concepts, and ways in which qualitative and quantitative methodologies can be employed in tandem. This is followed by a review of mixed methods studies in community-based research, with a particular focus on the specific techniques utilized and on how mixing methods can add to scientific rigor. Next, the benefits and challenges of integrating qualitative and quantitative data are discussed. The chapter concludes with an illustrative example of a mixed methods case study of a juvenile court system.

In Chapter 24, Brian Christens, Victoria Faust, Jennifer Gaddis, Paula Tran Inzeo, Carolina S. Sarmiento, and Shannon M. Sparks describe the orchestration of cyclical processes of action and research that mutually inform each other. This chapter elucidates the conceptual foundations of action research and demonstrates its utility as a framework for knowledge generation in collaboration with community organizations. Although action research is often conducted using qualitative methods, the authors make a case for methodological pluralism. Principles for designing and conducting mixed methods action research are provided, drawing specifically on an example of an ongoing collaboration with a community organizing network working on multiple issues, including immigration and transit.

Michael J. Kral and James Allen contribute Chapter 25 on community-based participatory research (CBPR). A defining feature of this perspective is the engagement, as co-researchers in the research process, of the people who are the community of concern. This act of engagement involves a sharing of power and a democratization of the research process, along with, typically, a social action component. The authors trace the historical roots of this approach, which is interconnected with concepts of community empowerment, ecology, social justice, feminism, and critical theory. Their example of the use of mixed methods in CBPR describes key events and outcomes from a collaborative project involving members of a grassroots Alaska Native sobriety effort and university-based researchers, in which a qualitative discovery-based research phase guided the development of measures for a quantitative second phase.

In Chapter 26, Emily J. Ozer's discussion on youth-led participatory action research (YPAR) presents a change process that engages students in identifying problems that they want to improve, conducting research to understand the nature of the problems, and advocating for changes based on research evidence. It explicitly focuses on the integration of systematic research implemented by young people with guidance from adult facilitators. The author describes YPAR's core processes, identifying similarities and distinctions between YPAR and other approaches to youth development, as well as factors that support YPAR projects' functioning and sustainability. She also makes links to the broader practice of CBPR (the approach discussed in Chapter 25), noting special considerations in conducting CBPR with youth. The chapter concludes with a case study in which qualitative and quantitative methods were used to assess the effects of participatory research on adolescents and their schools with respect to such dimensions as youth–adult power sharing and youth engagement.

Rebecca Volino Robinson, E. J. R. David, and Mara Hill write on participatory mixed methods across cultures in Chapter 27. Mixed methodology is particularly useful when researching in cross-cultural or cultural contexts, as it allows for both etic (i.e., between groups) and emic (i.e., within a group) investigations of phenomena. Participation occurs on a continuum from informal consultation with community representatives to fully integrated, participatory methodology that centralizes the community voice throughout all aspects of the research process and dissemination. Strengths and challenges faced when conducting participatory mixed methods research in a cultural context are discussed. As an example of this approach, they describe a participatory mixed methods investigation of resilience amid forced displacement in the context of Somali culture.

In Chapter 28, Katherine Cloutier presents (a) the utilization of performance ethnography within a CBPR framework and (b) the combination of this qualitative approach with quantitative methods. Performance ethnography considers such forms of performance as photo, video, fiction, and narrative histories (as well as other traditional or innovative formats that may fall under creative analytic processes) as integral components of an ethnographic research process. The author discusses the benefits and challenges of employing this approach within a CBPR framework. The chapter's case study describes the incorporation of elements of performance ethnography (specifically video creation and documentary work) into a sexual health education program in secondary schools in Barbados. The author demonstrates how this approach paved the way for a mixed methods, multiphase study that emerged as a result of initial fieldwork.

In Chapter 29, Gina Cardazone and Ryan T. Tolman focus on data visualization and its potential uses in participatory research, exploratory data analysis, program evaluation, and dissemination of research results. Although quite broad in scope, data visualization can be used in reference to ubiquitous items such as static bar charts or maps. User-friendly interactive data visualizations may enable people to manipulate large data sets, allowing for instant reconfiguration of the display based on specified variables. Participatory researchers with indigenous knowledge of their community who are able to interact effectively with data sets may generate predictions or research questions that may never occur to social scientists. Data visualization also has considerable potential with respect to the interpretation and dissemination of research results, enabling individuals, organizations, and policymakers to better understand complex concepts and relationships and make data-informed decisions. The case example presented explores how interactive data visualizations were employed in partnership with a Hawaii-based coalition targeting the prevention of child abuse and neglect.

Lisa M. Vaughn and Daniel McLinden discuss concept mapping in Chapter 30. This is an integrative mixed methods research approach that uses brainstorming and unstructured sorting combined with the multivariate statistical methods of multidimensional scaling and hierarchical cluster analysis to create a structured, data-driven visual representation of the ideas of a group. Concept mapping is uniquely suited to conducting research in a community and can be used within a participatory research framework. Unlike other group processes, concept mapping is not a consensus-building process but rather enables the multiple, diverse perspectives of various community stakeholders/participants to emerge. First, individuals work independently to generate ideas about a target issue. These ideas are then shared with the entire community and sorted into categories. Finally, results of the multivariate analysis visualize what the community members think about the issue. The authors present a project in which concept mapping was utilized to determine specific strategies to prevent teen suicide.

In Chapter 31, Yolanda Suarez-Balcazar and Fabricio Balcazar present a mixed methods approach to community development that combines the concerns report (a qualitative approach)—a survey that is developed in a participatory way by a group of community members—with a behavioral functional analysis (a quantitative approach). They describe how multiple factors play a role in the process of addressing community needs and ultimately can influence the success of the methodology's implementation. The chapter demonstrates how, taking into account contextual factors, the approach can help facilitate the skill development of community members leading action projects. The chapter's case study shows how these methods were utilized to aid a rural community in Mexico in promoting community and economic development.

Isidro Maya-Jariego, David Florido del Corral, Daniel Holgado, and Javier Hernández-Ramírez discuss network analysis and stakeholder analysis within mixed methods research in Chapter 32. Particular attention is paid to network visualization as a valuable tool for collecting, exploring, and analyzing data and as a way of presenting relational data. The chapter illustrates how such qualitative and quantitative analyses can be combined and integrated within the intervention process. The case example demonstrates the application of network analysis and stakeholder analysis to improving participation in organizations of fishermen and skippers in the Andalucia region of Spain.

In Chapter 33, Nicole E. Allen, Angela Walden, Emily Dworkin, and Shabnam Javdani discuss how qualitative approaches can be combined with quantitative ones (e.g., MLM) to enrich understanding of the contextual realities that shape the way that settings function and exert influence. A mixed methods approach to multilevel, multisetting inquiry allows examination of the strategic interplay of qualitative and quantitative methods at multiple stages of the inquiry process from data collection to interpretation. The chapter describes this interplay, drawing on theory in mixed methods regarding sequential design in the data collection process (in which one data collection method informs the next), analysis, and meaning making. This approach is illustrated by its application to a statewide network of family violence coordinating councils, which had a common mission and desired outcomes but were embedded within unique local community contexts.

In Chapter 34, Tres Stefurak, R. Burke Johnson, and Erynne Shatto describe dialectical pluralism, which is a process theory for dialoging across differences and effecting dynamic integration of divergent perspectives and methods to produce a more complex and meaningful whole. Recognizing that reality is dynamic, process theory provides a procedure, mechanism, and approach for obtaining desired outcomes, with equal participation and effective communication as key elements. The authors demonstrate how dialectical pluralism can be used to integrate the views of multiple stakeholders and findings from multiple methods. They also examine the benefits and costs of utilizing a values-based program evaluation lens based on dialectical pluralism. The approach is illustrated by a case study involving the evaluation of a community-based intervention program for juvenile offenders.

In the final chapter (Chapter 35), Caterina Arcidiacono, Teresa Tuozzi, and Fortuna Procentese describe the community profiling technique, a method that enables researchers and community members to identify the needs, resources, and deficiencies of communities and of local institutions and services. The approach involves the gathering of three types of data: (a) objective (e.g., demographic information and economic indicators), (b) subjective (mainly drawn from interviews with key informants from diverse contexts), and (c) symbolic (e.g., through dramatization and drawing). In this way, a community's strengths and weaknesses, as well as priorities and critical points for possible action plans and interventions, can be identified. The authors demonstrate the application of this approach with respect to a community development project in Naples, Italy.

We hope that the present work stimulates academically based social scientists, community-based professionals, and graduate students from various disciplines to contribute to the further maturation of community-based research and intervention by utilizing a wide array of methods that are theoretically sound, empirically valid, and creative. By addressing questions of import for the communities in which and with whom the authors work, community-oriented researchers and community-based organizations can facilitate ever more meaningful understanding and beneficial change within these communities.

REFERENCES

Gergen, K. J., Josselson, R., & Freeman, M. (2015) The promises of qualitative inquiry. *American Psychologist, 70*, 1–9.

Heller, K. (2014). Community and organizational mediators of social change: A theoretical inquiry. In T. P. Gullotta & M. Bloom (Eds.), *Encyclopedia of primary prevention and health promotion* (2nd ed., pp. 294–302). New York, NY: Springer.

Jason, L. A., & Glenwick, D. S. (2012). (Eds.), *Methodological approaches to community-based research*. Washington, DC: American Psychological Association.

Jason, L. A., Keys, C. B., Suarez-Balcazar, Y., Taylor, R. R., Davis, M., Durlak, J., & Isenberg, D. (2004). (Eds.). *Participatory community research: Theories and methods in action*. Washington, DC: American Psychological Association.

Jason, L. A., Stevens, E., Ram, D., Miller, S. A., & Beasley, C. R. (2016). *Theories and the field of community psychology*. Global Journal of Community Psychology Practice.

Kelly, J. G. (1985). The concept of primary prevention: Creating new paradigms. *Journal of Primary Prevention, 5*, 269–272.

Kelly, J. G. (1990). Changing contexts and the field of community psychology. *American Journal of Community Psychology, 18*, 769–792.

Kelly, J. G. (2006). *Becoming ecological: An exploration into community psychology*. Oxford, England: Oxford University Press.

Kloos, B., Hill, J., Thomas, E., Wandersman, A., Elias, M. J., & Dalton, J. H. (2012). *Community psychology: Linking individuals and communities*. Stamford, CT: Wadsworth.

Moritsugu, J., Vera, E., Wong, F. & Duffy, K. (2013). *Community psychology* (5th ed.). Upper Saddle River, NJ: Pearson.

Revenson, T. A., D'Augelli, A. R., French, S. E., Hughes, D. L., Livert, D., Seidman, E., . . . Yoshikawa, H. (Eds.).(2002). *A quarter century of community psychology: Readings from the American Journal of Community Psychology*. New York, NY: Kluwer Academic/Plenum.

Revenson, T. A, & Seidman, E. (2002). Looking backward and moving forward: Reflections on a quarter century of community psychology. In T. A. Revenson, A. R. D'Augelli, S. E. French, D. L. Hughes, D. Livert, E. Seidman, . . . H. Yoshikawa (Eds.), *A quarter century of community psychology: Readings from the American Journal of Community Psychology* (pp. 3–31). New York, NY: Kluwer Academic/Plenum.

Tolan, P., Keys, C., Chertok, F., & Jason, L. A. (Eds.). (1990). *Researching community psychology: Issues of theories and methods*. Washington, DC: American Psychological Association.

SECTION I

Qualitative Approaches

2

Introduction to Qualitative Approaches

ANNE E. BRODSKY, SARA L. BUCKINGHAM, JILL E. SCHEIBLER, AND TERRI MANNARINI

There is a natural fit between the work of interdisciplinary, community-based inquiry and qualitative methods. In the chapters on qualitative methods that follow in this section, readers will find a myriad of not only useful but also exciting approaches to community research and action. Community-based inquiry is often designed to question dominant, laboratory-based, so-called "scientific" findings and paradigms; to privilege external validity and local knowledge; to work with participants and communities; to value culture and context; and to lead to action and change. Qualitative methods provide the appropriate tools to do all this and more (Brodsky, Mannarini, Buckingham, & Scheibler, in press).

Many community-based research traditions and qualitative methods also share a modern history of having arisen in opposition to dominant social and scientific worldviews. Community psychology is one such example, as it developed alongside and was inspired by other movements of the 1960s to question the dominant paradigms of wellness promotion and illness prevention at multiple levels (Levine, Perkins, & Perkins, 2005). Thus, the connection between community-based research and qualitative methods is not merely incidental. Guba and Lincoln (1994) also elucidated how the methods we use are dependent on the paradigms and worldviews we hold. Qualitative methods are a natural partner of community-based research (Brodsky et al., in press).

Qualitative methods are adept at answering many of the questions that arise in community-based research in an ecologically valid way, given their premise on the belief that the control demanded by quantitative methods strips away the context that is central to life; their explicit attention to the disjunction between grand and local theory; and their focus on context, culture, and setting. Qualitative methods can be central to the effort to reframe dominant narratives, which seek causal pathways to and from individual-level problems, to a view that also takes into account individual- and community-level strengths and resources, which are active in responding to, and changing, systemic, broad-based issues. An important goal of qualitative methods is discovery, that is, developing holistic, comprehensive descriptions of systems, theories, and processes, as well as identifying factors and working hypotheses that warrant further research. In this way, qualitative methods are not solely focused on the type I and type II errors discussed in quantitative inquiry but also have concern for what Crabtree and Miller (1999) called type III (solving the wrong problem) and type IV (solving a problem not worth solving) errors. Moreover, qualitative researchers are willing to question prevailing notions of "scientific objectivity" and to be seen as "involved", as they are aware of the roles that researcher standpoint and the interaction between researcher and participant play in the production of data and findings (Glesne, 2011). Many qualitative traditions and researchers are also explicit in their aim for social justice, working alongside their community participants in the creation of knowledge and using research to inform and spur action (Guba & Lincoln, 1994).

The natural partnership between qualitative methods and community research has resulted in an exciting and longstanding history of work that has explored community needs and strengths in order to ultimately influence community action and change across a wide range of issues and settings. These include studies such as Berg, Coman, and Schensul's (2009) youth action research in Hartford, Connecticut, which used community ethnography and social action research to change individual and collective efficacy and prevent risky behaviors. Other qualitative researchers, Yoshikawa and Olazagasti (2011), used focus groups to study effective outreach and behavior change in preventing HIV transition in Asian/Pacific Islanders in New York City, which led to the development of culturally appropriate methods for addressing the influence of social oppression, immigration status, and cultural norms on HIV transmission. Other community researchers employ qualitative methods to examine and document community change efforts. For example, Speer and Christens (2012) partnered with citizens and utilized organizational and public documents, media coverage, and semistructured interviews to study local community action in holding organizations accountable for community development and housing improvements in Kansas City, Missouri. Yet another illustration is Kroeker's (1996) study of community functioning in agricultural cooperatives in Nicaragua. Her use of participant observation allowed her to discover the importance of mentoring and support for emerging leadership, which was then shared with and built into structures of these communities. In the remainder of the chapter, we first present an overview of qualitative methods and their salient aspects and then describe a case study that illustrates the use of such methods.

INTRODUCTION TO QUALITATIVE METHODS

The large umbrella of qualitative methods covers a vast array of research typologies, a number of which are described in the chapters that follow. These methods are shaped by various, and sometimes differing, theoretical and philosophical stances. However, the unifying features that bond the methods are their (a) use of nonnumerical data (e.g., words, pictures, observations) to explore, discover, and describe the experiences, meanings, processes, and purposes of the phenomenon under consideration from the perspective of those who are experiencing it and (b) value of the uniqueness, natural variation, diversity, and ambiguity in the findings. Qualitative methods also give attention to the iterative nature of processes and knowledge, as well as the standpoint of both the researcher and participants in the production and discovery of such knowledge. When designing community-based research and considering the use of qualitative methods, researchers must consider their worldview and that of their population of interest, their data collection methods and subsequent analysis, the trustworthiness of their research designs, and the multiple ethical issues that may arise during research. These considerations also play an important role in readers' and consumers' evaluation of community-based qualitative work.

Worldviews

The founders of community psychology and modern proponents of qualitative research have argued for the importance of articulating our worldviews. Malterud (2001, pp. 483–484) stated that researchers' backgrounds and positions "will affect what they choose to investigate, the angle of investigation, the methods judged most adequate for this purpose, the findings considered most appropriate, and the framing and communication of conclusions." Similarly, Sarason (1984, p. 477) noted that "we can never unimprison ourselves, except in small measure, from our world view." Our worldview is shaped by ontology (i.e., assumptions about the nature of reality), epistemology (i.e., beliefs about knowledge and knowing), and axiology (i.e., beliefs about values in the research process; Creswell, Hanson, Plano Clark, & Morales, 2007).

A researcher's ontological and epistemological views shape the work's paradigm and axiology, which can be broadly organized into four categories. *Positivists* believe in one "true" reality that can be perfectly apprehended. *Postpositivists* believe that, reality, while objective, is only imperfectly apprehendable, expressed only as a statistical probability. Neither positivists nor postpositivists believe that worldviews, often called "values" or "biases", should or do play a role in research. They work to eliminate or control the influence of worldviews, which more qualitatively aligned paradigms argue merely obscures our worldview and any possibility of apprehending "reality." *Constructivist-interpretivists* believe that reality is constructed in the interactions and minds of individuals; thus, there are multiple, equally valid realities. Constructivists believe that worldviews cannot be removed from research, and therefore researchers must acknowledge, describe, and fully consider their roles. Finally, *critical-ideologists*, or *criticalists*, believe that reality is constructed and cannot be separated from its socio-historical context and power imbalances. Criticalists believe that values should influence research and its outcomes, empowering participants to liberate themselves from oppression caused by these power structures (Ponterotto, 2005). Because paradigms dictate appropriate methods (Guba & Lincoln, 1994), most qualitative researchers ascribe to constructivist and/or critical paradigms and explore their biases, rather than control for them. Qualitative researchers reflect upon their worldview, lived experiences, values and beliefs, assumptions, theoretical predispositions, and roles as they pertain to the topic and setting. They then make these known to the reader in what is termed a statement of reflexivity (Crabtree & Miller, 1999; Glesne, 2011).

Participants and Communities of Interest

Aligned with the aims and understandings of community-based research, qualitative methods value the uniqueness of peoples and settings and do not aim for, nor claim, generalizability, nor are they bound by statistical necessities of random sampling strategies. Thus, their population of interest is usually localized. As such, sampling in qualitative research focuses on gaining rich, local information, as opposed to gleaning generalized, global summaries. The research question and paradigm dictate the sampling method, which might aim to increase or decrease variation, or explore extreme, typical, or particular cases of importance (Kuzel, 1999). Methods to access the population of interest include naturalistic, purposive, and snowball sampling strategies (Patton, 1990). In naturalistic sampling, researchers speak with a variety of participants whom they encounter within a setting. In purposive sampling, researchers aim to reach a specific population in terms of a specific characteristic (e.g., experience, demographic). In snowball sampling, participants and key informants suggest others who could participate in the research based on similar or different characteristics and/or experiences. Such sampling techniques are well suited for community-based research.

Data Collection

Qualitative methods in community-based research typically involve observing, listening, and engaging with people in their natural settings (Crabtree & Miller, 1999) in order to learn about particular phenomena in their lives. Data collection is usually accomplished through observations and interviews but could also involve photographs, video, personal or public historical records and other extant data, or data created with participants (see, for example, Chapter 9 on participatory action research).

Observational methods range along a continuum. One end of the continuum comprises structured approaches, such as preset surveys, rating forms, or logs to note predetermined structures, features, and activities in the setting (see, for example, Chapter 10 on geographic information systems); the other end comprises unstructured methods, such as many ethnographic field notes (see, for example, Chapter 8 on ethnographic approaches), descriptions of the setting's physical characteristics, individuals' overt and covert behavior, cultural artifacts, and more. Also included in observational data are the field and interpretative notes of the researchers, who are actively observing their own research processes via the recording of thoughts, feelings, experiences, working hypotheses, and/or reflexive statements throughout the entire research process (Emerson, Fretz, & Shaw, 2011; Glesne, 2011).

Interviews can be conducted with individuals, groups (e.g., focus groups), families, and other case sets, or within one case, such as an organization (see, for example, Chapter 5 on community narrative evaluation). The instruments used to gather interview data also fall along a continuum from structured, in which all questions are preselected and asked in a particular order to all participants, to unstructured, in which the researcher might use a single "grand tour" question (Fetterman, 1989) to start the interview, such as "tell me about [the subject of interest]," and then follow the natural course of the conversation. Many interview methods are semistructured, falling in the middle of the continuum; all participants are asked some form of preselected questions designed to touch on particular topics, but the questions are reordered, adapted, and interspersed with other questions based on the participant's responses. Interviews vary with respect to their techniques (i.e., objective, subjective, and even projective methods) and focus, which can be chronological, descriptive, action-oriented, or about the participant's process or essence (Creswell et al., 2007). They can differ in range, varying from one person's or community's entire history to a particular critical event experienced by many people or communities, and vary to privilege either depth or breadth. It cannot be overstated that, regardless of data collection method or focus, the most important "instruments" in qualitative methods are the researchers and their relationships with the participants (Glesne, 2011).

In addition to more traditional sources and types of data, researchers have begun to use photographs and art, and their related verbal and written descriptions, as primary data; much of this data is created in concert with participants (e.g., photovoice; see Chapter 9) and other visually based initiatives; Wang & Burris, 1997). Other methods of data collection include using extant data, such as newspaper articles, organizational and governmental records and notes, and old photographs and letters, as well as material traces (Hodder, 1992), such as accretion (e.g., grime to assess use of kitchen appliances) and erosion (e.g., dirt paths worn on grassy fields to determine where a new pathway should be created).

Data collection methods also range in terms of the level of participation in the setting. Some researchers fully participate in the setting (i.e., participant observation) and are insiders or become insiders through the course of their research. Other researchers are relatively disconnected from the community and phenomena they are studying, maintaining as much distance as possible while conducting the study. The researchers may choose to actively collaborate with the community, allowing the community to shape the research questions asked and the design and implementation of the data collection and analysis, or they may remain more distanced, conducting all of the research themselves. There are certainly benefits and drawbacks to each approach. Although participatory methods can provide a wealth of information and nuanced understanding about an issue, they are also time consuming, demanding of resources from settings and participants, and unpredictable, as researchers relinquish much of the control of the research process. On the other hand, although researcher-led studies can provide a useful outside perspective, may uncover knowledge that might not be gleaned by those immersed and involved in the issues and setting, and allow for control of the research design and method by a (hopefully) properly trained and experienced researcher, research without participants' active involvement might be impracticable in some settings, as well as miss the more subtle distinctions and deep understandings that only insider perspectives provide (Crabtree & Miller, 1999). Many qualitative researchers would argue for a balance of the two.

Data Analysis

Methods of analysis can vary considerably across types of community-based qualitative work and data types; however, they share an aim to organize, interpret, and present the collected data in order to shed light on the phenomena and settings of interest and to remain contextually grounded. Unlike in quantitative methods, data analysis is not entirely separate from data collection. Instead, an iterative process, in which the researcher begins informal analyses while collecting data, is commonplace. These initial thoughts and interpretations may impact the subsequent data collection process, as working hypotheses are explored through changes in the questions asked and inclusion of further participants and types of data collected. Such additional data may then impact the ongoing analytic process. At some more advanced point in the data collection process the researcher will begin a more in-depth analysis (detailed later), which is useful in identifying the point at which data collection should be stopped. Two processes that are often used for identifying this stopping point are *saturation*, the moment at which additional data collection yields little return because all additional data are only confirming the understanding that arose from the previous data collection, and *extension*, the point where additional data are starting to lead to tangential understandings and discoveries (Crabtree & Miller, 1999).

There are multiple perspectives and many classification systems relating to qualitative data analysis. Tesch (1991), for example, distinguished three basic orientations: "language-oriented" approaches (focused on the meaning of words and the ways in which people communicate); "descriptive/interpretative" approaches (aimed at providing descriptions and interpretations of social phenomena); and "theory-building" approaches. Regardless of orientation, the formal stage of data analysis typically begins with transcribing spoken data (which are usually audio or video recorded) and logging and organizing pictorial data, observations, and researcher field notes. Qualitative researchers then typically use some type of coding—marking certain content and processes that are linked to the research questions—to organize their data and highlight the most pertinent content, themes, processes, theoretical concepts, and so on. As coding is based on the specific method and research questions used, it varies greatly. At one end of the spectrum, codes are determined a priori, based on a theory, hypothesis, and/or extant literature (Crabtree & Miller, 1999). At the other end of the spectrum, codes are determined after many careful readings of the data and are based on the specific data content (e.g., grounded theory; Glaser & Strauss, 1967). Many methods lie between these two extremes. For example, researchers often combine the two, using *sensitizing concepts* (i.e., guiding constructs from the researcher's chosen discipline; Blumer, 1969) to inform coding but do not restrict coding to these concepts alone. Coding can focus on the meaning of the data as interpreted by the researchers, the exact content of the data as stated or "objectively" seen, or the way in which the content is communicated (e.g., the way something is said or a photograph is taken). Research teams may code data together or have multiple researchers code the same data separately, later coming together to determine the extent of agreement in their codes. Many teams maintain a qualitative mindset in this process, privileging the unique contributions of each research team member to the construction of understanding and thus striving to reach consensus, with all members presenting their reasoning for particular codes and the team coming to a mutual understanding and agreement (Brodsky et al., 2004). Other teams take a more quantitative approach, training all researchers to find a singular "truth" (which is often that of the principal investigator) and then recording the amount of agreement between codes, calculating reliability coefficients for their coding and striving for statistically shared understandings. Some researchers (e.g., Hill, 2012) recommend an approach that is somewhere in between.

Coding is nearly always an iterative process in which the codes and their application change as the data are analyzed, with the ultimate goal of creating contextually grounded working hypotheses and theories. All codes and working hypotheses are compared within and across "data points" (e.g., participants, interviews, observations, photographs, instances). During this process, researchers actively seek to identify outliers, or negatives cases that could refute their working hypotheses, leading to what Agar (1986, p. 25) called "breakdown". Unlike in quantitative work, these outliers are neither controlled nor rejected from the data set. Rather, they are treated as real and important examples of alternative perspectives and experiences whose contribution to understanding of the phenomenon in question need to be included. Breakdown leads to "resolution", in which further analyses reveal a better explanation of the data (Agar, 1986, p. 27). If it does not lead to a better explanation, researchers make it known that their working hypotheses and theories do not fit all of the data, and draw attention to these negative cases. Usually multiple researchers, participants, and community members are involved to "audit" or review the analyses and interpretations in order to ensure that they accurately represent multiple truths, experiences, and perspectives (Glesne, 2011).

Charmaz (2006) provided the analogy of a skeleton for explaining the analytic process in one particular qualitative method (constructivist grounded theory), but this analogy holds true across many types of analytic approaches. Analysis begins by setting the stage for the bones to be discovered or generated (i.e., prepping materials, such as compiling data and their related interpretations and initial thoughts). Next, the bones are discovered or generated as codes are assigned to segments of the data. Following this, the bones are assembled through additional analysis and connection, and built by comparing all of the bone segments and their connections to one another, corroborating multiple perspectives. Finally, the body is placed back into its context, as resulting theory is woven into a rich, descriptive narrative, so that the theory remains contextually grounded in the data. In this way, the data are analyzed, interpreted, and presented.

Rigor

The rigor of qualitative research, as with all research, is based on its design, enactment, and researcher competence, as well as the paradigms and associated beliefs (e.g., multiple "truths", respect for context over data control and manipulation). Although external validity is perhaps the most applicable and central to qualitative methods, a more appropriate way to think about rigor in qualitative methods is to replace quantitative standards of validity, reliability, and generalizability with standards to judge the *trustworthiness* of qualitative work. These include (a) *authenticity,* the fairness, sophistication, mutual understanding, and empowerment of participants and consumers of the knowledge to take action; (b) *credibility,* the accurate representation of multiple realities; (c) *transferability,* the applicability of the findings to other settings; (d) *dependability,* the consistency of findings; and (e) *confirmability,* objectivity in data collection, analysis, and presentation (Glesne, 2011; Lincoln & Guba, 1985). Trust in the rigor of qualitative methods is built and maintained through multiple decisions researchers make in the data design, collection, analysis, and presentation process, including researcher reflexivity. It is also strengthened by methodological consistency and transparency (i.e., making the path to conclusions clear to readers; Moisander & Valtonen, 2006), as well as triangulation, the use of multiple types of (a) data (e.g., observations and interviews), (b) collection time points (e.g., multiple interviews, several questions and follow-up prompts to ascertain the participants' viewpoints), (c) data sources, and (d) ways of analysis to be more certain that multiple realities are accurately captured and represented (Denzin, 1970). Analytic rigor is strengthened by involving participants, key informants, and other researchers in member checks, audits, and peer debriefing. Long-term and persistent involvement and observation during data collection and analysis are further believed to strengthen the study's trustworthiness. Finally, thick, rich, detailed description in data collection, including in field notes and in the writing process, all enhance the reader's ability to trust the accuracy and completeness of the findings presented and the interpretation made (Glesne, 2011; Lincoln & Guba, 1985).

Ethics

When embarking on community work, researchers must consider a myriad of ethical issues that may arise over the course of their involvement in the community. The American Psychological Association (2010) provided guidance for ensuring ethical research, including gaining informed consent from participants, providing adequate debriefing, reporting research results accurately, and sharing data for verification. However, these guidelines are often more clear cut when used in a laboratory or when conducting individual-level research. Thus, O'Neill (1989) aptly summed up two additional issues that community-based researchers must consider, namely, *to whom* they are responsible and *for what* they are responsible.

Regardless of discipline, it is crucial that qualitative researchers follow all applicable professional and personal ethical guidelines in order to protect the well-being, confidentiality, and dignity of those who choose to participate in studies, those who elect not to participate, and those who will receive the research products. First and foremost, researchers must be sure to have sufficient knowledge and skills to apply their chosen data collection and analysis methods. They especially must consider their role in relation to their participants, to the community, and to the topic of interest. Because qualitative researchers can occupy multiple roles vis à vis the research setting and participants (often in the same study) ranging from outside evaluators to inside community members, friends, advocates, and/or collaborators, these issues can be more complicated than in more traditional research relationships (Brodsky et al., 2004).

Issues of power, reciprocity, integrity, and expectations are also important to consider in qualitative research. Researchers must be aware of their power, that of the community, what imbalances exist, and what will be done to share power effectively. They must consider reciprocity and what the community gains in return for sharing its time, resources, and knowledge. Researchers must reflect upon their responsibility to the community and consider how they will enter the community, work with it, leave it, and represent it. They must also ascertain the expectations of the community, being open to hearing the needs, concerns, and perspectives of the participants and communities. At the same time, they must openly, skillfully, and honestly communicate their own roles and expectations, as well as their personal and professional guidelines so that misunderstandings can be better averted. In considering how they will provide feedback to and about the community, researchers must finally consider issues of honesty, applicability, harm reduction, and confidentiality. Davis, Olson, Jason, Alvarez, and Ferrari (2006) provided an excellent guide for developing and maintaining community partnerships, and Glesne (2011) covered other specific ethical considerations for qualitative researchers.

Challenges and Benefits

As with any approach, qualitative methods cannot perfectly address every research question or purpose, and, given its disparate methods and theoretical approaches, some argue that qualitative research does not represent a unified field (Denzin & Lincoln, 2000). Thus, researchers should be attuned to nuances of the qualitative method they choose and to its strengths and shortcomings and be wary of using any qualitative method for purposes for which it is not designed. The selection of the method should always be secondary to the research question and the paradigm in which the question is conceptualized. Most notably, qualitative methods are inherently not suitable for statistical hypothesis testing nor controlled intervention studies, given that their focus is on discovery rather than rejection of a null hypothesis. Qualitative methods are used to capture what is taking place in natural settings, rather than in controlled experiments; as such, causal statements cannot be firmly made from them. Furthermore, qualitative methods are not meant to be fully generalizable to a larger population; rather, they are meant to be "transferable" to similar cases; it is left to research consumers to evaluate the utility of the findings for their own settings and situations (Crabtree & Miller, 1999).

Because the paradigms underlying qualitative methods recognize the unalterable subjectivity of reality, qualitative researchers are not bound to the restrictions that quantitative methods demand to ensure "objectivity" and internal validity. Instrumentation, data collection, and analysis are all designed and utilized in such a way as to recognize the unique contribution of the researcher and the in vivo participants and setting of the research endeavor. This can lead to critique by researchers more wedded to and comfortable with more traditional paradigms and quantitative methods. Qualitative methods and researchers have also been critiqued for their efforts to recognize and examine how the researcher's worldview and values are inherent in the research endeavor and play a role in the design, data collection, analysis, interpretation, and presentation of research findings, as well as for using their research to directly inform action. However, many community-based disciplines, such as community psychology, with their roots in action research and social justice, obviously have a natural affinity for change-oriented qualitative work (Banyard & Miller, 1998). The fact that qualitative methods differ from quantitative in their approach to these critical issues does not undermine the scientific standards by which qualitative methods are judged or the scientific nature of qualitative work and product.

The final challenge for qualitative methods that we will mention here is a challenge that stems not from the methods themselves but from a lack of rigorous training in qualitative methods across disciplines. Although quantitative methods are taught at all educational levels, from elementary school through postgraduate education, qualitative methods are often treated as something that someone can simply learn and do without formal instruction, mentoring, or critique (Brodsky et al., in press). Thus, there are many examples of poor qualitative studies in a number of disciplines, which diminish the reputation of this method and the state of the research. Readers are cautioned to fully investigate the specific qualitative method that they aim to use in their research and to gain training and supervision in that method, beyond the material offered in this text, prior to embarking on their study design and implementation.

Overall, however, we believe, and the qualitative chapters that follow also make clear, that there are countless benefits to be gained through qualitative methods. These include that community-based qualitative researchers can convey and instill respect for, and protect the integrity of, context, culture, and setting; protect and present the voices, narratives, and perceptual frames of participants and communities; recognize the disjunction between grand and local theory; act in authentic ways with research participants and settings; produce knowledge that is not beholden to dominant theories, instrumentation, or narrative; and ultimately discover new knowledge, which, as Kuhn (1996) eloquently stated, can spark a scientific revolution.

CASE STUDY

Background and Aims

This example of qualitative community-based research is focused on understanding resilience and community in a high-risk cross-cultural context. It not only illustrates several of the concepts presented in the overview herein but also exemplifies how qualitative methods are particularly well suited for work in settings whose contexts present challenges to the use of standard methods and measures, theory, assumed cultural understandings, and processes. In such communities, there is an immediate assumption, or at least awareness of the possibility, that there exists a disconnect between the generalized understandings and approaches of Western social science and local theory. Although this example is extreme in many ways, it is important to note that it is possible that the challenges were just more obvious in this setting. It is likely that all settings contain vast amounts of unique understandings and processes that are too often glossed over by false assumption of familiarity and similarity.

This research was conducted with an underground women's humanitarian and political organization active in Afghanistan and Pakistan during and just after the 1996–2001 Taliban rule of Afghanistan. Their goal was to advocate for and promote women's rights and democratic society for men and women. The research goal was to explore resilience and resistance at the individual and organizational levels and the role of community in countering the risks Afghan women experienced across multiple decades of war and socio-religious-cultural repression. The ultimate action goal was to understand processes of "spontaneous resilience" (Brodsky & Faryal, 2006, p. 312) arising without outside intervention, which could improve internal and external policy and aid.

Method

The research was carried out over five 6- to 8-week-long trips to more than 10 locations, including refugee camps, orphanages, and boarding and day schools in Afghan and Pakistani cities and rural villages. Approximately 225 individual and group interviews with women, men, and children; participant observation; and archival and photographic review were conducted. The interviews utilized a semistructured, open-ended, and iterative framework to gain first-person narratives of participant experiences. These interviews were supplemented by formal and informal participant observations conducted during public and private activities ranging from group meals, meetings, and educational classes, to food distributions, protests, and community cultural gatherings. Records, publications, photographs, videos, and letters were reviewed to gain historical perspective on organizational activities.

The resulting 500-plus pages of interview and observation notes were coded using an open, recursive coding template built on extant research questions, researcher training, worldview, and reflexivity, as well as grounded theory. Findings and working hypotheses were discussed with research participants, key informants, and area experts. Multiple sets of analysis focused on various theoretical processes were conducted. Based on the research focus, some analyses were conducted by the primary researcher alone (e.g., Brodsky, 2003, 2014), some with area experts (e.g., Brodsky & Catteneo, 2013; Brodsky & Faryal, 2006), and some in a consensus-based research team approach (e.g., Brodsky, Welsh, Carrillo, Talwar, & Bulter, 2011).

Findings

Among the most noteworthy findings of this project were the in-depth, narrative description of the lives, experiences, and activities of this organization and its many Afghan members and supporters (Brodsky, 2003); articulation of a culturally sensitive, multilevel model of resilience (Brodsky et al., 2011); further conceptualization of the processes of multilevel psychological sense of community (Brodsky, 2009); exploration of the ways in which bridging diversity between inside and outside collaborators may be a false goal (Brodsky & Faryal, 2006); and description of the experiences of war, violence, and foreign intervention on women's lives (e.g., Brodsky, 2014). In addition to dissemination in scholarly and trade books and journal articles, the findings have been shared with participants and the public in Pakistan, Afghanistan, Europe, and the United States through newspaper and magazine interviews and articles; slideshows, talks, radio and TV interviews; and classroom lectures at the elementary through graduate school levels.

Discussion

Given the setting—a secretive, high-risk community organization situated in a cultural context that rarely produces or is represented in traditional social science research—a traditional quantitative approach would have been not only inappropriate but also practically impossible to carry out. Although trying to capture participants' experiences, beliefs, and values with established (mostly Western) psychology and social science measures might have resulted in "findings", their accuracy and applicability to local meanings and concerns would have been questionable, at best. Qualitative methods fit the exploratory and descriptive nature of the research question, the underlying values and principles of the researcher, and of community psychology epistemology and ontology. In a setting where women's voices are routinely silenced, open-ended interviewing was crucial to a goal to privilege their narratives and understandings rather than replicate oppressions. Furthermore, because survival in this context demands great caution in what is said, the researcher's ability to elicit narratives and observe actions in multiple settings provided crucial data triangulation that was essential to research rigor. Careful researcher reflexivity was also necessary to produce knowledge responsibly in a setting dissimilar from her "usual" research settings. This is a situation in which the standard positivist and postpositivist attempts to control researcher bias would have buried important insights that came from explicitly facing significant differences in worldview and understanding (Brodsky & Faryal, 2006). Finally, qualitative methods were ideal to explore the multiple, local cultural contexts that impacted participant experiences and are not just the "ground" but also, in their own right, central "figures" in community-based research (e.g., Brodsky, 2009).

CONCLUSION

As this introductory chapter and those that follow illustrate, qualitative methods provide a rich and robust approach to enhancing community-based research and action. It is incumbent upon researchers to not only choose the methods that fit their research question and theoretical paradigm (Guba & Lincoln, 1994) but also to be well trained in the pros, cons, and appropriate application of the methods they choose. Appropriate ethical and cultural considerations are also key to producing research and action that provides the necessary protection and respect to participating and nonparticipating members of a community. With these caveats in mind, we believe that qualitative methods can contribute immensely to the creation of contextually based, culturally relevant understandings and knowledge, enhanced well-being, and positive community change that are the ultimate hallmarks and goals of community-based research and action.

AUTHOR NOTE

The case study presented in this chapter was previously utilized in "Kindred Spirits in Scientific Revolution: Qualitative Methods in Community Psychology," by A. E. Brodsky, T. Mannarini, S. L. Buckingham, and J. E. Scheibler, in press, in *APA Handbook of Community Psychology*.

REFERENCES

Agar, M. A. (1986). *Speaking of ethnography*. Newbury Park, CA: Sage.

American Psychological Association. (2010). *Ethical principles of psychologists and code of conduct*. Washington, DC: Author. http://apa.org/ethics/code/index.aspx

Banyard, V. L., & Miller, K. E. (1998). The powerful potential of qualitative research for community psychology. *American Journal of Community Psychology, 26*, 485–505.

Berg, M., Coman, E., & Schensul, J. J. (2009). Youth action research for prevention: A multi-level intervention designed to increase efficacy and empowerment among urban youth. *American Journal of Community Psychology, 43*, 345–359.

Blumer, H. (1969). What is wrong with social theory? In H. Blumer (Ed.), *Symbolic interactionism: Perspective and method* (pp. 140–152). Englewood Cliffs, NJ: Prentice-Hall.

Brodsky, A. E. (2003). *With all our strength: The Revolutionary Association of the Women of Afghanistan*. New York, NY: Routledge.

Brodsky, A. E. (2009). Multiple psychological senses of community in Afghan context: Exploring commitment and sacrifice in an underground resistance community. *American Journal of Community Psychology, 44*, 176–187.

Brodsky, A. E. (2014). Narratives of Afghan childhood: Risk, resilience, and the experiences that shape the development of Afghanistan as a people and a nation. In J. Heath & A. Zahedi (Eds.), *Children of Afghanistan: The path to peace* (pp. 51–68). Austin: University of Texas Press.

Brodsky, A. E., & Cattaneo, L. B. (2013). A transconceptual model of empowerment and resilience: Divergence, convergence, and interactions in kindred community concepts. *American Journal of Community Psychology, 52*, 333–346.

Brodsky, A. E., & Faryal, T. (2006). No matter how hard you try, your feet still get wet: Insider and outsider perspectives on bridging diversity. *American Journal of Community Psychology, 37*, 311–320. doi:10.1007/s10464-006-9015-x

Brodsky, A. E., Mannarini, T., Buckingham, S. L., & Scheibler, J. E. (in press). Kindred spirits in scientific revolution: Qualitative methods in community psychology. In M. A. Bond, C. B. Keys, & I. Serrano-García (Eds.-in-Chief), M. Shinn (Assoc. Ed.), *APA handbook of community psychology: Vol. 2. Methods of community psychology: Research and applications*. Washington, DC: American Psychological Association.

Brodsky, A. E., Senuta, K. R., Weiss, C. A., Marx, C. M., Loomis, C., Arteaga, S. S., . . . Castagnera-Fletche r, A. (2004). When one plus one equals three: The role of relationships and context in community research. *American Journal of Community Psychology, 33*, 229–242.

Brodsky, A. E., Welsh, E., Carrillo, A, Talwar, G., & Butler, T. (2011). Between synergy and conflict: Balancing the processes of organizational and individual resilience in an Afghan women's community. *American Journal of Community Psychology, 47*, 217–235.

Charmaz, K. (2006). *Constructing grounded theory: A practical guide through qualitative analysis*. Thousand Oaks, CA: Sage.

Crabtree, B., & Miller, W. (Eds.). (1999). *Doing qualitative research* (2nd ed.). London, England: Sage Publications

Creswell, J. W., Hanson, W. E., Plano Clark, V. L., & Morales, A. (2007). Qualitative research designs: Selection and implementation. *Counseling Psychologist, 35*, 236–264.

Davis, M. I., Olson, B. D., Jason, L. A., Alvarez, J., & Ferrari, J. R. (2006). Cultivating and maintaining effective action research partnerships: The DePaul and Oxford House collaborative. *Journal of Prevention and Intervention in the Community, 31*, 3–12.

Denzin, N. (1970). *The research act in sociology: A theoretical introduction to sociological methods*. Chicago, IL: Aldine.

Denzin, N. K., & Lincoln, Y. S. (2000). (Eds.). *Handbook of qualitative research* (2nd ed.). Thousand Oaks, CA: Sage.

Emerson, R. M., Fretz, R. I., & Shaw, L. L. (2011). *Writing ethnographic fieldnotes* (2nd ed.). Chicago, IL: University of Chicago Press.

Fetterman, D. M. (1989). *Ethnography: Step by step* (2nd ed.). Thousand Oaks, CA: Sage.

Glaser, B. G., & Strauss, A. L. (1967). *The discovery of grounded theory: Strategies for qualitative research*. Chicago, IL: Aldine.

Glesne, C. (2011). *Becoming qualitative researchers: An introduction* (4th ed.). Boston, MA: Pearson Education.

Guba, E. G., & Lincoln, Y. S. (1994). Competing paradigms in qualitative research. In N. K. Denzin & Y. S. Lincoln (Eds.), *Handbook of qualitative research* (pp. 105–117). London, England: Sage.

Hill, C. E. (2012). *Consensual qualitative research: A practical resource for investigating social science phenomena*. Washington, DC: American Psychological Association.

Hodder, I. (1992). *Theory and practice in archaeology*. London, England: Routledge.

Kroeker, C. J. (1996). The cooperative movement in Nicaragua: Empowerment and accompaniment of severely disadvantaged peasants. *Journal of Social Issues, 52*, 123–138.

Kuhn, T. (1996). *The structure of scientific revolutions* (3rd ed.). Chicago, IL: University of Chicago Press.

Kuzel, A. J. (1999). Sampling in qualitative inquiry. In B. F. Crabtree & W. L. Miller (Eds.), *Doing qualitative research* (2nd ed., pp. 33–45). Thousand Oaks, CA: Sage.

Levine, M., Perkins, D. D., & Perkins, D. V. (2005). *Principles of community psychology: Perspectives and applications* (3rd ed.). New York, NY: Oxford University Press.

Lincoln, Y. S., & Guba, E. G. (1985). *Naturalistic inquiry*. Newbury Park, CA: Sage.

Malterud, K. (2001). Qualitative research: Standards, challenges and guidelines. *Lancet, 358*, 483–488.

Moisander, J., & Valtonen, A: (2006). *Qualitative marketing research methods: A cultural approach*. London, England: Sage.

O'Neill, P. T. (1989). Responsible to whom? Responsible to what? Some ethical issues in community intervention. *American Journal of Community Psychology, 17*, 323–341.

Patton, M. Q. (1990). *Qualitative evaluation and research methods* (2nd ed.). Newbury Park, CA: Sage.

Ponterotto, J. G. (2005). Qualitative research in counseling psychology: A primer on research paradigms and philosophy of science. *Journal of Counseling Psychology, 52*, 126–136.

Sarason, S. B. (1984). If it can be studied or developed, should it be? *American Psychologist, 39*, 477–485.

Speer, P. W., & Christens, B. D. (2012). Local community organizing and change: Altering policy in the housing and community development system in Kansas City. *Journal of Community and Applied Social Psychology, 22*, 414–427.

Tesch, R. (1991). Software for qualitative researchers: Analysis needs and programme capabilities. In N. G. Fielding & R. M. Lee (Eds.), *Using computers in qualitative research* (pp. 16–37). London, England: Sage.

Wang, C., & Burris, M. A. (1997). Photovoice: Concept, methodology, and use for participatory needs assessment. *Health Education and Behavior, 24*, 369–387.

Yoshikawa, H., & Olazagasti, M. R. (2011). The neglected role of community narratives in culturally anchored prevention and public policy. In M. S. Aber, K. I. Maton, & E. Seidman (Eds.), *Empowering settings and voices for social change* (pp. 173–192). New York, NY: Oxford University Press.

3

Grounded Theory

ANDREW RASMUSSEN, ADEYINKA M. AKINSULURE-SMITH, AND TRACY CHU

One of the basic tenets of community psychology is that researchers strive to capture participants' voices. Consistent with this are grounded theory approaches, which emphasize developing theoretical frameworks that arise from close examinations of participants' narratives and behavior (Glaser & Strauss, 1967). Such bottom-up qualitative approaches, in which findings are emergent from data (Glaser, 1992), have found receptive audiences in community-based research (Banyard & Miller, 1998; Stewart, 2000). In this chapter we provide an introduction to key methods in grounded theory and an example from a program of research with West African immigrant families.

INTRODUCTION TO GROUNDED THEORY

The several grounded theory approaches that exist in the literature all stem from the groundbreaking work by sociologists Barney Glaser and Anslem Strauss (1967), *The Discovery of Grounded Theory*. Glaser and Strauss (1967) were primarily concerned with (a) introducing the idea that theory can arise from data and (b) distinguishing the type of theory generated by grounded theory—"substantive," as opposed to "formal" (pp. 32–34). Consistent with the same 1960s ethos that brought community psychologists together at Swampscott, Massachusetts, the emphasis on substantive theory placed grounded theory at a more grassroots level than most of sociological theory to that point. Grounded theory has grown in the almost half century of its existence, but at the most basic level it remains an approach in which researchers use data to develop theory from the bottom up.

Maintaining Groundedness and Reflexivity

In order to build theory that is grounded, data must drive analytic processes. But of course, data are not agentic in any meaningful sense. Researchers set agendas for what kind of data they collect and use procedures to collect data that inevitably bias the content and form of their data. However, researchers can minimize these biases, and grounded theory researchers use a number of concepts and methods to stay as grounded as possible within the conceptual parameters in which they work.

For some, staying grounded means ignoring a priori knowledge of the topic of their research. They avoid literature reviews or discussion with like-minded researchers on topics relevant to the data prior to data collection or analysis. This becomes more difficult as they do more research in an area, as research projects usually build on one another. The role of *sensitizing concepts* (Blumer, 1969) is helpful here. Sensitizing concepts is a broad term referring to those interests, thoughts, and hunches that researchers have before they get started doing research. They spark researchers' thinking about a topic (van den Hoonaard, 1997), although they do not guide it per se. Charmaz (2014) clarified that sensitizing concepts "provide a place to *start* inquiry, not to *end* it" (p. 31, emphasis in original). The point with sensitizing concepts is that they are not formal theories, while at the same time they acknowledge that researchers are not without ideas and interests prior to examining data.

Another tool often used in grounded theory to minimize the effect of prior knowledge on theory building is reflexivity. Reflexivity has become a basic tenet of contemporary thinking throughout qualitative research. Reflexivity stems from the idea that researchers are the primary data collection tools—researchers design studies, ask questions, and even influence data collection in the way they present themselves and appear to participants during data collection. Reflexivity involves active self-reflection upon researchers' own subjectivity in an attempt to make biases explicit and examine how these biases might influence findings. Being reflexive might include journaling, documenting discussions with research collaborators, and noting personal preferences and biases prior to and during data collection and analysis. Reflexivity has been written about extensively (e.g., Watt, 2007), and any researcher serious about qualitative methodology should spend time with this literature.

Although not a method per se, working with research collaborators can also be important in keeping theory grounded. Collaborators may provide critical points of view that facilitate meaningful reflexivity and, if well trained, may even provide good models for becoming more reflexive. Collaborators become almost essential in identifying emergent codes and are, of course, indispensible in work that relies upon interrater reliability.

Qualitative researchers in general should pay close attention in the design stage to strategies designed to increase the rigor of their work. There is no qualitative analogy to the statistical summaries of data presented in Results sections of quantitative research articles. Qualitative researchers must therefore rely solely on rigorous research designs and well-crafted presentations of methods to convince readers that findings are reliable and valid. There are a number of techniques for strategies for rigor (for a review, see Padgett, 2008), but primary are triangulation, verification, and auditability. Triangulation refers to using multiple perspectives (e.g., of collaborators on a research team or of different sets of participants), data collection formats (e.g., interviews and observations), or more conventional uses of multiple points of view, like interrater reliability. Verification often involves reviewing findings and analyses with participants; the technique of member checking is a common form of verification. Auditability refers to the idea that others might follow the same research processes and come to similar conclusions, much like replicability in quantitative research. Keeping an "audit trail," a document with dates of meetings, decisions taken, notes, and even copies of correspondence between researchers, is an effective technique to ensure auditability.

Sampling

One of the hallmarks of grounded theory is theoretical sampling. Theoretical sampling is a purposive sampling process in which researchers select participants and groups for comparison in order to generate categories of meaning in their data. It is an iterative process based on researchers gauging what they know about these categories of meaning currently and sampling new participants who they think will be able to provide relevant information about what more they would like to know. This means that data analysis must begin as soon as data collection does. Theoretical sampling is "inductive and contingent" (Hood, 2007, p. 161) in that it is based on using initial analyses of data to direct further selection of participants. Participants are recruited until conceptual categories of data reach a point of "theoretical saturation," or a point where "no additional data are being found whereby the sociologist can develop properties of the category" (Hood, 2007, p. 161). Until theoretical saturation is reached, sampling proceeds.

Theoretical sampling implies that (a) the size and exact makeup of samples are unknown at the beginning of research and (b) analysis begins at the start of data collection. Not knowing the size and composition of samples can produce practical headaches that are, perhaps, unfamiliar to non-grounded theory researchers. For instance, not having a good sense of the number of participants in a research study *by design* presents a quandary when applying for research funding or submitting a research proposal to an institutional review board. In practice most grounded theory researchers estimate a number as if sample size were able to be determined beforehand.

Analysis

The primary analytical tool proposed by Glaser and Strauss (1967) was the constant comparative method (CCM). CCM is the driver of theoretical sampling and saturation, the basis of coding and memoing in grounded theory, and the process for building theory. Glaser and Strauss (1967, p. 105) described four stages: "(a) comparing incidents applicable to each category, (b) integrating categories and their properties, (c) delimiting the theory, and (d) writing the theory."

Coding

The first step of CCM begins by coding each incident or event in data with "as many categories of analysis as possible" (Glaser & Strauss, 1967, p. 105). To aid researchers in this task, Glaser and Strauss provided a "rule for constant comparative methods: *while coding an incident for a category, compare it with the previous incidents in the same and different groups coded in the same category*" (p. 106, emphasis in original). Coding is the process of applying a label for a category of meaning to a section of text (i.e., indicator). In grounded theory, coding is (a) bottom up, that is, not based on a priori categories, and (b) an iterative process proceeding from substantive to theoretical coding. Grounded theorists proceed from the relationships between indicators in the data, to the relation of these indicators to larger categories, and then to the properties of these larger categories (for an informative discussion, see Kelle, 2007). The distinction between substantive and theoretical codes is the difference between the content observed in the data and what researchers theorize about that content.

Substantive coding starts with open coding and ends with axial coding. Open coding begins line by line, with researchers reading their textual data (e.g., transcriptions, field notes) and summarizing each line of text with a few words (usually in the margins). It is here that the idea that theory actually can emerge from data is most credible. Line-by-line coding "forces the researcher to verify and saturate categories, minimizes missing an important category, and ensures relevance by generating codes with emergent fit to the substantive area under study" (Holton, 2007, p. 275). Early ideas generated by the close inspection of data are the fodder for theoretical codes and the basis of emergent theory. Time and effort spent using CCM at this point will pay off later.

Open coding of data should be performed on a reasonably diverse set of initial data and then discussed with research collaborators. Open codes can be listed and collapsed to account for different phrasing of categories (e.g., in a study of family roles, "childcare" and "taking care of children") and, following discussion, to account for some agreed-upon conceptual distance (e.g., "family caretaking" versus "childcare" and "eldercare"). At the end of open coding, researchers should have a list of codes that the research team agrees are relevant to the data and sensitizing concepts. These become axial codes.

Axial codes, sometimes referred to as thematic codes, are those codes that researchers apply to all of the data. They should be sufficiently broad enough to capture a range of indicators but specific enough not to cover overly large sections, or "chunks," of text. This means that time should be spent writing clear definitions. Clear definitions will aid in applying axial codes to data sources that follow those with which open coding was undertaken. Another practical aspect of axial codes is their number. Assigning codes to text chunks is a cognitive process requiring substantial sustained attention to the data, code definitions, and comparison of codes. Researchers must read content while at the same time remembering what categories to track. They must therefore consider carefully the number of codes that they can reasonably track at the same time.

An issue that invariably arises is the issue of how much text to code surrounding specific indicators. In qualitative lore, coders generally fall into two types: "chunkers," who code large pieces of text with material before and after the specific indicators of a category, and "splicers," who choose to code minimal material surrounding indicators. As qualitative research in general emphasizes context, it is generally better to err on the side of the chunkers. This is especially important when examining overlapping codes, which is a powerful technique for identifying interrelated categories in the service of developing theoretical codes. However, too large coded chunks of text can be unwieldy and lead to confusion surrounding which indicators indicate which categories.

Qualitative coding may be subject to interrater reliability analyses. One approach to interrater reliability in qualitative methods is to convert coded chunks of text into binomial variables and compare these across coders using statistics such as kappa. The primary challenge to this quantitative approach is the problem of different coding styles. A chunker may code a long passage of textual data with a specific code, whereas his or her collaborator, a splicer, will have two or three instances of that code in the same passage. Coders might decide that any overlap (regardless of number of instances agreed upon) is an indicator of agreement, or perhaps that only one of the splicer's coded text passages counts as overlapping with the chunker's. An alternative form of interrater reliability is to code text independently and then meet and come to consensus between coders. This should always be done for early data sources in order to develop open codes and train coders, but it can also be done throughout the study to ensure that indicators are coded consistently. Although this sort of consensus coding does not allow for retrospective judgment of whether two reasonable researchers would or would not agree, it does provide trustworthiness (see Morrow, 2005; Shenton, 2004) that the research team involved was consistent in its coding. Several qualitative software packages (e.g., Dedoose) allow for researchers to choose approaches to interrater reliability.

Memoing

Memoing has been described as "essential" (Hood, 2007, p. 156) and "*the* fundamental process of research/data engagement in grounded theory" (Lempert, 2007, p. 245, emphasis in the original). Memo writing is a critical step in the process through which substantive codes become theoretical codes and move on to theory. As such, memos are "the narrated records of a theorist's analytical conversations with him/herself about the research data" (Lempert, 2007, p. 247). Glaser and Strauss's (1967) description of memoing is refreshingly straightforward:

> After coding the category perhaps three or four times, the analyst will find conflicts in the emphases of his thinking. He will be musing over theoretical notions and, at the same time, trying to concentrate on his study of the next incident, to determine the alternate ways by which it should be coded and compared. At this point . . . *stop coding and record a memo on your ideas.* (p. 107, emphasis in original)

The researcher muses and stops to write down his or her thoughts. It is impossible to escape the sense that the authors meant "memo" in the simplest, most banal way—a brief note meant to capture someone's ideas.

Memos may appear in coded transcripts (e.g., on the margins), in audit trails, or in any other document the researcher may have access to during the analytical process. Memos should not be hampered by coherence, linear thinking, or the perceived gravity of generating theory. They are by nature somewhat creative, though in as much as they are written while reflecting on data they are based in empiricism.

Theoretical Coding to Grounded Theory

Arranging and rearranging substantive codes and memos results in theoretical codes. Unlike substantive codes' ground-level categories, the categories represented by theoretical codes are usually propositions that can be elaborated on and tested. Theoretical coding begins with examining overlap among substantive codes and sorting memos into categories. This process is facilitated by whatever techniques researchers find useful to concretize it. The first author prefers sorting techniques that are tactile and make use of spatial relationships, such as sorting exercises where slips of paper with substantive codes and memos are placed in piles on a large table and these piles are arranged in terms of conceptual proximity. Others might use lists on a whiteboard, post-it notes on a wall, or mapping features in qualitative software (e.g., ATLAS.ti). Any techniques that allow researchers to conceptualize relations between intersecting codes and memos will result in theoretical coding. Note that theoretical coding is a few levels "above" the data, "grounded" only in so much as the processes that preceded it were grounded.

At this point researchers integrate their theoretical codes into a theory. Theory resulting from grounded theory is a conceptually abstract narrative about how the elements of categories and concepts relate to one another. In order to have relevance, theory should speak to processes that go beyond the data, perhaps to similar populations or settings. Researchers should be explicit in the connections of their theory to existing theory and previous findings so as to situate their theory within the existing literature.

One particular practical implication of developing theory should be mentioned. Because the primary task of grounded theory is to elucidate broader relationships between indicators and categories of interest, grounded theory researchers are not as invested in describing every nook and cranny of their data in such a way as to draw strong conclusions. Glaser and Strauss (1967): "relationships among categories and properties . . . are suggested as hypotheses pertinent to the direction of relationship, not tested as descriptions of both direction and magnitude" (p. 63). Grounded theory is thus exploratory and generative, not confirmatory—or even particularly precise, for that matter. This puts grounded theorists at odds with other more general inductive qualitative researchers, who are usually more interested in obtaining a thick description of content in order to draw conclusions (Hood, 2007). Grounded theory is at its core about answering questions concerning processes, not describing phenomena or interpreting data in some more specific manner.

CASE STUDY

Overview

The present illustration of grounded theory in community-based research comes from a research study done under the auspices of the West African Families Project (WAFP). WAFP is a project with West African immigrant parents and children that uses stakeholder feedback to (a) develop theoretical perspectives on West African families in New York City and (b) present community members' voices to social service providers. WAFP has resulted in several publications; our (Rasmussen, Chu, Akinsulure-Smith, & Keatley, 2013) examination of the social ecology of West African families' problem solving is described here. In order to maximize opportunities for participants to share information about problem solving within families, we chose focus group interviews as our primary data collection mode. Group discussion is the preferred mode of discourse in many African cultures (Akinsulure-Smith, 2012). Because we also knew that there were topics that were often avoided in groups, we supplemented focus groups with individual interviews.

Maintaining Groundedness and Strategies for Rigor

We were conscientious about our particular social positions and histories in approaching the topics of family in West African communities in New York. In the spirit of reflexivity we were explicit in examining our interests, recognizing that they grew from two members' clinical work with asylum seekers, one of our experiences as an immigrant from Sierra Leone, and another's history as a second-generation immigrant from China. We kept these factors front and center while designing our research project and in analyses in order to check our assumptions about the communities we were entering. Another technique used to maintain groundedness concerned using multiple research team members. Team members triangulated disciplinary perspectives (psychology and sociology) throughout the process in order to help each other maintain close proximity to the data.

Other strategies for rigor not directly related to maintaining groundedness in the current study included triangulating data, verification, and auditability. Triangulating data included having (a) two interview formats (focus groups and individual interviews), (b) purposeful composition of groups across gender and parent/child roles, and (c) two coders per transcript. Verification involved conducting follow-up interviews with several participants and reviewing themes and preliminary conclusions with social service stakeholders. Auditability was ensured by keeping an audit trail—a detailed document that included dates and content of team meetings, interview schedules, memos taken during research processes, and details of stakeholder meetings.

Generating Sensitizing Concepts

We first met with advocacy groups and community-based organizations serving West African immigrants—the stakeholders—in order to generate sensitizing concepts. Salient topics directly related to the WAFP's aims included arguments between parents and children concerning United States culture and intimate partner conflict. In addition, we sought out media outlets oriented to African immigrants. In general, these media resources were generally disdainful of permissive "American" disciplinary practices, which were portrayed as the causes of rampant crime, recreational drug use, and premarital sex. Solutions emphasized respect for elders and educational accomplishment (e.g., Ogiehor-Enoma, 2010), and extolled the use of community processes—bringing in elders and religious leaders. These initial sensitizing concepts—permissive host culture, strict and idealized traditional cultures, and conflict resolution involving community structures—were documented in our audit trail and revisited during theory building.

Recruitment

Recruitment of the sample was purposive and done in three stages to allow for theoretical sampling.

Because we wanted to know about challenges, we drew initially from clinical settings and legal advocacy organizations. Stakeholders were asked to refer parents and adolescents who would be vocal about challenges. We believed that clients of these organizations would provide us with a good sense of the more difficult end of the problem spectrum from which we might reach out to other, perhaps less severe, cases.

Data collection took place at nine locations throughout New York City and northern New Jersey. In addition to clinical settings and legal advocacy organizations (Stage 1), we recruited from ethnically based community organizations and immigrant mutual aid societies (Stage 2), and a summer camp organized by a mutual aid society (Stage 3). Sampling at Stage 2 was theoretical sampling oriented toward following up on issues raised during Stage 1. Stage 3 recruitment was taken largely because Stage 2 failed to result in the number of youths we needed to triangulate adult perspectives.

Participants

We conducted 18 focus groups (of 2 to 12 participants, M = 3.50) and 8 individual interviews; 11 were follow-up sessions, and thus in total we interviewed 13 focus group cohorts and 5 individuals—59 different individuals. Ages of the 32 adults ranged from 22 to 83 (M = 37.33) and of the 27 children from 12 to 25 (M = 16.22). Arrival in the United States ranged from 3 months to 19 years (M = 7.86 years) prior to the interviews. The sample was majority Muslim (n = 34, 58%) and ethnically diverse (17 different groups). Eleven countries of origin were represented.

Interview Guide, Data Collection, and Data Transcription

Upon arrival, participants were asked for informed consent for themselves and their children; children were asked for assent. All those referred consented/assented. The focus group and individual interviews ran 75 to 90 minutes in duration. We began with a request to describe challenges in participants' families in the previous 2 weeks. Following these descriptions, moderators steered the conversation using probes based on sensitizing concepts. After about 20 minutes, moderators asked participants where they sought help for these challenges. After rephrasing the initial query without the 2-week time horizon and discussing potential solutions, the interviews concluded. Families received $40 for transportation following interviews

We took several measures to ensure that raw data were captured as reliably as possible. All interviews were audiorecorded using two digital audiorecorders (Olympus WS-400 S) with external table microphones. In addition to moderators, focus group interviews were attended by note-takers, who recorded the order of speakers and notable behaviors. Transcription of audiorecorded data was done by note-takers for focus group interviews and by either interviewers or research assistants for individual interviews. Moderators reviewed transcriptions while listening to audiorecordings and met with transcribers to finalize transcriptions.

Data Analysis

We began analyses immediately following the first focus groups, with researchers reviewing audiorecordings and identifying salient themes while they were being transcribed. Once transcribed, investigators returned to the first three focus groups to begin open coding. We open coded the first transcript by hand and then met to examine overlap in open codes. Open codes included events and objects (e.g., pregnancy, cell phone), conceptual categories (surveillance, stranger danger), and in vivo codes (codes indicated by the use of spoken phrases that indicated categories; e.g., "wrong place at wrong time," "racism").

Following agreement on codes, the team coded the second and third transcripts and then met again to reduce the number of open codes through categorizing and elimination and then finalized axial codes. Our final list included 22 axial codes. Going forward, two investigators independently coded and memoed each transcript using ATLAS.ti software, merged coded documents, and discussed each selection of coded text in order to come to consensus. In practice, 22 codes turned out to be too many to track simultaneously, and much of consensus coding sessions was spent pointing out missed sections of text that should have been coded with particular codes but were not. Following consensus coding, documents were merged into a single file that included transcriptions, coded text, and memos (a "hermeneutic unit," in ATLAS.ti terminology) for analysis.

Because we were particularly interested in problem-solving processes, we examined the intersection of codes signifying conflict and those signifying particular actors to come up with our theoretical codes. Initial codes for parent–child conflict included "parent/child," "disciplining and monitoring," and "interpersonal conflict," and, for intimate partner conflict, "spouses," "gender roles," and "interpersonal conflict" (for code definitions, see Rasmussen et al., 2013). Examining overlap between codes and relevant memos produced the theoretical codes that were then built into our theoretical model.

Results

The findings here illustrate how grounded theory data might be presented in publication. Within the WAFP data were four levels of problem-solving resources: individual/dyadic, extended family (i.e., microsystem; Bronfenbrenner, 1979), community leadership (mesosystem), and state-sanctioned authorities (exosystem). We organized our presentation of data by these levels, presenting data from parents and children (for parent–child conflict) and adult women and men (for intimate partner conflict). In the following excerpts, participants are identified by gender and age, and researchers by initials. (For a more complete illustration of our findings, see Rasmussen et al., 2013.)

A clear message from examining the overlap between relevant codes was that new economic and political realities of living in the United States affected more conservative, traditional ways of doing things. For instance, conflict between spouses was often presented as the result of traditional gender roles, in which men are primary providers and women did not earn money, being transposed across the Atlantic Ocean to a city where both spouses needed to be bread winners to survive and meet financial obligations to family in home countries. A 33-year-old woman from Sierra Leone described this dyadic-level conflict:

> F33: Back home, the women don't work. The women stay home. From the market to the kitchen. Not all of them are allowed to work.
>
> AR: M-hm.
>
> F33: And, so you don't complain, because over there, you don't pay house bill.... But over here, when the bill is too much and you come from the poor family—like me, I lost my father, I don't have nobody to take care of my mother. So I will not sit here and watch my mother dying with hunger, while I have the opportunity to do a job.

More extreme examples of traditional ways of problem solving clashing with new realities concerned responses to intimate partner violence. Intimate partner violence (IPV) was often addressed theoretically within extended family (the microsystem) or community (mesosystem) spheres, but these intersected with new host-country exosystem forces (i.e., state-sanctioned authorities). A 40-year-old Mauritanian man described how community leadership was supposed to operate in response to IPV:

> M40: In African community we have elders, we have people who come talk to the guy. Yeah, we can say, first step, go to them, tell them what's happen.... I know, these uh Guinean people, Sierra Leone people, they got a lot of people, the Imam or the people of... community organization they have, they can say to the guy, "You *wrong*."

Unfortunately, these interactions were not often resolved this way and instead were typically resolved by women choosing between acceptance by families and their own safety. The same 33-year-old woman from Sierra Leone explained that after she had sought police help following IPV, her extended family intervened to coerce her into apologizing to him and returning home: "So my uncle from the Bronx took me, go up to the shelter and pick me up. I stay with him for some month. They [raises voice:] get together, family talk, they give me, they say I'm [laughs] wrong, because why I do it."

In discussions of parent–child conflict we found similar thematic codes surrounding traditional modes of doing things paired with thematic codes concerning the challenges of living in the United States. Adult participants almost universally lamented the loss of collective responsibility for monitoring children (i.e., mesosytemic phenomena). Two women, a 70-year-old from Sierra Leone and a 47-year-old from Mali, noted this:

> F70: //I see with young families in this, in this country. Whereas, back home in Africa, you don't have that problem.

F47: [nods] Uh huh.
F70: Because, you have your neighbors//
F47: //Yeah. You have your neighbor//
F70: //You have your in-laws, you have your old parents.//
F47: //taking care your kids//
F70: //Even if your parents aren't there, your neighbors are there.

In contrast, children reported that their parents still monitored them through other adults. A 15-year-old Sierra Leonean girl reported that a friend of her father's called her father in Sierra Leone to tell him that she was out in the evening with a boy in New York:

F15: Oh my God, hold on, let me tell you a funny one first [laughs]. One day my mom, she wanted some—some food from outside, so she told me—it was like around 11:00—she told me to go get it for her, and my friend that came sleep over, so, she came with me//
TC: //M-hm.//
F15: //and then this guy, I don't know which one of his friends, call my dad all the way in Africa, telling him he saw me with a boy at night [laughs]. I was laughing, my dad called us the next morning, talking about how my mom letting me now have a boyfriend, and how [laughs], I couldn't help myself, it was funny. Like how did that happened? . . . . I mean, he's all the way in Africa!

Perceptions of the consequences of the results of interactions with public authorities was illustrated for parent–child conflict in discussions surrounding children's reactions to corporal punishment. An 18-year-old Liberian girl discussed the practice of sending children back to home countries in response to involving state authorities in disciplinary problems:

F18: If a person call the police on their parents [looks at TC]//
TC: //What did the parents do?
F18: Uh-m probably hit them, beat them, so . . . they call the police. If someone call the police on their parents//
TC: //Uh-uh//
F18: //If the parents don't go to jail, do you think that parent's gonna keep that child? No, they're going back [hand gesture].

During the process of interviewing and coding we wrote memos in our audit trail. The following memo, written by the first author following an interview with a woman living in a domestic violence shelter, is an example. Such reflections provided the fodder for developing our theoretical codes.

> As I was riding home this afternoon (on a 2 express train that was running local) I kept thinking about the "solving problems" theme and how it's a major part of why we're doing what we're doing. Several people have told us (in every adult interview/group anyways) that they either don't go to anyone for help or that they keep things inside their family and that they don't like it when outside forces (e.g., letters from school explaining that their children need special services) "intrude" upon their lives. This preference for insularity is seen as a real strength in some cases . . . and seen as a real problem in other cases—like the woman today. There are different levels of insularity, probably dependent on the type of problem and the resources available . . . but it's always about solving problems internally. For some, this is an extension of an emphasis on traditional culture, or at least the version of it that they remember or maybe some version that they are able to re-create here.

Building a Grounded Theory

From overlapping codes combined with memos, we built a multilevel theoretical model, our grounded theory. This theory described how immigrants from West African countries drew on resources within their social ecologies when trying to solve social problems and how these behaviors interacted with public authorities to reinforce suspicion of the public authorities and push the immigrant groups to become more conservative. Evident in the data was that traditional modes of solving family problems had been strained across migration. This strain seems to have resulted from attempts to recreate the model within a new setting in which (a) financial pressures translate into new family responsibilities, (b) the state has an interest in

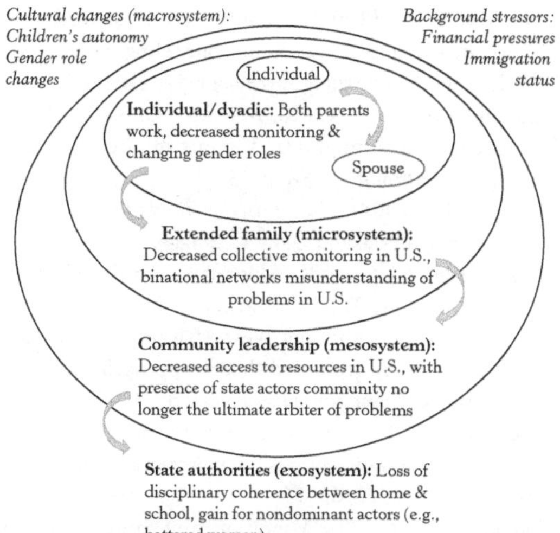

FIGURE 3.1: The social ecology of West African immigrants' problem solving.

Source: "The social ecology of resolving family conflict among West African immigrants in New York: A grounded theory approach.," by A. Rasmussen, T. Chu, A. M. Akinsulure-Smith, and E. Keatley, 2013, *American Journal of Community Psychology, 52(1-2)*, p. 193, Figure 1. Reprinted with kind permission from Springer Science and Business Media.

family functioning, and (c) the institutions that accompany this interest (e.g., child protective services, domestic violence shelters, police) ultimately hold power over traditional community structures.

Visual representations of data are particularly useful for representing theory. Figure 3.1 presents our theory on a background of stressors reported by participants that characterize their immigrant experience and cultural changes related to challenges to family well-being. Arrows indicate the paths by which participants seek out help in solving family conflict. The reluctance of actors to seek help beyond extended family networks because of the threat of shame and isolation is represented in Figure 3.1 by a thick line between micro- and mesosystems.

Integration With Existing Theory

Following the development of grounded theory from their data, researchers can then integrate existing theory and compare their findings to those in the extant literature. We believed that our multilevel model of solving family problems was best compared to Sluzki's (1979) stage model of conflict within migrating families. Parallel to decreasing family functioning a few years postmigration, the social ecology experiences instability. Also helpful was conservation of resources (COR) theory (Hobfoll, 2001), in which stress results from threats to existing resources. COR theory provided a more practicable interpretation for helping professionals interested in addressing the change in new immigrants' problem-solving social ecology. In the language of COR theory, the social ecological change represented in the model would reflect a loss spiral (Hobfoll, 2001), in which losses beget further losses, proceeding through the successive levels of analysis. Contextualizing our socio-ecological theory of solving family conflict within these grand theories allowed us to extend the model for future research with other immigrant populations that migrate from societies that are on balance more conservative than those they migrate to and have little sense that public institutions should be involved in family life.

CONCLUSION

Grounded theory is commensurate with many of the goals espoused by community psychologists: relying on empiricism, representing authentic voices, and developing theoretical models that remain faithful to those voices. To attain these goals, grounded theory eschews intensive review of research prior to engaging with participants, instead relying on sensitizing concepts and a specific set of processes to begin. Through the use of several key components—theoretical sampling, CCM, iterative coding, memoing, and theoretical saturation—researchers build substantive theory from their data. This theory is emergent in that it arises from granular examination of the data, substantiated and trustworthy by nature of a close reading—in a word, grounded.

REFERENCES

Akinsulure-Smith, A. M. (2012). Using group work to rebuild family and community ties among displaced African men. *Journal for Specialists in Group Work, 37*, 95–112.

Banyard, V. L., & Miller, K. E. (1998). The powerful potential of qualitative research for community psychology. *American Journal of Community Psychology, 26*, 485–505.

Blumer, H. (1969). *Symbolic interactionism: Perspective and method*. Englewood Cliffs, NJ: Prentice Hall.

Bronfenbrenner, U. (1979). *The ecology of human development: Experiments by nature and design*. Cambridge, MA: Harvard University Press.

Charmaz, K. (2014). *Constructing grounded theory* (2nd ed.). Thousand Oaks, CA: Sage.

Glaser, B. (1992). *Basics of grounded theory analysis: Emergence vs. forcing.* Mill Valley, CA: Sociology Press.

Glaser, B., & Strauss, A. (1967). *The discovery of grounded theory.* Chicago, IL: Aldine.

Hobfoll, S. E. (2001). The influence of culture, community, and the nested-self in the stress process: Advancing conservation of resources theory. *Applied Psychology: An International Review, 5*, 337–421.

Holton, J. A. (2007). The coding processes and its challenges. In A. Bryant & K. Charmaz (Eds.), *The Sage handbook of grounded theory* (pp. 265–290). Thousand Oaks, CA: Sage.

Hood, J. C. (2007). Orthodoxy v. power: The defining traits of grounded theory. In A. Bryant & K. Charmaz (Eds.), *The Sage handbook of grounded theory* (pp. 151–164). Thousand Oaks, CA: Sage.

Kelle, U. (2007). The development of categories: Different approaches to grounded theory. In A. Bryant & K. Charmaz (Eds.), *The Sage handbook of grounded theory* (pp. 191–213). Thousand Oaks, CA: Sage.

Lempert, L. B. (2007). Asking questions of the data: Memo writing in the grounded theory tradition. In A. Bryant & K. Charmaz (Eds.), *The Sage handbook of grounded theory* (pp. 245–264). Thousand Oaks, CA: Sage.

Morrow, S. L. (2005). Quality and trustworthiness in qualitative research in counseling psychology. *Journal of Counseling Psychology, 52*, 250–260.

Ogiehor-Enoma, G. (2010, May 15). Children of first generation immigrants: Victims of circumstances. *African Abroad—USA*, p. 35.

Padgett, D. (2008). *Qualitative methods in social work research.* Thousand Oaks, CA: Sage.

Rasmussen, A., Chu, T., Akinsulure-Smith, A. M., & Keatley, E. (2013). The social ecology of resolving family conflict among West African immigrants in New York: A grounded theory approach. *American Journal of Community Psychology, 52*, 185–196.

Shenton, A. K. (2004). Strategies for ensuring trustworthiness in qualitative research projects. *Education for Information, 22*, 63–75.

Sluzki, C. E. (1979). Migration and family conflict. *Family Process, 18*, 379–390.

Stewart, E. (2000). Thinking through others: Qualitative research and community psychology. In J. Rappaport & E. Seidman (Eds.), *Handbook of community psychology* (pp. 725–736). New York, NY: Kluwer Academic.

van den Hoonaard, W. C. (1997). *Working with sensitizing concepts: Analytical field research.* Thousand Oaks, CA: Sage.

Watt, D. (2007). On becoming a qualitative researcher: The value of reflexivity. *Qualitative Report, 12*, 82–101.

4

Thematic Analysis

STEPHANIE RIGER AND RANNVEIG SIGURVINSDOTTIR

Thematic analysis is a method for analyzing qualitative data that involves searching for recurring ideas (referred to as *themes*) in a data set. This chapter discusses the value of thematic analysis for community psychologists and describes, as an application of this method, a study of how a domestic violence court addressed substance abuse problems among both defendants and victims. In this study, we used an open-ended, inductive style of interviewing, typical of qualitative methods, that allowed us to capture the perspective of various actors in the court system, including judges, probation officers, victim advocates, and court administrators, as well as those who work in agencies that serve clients with a record of substance abuse and domestic violence. Thematic analysis enabled us to identify ideas common across these interviews.

INTRODUCTION TO THEMATIC ANALYSIS

Theoretical Basis of Thematic Analysis

Thematic analysis is a type of qualitative method. The APA PsychNET defines a qualitative study primarily as one that does not emphasize quantification: "a type of research methodology that produces descriptive data, with little emphasis given to numerical quantification" (Thesaurus of Psychological Index Terms, 2007). However, this defines qualitative research by what it is not, namely quantitative. Those who take a strictly methodological approach define qualitative research by the tools used to generate nonquantified data, such as case studies or focus groups, but that hardly captures the essence of interpretive qualitative methods, which involve a search for the meaning of phenomena to participants (Banyard & Miller, 1998). A basic assumption of this approach is that what is real is socially constructed. In other words, people attribute meaning to particular phenomena in interaction with those around them in context-specific settings. How people make sense of their experience is the focus of the research. Because various people may differ in their understandings, there is no single, fixed reality apart from people's interpretations. Researchers working from a critical theory perspective add a focus on the importance of power in shaping people's viewpoints, emphasizing the issues of dominance and control (Schensul, 2012). Thus, people's interpretations of phenomena may differ, perhaps as a function of their location in a social system's hierarchy, and multiple versions of reality may coexist.

The constructionist perspective conflicts with the postpositivist approach dominant in psychology today, which assumes that there is a measurable reality independent of our perceptions. The postpositivist perspective emphasizes hypothesis testing and a search for causal relationships among variables, while the constructionist approach seeks to understand the subjective meaning people put on their experience (Eagly & Riger, 2014). However, qualitative data may be used in a postpositive, deductive manner to test hypotheses. For example, qualitative data may be coded, counted, and then treated quantitatively in statistical analyses. Alternatively, qualitative data may be used as an adjunct to quantitative data, either to develop hypotheses then tested quantitatively or to expand on quantitative findings. In contrast, our focus here is on the interpretive, inductive process of identifying themes in a textual data set. In studying the domestic violence court, we sought to understand how actors in a specific context viewed the co-occurrence of domestic violence and substance abuse; we did not quantify the data or test preexisting theories. This approach to qualitative research is uncommon in many areas of psychology. Examination of psychology journal articles coded in PsycINFO as empirical found that only 8.7% were classified as qualitative-only, while that percentage shrank to 1.8% in the 30 journals considered most influential in psychology as identified by their 5-year impact factor scores (Eagly & Riger, 2014). There are signs, though, of increasing interest among psychologists in qualitative methods, including the establishment of a new journal, *Qualitative Methods*; the formation of the Society for Qualitative Inquiry in Psychology; and chapters on qualitative methods in psychology research methods handbooks.

Stages in Thematic Analysis

Thematic analysis involves proceeding through a series of steps that focus on the identification of recurring themes or ideas in a textual data set. Organizing information into themes is a process that forms the core of many qualitative approaches. For example, content analysis similarly may involve coding data but then treats the codes statistically, for example, looking at the frequency with which certain codes are present. In contrast, thematic analysis does not involve statistical analysis. Grounded theory also seeks to identify patterns in qualitative material, but ongoing analyses while data are being collected guide further data collection. In thematic analysis, data analysis does not begin until all data are collected. However, similar to grounded theory, thematic analysis seeks to develop theories that are based on the data.

Typically, a researcher conducting thematic analysis will work with interview data and inductively attempt to derive themes that are present (Pistrang & Barker, 2013). All themes in a given data set may be identified, or the focus may be on a specific theme, which allows examination in more detail (Braun & Clarke, 2006). Themes could be either implicit or explicit ideas that are present in the data set. They usually emerge multiple times within each interview as well as between interviews with different people. A theme also needs to capture something important in relation to the research question and something salient to participants. How exactly this is done depends on the purpose and theoretical framework of the study, but it is important to be consistent in identifying and developing themes.

Auerbach and Silverstein (2003) described the process of analyzing qualitative data as moving up a staircase, starting with raw text, then identifying relevant text, then finding repeating ideas, and then grouping these into themes. Once themes are identified, theoretical construction may begin. In thematic analysis, this process proceeds in a particular set of stages, as described by Braun and Clarke (2006):

Stage 1: Immersing oneself in the data. This stage involves transcribing interviews and reading the transcripts repeatedly. Transcribing is a time-consuming process but may be useful to become familiar with the data and offers the opportunity to begin to think about possible codes. While reading transcripts, a researcher should actively look for meanings and patterns. At this point, it may be useful to make notes on potential coding categories that could be further developed in subsequent analyses.

Stage 2: Generating initial codes. Once researchers are familiar with the data, they can identify an initial list of codes. Braun and Clarke (2006) contrasted data-driven codes that emerge inductively from the data set with theory-driven ones that respond to a specific question used to guide the analysis. Codes enable organization of the data into meaningful units, but they are not yet themes, which are broader and may capture several codes. Data may be coded manually or by computer. If one is coding manually, Braun and Clarke (2013) recommended writing notes or placing post-it notes on the texts, using highlighters or colored pens to enable the visual identification of repetitions. At this point, it is critical to code for as many potential themes as possible, as the value of some codes may become apparent later in the process, and more than one code may apply to portions of the data set.

Stage 3: Searching for themes. Once the data have been coded and material falling under the same codes has been brought together, a search for themes may begin. This stage involves considering how different codes may fit together into broader themes.

Themes may be organized hierarchically, with higher order themes and subthemes, or in networks of interlocking ideas (Attride-Stirling, 2001). Braun and Clarke (2013) suggested that visual representations such as tables or drawings may be helpful. At this point, a list of potential themes may exist, as well as codes that do not fit into any theme.

Stage 4: Reviewing themes. Once a set of potential themes is identified, they need to be reviewed and refined. Some potential themes may not be relevant to the research question, while others might be combined into broader ideas or divided into separate themes. There should be clear coherence of data within themes and equally distinct boundaries between themes. Two processes now occur: The first is to evaluate whether the coded extracts that make up a particular theme fit together, and the second is to assess whether the themes as a whole capture the entire data set. Braun and Clarke (2013) suggested rereading the entire data set at this point to capture any data that fit within themes but were omitted in earlier coding.

Stage 5: Defining and naming themes. Once a thematic map of the data exists, further refinement of the themes may occur. The critical task here is to identify the central idea in each theme and provide a name that concisely captures that idea. Subthemes may be described that capture dimensions of a theme. Braun and Clarke (2013) suggested writing a detailed analysis of each individual theme and how it fits into the overall picture of the data set.

Stage 6: Producing the report. Once themes and their interrelationships are fully identified, a research report may be written. The report should present the analysis in a way that the reader sees as trustworthy. This may involve including data extracts that distinctly illustrate the themes, as well as discussion of the decisions that were made during the process of the study. Braun and Clarke (2013) emphasized that the report of the study needs to go beyond simply a description of the data to make an argument. They raised critical questions that need addressing: "What does this theme mean? What are the assumptions underpinning it? What are the implications of this theme? What conditions are likely to have given rise to it? Why do people talk about this thing this particular way (as opposed to other ways)? What is the overall story the different themes reveal about the topic?" (p. 94)

The Value of Thematic Analysis

Banyard and Miller (1998) offered three reasons for the use of qualitative methods: (a) Such methods are consistent with the core values of community psychology; (b) they may be used to develop culturally anchored quantitative methods; and (c) they are useful for understanding the subjective meanings that people give to their experience that then give rise to certain behaviors. Thematic analysis meets all of these criteria.

Others argue that qualitative methods are valuable because the richness of qualitative data permits in-depth examination of nuances and contradictions, as well as the development of theory in underresearched areas (Pistrang & Barker, 2013). Perhaps most important is that qualitative methods allow access to meaning in context. They offer the opportunity to explore an issue in depth without the use of preordained analytic categories that may limit a participant's response or a researcher's investigation. Today there is a press for "evidence-based practice" that privileges randomized controlled methods and hypothesis testing, but such deductive methods may not be appropriate for all research questions. Not all people may respond to a situation in the same way and responses may vary depending on the setting. Particularly in a field such as community psychology where diversity is valued, inductive approaches such as thematic analysis allow an understanding of complexity and context-specific variation.

Qualitative methods such as thematic analysis are also valued as a means of giving voice to "the other," that is, of allowing those traditionally unrepresented or underrepresented in research to present their viewpoints in their own words, unhindered by predetermined response categories (Pistrang & Barker, 2013). Although quantitative research also may capture the responses of those who traditionally have been marginalized, qualitative methods may allow more unfettered communication. In addition, those who believe that research should include an action agenda, intended to address injustices and bring about social change, may prefer qualitative methods because of the relatively more equal relationship between researchers and participants (Creswell, 2007).

All of these apply to thematic analysis. Additionally, thematic analysis has one major strength over other qualitative approaches, which is its considerable flexibility while remaining rigorous. Moreover, thematic analysis can be used across a variety of different theoretical frameworks and worldviews. These may differ depending on the theoretical orientation of the researcher or vary by the question being asked (Braun & Clarke, 2006), yet thematic analysis as a method for examining qualitative data may be widely useful. In addition, thematic analysis is relatively straightforward and accessible.

Issues to Consider

Although analyzing qualitative data using the stages previously outlined may appear to be straightforward, there are several pitfalls that may occur (Braun & Clarke, 2013). The first is a failure to develop an overall analysis of the data and instead simply presenting extracts of the data set. The second is simply using the interview questions to organize the data, in which case no analysis has been done. The third is an analysis that is not sufficiently grounded in the data, misinterprets the data, or does not persuade the reader of the argument being made. The reader may be hesitant to accept the argument being made if there is no attempt to consider data that contradict the main argument. Finally, a weak thematic analysis is one that fails to consider the theoretical framework that guides the work. Perhaps most important is that there be a good fit between what one claims and the supporting evidence, that is, that the analysis is clearly supported by data.

Critics of qualitative work assert that it is anecdotal or that researchers can selectively pick the data elements they want to make an argument rather than systematically analyzing a data set. Furthermore, those trained in quantiative methods may raise concerns about validity and reliability in thematic analysis. Traditionally, validity refers to the extent to which researchers' claims about knowledge correspond to the reality they are studying (Eisner & Peshkin, 1990), while reliability refers to whether consistent results are obtained when the same measures are used repeatedly. These concepts pose challenges for all qualitative research methods, including thematic analysis. The interpretive perspective in qualitative research rejects the idea of a singular reality that is independent of our perception of it. Complicating validity still further, participants may see things differently over time or may fail to recall events, and the process of data collection itself may affect participants' views (Johnson & Waterfield, 2004). Consequently, the question of whether research findings conform to reality is inappropriate. Instead, Lincoln and Guba (1985) proposed four criteria for judging qualitative research: credibility, transferability, dependability, and confirmability. Credibility refers to whether the research participant finds the results believable. Because the aim is to describe the participant's worldview, participants are the best judge of accuracy in this case. Asking participants to comment on the researchers' interpretations and auditing field notes and other data by a researcher not directly involved in the study are ways of testing the credibility of the data (Barker & Pistrang, 2005). Transferability refers to the extent to which findings may apply to other settings, while dependability requires demonstrating that findings are consistent and could be repeated, perhaps by the inclusion in research reports of detailed description of data collection methods. Finally, confirmability refers to showing that the findings could be corroborated by others and are not biased by the researcher's values. For example, the researcher could describe a search for negative instances that challenge the interpretation of data or could keep an "audit trail" of work for others to review. These characteristics make up "trustworthiness," Lincoln and Guba's (1985) term for the rigor of research.

Some see these standards as unique to qualitative research, while others view these concepts as loosely parallel to those in quantitative research (Winters, 2013). For example, credibility may be seen as the parallel to internal validity, while transferability parallels external validity. Dependability is similar in concept to reliability in quantitative research, while confirmability is the counterpart of objectivity. However, the constructivist assumptions underlying qualitative research place boundaries on the extent to which these concepts overlap. Quantitative research typically is rooted in a realist epistemology, which assumes that there is a real world independent of our perceptions of it against which validity claims can be tested. Interpretive qualitative research such as thematic analysis, in contrast, is based in the constructionist view that because there is no objective reality independent of our perceptions of it, it is impossible to verify our perceptions against a "real" world (Pistrang & Barker, 2013). Although qualitative research may be conducted from a realist perspective, here we discuss interpretive qualitative research based on a constructionist view of the world.

All research is vulnerable to being swayed by the personal values and beliefs of the researcher. This is a particularly sensitive issue in qualitative research, as the researcher becomes the measurement instrument, asking questions and making observations. Thematic analysis is less structured than quantitative research, raising more opportunities for the researcher to influence the outcome. Researchers bring their worldviews, their values, and their life experience into the research process. Reflexivity, the process of critical reflection by researchers about their impact on their research, is designed to work against the possibility of undue influence. Reflexivity might include researchers' reflections on their choice of methods and their assumptions about the phenomena under study or discussion of how their identities or background might affect the research process. The purpose of reflexivity is not to reduce bias, which assumes that complete objectivity is possible. Rather, reflexivity requires researchers to consider how their way of looking at the world may shape the research process, in both detrimental and productive ways (Bailey, 2012). The critical issue is the extent to which the research process is transparent, not whether it is biased (Johnson & Waterfield, 2004).

Transparency may be increased by reviewing notes or memos that researchers write during the course of a study. Memos may include discussion of potential codes and themes, as well as decisions made while data are collected. Memos may also include discussion of any personal characteristics or experiences that might influence the research. These might go beyond personal demographics to include previous experience with the subject under investigation. Such factors may not necessarily be negative, as they may alert researchers to subtle distinctions of the phenomenon under study and may increase trust from research participants, facilitating the research process (Barker & Pistrang, 2005).

CASE STUDY

Domestic violence (DV) courts are based on a problem-solving approach to justice that aims not simply to punish but also to rehabilitate. A common obstacle to rehabilitation is substance abuse, as DV and substance abuse often co-occur among both victims and perpetrators (Brookoff, O'Brien, Cook, Thompson, & Williams, 1997; Campbell, 2002). Therefore, a number of people who come through a DV court are likely to also have a substance abuse problem. The goal of our study was to examine how a DV court treats substance abuse, both by offenders and victims. A detailed account of this study may be found in Riger, Bennett, and Sigurvinsdottir (2014).

We employed a constructionist perspective in our study. Because a DV court is a complex setting, it is unlikely that everyone in it will see an issue the same way. Our goal was to understand how different actors view the co-occurrence of DV and substance abuse in court and how those views are shaped by their roles and positions of power. We therefore interviewed people in a range of positions in the court and used thematic analysis to analyze the interviews because of its flexible yet rigorous nature, which would allow synthesis of different viewpoints into a coherent narrative.

The DV court in this study was located in a large Midwestern metropolitan area and was established in 1985. The court hears cases of violence by intimate partners and by family members or roommates who hit, choke, kick, threaten, harass, or interfere with the personal liberty of another family or household member. The court has connections with local batterer intervention programs and victim advocates but no formal connection with agencies that treat substance abuse. In 2011, the criminal side of the court conducted an average of 900 hearings per week (Office of the State's Attorney, 2011). A previous study of 899 offenders passing through the court showed that most (67%) were ethnic and racial minorities, few (17%) had postsecondary education, and the rate of full-time employment (57%) was low (Bennett & O'Brien, 2007).

In order to study the court in detail, we needed approval to gain access to the court and its workers. The two senior authors of the study had worked with local DV agencies for many years and knew the administrator of the court. After getting support from the administrator, we wrote to the Chief Judge describing the proposed study and requesting approval to conduct interviews with members of the court. The study was approved by the Chief Judge as well as by the university's Institutional Review Board. The administrator then notified members of the court about the study, and we recruited key informants located in various roles throughout the court. In addition, we also interviewed key members of batterer intervention programs and substance abuse and domestic violence agencies.

Sample

We used purposive sampling, which involves deliberate selection of participants who are knowledgeable about the topic under study (Johnson & Waterfield, 2004). To obtain a broad picture of the court, we interviewed judges, public defenders, state's attorneys, probation officers, the court administrator, advocates for victims, advocates for offenders, and a pro bono legal advocate. Most DV courts link to community agencies, such as programs for batterers or agencies that serve victims of domestic violence, and we also interviewed representatives from those agencies, totaling 22 key informant interviews, which usually lasted about 1 hour. All interviews were audiotaped with the participants' permission. The interviews were unstructured, but all participants were asked about how substance abuse becomes visible and is addressed by the court.

Procedure

We recruited participants by telephone; all those contacted agreed to be interviewed, although seven public defenders chose to submit written statements rather than be interviewed. Participants were asked how the court identifies substance abuse, how often they see substance abuse problems in court, how much of a problem they believe it is, how it comes up in court, and what they thought should be done about it, if anything. Each of these questions was tailored to participants' roles. An undergraduate assistant transcribed the interviews. In addition to the interview transcripts, we also observed the court in session several times and took notes during the process. These were not directly analyzed but informed our thinking about the data and emerging themes.

Analysis

Once the interviews were completed, data analysis proceeded according to the steps outlined by Braun and Clark (2006).

1. *Immersing oneself in the data.* During this phase, we became very familiar with the data. This happened in two phases. First, we conducted the interviews, asking the participants about substance abuse and the DV court. We listened to each participant, made notes during the interview. and informally discussed the content with each other during the data collection process. During the second phase, the two senior researchers read the interview transcripts repeatedly to understand not only the content of the interviews but also to identify nuanced differences in people's viewpoints.
2. *Generating initial codes.* The two senior researchers independently generated codes with the goal of organizing the data into meaningful units. Braun and Clark (2006) referred to coding done with specific research questions in mind as theory-driven coding, as opposed to more general data-driven coding in which specific issues to be examined in the data are not predetermined. It quickly became obvious in reading the interviews that a number of barriers prevent substance abuse from being identified and addressed within the court, and coding was done with an eye to examining those barriers. Each of the two senior researchers therefore went through the interview transcripts repeatedly to identify how and why substance abuse becomes apparent and is addressed in DV court. They also identified important differences in participants' views. For example, both of the researchers noticed that the issue of substance abuse came up in very different ways for those working with victims and those working with perpetrators in the court.

3. *Searching for themes.* After generating an initial set of codes, the two senior researchers compared their findings. For each code, they had identified quotes from the interviews to support their points. The researchers came up with slightly different, but significantly overlapping, themes. They discussed the themes, looking for commonalities in their analyses, and were able to integrate both of their coding schemes into one. The codes were reorganized into themes and subthemes.

   The combination of the two researchers' coding systems yielded the following themes: structural constraints (e.g., bounded role definitions precluding attention to substance abuse); economic constraints (e.g., lack of funds for substance abuse treatment); and negative attitudes of court and community personnel about the survivors of domestic violence (e.g., seeing the survivor as provoking violence).
4. *Reviewing themes.* At this point, Braun and Clark (2006) recommended reviewing and refining themes to see if some might be eliminated (as not sufficiently supported by the data) or combined. They recommended considering whether there is coherence within themes and sufficient distinctions among them. Up to this point, the two senior researchers had carried out all of the data analysis. The third researcher had read the transcripts but had not generated codes or themes. Now the third researcher read the entire data set with the three themes in mind in order to examine whether the themes fit the data closely and to assess coherence and distinction. The third researcher searched for quotes in the data that both supported and negated each of the themes. All three researchers then examined these findings and agreed that the themes represented the data and that all three themes were present across all the interviews.
5. *Defining and naming themes.* Next all three researchers met to discuss the themes, identify the essential features of each, and clarify the main point of each theme and any important subthemes. Each theme was given a name that captured its essential meaning. The researchers then reviewed a list of quotes drawn from the interview transcripts that were identified for each theme and chose the quotes that best exemplified the themes.
6. *Producing the report.* Braun and Clark (2006) emphasized that the report needs to contain an argument rather than merely describe the data. The argument that we made is that substance abuse is not identified or addressed in DV court because of specific barriers. For example, structural constraints, such as circumscribed roles, push legal actors to focus on violence and ignore substance abuse. Moreover, the court is an adversarial system, which prevents the identification of substance abuse because it would be harmful to both defendants and complainants. Negative attitudes toward victims can also prevent the identification and intervention of substance abuse. Finally, a lack of resources puts strain on the court and connected systems, making it even less likely that co-occurring DV and substance abuse among victims and perpetrators will be addressed. The report was written in the form of a journal article, which was published in an academic journal (Riger et al., 2014).

Reliability and Validity

Reliability checking takes a different form in a qualitative project than in a quantitative one. Lincoln and Guba's (1985) criteria of trustworthiness for judging qualitative research are to evaluate credibility, transferability, dependability, and confirmability. Credibility involves seeing whether the participants find the results believable. We had intended to present the report to the court and had asked for a meeting in which to do so, but such a meeting was never scheduled, so it was not possible to get participants' reactions to the report.

Transferability refers to whether the findings may apply to other settings. Some of the results found in this study are likely to be found in other DV courts because they are produced by overarching systemic factors, such as the organization of the legal system. Whether negative attitudes would also be found in other DV courts remains to be seen. Dependability refers to whether the findings are consistent and repeatable from the existing data, which is supported by the fact that two researchers independently found similar themes that were then reviewed by the third researcher. Finally, confirmability refers to whether findings can be corroborated by others and are not influenced by the researcher's values. To meet these criteria, the researchers looked for negative cases that challenged each of the themes. All of these factors support the study's reliability and validity.

Reflexivity

We approached the court as outsiders with no stake in the court system. The first two researchers are professors and the third is a graduate student; all identify as feminists. All three had worked with victims of domestic violence, the first two researchers for decades, and their sympathies lie with survivors of violence. Yet the researchers attempted to remain neutral during interviews so that respondents would express their opinions freely. No one, including victim advocates, hesitated to criticize victims. The researchers found themselves surprised and a bit shocked by the negative attitudes toward victims that were encountered in the court, but the negativity was not entirely clear until the data analysis was complete. Therefore, we do not think our attitudes affected data collection or analysis.

Limitations

Thematic analysis is a flexible method that allows analysis of qualitative data that is typically collected through interviews and observations. As with all qualitative research, as noted earlier, it is vulnerable to the beliefs and values of those who employ it. As is usual in qualitative studies, the results may be confined to the context in which they are gathered and may not generalize beyond this setting. The intention of this study was not to develop generalizable findings but rather to understand how actors in a particular context understood that situation. In addition to the possibility of skewed results, other problems potentially exist. The researchers obtained access to the court because of preexisting relationships with the court administrator; others may find access to a research site difficult. There are also practical problems in thematic analysis. Repeatedly reading interviews can be time-consuming and tedious, and consistent themes may not always emerge. Finally, this study required three people to do the analysis, which may not always be possible.

CONCLUSION

In this chapter, we have briefly reviewed the conceptual basis, purpose, and process of thematic analysis. In our example, we used thematic analysis to systematically identify patterns of meaning in data collected from many people who work in a DV court. This method allowed recognition of important differences in how people conceptualize DV and substance abuse, as well as how systemic factors in the legal system hinder the identification of these co-occurring problems.

Thematic analysis is a flexible and accessible method which we would encourage researchers to employ when they have complex qualitative data but want a systematic and rigorous approach to accurately represent those data. Qualitative data from studies that focus on people in context are typically rich and multifaceted, making thematic analysis an important addition to the toolbox of any community psychologist.

REFERENCES

Attride-Stirling, J. (2001). Thematic networks: An analytic tool for qualitative research. *Qualitative research, 1*, 385–405.

Auerbach, C. F., & Silverstein, L. B. (2003). *Qualitative data: An introduction to coding and analysis.* New York, NY: New York University Press.

Bailey, L. E. (2012). Feminist research. In S. D. Lapan, M. T. Quartarol, & F. J. Riemer (Eds.), *Qualitative research: An introduction to methods and designs* (pp. 391–423). San Francisco, CA: Josey-Bass.

Banyard, V. L., & Miller, K. E. (1998). The powerful potential of qualitative research for community psychology. *American Journal of Community Psychology, 26*, 485–505.

Barker, C., & Pistrang, N. (2005). Quality criteria under methodological pluralism: Implications for conducting and evaluating research. *American Journal of Community Psychology, 35*, 201–212.

Bennett, L.W., & O'Brien, P. (2007). Effects of coordinated services for drug-abusing women who are victims of intimate partner violence. *Violence Against Women, 13*, 395–411.

Braun, V., & Clarke, V. (2006). Using thematic analysis in psychology. *Qualitative Research in Psychology, 3*, 77–101.

Braun, V., & Clarke, V. (2013) *Successful qualitative research: A practical guide for beginners.* London, England: Sage.

Brookoff, D., O'Brien, K. K., Cook, C. S., Thompson, T. D., & Williams, C. (1997). Characteristics of participants in domestic violence: Assessment at the scene of domestic assault. *Journal of the American Medical Association, 277,* 1369–1373.

Campbell, J. C. (2002). Health consequences of intimate partner violence. *Lancet, 359,* 1331–1336.

Creswell, J. W. (2007). *Qualitative inquiry and research design: Choosing among five approaches* (2nd ed.). Thousand Oaks, CA: Sage.

Eagly, A. H., & Riger, S. (2014). Feminism and psychology: Critiques of methods and epistemology. *American Psychologist, 69,* 685–702.

Eisner, E. W., & Peshkin, A. (Eds.). (1990). *Qualitative inquiry in education: The continuing debate.* New York, NY: Teachers College Press.

Johnson, R., & Waterfield, J. (2004). Making words count: The value of qualitative research. *Physiotherapy Research International, 9,* 121–131.

Lincoln, Y. S., & Guba, E. G. (1985). *Naturalistic inquiry.* Newbury Park, CA: Sage.

Office of the State's Attorney. (2011). *Domestic violence division: 2011 statistics.* Chicago, IL: County of Cook.

Pistrang, N., & Barker, C. (2013). Varieties of qualitative research: A pragmatic approach to selecting methods. In H. Cooper (Ed.). *APA handbook of research methods in psychology* (Vol. 2, pp. 5–18). Washington, DC: American Psychological Association.

Riger, S., Bennett, L. W., & Sigurvinsdottir, R. (2014). Barriers to addressing substance abuse in domestic violence court. *American Journal of Community Psychology, 53,* 208–217.

Schensul, J. J. (2012). Methodology, methods, and tools in qualitative research. In S. D. Lapan, M. T. Quartarol, & F. J. Riemer (Eds.), *Qualitative research: An introduction to methods and designs* (pp. 69–107). San Francisco, CA: Josey-Bass.

Thesaurus of psychological index terms (11th Ed., 2007). Washington, DC: American Psychological Association.

Winters, K. (2013). *Reliability and validity in qualitative research and handling qualitative data examples.* Retrieved June 2015, from http://www.academia.edu/3004263/Reliability_and_validity_in_qualitative_research_and_handling_qualitative_data_examples

5

Community Narratives

BRADLEY D. OLSON, DANIEL G. COOPER, JUDAH J. VIOLA, AND BRIAN CLARK

Seymour Sarason, perhaps *the* formative community psychologist, reflected in his later years that community psychology research and practice had focused too exclusively on specialized psychological concerns (Sarason, 2000). As Sarason wrote, community psychology

> . . . has lost its vision, imaginativeness, and initial purpose, a commitment to an overarching, cohering sense of responsibility to study, understand, and to have impact on communities. (p. 923)

Neither community psychologists nor other community-based researchers, Sarason believed, tended to examine "whole communities." They did not work to find barometers to measure otherwise undetectable changes in whole communities. Sarason (2000) wrote:

> Nothing in our psychological background could serve as a compass for thinking and action. The one thing we knew was that we had been ignorant of how the communities we lived in and worked in changed . . . . we knew that our focus had to be that complexity we call a community. Not this or that segment, subgroup, or problem, but the whole of it and the way it works and changes for good and bad. (p. 925)

Although understanding the complexity of "whole communities" in a holistic way—across people, space, and time—may require volumes of books, there is something to be said for Sarason's striving toward more expansive psychological, cultural, and political methods of conducting community science. Evaluations of a community-based effort can lead to fuller, deeper, and richer understandings of a community's ecology. Such research approaches can tell us better what does and does not work in an initiative, comparing initial goals with what happens over time in the complex reality of a particular community.

Holistic understandings of communities can be aided by statistical techniques, although quantitative approaches alone are insufficient. The holistic nature of communities, we argue, can be captured best through qualitative methods, and here we focus on the use of community narratives to understand whole communities of place. In the chapter, we highlight the importance of eliciting narratives from community stakeholders to capture a diverse range of community perspectives. We first present a conceptual overview of the community narrative approach, followed by sections on its methodology and on its strengths and limitations. We conclude with a case study using community narratives to evaluate Habitat for Humanity International's Neighborhood Revitalization (NR) initiative.

INTRODUCTION TO COMMUNITY NARRATIVES

Conceptual Overview

Community narratives use qualitative research tools in a collaborative process with community members. The tools include "story" and "narrative" to draw out of stakeholders rich, holistic, and ecological understandings and to eventually paint a picture of a community context or initiative. Too often, quantitative approaches focus on change scores or other indices of improvement, stagnation, or loss, rather than the whole temporal process of life events. The real changes that transpire in whole communities occur qualitatively, in more complex ways than can be placed on a measurement scale or averaged in a statistic. Standardized "objective" measures struggle to capture the deeper psychosocial complexity that formative community-oriented theorists represent in their work (e.g., Rappaport, 2000; Sarason, 2000).

Formal, quantitative data—even the most complex statistical, inferential, and longitudinal techniques—have trouble capturing the most meaningful changes members of the community have experienced, which is often well represented in stories. Curvilinear time-series analyses do not capture well the phenomena of interest that Sarason (2000) had in mind when he called for better "barometers of change." Such barometers help trace a community's narrative history—the geographic, temporal, and interdisciplinary "whole" and all associated insights. Most keenly unique to this approach are the temporal sequences represented by story (i.e., narrative). Stories begin, progress, involve a middle, and often conflict, up through the end toward some form of resolution. This progression and these ends, as McAdams (2006) has extensively discussed, tend to be characterized by contamination or redemption.

A guiding concept for many community-based researchers has been that of empowerment (Rappaport, 1981, 1987). Empowerment involves all stakeholders in the research and change process taking a collaborative approach to the challenges at hand. Empowering research is about generating processes in neighborhoods that enhance people's control over their lives, their learning, and their growth, working together to open up niches and new opportunities (Rappaport, 1981). When a project is empowering, the roles among community members, practitioners, and researchers achieve a lateral status—mutual interventions and evaluations that are both valid and relational. Empowerment is both an individual stakeholder sense of control and a broader form of personal solidarity with all partners in a research project and the community.

A community narrative methodology captures an empowerment-oriented worldview. The method draws out a community's themes in solidarity with its needs, strengths, aspirations, challenges, and changes. The combination of narratives and empowerment helps community members spread, amplify, and give value to their experiences—to discover and create new stories. Research approaches have long been needed that value truth and objectivity while highlighting strengths.

Story-based questions often generate extensive qualitative responses, particularly compared to more abstract questions about beliefs, attitudes, and values. Participants absorb story-based interview questions and find them intuitively sensible. Stories are about people's lives and being human. Stories, as Rappaport (2000) noted, privilege the voices of the people studied. Compared to formal data, story-based questions send a metacommunication that turns research subject roles into that of co-participants (Rappaport, 2000).

Personal stories are elicited by asking story-based questions consistent with McAdams' (2006) life story methodology. A sample question might read:

> Imagine you are an autobiographer. Tell me about a high point episode in your childhood, a time you remember vividly where you felt extremely positive emotions. When did that episode happen in your life, who was there, what was said, how did the events progress, what were you feeling and thinking, and how does this episode relate to the person you are today?

Story-based questions often ask participants to provide full stories about low points or transitions in their lives. Once the interviewee has warmed up with the story-based questions, more abstract, value- or belief-based questions often follow.

Community narratives, beyond personal narratives, can be derived from a modification of the aforementioned questions, for example, "Tell us a high point in your community." Personal stories become community narratives in at least two ways. One is to ask community participants interview questions about the personal and historical narratives of their particular community. A second is to take a set of personal narratives from members of a community and code them; the themes that emerge across community residents are community narratives. Community narratives are, therefore, derived either from the interviewing process or from the analysis and interpretation process. In either case, they should be offered back to stakeholders and used to further community change efforts.

Through community narratives, researchers can uncover those features of communities that produce empowerment and, by communicating their findings, contribute to the empowerment process (Olson & Jason, in press; Olson & Jason, 2011; Rappaport, 2000). Community narratives help detect the barometers of change of whole communities: the history, structure, and social features of those communities (Sarason, 2000).

We have found this approach to be particularly useful in better understanding community development interventions. When a community attempts a total transformation of a neighborhood, whole-community change barometers in the form of narratives can help detect, analyze, and interpret positive changes. The approaches reveal features of the work that can be enhanced, replicated, and/or reconfigured in future efforts to benefit the whole community and all the residents within it.

Community Narrative Methods

There are several important components of the community narrative approach. They include (a) the choice and design of the interviews, (b) the participants chosen for the interviews, and (c) the methods of analysis. We have adapted story-based interview methods, created by McAdams (2006) within the personality field, to community narratives. Interviewing stakeholders from as many diverse perspectives and roles as possible represents the formative component of the whole community narrative technique.

The adaptation of the McAdams methodology to a community level enables questions about an organizing or change effort and about larger macro-level factors, but the techniques are very similar. The whole community method need not focus on a place-based community. The McAdams qualitative story-based technique varies greatly depending on the project's goals. The community-based adaptation interviews individuals or focus groups, asking (as in the personal narrative approach) about high points, nadir scenes, and transitions. When this methodology is adapted to personal life stories tied to a community effort, interviewees might be asked to provide stories about quality of life, low scenes in the community's history, transitions, strategies, positive experiences, or assets. The more diverse the stakeholders, the more history is revealed. The more interviewees can speak to the community's strengths and critique the community and change efforts being done, the better.

In essence, the researchers ask participants about personal and life histories of the community. Residents are asked to tell about their own lives, about their lives within the context of the community, and about the community's history, challenges, and changes perceived, as well as about the intervention itself. Barometers of change are discovered through dialogue about residents' stories, about family, organization, community, societal, and political interactions over time, all in discrete and vital episodes of their lives.

Even the most personal stories can be coded and triangulated to derive community narrative themes, from before the beginning of an initiative to the end. Any attempt to write up a whole community analysis requires moving back and forth, focusing on essential features of an individual's quality of life within the context of what is known about the broader community, in the hope of uncovering patterns that develop.

The next two phases of the community narrative approach involve data analysis and presentation back to community stakeholders. First, narrative quotes are coded by themes related to individual perceptions of community change. The narrative analyses can, as in any other qualitative study, be done inductively or deductively. Themes can even be quantified by the researcher, constructed either on existing theory or recurring themes in the early set of interviews, with the researcher then applying a numerical coding scheme to separate passages (McAdams, 2006; Olson & Jason, in press). What we have found to be most central in the analyses is to maintain the temporal sequences of the stories. We use the coded themes to help reconstruct the progression of the initiative itself and its important drivers. We find that, as will later be illustrated in the chapter, depicting those themes within a visual logic models is beneficial to discussion of the initial findings with multiple stakeholders.

Second, the rich narratives themselves are shared with stakeholders in order to facilitate greater dialogue and understanding about community aspirations, ecology, and change. The researcher can use narratives to help community members learn from and reflect on the stakeholders' varied perspectives and stories. Such learning and reflecting can, in turn, facilitate community empowerment and the initiative's future growth.

The rich qualitative data and its manifestation in the visual logic model can help stakeholders make sense of community dynamics, processes, and change efforts. For example, the creation of a logic model that is germane to an organizing or improvement initiative can validate or correct the effort and help stakeholders better understand and communicate what is successful in an approach. The visual logic model and narratives also can aid in uncovering challenges, unheard or missing voices, and areas where a change in the approach is necessary. Evaluation results should utilize community stories in a way that best moves a change effort forward. Thus, we believe that analyzing themes for, and presenting narratives to, community members is an engaging and empowering change process.

Strengths and Limitations of the Approach

The concepts of community narrative and whole communities speak to each other most because they are ecological (Kelly, 2006). The two concepts have great breadth and complexity compared to other measures and focus on communities over time. Whole stories of a community are complex, and the amount of data gathered through story-based interviews can be overwhelming, thus requiring focus on one piece—personal, organizational, historical—at a time. However, the approach, in line with Sarason's perspective described earlier, can help in identifying the otherwise invisible features of a setting, its social bonds, and changes in the community that reveal significant shifts. This approach is certainly not without its challenges and limitations.

Finally, we would note that this method is more impactful when triangulating with additional data sources in order to, as fully as possible, understand multilevel community phenomena or change. Capturing the diverse voices and stakeholders, particularly those with the least engagement or power, is always an important goal and challenge. Narrative interviews are time consuming and necessitate familiarity with a community, access to a broad set of stakeholders, and continued efforts to identify and engage disparate voices. This is not easily done without first establishing trust and taking the time to understand a community and its stakeholders. In the next section, we describe a neighborhood-based evaluation involving the application of the community narrative approach.

CASE STUDY

Background of the Evaluation

Habitat for Humanity International (HFHI) is one of the largest nonprofit organizations in the world, well known for its housing efforts in more than 87 countries. HFHI has a well-established model for bringing people together to build new homes and make affordable homeownership possible. Their work has served as a catalyst for family economic success and community improvement. In 2008 HFHI began encouraging affiliates to focus their efforts in smaller, more targeted neighborhoods, partnering with civic and business groups to establish community plans to improve quality of life across whole neighborhoods. This case study is derived from a larger evaluation of this broader national effort called the Neighborhood Revitalization (NR) initiative.

The shift to NR came from the realization that HFHI affiliates cannot transform neighborhoods alone, one house at a time, particularly in the wake of the 2007–2008 recession and foreclosure crisis. The NR initiative, therefore, strategically targets hard-hit neighborhoods, collaborating with diverse partners to comprehensively improve neighborhood quality of life. Guided by community stakeholder and resident participation, NR is about improving the quality of life for all residents of a neighborhood, whether they are HFHI homeowners or not. The case study that we provide here is an NR community intervention that took place in the West End neighborhood of Roanoke, Virginia. HFHI's NR mission exemplified empowerment values by engaging residents and stakeholders to exert greater control over neighborhood action and improvement. The goal was always for the HFHI affiliate, in this case Habitat for Humanity in the Roanoke Valley (more informally known as Roanoke Valley Habitat), to be one key partner, among others, playing a role in revitalizing the focus neighborhood.

When the effort started in 2008, the West End was struggling with disinvestment and the deterioration of an older housing stock. By 2014, this participatory mixed methods (see Olson & Jason, 2015) evaluation of the NR initiative indicated that it had significantly transformed this defined geographic community. Even in the stage of short-term outcomes, empowerment processes had led to other tangible and subjective increases in quality of life. Findings from property observation tools indicated that houses and streetscape appearances from NR work had changed the visual landscape of the West End. Community gardens had arisen as sources of pride and healthful forms of community building. Commercial interests in the area had grown. Consistent with the HFHI NR mission across the United States, the local partners, volunteers, and community residents had improved housing stock and neighborhood conditions, bringing about a greater sense of safety, community, and engagement. Eventually this led to increases in quality of life indicators, as evidenced in quantitative community resident surveys.

West End Community Narratives

The Narrative Interviewing Process

As part of the qualitative portion of the evaluation of the NR initiative, the researchers conducted narrative interviews with a diverse group of neighborhood stakeholders. More than 30 community stakeholders in the West End were interviewed individually and/or in small groups. A total of 20 narrative interviews were conducted. This included community residents—HFHI homeowners and longtime residents—and staff from local nonprofit community-based organizations and housing developers, HFHI staff members, local business owners, and city government partners. Each participant was asked about high points, low points, transitions experienced in the neighborhood, past history, relationships with the neighborhood, neighborhood revitalization strategies, and sequences of neighborhood transition. Additionally, interview questions were based on the larger NR initiative and partnership. Based on the original HFHI NR logic model, additional story-based and other questions were asked about initiative progression, partnerships, resources, home construction and repair, perceptions of neighborhood and housing, civic engagement, sense of community, commercial interest, and safety, all of which comprise aspects of neighborhood quality of life. A variety of questions were also spontaneously asked about personal, community, and project histories in the area in order to draw out the narratives.

Creating a Logic Model About Community Change Efforts

Visual logic models aid ecological thinking, helping strategists to appreciate multiple levels of community influence. The logic model is only one of many possible theoretical frameworks for this task, though it has proven useful to us in multiple evaluations. Visual logic models—temporally ordered conceptual diagrams—create simplified working maps of key community happenings that would otherwise be too much to take in and unwieldy to describe. Such models can help us understand the currents of the temporal sequences of stories, moving from beginnings to middles to endings, and interpret and navigate these sources of change and their causes.

Our approach used personal stories and derived community narratives whose collective themes provided a sense of the transformative changes occurring in the neighborhood, consistent with an original NR logic model. Yet it also led to the creation of an emergent logic model, based on narrative themes, of unique, whole neighborhood change that further articulated the intervention's neighborhood process and outcomes.

An emergent model is a combination of the concepts in the ideal/initial logic model and the reality-based and community narrative themes that have emerged from the evaluation. Much can be learned by comparing the ideal, original logic model—a hoped-for or generalized roadmap—with what has actually happened and worked. It also helps to compare how the original conception works differently in different settings. A visual logic model guides future dialogue about the project with participants and stakeholders. The on-the-ground, reality logic model—grounded in community narratives—helps stakeholders better understand which future strategies will help them solve their own community problems. Actively comparing pre- and postintervention logic models facilitates the use of past, current, and future potentialities.

Theme-driven visual logic models help partners identify the best combination of practices for certain contexts and which might generalize to future interventions or locations. Such logic models can be used to seed conversations among all stakeholders to better explain, understand, define, visualize, and act toward common and richer understandings of what has and is happening in a community. The models, along with the overall evaluation reports, can also be used for communicating with policy makers, funders, and the media.

The logic model in Figure 5.1 summarizes themes from community narratives related to the West End NR effort in Roanoke. Reading from left to right, the model summarizes (a) outputs, (b) short-term outcomes, (c) medium-term outcomes, and (d) long-term outcomes (see Fig. 5.1).

The West End logic model—grounded in community narratives—tells a story of a targeted effort and collaborative partnership. This logic model, along with other qualitative and quantitative findings, was presented back to community stakeholders and has since been used to further the HFHI NR effort in other US communities. Here we discuss how narrative themes from the interviews were used to create and summarize this model. The findings seen in this logic model indicate that, first, resources from multiple sources are obtained for the initiative, represented in the lower left corner of the model. Next, HFHI and its partners do what they do best, which is build and rehab homes, while other partners do additional improvement work. Property improvements and affordable housing bring greater homeowner stability and aesthetic improvements to the neighborhood. Moving farther to the right side of the model, under the medium-term outputs, we see changes on such social and psychological dimensions as social cohesion and civic engagement. We also see commercial development occurring in conjunction with residents' perception of neighborhood safety. Ultimately to the far right of the model, the long-term goal is met, namely, the areas in which community residents interviewed experience an improved quality of life. Given this overview, we now take a closer look at themes derived from the narratives, starting from the outputs and moving progressively through the short-, medium-, and long-term outcomes.

Outputs: Collaborative Partnerships

A consistent theme that emerged from the interviews was the strong importance and appreciation of local collaborations and partnerships. The underlying goal of the NR initiative is one of partnerships within a targeted neighborhood. Consistent with Rappaport's (1987) concept of empowerment, Roanoke Valley Habitat played one small role in a stronger set of high-quality and dedicated partners. The partnership included community residents (homeowners and residents) and landlords, as well as volunteers, such as the Habitat construction volunteers (e.g., retirees and active seniors, younger church group members, and

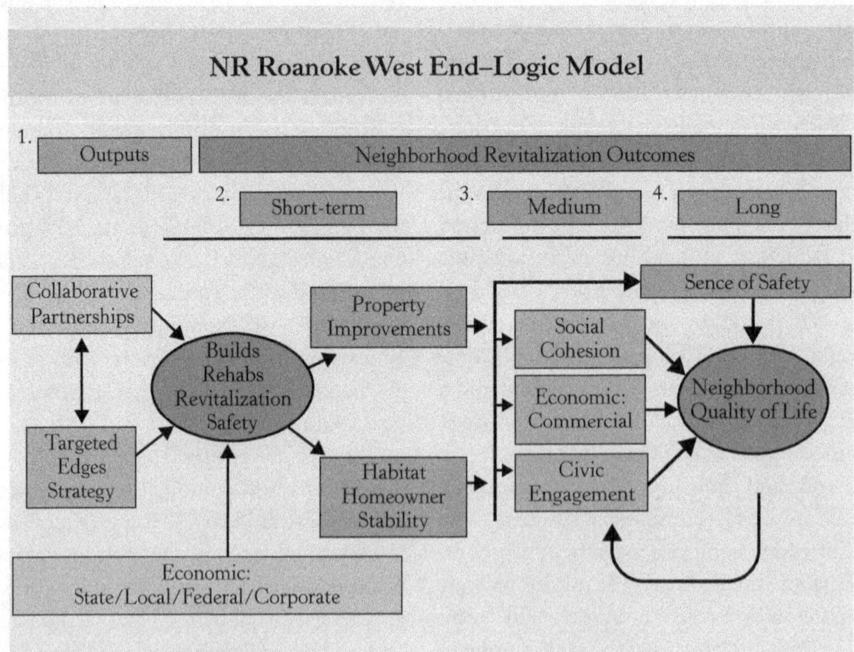

FIGURE 5.1: Roanoke West End narrative-derived logic model.

college students). Virginia Polytechnic Institute and State University (more colloquially known as Virginia Tech) faculty and student volunteers also provided specialized design plans and general landscaping and streetscape improvements within the West End. Also, students from local high schools participated, with the aims of building their skills and leadership capability while contributing to the community through service. Other major partners included Rebuilding Together, an organization that engaged more than 500 youth to rehab homes for seniors and people with physical disabilities, and social service agencies that provided safe and productive outlets for youth as well as wraparound services for neighborhood members.

Edges Strategy

Another consistent positive strategy that emerged was the importance of targeting neighborhood "edges" for improvement. The West End had long faced high rates of poverty and crime, a high proportion of rental units, and a promising but now dilapidated housing stock. And yet it sits on the "edge," or adjacent to two economically "healthy" sections of town, namely, downtown and a vibrant neighborhood called Grandin. The West End was an important transportation corridor that had the potential to attract Virginia residents seeking a shorter work commute into downtown Roanoke.

The progression from renting to affordable homeownership that Habitat makes possible did create new narratives. Residents found that, compared to renting, owning a Habitat home led to better places for children, a new ability to celebrate with larger families, and opportunities to invite neighbors over.

A broader community theme derived from stakeholder stories was *crisis turned into opportunity*. An existing, unsightly trailer park was located along the Roanoke River adjacent to both the West End neighborhood and the main transportation corridor through the neighborhood. The trailer park was on the geographic edge of the target area. One crisis to opportunity story was that several years earlier a flood had devastated the trailer park. The city took this newly abandoned, undevelopable area and turned it into a new section of the Greenway, a pathway where people could walk/bike through an attractive nature trail and thereby also travel through a portion of the otherwise too often ignored West End.

Economic Resources: State/Local/Federal/Corporate

Partners leveraged funds from the city and federal governments, including, for example, neighborhood improvement community development block grants from the city. Such grants guided immediate revitalization efforts, such as placing the police department on new bicycle patrols to increase a sense of safety, and more long-term revitalization efforts.

Short-Term Outcomes: Home Builds and Improvements

Roanoke Valley Habitat targeted home improvement areas in the West End. Roanoke Valley Habitat and other developers built new homes on vacant land, rehabbed other properties, and repaired small and major features inside and outside of the existing homes. Reflected in many stakeholder interviews and consistent with the NR initiative mission, increased economic resources, landscape improvements, and increased social interactions led to a greater sense of connection to the neighborhood.

Crises always arise in such an effort, and part of understanding the whole story of an initiative is understanding how such a complicated effort is actually accomplished and how variations of the initiative can be replicated elsewhere. Another story reflecting the crisis theme involved the fact that neglected, though excellent, housing stock stood within an historic district. Such historic stock is staunchly protected by Virginia's Department of Historic Resources, the city of Roanoke's Neighborhood Design District Guidelines, and the city's local Historic District requirements. Although the preservation policies cannot be said to be unimportant, they left little architectural flexibility for affordable housing development. Additionally, longtime residents were skeptical of HFHI's home-building efforts due to a perceived incompatibility with local character. Roanoke Valley Habitat embraced this challenge, hiring an innovative architect who developed a new, cost-effective "four square" design, a four-bedroom, two-story architectural design. The new designs were affordable, architecturally correct for the guidelines, and of higher quality than many had thought feasible at such prices. These new, larger homes were well received throughout the neighborhood and Roanoke, being seen as a better fit with the aesthetic structures within the historic neighborhoods. This flexibility on the part of the Habitat affiliate allowed the partners to weather this crisis and continue to revitalize the neighborhood in such a way that brought even greater respect for HFHI and Roanoke Valley Habitat among partners, local residents, and private investors.

In-depth stories from Habitat homeowners showed an appreciation for being part of this targeted neighborhood intervention. Many immigrant families were served by the program, becoming neighbors with other residents and thereby increasing feelings of social support and a sense of connectedness. Interviewees consistently described feeling fortunate to reside in this improving neighborhood. Simultaneously, partner organizations worked on a host of services and repairs for seniors and those with disabilities, such as curb fixing, nonaesthetic internal features of the houses, and land- and streetscapes. From the perspective of area residents and a variety of stakeholders, the combination of affordable housing and physical property infrastructure improvements led to an improved quality of life. As a reflection of these changes, we heard many stories of rehabs, repairs, and new houses in previously abandoned lots quickly leading neighbors on each side of these property improvements to take better care of their own properties.

Medium-Term Outcomes: Cohesion, Civic Engagement, and Commercial Interests

Stories from residents spoke to increases in neighborhood pride, empowerment, sense of community, social cohesion, and civic engagement. Stakeholders also relayed perceptions of increased neighborhood stability and new commercial and residential investment. Targeting a single neighborhood also led to new efficiencies in how Roanoke Habitat and other partners could build. Supervision could occur at multiple builds simultaneously, and, due to the concentrated proximity of the work, moving people and materials from one place to another became easier because of NR. Stories also made it clear that Habitat homeowners went together through similar education programs on financing and the maintenance and repair of new homes, which helped with relationship building. Another reflection of an improved quality of life was the already-mentioned stories of new homeowners, emphasizing the importance to their sense of community of a having larger, owned space to invite friends, family, and neighbors. Greater pride was also found where Habitat made home improvements. Homeowners, however, did not ignore in their stories continued challenges, such as neighborhood tensions between homeowners and renters, indicating the need to improve engagement with and cohesion among all neighborhood residents.

The NR initiative in the West End caught the attention of private developers, one of which contributed significantly to the initiative. After becoming aware of the partnership's focus on the West End, a private developer moved into the neighborhood and began to purchase and rehab more than a dozen properties in the area. Although collaborating extensively with Roanoke Valley Habitat and other partners, he started to develop higher-priced homes, which served the purpose of revitalization. Although this raised concerns about inclusion and affordability, gentrification remained a very small risk, and this developer did add to the engagement and revitalization in the neighborhood. Interviewees also reflected on the importance of attracting the neighborhood's first financial institution, a credit union whose opening was widely celebrated. A farmers' market soon followed, an event mentioned by interviewees as an important neighborhood symbol and an anchor for future community development.

Long-Term Outcomes: Overall Quality of Life and Sense of Safety

As noted earlier, the police gave early attention to the West End through bicycle patrols. Yet the improved sense of safety mentioned by interviewees was a lengthier, more complicated process. Safety was a clear priority of residents, and organizing efforts were viewed as being successful in bringing about better police responsiveness. Neighborhood associations and watches were perceived as being more alert over time. More pedestrian activity, a greater sense of pride, and increased social connections across neighbors were mentioned as leading to more "eyes on the street." The longer-term end of the collective story involved sustained signs of improvement in the community while recognizing that challenges remained.

CONCLUSION

Community narratives can help researchers and entire community partnerships better understand how interventions impact resident quality of life. The distillation of the stories, and the visualizations that arise, have worked toward better barometers and drivers of community change, often in change-resistant places. The aforementioned methods, derived from people's stories and community contexts, have helped us collectively play a meaningful supportive role in understanding and helping to facilitate resident-directed change. The steps have been helpful in Roanoke and other HFHI NR cities in which we have worked. We have no doubt that other researchers and evaluators who use the approach and adapt it to their own contexts will find the subsequent developments rewarding.

REFERENCES

Kelly, J. G. (2006). *Becoming ecological: An expedition into community psychology*. New York, NY: Oxford University Press.

McAdams, D. P. (2006). *The redemptive self: Stories Americans live by*. New York, NY: Oxford University Press.

Olson, B. D., & Jason, L. A. (2011). The community narration (CN) approach: Understanding a group's identity and cognitive constructs through personal and community narratives. *Global Journal of Community Psychology Practice, 2*, 1–7.

Olson, B. D., & Jason, L. A. (2015). Participatory mixed methods research. In S. Hesse-Biber & R. B. Johnson (Eds.), *The Oxford handbook of mixed and multimethod research inquiry*. New York, NY: Oxford University Press.

Rappaport, J. (1981). In praise of paradox: A social policy of empowerment over prevention. *American Journal of Community Psychology, 9*, 1–25.

Rappaport, J. (1987). Terms of empowerment/exemplars of prevention: Toward a theory for community psychology. *American Journal of Community Psychology, 15*, 121–148.

Rappaport, J. (2000). Community narratives: Tales of terror and joy. *American Journal of Community Psychology, 28*, 1–24.

Sarason, S. B. (2000). Barometers of community change: Personal reflections. In J. Rappaport & E. Seidman (Eds.), *Handbook of community psychology* (pp. 919–929). New York, NY: Kluwer/Plenum.

6

Appreciative Inquiry

NEIL M. BOYD

Participatory action research (PAR) is commonly used by consultants or facilitators when they inquire, intervene, and evaluate community-based organizations and community systems. However, a variety of important concerns exist when implementing PAR, such as how to involve multiple stakeholders in meaningful ways, how to take into account potential consequences to a whole community or organizational system, and how to develop genuine empowerment among participants. An additional concern, which will be this chapter's primary focus, is how to avoid the negative trappings of problem-based inquiry approaches.

In this chapter, appreciative inquiry (AI) is introduced as a *change* methodology that aims to create change through a focus on elevating strengths and helping to produce sustainable community-based organizations and communities (Boyd & Bright, 2007; Cooperrider & Srivastva, 1987; Ludema, Whitney, Mohr, & Griffin, 2003). Most often, PAR methodologies start with an attempt to solve community or organizational problems. By contrast, AI begins with the premise that organizations and communities have strengths that can be leveraged to reshape their image and function. The current chapter first presents the steps typically involved in the AI process. It then contrasts AI's opportunity-based orientation with the more traditional problem-based approach. It concludes with a case study illustrating AI's application in an organization concerned with injured workers' rights.

INTRODUCTION TO PROBLEM-BASED COMMUNITY/ ORGANIZATION DEVELOPMENT METHODOLOGIES

Problem-based PAR is rooted in the practices of Kurt Lewin, who developed the original conception of action research as a three-stage process for planned change (Lewin, 1951). The three stages consisted of *unfreezing* (reducing those forces maintaining resistance to change), *moving* (intervening with a change effort), and *refreezing* (stabilizing the change into a new state of equilibrium). Over time, Lewin's model was modified into what is commonly termed "traditional action research," which tends to be associated with the following basic steps (adapted from Boyd & Bright, 2007; Cummings & Worley, 2015; see also French & Bell, 1994; Schein, 1988):

Problem identification: This stage usually begins when an executive in an organization, or someone with power and influence, senses that the organization or system has one or more problems that might be solved with the help of a professional facilitator or organizational development and change (ODC) practitioner.

Consultation with a behavioral science expert: During the initial contact, the ODC practitioner and the client carefully assess each other. During this sharing stage, the client and consultant seek to establish an open and collaborative atmosphere.

Data gathering and preliminary diagnosis: This step involves gathering appropriate information and analyzing it to determine the underlying causes of organizational problems. Typically, interviews, process observation, questionnaires, and organizational performance data are collected.

Feedback to a key client or group: The feedback step, in which organizational members are given information by the ODC practitioner, helps them determine the strengths and weaknesses of the organization or department under study.

Joint diagnosis of the problem: At this point, members discuss the feedback and explore with the ODC practitioner whether they want to work on identified problems. A close relationship exists among data gathering, feedback, and diagnosis because the consultant summarizes the basic data from the client members and presents the data to them for validation and further diagnosis.

Joint action planning: Next, the ODC practitioner and client members jointly agree on further action implementation.

Action: This stage involves the actual change effort. It may include installing new methods and procedures, reorganizing structures and work designs, and reinforcing new behaviors.

Data gathering after action: Because action research is a cyclical process, data are collected after the action to measure and determine the effects of the action and to feed the results back to the organization. This, in turn, may lead to rediagnosis and new action.

One can see in these steps a focus on identifying and resolving problems. Notice the use of the terms "diagnosis" and "problem identification." This language assumes that something is wrong with the system, that the organization or community is ill and needs to heal. A consultant or facilitator who uses PAR would then take on the role of a physician who uses his or her positional role and skills to heal the system's ailments. In traditional PAR, data collection can generate skepticism and feelings of fear, concern, and venting. These reactions may increase if the process is controlled by a small group of people near the hierarchical top of the system. The leaders of the change event, including the facilitator, can then be in a role where they have to advocate and defend recommended changes to others. Understandably, this can increase anxiety and potential resistance to change.

OPPORTUNITY-BASED COMMUNITY/ ORGANIZATION DEVELOPMENT METHODOLOGIES

AI represents an opportunity-based PAR process as an alternative to a problem-based approach (Cooperrider & Avital, 2004; Cooperrider, Whitney, & Stavros, 2003; Ludema et al., 2003; Whitney & Trosten-Bloom, 2003). Consider the following assumptions of an AI process:

All organizations or communities are *centers of human connection* that can serve to magnify the best possibilities of the human condition.

Communities and organizations are *living organisms* filled with energy and potential.

All *questions are interventions*, and the focus of those questions, whether problem based or appreciative based, has serious implications for the tone and outcome of a planned change process.

The *entire system* needs to be involved in the change process.

Actual change is most likely when participants feel *trust and membership* and perceive that they are *psychologically safe*.

AI is different from problem-based PAR in a number of ways. First, AI includes an assumption of genuine questioning, as opposed to "diagnosis," as a critical first step in beginning a planned change process. AI also tends to enhance relationships between stakeholders during the inquiry, thereby aiding in reducing hierarchical boundaries between layers in a system.

In contrast to a traditional PAR approach, AI focuses on redefining problems as opportunities. For example, consider the problem of childhood obesity. Health is suppressed in this problem statement, and so are the associated images and language of positive health visions. A shift toward positive inquiry changes the focus of where the change process is directed because a different set of normative expectations are present at the onset of the process.

Although AI methods can vary, practitioners commonly use the 4-D cycle of discover, dream, design, and destiny (Cooperrider & Srivastva, 1987; Cooperrider & Whitney, 2001; Cooperrider et al, 2003; Ludema et al., 2003; Whitney, Cooperrider, Trosten-Bloom, & Kaplin, 2002). To demonstrate how AI works, a case analysis of a community-based organization is presented next.

CASE STUDY

Background of the Case

The author was involved as a consultant to a nonprofit organization whose mission was to promote and fight for the rights of injured workers. The organization is situated in a northeastern state of the United States, and at the time of the consultation had more than 2,000 members and was organized in 11 active regional statewide chapters. The organization also maintained a headquarters in a central location of the state that was operated by an executive director. Oversight of the executive director and the organization was maintained by a geographically dispersed group of board members.

The author entered the organization by invitation of the executive director, and, after a few preliminary meetings, a contract was established between the parties to create a steering committee that would manage the change process. The AI approach was selected as a general method to infuse change for two reasons: (a) The executive director wanted to try something new due to the fact that previous problem-based strategies had not worked in the past, and (b) the author wanted to test the efficacy of an opportunity-based change method in the field. For the purpose of evaluating the efficacy of the AI approach to change, qualitative and quantitative outcome measures were collected at the individual, change process, organizational, and community levels. Individual and AI process measures were collected via open-ended questionnaires of all stakeholders at the end of each AI stage. Organizational and community measures were collected via interviews with steering committee members and survey feedback from organization members immediately following the first consultation and at 6, 12, and 18 months post consultation.

The Case Begins

The following letter was sent to all members of the organization in order to create a steering committee for the change process:

> Hello. I am writing this letter to invite you to participate in an organizational development process that is currently being considered by our organization. During the past month, I have had a couple of preliminary meetings with a consulting team to discuss how we *can add to the great successes that we have already achieved*. As such, I would like you to consider participating in a steering committee that will be formed including board members, state directors, chapter leadership, members at large, and consulting team members.... As a final note, even if you are not able to participate in the steering committee work, you will likely have an opportunity at some time later to participate in the organizational development process. Take care and hope to hear from you soon.
>
> Sincerely,
> Executive Director

Notice that the AI approach was embedded in the call for action by highlighting a focus on past successes to serve as a guide for change. In addition, notice that the letter represents an attempt to create inclusiveness for all members of the organization. These statements were intentionally created for the purpose of setting a positive tone and direction of the change process. Future communications contained similar positive-oriented and inclusive statements. A few weeks later, a steering committee met at a neutral conference site for a half-day meeting. The steering committee was comprised of members from the entire organizational system and the external ecological system around the organization. The committee included the executive director, the author, three board members, eight chapter members, and state and local union officials. The steering committee designed a full-day session (referred to as an AI summit) in which participants would work through the 4-D cycle.

Discover

The underlying assumption of the discover phase is that people should create positive images of an ideal state about what the organization or community "should be." The primary goal is to create an awareness of images, stories, and capacities that are most likely to inspire future design of the organization or community. A well-executed opening activity uses questions to generate an atmosphere of energy, focus, and anticipation for positive possibilities in the future of the system.

In the case of the AI summit, approximately 50 organization and community members met for the full-day session. The day began with a warm-up period in which attendees introduced themselves and noted at least one positive thing that the organization had done for them or for injured workers. The warm-up served to orient the group to each other and was designed to identify and enhance the organization's "positive energy."

Immediately following the warm-up, attendees were randomly assigned to breakout groups and were charged with answering the following question: "What has the organization done in the past that made it successful?" The breakout session lasted approximately 45 minutes, and much dialogue and energy was present surrounding the stories of past organizational successes. Examples of successes included the following: (a) The organization helped to modify the latest version of the state workers compensation act. (b) The organization helped injured workers get access to important workers compensation information. (c) The organization increased awareness of the plight of injured workers. (d) The organization increased access to affordable and qualified attorney representation. The participants also reported that they noticed traits in others or in the community for the first time, as they became aware of previously unnoticed strengths (see Table 6.1 for additional individual and change process outcomes).

Dream

The dream phase moves the process from considering current system strengths to a focus on how current successes can be leveraged. In this phase, the focus is on practically discussing "what could be." Participants might work in groups to create artwork, poetry, or a skit to depict an ideal future, where the highest dreams, passions, and aspirations become clearly apparent. Participants might also summarize and prioritize key themes or ideas for action. In sum, the dream phase draws on the best of the past and present in a way that maximizes the capability for expansive thinking about a potential future.

In the present instance, a storytelling method was used in breakout groups to explore dreams for the organization's future. Facilitators invited participants to share personal stories of organizational successes. During the storytelling sessions, members brainstormed and recorded emergent themes from their stories on poster sheets. Emergent ideas were posted on the walls of the meeting hall, and a group moderator conducted content analysis, in real time, by organizing the themes of the conversation and creating a priority list of major positive successes. It was interesting to observe that the organization had created significant value to the participants' lives and the lives of injured workers, and there was a clear sense that the organization was an important and needed entity.

Next, in order to refine dreams of the future, the facilitator asked the breakout groups to answer the following question: "If you could look into the future 5 years from now, what are the successes that the organization has achieved?" Each member of a breakout team told his or her version of a futuristic story, and group members generated key themes from the content of these future visions. A moderator helped to summarize these key ideas for the future across all of the groups. Examples of dream statements included: (a) The state workers compensation act is repealed, and a new "worker-friendly" version is in place. (b) Injured workers are empowered by the organization to get access to the information and resources they need. (c) We are connected in a virtual communication network. (d) We have ample monetary resources to fund our mission. Notice that these ideas were stated in the present tense as a means to focus the mind on the possibility of an actualized reality.

Design

The design phase shifts the conversation from reflection to action. The major task is to identify specific actions that will move the organization or community closer to its envisioned future. In the AI summit, the facilitator asked breakout groups to design three specific actions that could meet

TABLE 6.1: A SAMPLE OF INDIVIDUAL, CHANGE PROCESS, ORGANIZATION, AND COMMUNITY OUTCOMES

Individual	"I'm feeling good about this organization"
	"I can see that lots of things are happening across the state"
	"My energy level is high today"
	"I learned how I can help make a difference with this organization"
	"I am excited to go back to my chapter and share with them what has happened here"
	"I have more faith in this organization than ever"
	"I think the sessions have shown me that people in this organization really care"
Change process	"This meeting has been the best thing that ever happened to this organization"
	"I especially like how we began the workshop with the good stuff about our work. I think it created a lot of energy for change"
	"The sessions showed us that we can take control of our organization, and get things done"
	"Being positive works! Two years ago, we held a conference for this organization, but most of the time was spent complaining about the politicians and laws. This time we could see that we are making a difference"
	"I would like to try this method with other organizations that I work with"
Organization	Central office disbanded and the organization structure changed from hierarchical to a virtual-systems orientation.
	Board of directors reconfigured to create majority control via the members
	New bylaws were created
	Eleven chapters reorganized into five regional chapters
	New web portal established
	New web portal connected the chapters, and members, together.
	"The New Web-Portal has significantly increased information flows between leadership and rank-and-file members"
	"We communicate in real time now"
	Average number of legislator contacts increased by 30% last year
	Average number of formal petitions to legislators increased by 33% last year
	Average number of rallies and protests increased by 20.5% last year
	Membership increased by 18% in the last year
	Revenues increased by 28% last year
Community	Number of community-based publications increased by 40% last year
	Number of community-based advertisements increased by 50% last year
	A State-Level Workers Compensation Advisory Council was established last year to accept public commentary
	A State Commission was established in this year for the purpose of initiating workers' compensation legislation reform
	The organization-supported bills introduced in the House or Senate has increased by 20% last year
	The organization-supported bills that became law increased by 15% last year

the major dreams of their group. After each group designed action plans, a few members of the steering committee moderated a session in which representatives from each group shared their action plans. These plans were then merged to create a single action plan. The collective action plan called for a new organizational structure change that would reduce the number of regional sites, interconnect the regional sites via an integrated computer network, and eliminate the executive director position. In addition, the plan suggested that a new board of directors should be created that better represented a cross-section of stakeholders to the organization. It was especially interesting that the AI Summit seemed to facilitate a moment in time where members realized they were in control of the organization's destiny (see Table 6.1 for additional individual and change process outcomes).

Destiny

The destiny phase is a transition from planning to action. In the case of the AI summit, the final 90 minutes included designing and assigning tasks for specific action plans to become a reality. Task assignments included, (a) designing a team to review and recommend changes to the bylaws of the organization, (b) creating a team to design a new election process to the board of directors, (c) having a team design a website for the organization so that members could stay connected, (d) creating a team to design the exit strategy of the executive director, and (e) creating a team to consider regional mergers and restructuring of the number of regional sites. At 6, 12, and 18 months after the AI summit, steering committee members monitored the change process. At each time segment, interviews were conducted with steering committee members, and survey feedback data were collected from organization members. Data showed significant increases in the ability to conduct legislative lobbying efforts, better communication between the regional sites, easier access to information through the web portal, and an increased sense of organizational control by the members. In addition, members thought that their mission was being achieved with greater effectiveness, fundraising was easier and amounts were increasing, and organization members felt a greater sense of community with each other (see Table 6.1 for additional organizational and community outcomes).

In conclusion, the 4-D cycle and the AI summit provided an opportunity for people to participate in a series of guided conversations that produced action steps and a new future. Moreover, stakeholders created a better network of relationships, stronger awareness of organizational strengths and resources, and greater leadership action among members throughout the system.

CONCLUSION

AI has the potential to assist change in community-based settings and is an approach that respects ecological analysis, diversity, prevention, and empowerment, which are factors that community-based organizers and organizational leaders commonly believe are important. First, AI is consistent with ecological analysis because it considers all members of the system who are internal and external to the boundaries of the entity of interest. Once a complete ecological stakeholder analysis is completed, the AI process helps to generate a consultative environment that has the potential to create real and lasting change because system-wide questions and issues have a chance to be fully considered.

Second, AI allows for stakeholder involvement that embraces diversity and individual differences. By its inherent nature, AI tends to create interventions that increase the power of diversity as an ongoing resource within organizations. AI approaches tend to help participants discover similarities with others, and participants often claim that they have a better respect for others when they are engaged in a positive-oriented change experience with multiple diverse stakeholders.

AI also promotes a preventive focus in community settings. AI is opposed to problem-based reactive change methods and instead attempts to capitalize on existing system strengths that can lead to a positive future. AI seeks to prevent a system from developing future problems by envisioning and implementing changes at the present time that could prevent future negative situations from occurring to the organization or community. In relation to the change process itself, AI helps prevent and reduce negative cognitions in individuals that could thwart the system's ability to reach desired outcomes and social changes.

AI also promotes an assumption of empowerment. AI requires a participative and empowering environment for all stakeholders where multiple positive voices are heard. When individuals and groups participate in problem-based change events, they can unconsciously develop states of "learned helplessness" that reduce their ability to envision a greater future (Seligman, 1992). AI can help ameliorate negative psychological states by preventing disempowering cognitions and instead create a sense of "learned optimism" for participants (Seligman, 1991).

In conclusion, this chapter highlights how opportunity-based approaches can help us rethink the latent assumptions that exist in traditional PAR methodologies. AI is an opportunity-based method that can help community professionals who are interested in facilitating organizational and social change. In addition, it is consistent with several underlying assumptions that community-based professionals believe are important.

AUTHOR NOTE

Portions of the case study in this chapter were previously published in Boyd and Bright (2007). Appreciative inquiry as a mode of action research in community psychology. *Journal of Community Psychology, 35*(8), 1019–1036. Reprinted with permission from John Wiley & Sons, Inc.

REFERENCES

Boyd, N., & Bright, D. (2007). Appreciative inquiry as a mode of action research in community psychology. *Journal of Community Psychology, 35*, 1019–1036.

Cooperrider, D. L., & Avital, M. (Eds). (2004). *Constructive discourse and human organization.* Boston, MA: Elsevier.

Cooperrider, D. L., & Srivastva, S. (1987). Appreciative inquiry in organizational life. *Research in Organizational Change and Development, 1*, 129–169.

Cooperrider, D. L., & Whitney, D. (2001). A positive revolution in change: Appreciative inquiry. *Public Administration and Public Policy, 87*, 611–630.

Cooperrider, D. L., Whitney, D., & Stavros, J. M. (2003). *Appreciative inquiry handbook: The first in a series of AI workbooks for leaders of change.* Bedford Heights, OH: Lakeshore Communications.

Cummings, T., & Worley, C. (2015). *Organization development and change.* Stanford, CT: Cengage Learning.

French, W. L., & Bell, C. H. (1994). *Organization development: Behavioral science interventions for organization improvement* (5th ed.). Englewood Cliffs, NJ: Prentice Hall.

Lewin, K. (1951). *Field theory in social science.* New York, NY: Harper & Row.

Ludema, J. D., Whitney, D., Mohr, B. J., & Griffin, T. J. (2003). *The appreciative inquiry summit: A practitioner's guide for leading large-group change.* San Francisco, CA: Berrett-Koehler.

Schein, E. H. (1988). *Process consultation.* Reading, MA: Addison-Wesley.

Seligman, M. E. P. (1991). *Learned optimism.* New York, NY: A. A. Knopf.

Seligman, M. E. P. (1992). *Helplessness on depression, development, and death.* New York, NY: W. H. Freeman.

Whitney, D., Cooperrider, D., Trosten-Bloom, A., & Kaplin, B. S. (2002). *Encyclopedia of positive questions.* Euclid, OH: Lakeshore Communications.

Whitney, D., & Trosten-Bloom, A. (2003). *The power of appreciative inquiry.* San Francisco, CA: Berrett Koehler.

7

The Delphi Method

SHANE R. BRADY

Qualitative research provides many methodological tools for understanding deeper meanings associated with complex phenomena and processes (Denzin & Lincoln, 2005). Qualitative research is thus regularly used, alongside quantitative and mixed methods, in the context of community-based research (Miles & Huberman, 1994). Qualitative methods provide community researchers and practitioners with tools that encourage community member participation and voice in addressing and understanding community strengths, histories, and challenges (Johnson, 2006; Minkler, 2005). One of the qualitative methods useful for promoting community participation in research is the Delphi method. The qualitative version of the Delphi is a flexible research method grounded in pragmatism and structured participation (Dalkey & Helmer, 1963). The Delphi method was developed to provide a structured mechanism to attain insights and perspectives from people with a specific expertise on a topic or issue in order to inform decision making about policy and practice (Dalkey & Helmer, 1963). The Delphi method utilizes structured anonymous communication between experts in order to gather consensus perspectives about an issue or topic that can then be translated or used to inform decision making about a specific issue or within a specific context (Birdsall, 2004; Dalkey & Helmer, 1963). Because the aim of community-based research is to generate knowledge that can directly improve community systems and the lives of residents through involving community members and stakeholders to some degree in the research process, the qualitative Delphi method is an essential tool for community researchers.

GUIDING THEORY AND PHILOSOPHY OF THE DELPHI METHOD

The qualitative Delphi method has roots in the philosophy of Locke, Kant, and Hegel (Turoff, 1970). Each philosopher emphasizes the importance of opinions and perceptions of groups of people, alongside other sources of empirical data, in considering what reality is or how to approach decision making. Additionally, because the Delphi method was designed for practical research that could be used to inform practice, the Delphi method was established in accordance with the philosophical assumptions consistent with Dewey's pragmatism (Dalkey & Helmer, 1963). Dewey's pragmatism has long been considered a practical bridge between theories and methods stemming from the interpretive paradigm concerned with subjective human experiences and contextual truths and the emphasis on generalizability and objectivity common in the postpositivist paradigm (Fay, 1996). Pragmatism is evident in the qualitative Delphi method in the following ways: (a) The Delphi method is flexible enough to be utilized with both quantitative- and qualitative-derived data; (b) the Delphi method is affordable, as it uses inexpensive questionnaires that vary from more open-ended to more structured and that can be easily disseminated to participants utilizing either traditional or electronic delivery; (c) the Delphi method is not concerned with having a generalizable sample but instead seeks input from a purposive sample of individuals with specific expertise on a topic; and (d) Delphi studies lack the complexity of many other research designs that demand highly specialized education, technology, and knowledge, which makes it a good tool for community-based research and decision making by community researchers and practitioners alike (Skulmoski, Hartman, & Kran, 2007). Finally, research questions and aims in Delphi studies must have direct bearing on informing practice, policy, or decision making (Alder & Ziglio, 1996; Dietz, 1987).

UTILIZING THE DELPHI METHOD IN COMMUNITY AND ORGANIZATIONAL SETTINGS

The Delphi method has been used in an array of different contexts, where expert knowledge is needed to inform decision making. Often, researchers and decision makers will want to solicit feedback from very different groups of people, each with a unique lens or expertise on an issue (Dietz, 1987). The Delphi method has been regularly employed in the context of public policy as a means of increasing understanding about how a specific policy should be developed or amended or as a tool for determining a policy's effectiveness and/or efficiency (Alder & Ziglio, 1996; Linstone & Turoff, 1975). Additionally, the Delphi method has been used in the area of management and organizational development as a catalyst for improving working relationships and making group decisions. The Delphi method has also been regularly utilized to inform the development of practice theories and models in a variety of fields and disciplines (Brady, 2012; Skulmoski et al., 2007). Finally, the Delphi method has been useful in conflict resolution and strategic planning within organizations and agencies (Hartman & Baldwin, 1998; Roberson, Collins, & Oreg, 2005). In one case, the Delphi method was included in participatory action research (PAR) in order to better inform health care policy and leadership in Canada (Fletcher & Childon, 2014). In that study, through this approach, community members from different geographic areas and of differing levels of power and vulnerability were able to provide stakeholders with direction about how to better deliver health care services, help with prioritizing health care issues, and insight into what was working and not working within the current system. Given the proven and practical utility of the qualitative Delphi method in informing decision making and practice, it provides a useful tool to those involved in conducting community-based research.

INTRODUCTION TO A STANDARD DELPHI METHOD

Although variations in qualitative Delphi studies exist, as is the case with most approaches to research (see Creswell, 1998; Denzin & Lincoln, 2005), certain consistent criteria apply to all qualitative Delphi studies, including purposive sampling, emergent design, anonymous and structured communication between participants, and thematic analysis (Linstone & Turoff, 1975). The expertise of participants on the topic of inquiry is the most important requisite in Delphi studies (Alder & Ziglio, 1996). Participant expertise must be defined with predetermined criteria (e.g., years of experience working in an area, years spent living in a community) in order for a sample to be properly identified and recruited. In a standard qualitative Delphi study, a sample of between 10 and 20 participants is recruited to participate. The range in sample size depends upon what is already known about an issue or topic and how broad or narrow the scope of expertise desired is on a topic. Frequently, in community settings gatekeepers may be called upon to help recruit and/or identify persons with a specific type of expertise. Individuals must not only have the type of expertise needed but also must have the time and desire to participate in the study. As with any other type of study, whether formal or informal, informed consent to participate is needed.

Questionnaires are the traditional data collection tool used in the Delphi method, as they provide an easy tool for soliciting and receiving honest expert opinions on a topic without fear of responses being impacted by unequal power dynamics, in-person groupthink, difference in social identities and values, or past history with one another (Bolger & Wright, 1994). Delphi studies collect data through questionnaires that may range from more open ended to closed ended, depending upon how much is already known about the topic (Dalkey & Helmer, 1963; Skulmoski et al., 2007). Questionnaires are usually sent out electronically to participants through e-mail, survey software, or a similar format; however, pen-and-paper questionnaires may also be sent out by mail.

In a typical Delphi study, three waves or rounds of data collection are undertaken. The first wave includes an initial questionnaire, usually between

7 and 10 questions, followed by a second wave that provides all participants the opportunity to provide feedback to the responses of others, and concluded by a final, third wave questionnaire that is developed from the consensus opinions analyzed in Wave 1 and 2 in order to arrive at a final consensus on a question, topic, or issue.

Qualitative Delphi studies utilize thematic analysis in order to identify the consensus opinions or themes present in participant responses to questions. Generally, more than one person on the research team will analyze responses in order to ensure consistency and accuracy in the analysis process. Prior to beginning data collection, members of the research team define what, numerically, will constitute consensus. Consensus in a Delphi study refers to the level of agreement between participants necessary to include an opinion, judgment, or insight into the final results or model. It is best thought of as the percentage of participants in agreement about a certain point or who respond similarly about something. The final results of a Delphi study may be sent back out to participants for a final vote on whether or not participant consensus was analyzed correctly by the research team.

Strengths of the Qualitative Delphi Method

The Delphi method has many positive attributes that make it an excellent option for community-based research studies. One positive is that it is relatively easy to learn and employ without any highly formalized education or a research-focused degree. Its pragmatic nature lends itself to use by community organizers and practitioners, who often already have relationships with stakeholders and understand the complex context of decision making in the community. Additionally, the Delphi method is low cost, as it generally relies on basic questionnaires that can be sent out electronically to participants. Also, it is very flexible and can be used with small to medium sample sizes of between 10 and 20 participants, whereas many other research methods are dependent upon medium to large sample sizes. Finally, in the context of community-based research, the Delphi method allows for community member voices and participation, especially from nonprofessionals and members of historically vulnerable groups, to be heard and included in community decision making.

Challenges to the Qualitative Delphi Method

Although the qualitative Delphi method has several beneficial qualities for use in community-based research, the method also has challenges that deserve mention. Because the Delphi method is rooted in pragmatic decision making, the method is limited to studies that seek expertise to inform decision-making purposes. Many community organizations employ satisfaction surveys, for instance, for which the Delphi method would not be appropriate, nor would it be useful in community decision-making processes that do not plan on utilizing feedback from those included in the study. Second, although the method is fairly easy to learn and utilize in most ways (e.g., sampling, data collection), analysis can be tricky, especially given the relatively little guidance provided in the literature. The Delphi literature speaks only to the fact that qualitative Delphi studies use thematic analysis, but it does not describe the process in much depth, which can be challenging to community practitioners not trained in research methods or analysis. In order to address this shortcoming, the author recommends that those using the qualitative Delphi consult other methodological resources, such as Bazeley (2009), Creswell (1998), or Strauss and Corbin (1998), for further help with analysis. Additionally, with respect to analysis, individuals using the qualitative Delphi should remember that consensus is always the most important criterion, so the more participants who mention or indicate a response, the more important it is in the final analysis and results. Lastly, the success of Delphi studies is tied directly to the anonymity of the communication; however, in small communities or neighborhoods, participants may know one another and may be tempted to talk about the study with one another. It is highly recommended that anyone seeking to use the Delphi method in community research formally discuss how to promote anonymity among participants and members of the research team.

CASE STUDY

Overview of the Community

During the past 30 years many rustbelt cities have experienced their share of economic, political, and social challenges, due, in part, to the recession, a decline in manufacturing jobs, instability in local governments, and a continued decline in population (Rugh, 2014). Despite these challenges, outside investors have begun to partner with local, state, and private leaders in redeveloping several areas and neighborhoods within communities. Although some of these processes have been touted as highly successful, many community organizers at the local neighborhood level have challenged whether or not the expertise and opinions of local residents have been taken into account during community development efforts (Dobbie & Richards-Schuster, 2008). This case study takes place in a community within a large rustbelt city.

In this study the private, government, and nonprofit sectors were working together to develop several at-risk neighborhoods and areas in the city with help from major foundations, federal grants, and for-profit investment. One of the major tasks that developers engaged in was establishing and prioritizing community needs. Despite some professionals being connected to the community through their professional or leadership roles, few were residents of the community. During some of the initial development processes, experts struggled to find creative ways to involve local residents in decision making and strategizing. Therefore, many of the early community development efforts lacked resident participation and input. Although many community organizers and researchers were aware of the lack of resident inclusion in community decision making, few knew exactly how to effectively involve community residents alongside professionals, academics, and other decision makers. As a result of the challenges associated with soliciting meaningful participation from local residents, new community-based research tools were needed. The qualitative Delphi method was one of the tools identified and successfully utilized in one community effort to attain feedback from long-time residents about development and planning.

Defining Community and Context

For the purpose of this case study, community was defined as an area of approximately 2 square miles inside the boundaries of a larger city that included approximately three different neighborhoods. The neighborhoods that comprised community in this case were similar with regard to race, with the majority of residents (85%) being African American, along with smaller percentages of Whites (8%) and Latinos (3%) (Staes, 2010). Residents had a mean age of 44 years old, with some diversity in families and older retirees living in the community. Because neighborhood residents had seldom been included in previous community development processes and were therefore distrustful of outside professionals and academics, it was imperative for the research team tasked with coming up with a community development plan to find a way to involve them in the research process.

Identifying and Recruiting Resident Experts

The Delphi method was chosen because it provided a way for local community members to be experts alongside other stakeholder groups. Because of the Delphi method's anonymous nature, a local resident would not know that he or she might be responding to the perspective of a city council member or business executive and vice versa. During the initial planning of the study, questions were raised about sample size, recruitment, and access to computers/technology needed to participate. The local community development corporation (CDC), along with a few local leaders, provided the perspective that we wanted to include a similar number of local residents as other stakeholder groups, which was determined to be best kept between 10 and12 residents out of 220 estimated residents living in the community.

The CDC had an existing group of local residents already engaged in neighborhood discussions and work, which would be a good source of potential participants. However, although the CDC was an important ally in recruitment, the research team thought that it was important to have another community organization involved in recruiting resident experts. Therefore, after carefully assessing the community, members of the research team identified a local church in close proximity to the community, which also had a resident-led group. Consequently, each of the two sources was asked to serve as a gatekeeper in order to recruit five members each for inclusion in the study. The use of gatekeepers in Delphi studies is important because, as noted earlier, participants must have the expertise, time, and willingness to participate. Both the CDC and the church received a basic overview of the study and scripts to use for recruitment purposes. Ten resident participants were recruited in this manner and were placed into a larger group with 10 decision makers from the business, government, education, and nonprofit sectors, for a total of 20 people included in the study. Out of the 10 residents who participated, 8 were African American, one was White, and one identified as Latino. Seven were female, and three were male; their ages varied from 22 to 67. These demographic characteristics were fairly representative of the community. Each resident had lived in the community for at least 10 years (a mean of 36.4 years), thus ensuring that resident participants had enough insider knowledge of the community to be considered experts for this study.

Engaging Community Members Using the Delphi Method

The overarching research question used to begin the study was "What does your ideal community look like?" The first questionnaire was based around major areas targeted for development. Ten open-ended questions were developed and included items about strengthening public transportation, improving and developing housing, types of businesses desired, parks and recreation, and city services (e.g., police, fire, trash). The aim of the first questionnaire was to gain insight and direction about how community needs should best be prioritized. The questionnaire was sent electronically to all 20 participations, with directions for completing them. The research team sent out the e-mails with all addresses and names hidden, so anonymity would be promoted. After all data were collected from this first round, the research team went through the responses to ensure that no names or other identifying information, such as titles, location, or places of employment, was used in responses. All responses for each of the 10 questions were then combined into one document, which was sent out again to participants for comments, feedback, and insights. This round of data collection was considered the study's second wave or round. Once participants had ample time to respond to the responses from the first questionnaire, each of the three members of the research team took the second-round document and began compiling responses and analyzing feedback to identify consensus about community priorities, as well as additional information needed to help clarify items not entirely clear in participant responses. The third-wave questionnaire consisted of five questions that were sent out to participants. After all questionnaires were returned from the third wave, the research team conducted final data analysis.

Finding Community Consensus Through Data Analysis

In Delphi studies, thematic analysis is used for qualitative data (Linstone & Turoff, 1975). Thematic analysis is a type of qualitative analysis that examines data for concepts, categories, and themes. In Delphi studies, consensus is the guiding factor in thematic analysis; however, although consensus concepts are often easy to identify in participant responses, as they will often be illustrated by concrete things such as housing, transportation, and recreation, developing categories and themes will often take more thinking on the part of the research team, as categories and themes provide links, categorization, and overall greater explanatory ability than concepts do on their own. However, because categories and themes are impacted more by how the research team interprets participants' responses, it is recommended that the final results be sent out to participants in order to ensure accuracy at capturing their consensus perspectives.

Each of the three researchers analyzed the data and placed the participants' responses into two major categories: tangible development wants/needs and nontangible development considerations. An example of a tangible development want might be the demolition of abandoned houses or the development of a major grocery store. An example of a nontangible consideration might include addressing crime better or neighbors getting to know one another better. After each researcher had analyzed all Wave 1 responses on his or her own, they then processed and discussed similarities and differences among themselves in order to reach a consensus about the major concepts and categories, which was defined as 50% or more participants listing or indicating the need or concern for an individual response to a question.

The third and final wave of questions was created from the analysis of the first two rounds. This third-round questionnaire asked residents to comment on the consensus priorities that had been expressed in the previous rounds, as well as how nontangible concerns could be addressed within each priority. For example, a consensus of participants had previously responded that in order to entice new residents to move into the community, city services must be increased and improved.

In the Wave 3 questionnaire, one question asked participants, "How could city services, such as police, tree removal, and lighting, be subsidized in long-term development plans to bring new residents to the community without putting added burden on existing community members that could force them to move out of the community?" This structure for third-wave questions allowed participants to consider how to concretely incorporate previous concerns that were more abstract or nontangible into the more tangible development priorities that they had come up with as a group. After all Wave 3 questionnaires were completed and returned, the research team again individually analyzed responses using rigorous thematic analysis. Final concepts, categories, and themes were compared among members of the research team. Points of difference were discussed until consensus could be reached among team members. The final themes that were identified were related to underlying values expressed by participants about what should guide community development in this neighborhood. These themes were diverse, affordable, safe, welcoming, and thriving. The final community priorities, suggestions/concerns, and values were sent out to all participants for a final check for trustworthiness. Out of 20 participants, 18 responded to the member check, and 100% of participants who responded agreed that the final priorities, suggestions, and values were a reflection of the group consensus. The final results were used to help developers guide the process of neighborhood development in this community. To date, the development efforts have been somewhat stalled due to funding challenges, but residents and developers continue to work together as additional funding is secured to complete the proposed development project. Although both residents and developers have expressed some frustration over the time it is taking to complete development, both groups believe the extra time and funding are worth these minor setbacks in order to ensure that the community is developed in a way in which local and professional expertise is taken into account.

CONCLUSION

In this case study, the Delphi method was an effective community-based research tool that allowed for the meaningful inclusion of community residents alongside decision makers and professionals. It provides a pragmatic method that is easy to use, minimally evasive, anonymous, and with the structure and rigor necessary to be useful in the context of community-based research. Researchers considering using the qualitative Delphi method in community development should consider how best to access community members with the given expertise to participate. Given the often conflict-prone nature of relationships among professionals, academics, and community members, gatekeepers and community-based organizations will frequently be important partners in helping to recruit community members to qualitative Delphi studies. Additionally, the use of the qualitative Delphi method to include local community members in decision-making processes should be considered only if developers, academics, and professionals are committed to using local expertise in the given project or to address community issues. However, if these caveats are met, community practitioners and researchers seeking a flexible approach for engaging community members in meaningful participation in development and other decision-making tasks should give serious consideration to using the qualitative Delphi method.

REFERENCES

Alder, M., & Ziglio, E. (1996). *Gazing into the oracle: The Delphi Method and its application to social policy and public health.* London, England: Jessica Kingsley Publishers.

Bazeley, P. (2009). Analyzing qualitative data: More than identifying themes. *Malaysian Journal of Qualitative Research, 6,* 6–22.

Birdsall, I. (2004). It seemed like a good idea at the time: The forces affecting implementation of strategies for an information technology project in the Department of Defense. *Digital Abstracts International, 65,* 2756.

Bolger, F., & Wright, G. (1994). Assessing the quality of expert judgment: Issues and analysis. *Decision Support Systems, 11,* 1–24.

Brady, S. R. (2012). *Discovering how community organizing leads to social change: Developing formal practice theory for social workers engaged in empowering community organizing.* Richmond: Virginia Commonwealth University.

Creswell, J. (1998). *Qualitative research and design: Choosing among five traditions.* Thousand Oaks, CA: Sage.

Dalkey, N., & Helmer, O. (1963). An experimental application of the Delphi methods to the use of experts. *Management Science, 9,* 458–467.

Denzin, N., & Lincoln, Y. S. (Eds.). (2005). *The Sage handbook of qualitative research* (3rd ed.). Thousand Oaks, CA: Sage.

Dietz, T. (1987). Methods for analyzing data from Delphi panels: Some evidence from a forecasting study. *Technological Forecasting and Social Change, 31*, 79–85.

Dobbie, D., & Richards-Schuster, K. (2008). Building solidarity through difference: A practice model for critical multicultural organizing. *Journal of Community Practice, 16*, 317–340.

Fay, B. (1996). *Contemporary philosophy of social science: A multicultural approach.* Malden, MA: Blackwell.

Fletcher, A., & Childon, G. P. (2014). Using the Delphi method for qualitative, participatory action research in health leadership. *International Journal of Qualitative Methods, 13*, 1–18.

Hartman, F., & Baldwin, A. (1998). *Leadership undertow: Project managers fears and frustrations.* Paper presented at the 29th Annual Project Management Institute Seminars and Symposium, Long Beach, CA.

Johnson, A. (2006). Privilege, power, and difference. In A. Johnson, *Privilege, power, and difference* (pp. 12–28). Boston, MA: McGraw-Hill.

Linstone, H. A., & Turoff, M. (1975). *The Delphi method: Techniques and applications.* Reading, MA: Addison-Weshley.

Miles, M., & Huberman, A. M. (1994). *Qualitative data analysis: An expanded sourcebook.* Thousand Oaks, CA: Sage.

Minkler, M. (2005). *Community organizing and community building for health* (2nd ed.). New Brunswick, NJ: Rutgers University Press.

Roberson, Q., Collins, C. J., & Oreg, S. (2005). The effects of recruitment message specificity on applicant attraction to organizations. *Journal of Business and Psychology, 19*, 319–340.

Rugh, P. (2014, 23-July). *Who bled Detroit dry?* Retrieved June 2015, from http://www.vice.com/read/who-bled-detroit-dry?utm_source=vicetwitterus

Skulmoski, G., Hartman, F. T., & Kran, J. (2007). The Delphi method for graduate research. *Journal of Information Technology Education, 6*, 1–21. Retrieved June 2015, from http://www.jite.org/documents/Vol6/JITEv6p001-021Skulmoski212.pdf

Staes, J. (2010, August 12). Comparing Detroit to other cities? Look at the map. *Detroit Unspun.* Retrieved June 2015, from http://blog.thedetroithub.com/2010/08/12/comparing-detroit-to-other-cities-look-at-the-map/

Strauss, A., & Corbin, J. (1998). *Basics of qualitative research.* Thousand Oaks, CA: Sage.

Turoff, M. (1970). The design for a policy Delphi. *Technological Forecasting and Social Change, 2*, 149–172.

8

Ethnographic Approaches

URMITAPA DUTTA

Ethnography as a social science methodology is by and large a 19th-century enterprise anchored in the discipline of anthropology. During the mid- to late 19th century, anthropologists increasingly recognized the value of knowledge acquired through direct participation and immersion in a culture. Anthropologists Franz Boaz and Bronislaw Malinowski are generally credited with the establishment of an ethnographic approach, or participant observation, as the principal method in anthropology (Tedlock, 2000). Ethnographic approaches have diverse philosophical origins, disciplinary traditions, and intellectual trajectories. This chapter focuses on critical ethnography as a community-based research approach. A civic, participatory, and collaborative project, critical ethnography is rooted in the social justice commitments of critical qualitative inquiry (Denzin & Giardina, 2011; Madison, 2005).

A number of shifts were instrumental in the development of critical ethnographic approaches in the United States. Leading these was the Chicago School of Ethnography, which emerged during the 1920s in the sociology department at the University of Chicago. Key proponents of the Chicago school, such as Robert Park, John Dewey, and Herbert Blumer, played a crucial role by shifting the ethnographic lenses from foreign, exotic cultures to a focus on urban landscapes in the United States. During the 1960s and 1970s, ethnographic approaches witnessed the emergence of ethnomethodologies (Garfinkel, 1967) and symbolic and interpretive anthropologies (Geertz, 1973; Turner, 1967). Clifford Geertz introduced the term *thick description* as a methodological device to get at the symbolic and interpretive import of what is documented during fieldwork. However, it was not until the 1980s that ethnographic approaches began to take a critical turn with the influence of feminist, indigenous, poststructural, and postcolonial scholarship. The most salient feature of the transformation was the unmasking of ethnographic authority, that is, the elucidation of colonial and imperialist underpinnings of classic ethnographic traditions (Conquergood, 1991). Critical ethnographic approaches shifted the focus of ethnographic inquiry from the objective study of other cultures to the reflexive study of social suffering and inequities (Angel-Ajani, 2006; Burawoy, 2003; Hale, 2008).

INTRODUCTION TO CRITICAL ETHNOGRAPHY

The salient feature of critical ethnography is its orientation to social justice and activism. Critical ethnography is rooted in critical realist philosophies that emphasize connections between structural inequities and the everyday realities of people (Carspecken, 1996). Critical ethnography begins with an ethical responsibility to address injustice and inequities in specific domains (Madison, 2005). Recognizing the disparities that stand between "what is" and "what could be" in many communities across the globe, critical ethnographers must disrupt the status quo and unpack the power structures underlying different forms of injustice. Madison (2005, p. 5) was unequivocal in her assertion that critical ethnographers must "resist domestication." This implies that we have to deploy the skills, resources, and privilege at our disposal to create spaces for voices that are systematically silenced or subjugated. The goal of critical ethnography ultimately is to contribute to emancipatory knowledge and decentered discourses of social justice. These fundamental principles align seamlessly with the guiding principles of community psychology and have the potential to enrich community-based research.

Critical Ethnography and Power

Critical ethnographic approaches are profoundly shaped by feminist, postcolonial, indigenous, and critical race scholarship (Comaroff & Comaroff, 2003; Tomaselli, Dyll, & Francis, 2008; Visweswaran, 2003), the common thread across these bodies of scholarship being a highly nuanced conceptualization of power. Although the potential of ethnographic approaches to generate deeply contextualized understandings is widely recognized (e.g., Banyard & Miller, 1998; Case, Todd, & Kral, 2014), these very understandings may reproduce existing dynamics of power, privilege, and subjugation. Interrogating the ebb and flow of power is fundamental to the emancipatory practice of critical ethnography and has significant implications for how community-based research is conceptualized, conducted, represented, and disseminated (Dutta, 2014). First, contemporary ethnography impels us to critically examine the positionality of the researcher in relation to community-based research. Second, it calls for a critical interrogation of "collaboration" between researchers and communities. Third, it impels us to examine and reenvision such dichotomies as global-local and universal-particular, which are often taken for granted in research.

Positionality and Reflexivity

A keystone of ethnography is the researcher's deep immersion in the community or context of inquiry. This immersion takes place in a particular sociopolitical and cultural milieu and is shaped by researchers' worldviews, values, biographies, and politics. The various intersections of these lived domains constitute the research horizon. Positionality refers to the explication of this horizon through a critical engagement with our power, privilege, biases, and insights vis-à-vis participant communities (Madison, 2005). Participant observation has a long and early history of scientific empiricism. Preoccupied with the notion of objectivity, early ethnographers, especially during the colonial period, failed to discern the values inherent in the categorizations they imposed on groups that were different from them. Along the lines of this postcolonial critique, critical race theorists have discussed how White privilege tends to be undetectable as neutral or normative, rendered so through institutional arrangements (Bonnet, 1999). Fine (1994) outlined an activist epistemological stance that requires the researcher to assume a clear position, one that is committed to disrupting hegemonic practices. It is precisely this activist stance that defines the positionality of the critical ethnographer. Although we do not presume to speak on behalf of marginalized voices, our research attempts to create conditions where such voices may be heard.

An activist stance calls for reflexivity, that is, the process of continually examining our roles and positions in relation to our multifaceted research contexts (Finlay, 2002). It is through a reflexive engagement that we strive to remain firmly anchored in the empirical world of our research participants (Dutta, 2014). The perfomative turn in ethnography played a crucial role in facilitating dialogues on reflexivity. Emerging from a critique of mainstream Western academic traditions that privilege written expressions, the performative turn privileged embodied practices and expressions, thus honoring and legitimizing diverse forms of knowledge and knowledge production (Madison, 2005; Mirón, 2008). Another example of reflexive practices is a decolonizing standpoint that entails assuming a transdisciplinary and political stance geared toward unpacking colonial and neocolonial legacies (Reyes Cruz & Sonn, 2011). Informed by feminist and postcolonial praxis, Lykes (2013, p. 777) clarified her positionality vis-à-vis communities affected by armed conflict in Guatemala as one of "passionate solidarity and informed empathy." These and other forms of reflexive practices are essential to a dialectical engagement among the researcher, research process, and research products.

Rethinking Collaboration

The *American Heritage Dictionary* (2014) defines collaboration as "working together, especially in a joint intellectual effort." Collaboration is considered foundational to community-based research and is typically viewed as a positive goal (e.g., Minkler, 2005). Many indigenous scholars, however, critique this assumption, arguing that the idea of collaboration typically embodies the desire and commitments of dominant groups (Jones & Jenkins, 2008; Smith, 2012). When the terms of collaboration are not interrogated, these efforts may unwittingly reinscribe the very imperialist impulses we wished to circumvent through collaboration (Fine, Tuck, & Zeller-Berkman, 2008; Lykes, 2013). Thus, instead of assuming that collaboration is inherently positive, critical ethnography demands a scrutiny of the power dynamics inherent in micropractices of collaboration. For example, who initiates the research and calls for collaboration? Who establishes the terms of the collaborative process? Who wishes to understand and to what end? What are the legitimate modes of expression? The rhetoric of inclusion associated with collaboration may easily disintegrate into exclusionary practices in the absence of a critical engagement with these questions (Smith, 2012). This critical engagement entails what Fine (1994, p. 72) referred to as "working the hyphen": "creating occasions for researchers and informants to discuss what is, and is not, 'happening between,' within the negotiated relations of whose story is being told . . . and whose story is being shadowed." Crucially, working the hyphen allows for uneasy or unsettled (non)relationships based on learning from the margins as opposed to learning about the other, thus allowing for decolonized alternatives to traditional collaboration (Jones & Jenkins, 2008).

Redefining Global-Local Relations

The global-local dichotomy serves as a referent for several common binary categorizations in research: Global North and Global South, center and periphery, universal and particular, colonizer and indigenous. These binaries are colonial and imperialist constructions, with one term representing the signifier and the other being signified (Jones & Jenkins, 2008; Nabavi, 2006). In addition to colonial and neocolonial forces, such binaries are promoted and reinforced through contemporary United States security lenses (Appadurai, 2000; Shome & Hegde, 2002). As a consequence, issues experienced by communities in the Global South and other regions of the world are discursively constituted as local, while issues and communities within the US context are viewed as embodying the global universal (Das, 2001). Drawing awareness to the symbolic violence inherent in these categorizations, we need to analyze how these terms and ultimately regions of the world are hierarchically interconnected (Gupta & Ferguson, 1992; Marcus, 1995). In order to fulfill its emancipatory promise, critical ethnographies strive to reestablish more reciprocal, nonhierarchical relations between the core and peripheries of knowledge production, within the Global North as well as between North and South (Appadurai, 2000; Ghamari-Tabrizi, 2005).

The Critical Ethnographic Research Process

This section presents some key considerations involved in critical ethnographic research. It should be noted, though, that the phases of the research typically play out in an iterative manner rather than progressing in a linear fashion. At the outset, we need to be aware of the philosophical and paradigmatic influences that shape our research agendas. Reflexivity of method is foundational to critical ethnography and helps us recognize the dynamic interplay between researchers and participants, critical theory and data, and research and action.

Data Collection and Analysis

The cornerstone of ethnography is immersive fieldwork in a territorially bound locale. Fieldwork typically involves participant (or nonparticipant) observation along with individual/group interviews and focus groups (Madison, 2005; Schensul & LeCompte, 2013). In order to examine the ways in which social structures and systems are instantiated locally, contemporary critical ethnographic approaches have expanded to include such methods as archival data, cultural products (e.g., books, television, music), spatial mapping, participatory action research, and multimedia techniques (Given, 2008). Some key considerations guiding decisions regarding specific methods are as follows: What are the goals of the research (e.g., gather exploratory data versus critical understanding)? Is the ethnography one of several components of the research or is the research primarily designed as an ethnographic project? Are there particular contingencies associated with research participants (e.g., hidden or hard-to-reach populations)? Are there risks associated with particular methods? As we explore the potential of various methods, it is important to keep sight of the centrality of the ethnographer as a critical, reflective tool in the research process (Schensul & LeCompte, 2013).

Sampling in ethnographic research relies primarily on purposive and criterion-based sampling techniques (e.g., critical case sampling, stakeholder sampling, and negative case sampling).

Such sampling techniques are designed to yield as information-rich data as possible. It is important to note that there is no one best sampling strategy because the most effective strategy is contingent on the community, context, and research objectives. The data collected may take a variety of forms. Primarily in the form of texts (e.g., fieldnotes, observations, or interview transcripts), data may also include cultural artifacts, photographs, and video. As much as data analysis is about seeking emerging patterns and themes, it is also about locating absences and irregularities. Analysis techniques may vary accordingly, although critical discourse analysis (Van Dijk, 1993), narrative analysis (Loseke, 2007), and cultural analysis (Strauss, 2005) are commonly used in critical ethnographic research. Methods of data collection and analysis are not mutually exclusive and may be creatively combined to illuminate the issues being studied.

Representational Issues in Critical Ethnography

The end product of traditional ethnographic research is the ethnographic text, although this scenario has altered considerably in recent times. The postmodern turn in qualitative inquiry brought about a crisis of representation, which challenged classic ethnographic norms based on objectivist represention of culture. The postmodern turn unveiled the complicity of conventional social science methods in reinscribing historical oppression (Denzin & Lincoln, 2011). Ethnographic approaches are increasingly used in conjunction with other methods to illuminate some contextual aspects of the phenomena or community of interest (e.g., Allen, Mohatt, Markstrom, Byers, & Novins, 2012; Greene, 2006). The production of detailed ethnographic texts is not central in these cases. Representational issues are core to critical ethnographic research, regardless of its scope. The distanced and disembodied stance of the researcher, typically venerated in social science research, is antithetical to the emancipatory foundations of critical ethnography (Jones & Jenkins, 2008; Reyes Cruz & Sonn, 2011). Reflexive practices are not limited to the formulation of research questions and collection of data. It is equally important for us to reflexively consider the implications of how we represent our findings. As Hammersley (2002, p. 74) argued, "representation must always be from some point of view which makes some features of the phenomenon relevant and others irrelevant." Given the multiplicity of explanations that are possible, it is vital for critical ethnographers to delineate the standpoint from which particular findings are understood and presented.

Quality Considerations in Critical Ethnographic Research

Critical ethnography reframes traditional notions of assessing research quality. This move is shaped by an awareness of the politics of evidence. Far from involving disinterested, cognitive acts, standards for assessing evidence are regulated by political and institutional apparatuses (Denzin, 2009). As critical ethnographers, we have to deconstruct the meaning of evidence vis-à-vis our research contexts by raising questions such as: Whose criteria and standards are used to assess evidence and about whom? Who determines what constitutes evidence? Who determines what methods produce the best forms of evidence? Critical ethnography moves away from truth claims–based authoritative norms or predetermined criteria in a bid to disrupt the status quo (Madison, 2005).

Considerations of quality in critical ethnographic research are inextricably tied to ethics (see Battiste, 2008, & Fine, 2006, for more elaboration). For example, Smith (2012) emphasized a justice orientation over a truth orientation in evaluating research, especially research involving historically disenfranchised communities. The concept of *psychopolitical validity*, introduced by Prilleltensky (2003), is particularly relevant for evaluating community-based critical ethnographic research. Psychopolitical validity is concerned with the extent to which research contributes to understanding, resisting, and addressing diverse forms of oppression. Prilleltensky discussed two kinds of psychopolitical validity. Epistemic validity evaluates the extent to which power dynamics are cognized in the research, while transformative validity assesses the extent to which research leads to social change. Another relevant validation principle is that of *ontological authenticity* (Lincoln, Lynham, & Guba, 2011). Applied to critical community-based ethnography, this means that our research should be evaluated on the extent to which it is able to provide a nuanced, discursively complex, and enriched conception of the issues of interest. A common thread uniting all these validation methods is an emphasis on the disruption of hegemonic understandings.

The next section draws upon the author's research in Northeast India to illuminate some methodological issues in critical ethnographic research. The author has been engaged in critical ethnographic investigations of ethnic conflict and peace building in Northeast India for over a decade. This example will illustrate how critical ethnographic research has been employed to explicate protracted ethnic conflict in the community. Consistent with a critical ethnographic approach, the case study illustrates a reflexive, first-person account of the ethnographic research.

CASE STUDY

Background and Aims

The site of this community-based critical ethnographic research is the Garo Hills region of Northeast India. Characterized by extraordinary ethnic and linguistic diversity, Northeast India has been the site of protracted ethnic conflicts, some of these spanning the entire postcolonial period since 1947. Much of the conflict takes the form of armed insurgencies. Northeast India shares almost 98% of its boundaries with neighboring countries and is connected to the rest of India (referred to as "mainland India" in popular discourse) by a narrow strip of land, approximately 12 miles wide. Thus, although the phenomenon of ethnic separatism is not unique to Northeast India, the strategic location of the region renders it critical from a national security standpoint. The Indian government relies on security-driven approaches to respond to conflicts in Northeast India, the most notable being the Armed Forces Special Power Act that grants extraordinary powers to the military and has been operational since 1958 in the region. Both public and scholarly attention focus on the spectacular confrontations between armed insurgent groups and the Indian military, obfuscating the violence that has become endemic to the region. The critical ethnographic project was an effort to move away from crisis-based politics and elucidate the ethnic violence from the vantage point of ordinary citizens. The project was guided by two main objectives: (a) to interrogate the everyday violence in order to understand the processes by which it is normalized and how it reconfigures identities and subjectivities of local youth and (b) to draw upon the emerging understanding to explore and facilitate community-based peace building in Garo Hills. Community-based research in contexts such as Garo Hills necessitates methods that create spaces for marginal or alternative narratives. Given the protracted violence in the community, I had to be mindful about refraining from depicting any final truth. Instead, the goal was to elucidate the complexity of ethnic identity politics, illuminating the diverse voices that are erased by powerful, security-driven discourses.

Methodology

I employed narrative inquiry and participatory action research methods within a broader critical ethnographic framework (Appadurai, 2006; McIntyre, 2000; Rappaport, 2000). Specific methods of data elicitation included interviews, group discussions, observations, and written materials collected over a year of intensive fieldwork in Garo Hills. The narratives of youth from diverse ethnic groups in Garo Hills formed the bulk of the materials, but I also conducted interviews with a range of stakeholders (e.g., members of insurgent groups, district administrators, police, educators) in order to gain an ecological understanding of the conflict. The interviews were complemented with participant observations of day-to-day life and community events, relevant public documents, and newspaper articles. Although I examined the data to discover thematic regularities in how my participants talked about everyday violence, I also conducted critical discourse analysis to understand the broader institutional contexts and societal narratives implicated in ethnic conflict in Garo Hills (Van Dijk, 1993).

Positionality and Reflexivity

My identity as a researcher is profoundly shaped by my experiences of growing up in the Northeastern borderlands of India. The gradually deepening ethnic faultlines in my home community sensitized me to complex layers of ethnic othering. The dominant ethnic group in Garo Hills is the Garo tribe, although other tribal and *non-tribal* (an official ethnic identity category) communities also live in the region. Much of the ethnic violence and exclusions are perpetrated against non-tribal minorities, considered to be outsiders in the region. Ethnically, I am "the other." Although this otherness was substantially mitigated by my family's longstanding involvement in local community organizing, there was always a disjuncture between my emotional experience of home and the sociopolitical conditions necessary to legitimize the relationship (Dutta, 2015). Growing up in Northeast India, I also became painfully aware of the deprecating lens with which the residents of the region are viewed by mainland India. The popular imagery of Northeast India tends to be associated with remoteness, insurgency, and underdevelopment. These characterizations, animating much intellectual debate and social policy, are immediate and tangible to the lives of those who call these locales home. Yet our voices are hardly ever part of the public discourse. These experiences and insights fundamentally shaped my research agenda, foregrounding the embodied experiences of ordinary citizens.

The particular configurations of my positionality—my ethnicity, community involvement, and current residence in the United States—made me a partial insider vis-à-vis Garo Hills. This status undermined my non-tribal ethnicity, allowing me to challenge local norms without the social or safety costs associated with being the ethnic other. Deep involvement with the larger community also enabled me to take advantage of serendipitous community events to advance inclusivity and civic engagement in Garo Hills. Through a reflexive use of autoethnography (e.g., utilizing experiences, memories, and my structural positioning), I tried to achieve greater intersubjectivity and representational richness in elucidating the fraught context of Northeast India (Dutta, 2015; Humphreys, 2005).

Critical ethnographic research requires us to be vigilant of our power and privilege as researchers. This meant being heedful of my emotional and structural positionality vis-à-vis my participants. My affiliation to a university in the United States conferred upon me privileged status in the local community. This privilege compounded my responsibility even as I leveraged it to secure social and material resources for my participants. I was cognizant that the shared histories with my participants did not erase the differences in our circumstances. This was never more evident than when youth talked about the limitations imposed on their mobility due to lack of social or financial capital. My privilege—to move across multiple contexts—was brought into sharp relief against the youths' efforts to reconcile with everyday violence. Ultimately, I was also in a position to produce knowledge about Garo Hills. Thus, democratizing the research process was imperative to avoid the reproduction of totalizing discourses about conflict in Garo Hills.

Recasting Ethnic Conflict Through a Critical Ethnographic Lens

The role played by hegemonic ethnic identity politics in producing and maintaining protracted ethnic violence in Northeast India became apparent early in my research. A critical ethnographic approach highlighted the importance of interrogating state-sponsored ethnic categorizations—the identity politics as well as the lived experiences associated with those categories. Divisive ethnic categorizations in Northeast India were created during the British colonial regime and subsequently reinforced through ethnocentric policies formulated by the postcolonial state (Baruah, 2003). A case in point is the Sixth Schedule of the Indian Constitution, which classifies residents of Northeast India into tribals and non-tribals, a distinction introduced by the British. The term *tribe* collapses over 400 heterogeneous groups into one broad classification distinguished from caste (Bhaumik, 2009). Similarly, the term *non-tribal* homogenizes all ethnicities that do not identify as tribals, whether they are long-term residents of the region or recent migrants. These ethnic divisions, however problematic and inadequate, constituted the lived realities of my youth participants and at times were embraced as politicized identities. Therefore, a constant challenge in this ethnography was to write about the embodied ethnic experiences without reinscribing the violence inherent in these categories.

Findings

I analyzed fieldnotes and transcripts from interviews and group discussions with youth to examine the everyday experiences associated with state-sponsored ethnic labels. Discourse analysis of interviews with stakeholders, such as educators, separatist groups, and district administrators, illuminated the social and institutional practices that reify and maintain ethnic divisions in Garo Hills. These analyses helped elucidate the different forms of everyday violence and othering that have become endemic to the local community. In particular, the analyses illuminated the ubiquity of ethnic violence experienced by non-tribal ethnic groups in Garo Hills and the processes by which it is normalized.

The analyses also underscored the marginality experienced by both dominant and minority ethnic groups in Garo Hills. These findings disrupted the victim-vicitimizer dichotomy, which is often implicated in intractable ethnic conflict.

The lives of non-tribal youth, the ethnic others in Garo Hills, are marked by routine acts of bodily harm, harassment, extortion, silencing, and humiliation. In the following excerpt, Kavi (a pseudonym, used to protect the participant's identity), a non-tribal youth participant, described the pervasive nature of ethnic violence against non-tribals:

> It (i.e., ethnic violence) happens everywhere—in offices, in banks, at the post office. But no one says anything. Everybody feels scorched, but there is nothing to be done. No one to complain to . . . . There is a continuous fear that some problem will occur. And it is not as if they (young Garo males) let people off after giving them one slap. They can do anything. Whatever comes to their mind, they do it. There is no limit.

This context, rife with violence, constitutes what Martín-Baró (1994, p. 125) referred to as "normal abnormality." The ubiquitous violence constrains the lives of non-tribal youth—their movement, the way they dress, and the way they talk; their ways of being in the world are mediated by the imperative to evade violence. These youth have come to anticipate the multiple forms of violence and marginality that shape their lives. Notably, more than the acts of physical violence, it is the constant threat of violence—"a continuous fear that some problem will occur" (as Kavi put it)—that creates a repressive environment. My critical ethnographic research uncovered the institutionalized social indifference to the everyday violence, illuminating processes that serve to normalize and naturalize everyday ethnic violence in Garo Hills. These processes included the absence of any social critique by influential Garo citizens, high levels of impunity enjoyed by those who perpetrate ethnic violence, and naturalization of the conflict by the district administration and state police. Collectively, these processes act to maintain the violence and impede individual or collective resistance (Scheper-Hughes, 2006).

The everyday violence is guided by a divisive logic where one's non-tribal ethnicity is often sufficient cause to elicit violence. Patrick, a Garo youth participant explained: "Honestly if I tell the truth then, yes, most of the Garo youth do not like non-tribals." Across multiple stakeholder narratives, there emerged a divisive master narrative positioning Garo tribals in opposition to non-tribals. This master narrative of tribal versus non-tribal acts powerfully to shape how issues of belonging and exclusion are negotiated in the local community. Embedded in narratives of ethnic othering is the theme of exclusion so that different ethnic groups have varying levels of access to civic and community life. Ethnic antagonism is also rooted in a deep-seated fear about the depletion of limited resources, with different groups vying for the same resources (Dutta, 2013). The master narrative is fueled by a purist stance, such that only those individuals who are born as Garos can stake a claim to Garo Hills and participate in civic life.

The numerical majority of the Garos, however, does not immunize them against experiences of marginality and exclusion. Garo youth feel excluded in relation to mainland India, which is a complex response to the historiographical and cultural marginalization of Northeast India. State-sponsored and mainstream Indian discourses of tribe frame them as culturally and developmentally inferior, contributing to widespread negative stereotypes about tribal groups (Dutta, 2015). This is illustrated by the following excerpt, where Rudy, a Garo youth participant, described his experience at a job interview in a highly cosmopolitan Indian city:

> At the interview, this person actually had the audacity to ask me: Do people in your place still live in jungles and wear animal skins? I mean what do you answer to people like that? I have seen that many Indians are more ignorant than us from the Northeast.

Along similar lines, James, another Garo youth, had pointed out: "While living in Garo Hills, we can live like kings! But once we go outside, it feels very awkward—as if we are someone from the slum." Using the allegory of slum dwellers, James tried to convey the stigma and social distance embodied in their tribal identity. Thus, both tribal and non-tribal youth struggle with experiences of marginality. Divisive identity politics have engendered victim identities among members of both groups, which is used to justify continued ethnic othering and violence. Being a responsible researcher in this context thus entailed explicating the multiple facets of violence—violence experienced by non-tribal minorities in Garo Hills as well as the structural violence perpetrated by the Indian State against tribal minorities such as the Garo tribe.

Implications and Actions

Critical ethnographic research is committed to moving from "what is" to "what could be." In this specific context, the process involved challenging victim-victimizer binaries and redefining the parameters of community in more inclusive terms. Thus, as much as this project was about interrogating everyday violence from the perspectives of ordinary citizens, it was also about exploring possibilities for resistance and change. Discourse analysis of the youth narratives suggested that individuals are not passive victims of these master narratives; rather, they demonstrated the potential to develop counternarratives when provided with a safe space to do so (Dutta & Aber, in press). Using research as intervention, I inititated and facilitated Voices, a youth participatory action research project on local community issues. The project engaged local youth from diverse ethnic groups in Garo Hills in a process whereby they collectively defined local community problems, framed research questions, conducted interviews and surveys with community members, analyzed the data, and represented local citizens' concerns to diverse audiences in a bid to inspire local action. Over the course of the project, the participating youth developed a strong researcher identity that took precedence over alliances based on ethnic identities. The project provided young people with opportunities to engage in social critique and to take deliberate action to enhance community well-being (Dutta & Aber, in press). The notion of everyday peace is rooted in these integrative community development processes. Violence that is entrenched in the social fabric of everyday life necessitates a notion of everyday peace. Embodied in the politics of possibility engendered by the community action project, the notion of everyday peace is captured in the following quote from Pansy, a youth member of Voices:

> After being a part of this project, discussing and working together for our community, it has become a part of our lives, something to look forward to .... The small project was so interesting and successful—imagine what we can do as a group!

CONCLUSION

This chapter has focused on critical ethnography as a conceptual and methodological framework for engaging in community-based research. A critical ethnographic approach is distinguished from traditional ethnographic approaches by its unequivocal commitment to public engagement and activism. These goals are advanced through a critical analysis of the power-knowledge nexus that shapes social realities. These analyses have major implications for community-based research, some of which, such as positionality and reflexivity, local-global relations, and representation, were discussed in this chapter. A case study illustrated how critical ethnographic approaches help us explicate a specific social problem–protracted ethnic conflict in Northeast India. A critical ethnographic approach illuminated the multiple narratives of marginality that are masked by dominant security-driven narratives. Doing so allowed us to generate community-level possibilities for peace building.

A salient feature of critical ethnography is the decolonization of knowledge production across all levels. At an interpersonal level, this engagement begins with an autoethnographic sensibility, or the recognition that we craft our scholarship in distinctive and personally meaningful ways. This meaningfulness has a range of consequences for community-based researchers engaged in social change. We do not merely describe the social world but also enact the social world through a complex set of assumptions made at every stage of the research process. A commitment to decolonization also entails attending to issues of representation. The way we represent social groups has serious consequences for how they are perceived and treated (Caplan & Nelson, 1973; Hall, 1997). At the level of knowledge production, critical ethnographic approaches call for a decolonization of the academy so as to create spaces for the production of counterhegemonic knowledge, otherwise reduced to local in scope. Critical ethnographic scholarship necessarily connects the personal to the social, cultural, and political.

The case study illustrates how critical ethnographic approaches may be employed to reframe protracted ethnic conflict in Northeast India and to disrupt the impasse created by divisive ethnic identity politics. This work tries to foreground the perspectives of ordinary citizens, which are systematically excluded from both public policy and scholarly discourses. These perspectives are represented through the researcher's specific relationship to the community. Rather than trying to bracket off preexisting relationships in a bid to achieve objectivity, the researcher makes a concerted effort to be reflexive about this engagement. This reflexivity has been crucial in highlighting the micropolitics of ethnic conflict in the local community. Although prioritizing local communities in Garo Hills, this work scrutinizes the ways in which transnational and globalized forces are embodied in everyday micropolitics of conflict. Specifically, it draws attention to forms of ethnic violence afflicting many postcolonial states across the world. Thus, the local or particular instance offers a window into a more universal phenomenon. The failure to elucidate these global-local nexus reproduces and reifies essentialized perspectives of developing nations. By providing a thorough analysis of the processes by which violence becomes endemic in social landscapes, critical ethnography also offers a conceptual framework to examine structural violence in community-based research.

In summary, critical ethnographic approaches represent considerable potential for community-based researchers committed to social justice and social change agendas. It is certainly one of many possible approaches, but its major strength lies in the deconstruction of categories viewed as foundational and taken for granted in academic research. The critical ethnographic research described here elucidates multivocality in communities, demonstrating that communities are rarely as bounded or homogenous as the concept might imply. In order to produce counterhegemonic knowledge, our research must explicate the diverse voices within a community and attend to power dynamics inherent in those contexts. Although particularly suitable for understanding and addressing protracted conflict, critical ethnographic approaches may be employed across diverse contexts where researchers are committed to local action—the kind that is informed by an elucidation of the complex interplay between local and macrosocial forces.

REFERENCES

Allen, J., Mohatt, G. V., Markstrom, C. A., Byers, L., & Novins, D. K. (2012). "Oh no, we are just getting to know you": The relationship in research with children and youth in indigenous communities. *Child Development Perspectives, 6*, 55–60.

Angel-Ajani, A. (2006). Expert witness: Notes towards revisiting the politics of listening. In V. Sanford & A. Angel-Ajani (Eds.), *Engaged observer: Anthropology, advocacy, and activism* (pp. 76–89). Piscataway, NJ: Rutgers University Press.

Appadurai, A. (2000). Grassroots globalization and the research imagination. *Public Culture, 12*, 1–19.

Appadurai, A. (2006). The right to research. *Globalisation, Societies and Education, 4*, 167–177.

Banyard, V. L., & Miller, K. E. (1998). The powerful potential of qualitative research for community psychology. *American Journal of Community Psychology, 26*, 485–505.

Baruah, S. (2003). *Durable disorder: Understanding the politics of Northeast India*. Oxford, England: Oxford University Press.

Battiste, M. (2008). Research ethics for protecting indigenous knowledge and heritage: Institutional and researcher responsibilities. In N. K. Denzin, Y. S. Lincoln, & L. T. Smith (Eds.), *Handbook of critical and indigenous methodologies* (pp. 497–510). Thousand Oaks, CA: Sage.

Bhaumik, S. (2009). *Troubled periphery: Crisis of India's North East*. Thousand Oaks, CA: Sage.

Bonnet, A. (1999). Constructions of whiteness in European and American anti-racism. In R. D. Torres, L. F. Mirón, & J. X. Inda (Eds.), *Race, identity and citizenship: A reader* (pp. 200–218). Oxford, England: Blackwell.

Burawoy, M. (2003). Revisits: An outline of a theory of reflexive ethnography. *American Sociological Review, 68*, 645–679.

Caplan, N., & Nelson, S. D. (1973). On being useful: The nature and consequences of psychological research on social problems. *American Psychologist, 28*, 199–211.

Carspecken, P. F. (1996). *Critical ethnography in educational research: A theoretical and practical guide*. New York, NY: Routledge.

Case, A. D., Todd, N. R., & Kral, M. J. (2014). Ethnography in community psychology: Promises and tensions. *American Journal of Community Psychology, 54*, 1–12.

Collaboration. (2014). In *The American Heritage dictionary of the English language online*. Retrieved June 2015, from https://www.ahdictionary.com/word/search.html?q=collaboration

Comaroff, J., & Comaroff, J. (2003). Ethnography on an awkward scale: Postcolonial anthropology and the violence of abstraction. *Ethnography, 4*, 147–179.

Conquergood, D. (1991). Rethinking ethnography: Towards a critical cultural politics. *Communications Monographs, 58*, 179–194.

Das, V. (2001). Violence and translation. *Anthropological Quarterly, 75*, 105–112.

Denzin, N. K. (2009). The elephant in the living room: Or extending the conversation about the politics of evidence. *Qualitative Research, 9*, 139–160.

Denzin, N. K., & Giardina, M. D. (2011). Introduction. In N. K. Denzin & M. D. Giardina (Eds.), *Qualitative inquiry and global crises* (pp. 9–27). Walnut Creek, CA: Left Coast Press.

Denzin, N. K., & Lincoln, Y. S. (Eds.). (2011). Introduction: The discipline and practice of qualitative research. In N. K. Denzin & Y. S. Lincoln (Eds.), *Handbook of qualitative research* (4th ed., pp. 1–20). Thousand Oaks, CA: Sage.

Dutta, U. (2013). Beyond the ethnicity question: Constructing and enacting more inclusive identities. In J. Prodhani & R. S. Thakur (Eds.), *Culture, ethnicity, and identity: A reader* (pp. 290–299). Guwahati, India: DVS Publications.

Dutta, U. (2014). Critical ethnography. In J. Mills & M. Birks (Eds.), *Qualitative methodology: A practical guide* (pp. 89–106). London, England: Sage.

Dutta, U. (2015). The long way home: The vicissitudes of belonging and otherness in Northeast India. *Qualitative Inquiry, 21*, 161–172.

Dutta, U., & Aber, M. S. (in press). Enacted cultural critique: Examining everyday violence in Garo Hills. *Journal of Prevention & Intervention in the Community.*

Fine, M. (1994). Working the hyphens. In N. K. Denzin & Y. S. Lincoln (Eds.), *Handbook of qualitative research* (pp. 70–82). Thousand Oaks, CA: Sage.

Fine, M. (2006). Bearing witness: Methods for researching oppression and resistance—A textbook for critical research. *Social Justice Research, 19*, 83–108.

Fine, M., Tuck, E., & Zeller-Berkman, S. (2008). Do you believe in Geneva? Methods and ethics at the global-local nexus. In N. K. Denzin, Y. S. Lincoln, & L. T. Smith (Eds.), *Handbook of critical and indigenous methodologies* (pp. 157–180). Thousand Oaks, CA: Sage.

Finlay, L. (2002). "Outing" the researcher: The provenance, process, and practice of reflexivity. *Qualitative Health Research, 12*, 531–545.

Garfinkel, H. (1967). *Studies in ethnomethodology.* Englewood Cliffs, NJ: Prentice-Hall.

Geertz, C. (1973). *The interpretation of cultures: Selected essays.* New York, NY: Basic Books.

Ghamari-Tabrizi, B. (2005). Can Burawoy make everybody happy? Comments on spublic sociology. *Critical Sociology, 31*, 361–369.

Given, L. M. (Ed.). (2008). *The Sage encyclopedia of qualitative research methods.* Thousand Oaks, CA: Sage.

Greene, J. C. (2006). Toward a methodology of mixed methods social inquiry. *Research in the Schools, 13*, 93–98.

Gupta, A., & Ferguson, J. (1992). Beyond "culture": Space, identity, and the politics of difference. *Cultural Anthropology, 7*, 6–23.

Hale, C. R. (2008). Introduction. In C. R. Hale (Ed.), *Engaging contradictions: Theory, politics, and methods of activist scholarship* (pp. 1–30). Berkeley: University of California Press.

Hall, S. (Ed.). (1997). The work of representation. In S. Hall (Ed.), *Representation: Cultural representations and signifying practices* (pp. 13–74). London, England: Sage.

Hammersley, M. (2002). Ethnography and realism. In A. M. Huberman & M. B. Miles (Eds.), *The qualitative researcher's companion* (pp. 65–80). Thousand Oaks, CA: Sage.

Humphreys, M. (2005). Getting personal: Reflexivity and autoethnographic vignettes. *Qualitative Inquiry, 11*, 840–860.

Jones, A., & Jenkins, K. (2008). Rethinking collaboration: Working the indigene-colonizer hyphen. In N. K. Denzin, Y. S. Lincoln, & L. T. Smith (Eds.), *Handbook of critical and indigenous methodologies* (pp. 471–486). Thousand Oaks, CA: Sage.

Lincoln, Y. S., Lynham, S., & Guba, E. G. (2011). Paradigmatic controversies, contradictions, and emerging confluences. In N. K. Denzin & Y. S. Lincoln (Eds.), *The Sage handbook of qualitative research* (4th ed., pp. 97–128). Thousand Oaks, CA: Sage.

Loseke, D. R. (2007). The study of identity as cultural, institutional, organizational, and personal narratives: Theoretical and empirical integrations. *Sociological Quarterly, 48*, 661–688.

Lykes, M. B. (2013). Participatory and action research as a transformative praxis: Responding to humanitarian crises from the margins. *American Psychologist, 68*, 774–783.

Madison, D. S. (2005). *Critical ethnography: Method, ethics, and performance.* Thousand Oaks, CA: Sage.

Marcus, G. E. (1995). Ethnography in/of the world system: The emergence of multi-sited ethnography. *Annual Review of Anthropology, 24*, 95–117.

Martín-Baró, I. (1994). *Writings for a liberation psychology* (A. Aron & S. Corne, Trans.). Cambridge, MA: Harvard University Press.

McIntyre, A. (2000). Constructing meaning about violence, school, and community: Participatory action research with urban youth. *Urban Review, 32*, 123–154.

Minkler, M. (2005). Community-based research partnerships: Challenges and opportunities. *Journal of Urban Health, 82*, ii3–ii12.

Mirón, L. F. (2008). Transnational, national, and indigenous racial subjects: Moving from critical discourse to praxis. In N. K. Denzin, Y. S. Lincoln, & L. T. Smith (Eds.), *Handbook of critical and indigenous methodologies* (pp. 547–562). Thousand Oaks, CA: Sage.

Nabavi, M. (2006). The power of oral tradition: Critically resisting the colonial footprint. In G. J. Dei & A. Kemph (Eds.), *Anti-colonialism and education: The politics of resistance* (pp. 175–192). Rotterdam, The Netherlands: Sense Publishers.

Prilleltensky, I. (2003). Understanding, resisting, and overcoming oppression: Toward psychopolitical validity. *American Journal of Community Psychology, 31*, 195–201.

Rappaport, J. (2000). Community narratives: Tales of terror and joy. *American Journal of Community Psychology, 28*, 1–24.

Reyes Cruz, M., & Sonn, C. C. (2011). (De)colonizing culture in community psychology: Reflections from critical social science. *American Journal of Community Psychology, 47*, 203–214.

Schensul, J. J., & LeCompte, M. D. (2013). *Essential ethnographic methods: A mixed methods approach* (2nd ed., Vol. 3). Lanham, MD: Altamira Press.

Scheper-Hughes, N. (2006). Dangerous and endangered youth: Social structures and determinants of violence. *Annals of the New York Academy of Sciences, 1036*, 13–46.

Shome, R., & Hegde, R. S. (2002). Postcolonial approaches to communication: Charting the terrain, engaging the intersections. *Communication Theory, 12*, 249–270.

Smith, L. T. (2012). *Decolonizing methodologies: Research and indigenous peoples* (2nd ed.). London, England: Zed Books.

Strauss, C. (2005). Analyzing discourse for cultural complexity. In N. Quinn (Ed.), *Finding culture in talk: A collection of methods* (pp. 203–242). New York, NY: Palgrave Macmillan.

Tedlock, B. (2000). Ethnography and ethnographic representation. In N. K. Denzin & Y. S. Lincoln (Eds.), *Handbook of qualitative research* (2nd ed., pp. 455–486). Thousand Oaks, CA: Sage.

Tomaselli, K. G., Dyll, L., & Francis, M. (2008). "Self" and "other": Auto-reflexive and indigenous ethnography. In N. K. Denzin, Y. S. Lincoln, & L. T. Smith (Eds.), *Handbook of critical and indigenous methodologies* (pp. 347–372). Thousand Oaks, CA: Sage.

Turner, V. W. (1967). *The forest of symbols: Aspects of Ndembu ritual.* Ithaca, NY: Cornell University Press.

Van Dijk, T. A. (1993). Principles of critical discourse analysis. *Discourse and Society, 4*, 249–283.

Visweswaran, K. (2003). Defining feminist ethnography. In K. N. Denzin & Y. S. Lincoln (Eds.), *Turning points in qualitative research: Tying knots in a handkerchief* (pp. 73–94). Walnut Creek, CA: Altamira Press.

9

Photovoice and House Meetings as Tools Within Participatory Action Research

REGINA DAY LANGHOUT, JESICA SIHAM FERNÁNDEZ, DENISE WYLDBORE, AND JORGE SAVALA

Participatory action research (PAR) is an epistemology where community members and researchers collaborate to (a) determine the problem to be researched, (b) collect data, (c) analyze data, (d) come to a conclusion, (e) determine an intervention, (f) implement the intervention, and (g) evaluate the intervention (Fals Borda, 1987). We refer to PAR as an epistemology rather than as a method because most PAR theorists view it as a way for those typically situated outside of science to insert their lived experiences and perspectives into the process of knowledge construction (Fals Borda, 1987). Specifically, PAR allows for the democratization of knowledge production by engaging multiple constituents. Through this PAR process, problem definitions shift, thus posing meaningful implications for community-based interventions and social action that focuses on addressing community members' needs. Indeed, some argue that PAR is an epistemology that is intimately connected to empowerment and social change (Fals Borda, 1987).

A paradigm that many PAR practitioners are embedded in is critical theory (Denzin & Lincoln, 2011). Critical theory considers knowledge as a constructed resource within social, historic, political, and economic structures. PAR, like critical theory, emphasizes engaging social justice and drawing from the skills and knowledge of multiple stakeholder groups to create structural change. Within this paradigm, social positioning is important because people who are situated differently in society based on their race, ethnicity, social class, gender, sexuality, citizenship status, and so on have access to different types of knowledge. The argument is that when people from different social positions work together, better science, interventions, and social actions are possible (Fine & Torre, 2006). Moreover, empowerment is engaged when subordinated groups can name their realities, or social condition, and determine which interventions are appropriate for their communities. Indeed, empowerment occurs when people have control over the resources that affect their lives; being in control over problem definition and interventions is an important resource (Rappaport, 1995).

There are many methods used within a PAR framework. Among these are photovoice and focus groups (Foster Fishman, Nowell, Deacon, Nievar, & McCann, 2005; Wallerstein & Duran, 2006; Wang & Burris, 1994). We focus on photovoice and house meetings—which are similar to, yet different from, focus groups. We used these methods for a year-long PAR project called Viva Live Oak! in an unincorporated area along the Central Coast of California.

We begin our chapter by discussing the two methods within the PAR process, specifically, how photovoice and house meetings work as tools toward social action and empowerment. We highlight some of the relevant literature where these tools have been used. For each method we discuss the steps involved in the process, as well as the benefits and challenges of each. Next, we provide reflections from two of our participant-researchers, who are also coauthors. We end the chapter with implications for community-based PAR and consider how photovoice and house meetings work as tools toward critical consciousness, empowerment, and social action.

PHOTOVOICE AS A TOOL FOR SOCIAL ACTION AND EMPOWERMENT

Photovoice involves participants taking pictures based on a prompt and then using a structured format to discuss photographs within the group. The goal is to involve community members in the study of their community and to move toward social action. Photovoice was developed as a feminist methodology (Wang & Burris, 1994). It was initially used in a rural community-based project that documented Yunnan Chinese women's health and work-related experiences (Wang, Burris, & Ping, 1996). Since its development, photovoice has been used in public health, psychology, education, and other social and applied sciences to highlight people's lived experiences via visual images and aesthetic representations.

Photovoice has been employed with varied populations for many purposes. Indeed, young people of color (e.g., Foster Fishman et al., 2005), immigrants (Rhodes et al., 2009; Stevens, 2010), Latinas (Mejia et al., 2013), and many others have used photovoice to investigate social inequalities and work toward social change. Uses have included needs assessments, asset mapping, and program evaluation (Wang, 1999), as well as community organizing (Wilson et al., 2007). The use and application of photovoice as a tool for research and action are varied, yet predominantly centered on engaging community members in the collection and analysis of data.

Although photovoice is utilized more broadly now, some characteristics of feminist methodologies and critical theory remain embedded in many photovoice projects. These include considering participants as collaborators and moving toward social action through the development of critical consciousness. Participants are collaborators because they control which pictures they take and share with the group. This allows them to highlight experiences that they choose, and it also provides them with the control to share based on their level of comfort. Moreover, critical consciousness is further developed when participants reflect critically on their lives and on how their experiences relate to others, including how structures shape subjectivity and everyday experiences (Carlson, Engebretson, & Chamberlain, 2006; Freire, 1970/1988).

Photovoice facilitates increased critical consciousness, empowerment, and social action through a process whereby participants are deeply examining their experiences in community with others who might share or differ in such experiences. The process of sharing and reflecting creates a space to have critical dialogues regarding how problems are defined. The images taken by participants and the stories they tell about them allow for the reassessment of what counts as problems. This is essential because subordinated communities often do not control the dominant hegemonic narratives about them, much less how problems that affect them are conceptualized. This is problematic because when powerful dominant groups define problems, they are typically defined in ways that blame subordinated communities for those problems (Rappaport, 1995).

Photovoice allows people to use photography as a tool to tell their own stories. This careful examination of reality opens up a decolonial space that allows people to systematically confront "the Social Lie," or stories authored by dominant groups that blame subordinated groups for their condition(s) (Martín-Baró, 1994). Furthermore, photovoice encourages participants to use art, in the form of images, to tell stories, or alternative narratives, that are grounded in their everyday lives. The method, therefore, provides a way for participants to take control of an important psychological resource—stories about them—and use those alternative narratives to shape civic life and discourses that (dis)empower them (Rappaport, 1995).

In addition to providing people from subordinated groups with resources such as cameras, photovoice has other foundational components that facilitate deeper critical consciousness, empowerment, and social action. Specifically, the method includes structured conversations designed to move dialogue from individual experiences to collective struggles to structural issues (Wang & Burris, 1994). In this way, photovoice facilitates social action by linking people's stories to broader structural issues embedded in systems of power (Jurkowski, Rivera, & Hammel, 2009).

Because photovoice involves visual and narrative representations to convey a message or highlight an issue, it is an appealing strategy to influence and engage with others. Policymakers, for instance, are often invited to photovoice exhibitions as a way for participants to influence policy (Wang, 1999). Indeed, the expression "a picture is worth a thousand words" is warranted when policymakers and power holders begin to think about issues represented in photovoice.

Photovoice Steps

The level of community collaboration in the setting of the problem definition can shape the steps involved in the photovoice process (Catalani & Minkler, 2010). In some cases, outside researchers have already set a problem definition. Although predetermining a problem might not be ideal for a fully collaborative process, it can sometimes be advantageous to have a problem already set. For example, when a problem has been set, those who have decision-making authority (e.g., elected officials, physicians) can be asked to serve on a photovoice board, with the intent of addressing the issue and supporting photovoice participants/community members. In this situation, after viewing photovoice results, the board could implement recommendations made by the participants, thus creating desired outcomes for community members (Wang, 1999).

On the other hand, when a problem definition is not set, participants can identify it. In this situation, various perspectives are taken into account in determining a problem, and collaboration among various community members can happen in a context where power is more equally shared. For example, in one photovoice project with African American teens in Baltimore, Maryland, youth decided to study love. This was surprising to many outsiders, who thought youth would study teen pregnancy, school dropout rates, or other topics deemed salient by power holders, including decision makers and academics (Downing, Sonestein, & Davis, n.d.).

Once a group has been established, the first photovoice session consists of introducing the project, as well as the PAR approach. Other topics that should be covered include the methodology, potential benefits and risks to participants, and confidentiality, as well as specific technicalities such as how to use the camera and take pictures safely, the ethics of taking pictures, and framing an image or scene to get the desired effect. A discussion on the ethics of photography is essential, including such issues as approaching people to take their picture(s), taking pictures of people without their knowledge, and determining when people should not be photographed. Related to this is being transparent about what might become of the pictures and whether these might be used for public display or research (Wang, 1999).

A prompt used for taking pictures (e.g., "What makes up your neighborhood? What do you like about it? What would you like to change?") can be determined or shared after establishing the purpose of the project and orienting participants, who will act as co-researchers. After a prompt is determined or agreed to, participants are then encouraged to take pictures and turn them in for development.

In subsequent photovoice sessions, participants discuss their photographs. They select one or two photos to share. The group discussion is then structured to follow the SHOWED method (Wang, 1999), which consists of the following questions: "What do you See here? What is really Happening here? How does this relate to Our lives? Why does this situation, concern, or strength exist? How could this photo be used to Educate policymakers? What can we Do about it?"

After several iterations of taking photographs and discussing these during photovoice sessions, participants are instructed on how to categorize photographs and narratives according to themes they have discerned from their pictures and conversations. Participants then plan activities, which are typically photo exhibitions. They select and agree upon several photos they would like to display in an exhibition or at a community event.

Some possibilities for photography exhibitions include slide shows, simple frames on walls, storytelling, and/or written narratives to accompany photos. Stakeholders and the public are then invited to the exhibition. The exhibition, in addition to providing participants with an opportunity to share their work, serves as an action or an opportunity to engage power holders and the broader community in a dialogue about issues depicted in their images. Although exhibitions are a common action, other actions, such as guerilla art or skits that dramatize themes, may be appropriate for community intervention and social change.

Benefits and Challenges of Photovoice

In the process of conducting photovoice, several benefits can arise for individuals and groups. Among these are facilitating the development of relationships across lines of difference by sharing photographs and stories that focus not only on individual experiences but also on representing a broader narrative that encompasses multiple perspectives. Through the use of photographs, photovoice can help generate dialogue and communication with others who might have differences in social status (e.g., race, class, gender, age, legal status), and in this way work toward building community (Carlson et al., 2006). Based on our experience, photovoice can create a venue for outsiders or newcomers to be integrated into their community. Additionally, it provides an opportunity for individuals to venture out of their comfort zone and engage their curiosities in a collective collaborative project. In all these ways, photovoice can facilitate the development and/or deepening of community bonds.

Generating conditions conducive to supporting participants' active community engagement is another benefit of photovoice. Through this process, community members can develop a collective imagination of possible social change. Photovoice therefore works as a tool toward catalyzing people into taking action(s) and creating social change because it provides them with an opportunity to inspect a condition, via a photograph, that might otherwise go unexamined.

Additionally, the use of photographs to initiate dialogue enables people to talk about topics or issues that might be difficult to discuss (Lykes, 2006). The depersonalization that often happens in the process of sharing a photograph allows an individual to share an experience in a way that feels safe because the person might choose to share it as a first- or third-person account. Such forms of photovoice have been used with people who have experienced racism, for example (Rhodes et al., 2009). Photovoice therefore presents several benefits that reinforce critical consciousness, empowerment, and social action.

Although photovoice is a powerful tool for engaging multiple stakeholders, the method presents several challenges. Among these is the level of commitment needed for the project, or the time the method requires. For example, participants are expected to take photographs and spend a significant amount of time reflecting on and discussing their photographs. Given that photovoice projects are often conducted with subordinated communities that might be struggling to make ends meet while juggling multiple jobs or responsibilities, participating in photovoice can be prohibitive or too demanding on their time. Yet this time is important because several photovoice studies have shown that critical consciousness-raising and empowerment processes require time; hence, any attempt at speeding up the process would be compromising to the goals of photovoice (Carlson et al., 2006; Catalani & Minkler, 2010).

Another challenge to conducting photovoice is the limited financial support to fund such projects. Researchers might compensate participants for their time by providing a small stipend, as well as a meal and child care during photovoice sessions. Researchers often struggle to find the financial support to provide participants with the necessary resources to help them engage in the research (Nykiforuk, Vallianatos, & Nieuwendyk, 2011). Related to this are the typically limited forms of institutional support and/or resources available to researchers who engage with paradigms such as critical theory and epistemologies such as participatory action research (Fals-Borda, 1987).

Similar to the ways in which researchers are often constrained by funders, or the lack of funding, the research process—despite all good intentions to be collaborative and transparent—might be abstruse to participants. That is, participants might not feel comfortable with the approach taken toward conducting research in their communities. These dynamics are further exacerbated by interpersonal group dynamics where different identities and social positionalities are made salient and, in some cases, threatened by other social identities (Cornwall, 2004).

Some group dynamics that might challenge the research process are language barriers and power hierarchies within the group (Cornwall, 2004; Wang & Burris, 1994). These challenges create difficulties when working toward more equal collaborations and building community. For example, some photovoice projects that include immigrants from diverse language-speaking communities might require additional forms of support to ensure that all voices are heard and that some are not privileged over others (Stevens, 2010). Yet adding support in the way of translation might generate other barriers, such as disrupting the flow of the conversations or limiting the possibility for in-depth discussions. Group dynamics are pivotal because participants often discuss their experiences as embedded within their relationships to one another and to the research process. Therefore, how people interact becomes an important process toward helping participants build a safer space where they can reflect and engage in dialogue (Clandinin & Connelly, 1994).

Creating a safer space can be a challenge for participants as well as researchers (Smith, 1999). In some cases, power dynamics can render some participants' experiences invisible, irrelevant, and insignificant because the more experienced people with academic credentials, such as researchers, might believe they know better (Smith, 1999; Wallerstein & Duran, 2006). That is, researchers might think they know more about particular issues and/or participants' experiences, even when researchers and participants have had longstanding collaborations (Wang & Redwood-Jones, 2001). On the other hand, it is also important that researchers not essentialize community members' experiences by assuming that all stories, beliefs, and so on are universally held within the community; researchers should be critical partners. Researchers must engage in their own process of reflection when engaging with community members in photovoice, and this might be a challenge for them as they move through the research process (Clandinin & Connelly, 1994; Lykes, 2006).

Photovoice might also present additional sets of challenges for communities, specifically for those where photography is often reserved for people in positions of power (e.g., people working with organizations) or who are community outsiders (e.g., tourists). Some research suggests that in certain communities, photography might be viewed as intrusive and thereby generate tensions within the members' cultural communities (Lykes, 2006; Stevens, 2010). That is, within some community contexts, photography might be viewed as culturally inappropriate and invasive (Wang & Redwood-Jones, 2001). Relatedly, participants may not take photographs as a way to safeguard themselves against reprisal (Stevens, 2010).

Although there are challenges to photovoice, there are several steps that can build generative relations with community members prior to initiating photovoice. Among these are developing relationships with the community by participating in events and organizations and taking on roles that facilitate the researchers' visibility within the community. Thus, when engaged in photovoice, it is imperative that researchers build relationships of rapport, transparency, and accountability in order to develop appropriate and culturally relevant participatory methods (Catalani & Minkler, 2010). In doing so, researchers must also take a strengths-based approach toward identifying not only community needs but also assets and how these can be leveraged toward facilitating deeper critical consciousness, social action, and empowerment.

HOUSE MEETINGS AS A TOOL FOR SOCIAL ACTION AND EMPOWERMENT

The house meeting is a tool used in Industrial Area Foundation (IAF) organizing groups (Cortes, 2006). House meetings are group deliberative conversations, with 6 to 12 participants, that are designed to lead to action (Cortes, 2006). They can happen in homes, places of worship, schools, recreation centers, or any mediating institution. A house meeting creates a public space in which to have a dialogue about issues that matter to a specific community (Kong, 2010). The technique was developed mostly in California in the 1950s, when César Chávez, Dolores Huerta, and Fred Ross were organizing farm workers in the Salinas Valley. Ross, who was with the IAF, taught Chávez how to run house meetings, and, later, Huerta was trained (Shaw, 2008).

There are many goals for house meetings. One is to agitate leaders into action (Kong, 2010). Agitation means that people's imaginations and curiosities are piqued and that their self-interest is visible (Toton, 1993). Also, a house meeting should help participants build relationships and come out of isolation by telling stories about their lives (Auerbach, 2009; Kong, 2010). In this way, participants develop a common narrative that is based in their everyday realities (Cortes, 2006). Moreover, in the course of the house-meeting process, the facilitator looks for potential leaders whose skills can be further developed. Furthermore, the facilitator should consider the meeting as a way to build a constituency around an issue through reflection and as a venue to mobilize for action (Kong, 2010). Finally, a house-meeting campaign can be used within a setting to initiate institutional culture shift; for example, people may get to know one another in ways that are not typical based on roles people have within the setting, and this can create shifts in bonding, relationships, and trust, or a democratic culture (Cortes, 2006; Toton, 1993).

House meetings share some similarities with focus groups but are also distinct in important ways. Considering similarities, house meetings and focus groups employ the strategy of a group conversation as a tool for understanding a phenomenon more deeply. With both methods, connections between participants are also encouraged, as is the telling of stories based on lived experience. Differences, however, include the intentions around organizing. With house meetings, an explicit goal is to agitate members to move toward action and to assess who might have an appetite to become a leader. Individual meetings are often set with potential leaders after the house meeting, in order to continue their engagement. Moreover, house meetings are frequently run with participants who know each other and are from the same institution.

House meetings have been deployed in different contexts with various issues. For example, they have been used in educational settings. Specifically, teachers ran house meetings in a Los Angeles school with parents; this created a shared bond and vision (Auerbach, 2009). Considering immigration as the main issue, house meetings were run in Sonoma County, California, for neighbors to discuss problems they were experiencing with the Sheriff's office regarding immigration raids, car impounds, and racial profiling (Kong, 2010). House meetings have also been used at the intersection of education and immigration. In one case, house meetings were a first step in developing a constituency to support funding for bilingual education in Texas (Cortes, 2006). House meetings were held with middle-class Whites and immigrants from Latina/o communities (both groups were members of congregations). What emerged from the sharing was a connection between both groups, a shift within this specific middle-class White community, and their movement to work toward supporting bilingual education (Cortes, 2006).

House meetings have also been utilized with people who were not part of the IAF or in IAF-member institutions. For example, after Hurricane Katrina hit New Orleans, IAF leaders taught other community leaders how to run house meetings, and many were run with evacuees. These house meetings resulted in community leaders working with decision makers to accelerate the elderly getting more stable housing and the creation of a playground for children (Cortes, 2006).

As is clear, house meetings are a means for achieving the goals of social action and empowerment. As the earlier examples indicate, house meetings have been effective in that they have altered role relationships among people within the same institutions, and they have facilitated changes in local policies and procedures, while creating opportunities for open dialogue and interaction among various constituencies and power holders.

House-Meeting Process

Once trained, members of the community usually run house meetings (Auerbach, 2009; Kong, 2010). House-meeting leaders recruit people to participate who they think will be interested in the topic (Cortes, 2006). There are several steps to a house meeting (IAF training materials, n.d.). The meeting begins with orienting attendees, via a culturally appropriate reading, to the purpose. Introductions are next. The house-meeting leader then explains that the goal is to share stories around a topic in order to understand how participants are experiencing the topic. The leader explains that everyone should contribute. Next, the leader explicates that someone will keep time and take notes. Sometimes this person is predetermined, and sometimes the leader asks for a volunteer. The leader then poses the discussion question to the group. An example of such a question is, "How has the economic downturn affected you, or someone you are close to?" When there are about 10 minutes left, the leader asks the note taker to summarize what was heard and checks in with participants to see if the summary is correct. After all are satisfied with the summary, the leader describes possible next steps, asks for the group's evaluation of how the meeting went, and ends with reading a passage, a prayer, or whatever is culturally appropriate for the group.

During the sharing part of the meeting, the facilitator has several roles (IAF Training Materials, n.d.). The leader ensures that people tell stories (that is, not give opinions) and that all have a chance to share, and also scans the group for agitation, in order to identify people who feel passionate about an issue. The leader also steers the group away from possible solutions, which is a common impulse for many participants.

Benefits and Challenges of House Meetings

Like all methods, house meetings have benefits and challenges. The benefits can be organized into two groups related to facilitating empowerment (i.e., group consciousness and connections) and facilitating social action. With respect to the former, house-meeting participants often learn that they are not alone. They come out of isolation and build bridges across status differences. For example, in house meetings with immigrant Latina/o parents and White teachers, almost everyone started crying when discussing why education was important to them (Auerbach, 2009). These connections across status differences can also enable groups in finding a common story or narrative that is grounded in lived experience rather than in dominant narratives, or overlearned stories, about "others" that are often based on stereotypes and deficits. In these ways, house meetings bring communities together, frequently despite little institutional support or few resources. Indeed, house meetings strive for inclusiveness. For example, the house meetings in which we participate and which we have run usually have real-time translation (i.e., everyone wears an earpiece and listens for simultaneous translation, as needed). This facilitates all people's participation. Because people rethink the meaning of their experiences and connect to one another in the development of a shared narrative, we label this as a form of empowerment. Indeed, people are taking control of some psychological resources, such as narratives, that affect their lives.

The house meeting structure also facilitates social action. For example, people take ownership over the process. Specifically, meetings are not led by outsiders (e.g., researchers or practitioners who are not members of the community), but by insiders who are passionate about and committed to the issues. Through the process, they identify leaders, who are then taught to lead house meetings. Subsequently, house meetings promote the development of leadership skills by all those who participate. Therefore, the house meeting structure is one that "gives away" knowledge production and democratizes knowledge through the practicing of local politics. Moreover, house meetings are expected to develop an agenda from the grassroots, as people talk about their experiences. The topics that arise from house meetings can drive what a group will do within its next organizing cycle; house meetings are structured to facilitate social action.

Although there are many benefits of house meetings, there are also challenges. Some challenges are related to logistics, some to the organizer, and some to participants. Considering logistics, it can be difficult to find a location to hold meetings if the community has little public infrastructure or intuitional spaces. This is often the case in unincorporated communities, or areas that have no municipal government. It can also be challenging to find a time that works for many people, especially when trying to bring together a heterogeneous group. With respect to the organizer, sometimes that person can push an agenda that is not shared by the participants; this can result in some stories being minimized and others given more attention. Finally, perhaps because the house-meeting organizer often has a relationship with the participants, it can sometimes be challenging to keep participants from digressing from the topic. Additionally, when participants know one another, sometimes existing group dynamics enter the space and some people speak much more than others. Finally, participants can become disengaged if they are not used to or comfortable with an organizing framework.

CASE STUDY

Viva Live Oak!

The director of the Live Oak Family Resource Center and the first author met to discuss a possible collaboration. The director was engaged in place-based community organizing (i.e., organizing people who live in Live Oak) and was frustrated that so few residents identified with Live Oak, which is an unincorporated area between Santa Cruz and Capitola. It was difficult to organize Live Oak residents when they did not identify with their community. Through discussions, the two agreed on a partnership whereby the first author and her team would begin a photovoice study to understand better how residents thought about their neighborhoods. The project was supposed to last for 7 weeks, but it continued for about a year, based on the desires of the participants. Community-based researchers learned about ethics, took photos for 5 weeks, analyzed data for 2 weeks, and then gradually took over the project. They mounted several exhibitions and ran house meetings. Their goal was to raise awareness and initiate community conversations around their photovoice themes (i.e., social justice, community pride, and historical and ecological preservation).

Denise's Experience

Photovoice

Before I joined the photovoice project, I was interested in my neighbors in a much different way. Although I have a job that requires me to speak regularly and sometimes personally with the general public, I do not think of my neighbors as acquaintances, let alone "friends." Yet I care very intentionally about humans and people with whom I am in relationship. Once my husband convinced me that it was worth my while since they gave us dinner and $20.00 instead of dinner for $20.00, I thought "what a deal" and tagged along willing.

The personal stories became my motivating factor. Our prompt was, "What makes up your neighborhood? What do you like about it? What would you like to change?" After attending a few meetings, I was drawn in to the stories and others' pictures. I opened my eyes to what others were seeing in my neighborhood. When walking or driving, I began to notice areas or places where others had taken pictures and would reflect on both the photographer and the story they shared. Sometimes I could not see the point of interest in a particular photo at first but would later grow a deeper appreciation as the group continued to share more of their personal stories.

As the group continued, I met people with whom I would not normally socialize and became engaged with them. I felt a sense of belonging and care. My care grew to include their families and eventually expanded to the neighborhood rather than the people with whom I live.

I realized that being involved in photovoice gave a clearer understanding of my neighbors' struggles and joys by means of a universal language similar to music and other art forms. I did not always feel commonality, but I did broaden my awareness of what others were experiencing. I decided I wanted to become more directly committed to what was happening in my community.

I did not feel uncomfortable, but I recognize that the organizers may have felt challenged by various issues. What comes to mind most specifically is the desire to involve a more diverse group of participants, although that creates additional challenges. I believe the experience could have been greater if more people had participated originally; however, as a group, we decided to strengthen our "voice." I think we moved from a self-serving group to an action committee.

Photovoice Exhibitions

Once the group was established, we spread our wings. We gave ourselves a name, Viva Live Oak! and expanded our audience by having some photos enlarged and matted, with our narratives. We grouped our photos into three categories that we determined: environmental and historical preservation, social justice, and community pride. The photos were then displayed throughout the community, including the library, the county building, the farmer's market, and coffee shops. We also made a free calendar that we distributed. Our farmer's market display included us talking with passersby, which stimulated interest with more of our unknown neighbors . . . and then we knew them, or at least had made a point to meet them. It was exciting, and I was grateful to have ventured out from my own place of comfort.

With time and encouragement, we developed ownership of the agenda, the group's direction, and what we wanted to accomplish. Our project was supposed to last seven weeks, but we decided to keep meeting for almost a year to achieve our goals. As we moved into action, we needed organizing tools. This provided us the opportunity to learn about house meetings.

House Meetings

We chose to utilize house meetings because they were already in use in our area, and Jorge had a lot of experience with them. He trained us to lead them. Our first house meeting was at a laundromat. We gave people quarters to wash and dry their laundry in exchange for their participation in a conversation about how they felt living in our neighborhood. We showed our pictures and discussed photovoice. We engaged several Spanish speakers and, fortunately, many from our group spoke Spanish. We used a device and provided real-time translation, so the lines of communication were open on several levels. I was grateful our group had bilingual speakers, so I was able to understand stories of all the participants, not just the English speakers. That was a subtle but pivotal moment in my life.

Actions Facilitated by Viva Live Oak!

At the time, our church was sponsoring a Spanish-speaking congregation. I became involved in the development of the Hispanic ministry. Although I spoke little Spanish, I attended meetings and worship services with Spanish speakers.

I strongly advocated for real-time translation equipment and translators to be provided whenever possible. Connecting with others on a more level playing field has always been important to me, but based on skills that I learned from attending house meetings, I found a way to verbalize better what I thought and felt. I found the importance of being able to share the stories of our lives.

Jorge's Experience

My brother and I joined the PAR project because it was a way to share our stories with the greater community. The middle school provided a welcoming place for the initial meeting, where the researchers explained the project. Sitting in a sunlit room under oak trees, we were provided with cameras and guidance. The thing that appealed most to me was the collective freedom a diverse group of people was provided to own the PAR project and the ability to meet neighbors with whom I would normally not associate.

My brother and I decided to take pictures of the neighborhood in which we grew up. Hidden and running parallel along the railroad was Kingsley Street, a cluster of single-family homes neighboring dilapidated apartment complexes. We saw kids playing a fierce soccer game in the alley where he and I once played. Circling around the apartment complex, I took a picture of a broken window, which seemed to be fixed with plastic due to the negligence of the property manager. This experience would later shape my civic engagement in the community. My brother and I were talking about our childhood and the lack of activities for kids of the working poor. We decided to organize a free Indoor Soccer Program for kids but did not know how. We did not want kids to be victims of gangs, drugs, and other negative influences readily available.

We all had different lives but connected in the middle school, and then the back room of the Live Oak Family Resource Center under the oak trees. Viva Live Oak!: Life between the S and the C was the name we gave the project (Live Oak is between Santa Cruz [the "S"] and Capitola [the "C"]). We printed our pictures with narratives in English and Spanish, alternating which language came first throughout the pictures. We did this to be inclusive of the growing Latina/o population. We set up displays and held house meetings in an effort to connect with the community and hear their stories of Live Oak.

I was trained by the IAF on how to conduct house meetings and have led many after participating in them. This grassroots organizing method was shared with and implemented within the Viva Live Oak! group at laundromats. With simultaneous translation, we were able to break down communication barriers and connect further with one another. At the end we identified two potential leaders, who experienced agitation after speaking of fear for their teenagers. We offered them an opportunity to participate in the Live Oak Family Resource Center's civic engagement component. The Live Oak Family Resource Center is involved in COPA (Communities Organized for relational Power and Action), a nonpartisan, broad-based organization affiliated with the IAF.

We continued having house meetings through the Live Oak Family Resource Center and connected with other community members and religious institutions. Members like Denise and others would later organize house meetings within their institution. These new relationships would later help carry out a Free Indoor Soccer Program (futsal), which led to a regional gang prevention strategy. Hundreds of house meetings were carried out by institutions, with a focus on community safety. Through the house meeting campaign, we heard stories of the need for free and enriching activities for minors but also a need for parent resources and relationships with law enforcement. We organized a nonpartisan Shared Prosperity Campaign, which contained this gang prevention strategy. COPA and the Catholic Diocese adopted this strategy, which led to the building of a Boys' & Girls' Club my brother and I always wanted in our neighborhood.

Follow-up

For Viva Live Oak!, the combination of photovoice and house meeting was effective in helping participants think about and reflect upon their lives more deeply, and take action both within the group and in other areas of their lives. Furthermore, the projects they began are still going strong. For example, futsal has completed five seasons and continues to be free for the children in the league. Because the futsal league has been so successful, free baseball and basketball leagues have also begun, with more than 500 children participating. Thus, because participants organized within their community to create resources that the community desired, we label this PAR project a success.

CONCLUSION

Photovoice and house meetings can be powerful tools for data collection, deep discussions, critical consciousness raising, empowerment, and social action. These tools can be easily used across settings, with various populations, and for different reasons. Furthermore, they have the potential to bring communities together in ways that few other methodologies can. For these reasons, we strongly recommend their consideration in participant-focused, community-based interventions.

AUTHOR NOTE

We dedicate this paper to Jorge's bother, Mario, who had the initial idea to start a free futsal league for children. He was a visionary and an organizer who made a lasting difference in the Live Oak community. We thank the Live Oak Family Resource Center and the Boys' & Girls' Club for their partnership. We also thank Edith Gurrola, Diana Arias, and the members of Viva Live Oak! for their participation and vulnerability. This project was made possible through a grant to the first author from the Center for Justice, Tolerance, and Community and a Social Sciences Junior Faculty Award. The second author was supported through a Cota-Robles Fellowship and a University of California Presidential Dissertation Year Fellowship.

REFERENCES

Auerbach, S. (2009). Walking the walk: Portraits in leadership for family engagement in urban schools. *School Community Journal, 19*, 9–32.

Carlson, E. D., Engebretson, J., & Chamberlain, R. M. (2006). Photovoice as a social process of critical consciousness. *Qualitative Health Research, 16*, 836–852.

Catalani, C., & Minkler. M. (2010). Photovoice: A review of the literature in health and public health. *Health Education and Behavior, 37*, 424–451.

Clandinin, D. J., & Connelly, F. M. (1994). Personal experience methods. In N. K. Denzin & Y. S. Lincoln (Eds.), *Handbook of qualitative research* (pp. 413–427). Thousand Oaks, CA: Sage.

Cornwall, A. (2004). Spaces for transformation? Reflections on issues of power and difference in participation in development. In S. Hickey & G. Mohan (Eds.), *Participation: From tyranny to transformation? Exploring new approaches to participation in development* (pp. 75–91). New York, NY: Zed Books.

Cortes, E. (2006). Toward a democratic culture. *Kettering Review, 24*, 46–57.

Denzin, N. K., & Lincoln, Y. S. (2011). Introduction: The discipline and practice of qualitative research. In N. K. Denzin & Y. S. Lincoln (Eds.), *Handbook of qualitative research* (4th ed., pp. 1–20). Thousand Oaks, CA: Sage.

Downing, R., Sonestein, F., & Davis, N. (n.d.). *Love though the eyes of Baltimore youth: Photovoice as a youth empowerment tool* [Recorded presentation]. Retrieved June 2015, from https://apha.confex.com/apha/134am/techprogram/paper_136310.htm

Fals Borda, O. (1987). The application of participatory action-research in Latin America. *International Sociology, 2*, 329–347.

Fine, M., & Torre, M. E. (2006). Intimate details: Participatory action research in prison. *Action Research, 4*, 253–269.

Foster Fishman, P., Nowell, B., Deacon, Z., Nievar, M. A., & McCann, P. (2005). Using methods that matter: The impact of reflection, dialogue, and voice. *American Journal of Community Psychology, 36*, 275–291.

Freire, P. (1970/1988). *Pedagogy of the oppressed.* (M. Bergman Ramos, Trans.). New York, NY: Continuum.

Industrial Areas Foundation (IAF) Training Materials. (n.d.). *Suggested agenda for house meetings.* Watsonville, CA: Communities Organized for relational Power and Action.

Jurkowski, J. M., Rivera, Y., & Hammel, J. (2009). Health perceptions of Latinos with intellectual disabilities: The results of a qualitative pilot study. *Health Promotion Practice, 10*, 144–155.

Kong, L. J. (2010). Immigration, racial profiling, and white privilege: Community-based challenges and practices for adult educators. *New Directions for Adult and Continuing Education, 125*, 65–77.

Lykes, M. B. (2006). Creative arts and photography in participatory action research in Guatemala. In P. Reason & H. Bradbury (Eds.), *Handbook of action research* (pp. 269–278). Thousand Oaks, CA: Sage.

Martín-Baró, I. (1994). *Writings for a liberation psychology.* (A. Aron & S. Corne, Trans.). Cambridge, MA: Harvard University Press.

Mejia, A. P., Quiroz, O., Morales, Y., Ponce, R., Chavez, G. L., & y Torre, E. O. (2013). From madres to mujeristas: Latinas making change with photovoice. *Action Research, 11*, 301–321.

Nykiforuk, C. I., Vallianatos, H., & Nieuwendyk, L. M. (2011). Photovoice as a method for revealing community perceptions of the built and social environment. *International Journal of Qualitative Methods, 10*, 103–124.

Rappaport, J. (1995). Empowerment meets narrative: Listening to stories and creating settings.

American Journal of Community Psychology, 23, 795–807.

Rhodes, S. D., Hergenrather, K. C., Griffith, D. M., Yee, L. J., Zometa, C. S., Montaño, J., & Vissman, A. T. (2009). Sexual and alcohol risk behaviors of immigrant Latino men in the South-eastern USA. *Culture, Health, and Sexuality, 11,* 17–34.

Shaw, R. (2008). *Beyond the fields: Cesar Chavez, the UFW, and the struggle for justice in the 21st century.* Berkeley: University of California Press.

Smith, L. T. (1999). *Decolonizing methodologies: Research and indigenous peoples.* New York, NY: Zed Books.

Stevens, C. A. (2010). Lessons from the field: Using photovoice with an ethnically diverse population in a HOPE VI evaluation. *Family and Community Health,* 33, 275–284.

Toton, S. C. (1993). Moving beyond anguish to action: What has Saul Alisnky to say to justice education? *Religious Education, 88,* 478–493.

Wallerstein, N. B., & Duran, B. (2006). Using community-based participatory research to address health disparities. *Health Promotion Practice, 7,* 312–323.

Wang, C. C. (1999). Photovoice: A participatory action research strategy applied to women's health. *Journal of Women's Health, 8,* 185–192.

Wang, C. C., & Burris, M. A. (1994). Empowerment through photo novella: Portraits of participation. *Health Education and Behavior, 21,* 171–186.

Wang, C. C., Burris, M. A., & Ping, X. Y. (1996). Chinese village women as visual anthropologists: A participatory approach to reaching policymakers. *Social Science and Medicine, 42,* 1391–1400.

Wang, C. C., & Redwood-Jones, Y. A. (2001). Photovoice ethics: Perspectives from Flint photovoice. *Health Education and Behavior, 28,* 560–572.

Wilson, N., Dasho, S., Martin, A. C., Wallerstein, N., Wang, C. C., & Minkler. M. (2007). Engaging youth adolescents in social action through photovoice: The youth empowerment strategies (YES!) project. *Journal of Early Adolescence,* 27, 241–261.

10

Geographic Information Systems

ANDREW LOHMANN

Geographic information systems (GIS) are computer-based programs designed for the storage, visualization, analysis, and display of data that contain spatial components (Chang, 2005). This chapter is devoted to discussing how GIS has been used to conceptualize neighborhoods and how it can be utilized to increase our understanding of neighborhoods' role in the ecological context of individuals, groups, and communities. I will be conceptualizing the current GIS mapping approaches on a number of dimensions, with the goal of guiding our approaches to neighborhood research, and then presenting several methodologies as exemplars of how these dimensions manifest in the extant literature.

INTRODUCTION TO GEOGRAPHIC INFORMATION SYSTEMS

The software for GIS allows for the visual layering of geographic detail (imagine one layer with city streets, another layer with locations of neighborhood watch programs, and a third layer with locations of crime) to assist in better understanding the relationships between spatial variables (Renger, Cimetta, Pettygrove, & Rogan, 2002). The data generally take one of three forms: points (e.g., the exact location of the crime), lines (e.g., the city streets), and polygons (e.g., the neighborhood watch area) (Chang, 2005). These categories contain some flexibility, however, because one could provide crime information in the form of a polygon (e.g., the number of crimes that occur in a specific area).

GIS also has numerous analytic tools to extract information concerning the spatial variables. Among the more basic of these are the capacity to analyze the distance and area of any geographic variable (e.g., the square mileage of neighborhood watch programs). More complex analytical operations involve *querying*—searching selected spatial variables for locations where specific criteria are met (e.g., selecting only neighborhood-watch programs where members have met in the past year and ignoring the other watch programs). By conducting queries for different spatial variables, areas of spatial correspondence can be located and analyzed (Chang, 2005).

The extant literature using GIS to study neighborhoods reveals two general approaches for neighborhood variables. The first approach focuses on using GIS to generate quantitative variables that are then incorporated into other analytical approaches, such as multiple regression or hierarchical linear modeling. The geographic variable in question is gleaned from the broader geographic data through queries and imported into a statistical software program where they are then analyzed. Demographic, consumer, health, or crime statistics within a geographic area are examples of variables that are often studied in this way, and GIS-calculated variables may be incorporated in the same fashion (e.g., commute distance, neighborhood geographic area). In this regard, GIS is often used for the production of quantitative variables.

The second approach is more qualitative, and it is some of these methodological approaches that will be summarized next. In the context of neighborhoods, these approaches seek to discern the nature of residents' understanding of and experience with their neighborhoods. Generally, they attempt to understand the meanings of neighborhoods for their inhabitants and how those residents generate that meaning through their interactions. This would include neighborhood boundaries, with the focus on their contexts and the social and spatial qualities that produce the social dynamics of neighboring and the significance of the spaces and relationships contained therein.

WHAT IS A NEIGHBORHOOD?

There has been concern for some time as to how to conceptualize neighborhoods accurately. Sweetser (1942) called attention to how neighborhoods provide a research challenge because they tend to be compositionally unique and spatially discontinuous. Since then, attempts at understanding the nature of that compositional uniqueness comprising neighborhoods has increased significantly, with the amount of research growing, presumably in part due to the accessibility of research tools such as GIS (Lohmann & Schoelkopf, 2009). At its most fundamental, the dimensions of neighborhoods can be broken down into the following factors: physical design (e.g., type of housing and architecture, streets and parks, geographic identity); social composition (e.g., psychological sense of community, familiarity, relationships and social support, identity); experiential (e.g., neighboring behaviors, shopping, playing); and symbolic, defined primarily based on the institutional connections or the shared meaning of the neighborhood (e.g., a neighborhood identification or history) (Aitken, Stultz, Prosser, & Chandler, 1993; Chaskin, 1997; Galster, 2001; Haeberle, 1988; Hunter, 1974).

In defining neighborhoods, the social and the spatial interact. Such geographic features as walls, railroad tracks, and main roads (Grannis, 1998; Lee, Tagg, & Abbot, 1975; Lynch, 1960) may act as barriers between neighborhoods, separating them not only spatially but also socially. Yet no definitive answer exists as to how these qualities contribute to an optimal operational definition of neighborhood. The reason for this is that local contexts—how the residents define their neighborhoods—may play the most crucial role (Cummins, Macintyre, Davidson, & Ellaway, 2005; Entwisle, 2007).

By way of example, in my own research (Lohmann & McMurran, 2009), the residents in two areas of a city were compared. One area that displayed the greatest consistency in defining itself as a neighborhood is a retirement community for former religious ministry members. The qualities of architecture, walkable streets, open spaces, geographic identity (i.e., clear demarcations of being in the neighborhood), and social components in that neighborhood are easily recognizable. On the other side of town, a residential area with no notable demographic differences from the first (other than age) possesses the same housing homogeneity, walkable streets, open spaces, and geographic identity and yet is clearly not a neighborhood (as described by the residents). Given that both areas comprise residents who chose to live there, and both have administrative entities (i.e., the retirement community administration and homeowners' association), it is notable that several in the second community referred to their administrative entity as "Big Brother." These two areas—in adjacent census block groups—appear to value differently the dimensions of neighborhood.

Ultimately, neighborhoods are at their core social-spatial entities (Cutchin, Eschbach, Mair, Ju, & Goodwin, 2011), a complex mix of geography and relationships that appears to vary with the demographic and psychological aspects of the residents and the built space. Changes in the built or the social environment may lead to changes in how residents define their neighborhoods (e.g., Lohmann & McMurran, 2009). Also, although obvious alterations in the built environment or demographics are easily identified, other changes—such as changes in social expectations, needs, or contexts as residents grow older—may be subtler.

NEIGHBORHOOD RESEARCH DIMENSIONS

It may be helpful to begin with a general framework in which to think about how neighborhoods are defined in community-based research. Given that neighborhoods are a blend of both social and spatial aspects, different methodological approaches seem to place differing emphases on the social versus the spatial. At one end of the spectrum, greater weight has been assigned to the phenomenological experiences of residents to formulate neighborhood boundaries, whereas, on the other end, neighborhoods are defined using pre-established and often administratively grounded boundaries, frequently taking the form of census tracts or block groups (hereafter referred to as census units). Other administrative units include school districts, also referred to as educational catchment areas (ECAs). We can conceptualize these two approaches as end points on a spectrum of operationalization (see Fig. 10.1). Given that administrative operational definitions of neighborhoods are by far the most

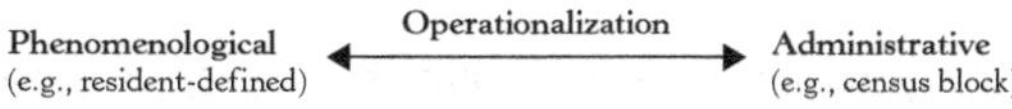

FIGURE 10.1: Spectrum of operationalization.

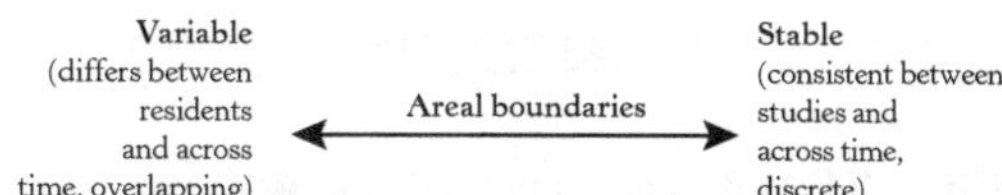

FIGURE 10.3: Spectrum of boundaries.

commonly used in research, this chapter focuses on the nonadministrative approach, highlighting the equally important but less often used phenomenological methodologies.

This tension between phenomenological versus administrative research approaches reveals the deeper dilemma that pervades neighborhood research, namely, the meaning of neighborhoods. To the degree that neighborhoods are social entities, the focus needs to be on the contextual settings as relevant to the residents—the symbols, neighborhood narratives, and interpersonal relationships that are considered crucial components in neighborhoods. In other words, most of the neighborhood-based research using GIS has been top-down and grounded in rational positivism (Aitken & Michel, 1995; Gauvin et al., 2007; Talen, 1999). These are the *etic* approaches, wherein definitions of neighborhood are established by researchers or entities outside the community. Less common are the *emic* approaches to defining neighborhoods, wherein the neighborhood boundaries are determined in a bottom-up approach, with the boundaries of the neighborhoods grounded in what they mean to the residents. This second approach could not only elucidate neighborhood dynamics that may not be captured using an etic approach but may also contribute to greater neighborhood interaction, depending on the means of data collection (see Parker, 2006; Sieber, 2006; Talen, 1999, for examples). Therefore, we may also consider the extant literature upon a second spectrum (see Fig. 10.2).

There are pragmatic methodological issues that need to be accounted for when engaging in neighborhood-based research. For example, should one opt to take a more phenomenological approach, he or she should be aware of the methodological challenges of disparate and potentially overlapping areal boundaries in the data. However, it is also quite possible that individuals living adjacent to each other would not identify themselves as living in the same neighborhood. This is not to say that stable, discrete boundaries (e.g., census units) are adequate surrogates for neighborhoods, but rather that overlapping neighborhoods create unique analytic challenges (see Fig. 10.3). For example, if one considers the impact of the spatial area on a resident living on the edge of a census unit as compared to one living in the center of it, it may be that the adjacent census unit, discretely defined but methodologically ignored, has more impact on the resident on the perimeter than on the one in the center (Hipp & Boessen, 2013).

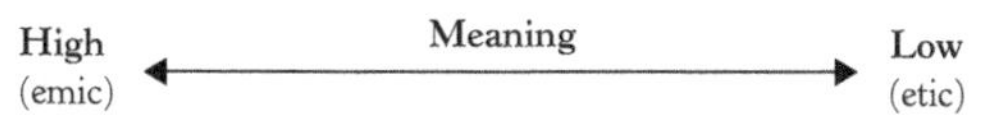

FIGURE 10.2: Spectrum of meaning.

The context in which residents are asked about their neighborhoods also manifests here: How people define their neighborhood in the context of their social networks of neighbors may indeed differ from their spatial definition when considering municipal public policy, which may differ when considering shopping and other commercial activities. This variability may also impact the capacity to study neighborhoods longitudinally because the spatial dimensions of the neighborhood would change given changes in the population; the sample or residents selected; and perceptions, relationships, and geographic environments of the long-term residents in these neighborhoods. In other words, even if one were to perform longitudinal research, tracking individuals over the years who lived at the same address, their neighborhood boundaries may indeed change, which may complicate analyzing data and providing reliable conclusions about the neighborhood. The benefit of defining neighborhoods from an administrative approach is that they are consistent and stable over time.

Perhaps the most significant reason why administratively defined spatial entities are so frequently used to define neighborhoods is the availability of data. The wealth of demographic data grounded in census units, ECAs, and others makes it a very attractive source for researchers and, given the expense and labor involved in conducting research, it is understandable that researchers would be attracted to the available demographic data to generate their research strategies. In contrast, when

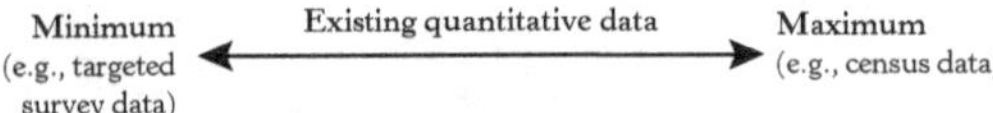

FIGURE 10.4: Spectrum of existing data.

researching from a contextual, phenomenological approach, the challenge is to find a functional means of defining neighborhood, incorporating meaningful resident perspectives, and collecting the data for analysis (see Fig. 10.4).

Why Not Just Use Administrative Neighborhood Definitions?

Although there are several benefits to using administrative units in neighborhood research, such usage is also problematic. A major concern is one of construct validity, that is, the degree to which an operational definition measures the concept it was intended to measure (Cook & Campbell, 1976). If you consider your current neighborhood, do you define it as the census unit in which you live, or rather is it a complex interaction of geographic space and social relationships that shapes its boundaries? The challenge facing the researcher involves making claims about neighborhood effects, as opposed to geographic effects. This tension between neighborhood and geography has been addressed repeatedly, with many suggesting (Brooks-Gunn, Duncan, Klebanov, & Sealand, 1993; Burton, Price-Spratlen, & Spencer, 1997; Cummins et al., 2005; Darling & Steinberg, 1997; Duncan & Aber, 1997; Entwisle, 2007; Korbin & Coulton, 1997; Mayer & Jencks, 1989; Sampson, Morenoff, & Gannon-Rowley, 2002) and several in fact demonstrating (Coulton, Korbin, Chan, & Su, 2001; Grannis, 1998; Lee, 1973; Lohmann, 2007) that the areas residents consider to be their neighborhoods appear to be both qualitatively and quantitatively different from administratively defined neighborhoods. Ultimately, a space may be a neighborhood only if the residents define it as a neighborhood.

For example, in his analysis of metropolitan areas, Grannis (1998) examined the impact of tertiary (that is, residential) streets on resident interactions and behaviors. Whereas the larger urban context did impact notions of neighborhood, it was the street networks—those "who lived down the street" (Grannis, 1998, p. 1531)—that appeared to be one of the driving forces that explained the racial segregation manifest in the urban areas. There is every reason to believe that the impact of those "who lived down the street" would be significantly greater on defining neighborhoods than those "who lived on the other side of the census unit." Yet the presence and effects of tertiary roads are generally ignored.

Therefore, the question we are left with is this: Do the operational definitions that we use for neighborhoods in our research actually do the job of defining neighborhoods and describing neighborhood effects? When closely examining the relevant variables, there is reason to believe that there often exists a significant degree of systematic error manifesting itself in our results. Given that the literature makes numerous conclusions about neighborhood impacts on residents (e.g., children, pregnant mothers, couples, elderly, those with serious mental illnesses), if we are systematically committing error in operationally defining the primary independent variable (i.e., neighborhoods), then, logically, the conclusions also probably possess systematic error. Without a solid means to operationalize neighborhood, our capacity to present quality inferences based on our findings is weakened (Mueller, 2003).

Given the noted shortcomings of geographically based operational definitions of neighborhoods, a brief synopsis of four alternative, GIS-based approaches will now be presented. They have been selected not for the results that they have produced but rather as illustrations of resident-oriented context-based approaches toward conceptualizing neighborhoods.

GEOGRAPHIC INFORMATION SYSTEMS CONTEXT-BASED APPROACHES TO CONCEPTUALIZING NEIGHBORHOODS

Resident-Defined Neighborhood Mapping

When it comes to assessing neighborhoods phenomenologically, perhaps the most direct approach is to ask residents to draw their neighborhoods. This approach has taken two forms, either (a) having residents draw the neighborhoods freeform (Appleyard, 1981; Appleyard & Lintel, 1971; Lynch, 1977) or (b) providing residents with maps of the local area and having them outline what they consider to be their neighborhoods (Coulton et al., 2001; Lee, 1973, Lee et al., 1975; Lohmann &

McMurran, 2009; Smith, Gidlow, Davey, & Foster, 2010). This is a methodology that has been particularly productive in the study of children and their construal of their neighborhoods. This freeform approach has been used to tap into how children perceive the excitement or stultification of neighborhood environments, as well as its relative safety (Hart, 1979; Lynch, 1977; Moore, 1990).

The discrepancy between resident-defined neighborhood boundaries and census tracts manifests itself in two ways: shape and size. As has already been suggested by the areal boundaries dimension, although there are some shared borders between the two geographic areas (e.g., major thoroughfares), resident-defined neighborhoods show much more interindividual variance. First, because neighborhoods incorporate meaningful social relationships, these social connections may differ even between people who live adjacent to each other. Indeed, residents living next door to each other may provide differing neighborhood boundaries (Chaskin, 1997; Lee, 1973) and may report neighborhoods that do not overlap at all (Lohmann, 2007). Part of the reason for this is that residents do not necessarily place their home in the center of their neighborhoods. Although some resident-defined mapping research has found a trend to locate the home near the centroid of residents' neighborhood polygon (Hipp & Boessen, 2013), others have found no such trend. In the research that produced the findings in Lohmann and McMurran (2009), residents placed the location of their home on the perimeter of their neighborhood polygon as frequently as its centroid (although most respondents locate their home at some point between these two extremes). Second, although there appeared to be general agreement on some boundaries of neighborhoods (e.g., major roads, parks, storm water causeways), there appeared to be differing interpretations as to the geographic features that constituted neighborhood barriers: Significant numbers of neighborhood boundaries ignored geographic features that are commonly considered neighborhood boundaries.

Behavioral Approaches

Instead of assessing the neighborhood from a predominantly cognitive perspective, others have attempted to extrapolate neighborhood boundaries using a behavioral approach by asking residents to describe their behavior within their local community. This activity spaces approach focuses on the interaction of individuals with identifiable places in their vicinity on a regular basis, that is, the locations where they shop, visit, and hang out and that are important to them (Gesler & Albert, 2000). The theoretical premise is that those areas frequented more often and for longer periods are more familiar to the individual and therefore more likely to be incorporated into his or her notion of neighborhood.

Residents are asked to either draw freehand maps or mark on a preprinted road map the places they frequent. These locations are geocoded, and from these points activity spaces are generated, often by creating an ellipse around the points of activity using a standard deviational ellipse method. This analytical tool available in a GIS calculates an areal shape that will include a specified proportion of the activity places (e.g., one standard deviation would include 68% of the points; two standard deviations, 96% of the points). Generally, it is recommended that one standard deviation be used (Sherman, Spencer, Preisser, Gesler, & Arcury, 2005). In this way, residents' range of repeated behaviors can be determined. Some findings suggest that larger spaces are positively associated with greater life satisfaction but negatively associated with a sense of community (Townley, Kloos, & Wright, 2009). It should be noted that activity space size is highly dependent upon the geographic dynamics of an area: Communities with meaningful spaces proximal to each other will naturally produce smaller activity spaces. Hence, there will likely exist different-sized spaces for urban, suburban, and rural residents.

The strength of this approach is its focus on behavior and on the conceptualization of neighborhood within the physical interactions one has with one's local surroundings. However, one weakness is that it does not provide clearly defined demarcations for neighborhoods. Additionally, its behavioral focus does not directly incorporate notions of social connectedness, instead focusing on interaction with spaces.

An approach that synthesizes social ties with behavior in generating neighborhood maps incorporates network analysis with GIS. By geocoding the social ties of adolescents, accounting for both location and frequency of contact with friends, Hipp, Faris, and Boessen (2012) identified network neighborhoods that showed greater agreement between adolescents and their parents regarding perceptions of crime, physical and social disorder, and collective efficacy compared to the use of census tracts. Interestingly, the research also suggested the potential for individuals to belong to a second, noncontiguous neighborhood.

All these approaches share the same conceptual foundation as qualitative neighborhood-based research using participatory photo mapping (PPM; Dennis, Gaulocher, Carpiano, & Brown, 2009). Similar to photovoice and photo-narratives, PPM has participants photograph those spaces that have meaning to them (in this case, the neighborhood context), either positive (places they like, engage with, or consider an asset) or negative (places they dislike, avoid, or deem a liability). However, residents could also be directed to photograph what they consider to be the boundaries of their neighborhood and to provide narratives to explain why they selected those locations. Those photographed locations could then be incorporated into a GIS to establish the boundaries of neighborhoods and the underlying rationale from the residents' perspectives.

For activity spaces, much of the research is still quantitative in nature—examining the distances that children can travel (e.g., Veitch, Salmon, & Ball, 2008) or the size of the activity space area. However, there is considerable potential for more qualitative analyses, such as examining the degree to which the activity space facilitates movement through social contexts and the subsequent impact on the development and maintenance of social relationships. Additionally, mapping activity and social ties could be incorporated into notions of *home range*, that is, the area around the home where the child engages in unsupervised activities, shaped by the child's age and disposition, neighborhood qualities, and parental permission (Gaster, 1995).

Experience Sampling Method

One approach toward defining neighborhood that has promise in providing geographic insight into neighborhood boundaries builds on the textually rich experience sampling method (ESM; Hektner, Schmidt, & Csikszentmihalyi, 2007). This approach often uses portable technologies that participants carry with them, prompts them to provide information regarding their thoughts, behaviors, and emotions at random times throughout the day (e.g., "As you were beeped, where were you?" "What else were you doing?" "Who were you with?") (Hektner et al., 2007). The data provide a daily ecological record of behaviors and feelings, and the rhythm of one's day can then be analyzed.

The ESM has been used to examine neighborhood effects. In seeking to understand the role of structured and unstructured activities outside of school hours for African American youth growing up in neighborhoods with differing crime rates, Bohnert, Richards, Kohl, and Randall (2009) collected behavioral and affective information from middle-school students seven times per day at random intervals. They examined whether unstructured activities led to higher rates of delinquency or depressive states. However, in that research, neighborhoods were operationally defined using ECAs and not neighborhoods as defined by the youth themselves. Incorporating a more phenomenological approach potentially leading to a better understanding of neighborhood boundaries and dynamics could certainly be done with very little additional effort. The questionnaire could ask whether participants felt they were in their neighborhood, as well as their assessment of crime rates in their neighborhood. If smartphones were used, the geographic position of the respondent could automatically be collected and imported into GIS. Although this approach would not provide a definitive geographic boundary for the neighborhoods, it certainly could provide both qualitative and quantitative richness to explain the experience of neighborhood. It would combine many elements of the behavioral approach with numerous emotional and cognitive perspectives of the residents.

Grid Methods

Grid approaches seek to merge phenomenological and administrative perspectives. These techniques generally begin with aerial photographs of the geographic area of interest and then break the area down into smaller units based on any number of (usually geographic) characteristics. Sometimes these units are identical squares, as if overlaying a sheet of graph paper over the map. One example of this approach examined residents' familiarity with the area around their home (Aitken et al., 1993). Overlaying a grid on aerial photographs of a community, residents reported their familiarity with each specific block-grid and how often they had been in that block-grid in the past week (other than driving). GIS then allows for residents' phenomenological neighborhood experiences on a block-by-block basis. The greater the reported familiarity with each cell presumably corresponded with areas that residents considered to be part of the neighborhood.

A variation of this approach—the socio-spatial neighborhood estimation method (SNEM)—involves a sequential strategy of taking an aerial photograph; creating a general grid, using compact geographic blocks that take into account street patterns, housing types and density, and parks and other natural and built barriers; and then engaging in field observations to confirm the validity of the boundaries established in the previous step (Cutchin et al., 2011). In follow-up surveys of the residents in each of these SNEM-generated neighborhoods, it was found that residents within each had greater agreement with each other with respect to sense of community, neighborhood satisfaction, and perceived crime (but not social embeddedness) compared to either census tracts or block groups.

Compared to the other methodologies considered in this section, such grid methods move the approach of neighborhood conceptualizing closer to the administrative side by establishing stable, discrete boundaries that incorporate more of an etic, top-down approach toward defining neighborhood. However, they still attempt to recognize the importance of resident perceptions in defining neighborhood. The issue of discrete boundaries, though, remerges with this approach. One variation that uses grids while avoiding discrete neighborhood units uses circular buffers of a fixed distance (1/4- to 3/4-mile radius) around each city block's center point. This creates patterns of overlapping neighborhoods, or *egohoods*, that manifest like "waves" throughout a geographic area, with each neighborhood/block impacting adjacent ones, with decreasing influence as distance increases (Hipp & Boessen, 2013). In their study, egohoods were better than either census block groups or tracts in predicting crime (Hipp & Boessen, 2013).

CASE STUDY

In our effort to examine the impact of a newly built freeway on sense of community (SOC) and neighborhood size in Claremont, California, we (Lohmann, 2007; Lohmann & McMurran, 2009) conducted a 6-year longitudinal study wherein we asked respondents to outline their neighborhoods on a map provided to them and to define their SOC within their neighborhood. The neighborhood outlines were entered in a GIS as polygons (essentially outlines), transformed into shapefiles (converting the outlines into solid shapes), and the individual resident SOC assessments were then assigned to the respective neighborhood shapes. The shapefiles of all the respondents were then aggregated and SOC scores averaged for every point on the city map. The resulting map displayed geographic hot and cold spots in the overall city for SOC.

There was significant contraction in the size of neighborhoods that abutted the newly built freeway such that they shrank 41%. They also exhibited a statistically significant drop in SOC that was visually recognizable using the maps. The maps allowed for the qualitative identification of areas of agreement on neighborhood boundaries and changes in patterns across space and time. In our analysis, the merging of resident-reported neighborhood areas with the corresponding SOC produced a map that was examined similarly to how one would view a medical magnetic resonance imaging (MRI) scan of the brain. Given the variability of neighborhood sizes, we found that the neighborhoods needed to be stratified based on size (smallest 25%, smallest 50%, smallest 75%, and then all neighborhoods); otherwise, smaller-sized neighborhoods could not be effectively analyzed. The maps were then analyzed, seeking changes or patterns of resident agreement or disagreement in neighborhood boundaries, both across and between geographic layers and over time (see Lohmann & McMurran, 2009, for a more detailed description).

The results highlight some of the strengths of this resident-defined approach to studying neighborhoods. First, the neighborhoods themselves may serve as meaningful variables beyond the quantitative data they provide. Some of the neighborhoods were quite contextually rich in and of themselves. Respondents on occasion reported neighborhoods with multiple polygons (e.g., one small circle around the home and a larger one around the local colleges), and yet others had unusually shaped polygons (e.g., a circular area around the home, a narrow corridor encasing the main road through the city, and a quite large circular area around a sizable nature preserve located to the north of the city). These unusual polygons suggested valuable data concerning the respondents' life, interests, and behaviors. Some neighborhoods were drawn with great precision, with evident care in including and excluding various parts of the surrounding area, and others were more haphazard, perhaps indicating a perception of neighborhood not specifically confined to a clear area with clearly conceptualized borders, but rather one more emotionally based and more generalized within a larger geographic context. Of course, more investigation of this approach toward neighborhood definitions needs to be conducted.

Lastly, and most interestingly, it appears that this methodology observed the "emergence" of a neighborhood. An area where in 1998 (the first data collection point) residents had little geographic agreement and low SOC, by 2004 had some of the highest SOC in the city, as well as more agreement by residents as to their neighborhood boundaries. It appeared that the cause of this change over the six years of the study's duration was the city's proposal to build an affordable housing complex in the vicinity of their neighborhood. This galvanized the residents to lobby against the housing plan and included a rather intense grassroots lobbying effort, including the development of a Web site. What is important to note is that when the same data were analyzed using census block groups instead of resident-defined neighborhoods, the resulting map showed no evidence of this neighborhood coming together across the same time period (Lohmann, 2007).

CONCLUSION

Given the dimensions discussed at the start of the chapter, a dilemma in neighborhood research becomes clearer. The greater the focus on defining neighborhoods in stable, concrete geographic terms, the more the social and relationship component of neighborhoods is sacrificed in the operationalization. Conversely, the more emphasis placed on experiential meaningfulness in defining neighborhoods, the more difficulty is created in analyzing and reporting the results in definitive ways, especially longitudinally. In the end, the dilemma focuses on the balance one strikes between these competing approaches.

It makes sense that researchers try to have as much congruence as possible in the operationalizing of neighborhood and the focus of their research question. Research examining the neighborhood impacts on academic achievement should define neighborhood using educational catchment areas. Studies interested in the impact of social relationships and neighborliness should rely on resident-defined neighborhood. Research questions oriented around behavioral integration among neighbors and local community-based action should consider conceptualizing activity spaces as neighborhoods.

It is evident that the most commonly used methods for conceptualizing neighborhoods, namely census units, produce spatial areas that are lacking in cognitive, emotional, and behavioral meaning to the residents who reside in them. The data also suggest that they appear to be too spatially large. The alternative, phenomenological approaches to conceptualizing neighborhoods have some traits in common. First, the distribution of neighborhood sizes, although exhibiting great variability, tends to be notably clustered, with the number of smaller neighborhoods far outnumbering the larger. For the resident-defined neighborhoods described earlier (Coulton et al., 2001; Lee, 1973; Lohmann & McMurran, 2009), the square mileage ranged from less than .01 to more than 25, with the majority of neighborhoods ranging from .15 to .35, and comparable census entity sizes ranging from 55% to 400% larger. Hipp and Boessen's (2013) egohoods were most predictive at roughly .44 square miles. In other words, the more emic methodologies produce neighborhoods significantly smaller than the census units that are often used in their stead. Therefore, if meaningful neighborhoods are smaller, and the geographic areas being studied are larger, the results manifesting in the smaller neighborhoods could likely be analytically "washed out" across the greater geographic space that is treated as the operational definition of neighborhood, thereby making it more likely that notable effects would not appear in the analyses when in fact they do exist (Hipp, 2007).

It is doubtful that there exists a "Holy Grail" of neighborhood conceptualization (Galster, 2001)—an operational definition for a concept that everyone knows exists and can identify but that behaves on the empirical level. Even if the residential population and the physical environment were unchanging (and they are not), and even if the impact of context was consistent (and it is not), the inherent variance in human relationships that generate the schema of what comprises a neighborhood is far too complex to account for all the permutations.

Hence, researchers are left with developing tools to understand neighborhoods contextually.

Each neighborhood methodology, even the ones grounded in administrative definitions, provides valuable insight into the question of how the social-spatial environment impacts people's lives. Ultimately, for neighborhoods to be studied effectively, there needs to be more methods blending the context-based methodological approaches with the wealth of data that exists in the more administrative spatial units. The lure of big data is not going away, nor is the growing evidence of the validity of the smaller, more phenomenological neighborhoods, as suggested by the converging evidence from multiple methods.

REFERENCES

Aitken, S. C., & Michel, S. M. (1995). Who contrives the "real" in GIS? Geographic information, planning and critical theory. *Cartography and Geographic Information Systems, 22*, 17–29.

Aitken, S., Stultz, F., Prosser, R., & Chandler, R. (1993). Neighborhood integrity and residents' familiarity: Using a geographic information system to investigate place identity. *Tijdschrift voor Economische en Sociale Geografie, 84*, 2–12.

Appleyard, D. (1981). *Livable streets*. Berkeley: University of California Press.

Appleyard, D., & Lintell, M. (1971). The environmental quality of city streets: The resident's viewpoint. *Journal of the American Institute of Planners, 38*, 84–101.

Bohnert, A. M., Richards, M., Kohl, K., & Randall, E. (2009). Relationships between discretionary time activities, emotional experiences, delinquency and depressive symptoms among urban African American adolescents. *Journal of Youth and Adolescence, 38*, 587–601.

Brooks-Gunn, J., Duncan, G. J., Klebanov, P. K., & Sealand, N. (1993). Do neighborhoods influence child and adolescent development? *American Journal of Sociology, 99*, 353–395.

Burton, L. M., Price-Spratlen, T., & Spencer, M. B. (1997). On ways of thinking about measuring neighborhoods: Implications for studying context and developmental outcomes for children. In J. Brooks-Gunn, G. J. Duncan, & J. L. Aber (Eds.), *Neighborhood poverty, Vol. 2. Policy implications in studying neighborhoods* (pp.132–144). New York, NY: Russell Sage Foundation.

Chang, K. (2005). *Introduction to geographic information systems* (5th ed.). New York, NY: McGraw Hill.

Chaskin, R. J. (1997). Perspectives on neighborhood and community: A review of the literature. *Social Service Review, December*, 521–547.

Cook, T. D., & Campbell, D. T. (1976). The design and conduct of quasi experiments and true experiments in field settings. In M. D. Dunnette (Ed.), *Handbook of industrial and organizational psychology* (pp. 115–136). Skokie, IL: Rand McNally.

Coulton, C. J., Korbin, J., Chan, T., & Su, M. (2001). Mapping residents' perceptions of neighborhood boundaries: A methodological note. *American Journal of Community Psychology, 29*, 371–383.

Cummins, S., Macintyre, S., Davidson, S., & Ellaway, A. (2005). Measuring neighbourhood social and material context: Generation and interpretation of ecological data from routine and non-routine sources. *Health and Place, 11*, 249–260.

Cutchin, M. P., Eschbach, K., Mair, C. A., Ju, H., & Goodwin, J. S. (2011). The socio-spatial neighborhood estimation method: An approach to operationalizing the neighborhood concept. *Health & Place, 17*, 1113–1121.

Darling, N., & Steinberg, L. (1997). Community influences on adolescent achievement and deviance. In J. Brooks-Gunn, G. J. Duncan, & J. L. Aber (Eds.), *Neighborhood poverty, Vol. 2. Policy implications in studying neighborhoods* (pp. 120–131). New York, NY: Russell Sage Foundation.

Dennis, S. F., Jr., Gaulocher, S., Carpiano, R. M., & Brown, D. (2009). Participatory photo mapping (PPM): Exploring an integrated method for health and place research with young people. *Health & Place, 15*, 466–473.

Duncan, G., & Aber, L. (1997). Neighborhood models and measures. In J. Brooks-Gunn, G. J. Duncan, & J. L. Aber (Eds.), *Neighborhood poverty, Vol. 1. Context and consequences for children* (pp. 62–78). New York, NY: Russell Sage.

Entwisle, B. (2007). Putting people into place. *Demography, 44*, 687–703.

Galster, G. (2001). On the nature of neighbourhood. *Urban Studies, 38*, 2111–2124.

Gaster, S. (1995). Rethinking the children's home-range concept. *Architecture & Comportment, 11*, 35–41.

Gauvin, L., Robitaille, E., Riva, M., McLaren, L., Dassa, C., & Potvin, L. (2007). Conceptualizing and operationalizing neighbourhoods: The conundrum of identifying territorial units. *Canadian Journal of Public Health/Revue Canadienne de Sante'e Publique, 98*, S18–S26.

Gesler, W. M., & Albert, D. P. (2000). How spatial analysis can be used in medical geography. In D. P. Albert, W. M. Gesler, & B. Levergood (Eds.), *Spatial analysis, GIS, and remote sensing application in the health sciences* (pp. 11–38). Chelsea, MI: Ann Arbor Press.

Grannis, R. (1998). The importance of trivial streets: Residential streets and residential segregation. *American Journal of Sociology, 103*, 1530–1564.

Haeberle, S. H. (1988). People or place variations in community leaders' subjective definitions of neighborhood. *Urban Affairs Quarterly*, 23, 616–634.

Hart, R. (1979). *Children's experience of place*. New York, NY: Irvington.

Hektner, J. M., Schmidt, J. A., & Csikszentmihalyi, M. (2007). *Experience sampling method: Measuring the quality of everyday life*. Thousand Oaks, CA: Sage.

Hipp, J. R., (2007). Block, tract, and levels of aggregation: Neighborhood structure and crime and disorder as a case in point. *American Sociological Review*, 72, 659–680.

Hipp, J. R., & Boessen, A. (2013). Egohoods as waves washing across the city: A new measure of "neighborhoods." *Criminology*, 51, 287–327.

Hipp, J. R., Faris, R. W., & Boessen, A. (2012). Measuring "neighborhood:" Constructing network neighborhoods. *Social Networks*, 34, 128–140.

Hunter, A. (1974). *Symbolic communities: The persistence and changes of Chicago's local communities*. Chicago, IL: University of Chicago Press.

Korbin, J., & Coulton, C. J. (1997). Understanding the neighborhood context for children and families: Combining epidemiological and ethnographic approaches. In J. Brooks-Gunn, G. J. Duncan, & J. L. Aber (Eds.), *Neighborhood poverty, Vol. 2. Policy implications in studying neighborhoods* (pp. 65–79). New York, NY: Russell Sage Foundation.

Lee, T. R. (1973). Psychology and living space. In R. M. Downs & D. Stea (Eds.), *Image and environment* (pp. 87–108). Chicago, IL: Aldine.

Lee, T. R., Tagg, S. K., & Abbott, D. J. (1975, September). *Social severance by urban roads and motorways*. Paper presented at the meeting of the Planning and Transport Research Ad Council, Canterbury, England.

Lohmann, A. (2007, June). *Conceptualizing neighborhoods as phenomenological versus census blocks: A comparison of methods*. Paper presented at the biennial meeting of the Society for Community Research and Action, Pasadena, CA.

Lohmann, A., & McMurran, G. (2009). Resident-defined neighborhood mapping: Using GIS to analyze phenomenological neighborhoods. *Journal of Prevention and Intervention in the Community*, 37, 66–81.

Lohmann, A., & Schoelkopf, L. (2009). GIS: A useful tool for community assessment. *Journal of Prevention and Intervention in the Community*, 37, 1–4.

Lynch, K. (1960). *Image of the city*. Cambridge, MA: Harvard University Press.

Lynch, K. (Ed.). (1977). *Growing up in cities*. Cambridge, MA: MIT Press.

Mayer, S. E., & Jencks, C. (1989). Growing up in poor neighborhoods: How much does it matter? *Science*, 243, 1441–1445.

Moore, R. C. (1990). *Childhood's domain: Play and place in child development*. Berkeley, CA: MIG Communications.

Mueller, C. W. (2003). Conceptualization, operationalization, and measurement. In M. S. Lewis-Black, A. Bryman, & T. F. Liao (Eds.), *The Sage encyclopedia of social science research methods* (pp. 161–165). Thousand Oaks, CA: Sage.

Parker, B. (2006). Constructing community through maps? Power and praxis in community mapping. *Professional Geographer*, 58, 470–484.

Renger, R., Cimetta, A., Pettygrove, S., & Rogan, S. (2002). Geographic information systems (GIS) as an evaluation tool. *American Journal of Evaluation*, 23, 469–479.

Sampson, R. J., Morenoff, J. D., & Gannon-Rowley, T. (2002). Assessing "neighborhood effects:" Social processes and new directions in research. *Annual Review of Sociology*, 28, 443–478.

Sherman, J. E., Spencer, J., Preisser, J. S., Gesler, W. M., & Arcury, T. A. (2005). A suite of methods for representing activity spaces in a healthcare accessibility study. *International Journal of Health Geographics*, 4, 24.

Sieber, R. (2006). Public participation geographic information systems: A literature review and framework. *Annals of the Association of American Geographers*, 96, 491–507.

Smith, G., Gidlow, C., Davey, R., & Foster, C. (2010). What is my walking neighbourhood? A pilot study of English adults' definitions of their local walking neighbourhoods. *International Journal of Behavioral Nutrition and Physical Activity*, 7, 34–41.

Sweetser, F. L. (1942). A new emphasis for neighborhood research. *American Sociological Review*, 7, 525–533.

Talen, E. (1999). Constructing neighborhoods from the bottom up: The case for resident-generated GIS. *Environment and Planning B: Planning and Design*, 26, 533–554.

Townley, G., Kloos, B., & Wright, P. A. (2009). Understanding the experience of place: Expanding methods to conceptualize and measure community integration of persons with serious mental illness. *Health & Place*, 15, 520–531.

Veitch, J., Salmon, J., & Ball, K. (2008). Children's active free play in local neighborhoods: A behavioral mapping study. *Health Education Research*, 23, 870–879.

11

Causal Layered Analysis

LAUREN J. BREEN, PETA L. DZIDIC, AND BRIAN J. BISHOP

Causal layered analysis (CLA) is an emerging qualitative methodology that allows the deconstruction of complex social issues. Originally a futurist's theory and method, CLA was designed to allow assessment of worldviews and cultural factors, as well as social, economic, and political structural issues to be considered in formulating alternative projections of the future. This assessment of deeper individual and collective processes should be inherently attractive to community-based researchers. In this chapter, we describe the theory underlying CLA, briefly outline the steps involved in conducting CLA, and describe its benefits and drawbacks. We then provide an example to demonstrate CLA's potential to deconstruct and analyze complex social psychological issues and argue that CLA is an important addition to the methodological armamentarium of community-based researchers.

INTRODUCTION TO CAUSAL LAYERED ANALYSIS

Valuing Context in Community-Based Research

The nature of community-based research requires a deep understanding of the social context. Unfortunately, positivism remains the dominant scientific epistemology for the social and behavioral sciences, despite a longstanding critique concerning its applicability to understanding the complexities of social and community phenomena (Breen & Darlaston-Jones, 2010; Polkinghorne, 1983, 1988). Pepper (1942) created a typology of scientific approaches, each with its own philosophical underpinning—mechanism (positivism), formism (trait and individual differences), organicism (holistic organic systems), and contextualism. Contextualism is one position that appears appropriate for community-based research.

In contextualism, people are not seen as discrete entities but are conceptualized as sharing similarities and differences with others in their contexts. Altman and Rogoff (1984, p. 24) defined this approach as "the study of changing relations among psychological and environmental aspects of holistic entities." There are a number of features to the epistemology of contextualism. First, it is assumed that the context, time, and a person's behaviors and actions are inseparable. Second, this approach acknowledges that notions of change in any direction are a continual process of all psychological phenomena. Third, it focuses on the contemporary events and determines the patterns and structure of phenomena. Fourth, it argues for the use of multiple observers who participate in different contexts and who investigate the same event. The complexity of this approach emerges not from the latter points but from the first point; the notion that people are not separable from context is contrary to lay understandings of what it means to be an individual and the central assumptions within mainstream understandings in disciplines such as psychology (Burr, 2002; Dashtipour, 2012; Hayes, 2002). This counterintuitive notion of people as part of context makes researching contextualism complex. Even in this previous sentence it is linguistically difficult to describe people as part of context, rather than being separate from context.

CLA emerged from futurists within the broad domain of planning and reflects postmodern thinking in the process of assessing the developments of future strategies and outcomes as part of community and societal planning (Inayatullah, 1998). Specifically, its development reflected concerns about traditional scientific planning whereby projections about what may occur in the future were based on what has happened in the past. This fundamentally linear approach to assessing potential outcomes was recognized to have shortcomings in that it does not reflect changing circumstances in societies and at international and national levels. In some ways, the critique parallels the rise within community-based research of concerns about the relevance of traditional treatment modalities based on positivism and the recognition of the need to be aware of social contexts. Users of CLA conceive of people as being part of context and not separable or meaningful outside of context, and, as such, the technique allows a holistic consideration of complex social issues.

LAYERS IN CAUSAL LAYERED ANALYSIS

One of the characteristics of CLA is that it forces the user to address more than the apparent factors involved in social change. In using CLA, researchers deconstruct discourses and narratives according to four conceptual layers (see Table 11.1). The first layer is Litany, which comprises the manifest and obvious events, contexts, and behaviors about which there is little dispute. The next layer is Social Causal, which is akin to a psychological analysis of the systemic social, political, economic, and governance factors that are involved in influencing the observed behavior at the Litany layer. The next layer is Worldview Discourse, in which the unacknowledged, value-based assumptions about the world (Sarason, 1981) are articulated. The fourth layer is Myth Metaphor, comprising glimpses of underlying cultural aspects that emerge through narratives and are the participants' attempts at explaining emotions and symbols in a language that is not available to abstract processes. This layer examines cultural archetypes, stories, symbols, imagery, fables, metaphors, and the social rules that may be so engrained in a culture that they go unnoticed. The complexity of cultural values, stories, and archetypes found at the Myth Metaphor layer often manifests across all of the layers, even the descriptive content depicted in themes at the Litany layer. In dealing with these two latter layers, then, it is important that we resist the temptation to individualize them. Instead, we adopt an approach that reflects Sarason's (1981) notion that worldviews are largely collective, and, as such, it is important that the Worldview Discourse and Myth Metaphor layers reflect these collective understandings.

Given the foci of each layer, the deconstructed discourse will vary in specificity from the largely personal and idiosyncratic descriptions within the Litany layer to the systemic issues within the Social Causal layer, to the cultural and collective layers of Worldview Discourse and Myth Metaphor (Bishop & Dzidic, 2014). An important strength, then, of this approach to analysis is that it does not limit the phenomena to being studied solely at an individual level (as Campbell, 1957, warned against) but instead incorporates an explicit examination of people within their social, structural, and cultural contexts. CLA allows us to make the assumption that people are both different but also the same. There is an inbuilt process that resists the temptation to treat people as discrete individuals, but rather sees people as both having some unique characteristics and histories (which are emphasized in the Litany and Social Causal layers) and being part of a broader society with common cultural understandings and histories (as depicted in the Worldview Discourse and Myth Metaphor layers). In this way, CLA has some conceptual similarities to the ecological systems theory of Bronfenbrenner (1979)

TABLE 11.1: LAYERS IN A CAUSAL LAYERED ANALYSIS

Layer	Focus of Concern
Litany	What we say—the overt or descriptive everyday experiences
Social Causal	What we do—the relationships between people and settings, social systems, and structures
Worldview Discourse	How we think—the perspectives, values, meanings, and positions that are often illustrated through one or more discourses
Myth Metaphor	Who we are—the deep, mythical stories and social/cultural archetypes relevant to the issue

Source: Compiled from the following: "Solving the Futures Challenge—All You Need Is a 3LA," by M. Barber, 2010, *Futures, 42*, p. 171; "Multiple Level Analysis as a Tool for Policy: An Example of the Use of Contextualism and Causal Layered Analysis," by B. J. Bishop, P. L. Dzidic, and L. J. Breen, 2013, *Global Journal of Community Psychology Practice, 4*, p. 5; and "Dealing With Wicked Problems: Conducting a Causal Layered Analysis of Complex Social Psychological Issues," by B. J. Bishop and P. L. Dzidic, 2014, *American Journal of Community Psychology, 53*, p. 17.

or the ecological approach of community-based disciplines (Jason & Glenwick, 2012; Kloos et al., 2012; Nelson & Prilleltensky, 2010).

Currently, the two dominant approaches are either an interpretative approach for analysis of nonnumerical (e.g., textual, visual) data or a facilitation approach for the collection of group-based data derived through workshops or focus groups (Bishop, Dzidic, & Breen, 2013). For example, CLA has been used as a method of analysis to examine a varied array of phenomena of interest to community-based researchers, including farmers' perspectives on land management policy in rural Australia (Bishop et al., 2015), traffic congestion in Bangkok, Thailand (Inayatullah, 2004), and natural resource management in the context of climate change in Australia (Green & Dzidic, 2013; Hofmeester, Bishop, Stocker, & Syme, 2012), and it has been used as a methodological framework in the areas of Aboriginal and Torres Strait Islander mental health, constructions of disability, and regional community needs.

Steps in Conducting a Causal Layered Analysis

Conducting a CLA typically involves five steps. The first step requires the conceptualization of a research question that inquires about the depth and complexity of the phenomenon of interest. The second step necessitates familiarization with the data and the context within which the data were generated. Third, excerpts from the data are coded according to the four increasingly complex layers (from the Litany, Social Causal, Worldview Discourse, and Myth Metaphor), capturing the surface issues all the way to the deep explanations. Next, the data are analyzed to identify themes within each layer. Thematic analysis can be used to achieve this within-layer analysis. The final step involves a narrative reconstruction of the phenomenon of interest. Existing theory and findings may be used to aid interpretation of the data. This reconstruction is driven by the research aim/questions and presents a consolidated interpretation of the complex underpinnings of the issue.

Strengths and Challenges of Causal Layered Analysis

A strength of CLA is that, by focusing on increasingly complex layers of interpretation, it promotes a depth of analysis that might not be apparent otherwise in other analysis methods. All too often, community-based researchers attempting to analyze qualitative data struggle with the need to identify discrete themes. CLA, on the other hand, facilitates the recognition that the emerging themes may be simultaneously linked but vary greatly in complexity. Specifically, some themes are more overt and descriptive, while others may be symbolic, metaphorical, or reflect broader cultural and historical influences.

Similarly, this attention to depth and complexity means that CLA provides a framework for analysis that allows (and expects) a contextual interpretation of the topic area. CLA may be especially useful when analyzing data where participants' reflections on the topic of inquiry are diverse, appear to reflect different contextual factors relating to values and worldviews, and include potentially illustrative discursive patterns, for example, common terms or group-specific jargon and imagery. Ultimately, the processes of deconstructing and reconstructing the issue lend CLA to understanding the real-world implications associated with the issue being explored.

Given the comparatively recent development and adoption of CLA as a methodological and interpretative approach within psychology, the approach may suffer from an apparent lack of familiarity from both potential users of the technique and the target audiences (e.g., policymakers, journal editors and reviewers, funding bodies), which may act to dissuade community-based researchers from its adoption. For instance, although many researchers, funders, and policymakers have some awareness of such techniques as thematic analysis or methodologies such as grounded theory or participatory action research, we find ourselves always having to explain even the basics of CLA. Furthermore, the analytical process takes time and requires the researcher to think critically and in greater depth than what might be expected for some other techniques for the analysis of textual data. This is particularly pertinent given the expectation that the researcher will be required to analyze transcripts with the purpose of identifying not only themes pertaining to individual experiences but also themes reflecting deeper cultural mythologies and collective understandings about the topic being explored. We are hopeful that these challenges involved in conducting a CLA will dissolve in time; familiarity with the approach may decrease anxiety associated with the unknown, assist in the analytical proficiency that comes with practice, and similarly assist in the uptake and translation of findings by the end users of such research.

CASE STUDY

Background

To illustrate the processes and potential applications of CLA, we focus on a relational women's sports community. The social, emotional, and physical health benefits that come from adopting a physically active lifestyle are well documented (Coleman, Cox, & Roker, 2008); so too are problematic trends associated with maintenance of physical activity as women age. For example, Australian women's level of participation in organized sport declines with age, with a noticeable decline as early as prior to their completion of high school. Participation in organized sports is noted again to decrease during years associated with childrearing, only for participation in physical activities to gain in popularity in retirement years. Noteworthy is that the participation changes with age, with women tending to engage in solitary and informal physical exercise (e.g., walking) as opposed to organized group activities. However, engagement in group exercise, which encourages social engagement between participants, is noted to result in better health outcomes for participants, both physically and psychologically (Jewson, Spittle, & Casey, 2008; Martin, Terence, & McCann, 2005).

One sport demonstrating a growing level of participation by women is the sport of flat track roller derby. Research that considers roller derby explicitly is somewhat limited, as are studies that capture the demography of the skaters in Australia. Research that does report on women in sport more generally and from health science and public health positions tends to explore women's participation in sports according to notions of body image, physical health and well-being, and for the promotion of physical activity and well-being during the life span (e.g., Krane, Choi, Baird, Aimar, & Kauer, 2004).

The limited research that considers roller derby explicitly tends to do so from a gender studies perspective (e.g., Finley, 2010) and is centered on exploring the gender roles and gender maneuvering of women who participate in the sport, but it does little to understand the contribution that the sport gives to the lives of women that participate. The analysis of women's participation in sports tends to be focused on sports that are traditionally male-dominated or draw on stereotyped masculine behaviors, such as aggression, physical strength, or competitiveness (Coleman et al., 2008; Ezzell, 2009). Such studies endeavor to make sense of how women negotiate their identities and conflicting expectations relating to their participation in the sport. There is a tendency within the literature to consider participation of children and adolescents, particularly adolescent females, and barriers associated with active lifestyles, with limited consideration of the motivating factors of women in their 20s and 30s and through to middle or later life. This is despite recognition of the physical, psychological, and social benefits of engaging in physical activity, particularly in later life (Stephan, Boiche, & Scanff, 2010).

Anecdotal information from roller derby publications, social networking sites, and league Internet home pages suggests that the roller derby community in Australia is strong and growing. Furthermore, references to strong, empowered women imply that there is "something" about roller derby that is attracting women to pursue the sport. The Women's Flat Track Derby Association (WFTDA) conducted annual participation surveys in 2010, 2011, and 2012 of roller derby skaters worldwide. In 2012, the average age of skaters polled was 31 years, with 59% between 25 and 34 years, and 27% were 35 years or older. Furthermore, 30% of the skaters reported a household composition that included children 18 years or younger (WFTDA, 2012). The age of skating participants in roller derby and the overall growth of the sport warrant further investigation. For example, is roller derby more than a sport, and if so, how? Understanding what it is that attracts women to participate in organized sports, particularly in the age bracket that suffers most from underrepresentation, may contribute to uncovering factors that can bolster and support women in their pursuit of physical activities at a group level.

Contemporary flat track roller derby is recognized as a grassroots, full-contact sport designed by women for women. As the sport is played on roller skates and requires high-level athletic endurance and agility, it differs from more traditional sports available to women. This is due not only to the level of physical contact and force demanded of players but also to the fact that the sport is not a variation or adaptation of an existing sport played by men. To illustrate, it is assumed that roller derby be played by women and that, therefore, male leagues will feature the prefix "male" and will follow the rules determined originally for women's participation. Unlike other organized sports in Australia, there is no specific governing body or formal competitive roster; rather, leagues are established and managed by groups of interested women at a grassroots level.

Methodology

The following excerpts were drawn from transcripts of interviews with 11 women roller derby players reflecting on their experiences of playing the sport. Due to the low participation rates of women in organized sports (for the reasons outlined earlier), the overarching aim of the research was to explore women's participation in roller derby.

The data were analyzed by first coding interview text into the four categories, line by line. It is worth noting here that not all of the text must be coded and multiple coding (i.e., coding to two or more layers) can occur. This initial coding to the four layers focused on "best fit" and allowed "mis-coding" to be identified to ensure that text coded to Litany only included uncontested observations and events, Social Causal only comprised structurally caused events and explanations, Worldview Discourse only encompassed individual and collective ways of viewing social action, and Myth Metaphor extracts only related to stories and emotional components of actions and events. Once we were satisfied with the categorization and coherence of coded text, we conducted a thematic analysis within each layer to identify common and contrasting themes. Given that the example we include here is for illustrative rather than definitive purposes, the thematic analysis is speculative and consistent with Polkinghorne's (2004) reflective understanding or Peirce's (1955) abductive reasoning.

As with any analysis technique, rigor and quality are essential. Bishop and Dzidic (2014) recommended the use of two primary strategies—reflexive journaling and peer coding. Reflexive journaling involves the identification of the researcher's epistemology, his or her own positions (including values and worldviews in relation to the research topic), and the ways in which these positions influenced the choice of topic, data collection, and analysis. Within the current research team, the second author was actively involved in roller derby as player and volunteer in a league, the first author has participated as a spectator at a few roller derby bouts, and the third author has no involvement in the sport. As a research team, we possess insider and outsider perspectives on the phenomenon of study. Throughout the project, we maintained written summaries of the research activity, ideas about coding and relationships between codes, and reflections on the data. Documenting our positions and perspectives on the data enabled a rigorous approach to reflexivity in interpreting the women's stories.

The second strategy, peer coding, involves working with one or more co-researchers to discuss the data and share preliminary interpretations of those data. We worked together as a team to independently read the transcripts and code to each layer. We then met several times to share codes and compare and contrast differences. Once we were satisfied with the coding to each layer, we worked together to identify the themes within each later. These discussions, particularly the sharing of alternate interpretations, are fruitful in the development of a strong and defensible CLA.

Findings

Table 11.2 provides an illustration of each CLA layer, the themes within each layer, and exemplary extracts. The women described roller derby as demanding on their time and relationships. They reflected on the degree to which players provided each other with mutual support, both within and outside of the game, and that existing relationships external to roller derby were often strained due to the level of commitment to the sport. The participants described roller derby as boosting their confidence and redefining who they were; this is particularly evident in the player's choice of "derby name." The name is typically a play on words, whereby phrases or names (e.g., of celebrities) are modified such that the result is "tougher." The name may also utilize humor, be overtly or covertly sexual, make reference to dynamics or qualities of the sport (e.g., rolling, wheels), and reflect qualities of the players' personalities or espoused identities. The discourse also identifies and formalizes the relationships between members (e.g., "Derby Wife" is a term used to describe a player's best friend in the league). The underlying grassroots and feminist

TABLE 11.2: THEMES ACCORDING TO THE CAUSAL LAYERS AND EXAMPLE EXTRACTS

Layer and Themes	Example Extracts
	Litany
Demands on time	Depending on what level and league you're skating at, it can be between anywhere between three or five nights training.
Identification as athletes	My personal best at the minute is 29 laps in five minutes of the derby track, so that is one every five and half seconds. . . . I would like to be able to do 31, which is one every, like, 4.9 seconds.
	Social Causal
Strong sense of community	At the beginning of the year, one of our skaters went down and she's kind of new to the league and she broke her arm, she broke both her bones in her arm, and she couldn't drive so we sort of organized obviously meals brought to her house, we had a "meals on wheels" sort of thing going on, and people drove her places particularly to doctor's appointments and things like that.
Complexity of relationships	In most leagues, everybody trains together and then on bout day there are two teams that play each other on the track, so people who you are friends with off the track and people you regularly socialize with become your competition on game day. Everyone has to kind of negotiate that in some way mentally, I guess, as preparation.
	Worldview Discourse
Transformation	At first it was all about becoming a "badass" derby skater who wore a tutu and fishnets and now it's all about the friendship and the fitness and . . . . I guess the personal growth it has given me; the fishnets and the tutu don't matter anymore.
A roller derby identity	It is kind of like my world is becoming roller derby. Like, people who play netball don't come to work, you know, and promote their netball games and talk about the bruises that they got . . . . Their netball friends are just sort of like one side of their friends but they're not a big part of their life as far as I can tell.
Space for all women	. . . and everyone is an individual and everyone is okay with the fact they're an individual. You know you've got your tattooed, pierced people who are really into their heavy metal and there's . . . we've got a lawyer . . . yeah we've got doctors and nurses and people whose job I don't actually know what she does but she has a pager and if it goes off she runs away um and there are mums and there are gay people and there are straight people and there are people who aren't quite sure what they are and just . . . it's really inclusive . . .
	Myth Metaphor
Having it all	. . . but I know that at some point, like, roller derby can't be such a big priority in my life forever because other things kind of get dropped, like, as you get more and more involved like, you know, um just seeing your friends outside of roller derby becomes a bit of an issue [laughs] or the ones that don't play, you know, so I can imagine, like, I'm glad that I don't have children because I can imagine that can be a huge hassle [laughs] if you play roller derby so imagine, like, later on in life um I would probably choose not to play roller derby and have a family or something like that instead.
Sport versus spectacle	There's never any sort of performance within the game but obviously you know you dress up and you wear fishnets and you sort of express that sort of side of yourself as well like . . . but in terms of performance as such there's not really any on the track.

ideology resonated with the participants' conceptualization of the sport as a domain of women.

As women, the multiple and competing roles meant personal sacrifice was required and that it was not possible for them to "have it all" at once. It was not uncommon for the participants to renegotiate their participation on an ongoing basis, particularly in instances where significant others or loved ones objected to the level of participation to the league. Additionally, they were aware of the risk of objectification, whereby players may be expected by the paying public to perform an ascribed sexualized role. The participants' stories illustrated how the legitimacy of women in sport, being skilled, having strength, and ultimately having power, is trivialized. Given this, although participation in roller derby may present within Western cultural contexts as an avenue in which the cultural construction of women could be challenged, the game continues to operate within a context that values dominant cultural constructions of gender.

As can be seen in Table 11.2, the process of coding within these layers of increasing depth and complexity prompts the consideration of the same issue from an individual (Litany) perspective, a systemic (Social Causal) perspective, a values (Worldview Discourse) perspective, and a cultural archetype (Myth Metaphor) perspective. Although not included in the present chapter because of space considerations, the final stage of a CLA typically involves a narrative reconstruction of the data from the four layers and the intralayer themes. In presenting the findings in the narrative reconstruction, each layer is described separately, with subheadings for each within-layer theme and the inclusion of interview or text extracts (Bishop & Dzidic, 2014).

CONCLUSION

CLA explicitly requires its users to take an ecological approach in examining phenomena and therefore is well suited to community-based researchers. However, CLA can be a daunting methodology, particularly to the novice or early career researcher. Typically, qualitative methods are about exploring the experiences of people within certain contexts. CLA offers community-based researchers the opportunity to delve deeply into context. In the case of women's participation in the organized sport of roller derby, the analysis using CLA revealed not only individual experiences of the sport and its demands, identity formation, and transformation but also a much more complex story about these same experiences embedded within the paradoxical nature of inclusion and community, and the at times conflicting social constructions of both "woman" and "athlete." As can be seen in the earlier example, CLA facilitated a deeper level of analysis and the uncovering of broader social and cultural understandings of the roles and expectations of women in modern Western societies.

It is through conducting an in-depth contextual analysis of data afforded by CLA that the community-based researcher is equipped with greater insights regarding the propensity for change and intervention. For example, if the intent was to explore mechanisms to support women's participation in sport, a less complex analysis may have led us to the conclusion that supporting the development of a sense of community within leagues and exploring women's empowerment might be options. Arguably, the deeper analysis achieved through conducting a CLA enabled the identification of more complex issues pertaining to broader cultural attitudes regarding the role and construction of women. The construction of women appeared to present operational and interpersonal challenges for the participants. This privileging of context places CLA as an important tool for community-based researchers.

AUTHOR NOTE

We thank the participants from the roller derby community in Western Australia for their time and the following students who assisted with data collection: Declan Mountford, Sasha Hayes, Melissa Zaha, and Daniel Northeast.

REFERENCES

Altman, I., & Rogoff, B. (1984). World views in psychology: Trait, interactional, organismic, and transactional perspectives. In D. Stokals & I. Altman (Eds.), *Handbook of environmental psychology* (Vol. 1, pp. 1–40). New York, NY: Wiley.

Barber, M. (2010). Solving the futures challenge–all you need is a 3LA. *Futures, 42*, 170–173.

Bishop, B. J., & Dzidic, P. L. (2014). Dealing with wicked problems: Conducting a causal layered analysis of complex social psychological issues. *American Journal of Community Psychology, 53*, 13–24.

Bishop, B. J., Dzidic, P. L., & Breen, L. J. (2013). Multiple level analysis as a tool for policy: An example of the use of contextualism and causal layered analysis. *Global Journal of Community Psychology Practice, 4*. Retrieved June 2015, http://www.gjcpp.org/pdfs/bishop-v4i2-20130619.pdf

Bishop, B. J., Dzidic, P. L., & Breen, L. J. (2015). Causal layered analysis as a tool for policy: The case of Australian agricultural policy. In S. Inayatullah & I. Milojevic (Eds.), *CLA 2.0: Transformative research in theory and practice* (pp. 163–171). Tapei, Taiwan: Tamkang University Press.

Breen, L. J., & Darlaston-Jones, D. (2010). Moving beyond the enduring dominance of positivism in psychological research: Implications for psychology in Australia. *Australian Psychologist, 45*, 67–76.

Bronfenbrenner, U. (1979). *The ecology of human development: Experiments by nature and design*. Cambridge, MA: Harvard University Press.

Burr, V. (2002). *The person in social psychology*. East Sussex, England: Psychology Press.

Campbell, D. T. (1957). Factors relevant to the validity of experiments in social settings. *Psychological Bulletin, 54*, 297–312.

Coleman, L., Cox, L., & Roker, D. (2008). Girls and young women's participation in physical activity: Psychological and social influences. *Health Education Research, 23*, 633–647.

Dashtipour, P. (2012). *Social identity in question: Construction, subjectivity and critique*. New York, NY: Routledge.

Ezzell, M. B. (2009). "Barbie Dolls" on the pitch: Identity work, defensive othering, and inequality in women's rugby. *Social Problems, 56*, 111–131.

Finley, N. J. (2010). Skating femininity: Gender manoeuvring in women's roller derby. *Journal of Contemporary Ethnography, 39*, 359–387.

Green, M., & Dzidic, P. (2013). Social science and socialising: Adopting causal layered analysis to reveal multi-stakeholder perceptions of natural resource management in Australia. *Journal of Environmental Planning and Management, 57*, 1782–1801.

Hayes, N. (2002). *Psychology in perspective* (2nd ed.). New York, NY: Palgrave Macmillan.

Hofmeester, C., Bishop, B., Stocker, L., & Syme, G. J. (2012). Social cultural influences on coastal governance in the context of climate change. *Futures, 44*, 719–729.

Inayatullah, S. (1998). Causal layered analysis: Poststructualism as method. *Futures, 30*, 815–829.

Inayatullah, S. (2004). Causal layered analysis: Theory, historical context, and case studies. In S. Inayatullah (Ed.), *The causal layered analysis reader* (pp. 1–52). Taipei, Taiwan: Tamkang University Press.

Jason, L. A., & Glenwick, D. S. (Eds.). (2012). *Methodological approaches to community-based research*. Washington, DC: American Psychological Association.

Jewson, E., Spittle, M., & Casey, M. (2008). A preliminary analysis of barriers, intentions, and attitudes towards moderate physical activity in women who are overweight, *Journal of Science and Medicine in Sport, 11*, 558–561.

Kloos, B., Hill, J., Thomas, E., Wandersman, A., Elias, M. J., & Dalton, J. H. (2012). *Community psychology: Linking individuals and communities* (3rd ed.). Belmont, CA: Wadsworth.

Krane, V., Choi, P. Y. L., Baird, S. M., Aimar, C. M., & Kauer, K. J. (2004). Living the paradox: Female athletes negotiate femininity and masculinity. *Sex Roles, 50*, 315–329.

Martin, P., Terence V., & McCann, T. V. (2005). Exercise and older women's wellbeing. *Contemporary Nurse, 20*, 169–179.

Nelson, G., & Prilleltensky, I. (2010). *Community psychology: In pursuit of liberation and wellbeing* (2nd ed.). Basingstoke, England: Palgrave Macmillan.

Peirce, C. S. (Ed.). (1955). *Philosophical writings of Peirce*. New York, NY: Dover.

Pepper, S. C. (1942). *World hypotheses: A study in evidence*. Berkeley: University of California Press.

Polkinghorne, D. E. (1983). *Methodology for the human sciences: Systems of inquiry*. Albany: State University of New York Press.

Polkinghorne, D. E. (1988). *Narrative knowing and the human sciences*. New York: State University of New York Press.

Polkinghorne, D. E. (2004). *Practice and the human sciences: The case for a judgment-based practice of care*. New York: State University of New York Press.

Sarason, S. B. (1981). *Psychology misdirected*. New York, NY: Free Press.

Stephan, Y., Boiche, J., & Scanff, C. L. (2010). Motivation and physical activity behaviors among older women: A self-determination perspective. *Psychology of Women Quarterly, 34*, 339–384.

Women's Flat Track Derby Association. (2012). *Roller derby demographics: Results from the Third Annual Comprehensive Data Collection on Skaters and Fans*. Austin, TX: Author.

12

Emotional Textual Analysis

RENZO CARLI, ROSA MARIA PANICCIA, FIAMMETTA GIOVAGNOLI, AGOSTINO CARBONE, AND FIORELLA BUCCI

In this chapter, we present a psychological methodology called emotional textual analysis (ETA; Carli & Paniccia, 2002). Much of this work is embedded within more psychoanalytic methods, which might be somewhat foreign to those involved in community-based research. In brief, when using ETA, texts are collected and analyzed with the aim of using the meaning of the words to provide knowledge to ultimately design culturally appropriate interventions. The method is based on the study of the association of *dense words*, that is, words that when taken out of the context of discourse have an immediate, very strong emotional sense (e.g., *bomb, mother, travel*). In this approach, language is thought of as an organizer of the relationship between the individual contributor of the text and his or her context, rather than just an expression of the individual's emotions. Tracks of these written representations are viewed within the complexity of relationships and settings.

ETA can be used to explore the culture of organizations in the production and service sectors, as well as the cultures characterizing many social and community groups. We refer to the culture identified using this methodology as *local culture*. ETA analyses are calibrated to the local cultures and have been used as a basis for bringing about interventions. Many examples of this method's use in Italy are described elsewhere (e.g., Paniccia, Giovagnoli, Bucci, & Caputo, 2014; Paniccia, Giovagnoli, & Caputo, 2014) and, more generally, in the e-journal *Rivista di Psicologia Clinica*.

In this chapter, we first provide the theoretical models upon which ETA is based. We discuss how, in its reliance on the assessment of both emotions and relationships, it differs from other qualitative approaches. We then provide a case example in which the application of ETA facilitated the explication of the employment situation of workers in Italy.

INTRODUCTION TO EMOTIONAL TEXTUAL ANALYSIS

Models Underlying Emotional Textual Analysis

ETA draws from specific traditions of psychological theories. Gestalt theory is one primary frame of reference. It stresses that we actively confer meaning to stimuli through a lens that depends on our culture, the context in which we grew up, and the context in which we perceive the world. Central to ETA is Freud's conceptualization of the unconscious. Matte Blanco (1975) suggested that the unconscious is a mode of thinking of the mind characterized by a *symmetrical* logic, unlike the logic of conscious thinking. According to Matte Blanco (1975), we operate continually with paradoxes, with schizophrenic thought being an extreme example. Schizophrenic thought seems strange to us, but it might be logical for symmetrical logic because external reality has been replaced by an inner, psychological reality. In this view, thought is always a compromise between these two forms of logic, unconscious and conscious thought. In the ETA approach, the unconscious is seen as the attribution of emotional meaning to social and contextual reality.

ETA also draws from another psychoanalytic tradition, object relations theory, which asserts that that we attribute emotional significance to every dimension of reality with which we relate and that we interpret these emotional experiences as being intentioned toward us. For example, a child may bang his or her head against the table and say "Bad table!" The table is viewed as having intentionally inflicted pain on the child. This process is present in adults as well as children. Adults sometimes get upset with a computer that does not obey their commands, despite knowing that the computer is inanimate and not capable of purposefully ignoring commands. We grow up giving emotional meaning to all aspects of reality that we encounter, such as the mother's nipple, light, sound, a voice, or a word.

The elaboration of ETA started in the 1970s within a multivocal cultural context. The publication of "The Unconscious as Infinite Sets" by Matte Blanco (1975) and the book *Symbol and Code* by Fornari (1976) were important contributions in the development of our theory of *emotional symbolization*. In this vein, in connection with French psycho-sociology and the journal *Connexion* (http://www.cairn.info/revue-connexions), we began to study social relationships and the dynamics of power in real social groups in the field, such as youth groups, national and international companies (e.g., electricity and communications companies, the Italian Banking Association), small and medium-sized enterprises, schools, and health services. The idea that thinking is always a compromise between the two forms of logic, that of the unconscious and that of the conscious, was applied to a psychological theory of social relationships.

In the ETA approach, the purpose of psychological interventions is to enable the client to conceive of and interpret the *collusive dynamics* that are operating in a particular context. By collusive dynamics, we mean the emotional symbolization of the context socially shared by those who belong to it. The social relationship originates from the shared emotional symbolization of the context, which forms the basis of sense making and behavior regulation in social groups. We attribute emotional significance to every dimension of reality with which we relate. However, because it is based on the symmetrical logic of the unconscious, emotional symbolization tends to assimilate and confuse external reality with internal, psychic reality. Only the thinking encompassed by emotional symbolization allows one to recover the distinction between external reality, on the one hand, and the multiple, different meanings that we can attach to it in our subjective representation, on the other. The process of thinking of the collusive dynamics—that is, the shared emotional symbolization of the context within, for example, a group, an organization, or a community—is the key goal of ETA and, more generally, of the psychological intervention. By exploring the most significant criticalities and resources which are present in the emotional dynamics that underlie social relationships—such as dynamics of power, dependency, and achievement (Carli & Paniccia, 2002)—ETA improves the client's organizational competence and supports social development.

In order to organize the research and interpret the collusive dynamics expressed by a text (e.g., a set of interview transcripts), it is essential to consider the relationships within which the text was produced. We need to consider in which social groups we collected the text and what goals we have for the analyses. In this method it is important to identify the people who requested assistance and to keep them in mind throughout the research process. In other words, when collecting and interpreting this type of data, a researcher needs to be clear about who will use them. The relationship is fundamental and influences the way in which research participants are approached, helps identify the models used to explore the data, and provides aid in interpreting findings.

The Double Impact of Language: Emotional and Cognitive

Within this context, words are an essential component of the ETA approach. If we use the subject and the object without the verb, we speak in ways that are hard to understand, such as by saying "I pasta." If the person had said, "I eat pasta," we would understand the meaning. It is evident that if our expressions are not complete, we cannot be understood. In addition, our language, like everything that we experience, has a double meaning, both emotional and cognitive. If a person says, "I devoured that book," we do not think that the person ate a book but that it was read avidly. We understand the meaning of "devoured" by understanding the emotional sense. Additionally, some words have a very strong emotional significance when expressed in specific settings. For example, at a sporting event, a famous soccer player who had an episode of tuberculosis and had just returned to play, heard a fan of the opposing team call him "Lung." The shouted word, in that context, had a clear-cut sense of aggression. It is clear that many words have strong emotional connotations. We can think of a continuum: On the extreme left side there are emotionally ambiguous words, which become effective only within their context; they are said to have low polysemy. On the opposite side, words have high polysemy, that is, a minimum of ambiguity because they are emotionally meaningful even when isolated from their discursive context. For example, the verb "to go" has a low emotional profile—"Where are you going tonight?"—and does not indicate emotions except, at times, within a sentence. Completely different is "to go away." Words such as "to go away," "hatred," "failure," and "ambition" are characterized by a maximum of emotional density and a minimum of ambiguity of meaning. We call these words *dense words* because they are emotionally dense. The emotionally dense sense is evident even when the word is taken out of the context of discourse.

Emotional Textual Analysis as a Methodology for Textual Analysis

In consulting work for organizations since the 1960s, Carli and Paniccia (1981, 2003) have developed a psychological theory and methodology of intervention called the *analysis of the demand*. This work is based on the analysis of cultures as mediators between individuals and context. The analysis of the demand proposes that interventions should not be focused on correcting deficits but rather on developing the client's resources. Using this approach, psychologists explore the emotional symbolization of problems in order to see how these relate to the client's goals and the possibility of achieving them. It is important to consider that by *client* we can mean an individual, a social organization, or a community requesting the intervention.

In the mid-1980s, consistent with the theoretical and methodological assumptions of analysis of the demand, Carli and Paniccia (2002) developed the methodology called ETA. This method uses the collection and analysis of texts in order to explore specific topics. Texts are analyzed based on writings, as well as on individual or group interviews. ETA aims to uncover how language expresses emotions—in other words, how language indicates emotional symbolization or the collusive dynamics of contexts. Because the aim is to approach the symmetrical unconscious logic of the text, ETA identifies the dense words within the text. To do this, ETA uses specific software, such as Alceste (Reinert, 1993) or T-LAB (Lancia, 2004), that divides the text collected by the researcher into units of meaning according to special algorithms (Benzècri, 1981).

Using this approach, we could, for example, ask the citizens of a city to provide a response to the question "What do you think of the traffic in your city?" There could be 50 people interviewed, each one having different structural characteristics (e.g., gender, age, socioeconomic level). Using the data collected, the software will generate a dictionary of all the words contained in the text. The researcher then chooses which words to be considered dense. Once the text has been divided into segments and only the dense words have been isolated, it becomes evident that there are segments within which some dense words and not others recur. By using multiple correspondence analysis and cluster analysis, text segments can be placed on the X-axis and the dense words on the Y-axis, allowing some clusters of dense words to be obtained and positioned in a factorial space (for more details, see Bucci, 2014). The clusters' interpretation is governed by the assumption that the co-occurrence of dense words within the text segments highlights the collusive dynamic expressed by the text. The collusive dynamic thus identified is historically situated and characterizes individuals defined within a specific context.

We came to elaborate ETA after years of intervention with organizations of various kinds and conducted research in order to verify if the clusters of dense words actually express the collusive process of the group interviewed. To verify correspondences and mismatches, the textual analysis should be conducted in parallel by more than one person. We have sufficiently communicable criteria, such as the notions of emotional polysemy and ambiguity. It is important to be aware that each person will take interpretative initiatives and declare one's own choices. The reading of the clusters and the dense words may invite intuitive interpretations. In this case, the researcher will find only what she or he already knows. To minimize this, specific models of the relationship formulated by the analysis of the demand which theoretically informs ETA are necessary in order to carry out the clusters' interpretation (Carli & Paniccia, 2002).

So far we have been speaking mainly about the clusters of dense words. It is important to consider, however, that the reading of the data cannot happen if there is no reference to two other parameters, namely, the factorial space and the relationship with the client who will utilize the research findings. When using ETA, one studies the clusters, then relates them to the factorial space, then goes back to the clusters, and so on, in a spiral process. The interpretation takes time. It is also important to keep in mind that the multivariate statistics adopted for ETA do not prove hypotheses but help to build them. This type of research produces interpretative hypotheses of the theme under investigation. It is important to share hypotheses, as well as the verification of these hypotheses, with the citizen or community group requesting the intervention. The following case study illustrates the application of ETA.

CASE STUDY

Since the end of the 1990s, the Italian labor market has been radically transformed. New forms of atypical employment spread, together with a multiplicity of nonstandard contracts (Fanelli et al., 2006). Atypical employment was meant to develop a flexibility that seemed to be advantageous, as it could accommodate the rapid change of companies' needs and enable people with obligations outside of the workplace (e.g., students, mothers of young children) to access the labor market. The aim was to overcome the excessive rigidity of the traditional employment contracts that hindered companies' hiring plans.

There has been tension within the Italian culture regarding this new form of employment. These new types of employment contracts often have lacked appropriate legal and trade-union protections traditionally important in Italian work culture. Consequently, the labor market has been divided into two parts, with protected workers on the one hand and marginal and insufficiently protected workers on the other. As a consequence, the atypical contracts have created workers who have precarious working conditions. Flexibility has been rapidly transformed into precariousness (Fanelli et al., 2006).

In the research presented here, we interviewed 97 employees having an atypical employment contract. It is important to note that, in ETA, those doing the interviews play an important role in presenting the research and its goals to the respondents. The interviewers are trained in how to select the research participants, share the interviews' aims with interviewees, and support the interviewees' associative process during the interview without interrupting them. In the study with atypical workers, the interviews were based on the following open-ended question: "As members of a university that is engaged in research and interventions concerning problems related to social coexistence, we are interested in flexible work. As you are engaged in flexible work, please tell us everything that comes to your mind when thinking about your work."

The open-ended question is actually not a simple question. During the training, the interviewers often want to know why they are to ask just one question. They frequently express concern that the interviewee's reply might last no more than 5 minutes. However, as part of this one-question process, interviewers also provide interviewees with information on who the interviewer is and why he or she is asking this question, and are trained to establish a relationship, one that offers the interviewee an opportunity to think about one's own experience by sharing thoughts with another. This method provides an invitation to say anything that crosses the interviewee's mind on the subject. Everything said will be considered relevant. The objective is to follow the thinking of the interviewee without guiding it beyond the initial approach. This procedure is consistent with the exploration of the emotional symbolization of the theme by the interviewee. An interviewer with little experience in this method might think that the interviewee would have no interest in replying for half an hour to "only one question." Conversely, one might also think that a theme could be so emotionally involving for the interviewee that it might be hard to deal with all the generated affect and issues. For example, if the atypical worker interviewed said, "I have had enough of this work, I have been doing this for a long time, I am very angry" and then fell silent, an inexperienced interviewer might be uncertain about what to do next and might ask: "How long have you been doing this job?" In this case, the interviewee might then answer "15 years" and fall silent again. This interviewer might find herself or himself asking one question after the other, steering the conversation to follow her or his own thoughts on the atypical employment. This would not be a good outcome for the interview. In contrast, a well-trained interviewer would wait before saying anything, without any impatience, looking in a friendly way at the interviewee. If the silence continued, the interviewer would repeat the interviewee's last word in a questioning tone: "Angry..." in order to reopen the exchange, without influencing the emotional tone of the interviewee's responses.

Data from the interviews explicated our understanding of the tensions experienced by atypical employees. Specifically, the data revealed which words held especial significance. In this particular study, a central word used by workers was *guarantee*. The etymological Germanic root of this word means to defend and to protect. A second key word that often appeared in the interviews was *future*; the use of this word inherently suggests unpredictability. At this point an emotional sense began to unfold. The third key word was the verb *project*, which means to think of the future. The lack of guarantee is connected to unpredictability when one looks ahead. In this example, we can grasp the fundamental principle of the analysis of the co-occurrences of dense words in the cluster. The co-occurrence of guarantee-future-project is what is meant by word clustering. Data analysis led to the positioning of this cluster on the right polarity of the first factorial axis. In contrast, another cluster ended up, by the data analysis, being positioned on the opposite polarity of the same factor. The first dense words characterizing the second cluster were *money* and *euro*. Thus, these two clusters expressed two different and contrasting symbolizations of work that were present in the respondents' discourse. The first emphasized the experience of unpredictability and lack of future associated with work, and the other instead presented work exclusively as a way to make enough money in order to support one's own family.

One soon realizes that within a specific text, some words have a higher relevance in relation to the particular context to which the text refers. For example, the word *queue* becomes dense if you analyze the culture of citizens with respect to banking services; *queuing up* at the counter can mark a specific cultural model according to which, for example, the bank is emotionally perceived as an enemy. This kind of research systematically requires the researcher to make specific interpretive choices. The emotional density of a word does not linearly coincide with the frequency of the word within the text. In some cases, for example, a high-frequency word can be so stereotypical for the group interviewed that it does not allow the exploration of any significant differences concerning the emotional symbolization of the investigated problem within the group interviewed.

Another application of ETA is research that we carried out for "Sapienza" University of Rome. The university is located in a working-class neighborhood where there has recently been a rise in anti-student feeling, with police patrolling the streets, students putting up posters, and so on. The aim of the research was to improve the relationship between the university and the neighborhood (Carli & Pagano, 2008). The knowledge of this local culture allowed us to find cultural resources to promote integration between the two. The ETA process, in such instances as this, enables us to longitudinally explore and potentially verify local cultural changes. Specifically, once a first analysis within a certain context has been made and discussed with those who commissioned it, it is possible to carry out a second analysis after a particular period of time.

This kind of research often generates follow-up initiatives by the organizations requesting the analysis. In such cases, the researcher can give advice on possible actions to be taken, with a new, subsequent ETA carried out to assess follow-up results, if desired. For example, in an ETA examination of the local culture of a mental health center, one cluster indicated the presence of service users presenting problems that could not be classified in psychiatric terms and required a more complex treatment with less predictable outcomes (Paniccia, Di Ninni, & Cavalieri, 2006). These findings helped initiate a discussion concerning what to do about this new group of patients. Before the ETA analysis there had been little awareness of the differences between clients, but, as a result of using this approach, the mental health center developed an appreciation of the problem.

Similarly, in an ETA assessment in another Italian mental health center, Paniccia, Dolcetti, Giovagnoli, and Sesto (2014) explored the culture of the reception service and investigated requests addressed to mental health services. Discrepancies were found between clients' needs and the services provided, as the mental health center often failed to recognize differences among service users' requests. To address the problems revealed by the study, the center is seeking support in the categorization and differentiation of service users' requests. When using ETA, investigators do not necessarily aim to solve a specific problem but rather to transform the situation or culture from which the problem arose. Illustratively, in this mental health center study, one of the foci of discussion of the results with the staff was a dense word cluster which indicated that service providers felt a sort of ideological obligation to give "the right answer" to everyone who came to the mental health center. After some months, the center asked us to extend the investigation through further interviews with service users. Frequently, ETA is able to shed light on minority cultures or points of view. Such analysis is possible if the organization acknowledges that it has a problem and is interested in understanding it instead of perpetuating the habitual collusive dynamics. The intervention is grounded in the possibility that in the relationship between the researcher and the client or citizen group, there is interest in the shared problem.

CONCLUSION

In this chapter, we have presented ETA as a distinctive way of collecting and interpreting textual data. By analyzing the co-occurrence of dense words within the text, ETA enables us to examine the emotional dynamics underlying relationships within social groups and local communities. As was illustrated by the case examples, the data collected through interviews and analyzed can be used to effect an intervention at a variety of levels.

Of course, one might ask why an investigator does not just keep all the words of the interviewee, rather than selecting from them, as is done in the ETA approach. Our approach aims to examine the symmetrical logic of the unconscious. With ETA we are placed in a space of mediation between the unconscious and the conscious. ETA methodology enables us, by investigating dense words and word clusters, to grasp the emotional sense of a text and thereby analyze the emotional symbolization that underlies the local culture of organizations and communities.

The products of the ETA method have pragmatic value. The majority of our emotional tensions, particularly the most dramatic, concern the experience of being confronted with the experience of impotence. If we have the power to intervene, or even to reformulate the problem in a new way, we feel alive. Insights generated by the ETA approach can help improve organizational competence and aid people in community settings in thinking about the emotional dynamics that underlie their relationships with each other. Thus, ETA empowers both researchers and community members and their organizations in sharing and reorganizing knowledge concerning specific problems that derive from collusive dynamics, thereby promoting the growth of community competence.

REFERENCES

Benzècri, J. P. (1981). *Analyse des donnée en linquistique* [Analysis of data in linguistics]. Paris, France: Dunod.

Bucci, F. (2014). Cultural representations of mental illness in contemporary Japan. *Rivista di Psicologia Clinica, 1*, 82–108.

Carli, R., & Pagano, P. (2008). *San Lorenzo: La cultura del quartiere e i rapporti con psicologia* [San Lorenzo: The culture of the neighborhood and the relationships with psychology]. Rome, Italy: Kappa.

Carli, R., & Paniccia, R. M. (1981). *Psicosociologia delle organizzazioni e delle istituzioni* [Psychosociology of organizations and of institutions]. Bologna, Italy: il Mulino.

Carli, R., & Paniccia, R. M. (2002). *L'analisi emozionale del testo: Uno strumento psicologico per leggere testi e discorsi* [Emotional textual analysis: A psychological tool for reading texts and discourses]. Milan, Italy: Franco Angeli.

Carli, R., & Paniccia R. M. (2003). *Analisi della domanda: Teoria e tecnica dell'intervento in psicologia clinica* [Analysis of the demand: Theory and technique of intervention in clinical psychology]. Bologna, Italy: il Mulino.

Fanelli, F., Terri, F., Bagnato, S., Pagano, P., Potì, S., Attanasio, S., & Carli, R. (2006). Il rapporto di lavoro atipico: Modelli culturali, criticità e linee di sviluppo [The relationship of atypical work: Cultural models, problems and development lines]. *Rivista di Psicologia Clinica, 1*, 61–79.

Fornari, F. (1976). *Simbolo e codice: Dal processo psicoanalitico all'analisi istituzionale* [Symbol and code: From the psychoanalytic process to institutional analysis.]. Milan, Italy: Feltrinelli.

Lancia, F. (2004). *Strumenti per l'analisi dei testi. Introduzione all'uso di T-LAB* [Tools for text analysis. Introduction to T-LAB]. Milan, Italy: Franco Angeli.

Matte Blanco, I. (1975). *The unconscious as infinite sets: An essay in bi-logic*. London, England: Gerald Duckworth.

Paniccia, R. M., Di Ninni, A., & Cavalieri P. (2006). Un intervento in un centro di salute mentale [An intervention in a mental health center]. *Rivista di Psicologia Clinica, 1*, 80–95.

Paniccia, R. M., Dolcetti, F., Giovagnoli, F., & Sesto, C. (2014). La rappresentazione dell'accoglienza presso un centro di salute mentale Romano a confronto con la rappresentazione dei servizi di salute mentale in un gruppo di cittadini Romani: Una ricerca intervento [The representation of the reception service in a mental health center of Rome confronted with the representation of mental health services in a group of Roman citizens: An intervention-research]. *Rivista di Psicologia Clinica, 1,* 186–208.

Paniccia, R. M., Giovagnoli, F., Bucci, F., & Caputo, A. (2014). Families with a child with a disability: The expectations toward services and psychology. *Rivista di Psicologia Clinica, 2,* 84–107.

Paniccia, R. M., Giovagnoli, F., & Caputo, A. (2014). In-home elder care. The case of Italy: The badante. *Rivista di Psicologia Clinica, 2,* 60–83.

Reinert, M. (1993). Les "mondes lexicaux" et leur "logique" à travers l'analyse statistique d'un corpus de récits de cauchemars ["Lexical worlds" and their "logic" through the statistical study of a body of nightmare narratives]. *Langage et Société, 66,* 5–39.

SECTION II

Quantitative Approaches

13

Introduction to Quantitative Methods

CHRISTIAN M. CONNELL

In recent years, there has been some debate in the field of community-based research regarding the use of quantitative methods. On the one hand, more action-oriented proponents in the field argue in favor of constructivist or relativistic paradigms to promote greater engagement with the contextual and community-based influences that impact our areas of study (Lincoln & Guba, 2000). From this perspective, there is concern about the potential limitations, or even the potential harms to those who are disenfranchised, of more objective experimental paradigms (e.g., positivism and postpositivisism). On the other hand, proponents of these quantitative methods argue that as a scientific discipline seeking to expand the influence of our field's perspective on the way social and community research is conducted, we should embrace the strengths of methods based on these paradigms to facilitate rigorous hypothesis testing, produce research that is both internally valid and externally generalizable, and assess cause-and-effect relationships between constructs (Johnson & Onwuegbuzie, 2004).

For many, this inherent tension suggests a need for the more pragmatic approach of methodological pluralism, or mixed methods research (Barker & Pistrang, 2005, 2012; Tebes, 2005). Barker, Pistrang, and Elliott (2002) defined methodological pluralism as a recognition that all research methods have relative advantages and disadvantages and that researchers should draw upon a variety of methods and use those most appropriate to the specific questions being studied. At its core, a mixed methods approach represents a call for the incorporation or integration of quantitative and qualitative methods in the same research study (Greene, Caracelli, & Graham, 1989; Langhout, 2003; Yin, 2006). Despite potential incompatabilities among these methods (Howe, 1988; Johnson & Onwuegbuzie, 2004), community-based research appears to be evidencing a growing affinity toward a mixed methods approach. A pragmatic justification for this approach is well grounded in both methodological and epistemological concerns (Kloos, 2005; Morgan, 2007; Tebes, 2005). This perspective recognizes that both quantitative and qualitative approaches have inherent strengths and weaknesses. Thus, researchers should draw from an array of methods and approaches, taking advantage of the strengths associated with each to better understand social phenomena. Furthermore, a pragmatitic perspective maintains that the research question should drive the methods to be used, with researchers selecting the most appropriate tool or method to answer the particular research question under investigation (Onwuegbuzie & Leech, 2005).

Although a mixed methods approach does expand the field's ability to incorporate greater contextual understanding of influences on the subject matter that we study, it is equally important (and not incompatible with a mixed methods approach) that the quantitative methods used by community-based researchers provide a strong framework for investigating complex and contextualized phenomena in their own right. To maintain pace with the field's complex theories of the "interplay between people and contexts" (Shinn & Rapkin, 2000, p. 185), community researchers should use data-analytic methods that best represent the relationship of ecological and contextual domains to the phenomena being investigated. This means that community researchers need to adopt measurement approaches that do a better job of capturing contextual information, such as social network analysis (SNA) or geographic information systems (GIS) methods (Luke, 2005), or "ecometric" approaches (Raudenbush & Sampson, 1999, p. 3) to the assessment of ecological contexts. Community researchers also must make greater use of data-analytic methods that incorporate contextual (i.e., setting-level) and cross-level (i.e., interactions between setting-level and individual-level) effects (Raudenbush & Bryk, 2002), as well as more complex processes (e.g., indirect or mediating effects, moderation effects) cross-sectionally, longitudinally, and across contextual settings (Bollen & Curran, 2006; Duncan, Duncan, & Strycker, 2006; Kline, 2006; Preacher, Zyphur, & Zhang, 2010; Raykov & Marcoulides, 2006; Tanaka, 2000). Finally, analytic methods should be dynamic and adaptable to the challenges of complex research designs and data structures. However, previous examinations of the state of the field's statistical methods (e.g., Luke, 2005) revealed that community researchers continue to rely on more traditional data-analytic methods (e.g., analysis of variance [ANOVA], regression, and correlation), rather than methods permitting greater complexity (e.g., structural equation modeling [SEM], cluster analysis, and SNA) or contextualization (e.g., multilevel modeling [MLM] and GIS analysis).

In the remainder of this chapter I frame the issue of what considerations should drive a researcher's selection of quantitative methods when conducting community-based research, including the nature of the research question. This overview is intended to set up the subsequent chapters of this section of the volume, which provide a more in-depth view of many of these advanced methods. In addition, I present an update of Luke's (2005) review of the state of statistical analyses in community-based research to assess the current use of methods that are able to incorporate greater complexity and contextualization relative to more traditional statistical methods. Luke's original review revealed that traditional analytic methods still predominated the field of community-based research. Luke argued that community researchers should embrace contemporary analytic methods (e.g., MLM, cluster analysis, GIS, and SNA) more consistent with the values and perspectives of the field with regard to the incorporation of contextual and community-based effects. This updated review will demonstrate the degree to which community researchers have heeded Luke's call to incorporate such methods within the field and where further efforts are necessary to expand their use.

FRAMING THE CHOICE OF QUANTITATIVE METHODS FOR COMMUNITY-BASED RESEARCH

In selecting the appropriate type of quantitative statistical methods to be used in a given study, there are a number of factors that need to be considered. Ideally, these considerations are made prior to the collection and analysis phases of a study (e.g., during the study conceptualization and design phases), but there are instances when the determination of data-analytic methods to be used occurs after data have already been collected (e.g., in the case of secondary analysis of existing data). A primary factor that should drive selection is the nature of the specific research questions to be answered. A secondary set of concerns relates to the nature of the data that have been collected to answer the research question (e.g., number and type of dependent and independent variables, inclusion of covariates, and whether the data are cross-sectional or longitudinal; Tabachnick & Fidell, 2013). For community-based research, an added set of concerns to be factored into the data-analytic planning process are the means by which contextual factors are measured and how their relationship to other study constructs is to be assessed. A frequent focus of community-based research is the understanding of people in context and the variability of behaviors or other phenomena across social contexts (Barker & Pistrang, 2005). Many community-based studies involve data collected at multiple levels to capture both individual and contextual processes. However, many traditional statistical procedures assume independence among our data elements. Thus, for community researchers, selection of appropriate data-analytic methods should also be informed by the contextual levels at which the researcher has designed the study and collected data.

As indicated, the nature of the research question is a primary factor in determining the type of data-analytic method to be used. In addition to questions of a primarily descriptive nature (e.g., the characteristics of a particular group or phenomenon), Tabachnick and Fidell (2013) identified five primary types of research questions requiring quantitative statistical methods that support hypothesis testing (i.e., inferential statistics). These include questions about (a) the degree of relationship among two or more variables, (b) the significance of group differences on a set of measures, (c) predictors of group membership, (d) measurement and structure of constructs, and (e) the time course of events.

The following sections briefly summarize the core aims of each of these types of research questions, indicating traditional statistical methods that are relevant to each and highlighting examples of more sophisticated methods that facilitate the incorporation of more complex or contextualized analyses relevant to community-based research. A number of these methods are described in greater detail in the chapters that follow. The specific types of analyses are meant primarily as a guide, as the lines between these different analytic methods are not necessarily fixed. Most can be considered variations of the generalized linear model, permitting skilled analysts and researchers to select from a wide array of data-analytic methods to answer the questions most appropriately (Onwuegbuzie & Leech, 2006; Tabachnick & Fidell, 2013). Muthén (2002) further extended the overlap among these methods through a general latent variable modeling framework implemented in the Mplus statistical software that facilitates even greater flexiblity to incorporate multilevel data, latent variable measurement models, and process-oriented structural models to address complex mediating and moderating relationships among variables within the context of an array of different types of variables (e.g., continuous, discrete, or count variables).

Degree of Relationship Questions

Degree of relationship questions focus on the extent to which two or more factors covary in a consistent manner; they are among the most common staticstical questions in psychological research. Traditional statistical methods include simple correlation (e.g., bivariate *r*) or standard regression techniques in the case of multiple continuous independent variables (IVs) or covariates and a single dependent variable (DV). For community-based research, these types of questions become more complex with the inclusion of setting-level data to contextualize effects. Delany-Brumsey, Mays, and Cochran (2014), for example, examined the extent to which neighborhood social capital (a contextual factor) serves as a protective buffer for family-related risks on child-level outcomes. Such a study asks not only about the direct effect of a contextual influence on an individual-level outcome but also about the extent to which that contextual influence interacts with a micro-level factor (e.g., family risk effects on child-level outcomes may vary by the level of social capital within a given neighborhood) to influence that outcome.

Traditional methods for assessing such a question (e.g., regression-based models) assume a single-level data structure in which data are collected only at the individual level, or any contextual information is disaggregated so that it is linked to individual participants (Duncan, Jones, & Moon, 1998). In addition, these methods assume independence among participants (i.e., that participants are not clustered within higher order structures such as neighborhoods). When these assumptions are violated, the resulting anslyses may produce elevated Type I error rates and biased parameter estimates (Peugh, 2010; Raudenbush & Bryk, 2002). Finally, disaggregation of group-level information to the individual level (e.g., treating contextual information about community settings as person-level data) also has the effect of treating all effects as fixed across contextual settings, a limitation that reduces the functionality of assessing for contextual effects in the first place (Duncan et al.,1998; Luke, 2005). Thus, for studies investigating the degree of relationship among variables it is critical that community-based researchers move away from traditional regression-based approaches to more appropriate multilevel models (Duncan & Raudenbush, 2001; Raudenbush & Bryk, 2002) that more accurately reflect the association among contextual factors and outcomes.

Significance of Group Differences Questions

Significance of group differences questions focus on the degree to which indicators of interest vary across meaningful groups (e.g., across experimental or quasi-experimental groups or across groups based on other criteria, such as status, context, or group affiliation). A number of traditional statistical methods are available for addressing such questions, including the *t* test, one-way ANOVA, and factorial ANOVA for continuous DVs with one or more discrete IVs; analysis of covariance

(ANCOVA) for the inclusion of covariates; and multivariate analysis of variance (MANOVA) or multivariate analysis of covariance (MANCOVA) when multiple DVs are included. For categorical indicators, contingency table methods (e.g., chi-square) can be used to detect group differences in distribution.

As with traditional regression-based models, ANOVA-based models also assume a single-level data structure that can lead to biased parameter estimates or increased rates of Type I error if the study design does not match the analytic approach. Hoffman and Rovine (2007) provided a thorough overview of specification procedures for multilevel models to test group differences in place of more traditional ANOVA models.

Cluster randomized trials (CRT; see Chapter 17) are one example of a community-based research design that poses a problem for traditional analytic methods when investigating group differences, as randomization occurs at the setting level rather than at the individual level. This design introduces a nested data structure in which individuals are grouped into settings, with treatment condition linked to the setting level and potential covarites available at both the individual and setting levels—the typical data structure of a multilevel model. In a recent example of a CRT, Hagelskamp, Brackett, Rivers, and Salovey (2013) randomly assigned 62 schools to a universal social-emotional learning intervention, with quality of classroom-level interactions as a primary outcome of interest. Given this data structure (i.e., classrooms clustered in schools, randomization at the school level), MLM was used to analyze intervention effects, providing less biased parameter estimates of these effects and also allowing for school-level variation in classroom-level effects associated with the intervention.

Prediction of Group Membership Questions

Prediction of group membership questions are similar in some respects to the more general question of the degree of relationship among constructs, except that the outcome of interest is typically discrete or categorical in nature. Rather than assessing the degree to which changes in a given construct result in changes in a continuous outcome variable, the focus is on the degree to which a given set of independent variables increases or decreases the likelihood of being classified into a particular group (a categorical dependent variable) among a range of possible group classifications. Simple examples of these types of outcomes might include identification of predictors of being a smoker, graduating from high school, or joining a self-help group, although more complex group-level outcomes are possible in which there are multiple competing group outcomes (e.g., being a nonsubstance user, engaging in social use, or engaging in problematic levels of use). The traditional statistical approach would typically involve logistic regression (for a binary outcome) or multinomial regression (for nominal outcomes with more than two categories), in the case of a single dependent variable, or discriminant function analysis for multivariate outcomes. As with standard regression methods, extensions of MLM permit the incorporation of higher level contextual effects into these types of research questions (Merlo et al., 2006). Gregory and Huang (2013), for example, were interested in understanding the unique predictive influences of student, parent, and math and English teacher expectations in the 10th grade on postsecondary status 4 years later. Using an extension of multilevel modeling that permits cross-classification of students in multiple settings (e.g., classrooms), the researchers demonstrated the unique effects of expectations at the teacher, family, and student levels, as well as interactions between teacher expecations and child and family-level factors (e.g., socioeconomic factors) on the likelihood of continuing to postsecondary education.

Another set of statistical methods that are beginning to be used more frequently by community-based researchers to investigate predictors of group membership is mixture modeling (e.g., latent class analysis [LCA] or latent transition analysis [LTA]; Lanza, Flaherty, & Collins, 2003). The goal of these methods are similar to that of cluster analysis, in that the aim is to identify homogeneous groups within a heterogeneous population based on similar patterns of response to a given set of indicators or on similar characteristics. These methods provide a way of recognizing the variability within a given sample and identifying subgroups that may have unique needs or characteristics. Once distinct groups are identified, researchers often try to identify those factors that predict likelihood of being in the particular groups that have been identified or understanding how group membership may influence subsequent outcomes differentially across groups. Fowler et al. (2013), for example, used multilevel LCA to estimate the prevalence of inadequate housing based on multiple indicators for families involved with child protective services. Through their analyses, they differentiated two groups, a normative group that did not show risk of housing instability and a smaller group of households (16%) that were more likely to exhibit risks for housing instability. Analyses identified a number of family and service-related factors that were associated with greater likelihood of membership in the housing risk group and showed that families in this risk group were nearly four times more likely to require housing-related services at 12-month follow-up.

Measurement and Structure Questions

Measurement and structure questions focus on the underlying latent structure of a set of variables. These types of questions are at the heart of how researchers operationalize a construct and demonstrate the validity of measurement strategies. These types of traditional measurement-related analyses typically involve either exploratory or confirmatory factor analytic methods (Floyd & Widaman, 1995; Preacher & MacCallum, 2003). Raudenbush and Sampson (1999, p. 3) argued that contextual measurement and structure questions need to evolve beyond traditional methods, or the result is a "serious mismatch . . . in studies that aim to integrate individual and ecological assessments." To correct for this limitation, they proposed an ecometric corollary to psychometric approaches that combines MLM with aspects of item response theory, generalizability theory, and factor analysis. Their example provides a framework for developing measures of ecological context, using both survey and observational methods, that capture within- and between-setting variation more accurately than traditional methods do. Barile, Darnell, Erickson, and Weaver (2012) engaged in a similar type of contextual measurement analysis, using multilevel confirmatory factor analysis (MCFA) to assess collaborative functioning among members of nearly 160 community-based collaboratives. MCFA, like the approach of Raudenbush and Sampson, addresses the clustering inherent in community-level measurement strategies with multiple informants but does so from a latent variable modeling perspective that permits identification of the underlying factor structure to facilitate examination of structural relationships after accounting for measurement error.

Measurement-related models often also examine more complex structural relationships (e.g., indirect or mediating relationships) among latent constructs, representing a combination of both structural and regression-based models to assess association. SEM is a widely used method for analyzing such questions that has been used with increasing frequency by community researchers (Luke, 2005). A more recent development that mirrors the use of MCFA described earlier is multilevel SEM (MSEM; see Chapter 16). MSEM capitalizes on the strengths of the SEM approach over traditional regression models, as well as those of more general MLM approaches that disentangle within- and between-person variance. An added advantage of the MSEM approach over general MLM methods is the ability to specify and test cross-level mediation effects to explicate the mechanisms by which contextual effects influence individual-level outcomes (Preacher, Zhang, & Zyphur, 2011; Preacher et al., 2010).

Time Course of Events Questions

Time course of events questions, the final analytic question type in the continuum presented by Tabachnick and Fidell (2013), focus on one of two aspects of longitudinal measurement, either (a) the amount of time to a given event or outcome or (b) the rate or trajectory of change in a dependent variable over time. Time to event analyses are traditionally analyzed using survival analysis, a type of statistical method that allows the user to assess both the likelihood of event occurrence over time (e.g., time to relapse in a treatment study or time to employment in a jobs program evaluation), as well as factors that influence the timing of event occurrence (Allison, 1995; Connell, 2012). With the adoption of a more general latent variable modeling framework (Muthén, 2002) described earlier, there have been significant advances in survival analytic methods to incorporate contextual effects through multilevel survival analytic models (Asparouhov, Masyn, & Muthén, 2006).

To assess changes in a dependent variable over time, traditional methods include repeated measures ANOVA as well as time-series analysis, an approach that has not been used frequently in community research (see Chapter 18). Due to restrictions in repeated measures ANOVA assumptions, repeated measures approaches also have been conceptualized from a multilevel framework, with time treated as a Level-1 variable that is nested within the individual, now treated as the Level-2 model (Hoffman & Rovine, 2007; Singer & Willett, 2003) or from a latent variable framework (Bollen & Curran, 2006; Duncan et al., 2006). Both approaches have some advantages and disadvantages, and each can accommodate additional contextual influences through higher order multilevel settings. Chapter 14 provides an overview of latent growth modeling methods as applied to community-based research from this latter perspective.

Alternative methods of examining longitudinal trajectories in outcomes over time are based on mixture modeling approaches described previously. LTA (Lanza et al., 2003) is a longitudinal extension of the LCA model that examines transitions of individuals between classes over time. In contrast, latent growth mixture modeling and its variants, such as latent class growth analysis (LCGA), identify subgroups within a heterogeneous population that follow more consistent trajectories of change over time. Lowe, Galea, Uddin, and Koenen (2014), for example, used LCGA to examine predictors of divergent trajectories of posttraumatic stress among urban residents, revealing four unique posttraumatic stress trajectories (low, high, increasing, and decreasing) and particular contextual risks associated with detrimental trajectories.

THE CURRENT STATE OF ANALYTIC METHODS IN COMMUNITY-BASED RESEARCH

With the recent advances in statistical methodology that incorporate more complex, contextualized data-analytic approaches to address community-based research questions, how is the field of community psychology moving to embrace these methods? It has been more than 10 years since Luke (2005) conducted a review of quantitative methods used in empirical papers within the *American Journal of Community Psychology (AJCP)*, the flagship journal of the Society for Community Research and Action (SCRA), for two 3-year periods (1981–1983 and 2001–2003) representing a 20-year period of research in the field of community science. This review provided a means of observing changes in the data-analytic practices of community-based researchers to move beyond traditional analytic frameworks (e.g., ANOVA, regression) toward more contemporary methods better suited to the particular research questions and types of data encountered by community researchers. A total of 215 empirical papers—126 from the early 1980s and 89 from the early 2000s—were examined.

Luke's analysis revealed a continuing reliance on traditional data-analytic methods into the early 2000s, including ANOVA (37% of manuscripts), regression (37% of manuscripts), psychometric analysis (45% of manuscripts), and categorical analysis (e.g., chi-square analysis, 26% of manuscripts), as well as a heavy reliance on descriptive analyses (75% of manuscripts) and correlational methods (35% of manuscripts). In addition, Luke's analysis revealed relatively infrequent use of more advanced analytic methods (e.g., SEM, 11% of manuscripts) or techniques that were specifically developed to incorporate contextually focused analyses, such as SNA, MLM, cluster analysis, or GIS. Each of these methods was used in fewer than 4% of manuscripts published in either the early 1980s or early 2000s. To encourage greater use within the field, Luke provided a brief overview of these latter methods (i.e., SNA, MLM, cluster analysis, and GIS), demonstrating their particular applicability to community-focused research.

To examine the degree to which the field of community research has advanced in its use of more sophisticated analytic methods to incorporate context in the past decade, I conducted a similar review of *AJCP* manuscripts from 2012 through 2014. Unlike Luke (2005), I focused this review on original research articles, including those in special issues, that included some level of quantitative or qualitative analysis. A total of 218 manuscripts were indicated as "Original Articles" by *AJCP* for this period, but 45 manuscripts were excluded that presented no data analyses (e.g., conceptual or review manuscripts). This resulted in a final sample of 173 manuscripts that were coded for the present chapter.

To code the primary data-analytic methods used in *AJCP* during the 3-year period, the abstract, methods, and results sections of each manuscript were reviewed to identify the primary analytic method (or methods) used to answer the primary research questions posed by the study. Most studies also included some level of descriptive or correlational analyses, but for purposes of this current review such methods were recorded only if they were used as a primary analytic method (as opposed to standard reporting of descriptive sample characteristics). After an intial round of coding, some categories were collapsed based on a common underlying focus to the analytic approach. For example, ANOVA, ANCOVA, MANOVA, and *t*-test analyses were combined because all have a common analytic purpose (e.g., to evaluate the significance of group differences), differing primarily on factors such as the number and type of DVs, IVs, and whether they accommodate additional covariates. MLM and other methods that were used to address hierarchical or nested data structures (e.g., generalized estimating equations [GEE]; generalized linear mixed models [GLMM]) were combined based on the primary emphasis of addressing a multilevel data structure. Similarly, multiple regression and logistic regression were combined (regression), as were exploratory and confirmatory factor analytic methods (factor analysis), and cluster analysis and various mixture modeling approaches (cluster/mixture). Finally, in addition to studies that included multiple distinct data-analytic methods, some types of analyses resulted in the application of multiple codes for a single analytic method. For example, although some repeated measures analyses were conducted using latent growth methods, there were also papers that used MLM to examine growth trajectories. For these papers both MLM and latent growth were coded. Similarly, some manuscripts involved latent growth mixture modeling and were coded for both mixture and latent growth modeling.

Figure 13.1 shows the frequency with which various analytic methods were used by papers published in AJCP during the period examined. The majority of manuscripts (59.5%) involved use of a single analytic approach to address the primary research question or questions. Approximately 29% used two different analytic methods, and 12% used three or four different analytic methods for primary analyses.

This review revealed some significant shifts in the data-analytic methods being used by the field in just the past decade. The most striking finding was a dramatic increase in the use of more sophisticated methods to incorporate contextual influences into research or to model more complex structural relationships among constructs. In particular, MLM and related methods (e.g., GLMM) have seen tremendous growth in their use among community researchers, with nearly a quarter (23.1%) of papers using these methods, compared to only about 5% in the early 2000s. This represents a nearly fivefold increase in the rate of use of these methods in the past 10-year period. Similarly, the use of SEM has continued to grow among community researchers in the past decade. As recently as the early 2000s, only about 11% of *AJCP* manuscripts used SEM, compared to 16% in the most recent 3-year period. In addition, latent growth modeling (which extends SEM to analyze repeated measures data) was used by an additional 6% of research papers, suggesting that the use of SEM-based methods has doubled in the past decade.

Another data-analytic method that showed a significant increase in use over the past decade is cluster analytic and mixture modeling analyses (e.g., LCA, LTA, and growth mixture modeling). Only 3% of papers used these methods in the early 2000s, while the current rates have tripled to more than 9%. Furthermore, there has been a shift to greater use of mixture modeling approaches compared to more traditional cluster analytic methods during that same period.

These increases in multilevel and SEM-based methods are mirrored by a corresponding decrease in the frequency of use of more traditional analytic methods, such as ANOVA-based group-level comparisons or of regression-based models (including both multiple regression and logistic regression methods). In the past 30 years, the use of ANOVA and related methods has declined from approximately 66% in the 1980s to 37% in the 2000s to 22% in the most recent 3-year period. Regression-based models, which had been fairly stable from the 1980s to the 2000s, declined fairly steeply, from nearly 48% to 20% in the most recent period.

These two parallel sets of changes in frequency of MLM and SEM, on the one hand, and ANOVA and regression modeling on the other, speak to an important shift in the ways in which community-based research studies are being analyzed and reported. As indicated, traditional ANOVA and regression-based models are appropriate for single levels of analysis but are not able to adequately incorporate contextual effects (as is done with MLM) or test more complex relationships among variables (as is done with SEM). These changes suggest that community-based research (as represented by *AJCP* publications in

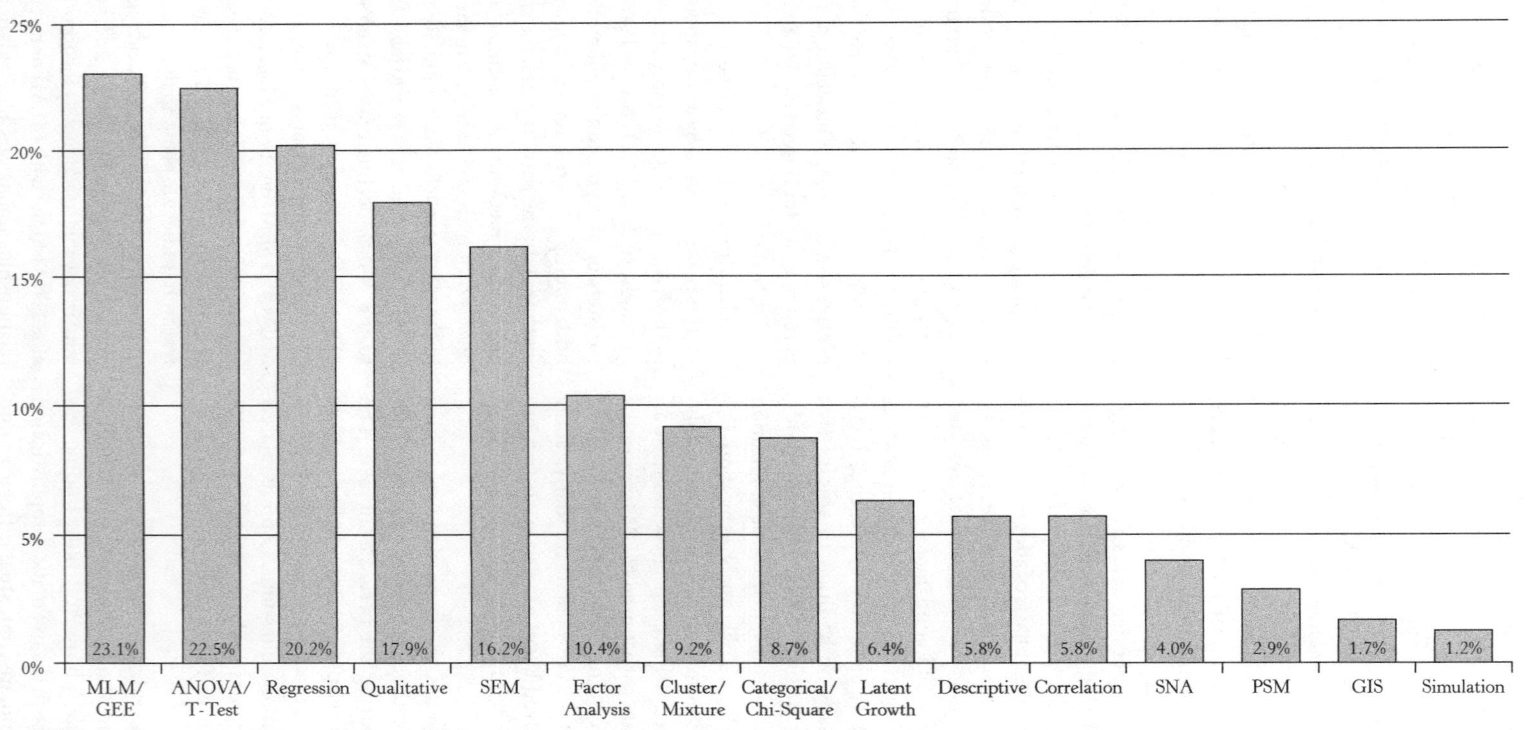

FIGURE 13.1: Primary analytic methods used in the *American Journal of Community Psychology*, 2012 through 2014 (N = 173 original papers reporting data analysis).

the field of community psychology for this review) is adopting statistical methods that are much more consistent with the questions that are being asked by researchers and the designs that are being used within the field.

In addition to these notable changes toward the greater integration of complex modeling, this review also revealed that some techniques remain underutilized despite their relevance to the types of research questions and data used by community researchers. In 2005, Luke highlighted four analytic approaches that were largely absent from the field in the early 2000s: MLM, cluster analysis, SNA, and GIS. As already indicated, the use of both MLM and cluster-related methods has increased significantly since the review conducted 10 years ago. However, the use of SNA and GIS continues to remain quite low (4.0% and 1.7%, respectively). Both SNA and GIS are reflected in chapters in this volume (SNA: see Chapters 21 and 22; GIS: see Chapter 10). Two additional methods, propensity score methods (PSM; Caliendo & Kopeinig, 2008; Rubin, 2001) and simulation-based methods such as agent-based modeling (ABM; Macy & Willer, 2002), were both utilized at relatively low rates as well (e.g., 2.9% and 1.2%, respectively). Luke and Stamatakis (2012) presented a useful overview of ABM in public health contexts that has significant implications for its use in community research, and Neal and Lawlor (see Chapter 20) provide a rich overview of their applications in a broader community context. PSM also has significant relevance to community researchers, providing a valuable means for removing selection bias and assessing group differences or causal effects in the context of quasi-experimental studies in which random assignment is not practical or possible. Given that many community researchers and evaluators frequently utilize these types of quasi-experimental conditions, PSM offers a valuable means of more rigorous testing of effects than do traditional comparative approaches.

Finally, although this chapter is primarily focused on the use of quantitative methods, the review of papers in *AJCP* also highlighted some interesting findings with respect to qualitative and mixed methods analyses. Luke's (2005) review revealed that the rates of qualitative analyses in *AJCP* increased from 4% in the early 1980s to 17% in the early 2000s. The rate of qualitative analyses appears to have remained steady at 18% in the most recent period. Of the 31 papers that included qualitative analyses, approximately one third also included quantitative analyses (i.e., had mixed methods analyses). Most frequently, the quantitative components included regression analyses (46%), ANOVA or *t* tests (36%), or categorical analyses (e.g., chi-square analyses; 27%) to assess group differences in the variables of interest. More sophisticated methods (e.g., SNA, MLM, GIS, or PSM) were used in conjunction with qualitative analyses for only one to two of the mixed methods papers reviewed.

CONCLUSION

Over the past 50 years, there has been a consistent call for advancement in the use of appropriate statistical methods to capture the complexity of community-based research questions. Such questions push the boundaries of traditional analytic methods, as they typically incorporate broader contextual influences on individual-level outcomes, examine complex processes as they unfold across person and context over time, or focus primarily on changes at the contextual level. These types of questions are critical to our central aim of understanding the complex relationships between person and context (Shinn & Rapkin, 2000). Unfortunately, our methods of statistical analysis have served as a potential limiting factor in realizing the full potential of community science to understand these phenomena, relying on traditional methods to test our hypotheses of these complex processes (Luke, 2005).

It does appear, however, that the field is beginning to make a significant shift in the use of more advanced statistical and data-analytic methods to appropriately model the complexity of our research questions and designs. In just a 10-year period, the level of methodological sophistication in our published research has made a seismic shift, particularly with respect to the use of MLM approaches as well as latent variable methods to capture complex processes (e.g., indirect effects), longitudinal effects, and population-level variation in phenomena of interest. This development is a critical stage in advancing community-based research, providing a strong foundation to test how theories and constructs operate within and across settings.

REFERENCES

Allison, P. D. (1995). *Survival analysis using the SAS System: A practical guide*. Cary, NC: SAS Institute.

Asparouhov, T., Masyn, K., & Muthén, B. (2006, August). *Continuous time survival in latent variable models*. Paper presented at the meeting of the American Statistical Association Section on Biometrics, Seattle, WA.

Barile, J. P., Darnell, A. J., Erickson, S. W., & Weaver, S. R. (2012). Multilevel measurement of dimensions of collaborative functioning in a network of collaboratives that promote child and family well-being. *American Journal of Community Psychology, 49*, 270–282.

Barker, C., & Pistrang, N. (2005). Quality criteria under methodological pluralism: Implications for conducting and evaluating research. *American Journal of Community Psychology, 35*, 201–212.

Barker, C., & Pistrang, N. (2012). Methodological pluralism: Implications for consumers and producers of research. In L. A. Jason & D. Glenwick (Eds.), *Methodological approaches to community-based research* (pp. 33–50.). Washington, DC: American Psychological Association.

Barker, C., Pistrang, N., & Elliott, R. (2002). *Research methods in clinical psychology*. Chichester, England: Wiley.

Bollen, K. A., & Curran, P. J. (2006). *Latent curve models: A structural equation perspective*. Hoboken, NJ: Wiley.

Caliendo, M., & Kopeinig, S. (2008). Some practical guidance for the implementation of propensity score matching. *Journal of Economic Surveys, 22*, 31–72.

Connell, C. M. (2012). Survival analysis in prevention and intervention programs. In L. A. Jason & D. S. Glenwick (Eds.), *Innovative methodological approaches to community-based research: Theory and application* (pp. 147–164). Washington, DC: American Psychological Association.

Delany-Brumsey, A., Mays, V. M., & Cochran, S. D. (2014). Does neighborhood social capital buffer the effects of maternal depression on adolescent behavior problems? *American Journal of Community Psychology, 53*, 275–285.

Duncan, C., Jones, K., & Moon, G. (1998). Context, composition and heterogeneity: Using multilevel models in health research. *Social Science and Medicine, 46*, 97–117.

Duncan, G. J., & Raudenbush, S. W. (2001). Neighborhoods and adolescent development: How can we determine the links? In A. Booth & A. C. Crouter (Eds.), *Does it take a village? Community effects on children, adolescents, and families* (pp. 105–136). Mahwah, NJ: Erlbaum.

Duncan, T. E., Duncan, S. C., & Strycker, L. A. (2006). *An introduction to latent variable growth curve modeling: Concepts, issues, and applications* (2nd ed.). Mahwah, NJ: Erlbaum.

Floyd, F. J., & Widaman, K. F. (1995). Factor analysis in the development and refinement of clinical assessment instruments. *Psychological Assessment, 7*, 286–299.

Fowler, P. J., Henry, D. B., Schoeny, M., Landsverk, J., Chavira, D., & Taylor, J. J. (2013). Inadequate housing among families under investigation for child abuse and neglect: Prevalence from a national probability sample. *American Journal of Community Psychology, 52*, 106–114.

Greene, J. C., Caracelli, V. J., & Graham, W. F. (1989). Toward a conceptual framework for mixed-method evaluation designs. *Educational Evaluation and Policy Analysis, 11*, 255–274.

Gregory, A., & Huang, F. (2013). It takes a village: The effects of 10th grade college-going expectations of students, parents, and teachers four years later. *American Journal of Community Psychology, 52*, 41–55.

Hagelskamp, C., Brackett, M. A., Rivers, S. E., & Salovey, P. (2013). Improving classroom quality with the ruler approach to social and emotional learning: Proximal and distal outcomes. *American Journal of Community Psychology, 51*, 530–543.

Hoffman, L., & Rovine, M. J. (2007). Multilevel models for the experimental psychologist: Foundations and illustrative examples. *Behavior Research Methods, 39*, 101–117.

Howe, K. R. (1988). Against the quantitative-qualitative incompatibility thesis, or dogmas die hard. *Educational Researcher, 17*, 10–16.

Johnson, R. B., & Onwuegbuzie, A. J. (2004). Mixed methods research: A research paradigm whose time has come. *Educational Researcher, 33*, 14–26.

Kline, R. B. (2006). *Structural equation modeling*. New York, NY: Guilford Press.

Kloos, B. (2005). Community science: Creating an alternative place to stand? *American Journal of Community Psychology, 35*, 259–267.

Langhout, R. D. (2003). Reconceptualizing quantitative and qualitative methods: A case study dealing with place as an exemplar. *American Journal of Community Psychology, 32*, 229–244.

Lanza, S. T., Flaherty, B. P., & Collins, L. M. (2003). Latent class and latent transition analysis. In J. A. Schinka & W. F. Velicer (Eds.), *Handbook of psychology, Vol. 2. Research methods in psychology* (pp. 663–685). Hoboken, NJ: Wiley.

Lincoln, Y., & Guba, E. (2000). Paradigmatic controversies, contradictions and emerging confluences. In N. K. Denzin & Y. Lincoln (Eds.), *Handbook of qualitative research* (pp. 163–188). Thousand Oaks, CA: Sage.

Lowe, S. R., Galea, S., Uddin, M., & Koenen, K. C. (2014). Trajectories of posttraumatic stress among urban residents. *American Journal of Community Psychology, 53*, 159–172.

Luke, D. A. (2005). Getting the big picture in community science: Methods that capture context. *American Journal of Community Psychology, 35*, 185–200.

Luke, D. A., & Stamatakis, K. A. (2012). Systems science methods in public health: Dynamics, networks, and agents. *Annual Review of Public Health, 33*, 357–376.

Macy, M. W., & Willer, R. (2002). From factors to actors: Computational sociology and agent-based modeling. *Annual Review of Sociology, 28*, 143–166.

Merlo, J., Chaix, B., Ohlsson, H., Beckman, A., Johnell, K., Hjerpe, P., . . . Larsen, K. (2006). A brief conceptual tutorial of multilevel analysis in social epidemiology: Using measures of clustering in multilevel logistic regression to investigate contextual phenomena. *Journal of Epidemiology and Community Health, 60*, 290–297.

Morgan, D. L. (2007). Paradigms lost and pragmatism regained methodological implications of combining qualitative and quantitative methods. *Journal of Mixed Methods Research, 1*, 48–76.

Muthén, B. O. (2002). Beyond SEM: General latent variable modeling. *Behaviormetrika, 29*, 81–117.

Onwuegbuzie, A. J., & Leech, N. L. (2005). On becoming a pragmatic researcher: The importance of combining quantitative and qualitative research methodologies. *International Journal of Social Research Methodology, 8*, 375–387.

Onwuegbuzie, A. J., & Leech, N. L. (2006). Linking research questions to mixed methods data analysis procedures. *Qualitative Report, 11*, 474–498.

Peugh, J. L. (2010). A practical guide to multilevel modeling. *Journal of School Psychology, 48*, 85–112.

Preacher, K. J., & MacCallum, R. C. (2003). Repairing Tom Swift's electric factor analysis machine. *Understanding Statistics, 2*, 13–43.

Preacher, K. J., Zhang, Z., & Zyphur, M. J. (2011). Alternative methods for assessing mediation in multilevel data: The advantages of multilevel SEM. *Structural Equation Modeling, 18*, 161–182.

Preacher, K. J., Zyphur, M. J., & Zhang, Z. (2010). A general multilevel SEM framework for assessing multilevel mediation. *Psychological Methods, 15*, 209.

Raudenbush, S. W., & Bryk, A. S. (2002). *Hierarchical linear models: Applications and data analysis methods* (2nd ed.). Thousand Oaks, CA: Sage.

Raudenbush, S. W., & Sampson, R. J. (1999). Ecometrics: Toward a science of assessing ecological settings, with application to the systematic social observation of neighborhoods. *Sociological Methodology, 29*, 1–41.

Raykov, T., & Marcoulides, G. A. (2006). *A first course in structural equation modeling*. Mahwah, NJ: Erlbaum.

Rubin, D. B. (2001). Using propensity scores to help design observational studies: Application to the tobacco litigation. *Health Services and Outcomes Research Methodology, 2*, 169–188.

Shinn, M., & Rapkin, B. D. (2000). Cross-level research without cross-ups in community psychology. In J. Rappaport & E. Seidman (Eds.), *Handbook of community psychology* (pp. 669–695). New York, NY: Springer.

Singer, J. D., & Willett, J. B. (2003). *Applied longitudinal data analysis: Modeling change and event occurrence*. New York, NY: Oxford University Press.

Tabachnick, B. G., & Fidell, L. S. (2013). *Using multivariate statistics* (6th ed.). Boston, MA: Pearson.

Tanaka, J. (2000). Statistical models for change. In J. Rappaport & E. Seidman (Eds.) *Handbook of community psychology* (pp. 697–723). New York, NY: Springer.

Tebes, J. K. (2005). Community science, philosophy of science, and the practice of research. *American Journal of Community Psychology, 35*, 213–230.

Yin, R. K. (2006). Mixed methods research: Are the methods genuinely integrated or merely parallel? *Research in the Schools, 13*, 41–47.

14

Latent Growth Curves

MEGAN R. GREESON

Studying change lies at the heart of community-based research and program evaluation. Community-based researchers frequently need to examine whether interventions did, in fact, create change and, if so, whether the change was sustainable. At times, they may also examine the natural fluctuation of community phenomena over time in order to understand how social problems and community assets unfold naturally. Yet all too often, the statistical models that are employed are much more simplistic than the ways in which we would actually expect changing community phenomena to behave. As a result, some advanced longitudinal statistical methods have received increased attention from the field (e.g., survival analysis, time-series analysis; Jason & Glenwick, 2012); however, thus far, latent growth curves (LGCs) have received less attention. LGCs are a tool that can capture more of the complexity of changing community phenomena. Therefore, the purpose of this chapter is to (a) provide a conceptual introduction to the use of LGC models in community-based research, including the models' contributions and drawbacks, and (b) present a case example of community-based research employing LGCs.

AN INTRODUCTION TO LATENT GROWTH CURVE MODELS

Growth curves are typically used to analyze longitudinal data in which the same construct is measured at multiple time points (i.e., repeated measures data). Rather than studying change in sample means over time, growth models are well suited to understanding within-person change as well as variability between people in within-person change. Growth curves analyses can be conducted within a structural equation modeling (SEM) or a multilevel modeling (MLM) framework (Bollen & Curran, 2006; Chou, Bentler, & Pentz, 1998; Curran, Obeidat, & Losardo, 2010). In both approaches, growth curves models have similar applications for community-based research. However, when discussing the construction of LGC models in the next paragraph, terms will be consistent with LGC models within an SEM framework (Bollen & Curran, 2006).

In an LGC model, the repeated measures data are used to create latent variables that capture two properties of the construct of interest, namely, a level and a slope. The level (or intercept) represents the baseline amount of the construct (Duncan & Duncan, 2004; McArdle, 2009). This baseline is typically set to be equal to participants' Time 1 scores. The slope, on the other hand, represents within-person change in the construct over time, or how much individuals changed (Duncan & Duncan, 2004; McArdle, 2009). There are different ways of creating the slope variable; this allows the analyst to test out different patterns of change (by modeling different *basis coefficients* that specify the weighting of each measurement occasion on the latent slope variable; Duncan & Duncan, 2004; McArdle, 2009). In this chapter, the term *pattern of change* refers to patterns related to the amount and direction of change across different time intervals within the same study (e.g., is the amount and direction of change always consistent across all time intervals?). This issue is discussed in more detail later in the chapter.

The level and the slope are modeled to have a mean and variance (McArdle, 2009). The mean of the level is the average baseline score in the sample. The variance of the level represents the amount that participants in the sample vary in their baseline scores, with some participants having higher baselines than others (between-person variability). Like the level, the slope is also modeled to have a mean and a variance (McArdle, 2009). The mean of the slope gives the average within-person change. The variance of the slope represents the variation among individual participants in how much they change, with some participants changing more than others over the course of the study (between-person variability) (McArdle, 2009). The researcher may also test whether baseline scores are related to how much change occurs over time (i.e., whether the level and the slope covary). Often, there is such a relationship—participants with high baseline scores tend to increase less than participants with low baseline scores—which is why it is important to consider this question for inclusion in the model.

Latent Growth Curves as Part of a Larger Model: What Relates to the Changing Variable?

Typically, the first step in an LGC analysis is to create the basic model of the level and slope and identify the model that best captures the pattern of change over time. Then, the researcher can add additional variables to the model to test whether they are related to participants' baseline scores (which becomes an intercept when it is a dependent variable) and their within-person change (the slope). In LGCs, there are a variety of options for examining relationships between the changing variable and other variables; the next section provides an overview of the basic options. Note that different options can be combined in the same model.

Growth as a Predictor of a Static Outcome Variable

Within-person change (i.e., the slope of the LGC) can be modeled as an independent variable that predicts a static (i.e., unchanging) dependent variable. An example of a research question would be, "Does within-person change in delinquency scores influence future substance abuse at one time point?"

Time-Invariant Predictors of Growth

A *time-invariant covariate* is defined as a variable that does not change in value as a function of time (Curran et al., 2010). These unchanging variables can be modeled as predictors of change (i.e., the slope of the LGC is the dependent variable). Conceptually, these variables may be of substantive interest or simply act as control variables (e.g., Does an intervention predict amount of change in delinquency scores?)

Time-Varying Covariates With Growth

The changing variable can be related to another variable that is also measured over time. The added variable is called a *time-varying covariate* when it is directly modeled as a predictor of the repeated measurement occasions (and is not a predictor of the latent slope) (Curran et al., 2010). This is appropriate when the time-varying covariate is believed to not have its own latent change process, but instead is believed to affect the measurement of the changing variable at each time point (e.g., Does English literacy at each time point affect delinquency scores on a self-administered survey at each time point?)

Covaration of Growth in One Variable With Growth in Another

In this instance, the researcher is interested in the relationship between multiple changing variables. When the second changing variable is believed to have its own latent growth process, a second LGC is added to the model and the growth curves are correlated with one another (a parallel process model) (Cheong, McKinnon, & Khoo, 2003; Curran et al., 2010; McArdle, 2009) The correlation between the two slopes tests whether change in one variable is related to change in the other. For example, does change in social support co-occur with change in delinquency? Or, in a multivariate LGC, the researcher can test whether multiple LGCs of different variables actually represent one common growth process (e.g., change in drug use and truancy as subcomponents of a second-order changing delinquency growth process) (Duncan & Duncan, 1996).

Extensions of These Basic Models

This provided an overview of the basic types of research questions about change that can be asked using LGCs. The researcher can then build from these basic types of relationships to test more complex relationships, such as mediation or moderation (Bollen, Curran, & Willoughby, 2004; Cheong et al., 2003).

THE IMPORTANCE OF NONLINEAR CHANGE IN COMMUNITY-BASED RESEARCH

Certain features of LGC models make them particularly useful for community-based research and program evaluation. One such advantage is that LGCs can capture a variety of patterns of change, including nonlinear change (McArdle, 2009; Ram & Grimm, 2007). Linear change means that the rate of change is constant over time. In other words, in any two time intervals of the same length, change occurs in the same direction and amount (see Fig. 14.1 for three examples of linear change). If a study measures sense of community every 3 months, an assumption of linear change would mean that sense of community is expected to increase or decrease in the same amount over each 3-month time interval. However, an ecological and systemic approach would suggest that, although this assumption may hold true in certain scenarios, it is too simplistic to capture many, if not most, patterns of change (Bronfenbrenner, 1979; Trickett, 2009). Instead, it is likely that, at least some of the time, the direction or rate of change over time may shift. To illustrate this, a series of patterns of nonlinear change that are likely to occur in community-based research and program evaluation will be presented.

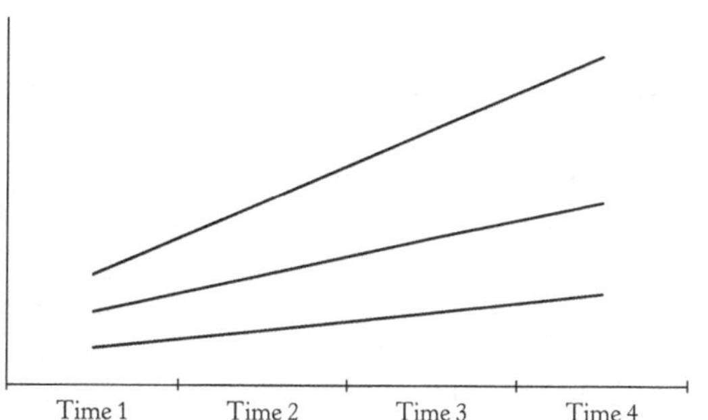

FIGURE 14.1: Three examples of linear change.

Patterns of Nonlinear Change

Incubation, or Delayed Change

One likely pattern of nonlinear change in community-based research and program evaluation is an "incubation effect" in which an intervention does not create change immediately: There is a lag between when the intervention occurs and when change begins. Such a pattern would be expected in "upstream" interventions that intervene in one part of a systemic process and are expected to create change that has to spread to another part of the system. Initially, there is no change in the targeted outcomes while the effects of the intervention flow through the system. Then, after a delay, improvement occurs (see Fig. 14.2).

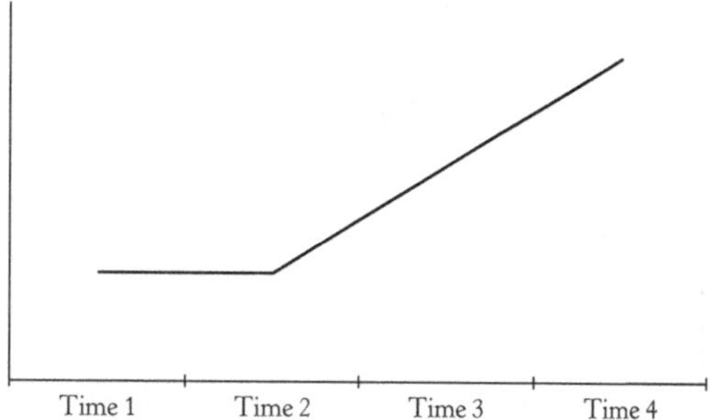

FIGURE 14.2: Delayed change.

Gains Followed by Maintenance

"Gains followed by maintenance" may occur for interventions that create a period of improvement followed by maintenance of the improved outcomes. Skill- and knowledge-building interventions that result in long-term retention would follow this pattern. From pre- to postintervention, you would expect an increase in skills/knowledge. After the intervention ends, you would expect that people's skills/knowledge would stay the same; improvement would not continue, but you would also not expect skills or knowledge to be lost (see Fig. 14.3).

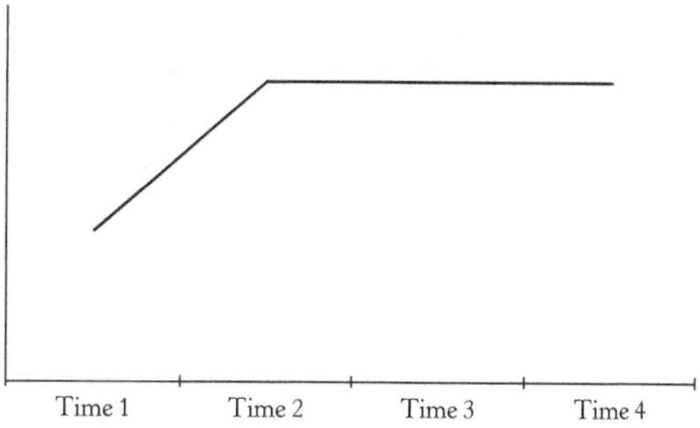

FIGURE 14.3: Gains followed by maintenance.

Lost Gains

Another pattern of nonlinear change that community-based researchers and evaluators may expect is "lost gains" in which change occurs after an intervention but is not sustained; all improvements are lost and outcomes return to preintervention levels. For example, an intervention may produce improvement only while resources are allocated to the issue, with outcomes dropping back to preintervention rates when those resources are gone (see Fig. 14.4).

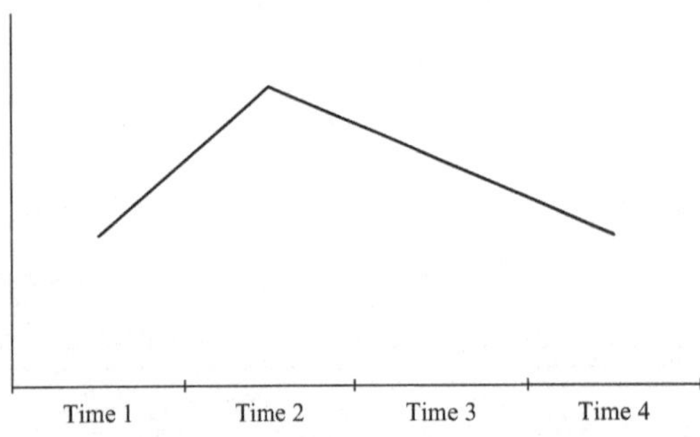

FIGURE 14.4: Lost gains.

Variation in the Rate of Change

In this pattern, the rate of change is not constant; change occurs more rapidly (acceleration) or less rapidly (deceleration; see Fig. 14.5). An example may occur in network-based adoption of innovations (Rogers, 2003). Change is initially less rapid when early adopters begin to adopt the innovation; then, as more people adopt the innovation, it spreads more rapidly to the people to whom they are connected; finally, once the network is almost saturated and there are few people in the network who have not adopted the innovation, adoption rates decelerate again.

Taken together, the different conceptual ways of thinking about change that have been presented highlight the importance of the flexibility of LGCs for community-based research and evaluation. By not being restricted to the simplistic assumption that change is linear, the analyst can choose the model that best fits the changing community phenomenon.

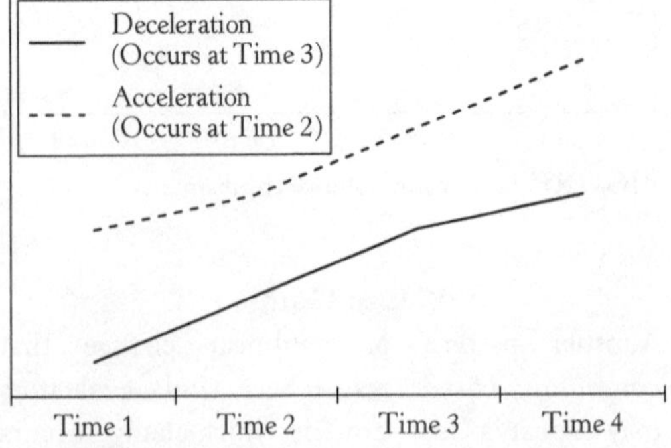

FIGURE 14.5: Variation in the rate of change.

Matching the Pattern of Change to the Appropriate Statistical Model

The literature provides some specific subtypes of LGC models that can be used to test different types of statistical models of nonlinear change. The analyst may include a linear growth slope term coupled with a polynomial slope term(s) to test for exponential growth (e.g., quadratic, cubic; Grimm & Ram, 2009; Ram & Grimm, 2007). Such models of exponential growth represent very specific types of variation in the rate of change. Spline growth curves are LGCs in which growth occurs at different rates within different periods of the study (also known as piecewise models; Ram & Grimm, 2007). Different spline models could be used to represent a wide variety of nonlinear types of change, including delayed change, gains then maintenance, lost gains, and certain forms of acceleration and deceleration. The broader latent growth curve literature provides specific guidance on how to implement these statistical models of nonlinear change appropriately (e.g., Grimm & Ram, 2009; Ram & Grimm, 2007).

Generally, researchers should use theory to inform the type of change they would expect to see in their study and then test how well that model fits the data. However, in community-based research and evaluation, there may not always be sufficient theory to determine how one would expect change to occur. For example, a researcher may expect an intervention to improve outcomes but not have a clear idea as to whether the gains would always occur at the same rate across different time intervals. In such instances, the researcher can create and test a specific type of LGC model called a *latent basis model* (McArdle, 2009; Ram & Grimm, 2007). In this model, rather than the researcher hypothesizing the pattern of change and then testing the data against his or her hypothesis, the data are used to figure out the best model of change. The results of the model reveal how rapidly change occurs in each time interval in the study.

Another feature of LGC models is useful when the researcher does not have sufficient theory to determine how exactly he or she expects change to occur. In some situations (specifically when two models are nested) the analyst can test different patterns of change against one another (using the chi-squared difference test) (McArdle, 2009). This test examines whether there is a statistically significant difference between the two models in how well the models fit the data. Suppose a researcher conducts an intervention study and believes that there has been a consistent improvement in outcomes. When the model is tested, statistical information (specifically, fit indices) will be provided to help evaluate how well the data fit the hypothesis of consistent change. However, testing this hypothesized pattern of change against other possible patterns of change provides more analytic rigor. In the same intervention study, the researcher could compare the model that represents consistent improvements (linear change) to a model that represents no improvements whatsoever (no change). A finding that the consistent (linear) change model is preferable to the no-change model would provide more statistical support for the initial hypothesis that outcomes have consistently improved. Thus, LGC models not only allow community-based researchers and evaluators to test for nonlinear change but also enable them to use their data to determine the pattern of change that appears to fit the data best.

These features of LGC are particularly important for conducting applied community-based research and evaluation. Other analyses that simply test for an effect of time, or assume that change is linear, can obscure how the process of change actually unfolds. Such an approach oversimplifies our understanding of interventions and the natural development of social problems and assets. Failing to understand the actual pattern of change may result in missing important issues related to the timing and sustainability of change; these, in turn, have significant implications for practice and future research and evaluation.

As an example, failure to capture nonlinear change could hamper the ability of a study to provide meaningful information on how to improve interventions. Suppose that an evaluation is conducted to see whether a neighborhood intervention led to significant improvements in residents' sense of community. In reality, the intervention led to an immediate improvement in sense of community scores, but the improvements were not sustained and sense of community scores slowly dropped back to preintervention levels. Testing only for linear change could lead to an erroneous conclusion that, overall, the intervention does not appear to work, when in reality it does produce improvement, but the improvement is not sustained. These two patterns of change have very different implications for program improvement and future research on similar types of programs. Concluding that there is no effect of the intervention suggests the need to seriously reconsider the intervention's design and implementation, while an intervention that is effective in the short term but the improvement is not sustainable suggests that the intervention design and implementation are generally working but the program needs adjustments to make changes sustainable in the long term. This highlights the importance of flexibility in testing for different patterns of change in applied, community-based research and evaluation.

Capturing Heterogeneity in Change

An additional advantage of LGC models for community-based research is that they allow the examination of heterogeneity in change. An ecological and diversity-oriented approach suggests that in community-based research there is likely to be heterogeneity within samples with respect to patterns of change (Trickett, 2009). Therefore, methods that capture within-person change (rather than change in means) are crucial. LGCs are such a technique. Specifically, in LGC models, rather than assuming that people change in a uniform way, participants may differ in the amount that they change. In other words, between-person variability in within-person change is captured (Duncan & Duncan, 2004; McArdle, 2009). Certain LGC models (including time-invariant covariates and parallel process models) allow the researcher to examine factors that are associated with differences in the amount of within-person change, potentially providing insight into why the heterogeneity exists. Furthermore, the researcher may use *multigroup LGCs* to test whether different groups of people differ in their patterns or trajectories of change over time (e.g., some groups may experience linear change, while others experience delayed change) (Curran et al., 2010; Ram & Grimm, 2009).

Examining heterogeneity in change has many potential applications in community-based research and evaluation. For example, researchers can use LGC models to test for differences in the amount of change and/or pattern of change between intervention and comparison groups (e.g., does the intervention group change more rapidly than the comparison group?). In a recent study, Darnell et al. (2013) employed LGC analysis to examine differences in change in counties' low infant birthweight rates over an 8-year period. They found that counties with community collaborative groups focused on low infant birthweight (the treatment group) had statistically similar baseline low infant birthweight rates in comparison to counties that did not have a community collaborative (the comparison group). Additionally, the data showed that over the 8-year period, low infant birthweight rates tended to increase, meaning that outcomes were worsening over time. However, the analyses revealed that the low infant birthweight tended to worsen less rapidly in the treatment group than in the comparison group. In other words, the intervention counties experienced less of an increase in low birthweights; although outcomes had a tendency to worsen, the intervention was effective at slowing this process. The intervention and comparison groups differed in the rate of change.

Testing for differences in the amount of change and pattern of change is also particularly useful for studying diversity, a core value in community-based research and program evaluation. LGCs allow researchers to test for differences in the amount and pattern of change between different demographic and social identity groups (e.g., race/ethnicity, gender, or age differences). Suppose a researcher is interested in racial differences in depression. Rather than simply testing whether different racial groups have different baseline depression scores, the researcher can also examine whether certain racial groups' depression scores improved more or less than others. This can be particularly useful in testing whether an intervention is equally beneficial to all groups that participated (e.g., Did racial minorities improve the same amount as European Americans in response to an intervention?).

Farrell and Sullivan (2004) employed such an approach to look at differences in witnessing violence between adolescent boys and girls over time. The study collected students' self-report data of how often they witnessed violence across five time points spanning the sixth through ninth grades. LGC analysis revealed that at baseline (sixth grade), boys, on average, witnessed more violence than girls. Moreover, the boys tended to have greater increases in witnessing violence over time than the girls did (Farrell & Sullivan, 2004). In other words, the boys and girls experienced inequality in witnessing violence at baseline and then experienced different amounts of change over the course of the study. Ultimately, this led to an even greater gender gap in witnessing violence at the last time point. Thus, rather than imposing a uniform model of change, LGC can test whether some groups of people change differently than others do.

An ecological focus also suggests that it is useful to understand a variety of other factors that relate to how much people change, beyond the issues that have been discussed so far. Researchers could test for differences in change between people with different contextual circumstances (e.g., participants from different types of neighborhoods, participants with different levels of social support). An ecological approach would also support testing for differences in change between groups of people with different individual-level characteristics that may make them more or less susceptible to change (e.g., differences in readiness).

Thus far, in this section, the examples have focused mostly on heterogeneity in the amount of change—do some groups change more than others? Advanced LGC models also allow for heterogeneity in the patterns of change. Such multigroup LGC models can test whether different groups have different patterns of change over the course of the study (Duncan & Duncan, 2004; Duncan et al., 2006; Ram & Grimm, 2009). For example, it may be that in response to an intervention to improve sense of community, neighborhoods with adequate resources experience a steady, consistent improvement in sense of community over the course of a study, while resource-poor neighborhoods experience a slower rate of change at first that then accelerates into more rapid improvements later in the study. This type of advanced model is more complex and is also much rarer in the literature.

Advanced Extensions of Latent Growth Curvess

More advanced extensions of LGCs are also likely to be useful to this audience. Because LGCs can be conducted within an SEM approach to modeling, LGC models can capitalize on other possibilities of SEM models. These include the ability to test mediation, the ability to have multiple dependent variables in the same analysis, and the use of measurement (structural) models that account for measurement error (Kline, 2011). Growth curve analysis can also be conducted within a multilevel modeling framework, which allows for growth curve models to be conducted when data are nested (meaning that the data violate the assumption of independent error terms; cases are nested in groups or settings that cause their errors to be correlated, such as individual children nested within classrooms) (Chou et al., 1998) (see Singer & Willett, 2003, for a discussion of longitudinal analyses within a multilevel framework).

As noted earlier in the chapter, multigroup LGC models can test whether known groups differ in their pattern (or trajectory) of change. Rather than testing for differences between known (i.e., measured) group membership (e.g., race and gender differences), growth mixture models can use the data itself to identify unobserved (latent) groups/classes that differ in their patterns of change (Muthén & Muthén, 2000; Ram & Grimm, 2009). For example, when analyzing data from an intervention study using growth mixture modeling, a researcher may test whether there is support for the existence of three different (unobserved) classes with different patterns of change: one that exhibits no change, one that significantly improves, and one that significantly gets worse. Finally, autoregressive model parameters can be added to LGCs to account for measurement error at one time point that is related to measurement error at the next time point (i.e., autoregressive residuals); autoregressive parameters can also be used in parallel process models to understand covariation of two changing LGCs over time, after controlling for their correlation at Time 1 (Bollen & Curran, 2004).

Drawbacks of Latent Growth Curves

The drawbacks of the LGC approach also warrant attention. In particular, LGCs should be employed only in specific circumstances. Like all models, LGC models require a sufficient sample size; larger samples may be required when the analyst is looking at heterogeneity in the pattern of change between different groups (Duncan & Duncan, 2004; Kline, 2011). Although Bollen (2002) stated that LGCs can be adopted for use with categorical data, LGCs are typically used with continuous data. Other methods, such as latent transition analysis, may be preferable when the longitudinal variable is categorical (Collins & Lanza, 2010).

Like all longitudinal data analyses, LGC models are best when the data are collected within a rigorous longitudinal study (for in-depth discussion, see Collins, 2006). In particular, the variable of interest should be measured at time intervals that are suited to capturing meaningful change in that variable. It is also important that the variable be measured consistently over time, so that the growth curve is not inadvertently capturing change that is due to measurement error. Despite these limitations, growth models are well suited to community-based research and evaluation. To illustrate their utility, a case study using LGC analysis will be presented next.

CASE STUDY

The case study comes from a 2013 study by Adams, Greeson, Kennedy, and Tolman. The lead author's program of research focuses on understanding the associations between women's experiences of intimate partner violence (IPV) and their financial well-being. Many survivors of physical IPV also experience economic abuse in which the batterer controls and/or exploits the victim's finances (e.g., damaging credit; interfering with work and school; Adams, Sullivan, Bybee, & Greeson, 2008). Despite a growing body of research on the impact of IPV on adult women's financial well-being, very little research had been done to understand the financial impact of IPV during adolescence. In the present study, we were interested in whether experiences of IPV during adolescence may influence women's financial well-being as adults.

Conceptualization of the Longitudinal Research Question

Prior research on adults shows that many batterers interfere with their partner's education (Adams et al., 2008). Because adolescence is a key developmental stage in which girls are contemplating and completing their education, we suspected that IPV during adolescence would influence the amount of formal education that women obtained and that, in turn, this would influence their earning potential as adults. This led to the following hypotheses:

Hypothesis 1: On average, women with a history of IPV during adolescence would have completed fewer years of formal education than would women with no adolescent IPV history.

Hypothesis 2: Women who completed fewer years of formal education would tend to earn less at Time 1 (T1) than women who completed more years of formal education.

Hypothesis 3: On average, women with a history of IPV during adolescence would earn less as adults at T1 than women without a history of IPV during adolescence; this relationship would be mediated by the number of formal years of education completed.

Because of the important role that education plays in earning potential, we believed that adolescent IPV and fewer years of education would not simply hinder women's earnings at T1; instead, we believed that these factors would also be detrimental to women's ability to increase their income over time. This led to the following longitudinal hypotheses:

Hypothesis 4: Women who completed fewer years of education would experience less growth in earnings over time.

Hypothesis 5: On average, women with a history of IPV during adolescence would experience less growth in earnings over time; this relationship would be mediated by the number of formal years of education completed.

Hypotheses 4 and 5 required repeated measurement of women's earnings as adults to understand growth in earnings over time. These hypotheses made LGCs a suitable analytic technique. The hypotheses were tested using data from Tolman and Wang's (2005) study of women's employment. The sample consisted of women who were single mothers and had received cash assistance. At the first interview, women reported retrospectively on whether they had experienced IPV during adolescence (at or before the age of 17) and the number of years of formal education they had completed prior to the study. Annual earnings from employment were assessed at T1 and at two follow-up interviews, with 1 year in between interviews.

Development and Results of the Latent Growth Curve Models

Our first step was to determine which pattern of change best fit the repeated measures data on women's earnings from employment. There was not strong prior research or theory to inform a very specific hypothesis about the pattern of change. We believed that women's earned income would likely increase somewhat over time, but we were unsure whether the change would be consistent (i.e., linear) or whether change from T1 to Time 2 (T2) would be different than change from T2 to Time 3 (T3) (that is, nonlinear). First, we tested a model that suggested no change—that women's earned income did not change at all over the course of the study. As we suspected, the model did not fit the data well, suggesting that there was significant change in individual women's earned income over time. Then, we tested two different models—a linear model and a latent basis model—against one another. The linear model posited that women would experience consistent change in their earnings (i.e., a woman's change from T1 to T2 would be functionally equal to her change from T2 to T3); the latent basis model allowed changes in a woman's income to happen at different rates (a woman's change from T1 to T2 would not be equal to her change from T2 to T3). Specifically, the latent basis model used the data to determine the best way to represent patterns of change. Statistical information (in the form of a significant chi-squared difference test) indicated the latent basis model fit the data well and was a better way of capturing within-woman change over time than was the linear model.

The results of the latent basis model showed that, on average, women's earnings increased a total of $4,115 from T1 to T3. The fact that the latent basis model was preferable to the linear model indicated that growth in women's earnings was not consistent over the different time intervals in the study. Rather, the results showed that the sample experienced much more rapid growth from T1 to T2 (62.9% of the total change over the course of the study occurred from T1 to T2) and slower growth from T2 to T3 (37.1% of the total change occurred from T2 to T3). Conceptually, this represents decelerating change. It may be that growth in income was much more rapid from T1 to T2 (in comparison to growth from T2 to T3) because the sample was limited to low-income women who had received welfare assistance.

We then added variables to the model to test whether adolescent IPV history and number of formal years of education completed were related to women's earnings at T1 and change in women's

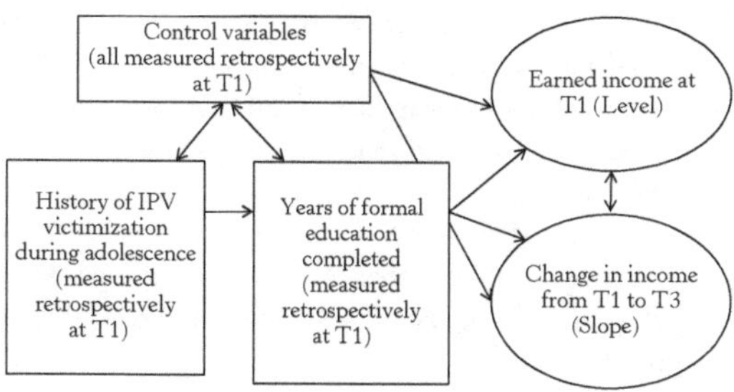

FIGURE 14.6: Case example of latent growth curve analysis to assess adolescent intimate partner violence (IPV) and education as predictors of change in women's earned income over time.

earnings from T1 to T3. The model also controlled for several covariates. Each of the covariates was measured retrospectively at T1. The conceptual model is provided in Figure 14.6.

The data supported our hypotheses. On average, women who had a history of IPV victimization during adolescence completed 0.5 fewer years of education than did women with no history of IPV during adolescence. Formal education was related to both T1 earnings (the intercept) and growth in earnings from T1 to T3 (slope). One additional year of education was associated with $855 more earnings from employment at T1 and a $664 greater increase in earnings from T1 to T3. Analysis of indirect effects (a technique used to test for mediation in SEM) suggested that a history of adolescent IPV contributed to fewer earnings at T1 (intercept) and less growth in earnings from T1 to T3 (slope) via fewer years of completed education.

Choosing LGC analysis provided several opportunities. We were able to capture the complexity of change in the earnings of these low-income women—the fact that the rate of change in income was not constant from one time interval to the next. In addition, by using LGC analysis, we were also able to capture and unpack heterogeneity in change over time. The model accounted for the fact that some groups of women had different amounts of change in their earnings than others. This variability in women's growth in earnings was partially explained by the number of formal years of education they completed and their history of IPV during adolescence. Finally, because the LGC was created in SEM, we were able to capitalize on the ability to conduct indirect effects analysis in SEM. This allowed us to test for a mediational relationship in which the dependent variable represented change over three time points.

One key limitation of this work was that we were able to analyze women's earned income at only three time points. LGC analyses are stronger when data are collected from more time points. With more data points, the analyses are able to tap into a more stable pattern of change. Although it is apparent that the rate of change was not linear, the rate at which income would continue to change is unclear. Data from additional follow-up time points would, therefore, provide a fuller picture.

Additionally, all of the control and independent variables were measured at only one time point (i.e., they were time-invariant covariates). Earned income was the only changing variable. One of the possibilities in LGC modeling is to examine covariation in two changing variables over time. The data set we analyzed did not have any relevant covariates that were measured with consistent repeated measures data. Therefore, another limitation of our study is that we could not examine whether change in a predictor variable may have related to change in our dependent variable (earned income). For example, in examining the relationship between adolescent IPV and growth in adulthood earning, it would have been helpful to control for changing adult IPV across all time points, rather than adult IPV victimization at T1 only. Future research in this area that accounts for changing covariates may be particularly beneficial.

CONCLUSION

LGC modeling is a flexible method for analyzing longitudinal data that is well suited to capturing the complexity of change in community-based research and program evaluation. The method enables evaluators and community-based researchers to capture nonlinear change and to examine heterogeneity in amount and patterns of within-person change over time. More advanced applications of this technique provide additional opportunities. These features are very well matched to the field's ecological and systems focus, interest in diversity, and use of research and evaluation to inform community practice.

REFERENCES

Adams, A. E., Greeson, M. R., Kennedy, A. C., & Tolman, R. M. (2013). The effects of adolescent intimate partner violence on women's educational attainment and earnings. *Journal of Interpersonal Violence, 28,* 3283–3300.

Adams, A. E., Sullivan, C. M., Bybee, D., & Greeson, M. R. (2008). Development of the Scale of Economic Abuse. *Violence Against Women, 14,* 563–588.

Bollen, K. A. (2002). Latent variables in psychology and the social sciences. *Annual Review of Psychology, 53,* 605–634.

Bollen, K. A., & Curran, P. J. (2004). Autoregressive latent growth trajectory models: A synthesis of two traditions. *Sociological Methods & Research, 32,* 336–383.

Bollen, K. A., & Curran, P. J. (2006). Unconditional latent curve model. In K. A. Bollen & P. J. Curran (Eds.), *Latent curve models: A structural equation perspective* (pp. 16–57). Hoboken, NJ: Wiley.

Bollen, K. A., Curran, P. J., & Willoughby, M. T. (2004). Testing main effects and interactions in latent curve analysis. *Psychological Methods, 9,* 220–237.

Bronfenbrenner, U. (1979). *The ecology of human development: Experiments by nature and design.* Cambridge, MA: Harvard University Press.

Cheong, J. W., MacKinnon, D. P., & Khoo, S. T. (2003). Investigation of mediational processes using parallel process latent growth curve modeling. *Structural Equation Modeling, 10*(2), 238–262.

Chou, C. P., Bentler, P. M., & Pentz, M. A. (1998). Comparisons of two statistical approaches to study growth curves: The multilevel model and the latent curve analysis. *Structural Equation Modeling, 5,* 247–266.

Collins, L. M. (2006). Analysis of longitudinal data: The integration of theoretical model, temporal design, and statistical model. *Annual Review of Psychology, 57,* 505–528.

Collins, L. M., & Lanza, S. T. (2010). *Latent class and latent transition analysis: With applications in the social, behavioral, and health sciences* (Vol. 718). Hoboken, NJ: Wiley.

Curran, P. J., Obeidat, K., & Losardo, D. (2010). Twelve frequently asked questions about latent growth curve modeling. *Journal of Cognitive Development, 11,* 121–136.

Darnell, A. J., Barile, J. P., Weaver, S. R., Harper, C. R., Kuperminc, G. P., & Emshoff, J. G. (2013). Testing effects of community collaboration on rates of low infant birthweight at the county level. *American Journal of Community Psychology, 51,* 398–406.

Duncan, S. C., & Duncan, T. E. (1996). A multivariate latent growth curve analysis of adolescent substance abuse. *Structural Equation Modeling: A Multidisciplinary Journal, 3,* 323–347.

Duncan, T. E., & Duncan, S. C. (2004). An introduction to latent growth curve modeling, *Behavior Therapy, 35,* 333–363.

Duncan, T. E., Duncan, S. C., & Strycker, L. A. (2006). *An introduction to latent variable growth curve modeling: Concepts, issues, and applications.* Mahwah, NJ: Erlbaum.

Farrell, A. D., & Sullivan, T. N. (2004). Impact of witnessing violence on growth curves for problem behaviors among early adolescents in urban and rural settings. *Journal of Community Psychology, 32,* 505–525.

Grimm, K. J., & Ram, N. (2009). Nonlinear growth models in Mplus and SAS. *Structural Equation Modeling, 16,* 676–701.

Jason, L. A., & Glenwick, D. S. (2012). *Methodological approaches to community-based research.* Washington, DC: American Psychological Association.

Kline, R. B. (2011). *Principles and practice of structural equation modeling* (3rd ed.). New York, NY: Guilford Press.

McArdle, J. J. (2009). Latent variable modeling of differences and changes with longitudinal data. *Annual Review of Psychology, 60,* 577–605.

Muthén, B., & Muthén, L. K. (2000). Integrating person-centered and variable-centered analyses: Growth mixture modeling with latent trajectory classes. *Alcoholism: Clinical and Experimental Research, 24,* 882–891.

Ram, N., & Grimm, K. (2007). Using simple and complex growth curves to articulate developmental change: Matching theory to method. *International Journal of Behavioral Development, 31,* 303–316.

Ram, N., & Grimm, K. (2009). Growth mixture modeling: A method for identifying differences in longitudinal change among different groups. *International Journal of Behavioral Development, 33,* 565–576.

Rogers, E. M. (2003). *Diffusion of innovations* (5th ed.). New York, NY: Free Press.

Singer, J. D., & Willett, J. B. (2003). *Applied longitudinal data analysis: Modeling change and event occurrence.* New York, NY: Oxford University Press.

Tolman, R. M., & Wang, H. (2005). Domestic violence and women's employment: Fixed effects models of three waves of women's employment study data. *American Journal of Community Psychology, 36,* 147–158.

Trickett, E. J. (2009). Community psychology: Individuals and interventions in context. *Annual Review of Psychology, 60,* 395–419.

15

Latent Class Analysis and Latent Profile Analysis

GLENN A. WILLIAMS AND FRAENZE KIBOWSKI

Latent class analysis (LCA) and latent profile analysis (LPA) are powerful techniques that enable researchers to glean insights into "hidden" psychological experiences to create typologies and profiles to provide better-informed, community-based policies and practice. These analytic methods have been used in a variety of domains, such as psychosis symptomatology in the general population (Kibowski & Williams, 2012; Murphy, Shevlin, & Adamson, 2007; Shevlin, Murphy, Dorahy, & Adamson, 2007); substance abuse (Cleveland, Collins, Lanza, Greenberg, & Feinberg, 2010; James, McField, & Montgomery, 2013), peer victimization (Nylund, Bellmore, Nishina, & Graham, 2007), and antisocial/self-defeating behavior (Rosato & Baer, 2012). LCA and LPA are versatile methods of dealing with data of interest to community-based researchers in a deep and psychologically grounded way. This chapter will address the nuances of how and when to use LCA and LPA. Case studies of LCA and LPA will also be presented to illustrate the applicability of these techniques.

INTRODUCTION TO LATENT CLASS ANALYSIS

The main aim of LCA is to split data that are apparently heterogeneous overall into subclasses of two or more different homogeneous groups or classes. Study participant responses to a questionnaire, structured interview, or behavioral checklist would be used as the basis for making probabilistic assessments of the likelihood of each participant being assigned to one of these classes. A participant's likelihood of belonging to any of the other latent classes would also be calculated, and then decisions would be made as to the ultimate class membership that each respondent would assume. The beneficial role that LCA can have is that, once class membership has been assigned to each participant in relation to the pattern of responses or behaviors, this class membership can be used to inform policies and practice-based interventions aimed at targeting a specific latent class that has emerged from the analysis. An example of the potential for this method can be seen in a study of the transportation-related attitudes and experiences of workers (Williams, Murphy, & Hill, 2008). In this study, latent class analysis was deployed to examine the role of multimodality (i.e., using more than one mode of transportation) versus single transport mode use on commuters' psychological well-being.

Other community-level analyses have utilized LCA to investigate how to encourage sections of the population to engage more in community-based arts activities (Biggins, Cottee, & Williams, 2012). LCA is also helpful for testing population-wide phenomena and epidemiological trends, such as the potential existence of psychosis symptom experiences being measured along a continuum throughout the general population (e.g., Murphy et al., 2007; Shevlin et al., 2007), rather than as a dichotomous, psychiatrically driven and rare phenomenon.

LCA is usually appropriate for samples of at least 100 participants, although there is evidence that Monte Carlo simulation could be used to model probable class solutions with data sets of smaller size and to thus extrapolate likely class numbers for hypothetical larger data sets (Nylund, Asparouhov, & Muthén, 2007). The method of LCA is grouped within the family of structural equation modeling (SEM) techniques, such as confirmatory factor analysis (CFA). In contrast to CFA, however, which could be construed to be primarily variable-centered, LCA is more of a person-centered approach because of its focus on participants' characteristics and on how a pattern of responding to questions can provide insight into different participant groups' experiences, behaviors, emotions, and cognitions. However, although LCA and LPA could be termed to be largely person-centered in orientation, it has been argued that person-centered and variable-centered methods are rarely independent of each other (Masyn, 2013).

LCA is exploratory in emphasis and concerns itself with unearthing homogeneity from seemingly heterogeneous samples. The drive to find this potential diversity also underpins why LCA is more generically labeled as "mixture modeling," as the analyst will use probabilistic techniques to draw inferences about the possible mix of subgroups within a population that can be "unmixed." This mixture can be explained by something the variables have in common or by something the subgroups of people have in common, or, alternatively, both persons and variables could share this commonality.

THE PROCESS OF UNDERTAKING A LATENT CLASS ANALYSIS

Extraction of homogeneous classes with LCA would adhere to the following process. Before conducting an LCA, the coding of the indicator variable data and the likely class type to be extracted should be borne in mind. Data coding is mainly categorical and often dichotomous, although LCA is sufficiently versatile to accommodate ordinal coding (e.g., Cleveland et al., 2010; LaFramboise, Hoyt, Oliver, & Whitbeck, 2006). Dichotomous coding could reveal the presence or absence of an occurrence (e.g., a traumatic event), a psychological phenomenon (e.g., a symptom of ill health, such as hallucinations), or a diagnosis (e.g., classing someone as having obsessive-compulsive disorder); the coding could encompass a feeling, either as a dichotomously (e.g., "satisfied" versus "unsatisfied") or differently (e.g., "never," "sometimes," and "often") scaled state. With LCA, the process is mainly exploratory, and, although the indicator variables could be coded as categorical or ordinal, the resultant latent classes will always be categorical. Although some studies seem to demonstrate the presence of latent classes that may be scale-like as if on a continuum (e.g., Murphy et al., 2007; Shevlin et al., 2007), this appearance can be deceptive, as LCA is primarily involved in extracting classes that are essentially categorical.

To achieve the aim of establishing categorical latent classes, one can employ the Expectation Maximization algorithm, which utilizes the full information maximum likelihood method of class extraction (Masyn, 2013) by randomly allocating people into classes and estimating a one-class solution, a two-class solution, and so on, until inspection of a range of fit statistics demonstrates the presence of a best-fitting solution. Model fit is evaluated with the Likelihood Ratio chi-square (LRχ^2), Bayesian Information Criterion (BIC), Sample Size Adjusted BIC (SSABIC), Akaike Information Criterion (AIC), Consistent AIC (CAIC), and the Lo-Mendell-Rubin adjusted Likelihood Ratio Test (LMR-LRT). Of all of these fit statistics, the BIC has been identified as performing the most reliably, although the Bootstrapped Likelihood Ratio Test (BLRT) has also been commended (Nylund, Asparouhov, et al., 2007).

Evaluation of the class solutions takes place by appraising when the class solutions have the lowest BIC, SSABIC, AIC, and CAIC values. Lower LRχ^2 values are also desired, and ideally these should be associated with a nonsignificant test value, although this is often a rare finding because the chi-square statistic is adversely affected by larger samples (Bollen, 1989; Tanaka, 1987), with a higher risk of committing a Type I statistical error. By contrast, a statistically significant LMR-LRT value is indicative of better fit. With the BLRT, this statistic helps to evaluate whether a model improves significantly from the model with $k - 1$ classes, where k is the number of classes for each analysis and there is an assessment as to whether a more parsimonious fit is available (Asparouhov & Muthén, 2012; Dziak, Lanza, & Tan, 2014). The entropy value (i.e., ranging from 0 to 1) for each class solution could be used, with higher entropy values indicating better probabilities of being able to successfully classify participants into a latent class, depending on the number of latent classes being extracted (Masyn, 2013). Finally, the ultimate decision on the optimal number of classes to be extracted rests on whether the class solutions make sense through inspection of the posterior probabilities for class membership in relation to each indicator variable. Higher posterior probabilities for some indicator variables (e.g., 70% likelihood or higher of endorsing an item/behavior) may offer clues as to the probable label to be given to the class and the persons who belong in it. Very low probability of endorsing certain indicator variables may also provide insights into what the class could be called. The posterior probabilities can be mapped out as a graphical plot (see Figure 15.1), with the likelihood of endorsing an item ranging from 0% to 100% and being marked from 0.00 to 1.00 on the y-axis or in tabular form.

As can be seen in Figure 15.1 (adapted from Williams et al., 2008), some respondents in this United Kingdom–wide study of work-related travel had a 100% likelihood of endorsing the "cycle" item and had a 10% chance of endorsing the "train" item. Another class was labeled the "rail" class, as there was a high chance of respondents endorsing the "train" item and (relative to those in the other classes) a higher probability of endorsing the "tram" or "tube" (i.e., the London Underground). There was also a "bus" class and a "car" class that represented higher likelihood levels of endorsing items relating to these modes of transport. It should be noted that this analysis took into account multimodality by entertaining the possibility that commuters may use more than one method of travel to get to and from work. This study was able to uncover whether data obtained from commuters could be split into a two-class solution (e.g., public transport class versus private transport class) or other potential solutions. The study found four latent classes in relation to commuting behavior, and we were able to see how certain latent classes of commuting could be related to greater risk of commuting-related stress.

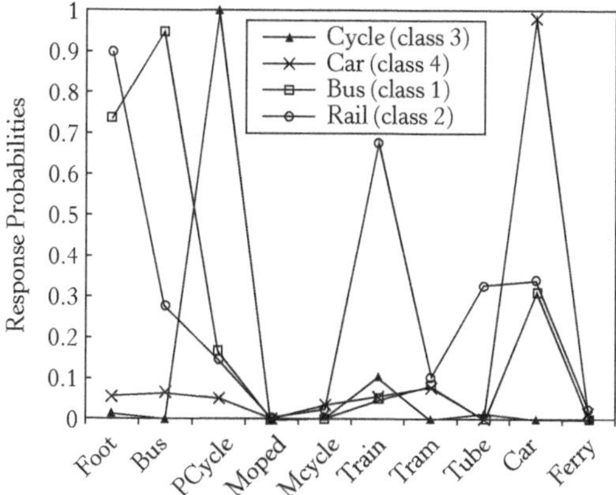

FIGURE 15.1: Probability of endorsing different commuting modes based on latent class membership.

With a tabular example of posterior probabilities in Table 15.1, which has been adapted from Ronzio, Mitchell, and Wang's (2011) study of witnessed community violence among African American mothers living in urban environments, we can see that a two-class solution was extracted from these 209 participants' data: (a) a "higher witnessed community violence exposure" class and (b) a "lower witness community violence exposure" class. Table 15.1 demonstrates that women in a "higher witnessed community violence exposure" class had a relatively higher probability of hearing a gunshot "often" when compared with the "lower witnessed community violence" class. In fact, although the probabilities of hearing a gunshot "sometimes" was similar for both groups (i.e., 56% vs. 49%), the differences between the two classes in hearing a gunshot "never" or "often" were quite stark (12% vs. 51% and 31% vs. 0%, respectively). This table also demonstrates the

TABLE 15.1: POSTERIOR PROBABILITIES IN RELATION TO LATENT CLASS FOR URBAN AFRICAN AMERICAN MOTHERS WHO HAD WITNESSED COMMUNITY VIOLENCE (WCV)

	Latent Class	
Type of Exposure	Higher WCV Exposure	Lower WCV Exposure
Heard a gunshot		
Never	0.12	0.51
Sometimes	0.56	0.49
Often	0.31	0.00
Saw an arrest		
Never	0.16	0.72
Sometimes	0.58	0.28
Often	0.26	0.00

Source: "The Structure of Witnessed Community Violence Amongst Urban African American Mothers: Latent Class Analysis of a Community Sample," by C. R. Ronzio, S. J. Mitchell, and J. Wang, 2011, *Urban Studies Research*, p. 5.

versatility of the LCA method in being able to accommodate differently coded indicator variables when comparing various categorical-type latent classes and the likely class membership in accordance with the probability of endorsing certain items at varying levels of agreement. The following section provides further insights into how to deploy LCA in community-based research, along with outlining the nuances involved in employing this method.

CASE STUDY OF LATENT CLASS ANALYSIS

An illustrative example of the potential for LCA in community-based research can be seen from the following study by the first author and his colleagues (Williams, Humberstone, & Harris, 2010) that was conducted with a sample of more than 4,000 participants drawn from one county in the East Midlands in England. This study was commissioned by the Derbyshire Arts Development Group and was aimed at inquiring into the reasons why some members of the general population did not engage with arts and cultural activities organized in the region. Respondents were asked about their participation in a number of arts and cultural activities and were also prompted to give reasons why they did not take part in these kinds of activities. The reasons for not taking part are depicted in Table 15.2.

After excluding "don't know" responses, there were 17 possible reasons that participants could choose. Respondents could endorse any (or none) of these reasons, so there were 2^{17} (i.e., 131,072) different response patterns that could be obtained (e.g., "yes" to all items was one possible response pattern; other permutations might be endorsing the first item out of the list of reasons and not endorsing any of the others). From this sample, 654 response patterns were elicited, but clearly we would not want to extract 654 different latent classes. A more parsimonious and manageable solution was needed. A six-class solution was chosen through inspection of the fit statistics (Table 15.3). This decision was attributed to the BIC value reaching its nadir at the six-class solution. The LMR-LRT also declined in value and was statistically significant up until the seven-class solution, which was when the value became non-significant ($p = 0.15$), which was interpreted as

TABLE 15.2: REASONS GIVEN FOR NOT ATTENDING ARTS AND CULTURAL EVENTS

Item	Number (% of Those Who Responded to Item)
It's difficult to find the time	1,494 (34.54%)
It costs too much	1,419 (32.80%)
Not enough information on what is available	1,123 (26.0%)
Not enough notice about the event	784 (18.1%)
It's not close enough to where I live/work	687 (15.9%)
Not really interested	653 (15.1%)
Nothing stops me from attending arts and cultural events	617 (14.3%)
I don't know enough about it	542 (12.5%)
Lack of transport	529 (12.2%)
Health isn't good enough	367 (8.5%)
I don't have anyone to go with	343 (7.9%)
Never occurred to me	185 (4.3%)
I might feel uncomfortable or out of place	171 (4.0%)
I wouldn't enjoy it	147 (3.4%)
Other reasons	156 (3.6%)
Don't know	77 (1.8%)
It is often too complex or confusing	63 (1.5%)
Against my religion/beliefs	25 (0.6%)

TABLE 15.3: REASONS GIVEN FOR NONPARTICIPATION IN ARTS AND CULTURAL ACTIVITIES—FIT STATISTICS FOR THE LATENT CLASS ANALYSIS

Model	Log Likelihood	Free Parameters	LR_{χ^2} (df) p	AIC	BIC	SSABIC	LMR-LRT (p)	Entropy
Two classes	−23,177.58	39	3,599.39 (262,040) 1.00	46,433.15	46,681.67	46,557.75	2,111.90 (0.00)	0.64
Three classes	−22,834.32	59	2,942.01 (262,023) 1.00	45,786.64	46,162.61	45,975.13	682.44 (0.00)	0.63
Four classes	−22,623.55	79	2,538.01 (262,005) 1.00	45,405.09	45,908.51	45,657.48	419.04 (0.00)	0.70
Five classes	−22,435.54	99	2,432.92 (262,003) 1.00	45,069.09	45,699.95	45,385.37	373.20 (0.0461)	0.68
Six classes	−22,283.91	119	2,186.01 (261,986) 1.00	44,805.83	45,564.14	45,186.01	301.46 (0.0035)	0.71
Seven classes	−22,201.58	139	2,045.14 (261,968) 1.00	44,681.17	45,566.93	45,125.25	164.04 (0.1456)	0.71

AIC, Akaike Information Criterion; BIC, Bayesian Information Criterion; LMR-LRT, Lo-Mendell-Rubin Likelihood Ratio Test; LR_{χ^2}, likelihood ratio chi-square; SSABIC, Sample Size Adjusted BIC.

the six-class solution being markedly better than the seven-class solution. The entropy value for the six-class solution also showed that 71% of the sample could be accurately categorized on the basis of their class membership. Although the entropy value for the seven-class solution was also 0.71, we have already uncovered with the LMR-LRT statistic that this solution is not significantly better than the six-class solution. As a result of the profile of these fit statistics, the six-class solution was chosen to be the most accurate representation of how people were responding in relation to reasons given for not taking part in the arts.

The posterior probabilities could have been mapped out in a profile plot, but this may have been difficult to interpret from visual inspection of the probability of endorsing 17 items in relation to being a member of any one of six latent classes. Instead, we examined the table of conditional probabilities, and inferences were made about what would be appropriate labels for each latent class. Through this process, we were able to identify the classes, which included an "arts-resistant" class (i.e., high likelihood of endorsing "not really interested" and moderate levels of probability of endorsing "don't really know enough about it," "It's difficult to find the time," and "I wouldn't enjoy it") and an "uninformed" class (i.e., high probability of endorsing "not enough information on what is available" and moderate levels of likelihood of endorsing "not enough notice about the event"), to name but a few of the latent classes that could be unearthed. Overall, this approach proved advantageous in modeling the mentalities and behaviors of a population within a certain region. After interventions addressing these types of hidden barriers uncovered through LCA, a follow-up study could be carried out to examine whether the latent classes still existed in the general population within a region and the prevalence of such barriers to participation. Such a follow-up study was indeed conducted with another sample of 4,000 participants within the same locality (Biggins et al., 2012) and showed reductions in some of the latent classes underlying barrriers to participation, such as the prevalence of an "isolated" class of respondents declining from 17.7% of the sample in 2008 to 5.0% in 2011. Clearly, LCA has the capacity to see if a typology of phenomena, such as barriers to arts participation, can exist over time when assessing data from two time points with two different samples studied with a cross-sectional design.

INTRODUCTION TO LATENT PROFILE ANALYSIS

LPA can also offer something new and useful to a community-based researcher. Community-based studies employing LPA have, for example, analyzed coping among ethnic minority youth (Aldridge & Roesch, 2008) and profiles of urban-based African American adolescents (Copeland-Linder, Lambert, & Ialongo, 2010) involving combinations of the three variables of violence exposure, parental monitoring, and parental involvement. The latter study examined how their obtained profiles differentially predicted depressive symptoms and aggressive behavior. Specifically, Copeland-Linder et al. (2010) were able to compile three class profiles (a "vulnerable" class, a "moderate risk/medium protection" class, and a "moderate risk/high protection" class), which could aid in the development of targeting at-risk youth and creating programs to help young people's well-being levels when violence in the community is salient and/or frequent.

Overall, LCA and LPA are two kinds of person-centred mixture modeling analyses that are used to identify subgroups of an underlying categorical latent variable with data obtained from cross-sectional designs. As such, the two types of analyses are very similar, and fit statistics that are scrutinized in LCA are also used in LPA. Rather than repeat for the reader what these statistics entail, we would note that the main difference between LCA and LPA is in the type of indicator variables used. While LCA is often undertaken on categorical indicator variables, LPA is used for continuous indicator variables.

In turn, there are some differences between LCA and LPA in the nuances of the analyses undertaken. In LCA, the shapes of the latent classes are defined by the assumption of local independence (i.e., the indicator variables are independent of each other within the latent classes), and the latent classes are described by the differing posterior probabilities (i.e., specified after the class solution has been extracted) of endorsing each indicator variable based on class membership. In contrast, the shape of the latent classes in LPA is not specified by the assumption of local independence, and the resultant best-fitting LPA solution is described by the different mean scores on each indicator variable, depending on class membership. With respect to the specification of what the latent classes are shaped like in LPA, Masyn (2013) suggested that four different specifications should be tested alongside the best-fitting solution. The first, most restrictive, specification describes a model in which the shapes of the resultant classes are constrained to be the same (i.e., variances and covariances are restricted to be the same across classes) and the assumption of local independence is implemented (i.e., the indicator variables are not allowed to covary within a class). The second and third specifications relax either one of these restrictions (i.e., local independence is assumed or not, and variances and covariances are restricted to be the same across classes, or not, respectively). The fourth, and final, specification relaxes both of these constraints; the variances and covariances are not restricted to be the same across classes (i.e., differing shapes across the classes), and the error variances of the indicator variables are allowed to covary (i.e., no local independence is assumed). Masyn (2013) suggested that these four specifications should be assessed alongside the different number of classes to arrive at a best-fitting solution of the LPA that takes into account both the best-fitting shape and best-fitting number of classes.

This best-fitting solution in LPA is described by the different mean scores on each indicator variable, depending on class membership. Figure 15.2 provides an example of how data from the National Comorbidity Survey of more than 8,000 participants in the United States were analyzed with LPA to elicit five homogeneous groups that were then compared on three different behaviors labeled as psychopathological and operating on continuous dimensions of "externalizing," "internalizing," and "psychosis" type profiles (Fleming, Shevlin, Murphy, & Joseph, 2014).

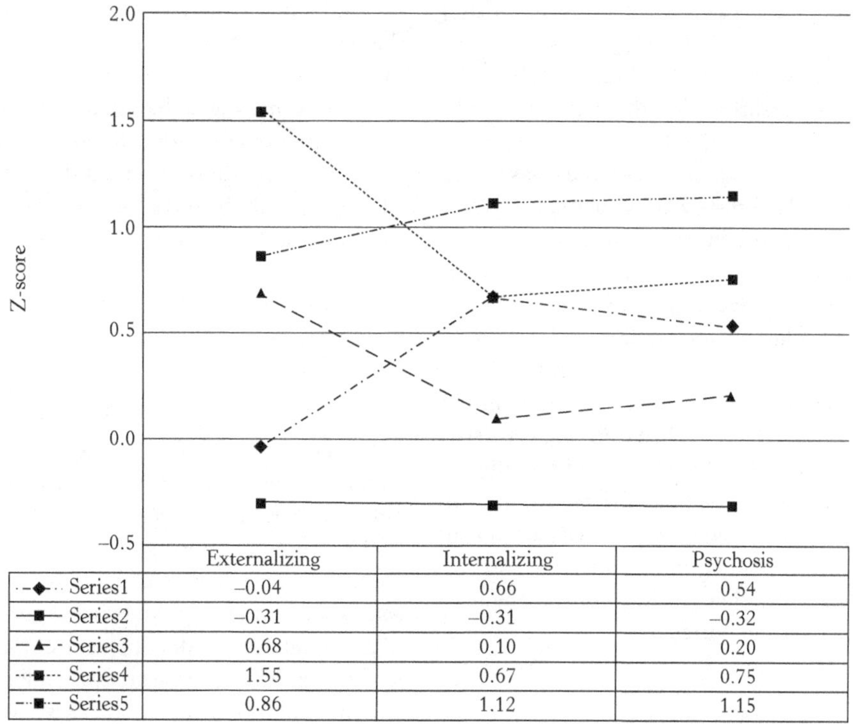

	Externalizing	Internalizing	Psychosis
Series1	−0.04	0.66	0.54
Series2	−0.31	−0.31	−0.32
Series3	0.68	0.10	0.20
Series4	1.55	0.67	0.75
Series5	0.86	1.12	1.15

FIGURE 15.2: Latent profile plot of psychopathological profiles across dimensions.

Adapted from "Psychosis Within Dimensional and Categorical Models of Mental Illness," by S. Fleming, M. Shevlin, J. Murphy, and S. Joseph, 2014, *Psychosis, 6* (1), p .8. Reprinted by permission of Taylor & Francis Ltd, http://www.tandfonline.com.

CASE STUDY OF LATENT PROFILE ANALYSIS

Geiser, Okun, and Grano (2014) provided an excellent applied example of LPA. They were interested in what motivates people to volunteer and provide unpaid services to the community at large. The study was specifically focused on how different forms of motivation (i.e., amotivation, extrinsic motivation, and intrinsic motivation) interact and predict frequency of volunteering. Furthermore, differences in sex and nationality were examined in this cross-national study of American and Italian participants.

Mean scores for six items (i.e., amotivation, intrinsic motivation, and four items for varying degrees of autonomy in extrinsic motivation) were evaluated. In order to undertake the LPA, it was assumed that there would be local independence (i.e., no covariance between indicator variables within the identified latent classes) and equal variances and covariances across the identified latent classes (i.e., same shape across classes). This is just one of the four specifications for the shapes and sizes of the latent classes that Masyn (2013) had advised to explore when deciding on the best-fitting class solution. However, the researchers were interested in inspecting the latent profile solutions for each of the two nationalities (American vs. Italian) and their respective sex (female vs. male). It would have added far too much complexity to take these four models (nationality paired with sex) and test each of them for the best-fitting shape and best-fitting class solution to test four specifications (i.e., local independence, or not, paired with equal variances/covariances, or not) for each number of classes examined. Checking a two-class through to a six-class solution would have meant 20 solutions (i.e., 5 × 4 specifications) solely based on the best-fitting shape and best-fitting class solution. These would then need to be checked for each model (nationality by sex), resulting in 80 solutions (i.e., 20 × 4 models).

Geiser et al. (2014) based their initial analyses on Nylund, Asparouhov, et al.'s (2007) recommendations that the BIC, SSABIC, BLRT, and LMR-LRT should be compared for a one- through to a seven-class solution for the four different models (nationality by sex). Due to these fit statistics not providing a consistent result for the best-fitting solution, Geiser et al. (2014) followed Marsh, Lüdtke, Trautwein, and Morin's (2009) recommendation of ensuring that the best-fitting solution described not only quantitative changes but also qualitative changes between the classes. The researchers judged the six-class solution to be the most interpretable with both qualitative and quantitative changes for all four models. A further multigroup LPA was undertaken to test similarities of the class solutions for the four different models (nationality by sex). A six-class solution was decided upon for the four models (nationality by sex), in which each model had differing class sizes for these six classes. The frequency of actually volunteering was then added to the model, and the researchers' original hypothesis—that participants who scored highly on intrinsic motivation and high in extrinsic motivation would volunteer the most frequently—was supported.

LIMITATIONS OF LATENT CLASS ANALYSIS AND LATENT PROFILE ANALYSIS

One of the main limitations of LCA and LPA is that the identified classes may not necessarily always (and without further validation) refer to existing subgroups within the population. Superfluous classes can be identified due to nonnormality of the data, nonlinear relationships between the indicator variables, or a misspecification of the model (Bauer & Curran, 2004). As both LCA and LPA are types of finite mixture modeling analyses, the assumption is that heterogeneous data can be explained by homogeneous subgroups that are mixed together. Thus, the nonnormality and nonlinearity that are observed in the heterogeneous data could be hypothesized as being attributed to the mixture of these subgroups that have been identified through the use of LPA and LCA. However, there are other possible explanations beyond the presence of latent classes as to why data may be distributed in a nonnormal and nonlinear fashion (Bauer & Curran, 2004). This may lead to the erroneous identification of classes that are meant to explain nonnormality or nonlinear relationships that are found within the data.

If the aim of community-based research that utilizes LCA or LPA is to make an explicit statement of having identified real subgroups in the population, then other possible explanations for nonnormality and nonlinearity of the data need to be investigated and potentially ruled out (Bauer & Curran, 2004). Simply deciding on a best-fitting solution by undertaking an LCA or LPA would not be sufficient to prove that these classes actually exist as tangible groups of people, so community-based researchers would still need to be cautious of reifying any classes that have been extracted.

CONCLUSION

LCA and LPA offer versatile solutions to community-based researchers for dealing with data obtained through cross-sectional designs, especially with large samples of data. These analytic methods can be powerful tools to guide theory generation and testing. Most important, LCA and LPA can inform the development of typologies of underlying behaviors, attitudes, and perceptions that may not be noticeable otherwise. These methodological approaches can help form the basis for informed decision making and the development of evidence-based policies, practices, and interventions aimed at improving people's quality of life and well-being.

REFERENCES

Aldridge, A. A., & Roesch, S. C. (2008). Developing coping typologies of minority adolescents: A latent profile analysis. *Journal of Adolescence, 31*, 499–517.

Asparouhov, T., & Muthén, B. O. (2012). *Using mplus TECH11 and TECH14 to test the number of latent classes.* Mplus Web Notes: No. 14. May 22, 2012. Retrieved June 2015, from http://www.statmodel.com/examples/webnote.shtml

Bauer, D. J., & Curran, P. J. (2004). The integration of continuous and discrete latent variable models: Potential problems and promising opportunities. *Psychological Methods, 9*, 3–29.

Bollen, K. A. (1989). *Structural equations with latent variables.* New York, NY: Wiley.

Biggins, A., Cottee, G., & Williams, G. (2012). *Arts audiences and participants research.* Nottingham, England: Nottingham Trent University.

Cleveland, M. J., Collins, L. M., Lanza, S. T., Greenberg, M. T., & Feinberg, M. E. (2010). Does individual risk moderate the effect of contextual-level protective factors? A latent class analysis of substance use. *Journal of Prevention and Intervention in the Community, 38*, 213–228.

Copeland-Linder, N., Lambert, S. F., & Ialongo, N. S. (2010). Community violence, protective factors, and adolescent mental health: A profile analysis. *Journal of Clinical Child and Adolescent Psychology, 39,* 176–186.

Dziak, J. J., Lanza, S. T., & Tan, X. (2014). Effect size, statistical power, and sample size requirements for the bootstrap likelihood ratio test in latent class analysis. *Structural Equation Modeling, 21,* 534–552.

Fleming, S., Shevlin, M., Murphy, J., & Joseph, S. (2014). Psychosis within dimensional and categorical models of mental illness. *Psychosis, 6,* 4–15.

Geiser, C., Okun, M. A., & Grano, C. (2014). Who is motivated to volunteer? A latent profile analysis linking volunteer motivation to frequency of volunteering. *Psychological Test and Assessment Modeling,* 56, 3–24.

James, S., McField, E. S., & Montgomery, S. B. (2013). Risk factor profiles among intravenous drug using young adults: A latent class analysis (LCA) approach. *Addictive Behaviors, 38,* 1804–1811.

Kibowski, F., & Williams, G. (2012, May). *Can latent classes of childhood trauma predict latent classes of psychosis-like experiences? Secondary data analysis using a nationally representative subsample of the NCS-R.* Paper presented at the annual conference of the British Psychological Society Northern Ireland Branch, Killadeas, Northern Ireland.

LaFramboise, T. D., Hoyt, D. R., Oliver, L., & Whitbeck, L. B. (2006). Family, community, and school influences on resilience among American Indian adolescents in the Upper Midwest. *Journal of Community Psychology, 34,* 193–209.

Marsh, H. W., Lüdtke, O., Trautwein, U., & Morin, A. J. S. (2009). Classical latent profile analysis of academic self-concept dimensions: Synergy of person- and variable-centered approaches to theoretical models of self-concept. *Structural Equation Modeling, 16,* 191–225.

Masyn, K. E. (2013). Latent class analysis and finite mixture modeling. In T. D. Little (Ed.), *The Oxford handbook of quantitative methods, Vol. 2. Statistical analysis* (pp. 551–611). New York, NY: Oxford University Press.

Murphy, J., Shevlin, M., & Adamson, G. (2007). A latent class analysis of positive psychosis symptoms based on the British Psychiatric Morbidity Survey. *Personality and Individual Differences, 42,* 1491–1502.

Nylund, K., Asparouhov, T., & Muthén, B. O. (2007). Deciding on the number of classes in latent class analysis and growth mixture modeling: A Monte Carlo simulation study. *Structural Equation Modeling, 14,* 535–569.

Nylund, K., Bellmore, A., Nishina, A., & Graham, S. (2007). Subtypes, severity, and structural stability of peer victimization: What does latent class analysis say? *Child Development, 78,* 1706–1722.

Ronzio, C. R., Mitchell, S. J., & Wang, J. (2011). The structure of witnessed community violence amongst urban African American mothers: Latent class analysis of a community sample. *Urban Studies Research, 2011.* Retrieved June 2015, from http://www.hindawi.com/journals/usr/2011/867129/

Rosato, N. S. & Baer, J. C. (2012). Latent class analysis: A method for capturing heterogeneity. *Social Work Research, 36,* 61–69.

Shevlin, M., Murphy, J., Dorahy, M. J., & Adamson, G. (2007). The distribution of positive psychosis-like symptoms in the population: A latent class analysis of the National Comorbidity Survey, *Schizophrenia Research, 89,* 101–109.

Tanaka, J. S. (1987). "How big is big enough?" Sample size and goodness of fit in structural equation models with latent variables. *Child Development, 58,* 134–146.

Williams, G. A, Humberstone, A., & Harris, T. (2010, April). *Participation in the arts and well-being: Constructing a typology of perceived barriers and benefits.* Paper presented at the Annual Conference of the British Psychological Society, Stratford-upon-Avon, England.

Williams, G. A., Murphy, J., & Hill, R. (2008, September). *A latent class analysis of commuters' transportation mode and relationships with commuter stress.* Paper presented at the Fourth International Conference on Traffic and Transport Psychology, Washington, DC.

16

Multilevel Structural Equation Modeling

JOHN P. BARILE

Multilevel structural equation modeling (MSEM), an analytical technique that combines traditional multilevel regression and structural equation modeling (SEM), offers many advantages compared to traditional approaches in understanding community-based data. MSEM enables researchers to assess individual-level and higher level data simultaneously, while minimalizing ecological, atomistic, psychologistic, and sociologistic fallacies commonly present in evaluation and intervention research. Utilization of MSEM is often necessary to understand the diverse web of ecological determinants of individual and community well-being. This chapter will present the basic tenets of MSEM and identify circumstances in which this approach is most appropriate. It will then present an example of the use of MSEM in an evaluation of community coalitions, in which data from multiple sources at both the individual and collaborative levels were utilized to better understand the processes and outcomes associated with successful collaboration.

Although researchers have stressed the need to consider context for many years (Lewin, 1935), the development and accessibility of analytic tools that can simultaneously assess individuals and their environment have only recently emerged. Shinn and Rapkin (2000) outline the need for cross-level modeling (i.e., multilevel modeling) when researchers are interested in (a) the direct effects of a higher level variable on a lower level variable, (b) the level of deviation an individual has from a group standard, (c) the study of variables at multiple levels simultaneously, with one controlling for the other, (d) the moderating effect of a variable at one level on a relationship at another level, and (e) the effects of person-environment fit.

Shinn and Rapkin (2000) made strong cases for the need to measure both individual and contextual constructs when doing community-based research. These ideas were further trumpeted by Luke (2005), who urged community scientists to "get the big picture" by utilizing analytical tools that capture context by using a variety of methods, including multilevel modeling. These calls have been answered by a growing number of publications that have utilized multilevel methods. This chapter builds upon community-based methodologies presented by Jason and Glenwick (2012) by introducing MSEM as a means to study context. The following sections review traditional multilevel regression and SEM and then show how MSEM addresses limitations of the former methods. The chapter concludes with an application of MSEM to data on community collaboratives.

INTRODUCTION TO TRADITIONAL MULTILEVEL REGRESSION MODELING

MSEM is a pairing of traditional multilevel regression modeling and structural equation modeling. Traditional multilevel regression modeling incorporates data that exist on two or more levels. (Multilevel modeling can also include longitudinal analyses of multiple scores nested within an individual but for purposes of this chapter, we will focus only on contextual modeling of multilevel data.) For something to be considered multilevel, individuals (or the lowest level of measurement) must be nested within (i.e., be part of) a larger construct or group. Most often, the lowest level occurs at the individual level. Individual-level data can include a person's background, such as his or her age, education, and/or ethnicity, as well as his or her responses to survey questions (e.g., attitudes, perceptions) or an inventory of behaviors. Contextual variables include measures that describe a specific unit in which individuals are nested. Examples of individuals within nesting units include residents within neighborhoods, students within classrooms, or members within spiritual groups. Contextual variables of neighborhood nesting units can include, for example, estimates of social capital, the nature of local policies, or the number of parks; contextual variables of classroom nesting units can include measures of teacher quality, lesson plans, or absence policies. Measures at the nesting unit level can include variables that occur only at this higher level, such as the nature of local polices, levels of school funding, and diversity indexes. They can also be represented by aggregated individual responses, such as average teacher ratings or average fear of crime. For the purposes of this chapter, the highest level of a multilevel model will be referred to as the *group level*, but other sources also refer to it as the *organization level, cluster level, between level*, or *level two*.

Historically, the majority of research in social sciences has been measured, analyzed, and reported on an individual level. Unfortunately, ignoring contextual influences associated with individuals' perceptions, actions, and outcomes can lead to biased results and inappropriate interpretations. Subsequently, a growing number of researchers have utilized multilevel modeling techniques to better address the limitations of single-level analyses. For example, Russo, Roccato, and Vieno (2011) conducted a study predicting perceived risk of crime. They found that individual factors, such as age, gender, and perceptions of disorder, were related to risk of crime, but county-level factors, such as collective perceptions of disorder, unemployment rates, and actual crime rates, also predicted individuals' perceived risk of crime.

Because individual attitudes and behaviors are shaped by both personal attributes and shared environment, one of the chief concerns of ignoring contextual influences is the potential to commit one or more inferential fallacies (Diez-Roux, 1998). Atomistic fallacies occur when researchers utilize individual-level data to make inferences at the group level. For example, a researcher could determine that IQ is the strongest predictor of academic achievement (both measured at the individual level) and consequently conclude that improving educational environments was unnecessary (group level). However, this analysis does not consider students circumstances; it could be that individuals found to have lower IQ were funneled into remedial classrooms with substandard teachers and resources, while those with high IQ were funneled into enriching classes with the best teachers (Gibbons, 2008). Similarly, ecological fallacies occur when researchers collect data at the group level but interpret them at the individual level. For example, a researcher may determine that there is no association between average household income and mortality at the county level (i.e., high-income counties and low-income counties, as aggregates, have comparable mortality rates), and consequently conclude that low-income individuals do not face any additional health challenges, compared to high-income individuals. Unfortunately, it is also plausible that within each county, individuals with the lowest incomes are at the higher risk of mortality when they live in higher income counties due to increased discrimination, but, on the aggregate, no associations are found. In the case of psychologistic and sociologistic fallacies, the researcher measures and analyzes data on the appropriate level but fails to take into account the impact that other levels of information have on the associations of interest. Here, if a researcher were interested in the association between student study habits and academic success (individual level), but the researcher did not take into account the school and home environment of the students (group level), the researcher would be at risk of committing a psychologistic fallacy (i.e., not taking into account contextual variables). Finally, if a researcher were interested in evaluating school policies that mandated the use of a curriculum (group level) but did not account for differences in the implementation of the curriculum by the teachers (individual level), he or she would be committing a sociologistic fallacy (i.e., not taking into account individual-level variables). Committing these fallacies can result in misidentifying the source of an influence, including whether it is at the individual or group level, which can lead to misidentification of problems and/or solutions.

Multilevel modeling helps limit the chance of committing each of these fallacies. Specifically, multilevel modeling can limit the chance of committing a fallacy by (a) estimating standard errors that account for the clustering of individuals within a higher order grouping, (b) evaluating the influence of contextual variables impacting individual-level variables, (c) evaluating the influence of individual-level variables influencing contextual variables, and (d) assessing cross-level interactions between associations at each level. Multilevel modeling is often necessary when data are nested within a higher grouping, regardless of whether or not the grouping variable is of any interest. For example, a researcher might be interested in evaluating individual risk factors for dangerous drinking within a sample of college students that belong to fraternities. In this case, the researcher will need to account for the clustering of students within fraternities even if he or she is not interested in any fraternity-level variables because the members of the same fraternity are not independent of one another. Not accounting for the clustering through the use of multilevel models (e.g., a random intercept models) often leads to biased estimates due to unaccounted dependency among individuals in the same cluster. The dependency occurs whenever individuals within the same cluster present more similarly than individuals in a different cluster, a violation of independence of observation (Kenny & Judd, 1986). The best and easiest way to determine whether multilevel modeling is necessary is to consider the intraclass correlation (ICC).

Determining the ICC of variables in one's analysis is a critical step in determining whether multilevel analyses are appropriate. The ICC is computed by examining the amount of variance that exists at the individual and at the group level. The ICC is computed by dividing the group-level variance (τ^2) by the total of the individual-level variance and group-level variance ($\tau^2 + \sigma^2$). This will result in a number ranging from 0 to 1 (ICC = ρ). This represents the percent of variance that occurs at the group level. For example, if a researcher determines that the ICC = .20 on a measure of student exam grades by classroom, we can assume that 20% of the variability in student grades was associated with the classroom a student was in and 80% of their grades was due to individual-level factors.

Assuming that researchers have accurately conceptualized the level at which their research questions lie and how they want to test their model, we can consider the other three purposes of multilevel modeling: (a) determining the influence of contextual variables impacting individual-level variables, (b) determining the influence of individual-level variables impacting contextual variables and (c) assessing cross-level interactions between associations at each level. Researchers are often interested in determining the amount of variance that occurs at each level and how each level uniquely predicts a dependent variable. For example, in a study by Vieno, Perkins, Smith, and Santinello (2005), school sense of community was regressed on students' perception of their school's democratic climate at the individual, classroom, and school level. They found that individual perceptions of the school climate was the strongest predictor of school sense of community, but that aggregates (averages) of student perceptions at the classroom and school levels were also positively related to sense of community. Also of note, they found that a school-level aggregate of socioeconomic status (SES) was a strong predictor of sense of community, but individual-level SES was not. This suggests that disadvantaged adolescents, concentrated in the same schools, likely experience climate-level factors that inhibit the development of a strong sense of community, but, within the same classroom, low-SES students do not perceive the sense of community any differently than high-SES students.

As in the earlier example, multilevel methods enable the researcher to model the same variable at more than one level. A common example of this is income. This is done by measuring the variable at the individual level (e.g., personal income) and aggregating these individual scores within a grouping variable, such as neighborhood, to create a group-level variable (e.g., average neighborhood income). Here, if we include both the individual-level variable (personal income) and the group-level variable (average neighborhood income) in the analysis, we can determine the level of association between income at both levels and an outcome (e.g., health). This type of analysis is sometimes referred to as compositional (individual-level factor) and contextual (group-level factor) effects analysis (Macintyre, Ellaway, & Cummins, 2002).

The final major purpose of conducting multilevel analyses is to determine whether associations between individual-level variables depend upon group-level predictors. This is a form of moderation across multiple levels of analysis commonly referred to as a *cross-level interaction*. For example, we may find that, although both individual income and neighborhood income predict health, low-income individuals have better health outcomes when they live in predominantly low-income neighborhoods and worse health outcomes when they live in high-income neighborhoods. In fact, associations such as these have previously been identified when strong cultural ties are more readily available in the lower income neighborhoods (Roosa et al., 2009). However, it is also possible that lower income individuals do worse in lower income neighborhoods due to a form of "double jeopardy," especially when there are not distinct cultural advantages to living in a lower income neighborhood compared to a higher income neighborhood (Barile, 2010; Williams, 1999). In each of these cases, the relationship between an individual-level predictor (individual income) and outcome (health) is moderated by a group-level variable (neighborhood income). Cross-level interactions are particularly useful when researchers are interested in determining whether an association is context dependent or examining issues associated with person-environment fit.

STRUCTURAL EQUATION MODELING

As stated previously, MSEM is a combination of traditional multilevel regression modeling and structural equation modeling (SEM). SEM is an analytic technique that enables researchers to estimate and model the relationships between latent variables. Latent variables (also described as latent factors, derived from confirmatory factor analysis) represent a construct of interest that cannot be directly observed. Instead, they are estimated by a set of manifest variables. Manifest variables, sometimes referred to as observed variables, are variables that are directly measured by the researcher. For example, we cannot directly measure depression, but we can measure symptoms of depression. With SEM, we would model depression (latent variable) as estimated by items from an inventory of symptoms (observed variables).

Structural equation modeling has a number of advantages over traditional ordinal least squares (OLS) regression. Unlike simple sum scores or the averaging of items from a scale, estimation of latent variables using SEM techniques takes into account measurement error associated with each item; only the common variance found between the indicators is used to define the construct (Anderson & Gerbing, 1988). Additionally, unlike the simple independent/dependent variable dichotomy found in OLS regression, SEM permits the researcher to test complicated models that include multiple mediators within a single model. Also, SEM provides greater flexibility in the types of indicators that can be used in the model (e.g., dichotomous, ordinal, categorical, count) and offers more advanced means for addressing missing data (e.g., full-information maximum likelihood, multiple imputation). (For additional information of missing data, see Graham, 2009.)

Within the SEM framework, researchers also have access to exact and approximate fit indices. Fit indices allow the researcher to compare statistically how well his or her model fares compared to an unconstrained model and/or alternative theoretical models. For most SEM models, exact model fit is assessed by a chi-square statistic (χ^2). The chi-square is a goodness-of-fit statistic that tests the magnitude of discrepancy between the sample covariance matrix and the estimated covariance matrix (Hu & Bentler, 1999). Approximate fit indexes (e.g., Comparative Fit index [CF]), Root Mean Squared Error of Approximation [RMSEA]) provide the researcher with additional indications of whether his or her model fits the data along a continuum (Hu & Bentler, 1999). For example, Hu and Bentler recommend that CFI values above .95 and an RMSEA below .06 correspond to a well-fitted model, although it should be noted that both the chi-square and approximate fit indices are sensitive to sample size (Browne, MacCallum, Kim, Andersen, & Glaser, 2002; Hu & Bentler, 1999). Further discussion of fit statistics are outside the scope of this chapter, but the simple availability of statistics to compare competing models directly is a distinct advantage of SEM over traditional OLS regression (see Hu & Bentler, 1999, and Vernon & Eysenck, 2007, for an in-depth examination of fit indices).

Finally, SEM also allows the researcher to detect measurement invariance, which OLS regression techniques do not. Measurement invariance addresses the extent to which individuals from different backgrounds interpret and report on survey questions in similar manners (Gregorich, 2006). Measurement invariance testing is particularly important when utilizing community-based data where individuals within a sample may come from a range of cultures and/or backgrounds. Measurement invariance is established by examining whether the strength of the association between an indicator (the observed variable) and its latent variable are similar across different populations, genders, cultures, etc. (See Gregorich, 2006, for an in-depth discussion of measurement invariance.)

MULTILEVEL STRUCTURAL EQUATION MODELING

Recent developments in statistical methodology have led to the growing use of MSEM, which combines the advantages of traditional multilevel regression modeling and SEM. MSEM has been found to be a particularly useful technique in studying such topics as social climates in schools (Barile, Donohue, et al., 2012; Marsh et al., 2012), community collaboratives (Barile, Darnell, Erickson, & Weaver, 2012; Brown, Hawkins, Arthur, Abbott, & Van Horn, 2008), and even factories (Brondino, Pasini, & da Silva, 2013). MSEM provides the measurement advantages associated with SEM and the research design advantages associated with traditional multilevel modeling. With this combination, MSEM aids researchers by (a) limiting the susceptibility for measurement bias common in multilevel regression models, (b) limiting the potential for fallacies often common in single-level SEM, and (c) accounting for the unreliability of individual-level reports of group-level constructs (Marsh et al., 2009; Mehta & Neale, 2005).

Multilevel data can include *compilation, composition,* or *fuzzy composition* variables (Dyer, Hanges, & Hall, 2005). Compilation variables, similar to individual-level formative variables (e.g., gender, income, age), are constructs that occur only at the group level and/or do not have any corresponding individual variables. These include such variables as policies, diversity indexes, and crime rates. Composition variables represent similar constructs at both the individual and group levels and are often measured by surveying individuals within groups. The group-level score is computed as an aggregate of individual scores. For example, if one were to ask students in a class how much they liked their teacher, the aggregate of all the student responses might be used to estimate an average score for the classroom. Unfortunately, it is difficult to know whether factor structures at the individual level correspond to the same factor structures at the group level. Fuzzy composition variables are variables that mean different things at different levels. For example, if individuals are asked a set of questions regarding dangers in their neighborhood, a researcher may get very different responses depending on whether they ask residents if they fear crime versus if residents in their neighborhood fear crime. Although it may be appropriate for researchers to ask about individuals' fear of crime, if modeled at the neighborhood level the resulting factors may mean something quite different than they do at the individual level. Consequently, a researcher may also find that constructs that are relatively independent at the individual level (e.g., fear of assault, fear of vandalism), fall under a single factor at the neighborhood level (e.g., climate of fear). One advantage of MSEM over traditional multilevel modeling is the ability for researchers to identify differences in factor structure across levels.

MSEM is a particularly useful analytic approach when survey data are collected from multiple respondents nested within multiple settings, a common scenario in the evaluation of such groups as students in classrooms or members of community collaboratives. In these cases, it would be unwise to simply aggregate these responses. Nowell (2009) noted that, although obtaining multiple reports from individuals within groups can be desirable, if these reports are simply aggregated, the researcher often loses critical individual perspectives. For example, if women are found to report a greater fear of assault (compared to men) but a similar fear of vandalism, important differences in perspectives would be unaccounted for. MSEM provides the unique opportunity to identify differences in perspectives at the individual level while also capitalizing on the shared knowledge of the group at higher levels. Marsh et al. (2009) dubbed models in which individual-level items (such as items on survey) are used to create latent variables at the individual (traditional SEM) and group levels (MSEM) *doubly latent models.*

Doubly latent models enable the researcher to address both sampling bias and measurement error (Marsh et al., 2009, 2012). Sampling bias can occur when the number or likelihood that certain individuals were sampled within one group differs from those sampled in another group. Sampling bias is a common occurrence in nonrandom samples. For example, if a researcher is interested in surveying members regarding their organization's leadership, it is likely that not all of the sampled members will have attended the same number of meetings or had similar roles within the organization, both of which could impact how they rate the leadership. Furthermore, it is unlikely that the researcher will be able to sample the same number of members within each organization. Using traditional regression techniques, the researcher would simply aggregate the responses of members within each group, and there would be no way to adequately address differences in who responded to the survey or how many people responded to the survey within each organization. Creating latent variables at the individual and group levels based on individual responses allows the research to correct for sampling bias due to nonrandom sampling and measurement bias associated with imperfect measurement of latent constructs.

Along with addressing sampling bias and measurement error, MSEM enables the researcher to test for measurement invariance of items at the individual and group levels. For example, if individuals within a group have different backgrounds or roles, they may interpret questions differently. An organization board member may interpret a question such as "Does the organization have a clear mission?" in a different way than a new volunteer does. This difference in interpretation can result in a latent variable (e.g., organizational vision) that has slightly different meaning for each individual and potentially across organizations. Like SEM, MSEM allows the researcher to test for these potential differences through a comparison of the strength of factor loadings for each construct and across organizations (see Jak, Oort, & Dolan, 2014, for more information on testing for measurement invariance in MSEM).

Practical Issues

Sample Size

In order to conduct a test of a multilevel model, the researcher must have an adequate sample size at both the individual and the group levels. The number of individuals and groups needed to obtain unbiased estimates and to ensure sufficient power for the analysis depends on the primary level of inquiry (individual, group, or cross-level interaction), the size of the ICCs, and expected effect sizes. Maas and Hox (2005) reported that using data with fewer than 50 group-level units can lead to biased estimates of the standard error, but this largely depends on the average number of participants within each organization. The bulk of the research on power and multilevel modeling (e.g., Heck & Thomas, 2009) suggests that maximizing the number of nesting units or groups, even at the expense of fewer individuals per group, may led to a greater chance of obtaining adequate power (see Maas & Hox, 2005, for more information on power and multilevel modeling).

Centering

Another important consideration when conducting multilevel modeling is how variables are centered within the model. In multilevel modeling, the researcher must decide whether to center predictor variables around their group mean, the mean of the sample as a whole (i.e., grand mean), or leave them in their raw metric. These decisions critically impact how a researcher should interpret his or her findings (see Enders & Tofighi, 2007, for an overview of this issue).

Model Building

Lastly, although MSEM is a powerful tool for community-based research, multilevel statistical models can quickly become large and computationally demanding. This is particularly true when researchers incorporate multiple factors, noncontinuous indicators and outcomes, or any other advanced analytical functions. It is wise to start with very simple models and slowly build up to more complete, ecological models. If not, researchers may have difficulties getting their models to converge and/or find their modeling programs running for hours (or days) on end (see Preacher, Zyphur, & Zhang, 2010, for more information on model-building techniques using MSEM).

CASE STUDY

The goals of the community-based study presented here were to (a) provide insight into the development of latent factors associated with collaborative vitality at the individual and group levels and (b) report on associations between manifest predictors at the individual and group levels. This case study is based on data obtained by the Georgia Family Connection Partnership (GaFCP). GaFCP is a public/private nonprofit that supports the Family Connection network of collaboratives that are focused on improving child and family well-being across the state of Georgia. Since 2002, these collaboratives have been operating in each of the state's counties. (One collaborative serves three counties.) Additional background on GaFCP can be found on their Web site (http://www.

gafcp.org/) and in previously published papers (Barile, Darnell et al., 2012; Darnell et al., 2013; Emshoff et al., 2007; Harper, Kuperminc, Weaver, Emshoff, & Erickson, 2014).

Members of 152 collaboratives completed a collaborative vitality survey. The survey included questions that assessed five a priori subscales: community (five items), communication (four items), participation (three items), productivity (four items), accountability (three items), and synergy (five items). Survey items queried whether, on a scale from 1 to 7, the member *strongly disagreed* (1) to *strongly agreed* (7) with 24 statements about his or her collaborative. Survey items included statements such as "There is a lack of communication among collaborative members" [communication], and "Collaborative members have a sense of pride in our collaborative's accomplishments" [community]. The survey also inventoried what survey respondents' position in the collaborative was (general member, board member, or staff), how many years they had been involved with the collaborative, and how many meetings (general, committee, and board) they had attended in the past year.

In order to determine whether multilevel modeling methods were appropriate, the ICC for each of the survey items was calculated. Based on 2,521 surveys (average of 16.59 surveys per collaborative), the ICCs for the items ranged from .08 (Item 4) to .24 (Item 6). This indicates that Item 4 (Conflict is freely expressed when it is felt in our collaborative) had the least amount of variability at the collaborative level and Item 6 (Family members are involved in our collaborative) had the most variability at the collaborative level.

To determine the best-fitting factor structure at both the individual and the collaborative level, four different multilevel confirmatory factor structures were estimated and evaluated with respect to their fit to the data. These models were used to determine how many factors the 24 items represented and whether the factor structure of the latent variables was similar at the individual and collaborative levels. Manifest individual- and collaborative-level predictors were included to determine whether there were any associations between collaborative vitality and (a) members' position in the collaborative (general member, board member, or staff); (b) how long members had been involved in the collaborative; and (c) how many general meetings they had attended in the last year. A graphic depiction of Model 2 appears in Figure 16.1.

Model fit indices and overall parsimony were considered to determine whether the six dimensions of collaborative vitality under study were differentially associated with one another, and whether they could be organized under a higher order factor of collaborative vitality. Model 1 specified a single global collaborative vitality factor underlying all 24 survey indicators at both the individual and collaborative levels. Model 2 specified the six a priori factors at both levels of analysis. Model 3 was constructed with restrictions on the latent factor covariances of Model 2 at both levels to test whether the six first-order factors were specified as indicators of a second-order global vitality factor. Model 4 included the higher order factor at the collaborative level only. Survey respondents' position in the collaborative, how many years they had been involved with the collaborative, and how many meetings they had attended in the past year were included as covariates at the individual level, and an aggregate of the number of meetings attended by respondents and the proportion of respondents that identified as a board member and staff were included as covariates at the collaborative level for all models.

Findings from the four models found that all fit the data well based on Hu and Bentler's (1999) criteria. Model 2, which included the six subscales at each level, fit the data best, χ^2 (690) = 1,546.47, $p < .001$, CFI = .98, RMSEA = .03 and Model 4, which included a second-order vitality factor at the collaborative level but not at the individual level, was the next best-fitting model and had the advantage of being more parsimonious, χ^2 (699) = 1,558.97, $p < .001$, CFI = .98, RMSEA = .03. Taken together, the four models suggest that there are likely multiple, semi-independent subscales that may also serve as indicators of a second-order collaborative vitality factor. In particular, these findings suggest that the six subscales form a cohesive second-order vitality factor at the collaborative level but not at the individual level.

Table 16.1 presents the associations between the predictors and the latent factors at both levels. At the individual level, the results do not indicate that staff or board members differ from general members in their responses on any of the six subscales. However, higher scores on a number of subscales were reported by members who were more

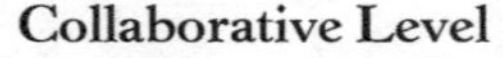

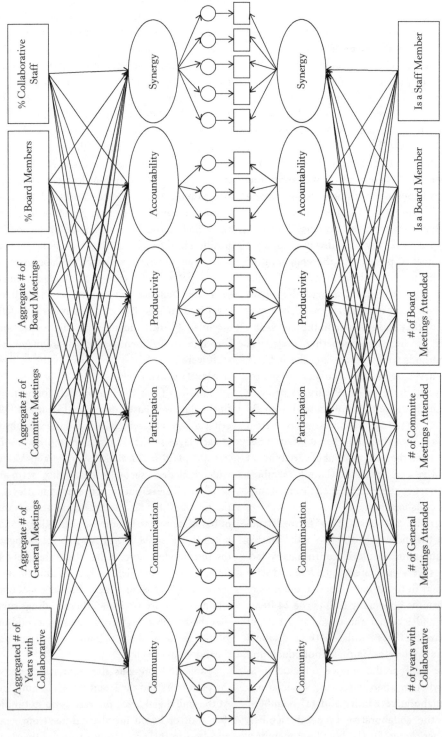

FIGURE 16.1: This represents the six latent factors at the individual and collaborative levels with six covariates at each level (Model 2). Boxes represent items from the collaborative vitality survey. Ovals represent latent variables that are estimated by the observed items.

TABLE 16.1: ASSOCIATIONS BETWEEN INDIVIDUAL AND COLLABORATIVE LEVEL PREDICTORS AND MULTILEVEL LATENT FACTORS

Covariates	Community		Communication		Participation		Productivity		Accountability		Synergy	
	b	*SE*	*b*	*SE*	*b*	*SE*	*b*	*SE*	*b*	*SE*	*b*	*SE*
Individual Level												
No. of years with collaborative	0.01	0.01	0.00	0.01	0.00	0.01	0.01	0.01	0.01	0.01	0.01	0.01
No. of general meetings	0.03**	0.01	0.01	0.01	−0.01	0.01	0.02	0.02	−0.01	0.01	0.00	0.01
No. of community meetings	0.03**	0.01	0.02	0.01	0.01	0.01	0.04*	0.02	0.01	0.01	0.04*	0.01
No. of board meetings	0.00	0.01	0.01	0.01	0.00	0.01	0.02	0.02	0.04*	0.02	0.01	0.01
Staff member 0/1	−0.13	0.12	−0.03	0.13	0.07	0.09	−0.12	0.19	−0.10	0.17	−0.02	0.14
Board member 0/1	0.12	0.08	0.07	0.09	0.07	0.07	0.05	0.15	0.18	0.13	0.08	0.10
Collaborative Level												
Aggregate years with collaborative	0.06*	0.02	0.13**	0.04	0.09**	0.03	0.12*	0.05	0.09*	0.04	0.04	0.03
Aggregate no. of general meetings	0.02	0.02	0.06	0.04	0.03	0.03	0.04	0.05	0.02	0.03	0.03	0.03
Aggregate no. of community meetings	−0.01	0.02	−0.01	0.04	0.02	0.04	0.01	0.05	0.05	0.04	0.03	0.04
Aggregate no. of board meetings	−0.01	0.03	0.03	0.06	0.02	0.05	0.04	0.07	−0.02	0.05	0.06	0.05
% Staff member	0.72*	0.37	1.08	0.62	0.97*	0.57	1.70*	0.85	1.04	0.56	1.47*	0.58
% Board member	−0.37	0.27	−0.89*	0.43	−0.74*	0.40	−1.21*	0.53	−0.52	0.40	−0.62	0.33

engaged in the collaborative through attending general meetings (community), committee meetings (community, productivity, synergy), and board meetings (accountability). At the collaborative level, the higher the average number of years members had been with the collaborative, the greater their scores on the community, communication, participation, productivity, and accountability subscales. This suggests that if collaboratives are able to keep the same members engaged over time, they will likely have greater collaborative vitality.

Additionally, the results suggest that the percentage of staff members responding (compared to general members and board members) was positively associated with higher scores on community, participation, productivity, and synergy. This is particularly interesting because at the individual level no differences between staff and general members were observed. It is possible that having a higher proportion of staff responding to the survey is indicative of collaboratives with greater funding (and subsequently more staff). This finding would support previous research on GaFCP that found positive associations between improved collaborative functioning (through systems change) and leveraged dollars. Finally, and interestingly, collaboratives with a higher percentage of board members reported lower scores on communication, participation, and productivity. This may suggest that collaboratives that are represented by fewer members (resulting in a higher percentage of board members reporting) are less able to develop strong indicators of collaborative vitality.

This example provides an illustration of how MSEM can be used with a simple community-based survey. In this example, multiple-factor structures were tested and compared. This process provides some indication of whether the factor structure at the collaborative level is similar to that on the individual level, providing some evidence of whether the survey items represent composition or fuzzy-composition factors. This example also tested associations with formative individual-level factors (number of meetings attended, years with the collaborative, role in the collaborative) and collaborative compilation variables (e.g., percent of staff members responding). This model could be expanded to include other county-level predictors of vitality (e.g., census data, measures of social capital), as well as other desired outcomes (e.g., child and family well-being). Additional invariance testing could also be undertaken to determine whether the factors identified on each level are consistent across all respondents and collaboratives.

CONCLUSION

MSEM techniques enable community-based researchers to disentangle individual and context-dependent variables using a robust methodology resistant to measurement and sampling error in ways that single-level regression, multilevel regression, and SEM do not. Furthermore, MSEM helps researchers avoid committing fallacies that can lead to inappropriate interventions and policies. MSEM techniques allow the researcher to incorporate individual- and group-level survey data, as well as archival data (e.g., census data), within the same model without having to choose whether to aggregate or not to aggregate. As such, MSEM is a flexible technique that allows the researcher to incorporate multiple predictors, mediators, moderators, and outcomes within a single model and can work in combination with other advanced techniques (e.g., latent class growth modeling). Community-based researchers interested in understanding the diverse web of ecological determinants of individual and community well-being should seriously consider this powerful tool when faced with nested data.

REFERENCES

Anderson, J. C., & Gerbing, D. W. (1988). Structural equation modeling in practice: A review and recommended two-step approach. *Psychological Bulletin, 103*, 411–423.

Barile, J. P. (2010). *Health disparities in a diverse county: Investigating interactions between residents and neighborhoods*. Unpublished doctoral dissertation, Georgia State University, Atlanta.

Barile, J. P., Darnell, A. J., Erickson, S. W., & Weaver, S. R. (2012). Multilevel measurement of dimensions of collaborative functioning in a network of collaboratives that promote child and family well-being. *American Journal of Community Psychology, 49*, 270–282.

Barile, J. P., Donohue, D. K., Anthony, E. R., Baker, A. M., Weaver, S. R., & Henrich, C. C. (2012). Teacher-student relationship climate and school outcomes: Implications for educational policy initiatives. *Journal of Youth and Adolescence, 41*, 256–267.

Brondino, M., Pasini, M., & da Silva, S. C. A. (2013). Development and validation of an Integrated Organizational Safety Climate Questionnaire with multilevel confirmatory factor analysis. *Quality and Quantity, 47*, 2191–2223.

Brown, E. C., Hawkins, J. D., Arthur, M. W., Abbott, R. D., & Van Horn, M. L. (2008). Multilevel analysis of a measure of community prevention collaboration. *American Journal of Community Psychology, 41,* 115–126.

Browne, M. W., MacCallum, R. C., Kim, C. T., Andersen, B. L., & Glaser, R. (2002). When fit indices and residuals are incompatible. *Psychological Methods, 7,* 403–421.

Darnell, A. J., Barile, J. P., Weaver, S. R., Harper, C. R., Kuperminc, G. P., & Emshoff, J. G. (2013). Testing effects of community collaboration on rates of low infant birthweight at the county level. *American Journal of Community Psychology, 51,* 398–406.

Diez-Roux, A. V. (1998). Bringing context back into epidemiology: Variables and fallacies in multilevel analysis. *American Journal of Public Health, 88,* 216–222.

Dyer, N., Hanges, P., & Hall, R. (2005). Applying multilevel confirmatory factor analysis techniques to the study of leadership. *Leadership Quarterly, 16,* 149–167.

Emshoff, J. G., Darnell, A. J., Darnell, D. A., Erickson, S. W., Schneider, S., & Hudgins, R. (2007). Systems change as an outcome and a process in the work of community collaboratives for health. *American Journal of Community Psychology, 39,* 255–267.

Enders, C. K., & Tofighi, D. (2007). Centering predictor variables in cross-sectional multilevel models: A new look at an old issue. *Psychological Methods, 12,* 121–138.

Gibbons, L. M. (2008). Nature+ nurture> 100%: Genetic and environmental influences on child obesity. *American Journal of Clinical Nutrition, 87,* 1968–1968.

Graham, J. W. (2009). Missing data analysis: Making it work in the real world. *Annual Review of Psychology, 60,* 549–576.

Gregorich, S. E. (2006). Do self-report instruments allow meaningful comparisons across diverse population groups? Testing measurement invariance using the confirmatory factor analysis framework. *Medical Care, 44,* S78–94.

Harper, C. R., Kuperminc, G. P., Weaver, S. R., Emshoff, J., & Erickson, S. (2014). Leveraged resources and systems changes in community collaboration. *American Journal of Community Psychology, 54,* 348–357.

Heck, R. H., & Thomas, S. L. (2009). *An introduction to multilevel modeling techniques* (2nd ed.). New York, NY: Routledge.

Hu, L., & Bentler, P. M. (1999). Cutoff criteria for fit indexes in covariance structure analysis: Conventional criteria versus new alternatives. *Structural Equation Modeling, 6,* 1–55.

Jak, S., Oort, F. J., & Dolan, C. V. (2014). Measurement bias in multilevel data. *Structural Equation Modeling, 21,* 31–39.

Jason, L. A., & Glenwick, D. S. (Eds.). (2012). *Methodological approaches to community-based research.* Washington, DC: American Psychological Association.

Kenny, D. A., & Judd, C. M. (1986). Consequences of violating the independence assumption in analysis of variance. *Psychological Bulletin, 99,* 422–431.

Lewin, K. (1935). *A dynamic theory of personality.* New York, NY: McGraw-Hill.

Luke, D. A. (2005). Getting the big picture in community science: Methods that capture context. *American Journal of Community Psychology, 35,* 185–200.

Maas, C. J., & Hox, J. J. (2005). Sufficient sample sizes for multilevel modeling. *Methodology: European Journal of Research Methods for the Behavioral and Social Sciences, 1,* 86–92.

Macintyre, S., Ellaway, A., & Cummins, S. (2002). Place effects on health: How can we conceptualise, operationalise and measure them? *Social Science Medicine, 55,* 125–139.

Marsh, H. W., Lüdtke, O., Nagengast, B., Trautwein, U., Morin, A. J. S., Abduljabbar, A. S., & Köller, O. (2012). Classroom climate and contextual effects: Conceptual and methodological issues in the evaluation of group-level effects. *Educational Psychologist, 47,* 106–124.

Marsh, H. W., Lüdtke, O., Robitzsch, A., Trautwein, U., Asparouhov, T., Muthén, B., & Nagengast, B. (2009). Doubly-latent models of school contextual effects: Integrating multilevel and structural equation approaches to control measurement and aampling error. *Multivariate Behavioral Research, 44,* 764–802.

Mehta, P., & Neale, M. (2005). People are variables too: Multilevel structural equations modeling. *Psychological Methods, 10,* 259–284.

Nowell, B. (2009). Profiling capacity for coordination and systems change: The relative contribution of stakeholder relationships in interorganizational collaboratives. *American Journal of Community Psychology, 44,* 196–212.

Preacher, K. J., Zyphur, M. J., & Zhang, Z. (2010). A general multilevel SEM framework for assessing multilevel mediation. *Psychological Methods, 15,* 209–233.

Roosa, M. W., Weaver, S. R., White, R. M., Tein, J. Y., Knight, G. P., Gonzales, N., & Saenz, D. (2009). Family and neighborhood fit or misfit and the adaptation of Mexican Americans. *American Journal of Community Psychology, 44,* 15–27.

Russo, S., Roccato, M., & Vieno, A. (2011). Predicting perceived risk of crime: A multilevel study. *American Journal of Community Psychology, 48,* 384–394.

Shinn, M., & Rapkin, B. D. (2000). Cross-level research without cross-ups in community psychology. In J. Rappaport & E. Seidman (Eds.), *Handbook of community psychology* (pp. 669–693). New York, NY: Kluwer Academic.

Vernon, T., & Eysenck, S. (2007). Structural equation modeling [Special issue]. *Personality and Individual Differences, 42*, 811–898.

Vieno, A., Perkins, D. D., Smith, T. M., & Santinello, M. (2005). Democratic school climate and sense of community in school: a multilevel analysis. *American Journal of Community Psychology, 36*, 327–341.

Williams, D. (1999). Race, socioeconomic status, and health the added effects of racism and discrimination. *Annals of the New York Academy of Sciences, 896*, 173–188.

17

Cluster-Randomized Trials

NATHAN R. TODD AND PATRICK J. FOWLER

Community-based researchers often are interested in implementing and evaluating interventions at the level of the community. Whether a community-wide intervention to decrease youth violence (e.g., Hawkins et al., 2012) or a classroom-based universal prevention program to promote behavioral regulation (e.g., Kellam et al., 2014), community interventions frequently are conceptualized, designed, and implemented for entire groups. Testing the effectiveness of the intervention and the mechanisms responsible for change is of paramount importance not only to community-based researchers but also to funders, policymakers, and others interested in how best to promote health and wellness. In this chapter we present (a) cluster-randomized trials (CRTs) as one useful research design for evaluating community-level interventions and (b) multilevel modeling as an efficient way to analyze the results of such trials. We present a general introduction to CRTs with a focus on design basics and strategies to increase power and precision. We then connect these designs to the appropriate multilevel model for analysis. Finally, a case study showcases the process of CRT design and analysis, as well as the benefit of using CRTs to understand whether and how community-based interventions achieve their goals.

DESIGN AND ANALYSIS OF CLUSTER- RANDOMIZED TRIALS

Overview of Cluster-Randomized Trials

Cluster-randomized trials (CRTs), also known as group-randomized trials, community trials, or cluster-randomized studies, are characterized by randomly assigning intact social groups (e.g., schools, neighborhoods, entire cities) to intervention and control conditions (Murray, 1998). The group, or "cluster," is the unit of randomization. For example, 20 schools may be randomly assigned to an intervention or control condition where all students in the same school receive the intervention (or not). CRTs enable researchers to study naturally occurring groups where the randomization of individuals is not possible due to ethical, logistical, political, or other reasons (Cook, 2005). For example, spillover (i.e., contamination) may be more of a concern if people within the same setting are randomly assigned to different interventions; however, randomizing groups minimizes spillover (because everyone in the same group receives the same intervention) and may be a more palatable option to communities.

Moreover, the purpose of community-based interventions often is to change something about the social environment, norms, community practices, or setting as the mechanism to shape individual behavior (Cook, 2005; Raudenbush, Martinez, & Spybrook, 2007). CRTs randomize at the same level of intervention deployment and offer a more ecologically valid approach to examining group-based interventions, such as randomizing entire classrooms to receive an intervention rather than dividing students within classrooms (Raudenbush, 1997). Also, the inclusion of randomization strengthens internal validity and begins to address bias of individuals self-selecting into preexisting groups, as well as other threats to internal validity (Cook, 2005; Murray, 1998). Clearly, there are many benefits to CRTs.

Although there are many benefits to CRTs, they also can be more costly and complex in scope, design, and analysis than other types of randomized experiments (Cook, 2005). CRTs require data collection on units within settings. Thus, considerations must account for reliable measurement, as well as adequate numbers of both individuals and settings to provide a feasible test of the intervention. In addition to data collection, necessary resources must be committed to monitor implementation of the intervention in order to assess threats to the validity of the design (e.g., uptake, compliance, contamination, attrition). For example, many CRTs have at least 20 unique groups to provide an adequate test of intervention effects, with substantial cost in implementing and monitoring the intervention in such a large number of groups. Also, because individuals are nested within groups, analytic methods that account for this clustering need to be used (Murray, 1998; Raudenbush, 1997). Importantly, ethical considerations, especially informed consent, become more challenging given that individuals may not be able to fully agree or avoid exposure to a setting-level intervention decided upon by representatives from the larger group (Sim & Dawson, 2012). The complexities require active collaboration with community gatekeepers and an engaged institutional review board to help ensure ethical practices.

The challenges of CRTs must be weighed with their potential benefits, addressing important research questions concerned with group-level processes. This chapter reviews a number of advances in theory and application that mitigate some of these complications, especially pertaining to the number of settings required to power the study and other adaptive design issues that make CRTs more feasible in terms of implementation and budget. We start with a presentation of CRT design basics. Although not exhaustive, these designs show possibilities and illustrate initial decisions that must be made by community-based researchers.

Design of Cluster-Randomized Trials

Cluster-Randomized Trial

Design Basics

Plans for implementation of a CRT begin with a clear articulation of the research questions. Deliberation must determine whether a CRT represents the most useful and practical design to address questions. Considerations must account for ethical practice, time, available resources, and threats to internal and external validity (Murray, 1998; Shadish, Cook, & Campbell, 2002). Although designs may include more than two conditions (e.g., factorial CRTs with a control group and multiple intervention conditions; e.g., Peters et al., 2003), we focus on a traditional intervention and control group design and use Murray's (1998) terminology to describe the different components.

An initial decision involves whether the design will include assessment only at the completion or endpoint of the trial (i.e., posttest-only control group design), will also collect pretest data (pretest-posttest control group design), or will include more than two assessment points. As with all experimental research designs (Shadish et al., 2002), the main weakness of the posttest-only design is the lack of information regarding selection bias and maturation (Murray, 1998). However, Murray noted that randomization of enough groups to conditions may begin to mitigate these concerns. The pretest design includes baseline or pretest data collection that allows conditions to be compared prior to the intervention and may also decrease other threats to internal validity. Importantly, baseline information also can be used to match groups prior to random assignment or as covariates in later analyses to increase power. As described later, availability of pretest assessment provides a number of benefits to testing intervention effects; however, time and resource limitations may influence feasibility. These tradeoffs should be carefully considered when planning a CRT.

Another early design decision pertains to sampling. Researchers must determine whether to collect data in a cross-sectional versus cohort design. As discussed by Murray (1998), a cohort design collects data on the same group of individuals followed over time and sampled at each measurement occasion, yielding longitudinal data. In a cross-sectional design, the group is sampled but different group members are assessed at each measurement occasion. For example, in a city-wide intervention to decrease smoking, at baseline a group may be randomly sampled from the city, whereas at the conclusion of the intervention a new group, not including any of the original members, would be sampled. The distinction between the cohort and cross-sectional designs is important, as it reflects different research questions. In a cross-sectional design the question is about change within the population, whereas a cohort design focuses on average individual change, requiring repeated observations of the same set (i.e., cohort) of individuals. Additionally, the cohort or cross-sectional nature of the design necessitates slightly different analytic models that influence the ability to detect program effects, as described later. Interested readers should consult Murray (1998) for other considerations when selecting a design and should be guided by the primary research question of interest.

Power

Power refers to the ability to detect an effect if the effect actually exists. It depends on such aspects of the design as size of the effect, number of participants, and level of statistical significance. However, there are more factors that influence power in CRTs compared with designs at the individual level (Murray, 1998). Power in CRTs also depends on the number of clusters and the variance between clusters on the outcome variables (Raudenbush et al., 2007). It should be no surprise that the additional considerations for power are directly connected to the nested nature of the CRT design, as nesting often creates correlated, dependent observations. Raudenbush (1997) noted that dependence may occur within a group for multiple reasons, such as people self-selecting into a group based on similar characteristics or having common experiences or mutual interactions once they are in the group. The intraclass correlation (ICC) is used as an index of the degree of dependence in a group or the proportion of variance that is between groups (Raudenbush, 1997). Dependence violates the independence assumption of ordinary least squares regression and tends to produce downward biased standard errors, which, in turn, results in a more liberal test of significance (Murray, 1998). Failure to account for this dependence increases the risk of committing a Type I error. However, appropriate methods of analysis (i.e., multilevel mixed models) account for this between-group variability and produce accurate estimates of the standard error of the treatment effect.

Holding other factors constant, CRTs tend to have less power than traditional individual-level randomized trials because the variance of the condition mean will systematically be higher in nested designs (Moerbeek & Terenstra, 2011; Murray, 1998). In fact, the stronger the dependence (i.e., the larger the ICC), the greater the variance of the condition mean. Scholars call this the design effect, or variance inflation factor, quantified as $(1+(n_1-1)ICC)$, where n_1 is the sample size per group (Moerbeek & Teerenstra, 2011; Murray, 1998). The intuitive implication is that increased dependence, as indexed by the ICC, increases the variance of the condition mean, which, in turn, decreases power. Thus, one strategy for increasing power is to lower the ICC (Murray & Blitstein, 2003). One way to do this is to select an outcome that tends to exhibit less variability between groups (Murray, 1998). Another is to include statistical controls that lower the ICC. Indeed, as noted by Cook (2005), it is the conditional ICC (i.e., the ICC conditioned on all variables in the model) that contributes to the design effect; thus, reducing the ICC through covariates may increase power. Both matching and covariates are ways to statistically reduce the ICC and noise in the study as well as to increase precision.

The general idea behind both matching and covariates is to include other variables in the model that are strongly related to the outcome of interest in order to reduce the unexplained variance, to decrease noise, and to decrease the ICC, all of which may increase power (Raudenbush, 1997; Raudenbush et al., 2007). Similar to other experimental designs (Shadish et al., 2002), matching involves selecting a variable that is correlated with the outcome of interest, ranking each group based on this variable, and then randomly assigning pairs of similar groups to the treatment or control condition. Raudenbush et al. (2007) showed that such matching may increase power when between-group variation is large and the variable is strongly related to the outcome. Matching in effect cuts down on the random noise among groups between conditions. Groups also may be matched on other characteristics to improve the face validity of comparing treatment and control conditions, such as balancing groups based on race/ethnicity or other demographic variables (Raudenbush et al., 2007). The drawback to matching is that this information also needs to be included in the analysis, which begins to cost degrees of freedom, which, in turn, decreases power (see Murray, 1998, for how to include matching as a random effect in the analytic model). Clearly, a balance exists between increasing power through matching with potential loss of power by losing degrees of freedom.

Similar to matching, covariates are collected before the intervention and should be strongly related to the outcome of interest. Covariates can be at the level of the cluster or individual, and an emerging literature (e.g., Konstantopoulos,

2012) examines the benefit of including covariates at different levels of analysis. For example, a study of school-based intervention could include individual student characteristics (e.g., pretest scores) and aspects of the school, such as size, teacher-student ratio, or socioeconomic status. Interestingly, a covariate will be more effective at increasing power the more the covariate helps to explain between-group differences, thus decreasing the ICC. Thus, carefully chosen covariates can dramatically increase power or alternatively decrease the number of groups needed to achieve desired power.

Inclusion of covariates requires additional assumptions. For instance, variables must demonstrate similar associations in treatment and control conditions, and residuals must be normally distributed with constant variance (Raudenbush, 1997). Also, there is a tradeoff involved including covariates, as this also lowers the degrees of freedom in the model; usually, though, the benefit to power is in favor of including the covariate. In general, the use of covariates tends to increase power more than the use of matching, although matching may help to increase face validity by balancing groups on certain characteristics (Raudenbush et al., 2007). As noted later, resources exist to calculate the exact benefit of including covariates to increase power.

In the planning stages of a CRT, estimates of key factors (e.g., ICC, potential variance explained by covariates) are needed to calculate power. Similar to other designs, researchers also must specify an effect size; they need to forecast how much the treatment groups will differ on outcomes as a result of the intervention. Such an effect may be based on previous research or on what constitutes practical differences. Also, scholars have compiled common ICCs found in educational research (Bloom, Richburg-Hayes, & Black, 2007; Hedges & Hedberg, 2007) and other types of community samples (Murray, Varnell, & Blitstein, 2004) that can inform estimates used to calculate power. Researchers also may be guided by previous research and experience to estimate the potential impact of covariates at both individual and group levels of analysis.

Based on this information, researchers can use free, intuitive programs like Optimal Design to calculate power (Raudenbush et al., 2007). As noted in the Optimal Design Documentation (Spybrook et al., 2011), the user can plot power charts versus the cluster size, the total number of clusters, the ICC, the effect size, and the amount of variance explained by covariates. One approach is to specify the minimum detectable effect size (MDES), or the smallest program effect in standard deviations of the outcome expected to be seen given other design considerations (i.e., number of clusters, conditional ICC, subjects, significance level, power). Optimal Design plots the MDES on the *y*-axis against the same information to provide a visual tool to aid researchers making design decisions. Outcomes can include continuous or binary distributions. This flexible program is a valuable resource for estimating power and gives community-based researchers the necessary resources to calculate power when designing a CRT.

Clearly, power costs resources. In order to maximize power for a given budget, the CRT literature (Moerbeek & Teerenstra, 2011; Raudenbush, 1997) has focused on determining the "optimal design" for a study. For example, there are differential costs and impacts on power for sampling more individuals within a setting versus recruiting an entire new setting. Calculating the optimal design usually focuses on minimizing the variance of the condition effect while considering the costs of modifying various aspects of the design (Raudenbush et al., 1997). Fortunately, the program Optimal Design includes a module to enter the total budget, cost per cluster, cost per cluster member, the significance level, the ICC, and the MDES. The program then calculates the optimal sample size per cluster and number of clusters as well as reports the power for such a design. This information may be a useful starting place to then use other modules in the program to examine the impact of including covariates or adjusting other design parameters. Clearly, resources such as the program Optimal Design provide the necessary tools for community-based researchers to design adequately powered CRTs.

Adaptive Designs

A number of modifications can be incorporated into basic CRT designs to address common questions in community research (Brown et al., 2009). Longitudinal designs that integrate multiple repeated measures allow investigation of change over time associated with group-based intervention. Beyond testing simple differences between groups, researchers can test hypotheses regarding whether treatment effects grow or diminish over time, as well as the shape of change in outcomes (e.g., linear, quadratic, exponential). Repeated measures also enhance the validity of CRTs; modeling within-person variation in outcomes provides more precise and, thus, more powerful estimates of program effects. Having more measurements also may provide information to test threats to internal validity, such as maturation, regression, and instrumentation. Likewise, the design enables the testing of mechanisms that may occur at the group level (e.g., social norms, social processes) to better understand how changing the setting or social ecology shapes individual behavior and attitudes (Fowler & Todd, in press). The increasing availability of administrative records provides an inexpensive way to leverage longitudinal designs.

Flexibility also exists around random assignment in CRTs. Studies may include multiple arms of an intervention, such as when testing dosage effects or multiple new interventions. For example, school-based prevention programs might stack intervention components such that schools within a district are randomized to receive a universal prevention program for all students, and intervention schools are further randomized to receive a selective or targeted intervention for at-risk students or both. Looking at school outcomes, the design simultaneously tests (a) the effects of the universal program versus treatment as usual; (b) the benefit of the universal program plus the selective component; and (c) effects of the combination of universal, selective, and targeted interventions. Interest in broad policy reforms common in community research makes CRT a useful tool; however, these designs require considerable forethought as to the degrees of freedom and number of groups needed to test research questions.

Researchers also may leverage CRT designs to study the rollout of new programs across units within a network of groups (Wyman, Henry, & Brown, 2015). The design works well when communities intend to make policy or program changes across groups but limited resources preclude making changes all at once. For instance, new procedures might require training across large numbers of geographic locations that are logistically impossible to do all at once. Relatedly, communities might be waiting to secure additional funding for new services before fully implementing the new intervention across the organization.

By randomly assigning when groups receive an intervention, researchers create a rigorous test of the short-term benefits of the program; that is, random assignment occurs for both groups and time. Groups waiting to receive the intervention serve as the randomly assigned control group until it is their "turn" to get the intervention, at which time they become part of the treatment group. Outcome data are collected at consistent time points across the entire rollout period, providing repeated measures before and after the intervention time point. By incorporating longitudinal outcomes into the CRT design, statistical power to detect small effects is greatly enhanced and makes the design very feasible with a relatively small number of groups (Brown, Wyman, Guoa, & Penab, 2006). The rollout design often appeals to community-based organizations because everyone receives the intervention and strong information is provided on the program. Importantly, the rollout CRT tests only the immediate effects of the intervention—the control group immediately transitions into the treatment. Thus, researchers must carefully consider the research questions of interest and the nature of the intervention. Delayed or compounding effects of the intervention will not be captured in rollout designs. Other adaptive features exist for CRTs, and interested readers are encouraged to review additional resources on the strengths and limitations of different components (Brown et al., 2009).

Analysis of Cluster-Randomized Trials Using Multilevel Modeling

This section provides an overview of multilevel modeling as an appropriate approach for analyzing data from CRTs, with a focus on connecting basic designs with analytic models. Multilevel models (MLMs; also known as multilevel linear models, mixed- or random-effects models, and hierarchical linear models) are an appropriate analytic strategy for analyzing CRTs because they use information about variance at multiple levels of analysis and produce accurate standard errors (Murray, 1998; Raudenbush, 1997). These models are now more accessible to understand and analyze within many statistical programs (Murray, 1998). Although a full treatment of MLM is beyond this chapter (see Fowler & Todd, in press, and Raudenbush & Bryk, 2002, for additional information), a presentation of the multilevel model illustrates applications to analyzing CRTs.

Multilevel models are unique due to the inclusion of random effects and other variables at both the individual and group levels of analyses. Usually the lowest level is called "Level 1" (such as students), and the cluster they are nested in is the higher level, known as "Level 2" (such as classrooms). Blending the notation of Raudenbush (1997) and Murray (1998), in the simplest posttest-only CRT design, the multilevel model (Model A) may be written as:

$$Y_{ij} = \gamma_0 + \gamma_1 C_j + \boldsymbol{\mu}_j + \boldsymbol{e}_{ij}$$

where the *ith* individual is nested within the *jth* group, γ_0 is the grand mean, γ_1 is the treatment contrast for condition (usually effect coded –.5 and .5), μ_j is the Level-2 error term (also known as the random effect for group), and e_{ij} is the Level-1 error term. Random effects are bolded in the model. This model also assumes that $\mu_j \sim N(0, \tau^2)$ and independent, and $e_{ij} \sim N(0, \sigma^2)$ and independent, where τ^2 is the between-cluster variance and σ^2 is the within-cluster variance (Raudenbush, 1997). The intraclass correlation (ICC) is $\frac{\tau^2}{\tau^2 + \sigma^2}$. What is important to note from this model are the separate random effects at Level 1 (i.e., e_{ij}) and Level 2 (i.e., μ_j) and that the ICC will increase the more variability there is between relative to within clusters. Also, the effect (i.e., γ_j) for C_j is of primary interest in determining the effect of the intervention.

As noted by Murray (1998), for a posttest-only design either a cross-sectional or cohort sample would be analyzed with this same Model A because data are collected only at the conclusion of the trial. The only difference is that in the cohort sample the only people included in the survey sample would be those who were present at the start of the intervention. In either case, covariates assessed at the beginning of the intervention (or that would not change due to the intervention, such as gender) also could be added to the model to increase precision and power.

If the design collected both pretest and posttest measures, for a nested cross-sectional design the model (Model B) would be as follows (Murray 1998):

$$Y_{ijk} = \gamma_0 + \gamma_1 C_j + \gamma_2 T_k + \gamma_3 CT_{jk} + \boldsymbol{\mu}_j + \boldsymbol{T\mu}_{jk} + \boldsymbol{e}_{ijk}$$

where T_k indicates if the person was in the first or second wave of data collection and CT_{jk} indicates the interaction between wave and condition. $T\mu_{jk}$ is the random effect for the interaction. In this design, the primary interest is in the CT_{jk} interaction as a way to determine the effectiveness of the intervention, with follow-up tests focusing on decomposing the interaction to understand how mean values on the outcome are similar or different for the control and intervention condition across time points. One would hope for differences in means from Time 1 to Time 2 for the intervention but not control condition, with similar means between conditions at Time 1. Covariates also could be added to this model to increase power.

A cohort design with pretest and posttest data would be analyzed with a very similar model to Model B, but individuals in this sample would be assessed at both time points and the model would add additional random effects for the person (see Murray, 1998). The addition of these random effects, and the ability of individuals to serve as their own control across time, serves to further increase power. Covariates also could be added to this model to increase power. Alternatively, as a special case, in a pretest-posttest cohort design, the outcome measured at Time 1 (e.g., reading score at Time 1) can serve as a covariate in the model predicting the outcome at Time 2 (e.g., Time 2 reading score). Thus, time is incorporated into the model (Model C) in a different way by including this covariate, such as:

$$(Time2Y)_{ij} = \gamma_0 + \gamma_1 C_j + \gamma_2 (Time1Y)_{ij} + \boldsymbol{\mu}_j + \boldsymbol{e}_{ij}$$

Model C is exactly the same as Model A, but information for Time 1 is introduced as a covariate in the model, while other covariates also could be added. The larger point is that the CRT design (posttest only, pretest-posttest, cross-sectional, or cohort) has direct implications for how to specify the analytic model. Power is likely increased when repeated observations and person- and group-level covariates are included. Covariates, such as Time 1 scores, may be especially potent in increasing power (Cook, 2005). Readers interested in further elaboration of these models, how to incorporate matching in the design and analysis, and SAS syntax for implementing such models are directed to Murray (1998).

A final advantage of multilevel modeling is the ability to generalize to other types of outcomes beyond continuous variables. Multilevel models fall under the broad umbrella of the generalized linear mixed model, which allows for outcomes that are discrete, binary, count, rates, and continuous. Scholars have discussed how MLM can incorporate such outcomes in general (Raudenbush & Bryk, 2002) and in particular for CRTs (Eldridge & Kerry, 2012; Murray, 1998; Murray et al., 2004). Such resources should be consulted to determine how power may be impacted by the type of outcome when planning a CRT.

Summary of General Steps in Designing a Cluster-Randomized Trial

As is clear from this description, careful planning of a CRT can help community-based researchers achieve adequate power while minimizing cost. However, there are many steps to consider beyond power, cost, and analysis (Murray, 1998). Among the most crucial are to clearly articulate the guiding research question, the theory underlying the intervention, and the mechanisms that are proposed to result in change (Cook, 2005). Such clarity informs whether the focus is on population change or individual change, which may help guide the researcher in selecting a cross-sectional or cohort design. In particular, clarity is needed in specifying theory and mechanism at multiple levels of analysis with respect to how processes may operate differently at individual versus group levels. If the social ecology or setting is the intervention target, the mechanisms of change expected to result in the desired outcomes should clearly be explicated. Statistical analysis cannot redeem an intervention that does not have a clear theoretical focus that produces testable hypotheses.

Given the high cost of a CRT, scholars also recommend conducting a pilot study to provide a general proof of principle that the intervention tends to work in the way that it is proposed (Murray, 1998). Such a pilot study may be conducted with only a few groups but also will provide an opportunity to refine the intervention and to anticipate further challenges with implementation. Even small effects in a pilot study may warrant a larger trial. Although beyond the scope of this chapter, plans also should be made to monitor the implementation of the intervention and to collect ongoing process data (Cook, 2005; Murray, 1998). Especially in the case of null findings, such information may be incorporated into the analysis (such as dose effects) or may further serve to contextualize why effects were present or not. A pilot study provides the opportunity to work out these details before investing in a larger CRT.

Early in this process a power analysis should be conducted to ensure that enough resources are available for an adequately powered CRT. As discussed earlier, estimates of the ICC from previous research can be used, along with thoughtful selection of variables for matching or covariates. As a part of this process, the optimal design should be calculated to ensure that there are enough resources to sample an adequate number of individuals and clusters. Also, before launching the CRT, the analytic method should be selected to ensure that all appropriate information is gathered during the CRT for use in analysis. Likely this will all be an iterative process (selection of design, power analysis, pilot study, determination of feasibility) in the planning of an adequately powered CRT.

Applications of Cluster-Randomized Trials

CRTs are increasingly being used in community-based research to test important questions regarding the influence of setting characteristics. In particular, prevention and intervention trials have examined the effects of programs, as well as strategies for implementing evidence-based practices to scale (i.e., with a larger number of settings or communities). Classroom-based interventions targeting low-income students demonstrate long-term effects on healthy child development (Kellam et al., 2014). Universal prevention programs that build coalitions to support the use of evidence-based practices show decreases in youth substance abuse and delinquency into high school (Hawkins et al., 2012). Moreover, studies compare implementation strategies to promote the use of evidence-based practices, including delivering parent training for youth in foster care across child welfare agencies in multiple states (Chamberlain et al., 2013) and addressing culture within community mental health agencies (Glisson, Hemmelgarn, Green, & Williams, 2013). The studies randomize intact groups—including classrooms, schools, counties, and states—in order to investigate theories of setting-level processes. To demonstrate the use and flexibility of CRT designs, we next examine a set of studies targeting adolescent suicide prevention.

CASE STUDY

Background

Adolescent suicide represents a key concern of communities in both the United States and internationally. Suicide represents the third leading cause of death among children and adolescents, with 9% completing suicide each year—a trend that has increased during recent decades (Brown, Wyman, Brinales, & Gibbons, 2007). Communities, and especially school leaders, seek information on practices that promote protective factors and reduce the risk of youth suicide. Evidence suggests the importance of active surveillance for warning signs, as well as immediate action to connect at-risk youth with appropriate mental health resources. Although schools engage with students and their social networks, teachers and staff struggle to provide systematic monitoring, and mental health resources often fail to meet demands. School-based efforts too often provide services haphazardly or revert to traditional one-on-one counseling models that inherently cannot generate reductions in suicide rates.

Challenges also exist in implementing and evaluating evidence-based programs. Individual-level random assignment is not a feasible option; effective surveillance requires participation by school staff interacting across student groups, and students interact within peer networks that extend beyond classrooms. Statistically, suicide represents a relatively rare event that requires considerable power to detect the true effects of prevention efforts; this means large samples followed over time. Brown et al. (2007) have quantified the scope of the challenge by calculating the number of person years (i.e., number of people in a study multiplied by the number of years the people are followed) needed to detect a 50% reduction in the incidence of youth suicide through a universal prevention program; 1 million person years would be needed to detect a 50% drop in the rate of adolescent suicide through a universal prevention program!

Methodology

To address these challenges, a coalition of researchers, school officials, program developers, and other community partners was formed to design a series of adaptive CRTs that would maximize statistical power and provide an adequate test of evidence-based prevention implementation within schools (Brown et al., 2007). An initial study tested a gatekeeper training model used within schools that educated school staff on (a) recognizing suicide warning signs and (b) communicating with students at risk (Wyman et al., 2008). All teachers and staff received 30-minute group trainings and a brief refresher. A pretest-posttest CRT design asked whether school staff increased their awareness of suicide risk indicators and if they were more likely to act on warning signs. To further test program theory, it was hypothesized that follow-up communications would occur more frequently among the staff who interacted with students around emotionally laden topics before the intervention. This tested whether education was enough to motivate behavior or if additional channels were needed to facilitate communication.

All secondary schools in a Georgia school district ($N = 35$) were stratified by middle versus high school, and by the number of crisis referrals made by schools in the previous academic year. Matched schools were randomized to gatekeeper training or a waitlisted control group. To assess staff awareness and communication, a random sample of staff in different roles (e.g., teacher, nurse) from each school were invited to complete surveys at baseline and 1 year later ($N = 249$). Because the same group was sampled at both time points, this was a cohort sample. Students ($N = 2{,}059$) also completed anonymous online assessments of suicidal ideation, help-seeking attitudes, and risk behaviors in order to further evaluate the effects of gatekeeper training. Balance of school and teacher characteristics existed across treatment conditions.

Results

Because the outcomes of interest focused on staff learning, and not on the relatively rare event of suicide, 1 million person years were not needed for this phase of the study. Analyses suggested adequate power to detect the anticipated moderate program effects (Cohen's $d = .60$) at a 95% significance level given a modest ICC (ICC = .06) among outcome variables within schools. Multilevel models regressed outcomes on treatment condition, baseline measures as covariates to increase power, school means for outcome variables, and treatment × baseline interactions, while also including school as a random effect. Intent-to-treat analyses suggested gatekeeper training improved awareness of risk behaviors among all types of school staff 1 year later, with staff who had reported lower baseline awareness showing the largest improvements. Overall rates of communication with distressed students increased, but the effects were driven by a small subset (14%) of school staff who regularly interacted with at-risk students. In addition, students who reported a history of suicidal behavior were less likely than other students to talk with adults about their distress. The findings supported the use of surveillance and identified primary mechanisms for prevention efforts to achieve reductions in suicide incidence.

Follow-Up

This initially successful CRT spurred follow-up studies that investigated modifications to the gatekeeper model based on initial findings, as well as tested short-term effects on adolescent suicide behaviors (Wyman et al., 2010). An adapted gatekeeper model leveraged adolescent leaders within high schools to deliver key prevention messages across peer networks. School staff nominated adolescent peer leaders, who received 4 hours of training on protective factors and on engaging with trusted adults. Schools also broadly disseminated messages of identifying and talking to a trusted adult through presentations, videos, and texts. Key research questions asked whether short-term changes occurred among peer leader attitudes and behaviors and in school norms around suicide protective factors.

In particular, one follow-up study used a CRT design to balance the needs of researchers and school officials. School officials wanted to implement prevention programming based on positive outcomes of the initial CRT and other piloting being done, while researchers wanted a rigorous test of implementation and outcomes of the program. Through a collaborative process, the team designed a multisite CRT that randomized schools to either the intervention or a 5-month waitlist. In particular, 18 high schools in three states (Georgia, New York, and North Dakota) were matched by state, region, and number of students; schools were randomized to treatment conditions on a one-to-one ratio within each state. Pretest-posttest assessments occurred with 453 peer leaders—half of whom received training during the intervention period—as well as other students at each school (N = 2,675). The MDES indicated an ability to detect the expected moderate effects on attitude changes among peers and across schools. Multilevel models included Level-1 covariates (gender, grade, ethnicity, baseline outcomes) and Level-2 fixed effects of intervention condition and school. The results of the CRT showed significant improvements in both peer and school-wide norms concerning suicide and engaging with adults.

The next phase of research required more innovative methodologies. Based on the accumulation of positive findings of fidelity and norm changes, school officials wanted to apply the intervention across all schools; however, program effects on the specific behaviors that reduce suicide rates had yet to be tested. To test impact on behaviors, more power would be needed than for the prior trials that focused on more easily detected attitude changes. This meant programming would need to be implemented across many more schools, with data collection occurring across hundreds of thousands of students. Given the unfeasibility of such a design, the team decided to focus on a more proximal outcome that would be easier to detect. The theory of change hypothesized reductions in suicide incidence when at-risk youth were identified and connected to needed resources. Gatekeeper training emphasized channels to refer at-risk youth for school-based mental health assessment. The team decided to examine gatekeeper training impact on crisis referrals for school mental health services. Ongoing record keeping of referrals provided readily accessible longitudinal data on all students within schools, which reduced the burden on survey data collection and provided information on the population of students.

A dynamic waitlist CRT optimized the number of schools needed to detect moderate program effects (Brown et al., 2007). The CRT randomized both schools and time to the intervention. In particular, 16 schools were blocked on school characteristics and then randomly assigned to start training at one of four designated time points over a 2-year academic period. Thus, the study started with four schools receiving the intervention, which increased incrementally until all schools had been trained. Data were collected for all students within all schools before and after receipt of the intervention. Across time the design balanced school characteristics that would systematically influence outcomes, and repeated measures of referrals increased efficiency to detect program effects. In particular, the MDES in a traditional waitlist design was powered to detect a 32% increase in referrals, while the dynamic waitlist was powered to identify a 23% increase. Change in referral rates was modeled over time with a time-varying indicator of whether the school received training. The results demonstrated a short-term effect of gatekeeper training after full implementation of the program (Wyman et al., 2015). The design addressed central research and practice questions; however, other methods would be needed to evaluate other relevant questions, such as maintenance of longer-term effects.

CONCLUSION

The CRT design provides a powerful and flexible approach for testing research questions that address setting characteristics through ecologically valid methods. However, the costs, complexities, and ethical considerations must be weighed when planning a study. Considerations must balance feasibility and accuracy, and a specific theory of change provides a necessary framework for guiding design and analyses choices. Using multiple methods provides greater opportunities to address important research questions. Moreover, community partnerships are key in all stages of designing and implementing CRTs. Deliberations among a wide range of stakeholders must consider issues of informed consent, prioritize questions of interest, ensure fidelity of interventions and their evaluations, and plan utilization of findings. Despite these challenges, CRTs offer much potential for addressing questions at the core of social interventions, as well as for developing truly community-engaged research.

REFERENCES

Bloom, H. S., Richburg-Hayes, L., & Black, A. R. (2007). Using covariates to improve precision for studies that randomize schools to evaluate educational interventions. *Educational Evaluation and Policy Analysis, 29*, 30–59.

Brown, C. H., Ten Have, T. R., Jo, B., Dagne, G., Wyman, P. A., Muthén, B., & Gibbons, R. D. (2009). Adaptive designs for randomized trials in public health. *Annual Review of Public Health, 30*, 1–25.

Brown, C. H., Wyman, P. A., Brinales, J. M., & Gibbons, R. D. (2007). The role of randomized trials in testing interventions for the prevention of youth suicide. *International Review of Psychiatry, 19*, 617–631.

Brown. C. H., Wyman, P. A., Guoa, J., & Pena, J. (2006). Dynamic wait-listed designs for randomized trials: New designs for prevention of youth suicide. *Clinical Trials, 3*, 259–271.

Chamberlain, P., Roberts, R., Jones H., Marsenich, L., Sosna, T., & Price, J. M. (2013). Three collaborative models for scaling up evidence-based practices. *Administration and Policy in Mental Health and Mental Health Services Research, 39*, 278–290.

Cook, T. D. (2005). Emergent principles for the design, implementation, and analysis of cluster-based experiments in social science. *Annals of the American Academy of Political and Social Science, 599*, 176–198.

Eldridge, S., & Kerry, S. (2012). *A practical guide to cluster randomized trials in health services research*. West Sussex, England: Wiley.

Fowler, P. J., & Todd, N. R. (in press). Methods for multiple levels of analysis: Capturing context, change, and changing contexts. In M. A. Bond, C. Keys, & I. Serrano-García (Eds.), *APA handbook of community psychology*. Washington, DC: American Psychological Association.

Glisson, C., Hemmelgarn, A., Green, P., & Williams, N. (2013). Randomized trial of the availability, responsiveness and continuity (ARC) organizational intervention for improving youth outcomes in community mental health programs. *Journal of the American Academy of Child and Adolescent Psychiatry, 52*, 493–500.

Hawkins, J. D., Oesterle, S., Brown, E. C., Monahan, K. C., Abbott, R. D., Arthur, M. W., & Catalano, R. F. (2012). Sustained decreases in risk exposure and youth problem behaviors after installation of the Communities That Care prevention system in a randomized trial. *Archives of Pediatric Adolescent Medicine, 166*, 141–148.

Hedges, L. V., & Hedberg, E. C. (2007). Intraclass correlation values for planning group-randomized trials in education. *Educational Evaluation and Policy Analysis, 29*, 60–87.

Kellam, S. G., Wang, W., Mackenzie, A. C., Brown, C. H., Ompad, D. C., Or, F., . . . Windham, A. (2014). The impact of the Good Behavior Game, a universal classroom based preventive intervention in first and second grades, on high risk sexual behaviors and drug abuse and dependence disorders in young adulthood. *Prevention Science, 15*, S6–S18.

Konstantopoulos, S. (2012). The impact of covariates on statistical power in cluster randomized designs: Which level matters more? *Multivariate Behavioral Research, 47*, 392–420.

Moerbeek, M., & Teerenstra, S. (2011). Optimal design in multilevel experiments. In J. Hox & J. Roberts (Eds.), *Handbook of advanced multilevel analysis* (pp. 257–281). New York, NY: Routledge.

Murray, D. M. (1998). *Design and analysis of group-randomized trials*. New York, NY: Oxford University Press.

Murray, D. M., & Blitstein, J. L. (2003). Methods to reduce the impact of intraclass correlation in group-randomized trials. *Evaluation Review, 27,* 79–103.

Murray, D. M., Varnell, S. P., & Blitstein, J. L. (2004). Design and analysis of group-randomized trials: A review of recent methodological developments. *American Journal of Public Health, 94,* 423–432.

Peters, T. J., Richards, S. H., Bankhead, C. R., Ades, A. E., & Sterne, J. A. C. (2003). Comparison of methods for analyzing cluster randomized trials: An example involving a factorial design. *International Journal of Epidemiology,* 32, 840–846.

Raudenbush, S. W. (1997). Statistical analysis and optimal design for cluster randomized trials. *Psychological Methods, 2,* 173–185.

Raudenbush, S. W., & Bryk, A. S. (2002). *Hierarchical linear models: Applications and data analysis methods* (2nd ed.). Thousand Oaks, CA: Sage.

Raudenbush, S. W., Martinez, A., & Spybrook, J. (2007). Strategies for improving precision in group-randomized experiments. *Educational Evaluation and Policy Analysis, 29,* 5–29.

Shadish, W. R., Cook, T. D., & Campbell, D. T. (2002). *Experimental and quasi-experimental designs for generalized causal inference.* New York, NY: Houghton Mifflin.

Sim, J., & Dawson, A. (2012). Informed consent and cluster-randomized trials. *American Journal of Public Health, 102,* 480–485.

Spybrook, J., Bloom, H., Congdon, R., Hill, C., Martinez, A., & Raudenbush, S. (2011). *Optimal design plus empirical evidence: Documentation for the "Optimal Design" software.* Retrieved June 2015, from http://hlmsoft.net/od/od-manual-20111016-v300.pdf

Wyman, P. A., Brown, C. H., Inman, J., Cross, W., Schmeelk-Cone, K., Guo, J., & Pena, J. B. (2008). Randomized trial of a gatekeeper program for suicide prevention: 1-year impact on secondary school staff. *Journal of Consulting and Clinical Psychology, 76,* 104–115.

Wyman, P. A., Brown, C. H., LoMurray, M., Schmeelk-Cone, K., Petrova, M., Yu, Q., . . . Wang, W. (2010). An outcome evaluation of the Sources of Strength suicide prevention program delivered by adolescent peer leaders in high schools. *American Journal of Public Health, 100,* 1653–1661.

Wyman, P. A., Henry, D. B., & Brown, C. H. (2015). Designs for testing group-based interventions with limited numbers of social units: The dynamic wait-listed and regression point displacement designs. *Prevention Science.* Epub ahead of print.

18

Behavioral and Time-Series Approaches

MARK A. MATTAINI, LEONARD A. JASON, AND DAVID S. GLENWICK

Behavioral community psychology attempts to understand and change community problems through the application of behavioral theory and technology (Bogat & Jason, 2000; Fawcett, Mathews, & Fletcher, 1980). Early on, several textbooks describing this field were published (e.g., Glenwick & Jason, 1980; Nietzel, Winett, MacDonald, & Davidson, 1977), as well as a special issue of the *Journal of Community Psychology* (Glenwick & Jason, 1984) and later updates (Glenwick & Jason, 1993). Also, in 1987 a reprint series from the *Journal of Applied Behavior Analysis* (Greene, Winett, Van Houten, Geller, & Iwata, 1987) on behavior analysis in the community was published.

During this early period, behavioral methods had been used in a wide variety of community interventions, such as increasing immunization of preschoolers (Yokley & Glenwick, 1984), providing peer tutoring in elementary schools (Jason, Frasure, & Ferone, 1981), establishing alternative environments for delinquent youth (Fixsen, Wolf, & Phillips, 1973), increasing blood donations (Ferrari, Barone, Jason, & Rose, 1986), reducing speeding and auto accidents (Van Houten et al., 1985), decreasing residential energy consumption (Winett, Leckliter, Chinn, Stahl, & Love, 1985), and encouraging individuals to dispose of their trash properly (Geller, Winett, & Everett, 1982). The power of the behavioral approach is that it translates problems into direct-action schemas where solutions are possible, even if they are of the "small win" category.

In this chapter we review the contemporary behavior analytic paradigm and its potential contributions to community-based research, as well as emerging work in behavioral systems science that expands those possibilities. This is followed by a review of behavior analytic methodology, with particular focus on the time-series designs characteristic of this approach. The discussion outlines the underlying natural science epistemology that supports those designs. Analysis in this paradigm usually involves the planned manipulation of contextual variables, and observations of the effects of that manipulation on the behaviors of interest under changing conditions over time, rather than the statistical procedures characteristic of social science. We also note, however, that there are situations when statistical procedures specific to time-series data can be useful within this paradigm. The chapter then describes and provides examples of reversal and multiple-baseline designs, two of the most widely applicable options for community-level intervention. Finally we present a detailed case study of an initially modest community intervention in Chicago using a reversal design that ultimately led to citywide policy change.

INTRODUCTION TO THE BEHAVIOR ANALYTIC PARADIGM

Although there are two major behavioral paradigms, behavior analysis and behavior therapy, we will focus on behavior analysis, which we believe has greater relevance to community interventions. The behavior analytic approach stresses the importance of the context of behavior (Skinner, 1971). It is ironic that although behavior analysts continually emphasized the importance of person–environment interactions, the behavioral community approach was never fully embraced by community psychologists (Bogat & Jason, 2000; Jason & Glenwick, 1984). Rappaport (1977), for example, argued that these types of behavioral technologies may not be applicable to applied settings or problems of concern to community psychology. In addition, community psychologists took issue with the behaviorist belief that there are specific and potentially generalizable solutions to problems, as the former believed that there are no simple solutions to complex social problems (Sarason, 1972), but rather divergent solutions that could not be generalized across communities.

It can be argued, however, that behaviorally oriented interventions can actually be better choices under such circumstances. Interrupted time-series research designs can be employed rigorously in each of several communities, without the need to randomize multiple only somewhat similar communities into contrast groups and apply the identical interventions across all communities in each group. As noted by Biglan, Ary, and Wagenaar (2000, p. 32), such comparison studies are limited by "(a) the high cost of research due to the number of communities needed in such studies, (b) the difficulty in developing generalizable theoretical principles about community change processes through randomized trials, (c) the obscuring of relationships that are unique to a subset of communities, and (d) the problem of diffusion of intervention activities from intervention to control communities." Behavioral time-series designs do not have these limitations, particularly when implemented with matched communities (Biglan et al., 2000; Coulton, 2005).

Within the contemporary behavior analytic community there is an emphasis on antecedent behavior change procedures as opposed to consequence-only procedures. Changing setting factors (i.e., aspects of the contexts and environments in which behavior occurs) can increase the likelihood of desirable behavior change—an approach often labeled as *ecobehavioral* (a term that came into common use in the 1980s; see Mattaini & Huffman-Gottschling, 2012). Contemporary behaviorists commonly provide participants with skills to act on and mold, rather than be passively shaped by, their environment. The process becomes a bidirectional one between individuals and their ecological contexts (Jason & Glenwick, 2002). Although historically the behavioral approach had been mostly applied at the individual level, higher order change has recently been much more strongly emphasized (e.g., Biglan, 1995; Bogat & Jason, 2000; Guerin, 2005). In addition, even interventions targeted at the individual level can help mobilize community concerns about a problem, increase attention to the problem, and become the first step toward tackling a larger social problem.

In recent years, a transnational group of behavior analysts has also begun to elaborate *behavioral systems science*, focusing on the interlocking sets of contingencies within and among behavioral systems. Behavioral systems science began with work in organizational behavior management but recently has moved into community, social policy, and social action work (Biglan & Sloane Wilson, 2015; Grant, 2011; Mattaini, 2013; Mattaini & Thyer, 1996; Todorov, 2013). Work focused on the selection of entire sets of interlocking behavioral contingencies and the dynamics of behavioral systems shows promise for understanding the functioning of large systems, moving well beyond a focus on the individual (Glenn, 2010; Houmanfar, Rodrigues, & Ward, 2010), and experimental work in these areas is beginning, particularly in Brazil. Most important contemporary problems are interdisciplinary in nature (National Academies, 2005). Therefore, collaboration with other professions and disciplines, which can produce synergistic effects and more potent intervention, is increasingly common in behavior systems work. Many recent contributions to the behavior analytic journal *Behavior and Social Issues* have thus been interdisciplinary in nature.

Community psychology has stressed the importance of involving the target populations for input concerning such aspects as problem identification, information on the problem, intervention design, and intervention acceptability (Jason & Glenwick, 2012). The result is a collaborative process in which the intervention is culturally relative and thus more sensitive to the local culture and environment. In a canonical article in the *Journal of Applied Behavior Analysis*, Fawcett (1991) drew behavior analysts' attention to these processes. He argued that community research and action required avoiding colonial relationships and establishing collaborative relationships with research participants (including communities), including collaboration in determining research goals and methods, designing and disseminating interventions, communicating research findings, and advocating for community change. As long as the issues of interest are well defined (which can be accomplished in a collaborative way), the behavioral approach can be a tool whereby researchers and citizens jointly plan and implement community interventions as true partners. A setting's ecology can often be better understood through the collection of ongoing time-series data, providing the community change agent as well as the participants with immediate feedback, a very different approach than the more typical collection of pretest and posttest outcomes.

BEHAVIOR ANALYTIC METHODOLOGY

Behavior analysts control and influence behavior by altering either antecedents (the environment or setting) or the consequences (rewards or punishments) associated with them (Fawcett et al., 1980). When evaluating their interventions, behaviorists collect time-series data that are objective and quantifiable using a variety of experimental designs, including reversal (ABAB) designs; multiple-baseline designs across time, individuals, settings, or situations; changing-criterion designs; and multiple-treatment designs (Kazdin, 2011).

Not surprisingly, the logic of such interrupted time-series experimental designs is distinct from that used in group designs. Behavior analytic research typically is conducted and analyzed using natural science, rather than social science, methods, in part due to differences in underlying philosophies of science. Most natural science research involves the direct manipulation of variables and observation of the effects over time, rather than the use of randomized group designs in which differences are explored using inferential statistics (Johnston & Pennypacker, 1993). These differences may be more important than they appear; Johnston and Pennypacker (1993) asserted the following:

> The natural sciences have spawned technologies that have dramatically transformed the human culture, and the pace of technological development only seems to increase. The social sciences have yet to offer a single well-developed technology that has broad impact on daily life. (p. 6)

In the basic time-series model, data are collected until a stable baseline rate for some dimension of behavior (such as rate, intensity, duration, or variability) has been established. Intervention is then introduced while data continue to be collected. If a change that is large, relatively immediate, and socially substantive is apparent, a stable change as a result of intervention is regarded as present. With multiple replications and increasingly rigorous designs with additional controls, confidence in such change increases. The standard form of analysis in behavioral designs is visual, accepting only clearly evident and reliable changes as depicted graphically (Parsonson & Baer, 1978). Weak or uncertain effects are usually dismissed as not large enough to be useful. When there is significant variability in the data, however, visual analysis can be unreliable (DeProspero & Cohen, 1979; Matyas & Greenwood, 1990).

In most situations where change is not clearly evident from visual analysis, behavior analysts then try to develop a stronger intervention. In some cases, however, there may be benefit in identifying more modest change if the issue is serious and a large population is involved. There is, therefore, a place for statistical methods in time-series research. For example, Kratochwill (1978) provided a series of data analytic methods, including time-series analysis, which emphasized repeated measurement during the baseline and treatment conditions. These techniques alerted investigators to possible internal and external validity threats and led to more sophisticated analyses (Glass, Willson, & Gottman, 1975). Such comparisons take into account differences in levels and slopes. However, because repeated observations from the same unit of interest are not independent from each other, traditional statistical tests that make the assumption of independence of errors are usually not appropriate. When the independence assumption is violated, time-series repeated observations follow an underlying integrated autoregressive moving average (ARIMA) model of order (p, d, q), where "p," "d," and "q" are integers that refer to the complexity of each of three explicitly differentiated types of variance in the time series.

Hoeppner and Proeschold-Bell (2012) described an interesting illustration of the use of this approach, where they found a decreasing trend in hepatitis C knowledge prior to the start of the intervention. After the start of an intervention, the data indicated an increase in patient knowledge, followed by another decrease in knowledge, although at a reduced rate, later in the intervention period. In another example of using these types of time-series analyses, Jason et al. (1999) found that, both within days and between days, perceived energy, physical exertion, and mental exertion were significantly related to fatigue in patients with chronic fatigue syndrome. Alvarez and Jason (1993) also employed time-series methods to show how significantly more infants were in safe car restraints after the passage of legislation requiring the use of proper restraints and a related educational program.

Todman and Dugard (2001) provided a practical guide to randomization tests in order to make sound causal inferences for single-case data. However, their guide requires that random assignment procedures be built into experimental designs. There are a number of other behavioral strategies for quantitative descriptions of environment–behavior relations, including matching theory (Dallery & Soto, 2013) and dynamic systems models that may be used to describe sequential dependencies in time-series data (Molenaar & Goode, 2013), but they are beyond the scope of this chapter.

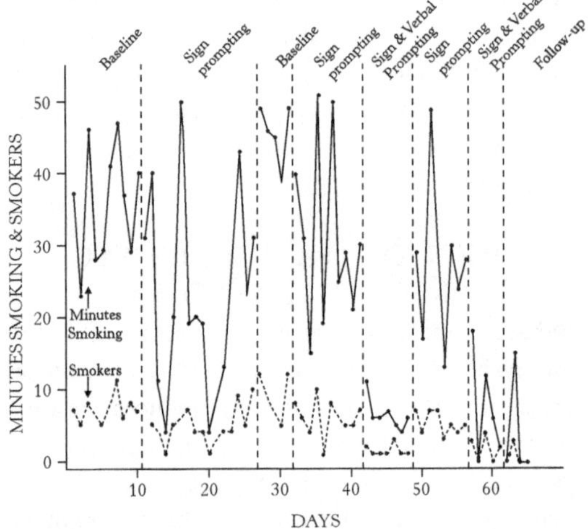

FIGURE 18.1: Smoking as a function of verbal prompting in a university cafeteria

Source: "Reduction of Cigarette Smoking in a University Cafeteria," by L. A. Jason and R. Liotta, 1982, *Journal of Applied Behavior Analysis, 15*, p. 576. Copyright 1982 by the Society for the Experimental Analysis of Behavior. Reprinted with permission from John Wiley & Sons, Inc.

BEHAVIORAL RESEARCH DESIGNS

In behavioral designs, data can be collected at the individual, group, community, or societal levels (Mattaini, 2010). We will focus here on two types of designs. The reversal design collects baseline data and then introduces an intervention to try to alter that behavior. Following successful behavior change, the intervention is then withdrawn to assess whether the behavior returns to the baseline condition. There are a number of variations on this design, but all assess combinations of baseline and interventions to see if the intervention is producing a meaningful and clearly evident effect on the participants' behavior. The following example of a reversal design demonstrates how interventions can be maintained over time. Smoking once dominated American culture, but this has changed dramatically over the past few decades. As part of the activism that helped to change smoking norms, in the early 1980s one group developed methods to evaluate the success of creating a nonsmoking section in a student cafeteria before there were laws restricting use (Jason & Liotta, 1982). The investigators first counted the number of smokers in a particular section of the cafeteria once a day. Next, no-smoking signs were posted. The number of smokers in the area did not change, indicating (see Fig. 18.1) that this intervention was not successful. The next intervention involved politely requesting people not to smoke in the nonsmoking area. This request, along with no-smoking signs, was effective in eliminating smoking in this designated area. However, when prompting stopped, the levels of smoking increased; when the researchers then reintroduced verbal prompting, the rates of tobacco use decreased.

At the end of this study, the director of food services assigned an individual responsible for collecting unreturned trays to continue the prompting (a polite request not to smoke). In addition, a permanent no-smoking section was established in the cafeteria. Follow-up data collected 3 months after the end of the formal intervention indicated that both the management and even customers continued the prompting procedures. It is possible that new social norms were established which helped nonsmokers become more fully integrated and comfortable in this new nonsmoking setting. From a transactional point of view, reductions in smoking in an area led management and customers to change their behaviors, which led to less smoking, and perhaps even more attempts at prompting.

In contrast, the multiple-baseline technique is useful when a reversal design would be unethical or when irreversible changes are likely. This design involves charting several behaviors until they stabilize during the baseline phase. There are several variations of multiple-baseline designs, including multiple baseline across systems (persons or communities), multiple baseline across behaviors, and multiple baseline across settings, as well as some that combine dimensions over time. In a multiple-baseline study across communities, several somewhat similar communities all struggling with the same issue can be selected. Baseline data are collected over a period of time for all. An intervention is then introduced in one community while the others continue to collect baseline data. After a predetermined time interval the intervention is introduced in a second community (the third community would continue to collect baseline data). After a similar interval of time, the intervention is introduced in the third community. If clearly evident change is observed in each community only at the time that the intervention is introduced there, the probability of genuine change is considered to be high (i.e., the probability of a Type 1 error would be low). If change is not apparent, immediate changes can be made to refine the intervention without wasting additional time or resources. Further replications and applications across other types of communities would gradually strengthen the effectiveness evidence while allowing analysis of community characteristics associated with greater or lesser response to the intervention.

Figure 18.2 shows the use of a multiple-baseline design in an investigation of ways to expand recovery homes (specifically, Oxford Houses) for

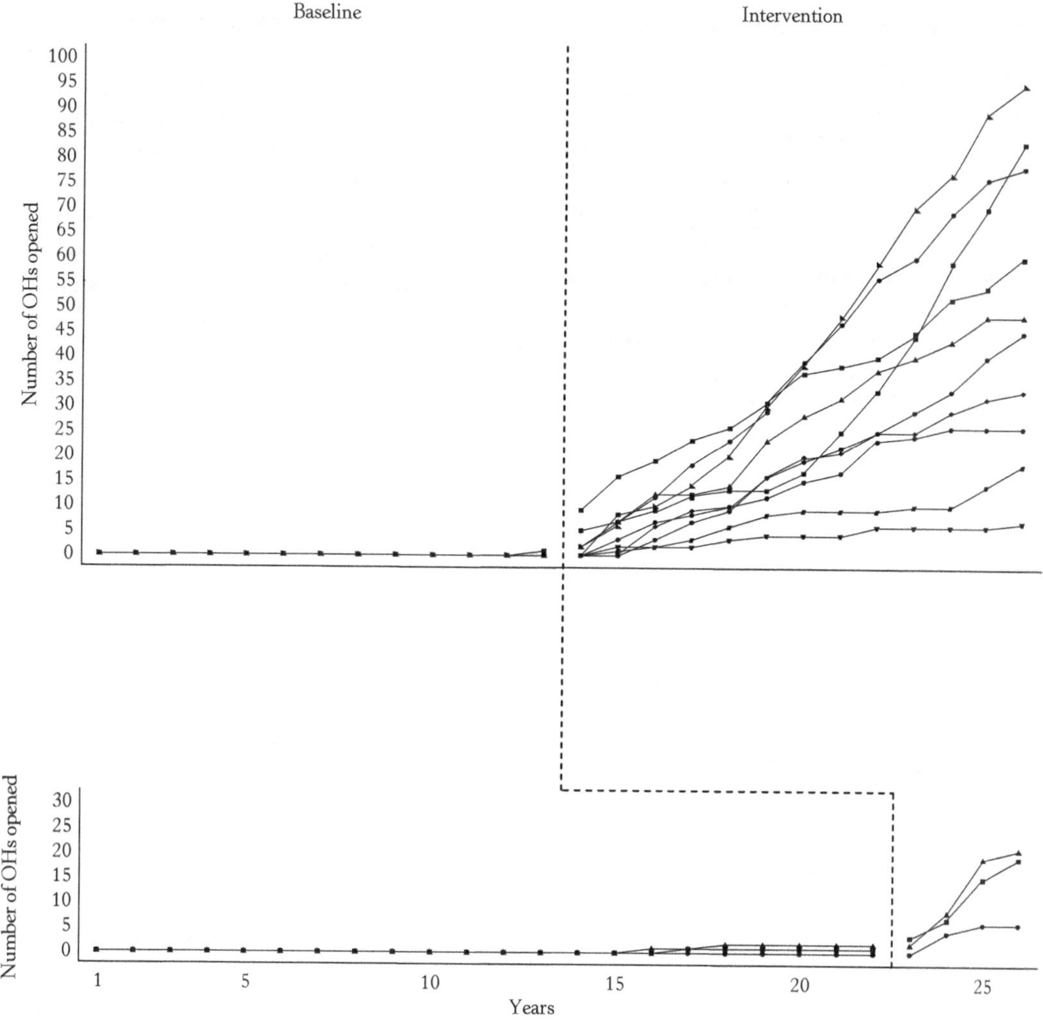

FIGURE 18.2: Recovery homes in two groups of states.

Reprinted from "Increasing the Number of Mutual Help Recovery Homes for Substance Abusers: Effects of Government Policy and Funding Assistance," by L. A. Jason, J. M. Braciszewski, B. D. Olson, and J. R. Ferrari, 2005, *Behavior and Social Issues, 14*, p. 76. Copyright 1982 by the authors.

people with substance abuse problems (Jason, Braciszewski, Olson, & Ferrari, 2005). The intervention involved providing a $4,000 loan program and a recruiter to open up new houses. Jason et al. utilized a multiple-baseline design to chart the expansion of Oxford Houses in different states. The horizontal axis indicates years, and the vertical axis refers to number of houses. Very few Oxford Houses were established during the years before the start of the intervention. Intervention onset (as indicated by the vertical dotted line at the top of the figure) first occurred in one group of states. A few years later the intervention was introduced in a second group of states (indicated by the vertical dotted line at the bottom of the figure). As states instituted the intervention (but not before), the number of houses expanded considerably, and the impact of the intervention was clearly evident.

CASE STUDY

In the late 1970s, the second author of this chapter (Jason) invited a representative from Chicago alderman Martin Oberman's office to speak to students in a community psychology course. When asked which problem was generating the most community dissatisfaction, the representative answered "uncollected dog feces." Jason and his graduate students decided to collect data on this problem. They selected a long block within the DePaul University area and recorded the following variables for 5 hours daily: the number of dogs, the number of dogs who defecated, and the number of dog defecations picked up by their owners. In addition, all defecations were picked up and weighed each morning. There were six phases in the study, each lasting 7 days (not consecutive days because Saturdays, Sundays, and rainy days were excluded).

Baseline 1: Regular patterns of dog and owner behavior were monitored from the top of a seven-story building.

Signs: During this phase, three black and white .3 m by .2 m signs reading "Protect Children's Health. Pick Up Your Dog's Droppings" were posted on trees and fences on each side of the street. At the end of 7 days, these six signs were removed from the street.

Prompting 1: Instructions and modeling were used in this phase. Every time dog owners entered the designated area, they were approached by a research assistant, who said: "Excuse me. Can I talk to you? I am a resident of this neighborhood and am very concerned about keeping this area clean. I would appreciate it if you would use this bag to pick up your dog's defecations." The research assistant then demonstrated how to use the bag. The plastic bag was then offered to the dog owner. If, after being given a bag, a dog owner left the designated area and then reentered it, the owner was not given another bag. During this phase, each owner was categorized by the prompter into one of the following five categories: missed (dog owner left the designated area before a bag was offered), pooper scooper visible (prompters were shown a receptacle owned by dog owners who indicated it would be used to pick up droppings), scooper in pocket (owners claimed a receptacle for picking up droppings was in their pocket), bag was accepted, or bag was refused.

Baseline 2: Observers again unobtrusively watched the street from the seven-story building, with no intervention.

Prompting 2: Prompting conditions identical to those described earlier were reintroduced.

Follow-up: Three months after the program ended, all defecations in the target area were counted. Two months later, defecations on seven random, nontarget streets (areas included in the preliminary study) were counted.

During the baseline phase, few dog owners picked up after their dogs, and more than 19 pounds of dog defecations were deposited in the target block. When antilitter signs were posted during the second phase, relatively few changes occurred on the criterion measures. However, during the next phase, when all dog owners were given instructions and a demonstration concerning how to use a plastic bag to pick up dog feces, 82% of the dog owners proceeded to pick up after their dogs (Jason, Zolik, & Matese, 1979). These findings indicate that the prompting intervention, which applied instructions and modeling, effectively motivated dog owners to dispose of their dogs' waste properly (see Fig. 18.3).

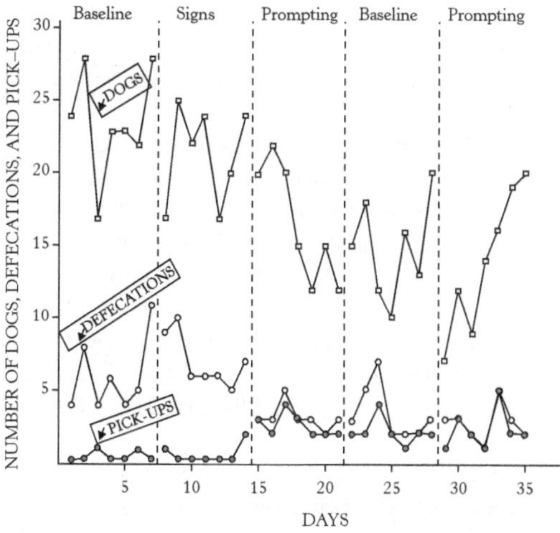

FIGURE 18.3: Dogs, dog feces, and pickups across experimental conditions.

Source: "Prompting Dog Owners to Pick Up Dog Droppings," by L. A. Jason, E. S. Zolik, and F. Matese, 1979, *American Journal of Community Psychology*, 7(3), p. 345. Copyright 1979 by the Society for Community Research and Action. Reprinted with kind permission from Springer Science and Business Media.

Following the study's completion, several community groups contacted Jason and his team for advice in setting up their own dog litter interventions. The team's next study involved a 9-month collaborative relationship between the researchers and a community group in another neighborhood. At a 13-month follow-up, the target block, as well as an area around the target block, had significant reductions in dog litter. The findings suggested that residents who participated in the program continued exerting pressure on dog owners to pick up after their dog even after the formal intervention ended. Thus, teaching skills to indigenous change agents might be an effective way to maintain gains following the termination of a behavioral intervention. In summary, the dog intervention studies documented effective approaches for combating the inveterate problem of dog waste in urban areas. To effect more substantial, enduring reductions in community dog droppings, working with community residents to implement procedures appears to represent the most promising approach.

This research was used to influence legislation, as the Chicago alderman asked Jason to present his findings at City Hall in order to support a proposed ordinance that would require dog owners to have in their possession a pooper scooper when walking dogs. The ordinance was passed by the City Council, making Chicago one of the first cities in the country to pass a pooper scooper ordinance.

CONCLUSION

Behavior analytic methods have been used with a wide variety of community issues. Although community researchers often focus much of their effort on self-report measures, behaviorally oriented investigators have pioneered innovative ways to document whether behavioral changes have occurred over time. Such behavioral interventions, just as with other community programs, compete with high-density alternative messages, which might overwhelm and nullify the interventions. That is, there are multiple ecological systems that impact health care systems and other human services, and their messages are often inconsistent. Illustratively, for many years smoking prevention interventions have been implemented in schools, and yet children report that they are almost always sold cigarettes by store vendors (Jason, Ji, Anes, & Birkhead, 1991). By sending youngsters conflicting messages (i.e., vendors selling minors cigarettes when school-based programs indicate that youths should not be smoking), our society diminishes the effectiveness of school-based smoking prevention interventions. Therefore, interventions have also been developed to reduce youth access to retail sources of tobacco (Biglan et al.,1995; Jason, Pokorny, Adams, & Hunt, 2008).

Behavior is influenced by multiple contingencies and setting features. For example, Herrnstein's hyperbola asserts that responding is governed by contingent reinforcement that is evaluated relative to all reinforcement provided by an environment (McDowell, 1982, 1988). Willems (1974) suggested that behaviorists need to examine second- and third-order consequences of interventions in order to better understand systems-like principles that permeate behavior and the environment. Ecobehavioral methods are designed to ensure that natural environmental contingencies can take over to sustain behavioral changes (Mattaini et al., 2012).

Finally, as we develop targeted interventions for particular problems, we need to be reminded that substance abuse, school failure, juvenile delinquency, and other social problems share many developmental roots (Biglan et al., 2015;

Biglan, Brennan, Foster, & Holder, 2004; Jason & Glenwick, 2002), thereby indicating that children and adolescents represent the most fertile population for preventively oriented behavioral interventions. Coordinating such youth-targeted interventions (and uncovering common environmental causes and interventive components) will hopefully increase both the scope and enduring impact of our interventions.

REFERENCES

Alvarez, J., & Jason, L. A. (1993). The effectiveness of legislation, education, and loaners for child safety in automobiles. *Journal of Community Psychology, 21*, 280–284.

Biglan, A (1995). *Changing cultural practices: A contextualist framework for intervention research.* Reno, NV: Context Press.

Biglan, A., Ary, D., & Wagenaar, A. C. (2000). The value of interrupted time-series experiments for community intervention research. *Prevention Science, 1*, 31–49.

Biglan, A., Brennan, P. A., Foster, S. L., & Holder, H. D. (2004). *Helping adolescents at risk: Prevention of multiple problem behaviors.* New York, NY: Guilford Press.

Biglan, A., Henderson, J., Humphrey, D., Yasui, M., Whisman, R., Black, C., & James, L. (1995). Mobilizing positive reinforcement to reduce youth access to tobacco. *Tobacco Control, 4*, 42–48.

Biglan, A., & Sloane Wilson, D. (2015). *The nurture effect: How the science of human behavior can improve our lives and our world.* Oakland, CA: New Harbinger.

Bogat, G. A., & Jason, L. A. (2000). Towards an integration of behaviorism and community psychology: Dogs bark at those they do not recognize. In J. Rappaport & E. Seidman (Eds.), *Handbook of community psychology* (pp. 101–114). New York, NY: Plenum.

Coulton, C. (2005). The place of community in social work practice research: Conceptual and methodological developments. *Social Work Research, 29*, 73–86.

Dallery, J., & Soto, P. L. (2013). Quantitative description of environment–behavior relations. In G. J. Madden (Ed.), *APA handbook of behavior analysis* (pp. 219–249). Washington, DC: American Psychological Association.

DeProspero, A., & Cohen S. (1979). Inconsistent visual analyses of intrasubject data. *Journal of Applied Behavior Analysis, 12*, 573–579.

Fawcett, S. B. (1991). Some values guiding community research and action. *Journal of Applied Behavior Analysis, 24*, 621–636.

Fawcett, S. B., Mathews, R. M., & Fletcher, R. K. (1980). Some promising dimensions for behavioral community technology. *Journal of Applied Behavior Analysis, 13*, 505–518.

Ferrari, J. R., Barone, R. C., Jason, L. A., & Rose, T. (1986). The use of incentives to increase blood donations. *Journal of Social Psychology, 125*, 791–793.

Fixsen, D. L., Wolf, M. M., & Phillips, E. L. (1973). Achievement Place: A teaching-family model of community based group homes for youth in trouble. In L. A. Hamerlynck, L. C. Handy, & E. J. Mash (Eds.), *Behavior change: Methodology, concepts and practice* (pp. 241–268). Champaign, IL: Research Press.

Geller, E. S., Winett, R. A., & Everett, P. E. (1982). *Preserving the environment: New strategies for behavior change.* New York, NY: Pergamon.

Glass, G. V., Willson, V. L., & Gottman, J. M. (1975). *Design and analysis of time-series experiments.* Boulder: University of Colorado Press.

Glenn, S. S. (2010). Metacontingencies, selection, and OBM: Comments on "Emergence and metacontingency." *Behavior and Social Issues, 19*, 79–85.

Glenwick, D. S., & Jason, L. A. (Eds.). (1980). *Behavioral community psychology: Progress and prospects.* New York, NY: Praeger.

Glenwick, D. S., & Jason, L. A. (1984). Behavioral community psychology: An introduction to the special issue. *Journal of Community Psychology, 12*, 103–112.

Glenwick, D. S., & Jason, L. A. (Eds.). (1993). *Promoting health and mental health in children, youth, and families.* New York, NY: Springer.

Grant, L. K. (2011). Can we consume our way out of climate change? A call for analysis. *The Behavior Analyst, 34*, 245–266.

Greene, B. F., Winett, R. A., Van Houten, R., Geller, E. S., & Iwata, B. A. (1987). *Behavior analysis in the community, 1968-1986, from the Journal of Applied Behavior Analysis.* Lawrence, KS: Society for the Experimental Analysis of Behavior.

Guerin, B. (2005). *Handbook of interventions for changing people and communities.* Reno, NV: Context Press.

Hoeppner, B., & Proeschold-Bell, R. J. (2012). Time series analysis in community-oriented research. In L. A. Jason & D. S. Glenwick (Eds.), *Methodological approaches to community-based research* (pp. 125–146). Washington, DC: American Psychological Association.

Houmanfar, R., Rodrigues, N. J., & Ward, T. A. (2010). Emergence and metacontingency: Points of contact and departure. *Behavior and Social Issues, 19*, 78–103.

Jason, L. A., Braciszewski, J. M., Olson, B. D., & Ferrari, J. R. (2005). Increasing the number of mutual help recovery homes for substance abusers: Effects of government policy and funding assistance. *Behavior and Social Issues, 14*, 71–79.

Jason, L. A., Frasure, S., & Ferone, L. (1981). Establishing supervising behaviors in eighth graders and peer-tutoring behaviors in first graders. *Child Study Journal, 11*, 201–219.

Jason, L. A., & Glenwick, D. S. (1984). Behavioral community psychology: A review of recent research and applications. In M. Hersen, R. M. Eisler, & P. M. Miller (Eds.), *Progress in behavior modification* (Vol. 18, pp. 85–121). New York, NY: Academic Press.

Jason, L. A., & Glenwick, D. S. (Eds.). (2002). *Innovative strategies for promoting health and mental health across the lifespan*. New York, NY: Springer.

Jason, L. A., & Glenwick, D. S. (Eds.). (2012). *Methodological approaches to community-based research*. Washington, DC: American Psychological Association.

Jason, L. A., Ji, P. V., Anes, M. D., & Birkhead, S. H. (1991). Active enforcement of cigarette control laws in the prevention of cigarette sales to minors. *Journal of the American Medical Association, 266*, 3159–3161.

Jason, L. A., & Liotta, R. (1982). Reducing cigarette smoking in a university cafeteria. *Journal of Applied Behavior Analysis, 15*, 573–577.

Jason, L. A., Pokorny, S. B., Adams, M., & Hunt, Y. (2008). A randomized trial evaluating tobacco possession-use-purchase laws. *Social Science and Medicine, 67*, 1700–1707.

Jason, L. A., Tryon, W. W., Taylor, R. R., King, C., Frankenberry, E. L., & Jordan, K. M. (1999). Monitoring and assessing symptoms of chronic fatigue syndrome: Use of time series regression. *Psychological Reports, 85*, 121–130.

Jason, L. A., Zolik, E. S., & Matese, F. (1979). Prompting dog owners to pick up dog droppings. *American Journal of Community Psychology, 7*, 339–351.

Johnston, J. M., & Pennypacker, H. S. (1993). Why behavior analysis is a natural science. In J. M. Johnston & H. S. Pennypacker (Eds.), *Readings for "Strategies and tactics of behavioral research"* (2nd ed., pp. 3–7). Hillsdale, NJ: Erlbaum.

Kazdin, A. E. (2011). *Single-case research designs*. New York, NY: Oxford University Press.

Kratochwill, T. R. (1978). *Single subject research: Strategies for evaluating change*. New York, NY: Academic Press.

Mattaini, M. A. (2010). Single-system studies. In B. Thyer (Ed.), *The handbook of social work research methods* (2nd ed., pp. 241–273). Los Angeles, CA: Sage Publications.

Mattaini, M. A. (2013). *Strategic nonviolent power: The science of satyagraha*. Edmonton, Canada: Athabasca University Press.

Mattaini, M. A., & Huffman-Gottschling, K. (2012). Ecosystems theory. In B. A. Thyer, C. N. Dulmus, & K. M. Sowers (Eds.), *Human behavior in the social environment: Theories for social work practice* (pp. 297–325). Hoboken, NJ: Wiley.

Mattaini, M. A., & Thyer, B. A. (Eds.). (1996). *Finding solutions to social problems: Behavioral strategies for change*. Washington, DC: American Psychological Association.

Matyas, T. A., & Greenwood, K. M. (1990). Visual analysis of single-case time series: Effects of variability, serial dependence, and magnitude of intervention effects. *Journal of Applied Behavior Analysis, 23*, 341–351.

McDowell, J. J. (1982). The importance of Herrnstein's mathematical statement of the law of effect for behavior therapy. *American Psychologist, 37*, 771–779.

McDowell, J. J. (1988). Matching theory in natural human environments. *Behavior Analyst, 11*, 95–109.

Molenaar, P. C. M., & Goode, T. (2013). Methods for sequential behavior analysis relations. In G. J. Madden, V. William, T. D. Hackenberg, G. Hanley, & G. P. Hanley (Eds.), *APA handbook of behavior analysis* (pp. 267–280). Washington, DC: American Psychological Association.

National Academies. (2005). *Facilitating interdisciplinary research*. Washington, DC: National Academies Press.

Nietzel, M. T., Winett, R. A., MacDonald, M. L., & Davidson, W. S. (1977). *Behavioral approaches to community psychology*. New York, NY: Pergamon.

Parsonson, B. S., & Baer, D. M. (1978). The analysis and presentation of graphic data. In T. R. Kratochwill (Ed.), *Single subject research: Strategies for evaluating change* (pp. 101–165). New York, NY: Academic Press.

Rappaport, J. (1977). *Community psychology: Values, research, and action*. New York, NY: Holt, Rinehart and Winston.

Sarason, S. B. (1972). *The creation of settings and the future societies*. San Francisco, CA: Jossey-Bass.

Skinner, B. F. (1971). *Beyond freedom and dignity*. New York, NY: Knopf.

Todman, J. B., & Dugard, P. (2001). *Single-case and small-n experimental designs: A practical guide to randomization tests*. Mahway, NJ: Erlbaum.

Todorov, J. C. (2013). Conservation and transformation of cultural practices through contingencies and metacontingencies. *Behavior and Social Issues, 22*, 64–73.

Van Houten, R., Rolider, A., Naw, P. A., Friedman, R., Becker, M., Calodovsky, I., & Scherer, M. (1985). Large-scale reductions in speeding and accidents in Canada and Israel: A behavioral ecological perspective. *Journal of Applied Behavior Analysis, 18*, 87–93.

Willems, E. P. (1974). Behavioral technology and behavioral ecology. *Journal of Applied Behavior Analysis, 7*, 151–165.

Winett, R. A., Leckliter, I. N., Chinn, D. E., Stahl, G., & Love, S. Q. (1985). Effects of television modeling on residential energy conservation. *Journal of Applied Behavior Analysis, 18*, 33–44.

Yokley, J. M., & Glenwick, D. S. (1984). Increasing the immunization of preschool children: An evaluation of applied community interventions. *Journal of Applied Behavior Analysis, 17*, 313–325.

19

Data Mining

JACOB FURST, DANIELA STAN RAICU, AND LEONARD A. JASON

Data mining, the subject of this chapter, has been most frequently used in the physical sciences (Kutz, 2013). However, as we shall show, it has also been successfully applied by social science investigators of community-level phenomena. Because they can be used to uncover patterns and relationships within large samples of people, organizations, or communities that would not otherwise be evident because of the size and complexity of the data, data mining methods are particularly appropriate for research on social problems.

Increasingly, as researchers, we are confronted with ever-larger data sets, and, as we bring diverse voices (e.g., consumers, community-based groups, government officials, and media and electronic sources) into our work, the complexity will inevitably increase (Dhar, 2013). With these vast new reservoirs of information, there is a need for us to develop methods to understand the dynamic transactions that occur between individuals and their social environments. Data mining is one method that helps us understand such voluminous data in new and more efficient ways. The IBM computer that was used on the television program *Jeopardy* in 2011 to defeat master human players had 16 terabytes of memory, an unimaginable amount of memory capacity at that time, but such an amount may be on desktop computers within the next 10 years (Harris, 2008). We are quickly having access to more and more powerful programs to process and search for solutions, ones in which computers actually learn and then provide us with ways of better understanding these large data sets. These processes are ones with which social scientists are now dealing and which could help solve some formerly intransigent social and community problems.

Social problems that could benefit from the use of data mining include detecting underlying communities, analyzing behaviors, and discovering evolutionary patterns in a community (Wang, Tong, Yu, & Aggarwal, 2012). For example, several studies (Davidson, Gilpin, & Walker, 2012; Ferdowsi, Settimi, & Raicu, 2010; Jiang, Ferreira, & Gonzalez, 2012) offered new perspectives for urban and transportation planning, as well as emergency response systems. Jiang et al. (2012) analyzed activity-based travel survey data from the Chicago metropolitan area to learn when, where, and how individuals interact with places in metropolitan areas. Ferdowsi et al. (2010) employed socioeconomic and housing data for the city of Chicago to help understand social changes of urban areas leading to the gentrification or abandonment of communities.

In this chapter, we will provide an overview of one method of data mining that uses decision trees to predict a classification (e.g., negative outcomes of high-risk neighborhoods in a community), based on successive binary choices of risk factors. At each branch point of the decision tree, a characteristic is examined (e.g., gang activity within a community), and the decision tree determines whether a characteristic is important in the outcome or classification. In data mining, multiple characteristics are reviewed, and an algorithm is ultimately developed that best predicts outcomes. We will then illustrate the application of this method to a chronic health condition, showing how computer-generated algorithms were developed to help guide community organizations and government bodies in arriving at more valid and less stigmatizing ways of characterizing patients.

INTRODUCTION TO DATA MINING AND DECISION TREES

Data mining is the process of discovering hidden, implicit, nontrivial, and useful patterns from large amounts of data. Figure 19.1 indicates that this process is an iterative and interactive sequence of steps that includes domain understanding, data collection, data preprocessing, data reduction, pattern discovery, and pattern evaluation for knowledge extraction. In the first step, domain experts and data mining experts formulate the research question or problem to be addressed using data mining. In the second step, the data are either collected or extracted from data resources, such as data warehouses, data marts, and databases. Third, because data rarely come in a clean format, a preprocessing step is required to do a number of functions, including, for instance, removing duplicates, filling in missing values, and solving any inconsistencies in the attributes. The process of collecting and preprocessing the data is time consuming and usually takes between 60% and 80% of the entire data mining process. Once the data are cleaned, a reduction in the number of attributes or number of cases may be necessary if the number of attributes is too large compared to the number of cases or the number of cases is too large to allow efficient modeling of the data. The next step, pattern discovery, employs such techniques as machine learning, artificial intelligence, and statistics to uncover patterns in the data.

Traditionally, these techniques can be *supervised* or *unsupervised*, depending on the availability of labeled data. If all the data samples have known labels, then supervised techniques can be used; supervised techniques use the known labels of existing data to create models to predict the unknown labels of new data. For example, a body of historical medical data, including patient symptoms and diagnosis, could be used to create a supervised learning model to diagnosis new patients based on their symptoms. If the data samples do not have known labels, then unsupervised techniques need to be applied to learn from the data based on the similarities among the cases; unsupervised techniques separate the data into similar categories based solely on relationships between the features of the data samples. To extend the earlier example, if the historical patient data had no diagnosis, unsupervised techniques could be used to separate the patients into similar symptom groups. Techniques for supervised learning include neural networks, decision trees, Bayesian classifiers, and support vector machines (Kotsiantis, 2007). Clustering techniques, including partitioning and hierarchical techniques (Ghahramani, 2004), are the most popular ones for unsupervised learning.

In the rest of this section, we will focus on decision trees as a machine learning technique for classification. Machine learning is one of the major disciplines used to support data-driven (i.e., empirical) research, research in which the data are too many for a reasonable hypothesis to be formulated a priori, making hypothesis-driven research impractical. A decision tree is a method of machine learning that is primarily focused on the task of data classification: predicting the category (or label) of data samples based on the attributes (or features) of the samples. Therefore, a decision tree is a supervised machine learner; that is, there must be samples with a known label from which to construct a

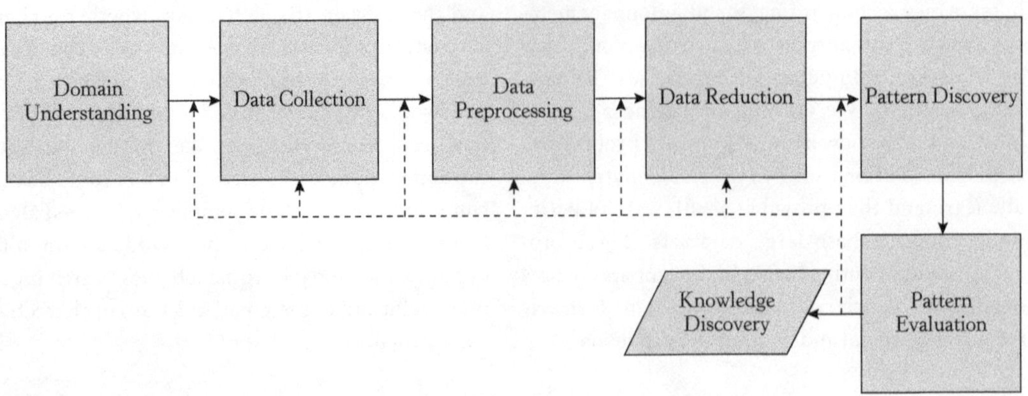

FIGURE 19.1: An overview of the data mining process.

model (the decision tree), on which future samples (with unknown labels) can be classified.

A decision tree is constructed by examining the features and labels of the data set and deriving a split of the data set based on a single feature and corresponding threshold of that feature that improves some measure of data consistency or classification accuracy. That is, the decision tree splits the data based on the value of some feature, such that the accuracy or consistency of the resultant subsets is better than the accuracy or consistency of the original data set. A decision tree will generally perform a comprehensive search of all features and all possible threshold values to determine the best split of the data. The measure of consistency or accuracy will depend on the kind of classification tree being used and the input of the user. The two most common methods of measuring "goodness of split" are Gini impurity and information gain (Breiman, Friedman, Olshen, & Stone, 1984). In most cases, the two metrics will behave similarly. After each split, the two subsets are recursively analyzed to determine if improvement can be made by splitting them. The tree will stop splitting when no further improvement can be gained. Consistent with the terminology used in general computer science data structures theory, subsets of data in the tree are called nodes, and the number of splits required to reach a node starting from the root is called the depth of the tree. The original data set has the special designation of root node and is at level zero.

Although accuracy, defined as the number of correctly classified cases over the total number of cases, is in general used to evaluate the performance of a classifier, there are other performance measures that can be employed as well. Specifically, in the biomedical and health care domains, when the interest is in the performance with respect to the positive class (it has the disease) versus the negative class (it does not have the disease), sensitivity and specificity are used. Sensitivity is the ratio between the number of correctly classified positive cases (true positives) over the total number of positive cases. Specificity is the ratio between the number of correctly classified negative cases (true negatives) over the total number of negative cases. A Receiver Operator Characteristic (ROC; Green & Swets, 1966) is used to visualize the relationships between specificity and sensitivity and to determine the best combination of parameters for the highest possible sensitivity and specificity.

Decision trees come in a variety of types, depending on the intended outcome and the method of building the tree. Classification trees are used to predict a discrete numerical or categorical label, while regression trees are used to predict a continuous numerical label. Frequently, the terms C&RT, CART, or Classification & Regression Tree (Breiman et al. 1984) are used to include both categories. CHAID (Kass, 1980) is a variation that allows for more than a single split at each node of the tree. It can be helpful if the data are missing values, as a split can involve a feature threshold value (or values), as well as a node for missing values (which cannot be determined to be above or below a threshold).

Among the most important advantages of decision trees is that they make no assumptions about the distribution of the underlying data. In particular, features do not have to be normally distributed for the tree to generate accurate and robust results. This can be especially important when the number of samples is very small. Decision trees are generally easy to understand and interpret. Using thresholding on feature values to split the data set into two more consistent data sets is an intuitive idea and easy to demonstrate. The features and their corresponding thresholds can also be stated as a Boolean logic decision rule, which can be easily and quickly applied to new cases.

Decision trees have built-in feature selection. A decision tree model can be easily analyzed to determine which features were important for the classification. This can refine and simplify further data collection and provide insights into properties of the data beyond the classification results.

Although decision trees require minimal data preparation, they do have a number of constraints that are important to remember when interpreting the results of classification: (a) They will generally overfit the data. (b) They use a "greedy" strategy. (c) They can be very sensitive to input parameters. (d) They can be sensitive to label sets of unequal size.

Overfitting is caused by the recursive nature of the construction of the decision tree. That is, because the tree stops splitting only when no further improvement on purity can be gained, a decision tree will always predict the known label set perfectly. If new (unclassified) elements do not match the original, labeled set perfectly, they will be misclassified. Thus, most decisions trees are limited in their growth, so as to find a balance between the predictive accuracy on the known set and the predictive accuracy on unknown elements.

There are generally three ways in which to limit the growth of a decision tree. The first method restricts the minimum size of a node before it can be split. The input parameter that restricts this is called the parent node size parameter. The second method restricts the minimum size of a child node resulting from a split. The input parameter that restricts this is called the child node size parameter. The third method limits the depth of the tree, not allowing nodes to split past a certain depth. There also exist pruning techniques, which do not limit the initial growth of the tree, but postprocess the finished tree to remove splits that are likely overfit. We used growth-limiting parameters, rather than pruning, in the case study to be presented.

A "greedy" strategy is an iterative solution that will always make decisions that are the best at the moment, without regard for previous or potential future decisions of the solution. With decision trees, this shows up in two significant ways. First, the decision tree will choose the single best feature on which to generate a split. If two features are highly correlated, and might produce very similar splits, the decision tree will choose the better of the two. The second feature may then not be optimal for subsequent splits and may not show up at all in the resulting decision rules, leading to an incorrect conclusion about the possible importance of the two correlated features. Second, the decision tree must choose a single feature for a split; the tree cannot choose, for instance, a pair of features and a double threshold that might be better than either of the features alone. There has been some initial unpublished work in the area of choosing feature pairs, but it has not yet established its value. In general, and for decision trees in particular, a "greedy" algorithm cannot guarantee a globally optimal solution.

As mentioned in the paragraph on overfitting, a typical tree will have three input parameters: parent size, child size, and depth. Although the depth parameter rarely needs to be used if set at a high level initially, the parent and child size parameters are important to prevent overfitting, and the classification results of a tree can be highly dependent on them. Also, there are no currently recognized solutions for finding the best pair of parent/child size parameters, and there are not even any common heuristics for choosing them. Most researchers choose parent and child size parameters initially as some fraction (e.g., 10% and 5%, or square root of the number of cases for the parent and half of that for the child node) of the total data set size and then try variations close to that fraction and compare results of models built on different parameter sizes. This can be a time-intensive and inconclusive approach to classification.

Finally, trees can be sensitive to disparities in the size of label sets, with greater disparities resulting in ever-worse decision tree models. In particular, a decision tree will almost always favor the classification of data items as belonging to the largest label set. There are two common techniques to overcome this bias: oversampling and undersampling (He & Garcia, 2009). In oversampling, the less-dominant label set provides multiple copies of each element to the creation of the model, such that the size of the two label sets is equal for the model. Some oversampling techniques create new elements from the smaller label set; this should be attempted only when one is confident about the underlying distributions of one's data features. Undersampling chooses a random, smaller set from the dominant label set, such that both label sets provide an equal number of samples to the decision tree model. To avoid undersampling bias, it is recommended that one run multiple trials, with a new, random undersample conducted in each trial.

Despite these shortcomings, a decision tree can produce very accurate and robust results on many data sets. There are a number of refinements to the basic strategy that can be used to gain more improvement from decision trees. The first of these involves the use of three subsets of the original data, termed the training set, the testing set, and the evaluation set (Fig. 19.2). The training set is used to create an initial model, which is then used to classify the elements of the testing set. Based on some comparison of performance (typically the difference between accuracies on the training and testing sets), a new set of input parameters will be used to create a new model on the training set, which will be used to again classify the elements of the testing set, leading to a new evaluation of parameters. This will cycle until the desired goal (typically near-equal accuracies on the training and testing sets) is attained, at which point the model will be tested on the evaluation set, that is, used to classify the elements of the evaluation set. This will provide

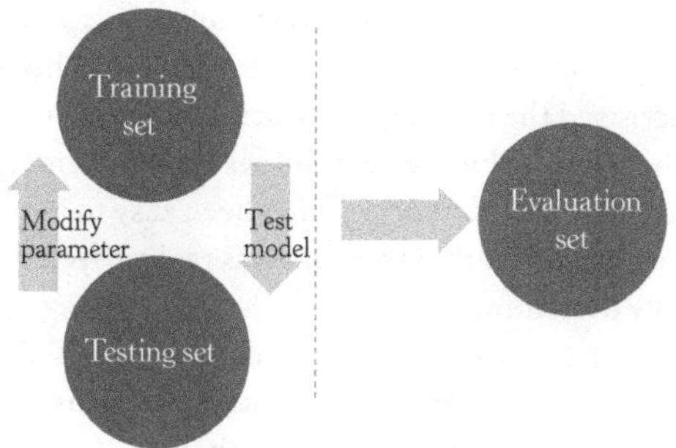

FIGURE 19.2: Block diagram of model creation.

the most robust predictor of the decision tree accuracy on unknown elements, as no elements of the evaluation test were used in the creation of the final model. The effectiveness of the predictor is suspect only if new elements come from a completely different data distribution than the original data. As mentioned earlier, in the creation of training, testing, and evaluation subsets, it is best to maintain a balance of labels in each set.

Although the method of testing, training, and evaluation can produce very reliable results, it can be difficult to implement if the size of the original data set is very small. In this case, a technique called *n*-fold cross-validation is typically used. In *n*-fold cross-validation, the original data set is broken into *n* distinct subsets of data. For any single fold, the remaining fraction of the data outside the fold is used as a training set, and the fold itself is used as a testing set. This is done for each fold, and results are typically reported as the average accuracy over all the folds. Where a final model is also presented, it is typically the model that performed the best on its training fold. Because there is no evaluation subset in cross-fold validation, it is recommended to use it carefully if one intends to tune parameters of the decision tree models.

The final variation on decision trees is becoming more common in machine learning in general, as improvements in technology allow ever-more complex models. The basic idea is to create an ensemble of classifiers (Dietterich, 2000), in which multiple different trees are created, with a final classification a result of the combination of the classification results from all members of the ensemble. Common ensemble techniques for decision trees are boosting and bagging, although both are beyond this chapter. Next, to illustrate the application of decision trees, we will present their usage in classifying patients with chronic fatigue syndrome (CFS) and myalgic encephalomyelitis (ME).

CASE STUDY

Data mining could be used to help legitimize a group of individuals who have been stigmatized by labels and inappropriate case definition criteria. In our case study, we will focus on CFS and ME, whose scientific validity many health care professionals continue to doubt. The social construction of this disorder as a psychogenic illness of neurotic women, similar to earlier depictions of multiple sclerosis, has contributed to the negative attitudes that health care providers have toward those with this syndrome (Jason et al., 1997). This has had a serious negative impact on patients with this illness. For example, investigators have found that 95% of individuals seeking medical treatment for CFS reported feelings of being misunderstood because of the illness or the treatment (Green, Romei, & Natelson, 1999). Patients had been characterized as predominantly European American, middle-to-upper class women, and this perpetuated a myth that CFS was a "yuppie flu" disease, affecting middle-class and affluent people. Epidemiological research has shown that is a myth, as those with this illness are more likely to be minorities and of lower socioeconomic status (Jason et al., 1999).

For now, we will focus on how to identify who has and who does not have ME or CFS. Data mining can help with this important objective. Although this might appear to be a topic appropriate for a more traditional clinical domain, rather than one within the community field, this question has important public-policy implications because, if ambiguities occur in case definitions, investigators might select samples of patients who are different on fundamental aspects of this illness. Impediments to replicating findings across different laboratories would make it exceedingly difficult to estimate the prevalence of the illness, consistently identify biomarkers, or determine which treatments help patients.

The issue of diagnosis becomes important because many patients have been considered by their health care professionals to have a primarily affective disorder, which patients feel has stigmatized them, just as patients with cancer would feel undermined if health care professionals felt that they only had a psychogenic disease. Major depressive disorder is an example of a primary psychiatric disorder that has often been confused with CFS. Some patients with major depressive disorder also have chronic fatigue and CFS-like symptoms that can occur with depression (e.g., unrefreshing sleep, joint pain, muscle pain, impairment in concentration). Because fatigue and such symptoms are also defining criteria for CFS, some health care professionals and scientists have used an inadequate CFS case definition to conclude that ME and CFS are really psychiatric illnesses (Barsky & Borus, 1999). However, several ME and CFS symptoms, including prolonged fatigue after physical exertion, night sweats, sore throats, and swollen lymph nodes, are not commonly found in depression. In addition, although fatigue is the principal feature of CFS, fatigue does not assume equal prominence in depression (Friedberg & Jason, 1998). Moreover, illness onset with CFS is often sudden, occurring over a few hours or days, whereas primary depression generally shows a more gradual onset. In summary, CFS and major depressive disorder are two distinct illnesses, although they share a number of common symptoms. If one uses appropriate measures, it is possible to successfully differentiate these two disorders (Hawk, Jason, & Torres-Harding, 2006).

It is also important for case definitions to have high sensitivity and specificity, particularly for disorders with low prevalence rates such as CFS (about 4.2 in a thousand) (Jason et al., 1999). As an example, in a city of 1,000,000, with a true CFS rate of 4.2 per thousand, there would be 4,200 CFS cases. According to Bayes' theorem (Jaynes, 2003), if a case definition had a 95% rate of sensitivity, it would correctly identify 3,990 of these cases. However, if the case definition had 95% specificity, there would be more than 49,000 individuals who did not have CFS but were identified as having it. Clearly, being able to identify true negatives with precision is of high importance with low prevalence illnesses, such as CFS.

Criteria for the current CFS (Fukuda et al., 1994) case definition required a person to experience 6 or more months of chronic fatigue of a new or definite onset, but it used polythetic criteria, that is, a set of symptoms in which all do not need to be present to make a diagnosis. Because the Fukuda et al. (1994) criteria require only four symptoms out of a possible eight, critical CFS symptoms such as postexertional malaise and memory and concentration problems were not required for a patient to receive a diagnosis of CFS. This has increased the heterogeneity of the population, and, when similar biological findings have not emerged in different laboratories, it has been easy to jump to the conclusion that this illness is really psychologically determined.

In part as a reaction against the vague Fukuda et al. (1994) criteria, another consensus clinical case definition was developed, called the Canadian Clinical ME/CFS criteria (Carruthers et al., 2003). This ME/CFS case definition does specify core symptoms, including postexertional malaise; impairment of memory and concentration; unrefreshing sleep; arthralgia and/or myalgia; and several autonomic, neuroendocrine, and immune manifestations. However, the Canadian ME/CFS criteria require seven specific symptoms or domains, and requiring larger numbers of symptoms can inadvertently increase the rate of psychiatric comorbidity of the group that meets criteria. In addition, these criteria were based on consensus rather than empirical methods. Domains have the disadvantage of being less precise, as symptoms of both high and low prevalence could exist within a particular domain (Jason et al., 2014). At the present time, both the Institute of Medicine and the Office of Disease Prevention have committees focused on this issue of what case definition is, and there is considerable controversy among the scientific community regarding how to proceed. Patients have been clamoring for change and have rejected the commonly used Fukuda et al. (1994) CFS criteria, preferring the Canadian ME/CFS criteria (Carruthers et al., 2004). However, there continues to be scientific skepticism regarding this case definition, with respect to both the theoretical justification for their seven domains and the measurement of the domains.

Statistical selection techniques can be used to develop an empirical case definition, which would go beyond current consensus-based approaches. The problem for investigators is that there are many possible symptoms that might be included in such a case definition, but it is unclear which ones best distinguish between patients and healthy people, and, therefore, which symptoms are most characteristic of the illness. Methods to resolve this issue have important policy implications, as all science is built on the construction of case definitions, and, if they are not reliable and valid, then the diagnostic criteria might not successfully identify patients, which will hamper efforts to estimate prevalence, etiology, prevention, and treatment. Data mining techniques can help compare and contrast case definitions, as well as determine the types of symptoms that may be most useful in accurately diagnosing illnesses. In particular, data mining can uncover patterns in the data that would not be evident to human observers because of the size and complexity of the data.

In our case study, decision trees were used to analyze 54 common symptoms among patients with CFS, with all variables being placed into the analyses, rather than one item or domain or a limited group of items or domains. In this effort, decision trees helped determine which symptoms (and, implicitly, which questionnaire items) were most effective at accurately classifying participants as patients or controls.

For our case study, decision trees consist of a series of successive binary choices (branch points) that ideally result in an accurate classification of participants. At each branch point of the tree, all of the symptom variables are examined to determine which symptom has the greatest effect on the entropy of the classifications. Here, entropy indicates the certainty of the diagnosis. The symptom selected at each branch point is the one that best predicts classifications at that point in the tree; it is used to split all of the cases into two groups. This process is repeated, and more symptoms are chosen, until the resulting series of branch points produces groupings of correctly classified participants.

SPSS Statistics software was used to build our decision tree models. To construct the models, a Classification and Regression Tree (CART) algorithm was applied to a training set consisting of 66% of the cases, stratified to reflect the distribution of patient and control groups. The value of the model was measured by evaluating its classification performance when applied to cases reserved for testing (34% of the data), allowing this technique the ability to be generalized to new data.

Given the unbalanced distribution of the two classes (CFS versus non-CFS) and the fact that learning algorithms are biased toward the majority class, we conducted an experiment with similar numbers of participants in groups by taking a random undersample of 80 patients with CFS along with the 80 controls. We created 100 sets of randomly chosen patient data to analyze. For most analyses, only three to five variables (symptoms) were needed to classify participants. The analyses suggested the selection of four symptoms: fatigue or extreme tiredness, difficulty finding words to express thoughts, physically drained/sick after mild activity, and unrefreshed sleep (Jason et al., 2015).

The findings of this study suggest that core symptoms of this illness are fatigue, postexertional malaise, neurocognitive issues, and unrefreshing sleep. These results are theoretically compatible with other studies, such as Hawk et al.'s (2006) investigation, which found that these domains were able to successfully differentiate patients with CFS from major depressive disorder. Other symptoms, such as pain, autonomic, immune, and neuroendocrine symptoms, are less prevalent, but still important, and scores on these domains could also be specified as secondary areas of assessment. This data mining study suggests that empirical methods can be used to help determine which symptoms to include in the case definition.

CONCLUSION

In this chapter, we reviewed data mining as a strategy to handle large amounts of data. In our case study, data mining methods were used to propose ways to develop a more empirical, rather than consensus-based, ME and CFS case definitions. The scientific enterprise depends on reliable, valid methods of classifying patients into diagnostic categories, and this critical research activity can enable investigators to better understand etiology, pathophysiology, and treatment approaches for ME and CFS, along with other disorders.

It is easy to become overwhelmed when confronting complex problems or power holders, such as in the case definitions of ME and CFS. However, by using advanced computational methods, and focusing on one small piece at a time, tangible change and success in the public-policy arena can be achieved. In part because of such research as that presented in the case study, the third author of this chapter was appointed the chairperson of the Research Subcommittee of the Chronic Fatigue Syndrome Advisory Committee, which makes recommendations regarding CFS to the US Secretary of Health and Human Resources. In this capacity, he was able to work on other policy-related issues, such as the inappropriate name given to this illness, an expanded case definition that the Centers for Disease Control (CDC) introduced, and leadership issues at the CDC regarding its program of CFS research. This policy work has taken more than 20 years, working with a number of coalitions involving patient organizations and scientific organizations.

Because of the third author's focus on sophisticated data-analytic methods with the case definition, he was invited to be a member of Health and Human Services' Department of Disease Prevention's Pathway to Prevention planning workshop that will focus on ME and CFS case definitions and has given an invited talk at the Institute of Medicine's commission to review the ME and CFS clinical case definitions. In each of these venues, the use of data mining strategies has been emphasized as one way to help investigators, patient organizations, and government bodies improve their decision making on complicated issues such as the ME and CFS case definitions.

In general, data mining provides a powerful tool to help both practitioners and researchers in uncovering patterns in the data that are not obvious to human observers and, consequently, cannot be analyzed using typical statistical analysis of hypothesis acceptance or rejection. In fact, data mining is opening up a new era of research, in which experimentation is data driven rather than hypothesis driven. Indeed, this new paradigm makes machine learning an ideal tool for community-based research for a number of reasons. First, unlike the exact sciences, community-based research rarely has easily discovered hypotheses, and the questions surrounding the interesting problems often cannott be represented simply using verifiable hypotheses. For instance, in our case, the question of "What symptoms are important for the definition and diagnosis of ME and CFS?" could be formulated as simply verifiable hypotheses, but we would have had to propose each possible subset of symptoms as the correct one and then use traditional statistical analysis to accept or reject each hypothesis. Given the existence of 54 symptoms in our survey instrument, this would have generated on the order of 10^{15} hypotheses to check. Instead, data mining provides a tool by which we can limit the number of possible hypotheses in a rigorous, empirical way. Second, where stigma or cultural avoidance issues enter into the research, data mining methods provide an objective method of investigation, in contrast to hypothesis-driven research, in which even the choice of hypothesis can have unfortunate social consequences. When the data determine your hypothesis, it is hard to argue that research bias exists. It is not the case that data-driven research is completely without bias, but it is harder to introduce bias when using automatic methods on source data. Third, despite the frequently intense algorithmic and analytical complexity of machine learning, faster and cheaper computers are becoming ever more prevalent, and one can confidently expect that data mining will be effectively available in mobile devices in the near future, either executed on one's phone or through quick and efficient cloud connections to powerful servers. For example, technological advances have allowed applying data mining to model public health on a population scale. Several studies have showed that, using large amounts of Twitter data, it is possible to track and predict influenza (Collier, Son, & Nguyen, 2011; Krieck, Dreesman, Otrusina, & Denecke, 2011) and also detect affective disorders such as depression (Golder & Macy, 2011).

Data-driven research is becoming increasingly more common. When the volume of data becomes so large that it is difficult for humans to discern patterns, then data-driven research can be effectively used to discover underlying issues in a relatively objective and empirical way. Note that it is not necessary to have an enormous sample in order to have a large volume of data; in community-based research in particular, it can be the case that the number of samples is relatively small, but the data on each sample are enormously rich. Although this can present a challenge to machine learning, the use of feature selection techniques, such as decision trees, can reduce the complexity of the sample data and allow for confident predictions on a small sample size. Furthermore, although much human data do distribute normally, much do not, and machine learning techniques, such as decision trees, that do not rely on assumptions about the distribution of the underlying data can effectively uncover patterns without normality.

Machine learning techniques, when used for classification, offer a number of other advantages that may be desirable in community-based research. Although classification typically predicts a categorical label, the underlying probability of prediction can be maintained, and probabilistic classification can be used. Thus, for example, rather that reading the output of a decision tree to say, "This patient has CFS," one can reference the underlying probabilities to suggest, "This patient has a 65% chance of having CFS." Such uncertainty can have positive impacts in human research, in which certainties may actually be detrimental to promoting cultural or policy change.

Furthermore, many machine learning techniques, and decision trees in particular, offer a variety of parameters that can be tuned for particular applications. Although such parameter tuning can contribute uncertainty to the final results, it does offer the possibility of leveraging the machine learning to focus on accuracy, specificity, or sensitivity. For example, in medical research, there is often a focus on specificity; the cost of missing a pathology in a diseased patient is much higher than the cost of misdiagnosing a healthy patient. Medical research will often sacrifice sensitivity for small increases in specificity. However, as we have seen in the case of CFS, and as is true in community-based research more generally, a focus on sensitivity might be more appropriate; allocating resources most efficiently or avoiding social stigma might argue in favor of not mislabeling pathology. The parameter tuning of machine learning allows us to generate models that focus on the best measure of effectiveness for a particular problem or situation.

In general, machine learning provides a powerful, flexible way of investigating data that allows researchers to uncover patterns that are not immediately obvious to human observers, in a way which preserves as much objectivity as possible and allows the data to directly determine results. Especially in the case of community-based research, in which standard methods from the physical sciences may not be directly applicable to the cultural environment of the richness of the data, machine learning can be a very effective method for discovery.

REFERENCES

Barsky, A. J., & Borus, J. F. (1999) Functional somatic syndromes. *Annals of Internal Medicine, 130*, 910–921.

Breiman, L., Friedman, J. H., Olshen, R. A., & Stone, C. J. (1984). *Classification and regression trees*. Monterey, CA: Wadsworth & Brooks/Cole.

Carruthers, B. M., Jain, A. K., De Meirleir, K. L., Peterson, D. L., Klimas, N. G., Lerner, A. M., . . . van de Sande, M. I. (2003). Myalgic Encephalomyelitis/chronic fatigue syndrome: Clinical working case definition, diagnostic and treatments protocols. *Journal of Chronic Fatigue Syndrome, 11*, 7–115.

Collier, N., Son, N. T., & Nguyen, N. M. (2011). OMG U got flu? Analysis of shared health messages for bio-surveillance. *Journal of Biomedical Semantics*, 2(Suppl 5), S9.

Davidson, I., Gilpin, S., & Walker, P. B. (2012). Behavioral event data and their analysis, *Data Mining Knowledge Discovery, 25*, 635–653.

Dhar, V. (2013). Data science and predictions. *Communications of the ACM, 58*, 64–73.

Dietterich, T. G. (2000). Ensemble methods in machine learning. J. Kittler & F. Roli (Ed.) *First international workshop on multiple classifier systems, lecture notes in computer science* (pp. 1–15). New York, NY: Springer Verlag.

Ferdowsi, Z., Settimi, R., & Raicu, D. S. (2010, July). *An application of clustering techniques to urban studies*. Paper presented at the 2010 International Conference on Data Mining, Las Vegas, NV.

Friedberg, F., & Jason, L. A. (1998). *Assessment and treatment of chronic fatigue syndrome*. Washington, DC: American Psychological Association.

Fukuda, K., Straus, S. E., Hickie, I., Sharpe, M. C., Dobbins, J. G., & Komaroff, A. (1994). The chronic fatigue syndrome: A comprehensive approach to its definition and study. *Annals of Internal Medicine, 121*, 953–959.

Ghahramani, Z. (2004). Unsupervised learning. In O. Bousquet, G. Raetsch, & U. von Luxburg (Eds.), *Advanced lectures on machine learning* (pp. 77–112). New York, NY: Springer Verlag.

Golder, S. A., & Macy, M. W. (2011). Diurnal and seasonal mood vary with work, sleep, and day length across diverse cultures. *Science, 333*, 1878–1881.

Green, D. M., & Swets, J. A. (1966). *Signal detection theory and psychophysics*. New York, NY: Wiley.

Green, J., Romei, J., & Natelson, B. J. (1999). Stigma and chronic fatigue syndrome. *Journal of Chronic Fatigue Syndrome, 5*, 63–75.

Harris, R. (2008). The 16 TB RAM PC: When? *ZDNet*. Retreived June 2015, from http://www.zdnet.com/article/the-16-tb-ram-pc-when/

Hawk, C., Jason, L. A., & Torres-Harding, S. (2006). Differential diagnosis of chronic fatigue syndrome and major depressive disorder. *International Journal of Behavioral Medicine, 13*, 244–251.

He, H., & Garcia, E. A. (2009). Learning from imbalanced data. *IEEE Transactions on Knowledge and Data Engineering, 21*, 1263–1284.

Jason, L.A., Kot, B., Sunnquist, M., Brown, A., Evans, M., Jantke, R., Williams, Y., Furst, J., & Vernon,

S.D. (2015). Chronic fatigue Syndrome and myalgic encephalomyelitis: Toward an empirical case definition. *Health Psychology and Behavioral Medicine: An Open Access Journal, 3,* 82–93..

Jason, L. A., Richman, J. A., Friedberg, F., Wagner, L., Taylor, R. R., & Jordan, K. M. (1997). Politics, science, and the emergence of a new disease: The case of chronic fatigue -syndrome. *American Psychologist, 52,* 973–983.

Jason, L. A., Richman, J. A., Rademaker, A. W., Jordan, K. M., Plioplys, A. V., Taylor, R. R., & Plioplys, S. (1999). A community-based study of chronic fatigue syndrome. *Archives of Internal Medicine, 159,* 2129–2137.

Jason, L. A., Sunnquist, M., Brown, A., Evans, M., Vernon, S. D., Furst, J., & Simonis,V. (2014). Examining case definition criteria for chronic fatigue syndrome and Myalgic Encephalomyelitis. *Fatigue: Biomedicine, Health, and Behavior, 2,* 40–56.

Jaynes, E. T. T. (2003). *Probability theory: The logic of science.* New York, NY: Cambridge University Press.

Jiang S., Ferreira, J., Jr., & Gonzalez, M. C. (2012). Discovering urban spatial-temporal structure from human activity patterns. In *Proceedings of the Association for Computing Machinery SIGKDD International Workshop on Urban Computing* (pp. 95–102). New York, NY: Association for Computing Machinery

Kass, G. V. (1980). An exploratory technique for investigating large quantities of categorical data. *Applied Statistics, 29,* 119–127.

Krieck, M., Dreesman, J., Otrusina, L., & Denecke, K. (2011). A new age of public health: Identifying disease outbreaks by analyzing tweets. In *Proceedings of Health WebScience Workshop, ACM Web Science Conference.* Koblenz, Germany: Association of Computing Machinery

Kotsiantis, S. B. (2007). Supervised machine learning: A review of techniques. *Informatica, 31,* 249–268

Kutz, J. N. (2013). *Data-driven modeling & scientific computation: Methods for complex systems and big data.* Oxford, England: Oxford University Press.

Wang, F., Tong, H., Yu, P., & Aggarwal, C. (2012). Guest editorial: Special issue on data mining technologies for computational social science. *Data Mining and Knowledge Discovery, 25,* 415–419.

20

Agent-Based Models

ZACHARY P. NEAL AND JENNIFER A. LAWLOR

The collection of methodological tools often called *system science methods* are rapidly gaining attention as useful in community-based research for their unique ability to capture ecological and contextual effects in a holistic way. Agent-based models are a specific variety of system science methods, which also include network analysis and system dynamics models (Neal, 2015). These models are designed to simulate the behaviors of agents (e.g., people) as they interact with one another in particular settings. Although they may be used in many ways, their most general purpose is to develop an understanding of how individual behaviors and features of the context can give rise to macroscopic social phenomena. In this chapter, we illustrate this through two extended examples. First, in introducing agent-based models, we describe how Schelling (1969) used an early version of agent-based modeling to understand how individuals' preferences to live nearby similar others (i.e., an individual behavior) and the diversity of a residential neighborhood (i.e., a contextual feature) give rise to patterns of residential segregation (i.e., a macroscopic social phenomenon). Second, in the case study, we describe how Neal and Neal (2014) examined how individuals' preferences to interact with similar and nearby others (i.e., individual behaviors) and the segregation of a residential neighborhood (i.e., a contextual feature) gives rise to sense of community (i.e., a macroscopic social phenomenon), and we adapt this model to explore how community public spaces (i.e., another contextual feature) may moderate this process. Interactive versions of several models discussed in this chapter are available on a companion Web site at http://www.msu.edu/~zpneal/communityabm.

Agent-based models have several features that make them especially useful for community-based research. First, they simultaneously incorporate individual behaviors, the contextual influence of other individuals in the setting, and the contextual influence of other setting characteristics like roads or parks. Thus, these models provide community-based researchers with a single analytic tool that takes a holistic perspective toward what communities are and how they work. Second, as a simulation method, agent-based models allow community-based researchers to study processes that might be impossible or unethical to investigate in real communities and, by simulating what-if scenarios, to anticipate otherwise unanticipated consequences of interventions. Thus, they can be a tool for ensuring that community-based research and community-based interventions are conducted and implemented in responsible ways. Third, as a highly interactive and iterative analytic strategy, agent-based models readily lend themselves to participatory research that seeks to engage community members, but they can also help community-based researchers clarify their thinking about what to do in communities before entering the field. Thus, these models can be a tool for ensuring that community-based work incorporates community members' perspectives while still being respectful of their time.

This chapter has several overarching goals. In the next section we introduce the basic features of agent-based models in a nontechnical way, focusing on the approach's epistemology, assumptions, and basic steps, using Schelling's (1969) simple model of residential segregation as an example. We then explore how agent-based models can be particularly useful for community-based research, focusing on a few key challenges that community-based researchers often encounter and considering the solutions that agent-based models offer. In the case study, we put these ideas into practice, describing the use of an agent-based model to evaluate the use of community public spaces as a potential intervention for cultivating sense of community. Finally, we offer some suggestions for getting started using agent-based models in community-based research.

INTRODUCTION TO AGENT-BASED MODELS

Agent-based models are embedded in an epistemological perspective known as methodological individualism, which views macrolevel social phenomena as arising or emerging from the microlevel interactions of individual agents (Agassi, 1960; Hodgson, 2007; Udehn, 2002). Methodological individualists contend that a complete understanding of a macrolevel social phenomenon requires explaining it in terms of the actions of the individual agents who caused it. This is a kind of reductionist epistemology, but one that innocently asks, if social phenomena are not caused by the actions and interactions of people and their environments, where else could we possibly look for an explanation? Accordingly, the goal of many agent-based models is to understand what microlevel interaction(s) could generate a given macrolevel social phenomenon, or what Epstein (1999) called the generativist's question. To answer this question, Epstein proposed that researchers conduct what he called the generativist's experiment: "Situate an initial population of autonomous heterogeneous agents in a relevant spatial environment; allow them to interact according to simple local rules, and thereby generate—or 'grow'—the macroscopic regularity from the bottom up" (p. 42).

A key feature of agent-based models is their flexibility: They can be used to explore nearly any macrolevel social phenomenon and nearly any kind of microlevel interactions, including those between two agents, or between an agent and its environment, or between different parts of an environment. For the sake of concreteness, we illustrate the basic principles of agent-based models in this section by using Schelling's (1969) model of segregation. Schelling (1969) was interested in understanding the macrolevel social phenomenon of residential segregation. He recognized that many mechanisms might explain the existence of residential segregation, including top-down institutional forces such as mortgage redlining and restrictive covenants, but was specifically interested in whether segregation would still emerge in the absence of these forces. If institutional forces do not impose segregation, is it likely to emerge anyway?

Basic Principles

Agent-based models begin with a population of autonomous, heterogeneous agents. The agents are the entities that act, interact, and react in the simulated world. In Schelling's model and in many other community-based models, the agents are people, but the agents could also be households, organizations, animals, and so on. These agents are assumed to be autonomous; that is, they act on their own and are not fully controlled by external forces. Importantly, the assumption that agents are autonomous does not imply that they have unrestricted autonomy; agents' actions may be heavily constrained by their environment or heavily influenced by other agents. In Schelling's model, people have autonomy to live where they wish, but their decisions are constrained by the availability of space and by the demographic characteristics of their neighbors. Agents are also assumed to be heterogeneous; that is, they are not interchangeable but differ from one another on any number of characteristics. In Schelling's model, people differ from one another in two ways: demographically (some are type A people, and some are type B people) and spatially (each person has his or her own residential location in the simulated world).

The population of agents is situated in a relevant spatial environment. In many agent-based models, the environment takes the form of a grid, where each square represents a location in the environment and may have its own unique characteristics. In Schelling's model, the environment is very simple: Each square represents a parcel of land where a person may choose to move and reside if it is unoccupied. In other models of a community, squares may represent parcels of land that differ in value or desirability, or some squares may represent residential opportunities while other squares represent parks or roads.

Once a simulated world of agents in an environment is created, the agents are allowed to interact according to simple, local rules. This closely mirrors Barker's (1968) behavior setting theory, which contends that people are essentially rule-following creatures who take cues about how to act from their setting. This component of agent-based models has three key features. First, the rules that agents follow are simple: People are not like computers that consider all possible actions and select the optimal one, but rather they follow heuristics and rules of thumb. In Schelling's model, people follow a single, simple rule when selecting a place to live: Find a place where at least X% of my neighbors are similar to me. The exact value of X can be adjusted by the researcher, thereby modifying the behavioral rule. Second, the rules that agents follow are local: People are not omniscient, but rather they selectively attend to the most salient features of their environment. In Schelling's model, when people consider whether a potential residential location meets their criteria, they consider only their immediate neighbors, not those living miles away. Finally, the agents are allowed to interact: The macrolevel social phenomena that emerge in the simulated world are strictly endogenous, arising purely from the agents' interactions with each other and their environment. In Schelling's model, people keep moving around according to their single behavioral rule, without any outside intervention, until they are all satisfied with their neighborhoods.

Perhaps the cardinal principle of agent-based models is simplicity. As Box and Draper (1987) explained, "all models are wrong, but some are useful" (p. 424). The goal is not to simulate reality in its full complexity and obtain the "right" model, which would be impossible, but rather to identify the minimal set of features necessary to "grow" the macrolevel social phenomenon of interest and thus be useful for understanding it. In Schelling's case, he showed that it was possible to observe the emergence of residential segregation in a world populated by two types of people both following the same plausible, simple rule. Although perhaps not realistic, he thus demonstrated that the emergence of segregation does not require top-down institutional forces, complex combinations of multiple demographic characteristics, a preexisting history of segregation, and so on. Perhaps even more noteworthy, he demonstrated that residential segregation would emerge even when the rule guiding peoples' neighborhood preferences was relatively weak (i.e., when the researcher makes X, the variable that controls the behavioral rule, small). For example, even when people are willing to be a minority in their own neighborhoods and merely want at least one third of their neighbors to be similar, fairly extreme segregation still develops. Here, the model is "wrong" because it omits many features of reality, including, for example, the role of streets (Grannis, 1998), school choice (Saporito, 2003), or mortgage foreclosure (Rugh & Massey, 2010). Nonetheless, it is still "useful" because it highlights how even subtle, innocuous preferences can make segregation nearly inevitable. It is also useful as a first step in a modeling cycle, which in subsequent iterations may incorporate some of these more complex phenomena.

The Modeling Cycle

The development of an agent-based model proceeds through a modeling cycle (Railsback & Grimm, 2011). As with most research projects, the first step involves clearly articulating the research question, which often takes the form: How does the researcher's macrolevel phenomenon of interest emerge from microlevel interactions? For Schelling, the goal was to understand how residential segregation emerges. Second, the researcher identifies the kind of agent(s) involved and the characteristics they have, the characteristics of the agents' environment, and the rule(s) that govern how the agents interact with each other and their environment. Schelling's model involved people with a single binary demographic characteristic, in a grid where squares represent possible residences, where people select residences by aiming to satisfy a preference for neighborhood demographic composition. The clearer, simpler, and more concrete the research question and model characteristics, the easier the third step: implementing the initial model using software. Once implemented, the model is checked for errors, run multiple times with experimental manipulations of features of the model, and the results examined to determine which interaction rules yield the macro-level phenomenon of interest. The goal of Schelling's analysis was to determine what percentage of similar neighbors (i.e., the value of X) people must prefer before segregation emerges; as noted earlier, the value is surprisingly low. At each stage in the modeling cycle, the researcher may refine or expand the model, incorporating additional elements (e.g., a new interaction rule or a new agent), making the process truly cyclical and iterative.

Just as agent-based model development proceeds through a cycle, running an agent-based model can also be viewed as involving a series of steps. Running a model usually begins with an initialization step, in which the simulated world (i.e., the agents and their environment) is created. This is followed by an interaction step, in which each agent takes a turn following one or more rules. In Schelling's model, during the initialization step, equal numbers of type A and type B people are each placed on random squares in the grid. During the interaction step, each person takes a turn counting the percentage of his or her neighbors that are similar. If this percentage exceeds the person's preference, the person is happy and stays, but if the percentage falls short of the person's preference, the person is unhappy and moves to a new location (i.e., an unoccupied square elsewhere in the grid). The interaction step can be repeated, allowing people to continually move and reevaluate their neighborhoods, until all people are happy with their location or until it becomes clear that universal satisfaction is impossible. At each step, the researcher can observe the current level of segregation and watch changes in the neighborhood's spatial patterns dynamically shift.

Software

There are a large number of specialty software programs designed for developing and running agent-based models. However, NetLogo (Wilensky, 1999) is particularly useful for a number of reasons. It is free to download (https://ccl.northwestern.edu/netlogo/) and use, and, as a Java-based program, will run on both PC and Macintosh computers. It is also accompanied by a tutorial, extensive documentation, and a library of example agent-based models to facilitate learning. Finally, it features a graphic interface that allows researchers to view and interact with models as they are running. An interactive version of Schelling's (1969) segregation model implemented in NetLogo (adapted from Wilensky, 1997) is available online. It helps illustrate the NetLogo interface and many of the features of Schelling's model discussed in this section. First, it includes an adjustable slider that allows the user to set the total population of the simulated world, which is created in the initialization step when the "1. Setup" button is pressed. Second, it includes an adjustable slider that allows the user to set the people's level of preference for similar neighbors, which people aim to satisfy in the interaction step when the "2. Go" button is pressed. Finally, it includes a graphic display of the simulated world and a line graph of the world's level of segregation over time, allowing the user to watch residential segregation emerge as agents move around seeking to satisfy their preferences.

APPLYING AGENT-BASED MODELS IN COMMUNITY-BASED RESEARCH

Although they have not yet been used extensively in community-based research, agent-based models offer a promising approach to addressing many of the challenges that emerge from conducting community-based research and can act as an important complement to data collected directly from community members. First, they can be used to guide community-based research and data collection without wasting researchers' or community members' time and resources. Second, they allow researchers to explore questions that would be impossible to examine in community settings. Third, they can help researchers anticipate the consequences of planned community interventions or efforts toward social change. Fourth, the cycle used to develop agent-based models provides many natural points to seek community input during model building and assessment, facilitating participatory inquiry.

Guiding Community-Based Research

Large-scale community studies and interventions can be challenging to plan and implement because there are often a bewildering array of individual and ecological characteristics that might be measured and examined. Agent-based models can be used as a first step, to inform the development of research questions and identify the most crucial data to collect, which can save researchers' and community members' time by helping them avoid unnecessary data collection and refine the scope of work to be done. Consider the case of developing a community-based intervention to reduce the spread of HIV/AIDS. A community-based researcher might consider measuring the prevalence of many different sexual behaviors within a population, including condom use, testing for HIV, frequency of sexual encounters, and duration of sexual relationships. However, each of these is costly for researchers to measure, requires invasive inquiry for community members, and is time consuming for all parties. A preliminary agent-based model might help the researcher ask, what do I really need to measure? An interactive AIDS model available online (adapted from Wilenski, 1997) simulates HIV/AIDS transmission in a community driven by these behaviors and can be used to see that testing frequency has a much greater impact on a community's rate of infection than other behaviors. This model-derived insight might provide a guide for data collection that not only makes the study more feasible for the researcher but also less burdensome for the community members.

Asking Unaskable Questions

Communities are real places, and community members are real people. These are the key reasons that community-based research is so important, but they also impose some substantial limitations on what community-based researchers can do. Many potential research questions or experimental manipulations would be unethical, impossible, or difficult to study in community settings. A study of how HIV/AIDS spreads in a particular community might benefit from exploring the impact of eliminating residents' access to condoms. It would surely be unethical to do this in a real community, but the AIDS model mentioned earlier provides the researcher a way of asking this otherwise unaskable question by simply instructing the agents (i.e., simulated community residents) to never use condoms and watching what happens as a result. In other cases, an experimental manipulation may not be unethical, but it may simply be impossible. In the mid-1990s, Hoffer (2006) ethnographically studied the local heroin market in Denver, Colorado. Examining the impact of police busts on the market would have been impossible for a variety of reasons, including the inability to experimentally control the timing and intensity of the busts and the inability to remain in the field after having done so. Instead, Hoffer, Bobashev, and Morris (2009) used the ethnographic findings to develop an agent-based model of the heroin market, within which they were able to simulate the effects of police busts. Finally, there are many cases where the data needed are ethical and possible, but not feasible, to collect. Social network data are a prime example because accurate network analysis requires high levels of participation and has a low tolerance for missing data (see Chapter 21), which severely limits the feasibility of collecting this type of data in (large) community settings. Rather than collect social network data from real community members, which can be very costly and time consuming, agent-based models can be used to simulate the dynamic formation of social networks among community members as they interact with one another according to certain rules (see Chapter 22). The resulting, simulated networks can give researchers a sense for the kind of network structures they might expect to find in real communities. We discuss an example of this type of model in the next section.

Perhaps one of the most pressing but unaskable questions in community-based research is the causal question. Community-based researchers are often relegated to the territory of association, left to conclude that X is associated with Y, but unable to push the epistemological envelope and conclude that X causes Y. However, the earlier AIDS, segregation, and social network examples highlight that agent-based models also allow community-based researchers to ask causal questions. Because the researcher has complete control over the simulated behaviors of the agents, and of the simulated environment in which they interact, agent-based models make it possible to conduct true (not merely quasi- or natural) experiments in simulated communities (Devine, Wright, & Joyner, 1994). Thus, whereas a field study may ultimately conclude that a community's lack of access to condoms is associated with higher rates of HIV infection in the community, an agent-based model may allow researchers to much more usefully conclude that, at least within the simulated community, lack of access causes higher rates of infection.

Anticipating Unanticipated Consequences

Community-based researchers often address complex problems, which makes it difficult to predict both how the problem will evolve over time and how different efforts to solve the problem might shift that evolution. Agent-based models provide one approach to anticipating the potential consequences of taking (or not taking) action in a community. This frequently takes the form of simulating a series of what-if scenarios in an agent-based model. For example, a community-based researcher might develop a model designed to simulate the formation of social networks among a community's stakeholders, which by itself may be useful for understanding stakeholder engagement. However, the researcher might subsequently use this model to explore the potential consequences of hosting monthly stakeholder meetings (e.g., what if I simulate all of the stakeholders interacting once per month?) or of an unanticipated community change (e.g., what if I simulate one of the stakeholders suddenly leaving the community?). By probing these what-if scenarios, community-based researchers can develop interventions and community change agendas with greater caution and confidence.

When paired with relatively fast and inexpensive computing resources (most agent-based models run quite fast on even modest personal computers), the range of what-if scenarios that can be examined is virtually unlimited. In practice, the examination of intended and unintended consequences in agent-based models often takes the form of a "parameter sweep." The researcher identifies one or more variables of particular interest (e.g., HIV testing frequency, intensity of residential preferences, likelihood of a stakeholder leaving) and conducts a simulation at each possible level of the variable(s), observing the outcome in each case. In this way, community-based researchers can examine all possible combinations of variable values, including those combinations that occur in real communities, as well as those that could plausibly occur but for which no real-world examples are available to study, to anticipate the outcomes that might be expected in both real and possible communities.

Engaging Community Members

Although nearly all community-based researchers see the value of engaging community members in their research, it is not always clear how or when this engagement should occur. The modeling cycle, through which agent-based models are developed, provides multiple ways and multiple opportunities for this type of engagement. During the model conceptualization phase, input from community members can illuminate which microlevel and macrolevel phenomena are valuable to investigate, while further community input during model design can define the kinds of agents and interaction rules that should be included to ensure the model accurately mirrors the setting. At the evaluation stage, engaged community members can interpret the results of the model alongside the researcher, providing feedback on whether outcomes make sense in the context of their experiences and identifying areas that need further development. Engagement can also foster a sense of community ownership of the model and increase the likelihood that participants will use the final model after the completion of the initial research project.

Often called participatory agent-based modeling, or PABM, these steps can help ensure that the model includes all appropriate phenomena and can bolster the models' validity. Moreover, unlike attracting community members' participation in more traditional forms of research, because agent-based models often look like "computer games" and community engagement often takes the form of "playing with" the model, participation can be easier to obtain. PABM remains somewhat rare, but the literature still contains several useful examples. Community members have used participatory modeling processes as tools for addressing issues such as resource allocation and land usage (Castella, Trung, & Boissau, 2005; Naivinit, Le Page, Trébuil, & Gajaseni, 2010). Castella et al. (2005) implemented PABM to understand changes in land usage over time among farmers in Vietnam. They collected data to inform model design by engaging community members in role-playing games and individual interviews to understand the kinds of simple rules that govern their land use decisions. Community members were ultimately able to employ the model as a tool for making decisions about how to move forward with sustainable practices that met the needs of all stakeholders involved in the local agriculture system. Naivinit et al. (2010) similarly used a role-playing game and follow-up interviews to build a participatory model of rice production and labor migration in Thailand. Participants then used the resulting model to understand and take collective action around issues related to labor migration. Although PABM remains relatively unexplored in community-based research, the ease of engaging participants in the modeling cycle and the benefits that emerge from its use make it a very promising approach to research.

CASE STUDY

Community-based researchers and activists often find themselves at the crossroads of conflicting goals in their work. A prime example is the twin goals of promoting community diversity and sense of community. An extensive literature around the dialectic of spatial integration and social cohesion has emerged, suggesting that as communities become more diverse and integrated, they experience declines in cohesion and sense of community (e.g., Portes & Vickstrom, 2011; Putnam, 2007;

Townley, Kloos, Green, & Franco, 2011). Neal and Neal (2014) sought to understand why this dialectic exists, or stated in terms of the generativist's question: What microlevel behaviors lead to the macrolevel social phenomena of integration and cohesion having a negative relationship?

To answer this question, they used an agent-based model to conduct a generativist experiment. Their model begins with a population of people who differ on a single unspecified demographic characteristic (Schelling, 1969), in a neighborhood with a specific level of spatial segregation. Some of their simulated neighborhoods were highly segregated, with people living only near demographically similar others, while other simulated neighborhoods were highly integrated, with people living among demographically mixed others. In the interaction step of the model, each person had the opportunity to form a relationship with each other person in the setting. The probability of a relationship forming between two people depended on two factors: (a) the tendency to have friends who are demographically similar (i.e., homophily) and (b) the tendency to have friends who live nearby (i.e., proximity). After a social network was formed in the simulated neighborhood, Neal and Neal computed the level of cohesion, which they operationalized as the average density of each person's personal social network (i.e., the clustering coefficient).

They simulated a large number of communities using range of possible values for segregation, homophily, and proximity (i.e., a three-parameter sweep), each time recording the level of cohesion observed in the community. This analysis showed that whenever social networks form through tendencies toward both homophily and proximity, there is a negative relationship between the community's level of integration and its level of cohesion. The more residentially integrated communities had less social cohesion, while the less integrated communities had more cohesion. Thus, answering the generativist's question, they found that the tendencies of homophily and proximity that are commonly observed in social network formation are sufficient to generate or "grow" the integration-cohesion dialectic. Interestingly, their parameter sweep also highlighted that a reversal in the tendency toward homophily (i.e., if people preferred dissimilar friends) or proximity (i.e., if people preferred friends who live far away) would eliminate the dialectic and make simultaneously integrated and cohesive communities possible. However, although reversing the tendency toward homophily or proximity is possible in an agent-based model, where the simulated people follow the researcher's instructions, it is likely not possible in reality and thus likely not a potential avenue for a community-based intervention.

Neal and Neal's (2014) study illustrates the use of an agent-based model to understand how a community phenomenon is generated by individual behaviors. Here, we build on their model to test a possible intervention to simultaneously cultivate community integration and cohesion and overcome the dialectic that they and others have observed. Specifically, we add to their model to explore a series of what-if scenarios that involve the construction of one or more community public spaces, like parks or community centers. We hypothesized that community public spaces can bring people together, including people who might not otherwise interact, and serve as a site for the formation of community relationships (Neal, 2013; Orum & Neal, 2009). These public space-based relationships may enhance community social cohesion, even in integrated neighborhoods where the community social network might otherwise be fragmented. However, parks and community centers are costly to build, and interventions are often accompanied by unanticipated consequences. Thus, a preliminary test of the intervention's hypothesized effect using an agent-based model offers a useful first step.

Our refined agent-based model includes several features not present in Neal and Neal's (2014) original model. First, we allow the simulated community to contain community public spaces, where each person in the community uses his or her nearest community public space. Second, in addition to the probability of a relationship between two people depending on homophily and proximity, we add one more: the tendency to have friends who use the same community public space. Finally, we allow minor adjustments in the location of the community spaces, including whether the spaces should be spread out or located near each other, and whether the spaces should be located randomly, in mostly integrated areas of the community, or in mostly segregated areas of the community. An interactive version of this model is available online.

To examine this model, we do not use a true parameter sweep because many possible parameter combinations would be unrealistic from the point of view of a feasible community intervention. For example, building 1,000 parks in a community, or encouraging people to exclusively make friends at community spaces but nowhere else, may enhance cohesion but are not viable intervention strategies. Instead, we examine a series of parameter combinations that match some plausible intervention scenarios. Figure 20.1 illustrates our findings from these what-if scenarios; each line represents a specific scenario and shows the expected relationship between community integration and cohesion. The solid line in both panels represents the baseline case, drawn from Neal and Neal's (2014) original model, in which people tend to form relationships with similar, nearby others and there are no community spaces. The dash-dotted lines indicate the expected relationship between integration and cohesion when one (the left panel) or two (the right panel) community public spaces are built in random, nonadjacent locations and when the impact of sharing a demographic characteristic and of using the same public space on relationship formation are equal. The remaining lines capture scenarios when the impact of sharing a demographic characteristic is slightly more important for relationship formation (dashed line), and when the impact of using the same public space is slightly more important for relationship formation (dotted line).

These results provide a number of insights into the potential consequences of a public space-building intervention designed to cultivate community integration and cohesion. First, in all of the intervention scenarios that we examine using the model (the 6 shown in Fig. 20.1, and 378 more), the same negative relationship between integration and cohesion observed by Neal and Neal (2014) persists ($-0.91 <$ Spearman's $\rho < -0.44$). This suggests that an intervention rooted in building community public spaces is unlikely to eliminate the much-lamented integration-cohesion dialectic. Second, although the dialectic persists in each intervention scenario, many yield increases in community cohesion compared to the baseline. For example, although an intervention that builds two community public spaces is expected to generate the greatest boost in cohesion in a segregated community, integrated communities would also be expected to experience increased cohesion. Thus, although a public space-building intervention cannot undo the dialectic, it may at least be an avenue toward greater social cohesion.

Finally, and perhaps most important for community-based research, these results help us to locate the intervention strategies that might be expected to work best. For example, an intervention that builds a single community public space,

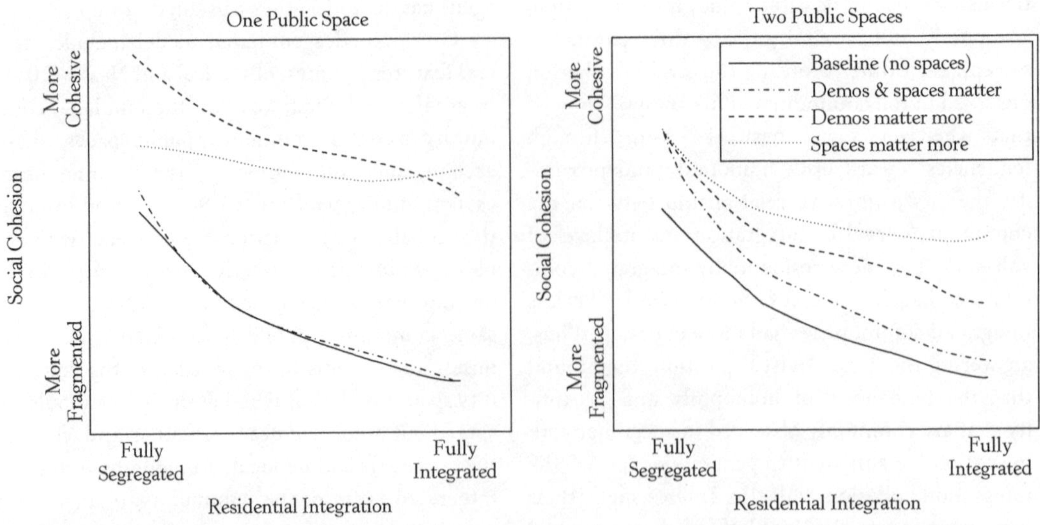

FIGURE 20.1: Results of a simulated public space building intervention.

Note: Baseline Scenario: Status Homophily = 1, Proximity = 3, Place Homophily = 0; Demos & Spaces matter scenario: Status Homophily = 1, Proximity = 3, Place Homophily = 1; Demos matter more scenario: Status Homophily = 2, Proximity = 1, Place Homophily = 1; Spaces matter more scenario: Status Homophily = 1, Proximity = 1, Place Homophily = 2. In the scenarios that include public spaces, the spaces were placed in random locations in the community; when two spaces were included, they were separated by at least five grid patches.

in a community where sharing a public space with another person has a slightly greater impact on the probability of forming a relationship than sharing a demographic characteristic with that person (dotted line in the left panel), seems to simultaneously minimize the dialectic and maximize the cohesion-boosting consequences. Reflecting on this finding, it may seem obvious; of course, social cohesion would be high in a community in which all residents use the same public space and for whom that public space is very important. However, it is obvious only in retrospect; note that a one-space intervention is substantially better than a two-space intervention. Although this does not guarantee that building a public space that is important to residents will yield a harmonious community, the finding at least allows us to focus our attention and refine our intervention before entering the field.

CONCLUSION

At first glance, agent-based models may seem to be quite different from more traditional methods used by community-based researchers and to require specialized technical skills in programming. However, in practice the learning curve for newcomers to agent-based modeling is actually quite shallow. Here, we offer a couple of suggestions for getting started. First, download the NetLogo software and complete the accompanying tutorial. This short tutorial takes a few hours to complete, walking the user through many of the software's most important features and the programming language's most important commands. At the end of the tutorial, the user will have written a complete agent-based model from scratch that includes agents interacting with each other and with their environment, which highlights how rapidly a model can be developed. Second, explore the built-in models that are bundled with NetLogo in its Model Library. Each model has a nontechnical description of what it does, as well as annotated programming code to understand how it works. There are a broad range of example models, including models on community-related topics such as urban sprawl, team building and collaboration, wealth distribution, and diffusion of resources through a network.

The tutorial and model library are helpful for getting acquainted with what agent-based models look like, how to interact with them, and what they are capable of. A particularly useful strategy for developing one's own model is to adapt an existing model. For example, the NetLogo model library includes an example model called Virus on a Network that simulates the classic epidemiological susceptible-infected-resistant (SIR) model of disease spread. This model might readily be adapted to investigate the spread of collective action through a community: Community members are "susceptible" to participation, and community change might be realized only after a sufficient number of people are "infected" with participation. However, it may require some minor changes: For example, the original model assumes that all people are susceptible to the virus, but perhaps only some people (i.e., those interested in a community issue) are susceptible to participation. Nonetheless, adapting existing models to new purposes and research questions provides a way to get started using agent-based models in community-based research very quickly.

A final suggestion, whether adapting existing models or building new ones, is to keep it simple. Communities and community-based research are complex, and agent-based models are not intended to capture the full complexity of reality. At each step, consider which aspects of the community are absolutely essential for understanding the core dynamics of the issue and leave everything else out (at first). Starting with a simple (albeit perhaps unrealistic) initial model and adding to it incrementally is more useful than starting with a very complex model that cannot be understood.

As this chapter has highlighted, although agent-based models are not widely used in community-based research currently, they have much to offer. First, they offer a single analytic tool that simultaneously integrates individual and ecological influences and that bridges the explanatory gap between microlevel processes and macrolevel outcomes. Second, they offer some solutions to several different challenges that frequently arise in community-based research, including allowing the researcher to refine research questions before entering the field, to ask unaskable questions, to anticipate unanticipated consequences, and to engage community members. However, agent-based models are not a replacement for other community-based methods, but rather they should be viewed as a useful supplement. Building a useful agent-based model still requires knowledge about the problems that are important to communities, about the microlevel processes that take place in communities, and about the constraints imposed on communities by internal (e.g., norms) and external (e.g., laws) forces. The AIDS model discussed earlier may be useful only in communities where HIV/AIDS is a pressing issue. Likewise, an AIDS model that simulates condom use behaviors may be appropriate only in communities where condoms are available, or one that simulates an abstinence-based intervention may be useful only in communities where local norms view abstinence as an acceptable behavior. However, when paired with at least a preliminary understanding of the research setting, agent-based models offer community-based researchers a powerful complement to other methods.

REFERENCES

Agassi, J. (1960). Methodological individualism. *British Journal of Sociology, 11*, 244–270.

Barker, R. G. (1968). *Ecological psychology: Concepts and methods for studying the environment of human behavior.* Stanford, CA: Stanford University Press.

Box, G. E. P., & Draper, N. R. (1987). *Empirical model-building and response surfaces.* New York, NY: Wiley.

Castella, J. C., Trung, T. N., & Boissau, S. (2005). Participatory simulation of land-use changes in the northern mountains of Vietnam: The combined use of an agent-based model, a role-playing game, and a geographic information system. *Ecology and Society, 10*, 27.

Devine, J. A., Wright, J. D., & Joyner, L. M. (1994). Issues in implementing a randomized experiment in a field setting. *New Directions for Program Evaluation, 63*, 27–40.

Epstein, J. M. (1999). Agent-based computational models and generative social science. *Complexity, 4*, 41–60.

Grannis, R. (1998). The importance of trivial streets: Residential streets and residential segregation. *American Journal of Sociology, 103*, 1530–1564.

Hodgson, G. M. (2007). Meanings of methodological individualism. *Journal of Economic Methodology, 14*, 211–226.

Hoffer, L. (2006). *Junkie business: The evolution and operation of a heroin dealing network.* Belmont, CA: Thompson Wadsworth.

Hoffer, L. D., Bobashev, G., & Morris, R. J. (2009). Researching a local heroin market as a complex adaptive system. *American Journal of Community Psychology, 44*, 273–286.

Naivinit, W., Le Page, C., Trébuil, G., & Gajaseni, N. (2010). Participatory agent-based modeling and simulation of rice production and labor migrations in Northeast Thailand. *Environmental Modelling and Software, 25*, 1345–1358.

Neal, Z. P. (2013). *The connected city: How networks are shaping the modern metropolis.* New York, NY: Routledge.

Neal, Z. P. (2015). *The Routledge handbook of applied system science.* New York, NY: Routledge.

Neal, Z. P., & Neal, J. W. (2014). The (in)compatibility of diversity and sense of community. *American Journal of Community Psychology, 53*, 1–12.

Orum, A. M., & Neal, Z. P. (2009). *Common ground? Readings and reflections on public space.* New York, NY: Routledge.

Portes, A., & Vickstrom, E. (2011). Diversity, social capital, and cohesion. *Annual Review of Sociology, 37*, 461–479.

Putnam, R. D. (2007). E Pluribus Unum: Diversity and community in the twenty-first century. *Scandinavian Political Studies, 30*, 137–174.

Railsback, S. F., & Grimm, V. (2011). *Agent-based and individual-based modeling: A practical introduction.* Princeton, NJ: Princeton University Press.

Rugh, J. S., & Massey, D. S. (2010). Racial segregation and the American foreclosure crisis. *American Sociological Review, 75*, 629–651.

Saporito, S. (2003). Private choices, public consequences: Magnet school choice and segregation by race and poverty. *Social Problems, 50*, 181–203.

Schelling, T. (1969). Models of segregation. *American Economic Review, 59*, 488–493.

Townley, G., Kloos, B., Green, E. P., & Franco, M. M. (2011). Reconcilable differences? Human diversity, cultural relativity, and sense of community. *American Journal of Community Psychology, 47*, 69–85

Udehn, L. (2002). The changing face of methodological individualism. *Annual Review of Sociology, 28*, 479–507.

Wilensky, U. (1997). *NetLogo segregation and AIDS models.* Retrieved June 2015, from http://ccl.northwestern.edu/netlogo/models

Wilensky, U. (1999). *NetLogo.* Retrieved June 2015, from http://ccl.northwestern.edu/netlogo/

21

Social Network Analysis

MARIAH KORNBLUH AND JENNIFER WATLING NEAL

Social network analysis (SNA) offers an innovative lens for conducting community-based research. It focuses on identifying patterns of relationships among sets of actors in a particular system (e.g., friendships among children in a classroom or collaboration among organizations in a coalition). In this chapter, we will describe how to collect network data and how to apply network measures to examine phenomena at multiple levels of analysis, including the (a) setting (i.e., characteristics of the whole network), (b) individual (i.e., an actor's position within the network), and (c) dyad (i.e., network characteristics of pairs of actors). Additionally, we use a case example to illustrate how SNA can be used to understand how the structure of teacher advice networks might facilitate or hinder the spread of classroom intervention practices.

INTRODUCTION TO SOCIAL NETWORK ANALYSIS

One of the pivotal differences between conventional data analysis and SNA is that the former focuses on individual actors and their attributes, while the latter extends beyond individual actors to quantify the structure of relationships between all actors in a setting (Hanneman & Riddle, 2005; Neal & Christens, 2014). Therefore, at its core, each social network includes a set of actors (e.g., individuals or organizations) and a type of relationship (e.g., friendship or collaboration).

Notably, SNA moves beyond an individual perspective and instead adopts a structural lens that is well suited for community-based research (Neal, 2008; Neal & Christens, 2014). In particular, researchers have stressed the importance of capturing whole networks to guide social action (Christakis & Fowler, 2009; Neal & Christens, 2014; Neal & Neal, 2013; see Chapter 22, this volume). To measure whole networks, researchers conduct SNA using a finite group of actors referred to as a system (e.g., students in a classroom or organizations in a coalition). Using whole network data, SNA can provide measures of the entire system (i.e., setting-level measures), individual actors' positions in this system (i.e., individual-level measures), or pairs of actors in the system (i.e., dyad-level measures). These measures can provide a rich array of information regarding interconnectedness in a community, distributions of power and centrality, and individual actors' perceptions of their surrounding community. Moreover, whole network analysis has been used to examine many phenomena of interest to community-based researchers, including coalitions, empowerment, dissemination, and implementation (Neal & Christens, 2014).

Network Data Collection and Management

SNA has been applied to diverse and unique communities, such as substance use recovery houses, coalitions, and schools (e.g., Jason, Light, Stevens, & Beers, 2014; Long, Harré, & Atkinson, 2014; Nowell, 2009). To conduct this type of research, it is necessary to identify a system and to determine a boundary that constrains which actors are included in the system (Wasserman & Faust, 1994). In many cases, these boundaries are natural and are often set by the actors under study (e.g., classrooms, clubs, organizations, or coalitions). Here, it may even be possible to find a roster of individuals who participate in the system. However, in other cases such as sexual networks or drug injection networks, system boundaries may be more fluid and, therefore, more challenging to determine. In these cases, researchers often employ snowball sampling methods or more rigorous respondent driving sampling methods to delineate the network (Hanneman & Riddle, 2005).

The accurate measurement of social networks requires much information. Therefore, methods for collecting network data diverge from the probabilistic sampling typically employed in more traditional forms of data collection. Because network methods focus on the relationships among actors, actors are not independent from one another. SNA analysts tend to study whole populations by means of census, which requires collecting data from every actor in a particular setting. Using a census in SNA is vital for holistically and accurately capturing every present relation within a network. For instance, if an actor's data are missing, the presence and absence of that actor's relations with every other actor in the network are absent. Notably, in SNA, data about nonrelationships are just as crucial for understanding the network structure as data about relationships. Thus, self-report measures require notably high response rates (i.e., greater than 80%–90%) (Neal, 2008).

In addition to specifying the set of actors to be included in a social network study, it is also necessary to specify the nature of the relationships that will be explored. Two features of relationships are particularly important to consider: directionality and value. First, it is important to determine whether the relationships should be specified as directed or undirected. Relationships should be specified as *directed* if it is important to understand who is sending and who is receiving a particular relationship. For example, in the case of advice relationships, one actor (the sender) provides advice to another (the receiver). Similarly, in the case of trust, one actor (the sender) may indicate that she trusts another (the receiver), but this relationship may not be reciprocated. However, relationships should be specified as *undirected* if they are assumed to be symmetric in nature. For example, hanging-out relationships often meet this assumption (i.e., if A hangs out with B, B logically must also hang out with A). Second, it is important to determine whether the relationships should be specified as binary or valued. Relationships should be specified as binary when it is sufficient to simply measure the presence or absence of a relationship at the nominal level. However, if researchers are interested in the strength or intensity of relationships, it may be necessary to use a valued measurement at the ordinal or ratio level.

Most commonly, researchers use sociometric surveys or interviews to collect social network data (Marsden, 1990, 2011). These sociometric surveys or interviews typically consist of name-generator questions (e.g., "In the last month, who have you gone to for advice?" "In the last 2 weeks, to which other organizations in the coalition has your organization made referrals?"). Each actor provides information about the presence of his or her own relationship (or his or her organization's relationship) with other actors in the system either through free recall or by selecting names from a roster. For example, Neal, Neal, Atkins, Henry, and Frazier (2011) used sociometric interviews to measure advice networks among teachers in three elementary schools. Teachers were asked name-generator questions about whom they socialized with and whom they went to for advice in three different areas (behavior management, family involvement, and instructional methods). In response to each question, teachers freely recalled as many or as few other teachers in their school as they wished. This is important because constraining actors' responses to a fixed number (e.g., "Name three people that you go to for advice") has been known to create serious measurement error. In particular, fixing the number of responses produces biased measurements of the network structure because it does not account for all possible relationships in the system (Holland & Leinhardt, 1973).

Although less common, structured observational methods can also be used to collect network data. For example, Schaefer, Light, Fabes, Hanish, and Martin (2010) conducted observations of social play among children in 11 preschool classrooms over the course of a school year. More specifically, they spent several hours in each of these classrooms on multiple days each week and conducted 10-second scan observations of random children to record their activities. These methods can provide rich longitudinal data on actors' behavioral interactions but are time and resource intensive to collect.

Finally, many researchers construct network data from archival sources, including meeting attendance records, Internet interactions, bill co-sponsorships, and scholarly publications (Marsden, 1990). For example, Wimmer and Lewis (2010) used Facebook friendship statuses to examine peer relations among college students. More specifically, they recorded the friendship lists from

TABLE 21.1: UNDIRECTED (SYMMETRIC) ADJACENCY MATRIX

	Actor 1	Actor 2	Actor 3	Actor 4
Actor 1	—	1	0	1
Actor 2	1	—	1	1
Actor 3	0	1	—	0
Actor 4	1	1	0	—

Note: All ties in this matrix are reciprocated.

participants' Facebook profiles. These preexisting data can provide detailed information about actors' relationships that are less prone to social desirability.

Once network data are collected, they are typically arranged in an adjacency matrix. Although quantitative data are usually organized in a rectangular case-by-variable matrix, an adjacency matrix is a square actor-by-actor matrix (Hanneman & Riddle, 2005). That is, the adjacency matrix contains the same number of rows and columns. Rows represent actor *i* (senders if relationships are directed), and columns represent actor *j* (receivers if relationships are directed). The two matrices in Tables 21.1 and 21.2 provide social network data about four actors (Actors 1–4), and thus each has four rows and four columns. Each cell in the adjacency matrix represents the relationship between actors *i* and *j*. If relationships are specified as binary, cells will be 0 if a relationship is absent and 1 if a relationship is present. In contrast, if relationships are specified as valued, cells will reflect the strength or intensity of each relationship. The example matrices in Tables 21.1 and 21.2 are both binary. In Table 21.1, the cell that corresponds to Actor 1 (row) and Actor 2 (column) has a value of "1," indicating that Actor 1 has a relationship with Actor 2. The diagonal of the matrix represents self-ties and is usually left blank. If relationships are specified as undirected, values above and below the diagonal will mirror one another (see Table 21.1). However, if relationships are specified as directed, values above and below the diagonal may be different. In Table 21.2, the cell that corresponds to Actor 1 (row) and Actor 2 (column) has a value of "1," indicating that Actor 1 sends a relationship to Actor 2. In contrast, the cell that corresponds to Actor 2 (row) and Actor 1 (column) has a value of "0," indicating that Actor 2 does not reciprocate by sending a relationship to Actor 1.

TABLE 21.2: DIRECTED ADJACENCY MATRIX

	Actor 1	Actor 2	Actor 3	Actor 4
Actor 1	—	1	0	1
Actor 2	0	—	1	1
Actor 3	0	1	—	0
Actor 4	0	1	0	—

Note: Actor 1 has nonreciprocated relationships.

Social Network Measures

Community-based researchers can apply SNA to understand the context of a particular setting or community using measures at multiple levels of analysis, including the (a) setting (i.e., characteristics of the whole network), (b) individual (i.e., an actor's position within the network), and (c) dyad (i.e., network characteristics of pairs of actors). Once whole network data are collected, any of these types of measures can be utilized, allowing community-based researchers to mix and match measures across these different levels of analysis depending on their research questions. Table 21.3 provides an overview of the setting-, individual-, and dyad-level social network measures discussed in this chapter.

Setting-Level Measures

Setting-level measures provide information about the structural characteristics of a whole system (i.e., the resource sharing ties among all organizations participating in a coalition). These measures can help researchers track and identify prominent relational patterns within the system. Although many different setting-level measures exist (e.g., density, reciprocity, transitivity) in SNA, here we concentrate on just one example: multiplexity measured using Jaccard similarity coefficients.

Multiplexity is a setting-level measure that focuses on types of relationships. Any set of actors can have multiple types of relationships with one another (e.g., friendship or advice), each forming a separate network. Researchers can examine these different networks to determine the extent to which these actors share different types of relationships (i.e., multiplexity). Specifically, researchers can use Jaccard similarity coefficients to examine the overlap between two networks representing

TABLE 21.3: SOCIAL NETWORK MEASURES

Network Measure	Example Measure	Case Example
Setting: Setting-level measures provide information about the structural characteristics of a whole system.	Jaccard similarity coefficients: Examine the overlap between two networks representing different types of relationships. They are calculated by dividing the number of present relationships that are reported in both networks by the total number of present relationships that are reported in either network. Scores range from 0 (no overlap in relationships across the two networks) to 1 (100% overlap in relationships across the two networks).	Jaccard similarity coefficients ranged from .19 to .42, indicating that the overlap between different types of networks was only moderate. Findings suggest the need to examine whether lead teachers are ideally located to provide support for all components of the intervention (e.g., Are they well situated in all advice networks?).
Individual: Individual-level measures focus on each specific actor's location within the network.	Degree centrality: Refers to the number of relations that an actor has in a network. It can be expressed as a raw number or can be normed to reflect the percentage of ties that an actor has out of all possible ties in the network.	Teacher 4's out-degree centrality shows that she or he gave advice about involving families to 42.11% of the other teachers, whereas Teacher 8 gave advice about involving families to only 5.26% of the other teachers. Findings suggest that Teacher 4 may be more ideally situated to support the dissemination of PAS strategies for involving families than Teacher 8.
Dyad: Dyad-level measurements explore network characteristics of pairs of actors in the network.	Geodesic distance: Calculates the shortest path between two actors within a network. A geodesic distance of 1 means that two actors in the network have an existing relationship, whereas a geodesic distance of 2 means that two actors can reach each other by going through one intermediary actor.	Teacher 4 was connected to 18 of 19 other teachers with a geodesic distance of three or less. In contrast, Teacher 8 was connected to only 1 of 19 other teachers. Findings suggest that Teacher 4 is more optimally situated to spread PAS strategies about involving families than Teacher 8.

different types of relationships. (Jaccard similarity coefficients are appropriate for examining multiplexity when relationships are specified as binary. If relationships are valued, Pearson correlation coefficients can be used.) Jaccard similarity coefficients are calculated by dividing the number of present relationships that are reported in both networks by the total number of present relationships that are reported in either network. Scores range from 0 (no overlap in relationships across the two networks) to 1 (100% overlap in relationships across the two networks).

Multiplexity has important implications for understanding communication structures that influence the diffusion of information in communities (Rogers, 1962). For example, Neal et al. (2011) compared teacher advice networks involving families with advice networks focused on classroom instruction and found Jaccard coefficients ranging from .28 to .36. In other words, only one third of advice-giving relationships in one network were present in the other network, indicating that teachers tended to get advice from different teachers depending upon the type of information they were seeking.

Individual-Level Measurements

Individual-level measures typically focus on each specific actor's location in the network. For social network analysts, centrality measures are common.

Centrality measures examine the extent to which an actor is embedded in a relational network (e.g., How many ties does an actor have with other actors?). In some cases, high centrality can be an asset. For example, occupying a central position in an advice-giving network can provide access to different sources of information. However, in other cases, high centrality is a detriment. For example, occupying a central position in a contact network may make an actor more susceptible to contracting the cold that is going around that season. Furthermore, actors' placement in the network can provide them with opportunities to exert control over other actors or, conversely, constraints placed upon by them by other actors. Although there are many ways to assess an actor's centrality in a network (Freeman, 1978/1979), here we will discuss the most common measure: degree centrality.

Degree centrality refers to the number of relations that an actor has in a network (Freeman, 1978/1979). Degree centrality can be expressed as a raw number or can be normed to reflect the percentage of ties that an actor has out of all possible ties in the network. In directed networks, degree centrality is reflected using two values, *in-degree* and *out-degree*. *In-degree* represents the number or percentage of ties that a particular actor receives in the network, while *out-degree* represents the number or percentage of ties that a particular actor sends in the network.

In friendship or advice networks, actors with higher degree centrality may have more information and resources at their disposal. Furthermore, in these networks, actors with many relations are less dependent on each particular tie for resources. For example, Neal (2009) found that children's use of relational aggression was associated with degree centrality in their classroom peer networks. The study indicates that, although relational aggression peaked for students with moderate levels of degree centrality, students with the highest levels of degree centrality were less likely to engage in relational aggressive behaviors.

Dyad-Level Measurements

Dyad-level measurements explore network characteristics of pairs of actors in the network. Typically, dyad-level measures are used by community-based researchers to examine the co-occurrence of attitudes, behaviors, and/or attributes (e.g., sense of empowerment, political activities, obesity) among pairs of related actors (Burk, Steglich, & Snijders, 2007). For instance, Burk et al. (2007) found that adolescents whose friends engaged in delinquent behaviors were more likely to engage in delinquent behaviors themselves. Dyad measures are also commonly applied to understand the mechanisms by which relationships influence the diffusion and adoption of innovations (e.g., health care practices, social media technology) (Rogers, 1962). Here, we focus on one mechanism of diffusion: cohesion (typically measured using geodesic distance).

Cohesion examines the diffusion of behaviors or innovations among actors with ties to one another, emphasizing that information, behaviors, and/or resources tend to spread among close directly or indirectly connected groups of individuals. Cohesion is often measured using geodesic distance, or the shortest path between two actors within a network. If two actors (A and B) have a geodesic distance of 1, it means that Actors A and B have an existing or direct relationship in the network. In contrast, if Actors A and B have a geodesic distance of 2, it means that Actors A and B can reach each other by going through one intermediary actor (e.g., Actor C). Coleman, Katz, and Menzel's (1966) classic study used geodesic distances to examine the doctors' adoption of a new pharmaceutical drug. They found that doctors who were less distant in the network to doctors utilizing the pharmaceutical drug were more likely to follow suit and prescribe the drug. In comparison, doctors who solely received information about the drug from advertisements or empirical research were less likely to prescribe it. Burt (1999) has since theorized that the mechanism of cohesion may be particularly important for diffusing information about new innovations.

Benefits and Drawbacks

The benefits of SNA for community-based research are numerous. Despite intentions to understand broader contextual forces, community-based researchers have struggled to locate methods that allow them to assess the structure of the settings and communities. As Luke (2005) noted, this has led to a disconnect where community-based researchers theorize about context but fall back on methods and analyses that measure individuals. Because SNA explicitly focuses on measuring the structure of relationships within a setting or community, it is inherently a contextual method and offers a potential avenue for remedying this disconnect. Moreover, the relational focus of SNA also permits community-based researchers to explicitly measure interdependence between actors in a setting, a key feature of ecological theories (Neal & Neal, 2013; Trickett, Kelly, & Vincent, 1985). Finally, once collected, whole network data are extremely flexible and allow researchers to move back and forth easily between multiple levels of analysis. Indeed, as illustrated in the previous section, community-based researchers can use the same whole network data to answer questions about the entire setting, actors' positions within this setting, or actors' relationships with one another.

Despite these major benefits, SNA also has some drawbacks. As noted earlier, community-based researchers who wish to analyze whole networks must have near-complete data on the relationships between actors in a setting. SNA is extremely sensitive to missing data, and even a small amount of missingness (e.g., greater than 20%) can lead to misleading and distorted results (Neal, 2008). Thus, community-based researchers who wish to collect whole network data must prioritize efforts to boost response rates or use alternate approaches to data collection that allow for more complete network data. For example, Neal (2008) has advocated using cognitive social structures (CSS) to collect whole network data in community-based settings where high response rates are typically not feasible (e.g., public school classrooms). CSS asks each respondent to identify the presence or absence of a relationship between each pair of actors in the setting. Thus, each respondent provides his or her perception of the entire network structure. These perceptions can then be aggregated across respondents to enumerate a whole network from only a subset of respondents in the setting. Although CSS is effective for collecting whole network data in settings where response rates are low, this method of data collection has a high response burden for participants and may not be feasible in settings with many actors.

There are ethical considerations that may also hinder community-based researchers' use of SNA. Because SNA requires researchers to know who is related to whom, it is not possible to collect data anonymously. Additionally, because actors are reporting on their relationships with other actors in the setting, secondary participation is common in SNA studies. Secondary participation occurs when an actor does not participate as a respondent in the study, but data are still collected from others about this actor. It is important for community-based researchers using SNA to take special steps to protect the confidentiality of both respondents and secondary participants and to provide explicit consent forms that clearly detail the unique nature of network data (see Borgatti & Molina, 2005).

CASE STUDY

In the earlier sections, we highlighted SNA's unique promise and flexibility for understanding the structure of relationships in community-based settings. However, to make these points more concrete, we now turn to an illustration of how SNA can be applied to inform the dissemination and implementation of community-based interventions, using the Promoting Academic Success Project (PAS) as a case example. PAS is a school-based intervention focused on improving the academic achievement of African American and Latino boys in elementary school. PAS is a multipronged intervention that includes mentoring, family involvement activities, and after-school programming. However, a critical component of the PAS program is a professional development series that targets classroom teachers, especially prekindergarten to third-grade teachers. Specifically, principals in each participating PAS elementary school selected one to two lead teachers who encouraged their colleagues' attendance at the PAS professional development series. These lead teachers also provided support for and promoted the use of teaching strategies designed to improve minority boys' academic, behavioral, and social outcomes (Burke et al., 2015). SNA proved to be a useful method for understanding (a) the implications of teachers' existing advice networks for the spread of PAS strategies and (b) the implications of lead teachers' positions within these advice networks for their ability to influence their colleagues (see Table 21.3).

Network Data Collection and Management in PAS

A team of researchers at Michigan State University (led by this chapter's second author) collaborated with five elementary schools implementing PAS to collect network data on teachers' advice and social relationships. Here, we present findings from one of these schools (Southlawn Elementary) as a case example. However, it is important to note that findings looked similar across the five schools. (Southlawn Elementary is a pseudonym. The real name of the school is protected to ensure the confidentiality of all participants.)

When collecting network data at each PAS school, our research team used staff rosters and bounded the network to include all regular and special education teachers. We collected social network data using brief 10- to 15-minute structured interviews with each of these teachers. During the interviews, a member of our team asked teachers to identify an unlimited number of teachers in their school from whom they received advice about certain issues related to minority boys' education, including (a) family involvement, (b) behavior management, (c) instructional methods, and (d) promoting positive relationships. Teachers were also asked to identify other teachers in their school with whom they socialized. Response rates using this method were very high. At Southlawn Elementary, we were able to interview 96% of the regular and special education teachers ($N = 19$). We used answers to these questions to create five separate self-reported network adjacency matrices (four advice and one social) for each school. Each of the five-adjacency matrices was directed and binary.

TABLE 21.4: JACCARD COEFFICIENTS FOR TEACHER ADVICE-GIVING NETWORKS

Networks	1	2	3	4	5
1. Instruction	—				
2. Involving families	.33	—			
3. Positive relationships	.42	.33	—		
4. Behaviors	.39	.32	.39	—	
5. Social	.35	.19	.33	.26	—

Results of the Analysis

What Are the Implications of Teachers' Existing Advice Networks for the Spread of PAS Strategies?

The social network data collected at Southlawn elementary school demonstrate how setting-level measures provide valuable insight into the topography of teachers' existing advice networks. Specifically, multiplexity (measured using Jaccard similarity coefficients) has implications for how strategies learned as part of the PAS program might diffuse among teachers at Southlawn. Looking at overlap between the five different types of networks measured at Southlawn, Jaccard similarity coefficients ranged from .19 to .42 (see Table 21.4). These coefficients indicate that the overlap between different types of networks at Southlawn was only moderate. For example, the Jaccard similarity coefficient between advice networks for involving families and behavior management was .32, indicating that only about a third of the relationships present in the advice network for involving families were also present in the advice networks for behavior management. These scores highlight that teachers at Southlawn tended to get advice from different teachers depending on the type of information that they were seeking. Thus, at Southlawn, the diffusion of PAS strategies will likely depend on the content that they impart.

These results have some general implications for selecting lead teachers to support dissemination and implementation of the PAS intervention. Specifically, because teachers tend to go to different individuals for different types of advice, it is crucial to examine whether lead teachers are ideally located to provide support for all components of the intervention (e.g., Are they well situated in all advice networks?). For example, certain teachers may hold influential positions for communicating about family involvement but may be more limited in their ability to communicate about behavior management. Alternatively, it might be helpful to consider selecting multiple lead teachers to assist with the PAS intervention, with each lead teacher exhibiting influential positions for disseminating information about different key components of the intervention.

Are the Lead Teachers Optimally Situated in the Network to Be Able to Spread PAS Strategies?

Although setting-level network measures provide general implications for the spread of PAS strategies at Southlawn, individual- and dyad-level network measures can help assess whether the two specific lead teachers selected by Southlawn's principal are optimally situated in the network to be able to spread PAS strategies. At Southlawn, Teachers 4 and 8 were designated by the principal as lead teachers for the PAS intervention.

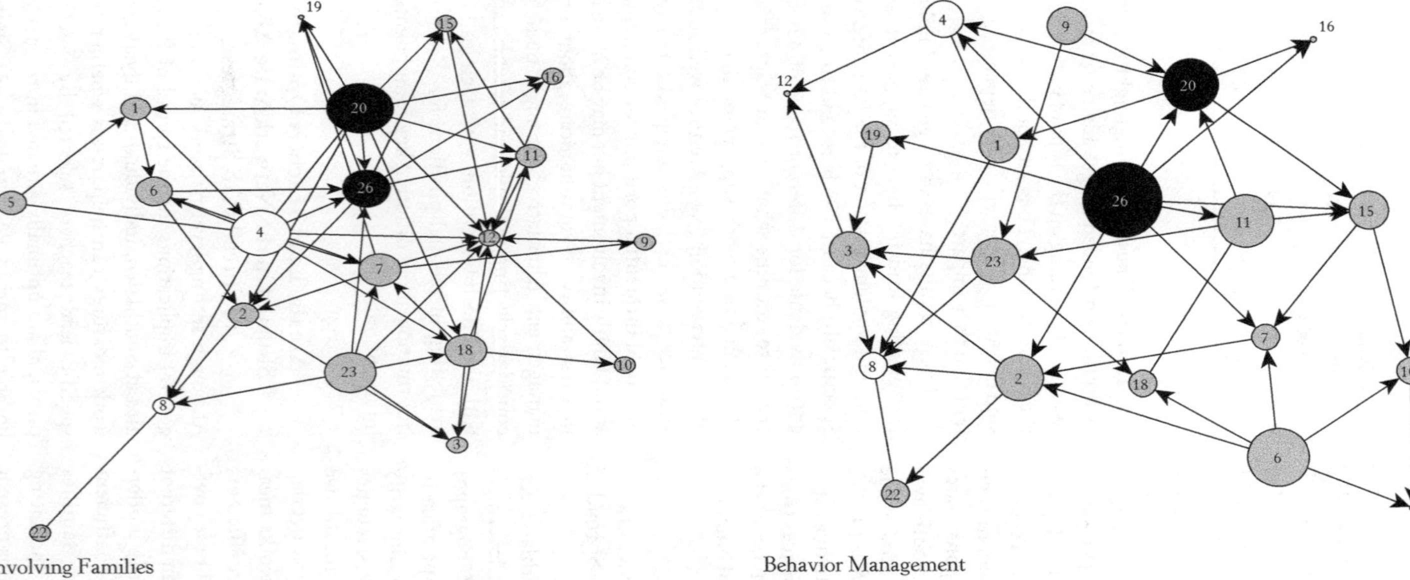

ID	Title	Involving Families		Behavior Management	
		Normed Out-Degree	Number of teachers ≤ 3 steps	Normed Out-Degree	Number of teachers ≤ 3 steps
4	Lead Teacher	42.11%	18	10.53%	4
8	Lead Teacher	5.26%	1	5.26%	1
20	Alternative Teacher	52.63%	18	21.05%	11
26	Alternative Teacher	26.32%	10	42.11%	17

FIGURE 21.1: Key: Actor-level measures of lead teachers (color-coded white) and alternative teachers (color-coded black).

Here we compare involving family and behavior management advice networks to assess the extent to which lead teachers at Southlawn were well situated to spread different types of information relevant to the PAS intervention. Figure 21.1 depicts two sociograms illustrating teachers' advice-giving networks for involving families (on the left) and behavior management (on the right). Each circle represents an actor (i.e., a teacher) and is color-coded. The principal's selected lead teachers are represented in white, potential alternative teachers discussed in this chapter are represented in black, and all other teachers are represented in gray. The size of the circles represents each teacher's out-degree centrality scores with larger circles reflecting larger scores. Each arrow in the sociogram represents the act of giving advice. For example, in the behavior management sociogram, arrows point from Teacher 3 and Teacher 4 to Teacher 12, illustrating that these teachers give behavior management advice to Teacher 12. Actor size (the node diameter) is based on out-degree centrality scores.

Centrality scores suggest that Teacher 4 may be more ideally situated than Teacher 8 to support the dissemination of PAS family involvement strategies. Specifically, Teacher 4 gave advice about involving families to 42.11%, while Teacher 8 gave advice about involving families to only 5.26% of the other teachers at Southlawn. Both Teachers 20 and 26 gave advice about involving families to more teachers at Southlawn (52.63% and 26.32%, respectively) and may have also been more effective at disseminating PAS family involvement strategies than Teacher 8. When examining the advice network for behavior management, the out-degree centrality scores of Teachers 20 and 26 (21.05% and 42.11%, respectively) reveal that they give advice about behavior management to more teachers at Southlawn than did Teachers 4 (10.53%) and 8 (5.26%). These findings suggest that Teachers 20 and 26 could serve as alternative lead teachers who may be more effective than the principal-selected lead teachers in disseminating PAS behavior management strategies.

Dyadic-level measures can also provide information about the extent to which the Southlawn principal's selected lead teachers are well positioned to spread PAS intervention strategies throughout the school. Teachers who have short geodesic distances to other teachers at Southlawn (i.e., a geodesic distance <3) are better positioned to spread information about PAS strategies rapidly and efficiently through the mechanism of cohesion. In the advice network for involving families, Teacher 4 is more highly connected to others teachers than is Teacher 8. Specifically, Teacher 4 was connected to 18 of 19 other teachers at Southlawn with a geodesic distance of three or less. In contrast, Teacher 8 was connected to only 1 of 19 other teachers at Southlawn with a geodesic distance of three or less. Thus, this dyad measure suggests again that Teacher 4 is more optimally situated to spread PAS strategies about involving families than is Teacher 8. However, in the advice network for behavior management, neither of Southlawn's lead teachers is particularly well positioned to spread PAS strategies. Specifically, Teacher 4 was connected to 4 of 19 teachers with a geodesic distance of 3 or less, while Teacher 8 was connected to 1 of 19 teachers with a geodesic distance of 3 or less. Other teachers at Southlawn (Teachers 20 and 26) would be much better positioned to spread PAS strategies about behavior management. These findings suggest that alternate teachers, other than the principal-selected lead teachers, may be influential in spreading PAS strategies through cohesion.

CONCLUSION

Community-based research emphasizes the relational and contextual nature of human behavior and social problems (Neal & Christens, 2014). SNA complements this perspective by providing a concrete method by which to assess the pattern of relationships between a set of actors (Luke, 2005). Perhaps one of the greatest advantages of SNA is the "bird's-eye view" that it provides of complex pattern of relationships between actors in a system. This bird's-eye view generally eludes individual community members and leaders and thus cannot easily be captured through more traditional survey or interview methods (Burke et al., 2015; Provan, Veazie, Staten, & Teufel-Stone, 2005). As a case in point, SNA analyses of the PAS project revealed that the lead teachers selected by the principal occupied positions that facilitated the diffusion of some types of PAS strategies but not others.

Despite the promise of SNA, researchers must be intentional and conscientious regarding the challenges that this method poses. First, SNA is vulnerable to missing data, which can greatly obscure the accuracy of a study's findings. Second,

SNA presents unique ethical considerations given the lack of anonymity and use of secondary participants in the data collection procedures. More specifically, community-based researchers have the challenge of presenting findings back to their community partners in a manner in which individual actors or organizations are nonidentifiable (see Klovdahl, 2005). To preserve confidentiality in our case study, we did not present analyses of lead teachers' position back to the schools participating in the PAS project. Instead, in our presentations to the schools, we highlighted setting-level measures that facilitated or hindered communication about PAS strategies and provided recommendations for strengthening communication networks among teachers.

Regardless of the challenges, SNA has exciting potential to examine complex social problems at multiple levels of analysis. We hope that this chapter inspires community-based researchers to use SNA to characterize community-based settings and to identify key points of intervention in community-level change efforts.

REFERENCES

Borgatti, S. P., & Molina, J. L. (2005). Toward ethical guidelines for network research in organizations. *Social Networks, 27*, 107–117.

Burk, W. J., Steglich, C. E., & Snijders, T. A. (2007). Beyond dyadic interdependence: Actor- oriented models for co-evolving social networks and individual behaviors. *International Journal of Behavioral Development, 31*, 397–404.

Burke, J., Hassmiller-Lich, K., Neal, J. W., Meissner, H., Yonas, M., & Mabry, P. (2015). Enhancing dissemination and implementation research using systems science methods. *International Journal of Behavioral Medicine*, 22(3), 283–291.

Burt, R. S. (1999). The social capital of opinion leaders. *Annals of the American Academy of Political and Social Science, 566*, 37–54.

Christakis, N. A., & Fowler, J. H. (2009). *Connected: The surprising power of our social networks and how they shape our lives*. New York, NY: Little, Brown and Company.

Coleman, J. S., Katz, E., & Menzel, H. (1966). *Medical innovation: A diffusion study*. Indianapolis, IN: Bobbs-Merrill.

Freeman, L. C. (1978/1979). Centrality in social networks conceptual clarification. *Social Networks, 1*, 215–239.

Hanneman, R. A., & Riddle, M. (2005). *Introduction to social network methods*. Riverside: University of California, Riverside.

Holland, P. W., & Leinhardt, S. (1973). The structural implications of measurement error in sociometry†. *Journal of Mathematical Sociology, 3*, 85–111.

Jason, L. A., Light, J. M., Stevens, E. B., & Beers, K. (2014). Dynamic social networks in recovery homes. *American Journal of Community Psychology, 53*, 324–334.

Klovdahl, A. S. (2005). Social network research and human subjects protection: Towards more effective infectious disease control. *Social Networks, 27*, 119–137.

Long, J., Harré, N., & Atkinson, Q. D. (2014). Understanding change in recycling and littering behavior across a school social network. *American Journal of Community Psychology, 53*, 462–474.

Luke, D. A. (2005). Getting the big picture in community science: Methods that capture context. *American Journal of Community Psychology, 35*, 185–200.

Marsden, P. V. (1990). Network data and measurement. *Annual Review of Sociology, 16*, 435–463.

Marsden, P. V. (2011). Survey methods for network data. In J. Scott & P. Carrington (Eds.), *The Sage handbook of social network analysis* (pp. 370–388). London, England: Sage.

Neal, J. W. (2008). "Kracking" the missing data problem: Applying Krackhardt's cognitive social structures to school-based social networks. *Sociology of Education, 81*, 140–162.

Neal, J. W. (2009). Network ties and mean lies: A relational approach to relational aggression. *Journal of Community Psychology, 37*, 737–753.

Neal, J. W., & Christens, B. D. (2014). Linking the levels: Network and relational perspectives for community psychology. *American Journal of Community Psychology, 53*, 314–323.

Neal, J. W., & Neal, Z. P. (2013). Nested or networked? Future directions for ecological systems theory. *Social Development, 22*, 722–737.

Neal, J. W., Neal, Z. P., Atkins, M. S., Henry, D. B., & Frazier, S. L. (2011). Channels of change: Contrasting network mechanisms in the use of interventions. *American Journal of Community Psychology, 47*, 277–286.

Nowell, B. (2009). Profiling capacity for coordination and systems change: The relative contribution of stakeholder relationships in interorganizational collaboratives. *American Journal of Community Psychology, 44*, 196–212.

Provan, K. G., Veazie, M. A., Staten, L. K., & Teufel-Stone, N. I. (2005). The use of network analysis to strengthen community partnerships. *Public Administration Review, 65*, 603–613.

Rogers, E. M. (1962). *Diffusion of innovations*. New York, NY: The Free Press.

Schaefer, D. R., Light, J. M., Fabes, R. A., Hanish, L. D., & Martin, C. L. (2010). Fundamental principles of network formation among preschool children. *Social Networks, 32*, 61–71.

Trickett, E. J., Kelly, J. G., & Vincent, T. A. (1985). The spirit of ecological inquiry in community research. In E. C. Susskind & D. C. Klein (Eds.), *Community research: Methods, paradigms, and applications* (pp. 283–333). New York, NY: Praeger.

Wasserman, S,. & Faust, K. (1994). *Social network analysis: Method and applications*. New York, NY: Cambridge Press.

Wimmer, A., & Lewis, K. (2010). Beyond and below racial homophily: ERG models of a friendship network documented on Facebook. *American Journal of Sociology, 116*, 583–642.

22

Dynamic Social Networks

LEONARD A. JASON, JOHN LIGHT, AND SARAH CALLAHAN

This chapter will provide an introduction to dynamic social networks. The first part of the chapter will present an overview of the theory and methodology of dynamic social networks, with particular attention to its usage in community-based research on friendship and mentoring. This will then be followed by a case study illustrating the application of this approach to the study of substance abuse recovery residences.

INTRODUCTION TO DYNAMIC SOCIAL NETWORKS

Personal Networks

Network studies in community-based research have typically been based on personal network data (also called "ego networks"). Personal networks are assessed by asking an individual ("ego") to identify his or her relationships ("alters"), which can be close friends, family members, and work associates. This identification allows the investigator to infer that the same person is being named in successive assessment occasions. Ego is also asked to rate each alter on various characteristics such as behaviors (e.g., substance use, current or past criminality). From such data, it is possible to calculate, for instance, the percentage of ego's friends who are using various substances and to track changes in this composition over time.

Personal network methodology offers greater detail in measuring social context compared to simple summary ratings. As an example, *turnover* describes the percentage of change in network composition for individuals from one time point to another. Although it is possible to assess this social context variable by a general question, such as "How much change has there been in your friendships since the last survey?," these measures are open to individual interpretation and may be unreliable. Alternatively, turnover can be *calculated* from personal network data. As an example, Stone, Jason, Stevens, and Light (2014) studied a sample of individuals in recovery from substance abuse and found less turnover in networks when alters were relatives of the person in recovery, abstinent from drugs, and had frequent contact with the person in recovery.

The personal network has a long history in our field (Groh, Jason, & Keys, 2008). Kornbluh and Watling Neal (see Chapter 21) identify network measures that characterize settings (e.g., density and reciprocity), actors (e.g., centrality and power), and actor dyads (e.g., structural equivalence and geodesic distance). This approach was used by Wrzus, Hänel, Wagner, and Neyer (2013), who found that the *sizes* of individuals' personal and employment networks varied with age and life events. Global networks decreased on average by about one person per decade after young adulthood, while the size of the family network remained stable. Divorce was associated with a decrease in the size of the family network, and death of a relative was associated with a decrease in global network size but an increase in the size of the closer personal network.

In the realm of substance use, Vaillant (1983) noted that environmental factors may be key contributors to maintaining abstinence after treatment. These factors include the amount and type of support one receives for abstinence. Individuals who participate in aftercare services sustain abstinence for a longer period of time (Laudet, Becker, & White, 2009). One study found that each additional month spent in aftercare led to a 20% increase in the odds of continued abstinence (Schaefer, Cronkite, & Hu, 2011). Supporting this line of research, Buchanan and Latkin (2008) examined the personal networks of heroin and cocaine users, finding that those who quit had a significant change in the composition of their social network from pre- to postcessation.

Whole Networks

With personal network research we are able to understand how one person perceives the relationships that comprise his or her network, but this provides only half of the story, as dyadic relationships are inherently concerned with both members. As an example, a child might rate how much support he or she feels from each friend for refraining from smoking. This is an important piece of information, but it does not tell us whether his or her friends actually support this youth's effort to not smoke, nor how they perceive the relationship. In contrast, a whole network approach would have every member of a network rate each other on relational issues, such as support for not smoking. Whole network approaches provide a relational map of an entire social ecosystem, capturing each individual's perspective, and it becomes possible to model how these potentially differing perspectives interact as time goes on. Thus, dynamic models of whole social networks focus on the mutual interdependence between relationships and behavior change over time, providing a framework for conceptualizing and empirically describing two-way transactional dynamics.

The Stochastic Actor-Oriented Model (Snijders, van de Bunt, & Steglich, 2010) provides a statistical framework for fully transactional models. In this modeling framework, social networks are conceptualized as a set of individuals whose relationships evolve over time according to an underlying probability structure. This process can depend on a linear combination of predictors, which are interpretable as hypothesized mechanisms that jointly predict network evolution. Model effects include both fixed (e.g., gender and ethnicity) and time-varying (e.g., attitudes and behaviors) measured characteristics of individuals, which are familiar from ordinary regression modeling. However, effects associated with dyads (pairs of individuals) are also possible, as well as effects associated with an individual's structural embedding (number of linkages with various alters, possibly with particular characteristics, or who lie along a similarity continuum on some behavior, for example). The latter effects exemplify a major contribution of the network perspective to the study of social relationships, namely, that relationship dynamics depend not only on individual characteristics, needs, and preferences but also on the state of the network and individuals' positions within it. There are many potentially important structural effects that can be examined with the Stochastic Actor-Oriented Model, depending on the substantive network being studied. For human relationships, two such effects are reciprocity (i.e., the tendency for relationships to become reciprocated or be dropped) and transitivity (i.e., the tendency for all members of triads to share the same relationship).

Although a transactional interchange between the individual and his or her social environment is an essential component of community psychology (Jason & Glenwick, 2012), methods for studying these systems are still quite limited. As an example, even advanced statistical techniques such as multilevel modeling are primarily useful for studying the effect of context on behavior and, despite some generalizations (e.g., Kenny, Mannetti, Pierro, Livi, & Kashy, 2002), does not extend to the effects of behavior on context naturally or broadly (e.g., Todd, Allen, & Javdani, 2012). A whole network approach can provide a methodological framework for thinking about and describing two-way transactional dynamics. Work in this area is part of what is considered systems research, in that interest centers on how microlevel mechanisms (e.g., how we both influence and are influenced by others) aggregate to the macrosystem level and then feed back to the microlevel in an ongoing causal loop.

Part of the reason for the popularity of personal network methodology in community psychology research is undoubtedly its tractability. In contrast, whole network data require the researcher to identify some relatively closed social ecology and assess all or nearly all of its members; these assessments must be carried on repeatedly over a substantively meaningful period of time in order to observe and model change. For many community-relevant units, especially geographical areas such as neighborhoods, this is obviously difficult. If no natural, fully assessable group of interest is available for a given network study, the personal network approach is attractive. It permits a more granular assessment of individuals' social contexts than do simple individually based summary ratings or perceptions, while still providing a tractable measurement strategy based on measurements from independent individuals.

Nevertheless, where whole network assessments are possible, such data confer considerable advantages. Examples of such situations include school-based child or adolescent friendships. In these settings, whole network models can separate effects of exposure to friends' behavior from the tendency to select behaviorally similar others as friends. As an example, using school-based longitudinal network data, Weerman (2011) found that exposure to delinquent friends had a significant (although small) effect on youths' own delinquency, but, contrary to common assumption, there was no tendency for friendship selection based on similarity of delinquent behavior. Another school-based network study by Mercken, Steglich, Sinclair, Holliday, and Moore (2012) found that similarity in smoking behavior among adolescent friends emerged from the linked mechanisms of selecting similar friends and the subsequent influence of those friends on behavior. Complete network methodologies are particularly well suited to measuring and explaining the dynamic interplay among friendship and other relationships, and attitude and behavior change, simultaneously identifying the active *social* mechanisms underlying these changes.

Friendship and Mentoring

Friendship and mentoring has become a major area of research in the field of community psychology (Rhodes & DuBois, 2008), and social network methodology represents a novel possibility for exploring these constructs. The study of friendship has a long tradition in group dynamics and social psychology research and theory. Friendship has, of course, also been a primary focus of network science since its inception (Moreno, 1934). In many of our social and community interventions, trust is a critical precursor of close relationships (Bonaventura et al., 2006; Horst & Coffé, 2012), and that trust is recognized as an essential ingredient of the development of friendships in a wide variety of settings (e.g., du Plessis & Corney, 2011; Way, Gingold, Rotenberg, & Kuriakose, 2005). Trust tends to develop in groups in part as a function of interindividual exposure (Patulny, 2011), especially when the individuals in the group are dependent on each other for desired outcomes (Schachter, 1951).

A body of classic literature explains how and why groups of different sorts experience conflict and how these groups can be brought together to develop friendships. For example, Sherif (1966) described two sets of boys at a summer camp who competed with one another in various events. Stereotypes developed, resulting in escalating hatred and aggressive behaviors. Sherif next attempted to reverse the rivalry by creating challenges that required cooperation between the two groups. In one instance, if either group wanted to see a movie on a particular evening, they had to pool their funds with the other group. These exercises were effective in reducing the negative feelings and aggression between the groups. Sherif interpreted these results in terms of superordinate goals, that is, goals that groups could share, even in the presence of ongoing differences. These superordinate goals bring individuals together and can counter other differences. Such research suggests that those community settings and groups that promote interdependence will foster friendship and trust, and these settings should mutually reinforce each other in a positive feedback loop. The key is to be able to have the methodological sophistication to capture these reciprocal feedback loops that occurred in Sherif's work and in much of the friendship and trust literature. This, we suggest, is exactly what the Stochastic Actor-Oriented Modeling framework offers: a method that can estimate transactional models from longitudinal, survey-based social network data.

In network studies of formal organizations, asymmetrical relationships are common due to recognized differences in expertise, even when rank is not formally designated within the group in question (e.g., a managerial hierarchy) (Snijders & Bosker, 2012). The mentor-friend distinction is well grounded in network and organizational theory and motivates a focus on conditions that promote the formation of each type of relationship. Because expertise asymmetry is typical of mentor relationships, it seems likely that these relationships will also tend toward asymmetry.

Mentorship relationships are conceptualized from the perspective of the social support literature. Close friendships are in most cases a source of mutual support. By contrast, mentors typically hold higher status positions, supplying mentoring and support in exchange for respect and gratitude, for example. According to social exchange theory (e.g., Blau, 1964), the asymmetric exchange of dissimilar goods or services is characteristic of hierarchical social relationships.

Such relationships are assumed to coevolve over time, affecting and affected by attitudes and behaviors and personal networks outside the group or setting. In recent years, whole network studies have opened a new level of insight into the social dynamics within a variety of areas, including substance use, especially among youth (e.g., Veenstra, Dijkstra, Steglich, & Van Zalk, 2013) but also in adult populations (Cruz, Emery, & Turkheimer, 2012). This approach has led to major advances in, for example, our understanding of the role of peer affiliations in substance use among adolescents (Brechwald & Prinstein, 2011; Dishion, 2013), for whom schools provide natural social laboratories because of their organization of youth into same-age cohorts, which often include nearly all such youth in a given community. Moreover, although studies of multiple types of network relationships are not new (e.g., White, Boorman, & Breiger, 1976), dynamic models of such "multiplex" networks have only just begun to appear (Snijders, Lomi, & Torló, 2013).

In the next section, we present a case study as an example of a multiplex dynamic social network study, using data from a small sample of recovery homes to examine some of the concepts discussed earlier. Because each recovery house is a complete network of relationships, it is possible to think of each as an independent set of relationships that coevolve over time with changing resident characteristics such as recovery-related attitudes and behaviors. Each house is treated as an independent network, but the Stochastic Actor-Oriented Model is used to create a model that is assumed to be driven by the same mechanisms across houses.

CASE STUDY

Drug abuse and addiction are among the costliest of health problems, totaling approximately $428 billion annually (National Drug Intelligence Center, 2011). In 2012, an estimated 23.9 million Americans aged 12 years or older were current illicit drug users (US Department of Health and Human Services, 2012), which represents 9.2% of the population aged 12 years or older. Unfortunately, many people who finish substance use treatment relapse within a few months (Vaillant, 2003), which might be due to the lack of longer term community-based housing and employment support (Jason, Olson, & Foli, 2008).

A number of self-help organizations, including Alcoholics Anonymous (AA), provide support to individuals following treatment, but such programs do not provide needed safe and affordable housing or access to employment. For these needs, a variety of professionally run and resident-run residential programs are available in the United States (Polcin, Korcha, Bond, Galloway, & Lapp, 2010). Although such recovery programs are important sources of housing and employment support, they do not work for everyone (Moos & Moos, 2006). For instance, early dropout from recovery homes often occurs due to a new resident's failure to become integrated into the house social ecology (Moos, 1994). The dynamics of social integration in recovery houses may be studied by conceptualizing them as social networks that evolve based on both structural tendencies and network members' characteristics.

It is plausible that a recovery house stay benefits residents in the same way as AA involvement, in being a source for alternative friendships, modeling, advice, and support. Thus, predictors of strong within-house relationships would be important to investigate. Relevant relationships would be those that promote discussion of recovery-threatening topics, for example, such negative feelings as stress, anxiety, and loneliness. Such people, which could be called confidants, are also important as a source of interactive problem solving that is less likely in 12-step meetings.

Some recovery houses, such as Oxford Houses (OHs), do provide comprehensive social environments for residents. OHs are the largest single network of recovery houses in the United States, with more than 10,000 individuals in some 1,700 houses at any given time. OHs are rented, single-family homes with a gender-segregated capacity for 6 to 12 individuals. Residents must follow three simple rules, namely, pay rent and contribute to the maintenance of the home, abstain from using alcohol and other drugs, and avoid disruptive behavior. The OH model of substance abuse aftercare is a standardized program with low start-up and maintenance costs (see Substance Abuse and Mental Health Services Administration's National Registry of Evidence-Based Programs and Practices, 2011).

The first author and his team have been studying recovery houses for over two decades. In our initial work, personal network data produced some intriguing results and led eventually to collecting data with whole networks. In one early study, we examined abstinence-specific social support and abstention from substance use in a national sample of OH residents. We found that only 18.5% of the participants reported any substance use over 1 year (Jason, Davis, Ferrari, & Anderson, 2007). Additionally, over the course of the study, the proportion of abstainers in individuals' personal social networks increased. Those with other OH residents as part of their social network were more likely to stay in OH at least 6 months and were less likely to relapse (Jason, Stevens, Ferrari, Thompson, & Legler, 2012). These findings provided us a hint of the importance of friendships within OHs as a mediator of positive outcomes.

In another study (Jason, Olson, Ferrari, & LoSasso, 2006), we successfully recruited 150 individuals who completed treatment at alcohol and drug abuse facilities in the Chicago metropolitan area. Half of the participants were randomly assigned to live in an OH, while the other half received community-based aftercare services (referred to here as Usual Care). At the 2-year follow-up assessment, the relapse rate for those individuals with 6 or more months of OH residency was 15.6%, while the rate was 45.7% for those individuals who stayed less than 6 months. For the UC group, the relapse rate was 64.8% (Jason, Olson, et al., 2007). In other words, staying in an OH for at least 6 months was critical for extremely high abstinence rates. For those residents who stayed 6 months or longer, the overall size of the personal network and the number of recovering alcoholics in that network increased, while the number of light drinkers decreased (Mueller & Jason, 2014). Significant changes occurred over those first 6 months with respect to likelihood of employment, change in median abstinence self-efficacy, and percentage of sober members in the individual's list of people considered of importance in their lives (Jason, et al., 2012). For example, the median abstinence self-efficacy for the OH sample increased significantly in the initial 6-month measurement period, the unemployment rate dropped by over 52 percentage points, and 100% of the most important people in their social network became sober.

Longitudinal network modeling methods were then utilized to help provide insight into house-level social dynamics that might affect length of stay. Although the time frame for this small study was too short to reliably estimate effects of dynamics on actual attrition, based upon prior studies we hypothesized that predictors of the tendency to form supportive relationships would provide useful input regarding this question. Our model postulated a set of relationships among recovery-related behaviors and attitudes, interpersonal trust, and both mentoring and friendship relationships. Risk-regulation theory (Murray, Gomillion, Holmes, Harris, & Lamarche, 2013) suggests that a resident will avoid other residents with low behavioral commitment to recovery because they threaten the residents' own recovery. In this model, trust develops from evidence of common recovery goals, as exemplified by similar recovery-related behaviors and attitudes, and then mediates the formation of close relationships (Rempel, Holmes, & Zanna, 1985).

We assume that a particular group to be studied can be meaningfully represented in terms of (a) a set of relationships of a particular type among group members—a "social network" N_r—with the added possibility that several such networks may be defined on a group, and some may be ordered, representing gradations of some abstract relationship; (b) a set of both fixed and time-variable characteristics that can be measured for each group member; and (c) a set of predictive interrelationships of the form $P(Y_t = y) = f(X_{t-\varepsilon})$, where X is a predictor, and $P(Y_t = y)$ is the probability that outcome Y has value y after the actor makes a decision (where y can be −1, 0, or +1, representing a change of at most 1 unit from the value of Y just prior to time t, that is, time t − ε). This conceptual formulation is consistent with the objective of modeling social integration processes (that is, changes in relationships) in recovery houses. We hypothesize that relationship closeness and trust will be positively and causally linked; if we let X be trust and Y be relationship closeness, then

$$P(Y_t = y) = f(X_{t-\varepsilon})$$

$$P(X_t = x) = g(Y_{t-\delta})$$

Thus, earlier trust $(X_{t-\varepsilon})$ predicts the probability of a change in later relationship closeness (Y_t), and vice-versa, net of other predictors that are included primarily to make causal inferences more plausible

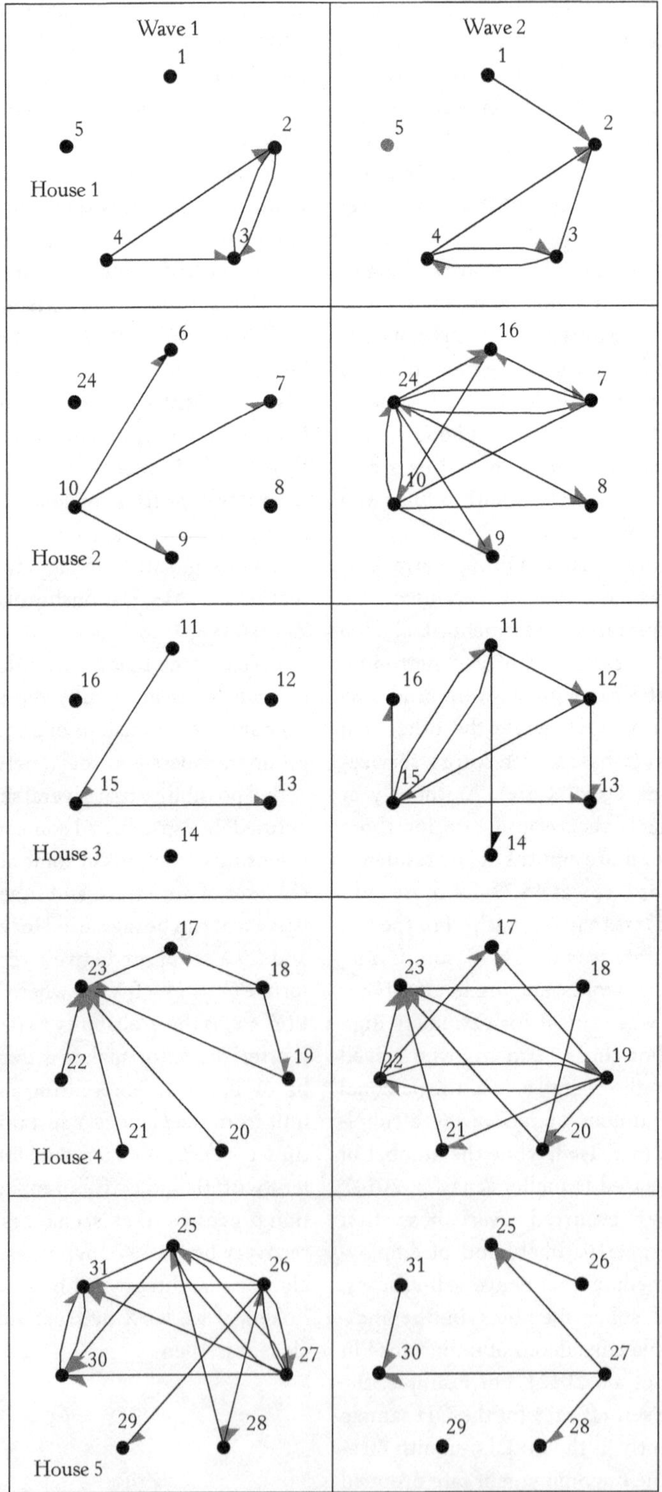

FIGURE 22.1 "Confidant" relationships for each Oxford House over time (Wave 1 and Wave 2).

Source: "Dynamic Social Networks in Recovery Homes" by L. A. Jason, J. M. Light, E. B. Stevens, & K. Beers, 2013, *American Journal of Community Psychology, 53*(3-4), p. 324–334, Figure 2. © Society for Community Research and Action 2013. Published with kind permission from Springer Science+Business Media.

(Fisher, 1934). It is important to bear this in mind as we present results that "predictors" do not predict the value of an outcome variable in this type of model; rather, they predict *change in* an outcome variable. This is a somewhat different perspective than the reader may be familiar with from ordinary regression and other covariance structure models.

We collected baseline and 3-month follow-up house-wide whole network data from five OH recovery houses with 31 participants (Jason, Light, Stevens, & Beers, 2014). Results from a Stochastic Actor-Oriented Model examining interrelationships among different levels of trust and formation of confidant relationships showed that (a) residents who had lived in the house for longer periods of time were more likely to be highly trusted, (b) high trust predicted formation of confidant relationships, and (c) confidant relationships were not regularly reciprocated. Confidant relationships showed no pattern of reciprocation, suggesting that they are not like friendships, which normally do evidence such a pattern. Figure 22.1 shows how confidant relationships were not necessarily likely to be reciprocated (Jason et al., 2014, p. 328). Of the 24 baseline dyadic confidant links among participants, only 12.5% were symmetrical; and at follow-up, only 10% were symmetrical. This suggests role specialization, and in confidant relationships, there is a confider and a listener. Friendships, by contrast, tended to become symmetrical, as a much higher percentage of trust relationships were reciprocated; at baseline, 59% of dyads trusted each other symmetrically, and at follow-up, 70% trusted each other symmetrically. In addition, trust relationships become increasingly likely the more one has them. These are called "outdegree" effects, and they suggest a threshold effect for trust, in the sense that once a person is trusted "somewhat," it is likely that he or she will eventually be trusted even more and that trusting others highly becomes self-reinforcing (Light, Jason, Stevens, & Stone, unpublished data).

That (a) formation of "high-trust" relationships is positively related to time in residence and (b) high trust is necessary to the formation of confidant relationships begins to sketch the outlines of a dynamic pathway to a successful residence experience. In other words, successfully finding a confidant or mentor may be a key pathway for continued sobriety. Although this model was necessarily simple, convergence for the model was excellent (Jason et al., 2014). All parameter *t* ratios were <0.05 (below 0.10 is considered good convergence; Snijders et al., 2010). Also, we obtained reasonable estimates of all parameter standard errors. Our study suggests that the innovative Stochastic Actor-Oriented Modeling approach is a feasible and promising empirical framework for studying evolving house social ecologies.

In the same data set, we also found that individuals who reported higher levels of general social support also reported higher levels of self-efficacy (Stevens, Jason, Ram, & Light, 2014). In addition, a larger social network predicted lower perceived stress. These findings merit further exploration regarding how and if social network size may be related to social support and the characteristics of social network size that relate specifically to promoting abstinence. They provide a strong basis for continuing to examine physical social network properties and their possible influence on an individual's psychological state.

CONCLUSION

This chapter has focused on dynamic social network models, a paradigm that is distinguished from other approaches by its emphasis on the mutual interdependence between relationships and behavior change over time. As such, it provides a framework for conceptualizing and empirically describing two-way transactional dynamics. The chapter reviewed studies using complete network data (i.e., where all possible dyadic relationships among individuals or other entities, such as organizations, are accessible), providing a structural map of an entire social ecosystem. We also provided an example showing how the dimensions of trust, friendship, and mentoring change over time in the relationships among persons living in substance abuse recovery residences.

There are several other frameworks available for modeling the coevolution of trust and relationship closeness. For instance, the Actor-Partner Interaction Model (Kenny et al., 2002) offers a way to estimate effects of personal characteristics apart from relationship partner effects on behavior change. On the other hand, it takes relationships as fixed, and hence cannot model behavioral and relational (dyadic) interdependence. Gottman, Swanson, and Murray's (1999) Linked Difference Equation model is an example of the differential (in continuous time) or difference (in discrete time) modeling approach originally applied to physical systems (e.g., Newton's laws of motion can be written in differential equation form). It has been useful for other scientific applications, for instance, mathematical biology (Murray, 2003) and child development (van Geert & Steenbeek, 2005). Structural equation modeling methods have been developed to estimate the parameters of such systems (Hu, Boker, Neale, & Klump, 2014; Voelkle, Oud, Davidov, & Schmidt, 2012).

The Stochastic Actor-Oriented Model is a specific application of differential equation modeling. It shares with such models an inherent "generative" nature, meaning that its temporal evolution can be simulated in a natural way (Snijders & Steglich, 2015). Unlike the deterministic models mentioned earlier, the underlying dynamics can be written as a set of stochastic differential equations, which is often substantively preferable for modeling complex, multidetermined systems. Conceptually, such systems are unlikely to evolve exactly the same way, given a particular set of initial conditions. The solution to a stochastic differential equation will be a stochastic process, which under the assumptions of a Stochastic Actor framework is a continuous-time Markov process. Abstractly, such models provide the type of continuous-time "transactional" representations required to realistically model relationship-behavior dynamics.

Pragmatically, moreover, such modeling has been well developed, extended, and thoroughly documented over the last several decades. Models may be estimated with publically available free software that is actively maintained and upgraded: the RSiena package for the statistical software environment R. Hundreds of relationship and behavioral effects can be modeled, and programming-oriented users can add their own. A suite of estimation methods based on tried and true statistical theory include Bayesian, maximum likelihood, and, for larger samples, a faster score function-based approach. Multilevel methods are built in, permitting variously pooled models across networks and other entities. Data requirements are clearly defined and based on familiar survey methods (although other data collection methods could also be used). This methodology is still developing, and some important aspects of it have yet to be evaluated, for example, the Markov assumption, which amounts to assuming that each "decision" made by an actor is unaffected by the history of the system prior to the time of the decision. Such weaknesses must be weighed against those of other available methods.

In this chapter we have presented a social network as both a theoretical/conceptual and an empirical entity. Conceptually, we think of it as a map of particular types of dyadic relationships in a bounded social group. Empirically, a network can be straightforwardly measured, for example by direct observation of interactions or, as in our example, by asking group members to nominate others as relationship partners. The network paradigm provides a particularly convenient framework for dynamic analysis of a set of developing social relationships.

This convenient grouping of a target population is not typical for adults; even studies of networks in organizations by no means include all relevant social contexts for organizational members, such as family and leisure companions. A limiting factor in whole network research is identifying a group where all the members of the network know each other, and another is having access to all these individuals for ratings. In contrast, personal network studies of substance use recovery have established the relevance of participant-reported associates as mediators of ongoing sobriety (Kaskutas, Bond, & Humphreys, 2002; Polcin et al., 2010). However, as mentioned earlier, personal networks are inherently limited by their reliance on the perceived relationships of a person and other network members, rather than on all of the relationships in a system.

The use of dynamic social networks provides a higher-magnification lens for understanding contextual influences on behavior and behavioral influences on context. For example, we can learn how an individual may influence the existing network, not just how an existing network may affect the individual's behavior. Questions that this approach will eventually help us understand may include the following: How do new individuals fit into this ecology—or fail to? What do they need to take away from it in order to succeed in settings? Are there more systematic ways individuals could prepare for entry into a setting? How do relationships within a setting, as well as within their own personal networks, interact? The answers to such questions lie in the study of the way setting cultures develop, are maintained, and are extended to new individuals, and how this process interacts with attempts to refashion personal networks to support a variety of personal goals. A novel adaptation of dynamic network modeling could help us answer questions such as these.

The work we have described in the case study was based on a complex system that involves those recovering from addiction and two social ecologies (their recovery house and personal network). Our perspective is naturally transtheoretical. At the level of the individual, Moos (2007) and Vaillant (2005) offer rationales for why integration into the house social system should be important to recovery house effectiveness, such as resultant bonding, monitoring, goal direction, modeling, positive reinforcement, rewarding alternatives to using, and advice and outlets for dealing with negative emotions and stress. Because relationships within the house (and/or in the personal network outside the house) are likely to be vehicles for these processes, integration can be viewed as relationship formation processes. Furthermore, as Valliant explicitly noted, many of these recovery-supportive processes are likely to be active in new, recovery-supportive friendship and mentoring relations. Dynamic social networks provide us with the ability to focus on processes whereby those relationships form in the house or support their formation in the personal network outside the house, and especially how friend and mentor relations affect recovery outcomes.

Our research has provided significant insight into house structure and dynamics as predictors of an individual's likelihood of maintaining a positive recovery trajectory. We have been able to identify contributions of external recovery behaviors (e.g., AA), external ego-centered networks (scope, composition, dynamics), and within-setting social networks. These mechanism-level effects are empirically verifiable and interesting in their own right, but the behavior of such a complex system as a whole is not immediately obvious. This sort of information can be obtained by simulation, however. Stochastic simulations will give rise to a distribution of outcomes of interest, such as the probability of developing a stable social support system within and outside the house, leaving the house prematurely, and relapsing. The models can also be studied to determine promising mechanisms that could be affected by changes in house operations, individual-level interventions, and so on, and possibly failure thresholds where the likelihood of poorer outcomes begins to accelerate. Thus, by identifying mechanisms through which social environments affect health outcomes and looking at system-level evolution, this approach could contribute to reducing health care costs by improving the effectiveness of the residential recovery home system in the United States and also restructuring and improving other community-based recovery settings. In addition, our work provides an initial framework for the study of network dynamics in recovery homes that may facilitate both the theoretical development and empirical investigation of the broader domain of recovery in community-based settings following treatment.

In summary, our social network design and resulting mathematical model provide a conceptually useful way to represent social system dynamics in relation to progress toward self-sustaining recovery. Substantively, our work using dynamic social network theory and methodology has addressed the longstanding question of how and why community-based settings support sobriety, perhaps moving this option more into the mainstream of substance abuse treatment protocols. This is but one example of the many social problems involving complex relationships between individuals and their social environments that could benefit from a dynamic social network approach.

REFERENCES

Blau, P. M. (1964). *Exchange and power in social life.* New York, NY: Wiley.

Bonaventura, M., Ames, K., Brumpton, R., Garratt, R., Hall, K., & Wilson, N. (2006). Human friendship favours cooperation in the Iterated Prisoner's Dilemma. *Behaviour, 143*, 1383–1395.

Brechwald, W. A., & Prinstein, M. J. (2011). Beyond homophily: A decade of advances in understanding peer influence processes. *Journal of Research on Adolescence, 21*, 166–179.

Buchanan, A. S., & Latkin, C. A. (2008). Drug use in the social networks of heroin and cocaine users before and after drug cessation. *Drug and Alcohol Dependence, 96*, 286–289.

Cruz, J. E., Emery, R. E., & Turkheimer, E. (2012). Peer network drinking predicts increased alcohol use from adolescence to early adulthood after controlling for genetic and shared environmental selection. *Developmental Psychology, 48*, 1390–1402.

Dishion, T. J. (2013). Stochastic agent-based modeling of influence and selection in adolescence: Current status and future directions in understanding the dynamics of peer contagion. *Journal of Research on Adolescence, 23*, 596–603.

du Plessis, K., & Corney, T. (2011). Trust, respect, and friendship: The key attributes of significant others in the lives of young working men. *Youth Studies Australia, 30*, 17–26.

Fisher, R. A. (1934). *Statistical methods for research workers* (5th ed.). Edinburgh, Scotland: Oliver and Boyd.

Gottman, J., Swanson, C., & Murray, J. (1999). The mathematics of marital conflict: Dynamic mathematical nonlinear modeling of newlywed marital interaction. *Journal of Family Psychology, 13*, 3–19.

Groh, D., Jason, L. A., & Keys, C. B. (2008). Social network variables in Alcoholics Anonymous: A literature review. *Clinical Psychology Review, 28*, 430–450.

Horst, M., & Coffé, H. (2012). How friendship network characteristics influence subjective well-being. *Social Indicators Research, 107*, 509–529.

Hu, Y., Boker, S., Neale, M., & Klump, K. L. (2014). Coupled latent differential equation with moderators: Simulation and application. *Psychological Methods, 19*, 56–71.

Jason, L. A., Davis, M. I., Ferrari, J. R., & Anderson, E. (2007). The need for substance abuse after-care: Longitudinal analysis of Oxford House. *Addictive Behaviors, 32*, 803–818.

Jason, L. A., & Glenwick, D. S. (2012). Introduction: An overview of methodological innovations in community research. In L. A. Jason & D. S. Glenwick (Eds.), *Methodological approaches to community-based research* (pp. 3–10). Washington, DC: American Psychological Association.

Jason, L.A., Light, J. M., Stevens, E. B., & Beers, K. (2014). Dynamic social networks in recovery homes. *American Journal of Community Psychology, 53*, 324–334.

Jason, L. A., Olson, B. D., Ferrari, J. R., & Lo Sasso, A. T. (2006). Communal housing settings enhance substance abuse recovery. *American Journal of Public Health, 96*, 1727–1729.

Jason, L. A., Olson, B. D., Ferrari, J. R., Majer, J. M., Alvarez, J., & Stout, J. (2007). An examination of main and interactive effects of substance abuse recovery housing on multiple indicators of adjustment. *Addiction, 102*, 1114–1121.

Jason, L. A., Olson, B. D., & Foli, K. (2008). *Rescued lives: The Oxford House approach to substance abuse*. New York, NY: Routledge.

Jason, L. A., Stevens, E., Ferrari, J. R., Thompson, E., & Legler, R. (2012). Social networks among residents in recovery homes. *Advances in Psychology Study, 1*, 4–12.

Kaskutas, L. A., Bond, J., & Humphreys, K. (2002). Social networks as mediators of the effect of Alcoholics Anonymous. *Addiction, 97*, 891–900.

Kenny, D. A., Mannetti, L., Pierro, A., Livi, S., & Kashy, D. A. (2002). The statistical analysis of data from small groups. *Journal of Personality and Social Psychology, 83*, 126–137.

Laudet, A., Becker, J., & White, W. (2009). Don't wanna go through that madness no more: Quality of life satisfaction as predictor of sustained substance use remission. *Substance Use and Misuse, 44*, 227–252.

Mercken, L., Steglich, C., Sinclair, P., Holliday, J., & Moore, L. (2012). A longitudinal social network analysis of peer influence, peer selection, and smoking behavior among adolescents in British schools. *Health Psychology, 31*, 450–459.

Moos, R. H. (1994). *The Social Climate Scales: A user's guide* (3rd ed.). Palo Alto, CA: Mind Garden.

Moos, R. H. (2007). Theory-based active ingredients of effective treatments for substance use disorders. *Drug and Alcohol Dependence, 88*, 109–121.

Moos, R. H., & Moos, B. S. (2006). Rates and predictors of relapse after natural and treated remission from alcohol use disorders. *Addiction, 101*, 212–222.

Moreno, J. (1934). *Who shall survive?* Washington, DC: Nervous and Mental Disease Publishing.

Mueller, D. G., & Jason, L. A. (2014). Sober-living houses and changes in the personal networks of individuals in recovery. *Health Psychology Research, 2*, 5–10.

Murray, J. D. (2003). *Mathematical biology II: Spatial models and biomedical applications*. New York, NY: Springer.

Murray, S. L., Gomillion, S., Holmes, J. G., Harris, B., & Lamarche, V. (2013). The dynamics of relationship promotion: Controlling the automatic inclination to trust. *Journal of Personality and Social Psychology, 104*, 305–334.

National Drug Intelligence Center. (2011). *The economic impact of illicit drug use on American society*. Washington, DC: United States Department of Justice.

Patulny, R. (2011). Social trust, social partner time and television time. *Social Indicators Research, 101*, 289–293.

Polcin, D. L., Korcha, R., Bond, J., Galloway, G., & Lapp, W. (2010). Recovery from addiction in two types of sober living houses: 12-month outcomes. *Addiction Research and Theory, 18*, 442–455.

Rempel, J. K., Holmes, J. K., & Zanna, M. P. (1985). Trust in close relationships. *Journal of Personality and Social Psychology, 49*, 95–112.

Rhodes, J. E., & DuBois, D. L. (2008). Mentoring relationships and programs for youth. *Current Directions in Psychological Science, 17*, 254–258.

Schachter, S. (1951). Deviation, rejection, and communication. *Journal of Abnormal and Social Psychology, 46*, 190–207.

Schaefer, J. A., Cronkite, R. C., & Hu, K. U. (2011). Differential relationships between continuity of care practices, engagement in continuing care, and abstinence among subgroups of patients with substance use and psychiatric disorders. *Journal of Studies on Alcohol and Drugs, 72*, 611–621.

Sherif, M. (1966). *In common predicament: Social psychology of intergroup conflict and cooperation*. Boston, MA: Houghton-Mifflin.

Snijders, T. A. B., & Bosker, R. J. (2012). *Multilevel analysis: An introduction to basic and advanced multilevel modeling* (2nd ed). Thousand Oaks, CA: Sage.

Snijders,T. A .B., Lomi, A., & Torló, V. J. (2013). A model for the multiplex dynamics of two-mode and one-mode networks, with an application to employment preference, friendship, and advice. *Social Networks, 35*, 265–276.

Snijders, T. A. B., & Steglich, C. (2015). Representing micro-macro linkages by actor-based dynamic network models. *Sociological Methods and Research, 44*(2), 222–271.

Snijders, T. A. B., van de Bunt, G.G. & Steglich, C. E. G. (2010) Introduction to stochastic actor-based models for network dynamics. *Social Networks, 32*, 44–60.

Stevens, E., Jason, L. A., Ram, D., & Light, J. (2014). Investigating social support and network relationships in substance use disorder recovery. *Substance Abuse*. Epub ahead of print.

Stone, A., Jason, L.A., Stevens, E., & Light, J. M. (2014). Factors affecting the stability of social networks during early recovery in ex-offenders. *American Journal of Drug and Alcohol Abuse, 40*, 187–191.

Substance Abuse and Mental Health Services Administration's National Registry of Evidence-Based Programs and Practices. (2011). *Oxford House*. Retrieved June 2015, from http://www.nrepp.samhsa.gov/ViewIntervention.aspx?id=223

Todd, N. R., Allen, N. E., & Javdani, S. (2012). Multilevel modeling: Method and application for community-based research. In L. A. Jason & D. S. Glenwick (Eds.), *Methodological approaches to community-based research* (pp. 167–186). Washington, DC: American Psychological Association.

US Department of Health and Human Services. (2012). *Results from the National Survey on Drug Use and Health: Summar of national findings*. Retrieved June 2015, from http://www.samhsa.gov/data/nsduh/2012summnatfinddettables/nationalfindings/nsduhresults2012.htm

Vaillant, G. E. (1983). *The natural hstory of alcoholism*. Cambridge, MA: Harvard University Press.

Vaillant, G. E. (2003). A 60-year follow-up of alcoholic men. *Addiction, 98*, 1043–1051.

Vaillant, G. E. (2005). Alcoholics Anonymous: Cult or cure? *Australian and New Zealand Journal of Psychiatry, 39*, 431–436.

van Geert, P. L. C., & Steenbeek, H. W. (2005). Explaining after by before: Basic aspects of a dynamic systems approach to the study of development. *Developmental Review, 25*, 408–442.

Veenstra, R., Dijkstra, J. K., Steglich, C., & Van Zalk, M. H. W. (2103). Network–behavior dynamics. *Journal of Research on Adolescence, 23*, 399–412.

Voelkle, M. C., Oud, J. H. L., Davidov, E., & Schmidt, P. (2012). An SEM approach to continuous time modeling of panel data: Relating authoritarianism and anomia. *Psychological Methods, 17*, 176–192.

Way, N., Gingold, R., Rotenberg, M., & Kuriakose, G. (2005). Close friendships among urban, ethnic-minority adolescents. *New Directions for Child and Adolescent Development, 2005*, 41–59.

Weerman, F. M. (2011). Delinquent peers in context: A longitudinal network analysis of selection and influence effects. *Criminology, 49*, 253–286.

White, H. C., Boorman, S., & Breiger, R. (1976). Social structure from multiple networks. I. Blockmodels of roles and positions. *American Journal of Sociology, 81*, 730–779.

Wrzus, C., Hänel, M., Wagner, J., & Neyer, F. J. (2013). Social network changes and life events across the life span: A meta-analysis. *Psychological Bulletin, 139*, 53–80.

SECTION III

Mixed Methods Approaches

23

Introduction to Mixed Methods Approaches

VALERIE R. ANDERSON

Community-based research, and the field of community psychology in particular, has increasingly embraced and called for the use of multiple methods (Barker & Pistrang, 2005; Tebes, 2005). Mixed methods research—also referred to as methodological eclecticism or methodological pluralism—involves combining quantitative and qualitative methods in a study in which multiple quantitative and/or qualitative methods are used in tandem (APA Task Force, 2006; Creswell & Plano-Clark, 2007; Molina Azorin & Cameron, 2010; Wiggins, 2011). Although mixed methods research typically refers to a single study, it also can encompass a series of studies addressing the same research questions that use multiple methods for inquiry.

This chapter is organized into four sections. The first section provides an overview of mixed methods research by providing a brief review of the history of mixed methods research, definitions, and key concepts. The second section focuses on how quantitative and qualitative methods have been integrated in research. In particular, it focuses on how methods can be integrated, as well as the benefits and challenges involved in conducting mixed methods research. The third section highlights several community-based research studies that utilized mixed methods, with a focus on the specific techniques for integration and how mixing methods can add to scientific rigor in such research. The chapter concludes with an example of a mixed methods study of a juvenile court system that illustrates these concepts.

INTRODUCTION TO MIXED METHODS RESEARCH

As there has been an increase in the development and use of diverse types of community-based research methods, there has also been an increase in debates around methodological pluralism and what scholars refer to as the *paradigm wars*—the inherent opposition of quantitative and qualitative methods (Howe, 1988; Wiggins, 2011). A *paradigm* refers to a worldview and its accompanying assumptions of how the world works (Kuhn, 1962). Paradigms and their sets of assumptions guide the structure and nature of questions and are so engrained that they are not usually examined in any great detail (Kuhn, 1962). In addition, for the purpose of clarity in this overview, *method* refers to the technical aspects of research (e.g., the procedures for collecting data), whereas *methodology* refers to the study of methods. Thus, regardless of the approach, the paradigm will influence the methodology that ultimately influences the choice of method for a study.

Historically, scholars have taken an either/or approach to using quantitative or qualitative methods, which has led many researchers to abstract that they are inherently opposed methodologies (Molina Azorin & Cameron, 2010; Wiggins, 2011). For example, quantitative research methods are born out of a positivistic/postpositivistic paradigm, whereas qualitative research methods belong to an interpretivist or constructivist paradigm. Thus, each is viewed as having a distinct epistemology, ontology, and axiology (see Dixon-Woods, Agarwal, Young, Jones, & Sutton, 2004, and Wiggins, 2011, for a more detailed review of the paradigmatic wars and discussion of the perceived incompatibility of methodologies).

Why Mix Methods?

There are a number of reasons and rationales for mixing methods. First, all research methods have their limitations. Most mixed methods studies attempt to use both quantitative and qualitative methods to offset each other's strengths and weaknesses or mix methods to answer a research question or questions by all means available (Tashakkori & Creswell, 2007; Wiggins, 2011). In mixed methods research, methodological approaches are not necessarily seen as that rigid in terms of differences in how methodology should play out based on worldviews (Wiggins, 2011). In fact, some scholars would argue that methods should be mixed to utilize different perspectives to understand a phenomenon (Tashakkori & Creswell, 2007). Additionally, mixed methods can provide a more nuanced understanding of research questions than a single method can accomplish on its own (Molina Azorin & Cameron, 2010). For example, Palikas, Horwitz, Chamberlain, Hurlburt, and Landsverk (2011) identified that researchers tend to use qualitative methods for a topic with currently little research and/or for a more in-depth examination, but tend to use quantitative methods to test hypotheses and/or for generalization.

Over time there has been a greater acceptance and value of the use of both approaches, but the relationship between them and how to engage in meaningful integration has remained unclear due to each being born out of divergent philosophies of science (Wiggins, 2011). Other scholars have identified that the divergent philosophies of science from which methods are born is actually a strength of mixed methods research, because it can employ a dialectical perspective through engaging multiple worldviews (Greene & Caracelli, 1997). However, there is still not a consensus among methodological camps as to whether or not mixed methods research can—or should—utilize multiple worldviews or a single paradigm in a study (Creswell & Creswell, 2005).

INTEGRATING QUANTITATIVE AND QUALITATIVE METHODS

In mixed methods research, integration can occur at the level of the paradigm, the methodology, or the method. In determining mixed methods design, or type of integration, first the implementation and priority of data collection need to be considered (Molina Azorin & Cameron, 2010). In this context, implementation refers to the sequence in which data is collected (e.g., concurrently, sequentially), and priority refers to the emphasis each method is given (e.g., one method is dominant or both methods are equally emphasized) (Molina Azorin & Cameron, 2010). Second, the design can be predetermined or be emergent (e.g., evolving based on new opportunities or developments in a research project), but researchers should be explicit about why they are mixing methods (Molina Azorin & Cameron, 2010). Palinkas et al. (2011) outlined four key questions researchers can ask themselves when designing a mixed method study:

1. What is the rationale? Is the study dictated by data, by objectives, by research questions, and/or to complement the strengths/weaknesses of the various methods utilized?
2. What is the structure? How are the methods integrated together (see Morse's 1991 taxonomy)?
3. What is the function? Is the goal convergence of findings, providing complementary explanations, expanding upon previous findings, the development of an instrument, or for sampling purposes?
4. What is the process? Will data sets be merged together, connected in some type of sequence, or is one data set embedded within another?

Answering these questions up front will provide researchers with a framework for their research design and more meaningful integration of their methods.

Types of Integration

Most commonly mixed methods studies involve within-study integration of quantitative and qualitative methods to examine a research question (Wiggins, 2011). Traditionally, methods are mixed hierarchically, with one method usually being the dominant or more central method to the study—whether done implicitly or explicitly—while the other method acts in a supporting role (Molina Azorin & Cameron, 2010). Methods may also be mixed sequentially by first using an exploratory method for discovery and later using a confirmatory method for justification (Wiggins, 2011). For example, in a typical sequential mixed methods design, qualitative methods might be used first as an exploratory method to help develop survey items, and then quantitative methods would be used to explore the survey's psychometric properties and utilize the survey to test a hypothesis.

Morse (1991) was the first scholar to develop a typology of mixed methods research designs using notation to represent each of the designs. In Morse's system the dominant method is represented using all capital letters (e.g., QUAN, QUAL) and the complementary method is represented using all lowercase letters (e.g., quan, qual). An arrow (→) is used to denote a sequential design, and a plus sign (+) is used to denote a concurrent design. Given Morse's typology, there are four types of mixed methods designs, with the potential for nine different combinations:

1. Equivalent, simultaneous designs (QUAL + QUAN)
2. Equivalent, sequential designs (QUAN → QUAL; QUAL → QUAN)
3. Dominant, simultaneous designs (QUAN + qual; QUAL + quan)
4. Dominant, sequential designs (QUAN → qual; quan → QUAL; qual → QUAN; QUAL → quan)

Wiggins (2011) outlined three ways in which mixing occurs at the level of method: (a) triangulation, (b) demarcation, and (c) reclassification. Triangulation has a long history in research using multiple methods. The purpose of triangulating is, by converging findings, to use multiple methods to increase the study's validity (Webb, 1966). Demarcation refers to how the methods are related (e.g., quantitative as the dominant method and qualitative as the secondary method). Reclassification refers to how both methods can be used in exploratory and confirmatory ways (Wiggins, 2011). Finally, Wiggins noted that methodological appropriation often occurs, deliberately and unintentionally, via blending the two methods within a single worldview. For example, methodological appropriation occurs in a postpositivistic paradigm where researchers transform qualitative data into numbers for statistical analysis or only use qualitative methods to lay the groundwork for a quantitative study.

Building upon Wiggins's (2011) overview of the paradigmatic issues in mixed methods research, Creswell and Plano Clark (2007) also provided a detailed account of multiple formats for mixing methods: (a) concurrent triangulation, (b) sequential/multiphasic designs, and (c) embedded designs. Concurrent triangulation involves simultaneous data collection and analysis allowing for the examination of convergent and divergent findings. For example, transforming qualitative data for quantitative analysis can reveal the ways in which findings do or do not fit. Sequential/multiphasic designs—the most prominent mode of mixing methods—focus on explanatory (quantitative data collection and analysis → qualitative data collection and analysis) and/or exploratory (qualitative data collection and analysis → qualitative data collection and analysis) processes. One rationale for an explanatory design is that qualitative methods can be used to strengthen the study by providing a deeper explanation and contextual analysis of the quantitative findings, whereas the rationale for an exploratory design might include strengthening the development of an instrument or exploring a phenomenon in depth before attempting to quantify it (Creswell & Plano Clark, 2007). A multiphasic sequential design may integrate different methods across multiple points in time (qualitative → quantitative → qualitative → quantitative → etc.) to converge the data (Creswell & Plano Clark, 2007). In both types of sequential/multiphasic designs, quantitative and qualitative results are usually reported separately (see Bartholomew & Brown, 2012, for a review). Finally, an embedded design involves using one data set to support the other data set either concurrently or in phases (Creswell & Plano Clark, 2007).

Tashakkori and Teddlie (2003) noted that other researchers have identified at least 35 distinct types of mixed method designs. This plethora leaves researchers with the challenge of figuring out, from this abundance of design choices, the optimal design for their research questions. Leech and Onwuegbuzie (2007) created a three-dimensional typology of mixed methods designs in order to address this issue to simplify design choices. The three dimensions include identifying (a) the level of mixing (e.g., fully mixed or partially mixed), (b) the timeframe for mixing (e.g., concurrent or sequential), and (c) the emphasis of each method (e.g., are they equal or is one method dominant?). Each of these integration techniques is useful for guidance in design choices and enables mixed methods researchers to speak a common language.

Finally, scholars should assess the quality of mixed methods research based on research planning, design, data, and interpretation (O'Cathain, 2010). Given the history of these distinct types of research methods and the amount of integration techniques identified in the mixed methods literature, there are a number of benefits and challenges involved in mixing methods.

Benefits

There are multiple benefits that mixed methods research provides over and above a monomethod approach. First, using both quantitative and qualitative methods in a single study can address and combat each other's strengths and weaknesses (Wiggins, 2011). In particular, mixing methods can enhance the validity or trustworthiness of inferences and assertions by providing mutual confirmation of findings. For example, does one method facilitate our understanding of the results generated by another method (Molina Azorin & Cameron, 2010)? Mixed methods designs can provide deeper exploration of causal mechanisms, interpretation of variables, and contextual factors that may mediate or moderate the topic of study (Bartholomew & Brown, 2012; Molina Azorin & Cameron, 2010). Mixed methods research can facilitate the development of culturally appropriate instruments and foster a deeper understanding of the phenomenon of interest (Bartholomew & Brown, 2012). Finally, mixed methods designs can strengthen evaluations of interventions across disciplines and foster team-based research in which researchers can bring their own strengths and areas of expertise to the table (Bartholomew & Brown, 2012).

Challenges

Mixed methods research also poses a number of challenges to scholars interested in addressing a research question using both qualitative and quantitative approaches. Currently, although frameworks exist in different fields, there are no definitive guidelines for how to conduct a mixed methods study (Palinkas et al., 2011; Wiggins, 2011). In addition, there is great ambiguity in addressing the paradigm wars—incompatibility issues of mixing methods—and there are a number of challenges for synthesis of both across and within methods (Bartholomew & Brown, 2012; Dixon-Woods et al., 2004; Palinkas et al., 2011; Wiggins, 2011). For example, triangulating findings occurs at the level of method, which ignores the worldview issue (Wiggins, 2011).

There have been consistent calls both within psychology and across other disciplines for the development of a more comprehensive framework for the integration of methods (Wiggins, 2011). However, there are multiple technical limitations that need to be addressed in the mixed methods literature. For example, integrating multiple data sets is a complex task, especially when they come from different methodological traditions (Bartholomew & Brown, 2012; Molina Azorin & Cameron, 2010). There are also challenges in publishing due to page and word limits in journals (Molina Azorin & Cameron, 2010). There is a lack of in-depth training by scholars in both methodologies—mixed methods research requires a larger skill set than a researcher who only uses quantitative or qualitative methods (Bartholomew & Brown, 2012; Molina Azorin & Cameron, 2010). Also, by incorporating multiple methods in the design, mixed methods research takes longer to complete than a monomethod study, and typically more resources (e.g., time, financial) are needed to conduct such studies (Molina Azorin & Cameron, 2010). Additionally, researchers have noted that there is a need for greater specification of the types of qualitative methods utilized (Bartholomew & Brown, 2012). For example, in Palinaks et al.'s (2011) review, many of the studies did not provide detailed procedures regarding the type of qualitative analysis conducted. As with quantitative methods, there are multiple types of qualitative data analysis (e.g., grounded theory, analytic induction, narrative analysis, content analysis), and those types need to be expanded upon in the methodological literature and in empirical studies using multiple methods.

MIXED METHODS RESEARCH IN COMMUNITY-BASED RESEARCH

The use of multiple methods in community-based research has increased in recent years. This section provides four examples of such studies and how those studies integrated quantitative and qualitative data using the frameworks outlined in the previous section.

Campbell (1995) studied police perceptions of date rape using an integrated quantitative and qualitative design. First, she utilized quantitative structural equation modeling to identify relationship patterns of police perceptions of rape. She identified a direct path between amount of officer experience and more sympathetic feelings about date rape victims, and found that trainings on rape mediated this relationship (e.g., police who received trainings had greater sympathy); this relationship then predicted less victim-blaming ideologies. Second, Campbell qualitatively examined police officer narratives in which content analysis was used to validate the findings from the quantitative portion of the study. For example, police officers with more experience and who received trainings on rape had less victim-blaming narratives on date rape. Campbell used quantitative and qualitative methods in tandem primarily for convergence of findings (e.g., the qualitative content analysis findings confirmed the quantitative structural equation modeling findings).

Salem, Foster-Fishman, and Goodkind (2002) studied collective action organizations' openness to innovation and organizational change using a quant → qual design. Phase I (the quantitative portion) examined leadership perspectives across 63 organizations. The organizations were surveyed to identify factors related to the organizational environment (e.g., perceptions/attitudes), the external environment (e.g., organizational network, funding requirements), chapter activities, and philosophies of service delivery. Phase II (the qualitative portion) involved interviews with chapter leaders using a modified grounded theory approach to identify emergent themes. Salem et al. primarily used a mixed methods approach to triangulate the different sources of data for convergent and disconfirming evidence (e.g., negative case analysis).

Using a quant → qual design, Ellis, March, and Craven (2009) examined the effectiveness of a peer support program for youth transitioning into high school. With respect to quantitative methods, the researchers utilized a longitudinal, experimental design with a control group and baseline measures to assess the program's effectiveness. They found that the program enhanced students' connectedness, resourcefulness, and self-concept as it related to school. After obtaining these results, Ellis et al. recruited a subsample of program participants for focus groups and open-ended surveys to understand the program from students' perspectives. The qualitative data were content analyzed to identify themes. As the qualitative data were used to confirm and expand upon the quantitative findings that indicated that the program provided benefit to youth transitioning into high school, qualitative methods were the supplemental method employed to enrich the quantitative findings.

Finally, Knox, Guerra, Williams, and Toro (2011) combined two studies to evaluate an evidence-based program, Families and Schools Together (FAST). The first study was a quantitative evaluation using linear growth models to assess the reduction of aggression in children up to 12 months following the program. The researchers found no differences between the treatment and control conditions with respect to reducing children's aggression, but the treatment condition did produce greater improvements in problem-solving skills and collective efficacy. To follow up the quantitative evaluation, the researchers conducted two focus groups to explore other potential outcomes that were not captured in the quantitative evaluation, through which they found that the intervention positively impacted family communication. In this design, Knox et al. utilized the qualitative data to enhance and expand upon the quantitative findings within a quant + qual framework. Both studies supported the finding that the intervention was not effective in reducing aggression but that there were other beneficial outcomes.

In summary, this brief highlighting of community-based studies suggests that the dominant mode of mixing methods is a quantitative → qualitative sequential design, with varying levels of emphasis on each method. Each of the studies reported the findings separately (e.g., separate sections in the results for reporting the data). Primarily, the qualitative data were used to supplement or expand upon the quantitative findings.

CASE STUDY

In recent years female juvenile offenders have comprised a growing proportion of juvenile court caseloads (Chesney-Lind & Shelden, 2004; Stevens, Morash, & Chesney-Lind, 2011). In particular, the greatest increase has been in violent offenses among girls (Puzzanchera, Adams, & Sickmund, 2010). This increase in official female juvenile delinquency is largely seen as a reflection of the change in system-level policies and practices (Javdani, Sadeh, & Verona, 2011; Stevens et al., 2011) and changes in arrest patterns through the "upcriming" of girls' offenses rather than an increase in actual criminal behavior (Schwartz & Steffensmeier, 2012).

Thus, there is a growing interest and investment in gender-responsive services among juvenile justice practitioners and researchers (Chesney-Lind & Irwin, 2008; Chesney-Lind & Shelden, 2004). Furthermore, there have been consistent calls for more rigorous evaluation studies on the effectiveness of gender-specific programming (Chesney-Lind, Morash, & Stevens, 2008; Kerig & Schindler, 2013; Zahn, Day, Mihalic, & Tichavsky, 2009).

Given the increased visibility of girls in the juvenile justice system, it is important to (a) examine how juvenile court personnel understand and respond to girls and (b) rigorously evaluate gender-responsive programming for girls. These foci informed the current mixed methods study. An emergent, mixed methods design was used to answer two research questions sequentially. The first question (quantitative) was developed within the context of a collaborative research team between Michigan State University and a juvenile county court system. The second question (qualitative) was developed after the quantitative study was completed as part of a broader qualitative study on how practitioners understand and utilize the construct of gender-responsivity in their service provision. Thus, this is a case example of a sequential explanatory mixed methods design.

Girls' Group Home Intervention Effectiveness With Propensity Score Matching

Given the calls for more rigorous program evaluation of gender-responsive services for girls in the juvenile justice system, an evaluation was conducted using archival court data regarding an out-of-home placement intervention designed to address the unique needs of girls involved with the system. The main research question asked what the effectiveness of this intervention was for girls who received the program compared to girls who did not receive the program with respect to their reoffense outcomes

The quantitative study compared reoffense outcomes for girls who received treatment in group homes ($n = 172$) and girls who received standard probation services ($n = 816$) for adjudicated females in a midsized, Midwestern county court between 2005 and 2012. Preliminary examination of sociodemographic and risk assessment variables indicated that the girls who received the group home placement had significantly higher baseline scores on the Youth Level of Service/Case Management Inventory (YLS/CMI)—the criminogenic risk measure that the court administers to youth—than the girls on standard probation. The two samples also significantly differed in age, with the group home girls being younger on average than the girls not receiving the treatment. Given these differences, it was important to compare girls in the two samples who had similar demographics and criminogenic risk profiles. To accomplish this goal, girls were propensity score matched on 11 theoretically salient variables (e.g., age, criminogenic risk assessment scores, race/ethnicity, initial offense type). Propensity score matching is a quantitative method to control for potential selection effects in a nonrandomized design and produces a statistical balance in the observed covariates used for analysis (see Stuart, 2010; Thoemmes & Kim, 2011).

The dependent variable for the study was recidivism and was collected via the court data management system. Recidivism was defined as any new petition to court 24 months following their initial YLS/CMI assessment for the comparison group and 24 months following exit from group home placement for the treatment group. If the girl aged out during the follow-up period, adult records were checked as well.

The group homes incorporate theoretically informed gender-responsive elements, such as girls' pathways into the system (e.g., addressing trauma, abuse, and neglect) and relationships (e.g., focusing on the centrality of relationships, inclusion of girls' voice, and sense of connection to others). Of particular interest was the group homes' use of the Girls Moving On (GMO) gender-responsive curriculum. GMO is a gender-responsive cognitive-behavioral treatment program for at-risk girls between the ages of 12 to 21 years old (Orbis Partners, 2014). The program's main goal is to provide girls with skills and resources, increase girls' capacity for healthy relationships, and to reduce girls' risk for juvenile and criminal justice system involvement.

After the propensity scores were created, group home girls were matched to non–group home girls having the closest possible propensity by using a 1:1 nearest neighbor ratio. In other words, this procedure created a probability variable for receiving treatment based on the selected covariates and created a group of 172 non–group home girls with near-identical demographic and risk profiles as the comparison sample. Analysis of the outcome data indicated that the girls' group home sample had significantly lower recidivism rates at both 1-year (20% vs. 27%) and 2-year (27% vs. 37%) follow-up than did the comparison sample. Thus, it is likely that the group home intervention reduced girls' recidivism rates two years following release from the program.

Gender-Responsivity in the Juvenile Justice System

The qualitative portion of the study came from a larger study on how juvenile court practitioners detect and respond to the needs of girls. In particular, the researchers were interested in addressing the ambiguity in what gender-responsivity entails and means to those implementing the services. Data collection involved interviewing juvenile court personnel (n = 39), including court officers, programs/services managers, judges, and administrators, about their experiences working with girls and the services the court and the community provide to youth. The second part of the qualitative study included case discussions with juvenile court officers (n = 24). The purpose of the case discussions was to provide an in-depth illustration of current cases of girls involved in the system. The interviews and case discussions provided rich, detailed data for understanding the context of why girls are involved in the system, the services they receive, and the perceived successes and failures of those services.

Because data collection began after the quantitative evaluation was complete, the lead author on both projects was able to add additional questions in the semistructured qualitative interviews and case discussions about the girls' group homes. In particular, given that the findings from the quantitative study had revealed that group home girls fared better two years following release from the program than girls with similar risk and demographic profiles who did not receive treatment, the next question to ask was why is this the case? Why did court practitioners send girls to the group home? What makes this program gender-responsive? Why is this program more effective for higher risk girls over and above standard best practices in juvenile justice treatment?

The qualitative data were analyzed using directed and conventional content analytic approaches (see Hsieh & Shannon, 2005, for a review of types of qualitative content analysis). The directed approach allowed the researchers to examine how elements of gender-responsivity, as defined in the literature, were or were not integrated into treatment and to what extent they were integrated (e.g., how frequently were court personnel discussing each element, such as using trauma-informed approaches to intervention, helping girls build healthy relationships with their families, etc.). The conventional content analytic approach revealed more information related to why practitioners view the group homes as effective for girls. For example, juvenile court officers frequently mentioned that girls have different needs than boys and that those different needs should be reflected in programming. The group homes are the only programs in the county specifically designed for girls in which they focus on addressing girls' trauma in a safe environment. The qualitative findings provided rich descriptions of program elements, success stories about girls who went to the group homes, and other very detailed information that could not have been obtained with the archival data used for the quantitative evaluation.

Integrating Methods

This study utilized a sequential explanatory mixed methods design (with quantitative data collection and analysis leading to qualitative data collection and analysis) in an attempt to understand (a) the effectiveness of a gender-responsive intervention for girls in the juvenile justice system, and (b) why this type of intervention modality is needed for girls in the juvenile justice system, and (c) the underlying mechanisms that make the intervention gender-responsive. The four questions that Palinkas et al. (2011) called for researchers to ask when designing a mixed methods study (see earlier) were addressed as follows:

1. What is the rationale? The study was primarily dictated by data (i.e., archival data for the quantitative piece and interviews for the qualitative piece). The secondary rationale was to address the emergent research questions in the qualitative study that evolved based on opportunities and new developments throughout the research process.
2. What is the structure? The methods were integrated in an equivalent sequential, explanatory design (QUAN $\rightarrow$ QUAL) in

which the quantitative data were collected and analyzed prior to the data collection and analysis of the qualitative data (Creswell & Plano Clark, 2007; Morse, 1991).
3. What is the function? The study's primary goal was to expand upon the previous quantitative findings using the qualitative data for explanatory purposes.
4. What is the process? The process of integration involved connecting the two data sets in a sequence (e.g., quantitative evaluation first, qualitative exploration second).

This case study demonstrated how mixed methods research can utilize qualitative findings to build upon quantitative findings. The qualitative study was able to identify other areas where the quantitative data set was limited. For example, the quantitative study was limited by measuring only recidivism as the outcome of interest. The qualitative findings revealed that the group home increased girls' safety in general, provided them with additional treatment hours to address trauma-related issues, and worked at helping girls either (a) reunite with their family by focusing on building and restoring positive relationships or (b) transition to independent living if going back to their family was not the best option.

CONCLUSION

In summary, this chapter has attempted to show how researchers can integrate quantitative and qualitative data, to present the benefits and the challenges of mixing methods, and some illustrations of mixed methods community-based research. There are certainly multiple directions (e.g., exploring different typologies for mixing methods beyond the typical quant → qual sequential design used in the literature) for researchers to take in order to expand the empirical literature on mixed methods approaches. We look forward to continued developments in this area in the coming years.

REFERENCES

American Psychological Association Presidential Task Force on Evidence-Based Practice. (2006). Evidence-based practice in psychology. *American Psychologist, 61*, 271–285.

Barker, C., & Pistrang, N. (2005). Quality criteria under methodological pluralism: Implications for conducting and evaluating research. *American Journal of Community Psychology, 35*, 201–212.

Bartholomew, T. T., & Brown, J. R. (2012). Mixed methods, culture, and psychology: A review of mixed methods in culture-specific psychological research. *International Perspectives in Psychology: Research, Practice, Consultation, 1*, 177–190.

Campbell, R. (1995). The role of work experience and individual beliefs in policy officers' perceptions of date rape: An integration of quantitative and qualitative methods. *American Journal of Community Psychology, 23*, 249–277.

Chesney-Lind, M., & Irwin, K. (2008). *Beyond bad girls: Gender, violence and hype*. New York, NY: Routledge.

Chesney-Lind, M., Morash, M., & Stevens, T. (2008). Girls' troubles, girls' delinquency, and gender responsive programming: A review. *Australian and New Zealand Journal of Criminology, 41*, 162–189.

Chesney-Lind, M., & Shelden, R. G. (2004). *Girls, delinquency and juvenile justice* (3rd ed.). Belmont, CA: Wadsworth.

Creswell, J., & Creswell, J. (2005). Mixed methods research: Developments, debates, and dilemmas. In R. Swanson & E. Holton III (Eds.), *Research in organizations: Foundations for methods of inquiry* (pp. 315–326). San Francisco, CA: Berrett-Koehler.

Creswell, J. W., & Plano Clark, V. L. (2007). *Designing and conducting mixed methods research*. Thousand Oaks, CA: Sage.

Dixon-Woods, M., Agarwal, S., Young, B., Jones, D., & Sutton, A. (2004). *Integrative approaches to qualitative and quantitative evidence*. London, England: Health Development Agency.

Ellis, L. A., Marsh, H. W., & Craven, R. G. (2009). Addressing the challenges faced by early adolescents: A mixed method evaluation of the benefits of peer support. *American Journal of Community Psychology, 44*, 54–75.

Greene, J. C., & Caracelli, V. J. (1997). Advances in mixed methods evaluation: The challenges and benefits of integrating diverse paradigms. *New Directions for Evaluation, 74*, 5–17.

Howe, K. (1988). Against the quantitative-qualitative incompatibility thesis (or dogmas die hard). *Educational Researcher, 17*, 10–16.

Hsieh, H., & Shannon, S. E. (2005). Three approaches to qualitative content analysis. *Qualitative Health Research, 15*, 1277–1288.

Javdani, S., Sadeh, N., & Verona, E. (2011). Gendered social forces: A review of the impact of institutionalized factors on women and girls' criminal justice trajectories. *Psychology, Public Policy, and Law, 17*, 161–211.

Kerig, P. K., & Schindler, S. R. (2013). Engendering the evidence base: A critical review of the conceptual and empirical foundations of gender-responsive interventions for girls' delinquency. *Laws, 2,* 244–282.

Knox, L., Guerra, N. G., Williams, K. R., & Toro, R. T. (2011). Preventing children's aggression in immigrant Latino families: A mixed methods evaluation of the families and schools together program. *American Journal of Community Psychology, 48,* 65–76.

Kuhn, T. S. (1962). *The structure of scientific revolutions.* Chicago, IL: University of Chicago Press.

Leech, N. L., & Onwuegbuzie, A. J. (2007). A typology of mixed methods research designs. *Quality and Quantity, 43,* 265–275.

Molina Azorin, J., & Cameron, R. (2010). The application of mixed methods in organizational research: A literature review. *Electronic Journal of Business Research Methods, 8,* 95–105.

Morse, J. (1991). Approaches to qualitative-quantitative methodological triangulation, *Nursing Research, 40,* 120–123.

O'Cathain, A. (2010). Assessing the quality of mixed methods research: Towards a comprehensive framework. In A. Tashakkori & C. Teddlie (Eds.), *Handbook of mixed methods in social and behavioral research* (pp. 531–558). Thousand Oaks, CA: Sage.

Orbis Partners. (2014). *Girls . . . Moving on: A program for criminal justice involved girls.* Retrieved June 2015, from http://orbispartners.com//wp-content/uploads/2014/07/GirlsMovingOn-DataSheet.pdf

Palinkas, L. A., Horwitz, S. M., Chamberlain, P., Hurlburt, M. S., & Landsverk, J. (2011). Mixed methods designs in mental health services research: A review. *Psychiatric Services, 62,* 255–263.

Puzzanchera, C., Adams, B., & Sickmund, M. (2010). *Juvenile court statistics 2006-2007.* National Center for Juvenile Justice: Pittsburgh, PA.

Salem, D. A., Foster-Fishman, P. G., & Goodkind, J. R. (2002). The adoption of innovation in collective action organizations. *American Journal of Community Psychology, 30,* 681–710.

Schwartz, J., & Steffensmeier, D. (2012). Stability and change in girls' delinquency and the gender gap: Trends in violence and alcohol offending across multiple sources of evidence. In In S. Miller, L. D. Leve, & P. K. Kerig (Eds.), *Delinquent girls: Contexts, relationships, and adaptation* (pp. 3–23). New York, NY: Springer.

Stevens, T., Morash, M., & Chesney-Lind, M. (2011). Are girls getting tougher, or are we getting tougher on girls? Probability of arrest and juvenile court oversight in 1980 and 2000. *Justice Quarterly, 28,* 718–744.

Stuart, E. A. (2010). Matching methods for causal inference: A review and a look forward. *Statistical Science, 25,* 1–21.

Tashakkori, A., & Creswell, J. W. (2007). The new era of mixed methods. *Journal of Mixed Methods Research, 1,* 3–7.

Tashakkori, A., & Teddlie, C. (2003). *Handbook on mixed methods in the behavioral and social sciences.* Thousand Oaks, CA: Sage.

Tebes, J. K. (2005). Community science, philosophy of science, and the practice of research. *American Journal of Community Psychology, 35,* 213–230.

Thoemmes, F., & Kim, E. S. (2011). A systematic review of propensity score methods in the social sciences. *Multivariate Behavioral Research, 46,* 90–118.

Webb, E. J. (1966). *Unobtrusive measures: Nonreactive research in the social sciences.* Chicago, IL: Rand McNally.

Wiggins, B. J. (2011). Confronting the dilemma of mixed methods. *Journal of Theoretical and Philosophical Psychology, 31,* 44–60.

Zahn, M., Day, J. C., Mihalic, S. F., & Tichavsky, L. (2009). Determining what works for girls in the juvenile justice system: A summary of evaluation evidence. *Crime and Delinquency, 55,* 266–293.

24

Action Research

BRIAN D. CHRISTENS, VICTORIA FAUST, JENNIFER GADDIS, PAULA TRAN INZEO, CAROLINA S. SARMIENTO, AND SHANNON M. SPARKS

Kurt Lewin (1946) introduced the term *action research* as a practical response to complex and intractable social issues. He defined it as comparative research on social action and its effects that could lead to further social action. Social research, he argued, had made noteworthy progress at discovering general laws that governed behavior such as racism and at what he called "diagnosis" (p. 37) of the specific character of situations. There was a need, however, for a complementary area of research that was engaged every step of the way with social planning and social action processes. Drawing on examples of research collaborations with civic and institutional actors seeking to improve intergroup relations, he explained that this form of social research "proceeds in a spiral of steps each of which is composed of a circle of planning, action, and fact-finding about the result of the action" (p. 38). Action research could demonstrate the potential for synergy between practitioners and social scientists for achieving social progress, although he recognized that it would require "training large numbers of social scientists who can handle scientific problems but are also equipped for the delicate task of building productive, hard-hitting teams with practitioners" (p. 42).

This chapter defines action research as an approach that orchestrates cyclical processes of action and research that are simultaneously contributing to addressing practical concerns related to social issues and to the goals of social science. We believe that action research is especially well suited for community-based research designed to contribute to community capacity building and democratic social change efforts. Our chapter begins with an introduction to action research in which we provide brief examples of action research projects conducted on a variety of issues and in a variety of contexts. The next section focuses on the design and conduct of action research. In that section, we offer design principles for conducting action research in community and organizational settings. This is followed by a case study of an action research partnership with a community organizing network working on multiple issues, including mass incarceration, immigration, and transit. We conclude with a call for more transdisciplinary action research on pressing social issues.

INTRODUCTION TO ACTION RESEARCH

In introducing and developing the concept of action research, Lewin (1946) could sense that he was on to something big: "I could not help but feel that the close integration of action, training, and research holds tremendous possibilities for the field of intergroup relations. I would like to pass on this feeling to you" (p. 43). The fact that similar models for action research have emerged in many disciplines and in different parts of the world suggests that his enthusiasm was well founded. Although all of these models have themes in common—for instance, a focus on collaborative efforts to identify solutions to social problems—there is substantial variation in the relative emphases of these models.

For example, models for participatory action research that have been influential in South America (e.g., Fals-Borda & Rahman, 1991) have tended to emphasize empowerment and critical consciousness of participants in the service of societal transformation and liberation of oppressed groups. Some strands of action research in North

America, such as those commonly described as community-based participatory research (e.g., Wallerstein & Duran, 2006), have tended to emphasize democratization of the research process, with a critical eye on the mutuality of relationships between community members and (typically academic) research partners. Some position participatory action research as a vehicle for elevating alternative knowledge systems: "an epistemology that values the intimate, painful and often shamed, knowledge held by those who have most endured social injustice" (Torre & Fine, 2011, p. 116). Others emphasize the utility of a different epistemology for applied research and the need for an action science to deal with the complex systems that perpetuate longstanding social problems. These strands sometimes echo Lewin in arguing for an approach to social science that is more akin to the practical problem solving that takes place in engineering than it is to the controlled experiments conducted in basic physical sciences (e.g, Livingood et al., 2011). Still others (e.g., Nyden & Wiewel, 1992) emphasize the potential impact of equipping less-resourced community-based organizations with research that can strengthen their hand in policymaking processes.

As a broad overarching concept, then, action research can be defined as an approach that "aims to contribute both to the practical concerns of people in an immediate problematic situation and to the goals of social science by joint collaboration within a mutually acceptable ethical framework" (Rapoport, 1970, p. 499). When compared with the more common philosophical grounding of social science, logical positivism, action research represents not only a difference in research setting, design, or method but also a difference in epistemology. The epistemological underpinnings of action research can be located in the Aristotelian concept of praxis, in the philosophical pragmatism exemplified by the writings of William James and John Dewey, in existentialism and phenomenology, and in critical theory (Brydon-Miller, 1997; Susman & Evered, 1978). Again, variation exists among models or strands of action research, with some applications drawing on multiple methods and epistemologies, sometimes including positivism, and others more strictly applying singular theories and methods.

It is certainly possible for action researchers and other social researchers operating in a positivist framework to collaborate. There have often been tensions, however, between the two. This is primarily because of the differing standards for evaluating the results of research, which are linked to the deeper differences in the fundamental goals of research pursuits. Many advocates for action research (e.g., Greenwood, 2007; Hoshmand & O'Byrne, 1996) have pointed out that conducting action research can present challenges to researchers attempting to operate or build careers in institutions that assess impact and productivity according to standards for positivist social science. These challenges include a lack of understanding of the action research process and the types of outputs that it produces, as well as a lack of a supportive and collegial climate for sustaining programs of action research.

Although we readily acknowledge that it is challenging to design and conduct action research, and to sustain programs of action research in institutions where most social research is carried out in other traditions, we wish to provide an alternative perspective, especially as this type of work is particularly timely. Information on the large number of social, political, economic, and environmental justice issues facing our communities and societies can tend to inundate us. Many of us feel compelled to direct our efforts not only toward greater understanding of these phenomena but also toward action and progress. At the same time, academic disciplines and research-oriented institutions are questioning and critically examining their relevance to communities near and far. Many are examining and investing in new models for outreach and engagement, including action research. It is, therefore, an important time to demonstrate the possibilities for action research to bridge research and practice and contribute to both the current state of knowledge in the social sciences and to progress on pressing community and social issues.

There are a wide variety of topics and disciplines engaged in different forms of mixed methods action research. For example, action research is often conducted in pursuit of health equity. Within this domain, it is sometimes referred to as community-based participatory research and strives for true partnership between researchers and communities and a balance between research and action, with the goal of ending health disparities. These approaches tend to prioritize health concerns of local relevance to communities and utilize an ecological framework that recognizes and attends to multiple determinants of health, illness, and disease. As noted earlier, such partnerships emphasize collaborative, equitable relationships and participation of all partners—community and academic—throughout all stages of the research process (Israel et al., 2008; see Chapter 25, this volume).

The specific methods utilized in action research projects in pursuit of health equity are variable and determined by the specific needs and capacities of community partners. There are numerous examples of partnerships employing mixed methods approaches. For instance, several of this chapter's authors have collaborated on a project utilizing mixed methods that emerged out of a community's desire to understand a significant and unexpected improvement in the African American infant mortality rate in Dane County, Wisconsin. Leaders in neighborhoods, local nonprofit organizations, and local government agencies posited that changes in interorganizational networks operative in the county might have impacted mothers' ability to access health services, information, social services, and other resources of importance for assuring positive birth outcomes. The community-academic partnership investigated this hypothesis using a multistage mixed methods design that began by conducting semistructured qualitative interviews of representatives of key social service, health care, and advocacy organizations. Preliminary analyses of these interview data were used to inform survey data collection, which included an interorganizational network analysis to capture specific changes at the organizational and systemic levels thought to have impacted infant mortality rates. Finally, to triangulate findings from the first two (i.e., the qualitative and quantitative) phases of data collection and analysis, focus groups were conducted with women who had experienced these organizations and systems as clients and patients (Sparks, Faust, Christens, & Hilgendorf, 2015).

Action research can also be applied in urban planning and community development efforts. As a response to the lack of community input in the urban planning and development process, residents and organizations can come together to build community-based coalitions to support and represent the interests and benefits of low-income communities of color (Baxamusa, 2008). One such community is Santa Ana, California, a city whose population is nearly 80% Latino. Almost half of the population (47.3%) is foreign born, and 21.5% of persons live below the poverty line. A group of organizations and residents helped create the Santa Ana Collaborative for Responsible Development (SACReD) to advocate for development that meets the needs of the local community and is accountable to those who are impacted by the development. The SACReD coalition is comprised of neighborhood-based and nonprofit organizations focused on housing, economic justice, health, culture, and historic preservation.

In 2009, SACReD became aware of a plan between the city council and a developer for a housing development that would impact a historic Latino barrio and began organizing to include community benefits into this specific development (González, Sarmiento, Urzua, & Luévano, 2012). As part of a larger political grassroots strategy, action research was led by community organizers, residents, engaged scholars, and community-based planners. This model involved using data from various community organizing strategies, including home visits, community forums, meetings, and community actions. It also included gathering and analyzing data from various sectors, such as housing, culture and the arts, open space, historic preservation, and labor. The collaborative produced several documents, including the proposed community benefits agreement, outreach materials, and alternative project proposals. SACReD built the necessary political power to bring the city council to the negotiating table and include some community benefits within the development.

Action research can also be a tool for economic and labor justice and for food systems change. From campaigns to raise federal and state minimum wage levels across all sectors, to nationwide fast-food protests, food chain workers are organizing against social and economic injustices of the dominant industrial food system (e.g., Jayaraman, 2013; Lo, 2014). Mixed methods action research is a core tool used to build this cross-sector movement across local and national scales. The Food Chain Workers Alliance (FCWA) seeks to build solidarity among roughly 20 million food chain workers in order to improve wages and working conditions for all food systems workers. One member organization, Restaurant Opportunities Center United, has created extensive action research partnerships between workers, organizers, and academic researchers. Another member organization, UNITE HERE, has used mixed methods action research to launch Real Food, Real Jobs (http://www.realfoodrealjobs.org/) campaigns in numerous K-12 schools, college campuses, and international airports. To reach broader audiences and generate public support, some of these organizations also rely on mixed methods (e.g., maps, text-based reports, videos) for disseminating research findings (e.g., Food Chain Workers Alliance, 2014).

These initiatives typically involve workers not only as future beneficiaries of specific policy and systems changes but also as key contributors to the research process. For instance, in New Haven, Connecticut, school cafeteria workers belonging to Local 217 of UNITE HERE used mixed methods action research for their successful campaign to bring more scratch cooking (i.e., preparing meals with raw and minimally processed ingredients instead of reheating premade frozen foods) and local foods to New Haven's public schools. The action research that made this possible—conducted in partnership with one of this chapter's authors—began with a series of qualitative interviews with key members of the K–12 cafeteria labor force. These preliminary data served as the basis for quantitative survey research. Local 217 organizers leveraged the survey collection process as a means for developing union leadership. Specifically, they asked core members to take ownership of the campaign by actively (and in some cases repeatedly) encouraging their coworkers to complete the questionnaire. This peer-to-peer model, which resulted in a 70% survey response rate, also provided workers with a conversational platform for envisioning and verbalizing what the "lunch ladies' vision" of school food would be. Their vision entailed cooking healthy fresh foods of high gustatory quality ("real food") and increasing the work hours and number of skilled positions within the school food service sector ("real jobs").

Mixed methods data—workers' personal stories combined with aggregate statistics from the survey questionnaires—provided a holistic picture of the importance of improving school food. The research team packaged analyses of these data into an accessible, highly visual report that cafeteria workers shared with neighbors, parents, and other community members (Gaddis & Cruz-Uribe, 2013). Local 217 built the necessary political support to negotiate a new contract that makes significant strides in improving cafeteria workers' ability to earn a livable wage and feel proud of the taste and nutritional quality of the meals they serve. After this win at the bargaining table, academic partners were drawn back into the action research cycle to assist Local 217 in designing new pilot programs and evaluation protocols.

DESIGNING AND CONDUCTING ACTION RESEARCH

The examples described earlier provide a sense of the varied social issues and policy domains that can be targeted by action researchers and their community and organizational partners. They also exemplify the breadth of disciplinary perspectives, methodologies, collaborations, and partnership structures that can be employed in the conceptualization, design, and implementation of action research projects, as well as the actions associated with the research. Clearly, design of action research must take a variety of complex issues into account. Nevertheless, in seeking to simplify and unite the field, or introduce it to others, many action researchers (e.g., Acosta & Goltz, 2014) often cite a basic cycle involving four phases: (a) assessment, (b) planning, (c) action, and (d) reflection. This cyclical notion harkens back to Lewin's (1946) idea that action research proceeds in a "spiral of steps" (p. 38), with each step including planning, action, and evaluation of the results of actions. A spiral or helical representation of this process emphasizes that the process should build on the knowledge gained from the previous step. Although this process model can be useful for heuristic and descriptive purposes, its simplicity can mask some of the complexity and nuance involved in designing and conducting action research for maximal impact on social issues. Here, we offer several principles for designing and conducting action research in community and organizational settings that shed some light on the complexities involved.

Bridge Research and Action

The questions that animate social scientific research do not always run parallel to those that pique the curiosity of those involved in social action and community practice. Action research that is designed and conducted well, however, can contribute both to the research literature in the social sciences and to social action through identifying commonalities and foundations on which to build bridges between the two. This requires an ability to translate not just research to practice (a translational skill that is stressed in many forms of research) but also action or practice to research. Furthermore, in addition to the ability to interpret, describe, and translate each field for the other, it requires the ability to creatively imagine ways in which the two could harness each other's strengths for improved outcomes on both sides. When action research is designed and conducted in ways that do not effectively build these bridges, it can become either (a) social action or community practice with some research or evaluation being conducted on it or its effects that is largely disconnected from theory or (b) social science research that is theoretically driven and conducted with some degree of involvement or buy-in from participants in community and organizational settings. It is important to distinguish these more lopsided versions of integration of research and action from action research that builds bridges that are firmly anchored on both the research side and the action side. One principle that we propose for action research design is, therefore, to maximize the aspects of a project that can contribute to theory in social science while also informing and influencing action in community and organizational settings.

Bridge Disciplines

Problems that communities and organizations face rarely confine themselves neatly to a single discipline. It is possible for action researchers to design research that draws upon and contributes to multiple disciplines and simultaneously provides more meaningful insights for social action or community practice. Sometimes, a single researcher can become familiar with theory, methods, and evidence from several disciplines. In many cases, however, it is advantageous for teams of researchers from different disciplines to collaborate to design and conduct research that can more holistically address the various substantive phenomena, processes, and outcomes of interest to communities and organizations. The example described earlier of mixed methods action research on declines in the African American infant mortality rate in Dane County, Wisconsin, is illustrative. A project team was formed specifically to pair the substantive and methodological expertise of a medical anthropologist with that of a community psychologist. The resulting design for the research project incorporated insights from several disciplines to respond to the hypotheses of community partners in a way that was more fully informed in terms of theory and methodology. Such transdisciplinary collaborations have been proposed and studied as promising strategies for achieving the potential of action research (Stokols, 2006). A second proposed principle for designing and conducting action research is, therefore, to optimally match and mix the substantive and methodological strengths of researchers with the hypotheses emerging from ongoing social action.

Build Powerful Partnerships

A number of factors must be considered when establishing partnerships for designing and conducting action research. The partnerships that were described earlier, between social researchers and the SACReD collaborative and between researchers and Local 217 of UNITE HERE, provide examples of powerful partnerships in which intentional and mutually advantageous relationships have been developed between social researchers and organizations and community residents leading social action efforts. In seeking to develop such partnerships for designing and conducting action research, researchers should seek to partner with entities that can build and exercise power and who are committed to improving their practices through implementation of research findings. Action researchers, in turn, should examine hypotheses that are emerging from the partner organization or community, should use multiple methods, and should provide regular, thoughtful feedback of analyses of data that are collected. Speer and Christens (2013) highlighted these as key elements in strategic engagement in action research for impact on social issues. A third proposed principle for designing and conducting action research is, therefore, that in order to achieve maximum impact, action researchers should seek to develop partnerships with communities and organizations capable of exercising social power.

CASE STUDY

We now turn to an example of the application of action research that involves several of the authors of this chapter and WISDOM, a Wisconsin statewide federation of congregation-based community-organizing initiatives. Across multiple projects, the WISDOM organizing network serves as a partner in making social science matter through action research. Community organizing is a field of practice in which residents collaboratively investigate and undertake sustained collective action regarding social issues of mutual concern (Christens & Speer, 2015). WISDOM empowers people throughout Wisconsin to be a part of political, social, economic, and environmental decision-making processes that impact their lives. As an interfaith, nonpartisan organization, nearly 160 congregations representing more than 19 religious traditions are members of WISDOM. Congregations engage through the federation's 11 affiliates located in regions across the state. WISDOM affiliates establish local campaigns to address economic, racial, and social disparities throughout Wisconsin. Most local organizing federations are also involved in statewide issue campaigns that mobilize broad bases of people around mass incarceration, immigration, public transportation, access to health care, and a fair economy.

WISDOM functions as a powerful strategic partner for action research because of its ability to exercise social power for the purposes of social change, as well as its clarity in mission and process toward these ends. Its affiliates come together in support of WISDOM's primary goals:

1. To build a powerful, values-based community that bridges the divides of race, class, religious denomination, geography, and partisan political affiliation.
2. To develop the leadership capacities of its members and, especially, to encourage the leadership capacity of members who belong to groups that have been marginalized by the larger society.
3. To build the capacity to be able to bring about real, effective systemic change that aligns with our shared values on the local, state, and even national levels.

To meet these goals, WISDOM members are continuously involved in ongoing training and leadership development and continual cycles of community organizing, which include relationship building, research, action/mobilization, and evaluation/reflection. Organizing norms, such as listening, critical reflection, and shared analysis of social issues, cut across phases of the organizing cycle to build powerful organizations by creating a foundation of accountable relationships, interconnected collective interests, and a shared commitment to address root causes of social issues (Christens, Inzeo, & Faust, 2014). Through these processes, WISDOM affiliates not only engage new potential members but also build strategic partnerships with other organizations in order to advance social and systems changes.

The cycle of organizing generates a wide range of hypotheses of interest to WISDOM leadership with respect to the dynamics of the social issues it seeks to impact, as well as the process of mobilizing empowering relationships for social change. For example, since 2006, WISDOM had been working on a campaign to advance alternatives to incarceration as a means to rehabilitate those suffering from mental health and alcohol and other drug misuse issues. Through early phases of research and discussions with community members about common concerns, organizers and leaders suspected that increasing levels of incarceration were exacerbating health inequities in the state. To further investigate these impacts through a participatory research project, they sought out partnerships with Human Impact Partners, the Wisconsin Center for Health Equity, and researchers at the University of Wisconsin.

With support from these researchers, WISDOM engaged in a mixed methods health impact assessment (HIA) to evaluate the impacts of the policy option on the health of Wisconsin's residents. The purpose of the HIA was to predict future health impacts of a proposal in the state budget to provide $75 million per year to Treatment Alternative and Diversion (TAD) programs. The study utilized data from the Department of Health Services; evaluations of previous TAD program implementation in the state from the University of Wisconsin–Madison's Population Health Institute; focus groups with formerly incarcerated individuals, judges, TAD program participants, and TAD program service providers; and a review of best-available science. The HIA report, *Healthier Lives, Stronger Families, Safer Communities: How Increasing Funding for Alternatives to Prison Will Save Lives and Money in Wisconsin*, was published in November 2012.

Through WISDOM's mobilization and collective action, those most affected by the issue—many of them formerly incarcerated people—were engaged as experts throughout the HIA. Others included professors, clergy, treatment providers, judges, and residents involved in shaping the scope of the HIA, as well as in collecting the quantitative and qualitative information that went into the final product. These individuals were a part of a daylong scoping meeting to identify specific TAD program interventions and impacts for further study. The HIA team drafted pathway diagrams based on this input and further refined them with feedback from participants. An advisory team made up of researchers, individuals from the State Public Defender's Office, and WISDOM and affiliate leaders finalized the scope, assisted in gathering and analyzing secondary data, shaped focus group data collection questions, and identified participants.

The HIA found that treatment alternatives reduce economic costs, reduce crime, increase recovery, strengthen families, and improve economic opportunity through employment. After the HIA was completed, nearly 60 people testified at various budget hearings, and more than 1,000 people attended a rally in Madison, followed by constituent visits to legislative offices. Every major media outlet in the state covered the release of the HIA findings, and many Republican and Democratic legislators pledged public support to an increase in funding for treatment alternatives in the state budget. As a result of this work, the budget for Treatment Alternatives and Diversions went up by 150%—from $1 million/year to $2.5 million/year—with continued increases anticipated. More generally, the HIA influenced Community Justice Reinvestment agendas at the state level to include discussions of mental health needs and shifted the state narrative from being "tough on crime" toward being "smart on crime." The HIA partnerships demonstrated WISDOM's ability to bring social and behavioral science research to bear on policy issues through a commitment to building social power to address root causes of disparities.

In addition to providing targeted research support on community impacts and health outcomes of social issues, opportunities for bridging research and action arose from WISDOM's focus on relationship building, civic engagement, and empowerment through cycles of relational organizing. With an interest in learning more about how its organizing processes sustain civic participation, WISDOM partnered with the University of Wisconsin–Madison's Center for Community and Nonprofit Studies to collect and analyze longitudinal information about its organizing settings and the participants who engage in these settings. Researchers specializing in civic participation, empowerment, and networks developed and implemented mobile participation data collection mechanisms and surveys, gathering individual- and setting-level data on patterns of involvement and impacts of participation. Although collection of participation data has only recently begun for this aspect of the research, the collaboration includes researchers with expertise in quantitative longitudinal and multilevel models in order to explore setting-level dynamics, such as neighborhood characteristics, social networks, and dynamics of local organizing initiatives, that promote civic participation.

Analyses of participation dynamics will assist WISDOM organizers in building more effective organizing environments—those that foster participation and the development of social power—and will simultaneously contribute to social science research on civic participation. For example, as part of a similar collaboration with community organizing groups, Christens and Speer (2011) reported an analysis of the influence of attendance at particular types of meetings as predictors of continued participation in organizing in successive years, finding that two particular types of meetings were predictive of continued engagement. This multilevel longitudinal model controlled for numerous other factors, including the influences of neighborhood-level variables, social networks, individual-level characteristics, and participants' overall levels of involvement in previous years. These findings have not only been published for a social scientific audience but also have been broadly disseminated among community organizers, who value the insights that this type of evidence-based approach to their craft can yield. The tools and supporting analyses generated through this action research will help improve the internal processes of WISDOM that establish and support relationship and leadership development, increasing its capacity to build and exercise the social power needed to champion solutions that enhance community well-being.

The mixed methods action research partnership between WISDOM and the University of

Wisconsin–Madison Center for Community and Nonprofit Studies now undergirds ongoing efforts to enhance community health and well-being. Together, organizing and academic partners have built the capacity of health promotion leaders and coalitions to increase their ability to equitably pursue policy, systems, and environmental changes to advance community health and health equity. The two groups have worked together to develop and provide training, technical assistance, and evaluation of 28 local coalitions across the state of Wisconsin pursuing changes to make their communities healthier places to live. They have also collaborated on building a statewide alliance between the field of community organizing and the field of public health, broadly defined.

The aforementioned efforts laid the groundwork for ramping up actions to build collective impact and community organizing initiatives to address the systems that have led to increases in obesity in Wisconsin. WISDOM and the University of Wisconsin–Madison Center for Community and Nonprofit Studies are significantly involved in a 5-year statewide targeted obesity prevention initiative that began in 2014. This initiative seeks to prevent obesity through building local community capacity to pursue actions to effect systemic change so that healthier choices (e.g., active transportation, healthy eating) are easier to make. The initiative involves academic researchers from medicine, public health, urban planning, nutrition, landscape architecture, human ecology, and other disciplines. WISDOM is playing a key role in the project, including mentoring and supporting local community organizers who are leading efforts in local communities in collaboration with researchers. The research team is using multiple methods for research and evaluation, ranging from participant observation and qualitative interviews to the establishment of a statewide surveillance system to monitor changes in health behaviors and outcomes.

The action research partnership between this statewide network for community organizing and academic researchers continues to grow in breadth and depth. The projects described here reflect a variety of issue domains and involve basic cycles commonly associated with action research. More important, however, features of this case example highlight and reinforce the principles we proposed for designing and conducting action research earlier in the chapter. First, WISDOM's local federations are not implementing an organizing model that was conceived by academics; they are independent entities that have developed expertise at building community power for systems change. Their organizing efforts align with some of the priorities and research interests of action-oriented researchers in the university, setting the stage for a community-academic partnership that generates additional opportunities for social action, as well as new paths of research. Second, University of Wisconsin–Madison researchers from various disciplines are engaged in different aspects of projects and working on teams as part of this action research partnership. Although it is not always easy to forge collaborations and synthesize work across disciplinary lines, it is often worth the effort to be able to more comprehensively address complex issues such as obesity and health equity. Third, both the researchers and community organizers involved in the partnership have built an understanding of the practical and theoretical aspects of the collaborative work. Community organizers in WISDOM have considerable capacity for integrating research into organizing processes. Researchers at the Center for Community & Nonprofit Studies have an interest in collaboratively designing action research. These facts create the potential for a powerful partnership to maximize impact on social issues.

CONCLUSION

Action research is an approach to generating knowledge and addressing social issues in pursuit of social justice. It can be conducted in many disciplines and even across disciplines. Those who conduct it cite a variety of influences and traditions but commonly identify both a desire to bring about change through conducting research and the view that theory and research can be enhanced through close proximity to action and/or practice. Action research can, therefore, be seen as a testing ground for the utility of theory, for new methods in the social sciences, and for new combinations of ideas and methods from various disciplines and fields of practice.

Many intellectual and practical challenges exist for those seeking to build and sustain programs of action research. Nevertheless, we would urge more researchers to take up these challenges and launch collaborative action research projects with community and organizational partners. We believe that action research can play a key role in producing scientific evidence needed to tackle persistent social problems. Furthermore, we believe that action research is a promising strategy for multiplying the direct roles that social science can play in the resolution of social issues and promotion of community well-being.

REFERENCES

Acosta, S., & Goltz, H. H. (2014). Transforming practices: A primer on action research. *Health Promotion Practice, 15*, 465–470.

Baxamusa, M. H. (2008). Empowering communities through deliberation: The model of community benefits agreements. *Journal of Planning Education and Research, 27*, 261–276.

Brydon-Miller, M. (1997). Participatory action research: Psychology and social change. *Journal of Social Issues, 53*, 657–666.

Christens, B. D., Inzeo, P. T., & Faust, V. (2014). Channeling power across ecological systems: Social regularities in community organizing. *American Journal of Community Psychology, 53*, 419–431.

Christens, B. D., & Speer, P. W. (2011). Contextual influences on participation in community organizing: A multilevel longitudinal study. *American Journal of Community Psychology, 47*, 253–263.

Christens, B. D., & Speer, P. W. (2015). Community organizing: Practice, research, and policy implications. *Social Issues and Policy Review, 9*, 188–216.

Fals-Borda, O., & Rahman, M. A. (1991). *Action and knowledge: Breaking the monopoly with participatory action research.* New York, NY: Apex.

Food Chain Workers Alliance. (2014). *Maps: Food workers organizations.* Retrieved June 2015, from http://foodchainworkers.org/?page_id=2443

Gaddis, J., & Cruz-Uribe, C. (2013). *Healthy Kids First: Why cafeteria workers want to cook fresh meals in New Haven public schools.* Retrieved June 2015, from http://www.realfoodrealjobs.org/wp-content/uploads/NH-Cafeteria-Report-for-web.pdf

González, E. R., Sarmiento, C. S., Urzua, A. S., & Luévano, S. C. (2012). The grassroots and new urbanism: A case from a Southern California Latino community. *Journal of Urbanism, 5*, 219–239.

Greenwood, D. J. (2007). Teaching/learning action research requires fundamental reforms in public higher education. *Action Research, 5*, 249–264.

Hoshmand, L. T., & O'Byrne, K. (1996). Reconsidering action research as a guiding metaphor for professional psychology. *Journal of Community Psychology, 24*, 185–200.

Israel, B. A, Schulz, A. J., Parker, E. A., Becker, A. B., Allen, A. J., & Guzman, J. R. (2008). Critical issues in developing and following CBPR principles. In M. Minkler & N. Wallerstein (Eds.), *Community-based participatory research for health: From process to outcomes* (pp. 47–66). San Francisco, CA: Jossey-Bass.

Jayaraman, S. (2013). *Behind the kitchen door.* Ithaca, NY: Cornell University Press.

Lewin, K. (1946). Action research and minority problems. *Journal of Social Issues, 2*, 34–46.

Livingood, W. C., Allegrante, J. P., Airihenbuwa, C. O., Clark, N. M., Windsor, R. C., Zimmerman, M. A., & Green, L. W. (2011). Applied social and behavioral science to address complex health problems. *American Journal of Preventive Medicine, 41*, 525–531.

Lo, J. (2014). Social justice for food workers in a foodie world. *Journal of Critical Thought and Praxis, 3*, 7.

Nyden, P., & Wiewel, W. (1992). Collaborative research: Harnessing the tensions between researcher and practitioner. *American Sociologist, 23*, 43–55.

Rapoport, N. (1970). Three dilemmas of action research. *Human Relations, 23*, 499–513.

Sparks, S. M., Faust, V., Christens, B. D., & Hilgendorf, A. E. (2015). The effects of changes in organizational ecology on racial disparities in infant mortality. *Journal of Community Psychology, 43*, 701–716.

Speer, P. W., & Christens, B. D. (2013). An approach to scholarly impact through strategic engagement in community-based research. *Journal of Social Issues, 69*, 734–753.

Stokols, D. (2006). Toward a science of transdisciplinary action research. *American Journal of Community Psychology, 38*, 63–77.

Susman, G. I., & Evered, R. D. (1978). An assessment of the scientific merits of action research. *Administrative Science Quarterly, 23*, 582–603.

Torre, M. E., & Fine, M. (2011). A wrinkle in time: Tracing a legacy of public science through community self-surveys and participatory action research. *Journal of Social Issues, 67*, 106–121.

Wallerstein, N. B., & Duran, B. (2006). Using community-based participatory research to address health disparities. *Health Promotion Practice, 7*, 312–323.

25

Community-Based Participatory Action Research

MICHAEL J. KRAL AND JAMES ALLEN

"There must exist a paradigm, a practical model for social change that includes an understanding of ways to transform consciousness that are linked to efforts to transform structures" (bell hooks, 1995, p. 193). The transformative role of knowledge production in structural change, summarized in the preceding quote, highlights ways broadening understanding of the circumstances of one's oppression can kindle transformations on the individual and group levels, and how these transformations of consciousness regarding one's circumstances can drive structural change. This type of change is of central concern in participatory research, a research perspective that has social action and structural change as its ultimate goals.

From its earliest roots, community psychology has enjoyed a rich history of participatory, collaborative research efforts. This history predates the advent of the term *community-based participatory research* (CBPR), as advanced by public health, a term that has also been variously described as collaborative research, participatory research, social action research, community-engaged research, and participatory action research (PAR). A defining feature of CBPR involves engagement of the people who are the community of concern as co-researchers in the research process. This act of engagement involves a sharing of power, a democratization of the research process, and an action component. Typically, adherents are engaged in social change, program development, and policy change efforts. Understood as a perspective rather than as a research method, participatory research has taken on multilayered and different meanings and forms, ranging from community members acting as consultants to academic researchers working at the direction of community members on research questions defined by the community.

There are two primary terms used for participatory research. One is community-based CBPR, and the other is PAR. One definition of CBPR involves the equitable involvement of community members, organizational representatives, and researchers in the entire research process, identifies the community as a unit of identity, builds on strengths and resources within the community, promotes co-learning and capacity building among everyone involved, and achieves a balance of research and action (Israel et al., 2008). CBPR links science with social activism, is based in action research, and sees community members as active, decision-making participants (Wallerstein & Duran, 2008). Definitions of PAR focus on concerns with community empowerment (Zimmerman, 1995) and a commitment to democratic social change, a participatory worldview, and practical solutions to pressing needs of communities (Brydon-Miller, Greenwood, & Maguire, 2003). Thus, CBPR and PAR are similar in approach and seek to achieve similar ends, which is why we combine them in our title through the term *community-based participatory action research* (CBPAR).

This chapter provides an introduction to mixed methods participatory research. Mixed methods refer to research that integrates rigorous quantitative and qualitative research to draw on the strengths of each (Creswell & Plano Clark, 2011). To set the stage, we provide a brief history of participatory research, tracing its historical evolution and theoretical roots to define its essential characteristics. These roots include community empowerment, ecology, social justice, feminism, and critical theory. With this in place, we next provide two case studies that used mixed methods to advance a participatory research agenda. We conclude using Arnstein's (1969) framework as a guide to consider some current controversies in the application of participatory principles and their interface with mixed methods research.

INTRODUCTION TO COMMUNITY-BASED PARTICIPATORY ACTION RESEARCH

In most areas of human research, the person who is the subject of research never participates. Why should subjects participate? If a researcher is interested in studying memory functioning, conceivably one could argue that memory is the subject, and its evaluation becomes decontextualized from the experience of the person under study. Is this best scientific practice for research that involves communities of people? Is this viewpoint even relevant to research in the community? Moreover, how might such a viewpoint, applied to communities of historically and currently oppressed groups, perpetuate inequity, discrimination, and other forms of structural violence? Is there another way?

Participatory research, also referred to as collaborative inquiry, is a paradigm-shifting approach to research. It involves varying degrees of participation of the researched as coresearchers. The approach involves studying *with*, rather than about. For many of its adherents, it is also a moral perspective, an ethical stance bringing social justice considerations into research practice (Shore, 2008). Pursuit of social justice objectives has led participatory researchers to often creatively bridge quantitative-qualitative ideological divisions, using both quantitative and qualitative methods as research tools. In doing this, participatory approaches adopt a methodological pluralism, driven by pragmatism to advance both coresearcher involvement common and structural and policy change.

Communities are collectives. They are people who know each other, love each other, take care of each other, and communicate with each other. When a researcher shows up, communities take notice. They talk about and evaluate the researcher and decide if they want to participate. They ask how they and their community might benefit from such participation. Communities are active agents. What is needed is a science and perspective that acknowledges these realities. Moreover, in research with oppressed communities, there is an added imperative for approaches that include a social action element whose end goal is structural change.

A quarter century before bell hooks envisioned an idea of transformative change, Arnstein (1969) wrote about citizen power as a model for achieving these types of change. Arnstein described ways "[the] 'nobodies' in several arenas are trying to become 'somebodies' with enough power to make the target institutions responsive to their views, aspirations, and needs" (p. 217). Participatory, for Arnstein, meant making a difference; this required both being heard *and* precipitating action coming out of being heard. Token membership on a decision-making board is not the same as citizen participation, which she viewed as the power to make institutions responsive. Out of this conviction, she developed a ladder of citizenship participation as a framework to assist understanding of the variety of approaches to participatory research.

This ladder of citizen participation comprises eight levels of participation, moving from nonparticipation to degrees of tokenism to degrees of citizen power. The bottom two rungs are (1) manipulation and (2) therapy. These describe levels contrived to substitute for genuine participation that enable entrenched interests to maintain power. An example of manipulation would be a citizen advisory board with no real decision-making input. Therapy includes the ways that grassroots citizens groups sometimes are enlisted as vehicles to change participants. Illustratively, an early childhood program developed to serve an immigrant group might instead function to assimilate the group's values and attitudes to those of the mainstream dominant group through parenting classes largely based on dominant culture parenting practices. (3) Informing and (4) consultation describe a form of tokenism where participants may be heard but lack power to ensure that their views are heeded, while (5) placation allows participants to advise but not to decide. Degrees of citizen power include (6) partnership, characterized by negotiation and trade-offs; (7) delegated power, where citizens enjoy a majority of decision-making seats; and (8) citizen control, or full managerial power at its highest point. Arnstein examined primarily urban renewal and antipoverty programs. However, she also saw how citizen power could be applied to other institutional structures, and her model has influenced policymakers more broadly, especially in health care (Tritter & McCallum, 2006). In the conclusion of this chapter, we will return to Arnstein's model as a means of evaluating and critiquing implementations of participatory research, the relative merits of qualitative and quantitative methods in participatory work, and efforts that blend the two methods.

BACKGROUND OF PARTICIPATORY RESEARCH

Although participatory approaches have existed for well over a century (Hall, 2005), current manifestations can be traced to the 1960s, most notably in work from Latin America, including Fals Borda's work with peasant movements (Fals Borda, 2001) and Freire's reframing of adult education as democratic empowerment (Freire, 1970). Research from Europe, Asia, and Africa aimed at helping the marginalized in society (Hall, 2005) contributed as well. Some of this movement developed out of literacy work (Kemmis & McTaggart, 2005), as well as youth participation and the rise of activist scholarship in the academy (Fine & Torre, 2005). Participatory research became an international method (Kapoor & Jordan, 2009) involving work with marginalized peoples, with active community participation on research questions coming from the community and a goal of transforming social reality (Hall, 2005).

Similar notions emerged historically from a number of sources in the United States, including early settlement and land ownership, the property rights movement, and, later, a reframing of environmental issues (Dukes, Firehock, & Birkoff, 2011). Traditions such as Kurt Lewin's (1970) action research also focused on social change; central to this approach was a view of research as intervention and a community perspective.

WHAT IS PARTICIPATORY RESEARCH?

When a researcher meets a community, a relationship is formed (Kral, 2014). Relationships are at the core of community research. Communities often look for reciprocity in their relationships with researchers; participatory research emphasizes reciprocity in a respect for local knowledge, belief in democratic principles, and commitment to social justice that leads to positive change. Like jazz, participatory research is a collaborative process whereby everyone respects each other's contributions, is willing to innovate and explore, and views every contribution as essential (Brydon-Miller, Kral, Maguire, Noffke, & Sabhlok, 2011). The participatory perspective draws from work in feminist theory and social reconstruction (Mies, 1996); multicultural theory (Sue, 1999); critical theory (Kagan, Burton, Duckett, & Lawthom, 2011); critical race theory (Brydon-Miller, 2004); social theory emphasizing agency, subjectivity, and power (Ortner, 2006); and indigenous/decolonization perspectives (Smith, 2012).

Community members have typically been the objects of research that generates representational knowledge, with the research problems studied being ones identified by individuals from outside of the community. In participatory approaches, community members transform representational knowledge into relational and reflective knowledge through the establishment of a democratic dialogue with the researcher (Gustavsen, Hanson, & Qvale, 2008). Community members shape and construct the research questions, methods, interpretations, and conclusions. The process imbues knowledge generated through the research with the meaning of participants to build *conscientization* (Freire, 1970), wherein knowledge becomes emancipatory (Fals Borda, 2001), generated through a process that empowers communities to solve concrete problems (Brydon-Miller et al., 2011). Rather than being a specific research methodology, participatory research is an attitude, a perspective, and a philosophy of practice (Kidd & Kral, 2005).

Participatory research focuses on multiple ways of knowing based on relationships of reciprocal responsibility, collaborative decision making, and the sharing of power. The perspective rests on a covenantal ethics, "an ethical stance enacted through relationship and commitment to working for the good of others" (Brydon-Miller, 2008, p. 244). CBPAR has improved programs through improved efficiency, sustainability, and equitable service delivery (Wallerstein & Duran, 2010) and has often resulted in positive research outcomes (Jason, Keys, Suarez-Balcazar, Taylor, & Davis, 2004).

The approach is well suited to a community-based research focus on what Tolan, Chertok, Keys, and Jason (1990, p. 4) called "ill-structured" problems that are defined in local terms, with solutions dependent on particular elements of the local context. A participatory action perspective is increasingly being used in such research (Jason et al., 2004) and is a common global theme

(Reich, Riemer, Prilleltensky, & Montero, 2007). Although participatory research is common in community psychology, other disciplines also use it to focus on health disparities and social justice, including public health (Cargo & Mercer, 2008; Wallerstein & Duran, 2010), social work (Baffour, 2011), nursing (Savage et al., 2006), and medicine (O'Toole, Aaron, Chin, Horowitz, & Tyson, 2003).

Community participation in research can mean different things. Some may say that consent is participation; however, we view participation instead as deep collaboration. This means a more meaningful partnering with a community agency, organization, or group. No studies have yet explored how various types and levels of partnership may be differentially beneficial (Jason et al., 2004). Within partnership, given the needs of the partnership, the research question, the strengths and challenges in the context and setting, and the problem at hand, participation can take on many forms, and partnership can take place at different times and at different levels.

MIXED METHODS AND PARTICIPATORY RESEARCH AS PARADIGM SHIFTS

As sociologists began identifying social factors in mental health in the late 19th century, they developed the methods of the social survey, which reached ascendency between 1940 and 1960, and with it quantitative methods for the analysis of survey data in the social sciences, including psychology. Beginning in the 1970s, a paradigm war erupted in the social sciences between adherents to quantitative versus qualitative methodological approaches. The civil rights and feminist movements of this period had formed what Staller, Block, and Horner (2008) called a methodological revolution in which the role, responsibility, and authority of the researcher were questioned. These paradigm wars included a "politics of evidence" (Denzin & Giardina, 2008, p. 9), where qualitative researchers railed against the preferred methods of experimental design, psychometric theory, and biomedical models of research. The goal of adherents of qualitative, interpretive research was not to create a mirror of nature, or even constructs by which to describe it, but instead to provide an understanding of social reality created by human actors in context (Yanow, 2006).

Accompanying the paradigm conflict was a diffusion of methodological approaches aligned with the qualitative movement (Alastalo, 2008), including critical and indigenous methodologies (Denzin, Lincoln, & Smith, 2008; Kovach, 2009). We are currently in a period of emergent methods, wherein the traditional research process has been challenged and disrupted (Hesse-Biber & Leavy, 2008). This diffusion in methodology has now come full circle and includes the integration of quantitative and qualitative methods, or mixed methods.

Mixed methods research combines what Shweder (1996) described as *quanta*, data that are consistent, replicable, comparable, able to be counted, and generalized, with *qualia*, where the objects of inquiry are subjectivity, meaning making, signification, and local discourse. It involves pragmatism in problem solving, with an emphasis on practical consequences and research questions over methods, through a blend of deductive and inductive reasoning (Hanson, Creswell, Plano Clark, Petska, & Creswell, 2005). Greene (2007, p. 199) described mixed methods as crossing "borders and boundaries once fenced and defended," which "invites diverse ways of thinking to dialogue one with the other." Mixed methods research is a conversation, a mixing of mental models involving multiple philosophies, values, theories, methods, and analyses. This pluralism in methodologies can be understood as a dialectical stance bridging postpositivist, postmodernist, and social constructivist worldviews, as well as pragmatic and transformative perspectives. Mixed methods can provide a "more comprehensive understanding . . . [and] highly informative, exhaustive, balanced and useful research results" (Krivokapic-Skoko & O'Neill, 2010, p. 279). Through mixed methods, the concept of triangulation across multiple methods, as introduced to psychology by Campbell and Fiske (1959), moves a step further, encouraging researchers to adopt a more critical view toward their data and to extract their interpretations from multiple sources and methods, seeing this as a form of convergent validity (Fielding & Fielding, 2008). Like participatory research itself, mixed methods research involves a shift in, and perhaps an inversion of, paradigms (Park, 1992).

Creswell, Klassen, Plano Clark, and Smith (2011) summarized definitions, methods, and strengths of qualitative and quantitative research and of the major approaches to combining the two. Qualitative approaches include ethnography, case studies, life history interviews, and structured interviewing. Quantitative research is deductive, tests theories or hypotheses, and studies the relationship among variables or gathers descriptive knowledge. Measurement leads to numeric data, to statistical analysis to establish causality, and generalization to populations or group comparison. Quantitative approaches include randomized controlled trials, time-series and other quasi-experimental designs, observational studies, case-control studies, and descriptive surveys. Mixed methods research combines an intentional collection of both quantitative and qualitative data with an intentional integration of the data. This integration seeks to minimize the weaknesses and maximize the strengths of each approach.

Creswell and Plano Clark (2011) identified three general mixed methods approaches involving merging, connecting, and embedding data. Merging data is achieved by reporting results together. Examples include reporting quantitative statistical results with qualitative quotes or themes that support or refute the quantitative results, or transforming qualitative to quantitative data (such as by reporting counts of occurrence of qualitative codes). Connecting data involves analysis of one data set (for example, a quantitative survey) to inform a subsequent project (an in-depth qualitative interview study). Embedding data occurs when data collection of secondary importance is implanted within a primary research design, as in the case of a qualitative descriptive study that elucidates the subjective experience of treatment among the participants within a randomized controlled trial. The case studies that follow provide examples of connecting and embedding data, respectively.

CASE STUDIES

People Awakening Project

Alcohol research with Alaska Native communities has had a history of conflict, resulting in community suspicion of research (Manson, 1989). At the same time, there is a critical need for research to guide alcohol abuse prevention and treatment with Alaska Native people. The People Awakening research group of grassroots members of the Alaska Native sobriety movement and university researchers addressed this need together (see Mohatt, Hazel, et al., 2004, for greater detail). The group of community members who formed the research coordinating council for the project began its work by choosing a methodology that honored the oral traditions of Alaska Native cultures through the use of life history interviews. It then redefined the research question itself from alcoholism to sobriety. Interview protocols were developed collaboratively, emphasizing protocols that facilitated shaping the study methodology toward the empowerment of participants. The research coordinating council members were trained in the coding process, discussed data interpretation, and coded and interpreted a sample of the life histories in order to provide an audit of the university researcher's data coding efforts from the perspective of local cultural understandings. The work identified protective factors, capturing hidden and unheard narratives of Alaska Native strength and resilience (Mohatt, Rasmus, et al., 2004).

These qualitative findings were connected to culturally adapted existing instruments and developed into new, culturally grounded ways of measuring these salient factors in quantitative work with a Yup'ik (an Alaska Native Indigenous population) coresearcher group who assisted in the direction of this instrument development. The qualitative findings culminated in a culturally grounded heuristic model of protection to guide intervention (Allen et al., 2006). The qualitative findings were connected to the quantitative survey methods, where they guided development and testing of a protective factors measure through contributions to item content and construct composition. Through seminar training meetings and commentary at team meetings, the Yup'k coresearchers, who did not initially possess specialist measurement training, provided key input into the design, implementation, and interpretation of the findings.

This and similarly developed measures were tested as part of a complex model of protection made possible only through the detailed, rich qualitative data and the heuristic model developed out of the Phase 1 life history research (Allen et al., 2014). The results of Phase 2 suggested important alterations to the original heuristic model, displaying how mixed methods research draws on complementary strengths in methods. One finding refined the team's understanding of the role of family characteristics as moderating peer influences on alcohol beliefs. Another contribution was structural equation modeling's ability to assign relative weights to different protective factors within the model, suggesting particularly important areas for intervention. A culturally patterned finding with implications for prevention emerged in young people's preference for problem solving using communal mastery over self-mastery strategies. Although this preference was anticipated through the qualitative findings, the extent of that preference that these communal strategies to achieve mastery would draw on family relationships over adolescent peer friendships was not predicted.

In the quantitative interplay with qualitative data, methods limitations also emerged. Foremost was what was lost in the transition from a heuristic model based on rich, narrative data embedded in deep cultural structures to a model based on self-report quantitative data. Each level of the original heuristic model included nuanced description that was reduced in the measurement instruments to only a few salient factors. Clearly, the creation of brief measures developmentally appropriate for youth as young as age 12 required simplification. However, there were also issues related to the nomothetic method. For example, although the existence of a safe place growing up was reported to be of critical importance by a small high-risk group of qualitative research participants, it was not an issue for the larger overall group, and, in the aggregated data, safe places did not exhibit a significant relationship to outcomes.

Researcher experience with community cultural norms regarding direct questions about trauma provides an even more far-reaching case example in comparative strengths and weaknesses of method (Gonzalez & Trickett, 2014). Trauma exposure, protection from trauma, and response to traumatization emerged as important elements in the original qualitative heuristic model (Allen et al., 2006). However, discussion of trauma during the life history interviews occurred at the disclosure, discretion, and choice of the individual. Interviewers did not ask direct questions about trauma. Instead, interviewers asked about important transformative events, both positive and negative, and followed up with careful yet respectful inquiry if trauma experience was revealed. In developing measurement strategies for the protective factors study, many community members were not comfortable with researchers asking youth direct questions of the type found in trauma self-report measures. Within the Yup'ik cultural context, given the respect afforded to individual autonomy, direct questions of this type by their very nature can be intrusive and culturally inappropriate. Therefore, in the quantitative work it was not possible to explore this component of the model. In summary, connecting qualitative to quantitative methods led to increased specificity and generalizability but at a cost in nuance, description of individual- and community-level differences, and appreciation of the deeper structure of several cultural elements.

Developing Communities Project of Greater Roseland

A research collaboration between the University of Illinois at Chicago and the Developing Communities Project of Greater Roseland (DCP), a local church-related community organization, provides an embedded mixed methods case study. A key component of this participatory intervention was leadership development of community members who were delivering substance abuse education and prevention programming in their community. A primary aim was to identify issues, processes, and motivating influences behind the emergence of community leaders that the intervention drew upon and to present the findings in a way that would be of maximum usefulness to the community organization. Semistructured interviews with the community leaders explored leadership influences around four topics: (a) social support for the community leader, (b) skills learned and skills to be learned in future training, (c) communications with other community organizations, and (d) personal visions of the community leaders.

The process of qualitative data collection, coding, and interpretation for 77 interviews is presented in Tandon, Azelton, Kelly, and Strickland (1998). Through the process of its analysis, the research team concluded that the 56 codes generated could be grouped into five dimensions describing social processes of community leadership: (a) reasons for community involvement and activities, (b) the organization's impact on the leaders, (c) factors promoting continued and active involvement, (d) religious influences affecting leaders' commitment, and (e) personal visions. Community dissemination of the results used a graphic representation of five trees; each tree represented one of these five dimensions, with the codes organized according to each dimension as a branch of one of the trees. In providing individual feedback to participants, the codes that emerged in each individual interview were plotted on each participant's own five trees of leadership so that the citizen leader could examine his or her profile and even compare it with group data.

The executive director of DCP was interested in whether the community leaders in their program formed subgroups based on their motivations to take on the leadership responsibilities the DCP depended upon. The executive director believed that better understanding of the types of motivations could guide recruitment and improve leader training. Henry, Dymnicki, Mohatt, Allen, and Kelly (2015) described and then explored the utility of three different cluster analysis approaches in assisting with the identification of these subgroups.

The interpretation of the meaning of the different clusters of leadership subgroups and their implications for recruitment and retention was facilitated through the active involvement of the coresearcher group. The coresearcher team identified the leaders comprising the first cluster as being motivated by the desire to create community change, those in the second cluster by the prospect of gaining personal knowledge and exchanging information with others, and those in the third cluster by an agenda for systemic community change via economic development. The DCP organization and its board felt that the cluster analysis provided helpful information to guide enhancement of the organization's recruiting and training activities.

Embedded approaches involve more transformation of data from one approach into another than is the case in merging or connecting data approaches. In the DCP study, the quantitative findings were secondary and were used as a tool yielding new interpretative information from the qualitative data that were primary in importance for analytic yield. These clustering methods can guide qualitative analysis using complex coding systems and can support more systematic exploration of the meaning of relational configurations of code structures. This can provide qualitative researchers with new tools to explore their data beyond individual code types in isolation. However, embedded mixed methods can be used effectively only by researchers with grounding in theory and context, and through rich immersion in narrative data made possible through qualitative work combined with coresearcher involvement and collaboration. Such mixed methods approaches move the field closer to the concept of triangulation as convergent findings from multiple methods envisioned by Jick (1979).

CONCLUSION

Arnstein's (1969) citizen participation framework provides a useful tool for describing the implementation of participatory research and the contribution of mixed methods. Clearly, some projects foster citizen power, while others, although described as CBPAR, may represent tokenism or even nonparticipation. The framework allows us to think about what is participation and to what extent a CBPAR project embodies it. An important element of the qualitative component in mixed methods may be the avenues by which it makes research approachable and relevant to the coresearcher team and community, creating portals for introducing local meaning and direction, while including elements of precision and generalizability associated with quantitative work persuasive to the policymakers whom a community hopes to influence. The utility of mixed methods in participatory research thus involves the ways in which it moves the project up the ladder of participation.

This issue is discussed by Trickett (2011), who described the worldview of participatory research as involving the community as the unit of solution and practice, community involvement in decision making, social change as goal, a constructivist approach, and sustainability as a concern. Trickett noted that elements of the participatory research perspective can be selectively bracketed and invoked to accomplish aims that are not collaboratively defined. For example, a research team may use participatory elements in implementing a randomized controlled trial of an adapted intervention. Yet it may be the case there was limited community input and choice in selection of which intervention to adapt, and deeper still, the general approach to the solution of the social problem, and even the selection of the research problem itself as an area of community concern. In such cases, local knowledge is relegated to carrying out science as conceived within a framework devised by experts from outside the community, and without empowerment and community capacity development as explicit goals. Mixed methods research provides one additional portal for critical insertion of the local knowledge, concerns, frameworks, and aims that distinguish CBPAR as a worldview, as opposed to a set of instrumental strategies in the service of implementation of an outside research agenda.

In summary, mixed methods research's utility in participatory research can be judged by the degree to which it maximizes engagement, voice, *and* influence in facilitating structural change. Qualitative research elucidates local meaning, understandings, and a narrative defined by participants. Quantitative research can be influential in the process of structural change. Judged by the criteria of influence, mixed methods is a valuable way of facilitating higher levels of citizen participation in research.

REFERENCES

Alastalo, M. (2008). The history of social research methods. In P. Alasuutari, L. Bickman, & J. Brannen (Eds.), *The Sage handbook of social research methods* (pp. 26–41). Thousand Oaks, CA: Sage.

Allen, J., Mohatt, G. V., Hazel, K., Rasmus, M., Thomas, L., Lindley, S., & People Awakening Team. (2006). The tools to understand: Community as co-researcher on culture specific protective factors for Alaska Natives. *Journal of Prevention and Intervention in the Community, 32*, 41–59.

Allen, J., Mohatt, G. V., Fok, C. C. T., Henry, D., Burkett, R., & People Awakening Team. (2014). A protective factors model for alcohol abuse and suicide prevention among Alaska Native youth. *American Journal of Community Psychology, 54*, 125–139.

Arnstein, S. R. (1969). A ladder of citizen participation. *Journal of the American Institute of Planners, 35*, 216–224.

Baffour, T. D. (2011). Addressing health and social disparities through community-based participatory research in rural communities: Challenges and opportunities for social work. *Contemporary Rural Social Work, 3*, 4–16.

bell hooks. (1995). *Killing rage: Ending racism*. New York, NY: Henry Holt.

Brydon-Miller, M. (2004). The terrifying truth: Interrogating systems of power and privilege and choosing to act. In M. Brydon-Miller, P. Maguire, & A. McIntyre (Eds.), *Traveling companions: Feminism, teaching, and action research* (pp. 3–19). Westport, CT: Praeger.

Brydon-Miller, M. (2008). Covenantal ethics and action research: Exploring a common foundation for social research. In D. Mertens & P. Ginsberg (Eds.), *Handbook of social research ethics* (pp. 243–258). Newbury Park, CA: Sage.

Brydon-Miller, M., Greenwood, D., & Maguire, P. (2003). Why action research? *Action Research, 1*, 9–28.

Brydon-Miller, M., Kral, M. J., Maguire, P., Noffke, S., & Sabhlok, A. (2011). Jazz and the Banyon tree: Roots and riffs on participatory action research. In N. K. Denzin & Y. S. Lincoln (Eds.), *The Sage handbook of qualitative research* (4th ed., pp. 387–400). Thousand Oaks, CA: Sage.

Campbell, D. T., & Fiske, D. W. (1959). Convergent and discriminant validation by the multitrait-multimethod matrix. *Psychological Bulletin, 56*, 81–105.

Cargo, M., & Mercer, S. L. (2008). The values and challenges of participatory research: Strengthening its practice. *Annual Review of Public Health, 29*, 325–350.

Creswell, J. W., Klassen, A. C., Plano Clark, V. L., & Smith, K. C. (2011). *Best practices for mixed methods research in the health sciences*. Bethesda, MD: National Institutes of Health.

Creswell, J. W., & Plano Clark, V. L. (2011). *Designing and conducting mixed methods research* (2nd ed.). Thousand Oaks, CA: Sage.

Denzin, N. K., & Giardina, M. D. (2008). The elephant in the living room, or advancing the conversation about the politics of evidence. In N. K. Denzin & M. D. Giardina (Eds.), *Qualitative inquiry and the politics of evidence* (pp. 9–51). Walnut Creek, CA: Left Coast Press.

Denzin, N. K., Lincoln, Y. S., & Smith, L. T. (2008). *Handbook of critical and indigenous methodologies*. Los Angeles, CA: Sage.

Dukes, E. F., Firehock, K. E., & Birkoff, J. E. (Eds.). (2011). *Community-based collaboration: Bridging socio-ecological research and practice*. Charlottesville: University of Virginia Press.

Fals Borda, O. (2001). Participatory (action) research in social theory: Origins and challenges. In P. Reason & H. Bradbury (Eds.), *Handbook of action research* (pp. 27–37). London, England: Sage.

Fielding, J., & Fielding, N. (2008). Synergy and synthesis: Integrating qualitative and quantitative data. In P. Alasuutari, L. Bickman, & J. Brannen (Eds.), *The Sage handbook of social research methods* (pp. 555–571). Thousand Oaks, CA: Sage.

Fine, M., & Torre, M. (2005). Resisting and researching: Youth participatory action research. In S. Ginwright, J. Cammarota, & P. Noguera (Eds.), *Social justice, youth, and their communities* (pp. 269–285). New York, NY: Routledge.

Freire, P. (1970). *Pedagogy of the oppressed*. New York, NY: Seabury.

Greene, J. C. (2007). *Mixed methods in social inquiry*. San Francisco, CA: Wiley.

Gonzalez, J., & Trickett, E. J. (2014). Collaborative measurement development as a tool in CBPR: Measurement development and adaptation within the cultures of communities. *American Journal of Community Psychology, 54*, 112–124.

Gustavsen, B., Hanson, A., & Qvale, T. U. (2008). Action research and the challenge of scope. In P. Reason & H. Bradbury (Eds.), *Handbook of action research* (2nd ed., pp. 63–76). Thousand Oaks, CA: Sage.

Hall, B. L. (2005). In from the cold? Reflections on participatory research from 1970-2005. *Convergence, 38*, 5–24.

Hanson, W. E., Creswell, J. W., Plano Clark, V. L., Petska, K. S., & Creswell, J. D. (2005). Mixed methods research designs in counseling psychology. *Journal of Counseling Psychology, 52*, 224–235.

Hesse-Biber, S. N., & Leavy, P. (Eds.). (2008). *Handbook of emergent methods*. New York, NY: Guilford Press.

Henry, D., Dymnicki, A. B., Mohatt, N. V., Allen, J., & Kelly, J. (2015). Clustering methods with qualitative data: A mixed methods approach for prevention research with small samples. *Prevention Science*. Epub ahead of print.

Israel, B. A., Schulz, A. J., Parker, E. A., Becker, A. B., Allen, A. J., & Guzman, J. R. (2008). Critical issues in developing and following CBPR principles. In M. Minkler & N. Wallerstein (2008), *Community-based participatory research for health: From process to outcomes* (pp. 47–63). Hoboken, NJ: Wiley.

Jason, L. A., Keys, C. B., Suarez-Balcazar, Y. E., Taylor, R. R., & Davis, M. I. (2004). *Participatory community research: Theories and methods in action*. Washington, DC: American Psychological Association.

Jick, T. D. (1979). Mixing qualitative and quantitative methods: Triangulation in action. *Administrative Science Quarterly, 24*, 602–611.

Kagan, C., Burton, M., Duckett, P., & Lawthom, R. (2011). *Critical community psychology*. Hoboken, NJ: Blackwell.

Kapoor, D., & Jordan, S. (Eds.). (2009). *Education, participatory action research, and social change: International perspectives*. New York, NY: Palgrave Macmillan.

Kemmis, S., & McTaggart, R. (2005). Participatory action research: Communicative action and the public sphere. In N. K. Denzin & Y. S. Lincoln (Eds.), *The Sage handbook of qualitative research* (3rd ed., pp. 559–603). Thousand Oaks, CA: Sage.

Kidd, S. A., & Kral, M. J. (2005). Practicing participatory action research. *Journal of Counseling Psychology, 52*, 187–195.

Kovach, M. (2009). *Indigenous methodologies: Characteristics, conversations, and contexts*. Toronto, ON: University of Toronto Press.

Kral, M. J. (2014). The relational motif in participatory qualitative research. *Qualitative Inquiry, 20*, 144–150.

Krivokapic-Skoko, B., & O'Neill, G. (2010). Doing mixed methods research. In J. Higgs, N. Cherry, R. Macklin, & R. Ajjawi (Eds.), *Researching practice: A discourse on qualitative methodologies* (pp. 279–288). Rotterdam, The Netherlands: Sense.

Lewin, K. (1970). Action research and minority problems. *Journal of Social Issues, 2*, 34–46.

Manson, S. M. (1989). Barrow alcohol study: Emphasis on its ethical and procedural aspects. *American Indian and Alaska Native Mental Health Research, 2*(3), 5–6.

Mies, M. (1996). Liberating women, liberating knowledge: Reflections on two decades of feminist action research. *Atlantis, 21*(6), 10–24.

Mohatt, G. V, Hazel, K. L., Allen, J., Stachelrodt, M., Hensel, C., & Fath, R. (2004). Unheard Alaska: Culturally anchored participatory action research on sobriety with Alaska Natives. *American Journal of Community Psychology, 33*, 263–273.

Mohatt, G. V., Rasmus, S. M., Thomas, L., Allen, J., Hazel, K., & Hensel, C. (2004). Tied together like a woven hat: Protective pathways to Alaska Native sobriety. *Harm Reduction, 1*(10), 1–12.

Ortner, S. B. (2006). *Anthropology and social theory: Culture, power, and the acting subject*. Durham, NC: Duke University Press.

O'Toole, T. P., Aaron, K. F., Chin, M. H., Horowitz, C. & Tyson, F. (2003). Community-based participatory research: Opportunities, challenges, and the need for a common language. *Journal of General Internal Medicine, 18*, 592–594.

Park, P. (1992). The discovery of participatory research as a new scientific paradigm: Personal and intellectual accounts. *American Sociologist, 23*, 29–42.

Reich, S. M., Riemer, M., Prilleltensky, I., & Montero, M. (Eds.). (2007). *International community psychology: History and theories*. New York, NY: Springer.

Savage, C. L., Xu, Y., Lee, R., Rose, B. L., Kappesser, M., & Anthony, J. S. (2006). A case study in the use of community-based participatory research in public health nursing. *Public Health Nursing, 23*, 472–478.

Shore, N. (2008). Introduction to special issue: Advancing the ethics of community-based participatory research. *Journal of Empirical Research on Human Research Ethics, 3*, 1–4.

Shweder, R. A. (1996). Quanta and qualia: What is the "object" of ethnographic method? In R. Jessor, A. Colby, & R. A. Shweder (Eds.), *Ethnography and human development: Context and meaning in social inquiry* (pp. 175–182). Chicago, IL: University of Chicago Press.

Smith, L. T. (2012). *Decolonizing methodologies: Research and indigenous peoples* (2nd ed.). London, England: Zed.

Staller, K. M., Block, E., & Horner, P. S. (2008). History of methods in social science research. In S. N. Hesse-Biber & P. Leavy (Eds.), *Handbook of emergent methods* (pp. 25–51). New York, NY: Guilford Press.

Sue, S. (1999). Science, ethnicity, and bias: Where have we gone wrong? *American Psychologist, 54*, 1070–1077.

Tandon, S. D., Azelton, L. S., Kelly, J. G., & Strickland, D. (1998). Constructing a tree for community leaders: Contexts and processes in collaborative inquiry. *American Journal of Community Psychology, 26*, 669–696.

Tolan, P., Chertok, F., Keys, C., & Jason, L. (1990). Conversing about theories, methods, and community research. In P. Tolan, C. Keys, F. Chertok, & L. Jason (Eds.), *Researching community psychology: Issues of theory and methods* (pp. 3–8). Washington, DC: American Psychological Association.

Trickett, E. J. (2011). Community-based participatory research as worldview or instrumental strategy: Is it lost in translation(al) research? *American Journal of Public Health, 101*, 1353–1355.

Tritter, J. Q., & McCallum, A. (2006). The snakes and ladders of user involvement: Moving beyond Arnstein. *Health Policy, 76*, 156–168.

Wallerstein, N., & Duran, B. (2008). The theoretical, historical, and practice roots of CBPR. In M. Minkler & N. Wallerstein (Eds.), *Community-based participatory research for health: From process to outcomes* (pp. 25–46). Hoboken, NJ: Wiley.

Wallerstein, N., & Duran, B. (2010). Community-based participatory research contributions to intervention research: The intersection of science and practice to improve health equity. *American Journal of Public Health, 100*, 40–46.

Yanow, D. (2006). Neither rigorous nor objective? Interrogating criteria for knowledge claims in interpretive science. In D. Yanow & P. Schwartz-Shea (Eds.), *Interpretation and method: Empirical research methods and the interpretive turn* (pp. 67–88). Armonk, NY: M. E. Sharpe.

Zimmerman, M. A. (1995). Psychological empowerment: Issues and illustrations. *American Journal of Community Psychology, 23*, 581–599.

26

Youth-Led Participatory Action Research

EMILY J. OZER

This chapter discusses youth-led participatory action research (YPAR), a change process that engages students in identifying problems that they want to improve, conducting research to understand the nature of the problems, and advocating for changes based on research evidence. After providing an overview of YPAR and its core processes, the chapter reviews the literature regarding the effects of YPAR on youth and their settings and identifies the benefits of YPAR. This is followed by a multimethods case study of YPAR projects involving more than 25 urban classrooms. Lastly, I consider existing resources and new resources in development to support the dissemination of YPAR as a community research and intervention method.

INTRODUCTION TO YOUTH-LED PARTICIPATORY ACTION RESEARCH

What Is YPAR?

Youth-led participatory action research (YPAR) involves the training of young people to identify major concerns in their schools and communities, conduct research to understand the nature of the problems, and take leadership in influencing policies and decisions to enhance the conditions in which they live (London, Zimmerman, & Erbstein, 2003). It is a specialized form of community-based participatory research (CBPR; see Chapter 25). YPAR shares CBPR's emphases on promoting the power of marginalized groups via an iterative process of inquiry and action (Minkler & Wallerstein, 2003) and democratizing research to include the expertise and voice of those affected by it (Langhout & Thomas, 2010). Issues of power are central to YPAR in promoting the influence of young people in systems and communities—especially as they do not exercise the same rights as adults—as well as in considering how adult facilitators share ownership and decision making with youth in implementing YPAR projects (Ozer, Newlan, Douglas, & Hubbard, 2013).

YPAR shares some goals and advocacy methods with youth-organizing approaches aimed at promoting the critical consciousness and power of young people to improve their lives and communities (Brown & Rodriguez, 2009; Cammarota & Fine, 2008; Freire, 1994; Ginwright, Noguera, & Cammarota, 2006; Kirshner, 2007; McIntyre, 2000). YPAR, however, is distinctive with respect to its focus on an iterative process of systematic *research* and action conducted by the young people themselves. The data generated by the youth inform their actions and advocacy in dialogue with their own social position and experiences.

Paradigmatic Considerations

Although YPAR offers valuable methods to community researchers, it is important to note that YPAR also embodies a deeper epistemological approach in asserting that young people are experts who can create knowledge leading to empowerment and social justice (Langhout & Thomas, 2010). In considering the intellectual basis and value of YPAR, Fine (2008) made a compelling case for how what is often narrowly defined as research "rigor" can be broadened and strengthened by YPAR in its honoring of the distributed nature of expertise. Key expertise is viewed as residing within marginalized youth and others who directly experience the research "topics" in their lives but have historically been the objects rather than subjects of research. YAR as a field of scholarly inquiry and practice has grown markedly in the past decade; as of 2015, a

PsycINFO search for "CBPR and youth" yielded 570 citations across many disciplines (e.g., psychology, public health, education, nursing), languages, and countries.

Key Processes

In prior work, we proposed a framework for core processes of YPAR, mindful that the implementation of projects requires flexibility and will differ across contexts. Ozer, Ritterman, and Wanis (2010) identified core YPAR processes, including (a) iterative integration of research and action, (b) training and practice of research skills, (c) practice of strategic thinking and strategies for influencing change, and (d) adults' sharing of power with students in the research and action process. Other processes that are important for high-quality implementation of YPAR but are not unique to it include opportunities and guidance for working in groups to achieve goals, expansion of the social network of the youth, and the development of skills to communicate with other youth and adult stakeholders (Ozer & Douglas, 2015).

Power sharing is a theoretically central dimension of YPAR and typically a challenging one to enact given the inherent inequality of adult–youth relationships. In principle, the youth-led approach entails the young people exerting power over key aspects of the research and action process (e.g., defining the problem/topic to be addressed, research methods, data analysis and interpretation, action steps), with adults in a support role. Skillful scaffolding from adults is needed to promote young people's sense of ownership while helping them manage demands such as deadlines and conflicts (Larson, Walker, & Pearce, 2005; Mitra, 2004; Vygotsky, 1978). This process of sharing power is a nuanced "dance" in hierarchical settings, such as schools, characterized by institutionalized power differentials, with adults holding the power, deciding the rules, and determining what counts as knowledge (Kohfeldt, Chhun, Grace, & Langhout, 2011; Ozer et al., 2013). As Sarason (1996, p. 363) observed, the typical classroom is one in which teachers rather than students ask questions, adults are rendered "insensitive to what their [children's] interests, concerns and questions are . . . and children are viewed as incapable of self-regulation." Thus, YPAR disrupts the status quo by its very nature of generating youth-driven inquiry and knowledge. This is especially so if the young people generate problems to address and solutions to consider that are not viewed as similarly important by adult staff or if both youth and adults see a high-priority problem but have a different analysis of causes.

It is important to note that the concept of young people having power over key decisions and processes in YPAR does not mean in practice that all ideas, methods, or data interpretations generated by the youth researchers should be supported uncritically by the adult facilitators or peers. Rather, it means that a dialogic and iterative process is intentionally enacted in which the young people's ideas are voiced and respected and that they get a chance to see the strengths and limitations of their ideas rather than being shut down by the power of the adult. Kohfeldt et al. (2011) provided an in-depth example of this complex process of how adult staff in an elementary school eventually understood and valued the process of youth-led inquiry as distinctive from their regular teaching practices. In a similar vein, Ozer et al. (2013) identified the types of constraints experienced by multiple YPAR cohorts in high-school settings, as well as the strategies used by the students and teachers to enhance student power and action despite the constraints of "bounded empowerment."

Sociopolitical and Developmental Relevance of YPAR

YPAR can be viewed as an intervention approach intended to address inequalities in health and education; create and strengthen opportunities for youth to enhance their own knowledge, skills, and motivations; and expand the opportunities for meaningful influence or voice in the settings in which youth live (Berg, Coman, & Schensul, 2009; Cargo, Grams, Ottoson, Ward, & Green, 2003; Mitra, 2004; Nieto, 1996; Ozer & Wright, 2012; Shor, 1996). For example, youth researchers have advocated for policy changes to reduce diesel bus emissions (Minkler, Vásquez, & Shepard, 2006) and improve neighborhood food access (Breckwich Vásquez et al., 2007), educated communities regarding the judicial system (Stovall & Delgado, 2009), worked to prevent childhood obesity (Findholt, Michael, & Davis, 2011), and participated in urban planning processes (Horelli & Kaaja, 2002).

The potential benefits of YPAR suggested by theory and research include key attitudinal and behavioral aspects of psychological empowerment, such as perceptions of control and efficacy in relevant domains; motivation to influence involved youths' schools or communities in constructive ways; decision-making and problem-solving skills; critical understanding of the sociopolitical environment; and participatory behaviors (Holden, Evans, Hinnant, & Messeri, 2005; Zimmerman, 2000). Other individual-level gains observed in qualitative YPAR research include increases in adolescents' sense of purpose, perceived support from caring adults, and more positive attitudes toward education and school (Mitra, 2004; Wilson et al., 2007).

Several studies in public health have examined if youth researchers who study a particular health issue actually change their own attitudes and behavior regarding the issue. For example, effects have been found with respect to reductions in marijuana use (Berg et al., 2009). Research on alcohol use found positive effects for empathy, positive control, and domains of self-efficacy but not for behavioral outcomes related to alcohol or violence (Wallerstein, Sanchez, & Velarde, 2005). Gibson, Flaspohler, and Watts (2015) examined whether a YPAR project on bullying in three middle-school sites affected bullying attitudes and behavior at the school level; the research found positive effects at the one site that actively engaged the school community via a bullying prevention message contest but not for the sites in which the youth research project culminated in presentations to the school community about bullying.

There are a number of reasons why YPAR is particularly relevant for adolescents and their schools. In the United States, K–12 education has been a major site of YPAR inquiry and action, as exemplified in our case examples highlighted in this chapter and in that of multiple other scholars. Much of this school-oriented work has focused on addressing rampant inequalities by race and class in educational opportunities, safety, and resources, as well as disproportionate discipline and special education placements for youth of color (Gregory & Weinstein, 2008). In Ozer, Ritterman, and Wanis (2010), we considered how YPAR can help address the developmental mismatch between adolescents and typical public secondary schools (Eccles, Midgley, Wigfield, & Buchanan, 1993; Simmons, 1987). Although older children and young adolescents demonstrate growing capacity and desire for autonomy, longitudinal research indicates that youth perceive fewer opportunities to exercise autonomy and participate in making decisions and rules in junior high than they did in elementary schools (Midgley & Feldlaufer, 1987).

Furthermore, YPAR holds particular promise for adolescents because this developmental period is a time of fluidity and transition for individual and collective sense of identity and purpose (Damon, 2003; Ozer, Ritterman, & Wanis, 2010). Developmental theories focused on youth of color emphasize the influences of social position, racism and discrimination, and immediate environments (García Coll et al., 1996). YPAR that involves youth of color in analyzing and having an impact on the social, economic, and political conditions that shape their schools and communities thus provides developmental opportunities for youth to see themselves as leaders with a sense of purpose (Damon, 2003; Spencer, Fegley, & Harpalani, 2003) rather than internalizing negative stereotypes held by others (Cahill, Rios-Moore, & Threatts, 2008). Also, YPAR is intended to promote critical consciousness—critical reflection, motivation, and action—that pushes youth beyond individual-level explanations of problems faced by communities of color to investigate broader factors (Watts, Diemer, & Voight, 2011).

In their analysis of the integration of developmental psychology and liberation psychology, Watts and Flanagan (2007) raise the issue of a politically "sensitive" period for identity formation regarding civic engagement, making the case for sociopolitical activism as an important pathway to critical consciousness and civic engagement for youth of color beyond the traditional routes of civic engagement such as volunteer service. In addition to promoting civic and political engagement—and relevant skills in inquiry and advocacy—being youth researchers can also promote young people's view of themselves as researchers and scientists, opening up possible pipelines into these fields when there are actual opportunities provided.

YPAR and Research Validity

With respect to research validity, YPAR can be viewed as a special approach to address research questions that young people are particularly well equipped to define and investigate. Fine (2008) challenged the field to consider how YPAR enhances the quality and trustworthiness of research, even from the standpoint of classic psychological traditions, with respect to expanding the constructs of objectivity, construct validity, and generalizability (Cook & Campbell, 1979). For example, in a collaborative project with high-school students, Fine (2008) observed that YPAR enhanced construct validity when youth researchers responded to the adult researchers' focus on the "achievement gap" by redefining the problem as the "opportunity gap," thereby strengthening the construct and causal conceptualization to fit the phenomenon.

YPAR can improve the rigor (in the expanded sense noted earlier), relevance, and reach of science (Balazs & Morello-Frosch, 2013) by affording insider expertise not only in the identification of questions that are important to study but also in enhancing the quality and validity of data and interpretation. Insider expertise is important generally and even more salient in the investigation of youths' experience of sensitive, hidden, or hard-to-report phenomena in which the presence of an adult observer would change the nature of the phenomena. Many key topics for research and health promotion regarding adolescent health and well-being relate to social phenomena that are less accessible to adult inquiry and/or affected by the presence of adult observers, such as bullying, dating relationships, substance use, aggression, and disproportionate discipline by teachers.

Relevance

As indicated earlier, a core early step in the YPAR process is the young people's identification of the topics to be addressed, but importantly also strengths or resources that run counter to stereotypically negative narratives of their communities (Dill, 2015). Thus, the relevance of the research process should be inherently strengthened by YPAR insofar as there are authentic opportunities for the youth researchers to determine their questions or to refine the focus of questions in situations in which the overall topic might already be constrained by prior cohorts or other factors that establish parameters for their inquiry (Ozer et al., 2013). There are multiple methods that youth researchers use to generate issues of concern and then select from as an area of focus. In addition to interviews and observations, PhotoVoice and mapping are two specific methods that have been used to provide contextualized material for issue identification and selection (Catalani & Minkler, 2010). For example, both McIntyre (2000) working in the US Northeast and Vaughan (2014) in Papua, New Guinea, discussed how young people's photos of garbage in their communities became a focus of YPAR efforts.

Rigor

YPAR can enable situations in which youth insiders study phenomena that are accessible to them in ways that would likely not be accessible to adults in their communities or to academic researchers. Although there are important examples of adult ethnographers gaining the trust of young people to study hidden or stigmatized phenomena, such as racially motivated violence and the experience of structural inequalities for youth of color (Pinderhughes, 1997; Seyer-Ochi, 2006), ethnographies are relatively rare and extremely time-intensive research projects that are typically focused on generating novel social science theory. In contrast, YPAR can afford an insider phenomenological perspective on practical, relevant, and often time-sensitive issues for the improvement of young people's life conditions, nurturing the capacities of youth themselves to generate critical inquiry and empirical findings.

There are many examples in the YPAR literature that demonstrate the value of youth insider expertise. For example, Ozer, Ritterman, and Wanis (2010) engaged a group of female adolescents at a majority-Latino middle school as part of a classroom-based YPAR project. In the YPAR process, the students generated a range of problems to address, including the perceived pressure to join gangs or "claim colors." Although the school had a strict dress code that excluded gang colors, students shared the small ways that they noticed colors being claimed, an example of peer expertise about the trajectory of the process that was likely "under the radar" for adults. The youth researchers also identified important causal factors regarding why their peers joined gangs.

With respect to rigor on the applied intervention side, YPAR also provides important opportunities for evaluation of programs in which youth participate (Youth Impact, 2001) as well as the adaptation of programs to be more relevant to their lives, strengths, and needs (Chen, Weiss, & Nicholson, 2010; Ozer, Wanis, & Bazell, 2010). Local tailoring of school and community-based interventions is a highly challenging effort, especially when we consider the many diversities inherent in the classrooms, schools, and communities meant to be served by such programs. Engaging the local expertise of young people in adaptation can help avoid relying on overgeneralization and untested assumptions about group differences in enhancing the relevance of community-based programs.

Reach

Recent work in public health has focused on YPAR's role in policy change as well as in reducing the research-practice gap. In an interview study of the utilization of YPAR versus academic research in five public health departments in California, Wanis and Ozer (unpublished data) found that "research-friendly" public health departments utilized evidence generated by both academic research and YPAR but that some departments that did not tend to value or utilize academic research did utilize the findings of YPAR to inform policies and practices because it was seen as relevant to the youth they serve. Thus, in this case, YPAR demonstrated a potential for enhancing the utilization of research by practitioners, relative to academic research.

Garcia, Minkler, Cardenas, Grills, and Porter (2014), in their analysis of an effective partnership between academic partners, a community-based organization, and youth researchers living in an economically marginalized neighborhood of Los Angeles, identified how the YPAR project utilized neighborhood surveys as well as youth panels and videos to gather data about the young people's experiences and needs. They also successfully used these methods to redefine public opinion about who lived in the neighborhood and to advocate for accessible and safe playgrounds as well as other resources.

CASE STUDY

Overview of Study

The case study presented here was part of a 5-year, mixed methods intervention that investigated the effects of YPAR on participating youth and their school settings (Ozer & Douglas, 2015).The within-school design at five urban high school sites included 29 classes of high-school students who conducted YPAR projects; these were compared with 34 classes of students who participated in a direct service peer education class that did not include training in YPAR. The sample was ethnically diverse, with 35% of the adolescents being of Asian American ethnicity, 31% Latino/Hispanic, 14% African American, 7% European American, and 10% from other minority groups such as Native American or Arab American. The overall sample was 65% female and 35% male with an average age of 16 years.

The study represented a collaboration of University of California-Berkeley researchers with the high schools and a community-based organization (SF Peer Resources). Classroom teachers coordinated the YPAR projects in a daily elective class, with technical assistance from their supervisor and the university team (Ozer et al., 2008). The study assessed individual-level quantitative outcomes of psychological empowerment for young people who participated in the YPAR projects and gathered extensive qualitative data from students regarding the YPAR projects via interviews and participant observation. Qualitative methods were used to assess school-level effects of YPAR (Ozer & Wright, 2012), to analyze constraints on student power in schools, and to identify processes to help promote student power (Ozer et al., 2013).

YPAR Projects

The problems addressed in the YPAR projects were decided by the students, with facilitation from their teachers. Topics included the prevention of school dropout; smoothing the transition to grade; stress related to family, academics, or peers; improving the school lunch; cyber-bullying; sexual health; safety and hygiene in the school bathrooms; improving teaching practices to engage diverse students; and improving interethnic friendships at the school. Each project lasted at least one semester; some continued for the year. At two sites, the subsequent year's cohort decided to continue with the same topic. The curriculum used by the teachers was adapted by SF Peer Resources, based on existing YPAR curricula (Silva, Zimmerman, & Erbstein, 2001; Sydlo, 2000).

Intended Outcomes

The intended outcomes, with respect to the school setting, were to establish opportunities for students to participate in school governance and shape school practices by sharing with administrators research-based recommendations aimed at improving the school in areas of concern to the students. Other intended school-level effects included improving alliances between students and adult staff, creating opportunities for students and adults to engage together in inquiry relevant to the school and to students, and enhancing students' collective efficacy to enact thoughtful and high-quality research and advocacy activities. The intended outcomes for students included (a) strengthening knowledge and skills regarding research, communication, strategic thinking, collaborative group work, and advocacy and (b) enhancing positive ethnic identity, sense of purpose, connection to school, and motivation to influence the school.

Overview of YPAR Processes

In the issue selection phase, the teacher-facilitators led multiple class sessions intended to help students decide on a topic as a group and to pick a topic that was within the scope of feasible action. The issue selection process started with students' creation of an "issue tree," consisting of branches of "leaves," that is, post-it notes representing problems that were organized in terms of domains and hypothesized "root" causes. These issues were generated by the students, based on their experiences and informal interviews with students, teachers, and parents. In structured activities, students advocated and voted for their choice of topics, with the teacher-facilitator assisting the group in respecting differing views and working together to achieve consensus. Students also looked for ways to combine topics or identify cross-cutting themes, for example, peer pressure being related to several topics, including sex and drugs.

With training and guidance from their teachers and the university team, students then engaged in a research phase to study and understand the problem, using a range of survey, interview, observational, and multimedia approaches for data collection. Following this, in the action phase, the teacher-facilitators helped students to identify specific and feasible actions that they could take to start to address the problem, with the understanding that it was likely beyond the scope of the project to fully solve it.

Students' Use of Multiple Methods

The training of the teacher-facilitators and the curricula used in the YPAR projects emphasized the value of multiple types of research methods for data gathering. In one of the first training exercises, students engaged in a "research roundtable" in which they walked around the room to different "stations" with examples of data generated by surveys, interviews, observations, or photovoice and were invited to reflect on the strengths and limitations of each form of data. In their actual projects, after the YPAR students identified their topic, they engaged in parallel discussions to determine the methods they would use to gather data. As in professional multimethods research projects (Yoshikawa, Weisner, Kalil, & Way, 2008), the students sometimes used multiple methods sequentially, for example, starting with a survey to assess the major concerns of students in the school and then moving into using other methods, such as observations, to obtain more fine-grained data regarding their specific topic.

One example of the sequential multimethods approach was the Best Practices Club, a project in which students focused on how to improve the teaching at a majority-Latino school with low graduation rates (Ozer & Wright, 2012). With guidance from their teacher-facilitator, the students decided to focus on "boring teaching" as a reason why some students did not attend and stay engaged in class. They developed an observation method (observing in pairs in order to compare notes) and conducted interviews with teachers before and after the observations to identify issues of concern for the teacher and provide feedback to teachers on practices that seemed to work to engage diverse learners.

In interviews conducted with the school principal and staff about the effects and challenges of this Best Practices Club project, a strong theme that emerged was that the students' observations were actually more valid than the principal's own observations of classroom practice. The teachers noted that they "forgot" that the student was an observer and therefore acted more naturally than they did when the principal or other adults conducted observations in their classroom. Our study findings also indicated that the transition to seeing students, especially low-performing students, as "experts" who had important perspectives and data that related to the issues of student engagement and academic performance was a major shift in how the adult staff viewed the students and in how the students viewed themselves (Ozer & Wright, 2012). Lastly, we noted that the ways that students were able to contribute to the school as youth researchers differed from the role of student leaders on an existing principal advisory board;

the teacher who led both efforts noted that students' advisory board input tended to be simplistic and punitive of students (e.g., steeper punishment for lateness), whereas the YPAR process led to nuanced, data-informed recommendations from students that considered multiple perspectives.

Research Team's Use of Multiple Methods to Study YPAR

In addition to students' use of multiple methods within their YPAR projects, our research team developed and utilized a range of methods to study the processes and outcomes of YPAR on both the individual student and the school setting levels. Our integration of qualitative and quantitative methods occurred in multiple ways over the course of the project, with the relative dominance of quantitative versus qualitative data varying with the research questions and the stages of the project (Yoshikawa et al., 2008).

YPAR Outcomes

For the assessment of outcomes with respect to psychological empowerment, we used group interviews with students, interviews with teachers, and observations in the early stages of the project to develop items to pilot new subscales of psychological empowerment and adapt existing measures (Ozer & Schotland, 2010). We used this formative research to consider the question of the potential effects of YPAR on the students, beyond what might be captured by existing psychological measures. Even after developing and testing the quantitative measure, however, we continued to conduct group interviews with all of the YPAR classes and with the teachers at the end of each semester to make sure that we captured the narrative of the project, as well as how the impact (or lack thereof) was understood and experienced by the students themselves.

YPAR Processes

Having in-depth process data regarding what was happening in the YPAR projects was critical to avoiding a "black box" evaluation of YPAR. Because classroom and school contexts differed, and the projects' topics also varied, it was essential to assess rather than assume implementation with respect to YPAR processes and their degree of intensity and quality. To address these questions, we used initial open-ended field notes gathered by the research team to generate an observational rating scale with illustrative quotes. This observational rating scale was based on our theory of change and integrated existing observational quantitative scales to assess general classroom practices (e.g., student engagement) as well as specialized scales we developed to capture the core YPAR processes discussed earlier (Ozer & Douglas, 2015). The research team then used this hybrid rating scale to generate implementation quality ratings in weekly observations of the YPAR classes at each site.

Although this in-depth assessment of classroom interactions was necessary, we found that it was not sufficient to capture larger intervention processes that occurred over the course of the project. Examples of what we termed "metalevel processes" included the degree of shared power between the teacher-facilitator and students and the integration of research and practice. These were assessed by the research group via a consensus coding process, based on triangulation of the range of quantitative and qualitative process data for each semester cohort (i.e., teacher interviews, teacher meeting notes, student interviews, and observational ratings).

CONCLUSION

This chapter has provided an integrative overview of the practice, evidence, and promise of YPAR as a multidimensional approach to community research and youth development with an explicit focus on reducing inequalities in schools and communities. YPAR serves as a potential pathway for schools and communities to benefit from youth's expertise and as a pipeline for economically and politically marginalized youth into community-engaged inquiry and action. Furthermore, we note that the critical inquiry and communication skills emphasized in YPAR are consistent with the new Common Core standards that have been adopted in almost all US states (Kornbluh, Ozer, Kirshner, & Allen, unpublished data).

With respect to YPAR resources, there are excellent curricula for conducting YPAR that are available at little or no cost that schools and organizations can access (Silva et al., 2001; Sydlo, 2000) In addition, Web sites exist that provide rich photographic and video examples of the products of YPAR for adult facilitators, as well as models for young people to see what is possible (Center for Regional Change, Public Science Project, The Institute for Community Research). Notably, a 2014 Emmy-nominated documentary, *The Revolutionary Optimists*, provided an in-depth narrative of a project conducted by youth researchers seeking to bring drinking water and promote immunizations in their slum neighborhood of Kolkata, India (Grainger-Monsen & Newnham, 2013). Finally, I am in the process of developing an interactive Web platform, the YPAR Hub, to support and highlight the findings of YPAR (please contact me for further details).

Despite the existence of many exemplary YPAR projects, there has been little discussion in the YPAR literature about how to support networks of YPAR projects so that youth researchers learn from each other and potentially work together to maximize their impact on issues of shared concern. Several big questions currently facing the field include the following: (a) How can YPAR diffuse beyond specific sites to grow into a practice that can benefit youth and communities more broadly? (b) What are the potential opportunities and "spaces" to embed YPAR within other large-scale efforts, such as the reform of schools and other youth-serving systems? (c) How do we support the capacity to do YPAR well, particularly as it is a flexible process rather than a fixed, manualized curriculum? As has hopefully been evident throughout this chapter, the challenge of doing YPAR well is concerned not only with the quality and trustworthiness of the research inquiry and products but with the intentionality and skills in promoting the core empowerment and youth development goals of YPAR. Thus, supporting the high-quality diffusion of YPAR goes beyond the training of specific skills or tools and encompasses an equity and youth development framework.

YPAR is an important and growing approach to community research. Key challenges for YPAR researchers to address in the coming years are the promotion and assessment of YPAR's impact beyond the relatively small projects conducted to date and the identification of opportunities for YPAR and other forms of youth-generated data to inform youths' school systems and the communities in which they live.

AUTHOR NOTE

The research described in this chapter was supported by a William T. Grant Scholars' Award and funding from the Centers for Disease Control and Prevention. The YPAR Hub Web platform project is funded by an award from the Peder Sather Center for Advanced Study at University of California-Berkeley. The author thanks Jackson Masters and Christine Kyauk for assistance in manuscript preparation; the high school students who participated in the projects; San Francisco Peer Resources (especially Elizabeth Hubbard, Gary Cruz, Adee Horn, Morgan Wallace, and Pui Ling Tam) and SFUSD for collaboration in the research projects; and Laura Douglas, Miranda Ritterman, Marieka Schotland, Yolanda Anyon, Maggie Wanis, Eddy Jara, Sami Newlan, and the University of California-Berkeley graduate and undergraduate research teams who assisted with the research.

REFERENCES

Balazs, C. L., & Morello-Frosch, R. (2013). The three R's: How community based participatory research strengthens the rigor, relevance and reach of science. *Environmental Justice, 6*(1), 9–16.

Berg, M., Coman, E., & Schensul, J. J. (2009). Youth action research for prevention: A multi-level intervention designed to increase efficacy and empowerment among urban youth. *American Journal of Community Psychology, 43*, 345–359.

Breckwich Vásquez, V., Lanza, D., Hennessey-Lavery, S., Facente, S., Halpin, H. A., & Minkler, M. (2007). Addressing food security through public policy action in a community-based participatory research partnership. *Health Promotion Practice, 8*, 342–349.

Brown, T. M., & Rodriguez, L. F. (2009). *Youth in participatory action research*. San Francisco, CA: Jossey-Bass/Wiley.

Cahill, C., Rios-Moore, I., & Threatts, T. (2008). Open eyes-different eyes: PAR as a process of personal and social transformation. In J. Cammarota & M. Fine (Eds.), *Revolutionizing education: Youth participatory action research in motion* (pp. 89–124). New York, NY: Routledge.

Cammarota, J., & Fine, M. (Eds.). (2008). *Revolutionizing education: Youth participatory action research*. New York, NY: Routledge.

Cargo, M., Grams, G., Ottoson, J., Ward, P., & Green, L. (2003). Empowerment as fostering positive youth development and citizenship. *American Journal of Health Behavior, 27*(Suppl 1), S66–S79.

Catalani, C., & Minkler, M. (2010). Photovoice: A review of the literature in health and public health. *Health Education & Behavior, 37*, 424–451.

Chen, P., Weiss, F. L., & Nicholson, H. J. (2010). Girls Study Girls Inc.: Engaging girls in evaluation through participatory action research. *American Journal of Community Psychology, 46,* 228–237.

Cook, T., & Campbell, D. (1979). *Quasi-experimentation: Design and analysis issues for field settings.* Chicago, IL: Rand-McNally.

Damon, W. (2003). The development of purpose during adolescence. *Applied Developmental Science, 3,* 119–128.

Dill, L. J. (2015). Poetic justice: Engaging in participatory narrative analysis to find solace in the "killer corridor." *American Journal of Community Psychology, 1-2,* 128–135.

Eccles, J. S., Midgley, C., Wigfield, A., & Buchanan, C. M. (1993). Development during adolescence: The impact of stageenvironment fit on young adolescents' experiences in schools and in families. *American Psychologist, 48,* 90–101.

Findholt, N. E., Michael, Y. L., & Davis, M. M. (2011). Photovoice engages rural youth in childhood obesity prevention. *Public Health Nursing, 28,* 186–192.

Fine, M. (2008). An epilogue, of sorts. In J. Cammarota & M. Fine (Eds.), *Revolutionizing education: Youth participatory action research in motion* (pp. 213–234). New York, NY: Routledge.

Freire, P. (1994). *Pedagogy of hope: Reliving pedagogy of the oppressed.* New York, NY: Continuum Press.

Garcia A.P., Minkler, M., Cardenas, Z., Grills, C, & Porter C. (2014). Engaging homeless youth in community-based participatory research: A case study from Skid Row, Los Angeles. *Health Promotion Practice, 15,* 18–27.

García Coll, C. T., Lamberty, G., Jenkins, R., McAdoo, H. P., Crnic, K., Wasik, B. H., & Vazquez García, H. (1996). An integrative model for the study of developmental competencies in minority children. *Child Development, 67,* 1891–1914.

Gibson, J. E., Flaspohler, P. D., & Watts, V. (2015). Engaging youth in bullying prevention through community-based participatory research. *Family and Community Health, 38,* 120–130.

Ginwright, S., Noguera, P., & Cammarota, J. (Eds.). (2006). *Beyond resistance! Youth activism and community change: New democratic possibilities for practice and policy for america's youth.* New York, NY: Routledge.

Grainger-Monsen, M., & Newnham, N. (Producers) & Grainger-Monsen, M., & Newnham, N. (Directors). (2013). *The revolutionary optimists* [Motion picture]. India: Zoetrope Aubry Productions.

Gregory, A., & Weinstein, R. S. (2008). The discipline gap and African Americans: Defiance or cooperation in the high school classroom. *Journal of School Psychology, 46,* 455–475.

Holden, D., Evans, W. D., Hinnant, L., & Messeri, P. (2005). Modeling psychological empowerment among youth involved in local tobacco control efforts. *Health Education and Behavior, 32,* 264–278.

Horelli, L., & Kaaja, M. (2002). Opportunities and constraints of internet-assisted urban planning with young people. *Journal of Environmental Psychology, 22,* 191–200.

Kirshner, B. (2007). Supporting youth participation in school reform: Preliminary notes from a university-community partnership. *Children, Youth and Environments, 17,* 354–363.

Kohfeldt, D., Chhun, L., Grace, S., & Langhout, R. D. (2011). Youth empowerment in context: Exploring tensions in school-based YPAR. *American Journal of Community Psychology, 47,* 28–45.

Langhout, R. D., & Thomas, E. (2010). Imagining participatory action research in collaboration with children: An introduction. *American Journal of Community Psychology, 26,* 60–66.

Larson, R., Walker, K., & Pearce, N. (2005). A comparison of youth-driven and adult-driven youth programs: Balancing inputs from youth and adults. *Journal of Community Psychology, 33,* 57–74.

London, J., Zimmerman, K., & Erbstein, N. (2003). Youth-led research and evaluation: Tools for youth, organizational, and community development. *New Directions in Evaluation, 98,* 33–45.

McIntyre, M. (2000). Constructing meaning about violence, school, and community: Participatory action research with urban youth. *Urban Review, 32,* 123–154.

Midgley, C., & Feldlaufer, H. (1987). Students' and teachers' decision-making fit before and after the transition to junior high school. *Journal of Early Adolescence, 7,* 225–241.

Minkler, M., Vásquez, V., & Shepard, P. (2006). Promoting environmental health policy through community based participatory research: A case study from Harlem, New York. *Journal of Urban Health, 83,* 101–110.

Minkler, M., & Wallerstein, N. (2003). *Community-based participatory research for health.* San Francisco, CA: Jossey-Bass.

Mitra, D. L. (2004). The significance of students: Can increasing student voice in schools lead to gains in youth development? *Teachers College Record, 106,* 651–688.

Nieto, S. (1996). Lessons from students on creating a chance to dream. *Harvard Education Review, 64,* 392–426.

Ozer, E. J., Cantor, J. P., Cruz, G. W., Fox, B., Hubbard, E., & Moret, L. (2008). The diffusion of youth-led participatory research in urban schools: The role of the prevention support system in implementation and sustainability. *American Journal of Community Psychology, 41,* 278–289.

Ozer, E. J., & Douglas, L. (2015). Assessing the key processes of youth-led participatory research: Psychometric analysis and application of an observational rating scale. *Youth and Society, 47,* 29–50.

Ozer, E. J., Newlan, S., Douglas, L., & Hubbard, E. (2013). "Bounded" empowerment: Analyzing tensions in the practice of youth-led participatory research in urban public schools. *American Journal of Community Psychology, 52,* 13–26.

Ozer, E. J., Ritterman, M., & Wanis, M. (2010). Participatory action research (PAR) in middle school: Opportunities, constraints, and key processes. *American Journal of Community Psychology, 46,* 152–166.

Ozer, E. J., & Schotland, M. (2010). Psychological empowerment among urban youth: Measure development and relationship to psychosocial functioning. *Health Education and Behavior, 38,* 348–356.

Ozer, E. J., Wanis, M. G., & Bazell, N. (2010). Diffusion of school-based prevention programs in two urban districts: Adaptations, rationales, and suggestions for change. *Prevention Science, 11,* 42–55.

Ozer, E. J., & Wright, D. (2012). Beyond school spirit: The effects of youth-led participatory action research in two urban high schools. *Journal of Research on Adolescence, 22,* 267–283.

Pinderhughes, H. (1997). *Race in the hood: Conflict and violence among urban youth*: Minneapolis: University of Minnesota Press.

Sarason, S. B. (1996). *Revisiting "The culture of the school and the problem of change."* New York, NY: Teachers College Press.

Seyer-Ochi, I. (2006). Lived landscapes of the Fillmore. Innovations in educational ethnography: Theory, methods, and results. In G. D. Spindler & L. A. Hammond (Eds.), *Innovations in educational ethnography: Theory, methods, and results* (pp.162–232). Mahwah, NJ: Psychology Press.

Shor, I. (1996). *When students have the power: Negotiating authority in critical pedagogy.* Chicago, IL: University of Chicago Press.

Silva, E., Zimmerman, K., & Erbstein, N. (2001). *Youth rep: Step by step: An introduction to youth-led evaluation and research.* Oakland, CA: Youth in Focus.

Simmons, R. (1987). *Moving into adolescence: The impact of pubertal change and school context.* Hawthorne, NY: Aldine de Gruyter.

Spencer, M. B., Fegley, S. G., & Harpalani, V. (2003). A theoretical and empirical examination of identity as coping: Linking coping resources to the self processes of African American youth. *Applied Developmental Science, 7,* 181–188.

Stovall, D., & Delgado, N. (2009). "Knowing the ledge": Participatory action research as legal studies for urban high school youth. *New Directions for Youth Development, 2009,* 67–81.

Sydlo, S. J. (2000). *Participatory action research: Curriculum for empowering youth.* Hartford, CN: National Teen Action Research Center, Institute for Community Research.

Vaughan, C. (2014). Participatory research with youth: Idealising safe social spaces or building transformative links in difficult environments? *Journal of Health Psychology, 19,* 184–192.

Vygotsky, L. S. (1978). *Mind and society: The development of higher mental processes.* Cambridge, MA: Harvard University Press.

Wallerstein, N., Sanchez, V., & Velarde, L. (2005). Freirian praxis in health education and community organizing: A case study of an adolescent prevention program. In M. Minkler (Ed.), *Community organizing and community building for health* (2nd ed., pp. 218–236). New Brunswick, NJ: Rutgers University Press.

Watts, R. J., Diemer, M. A., & Voight, A. M. (2011). Critical consciousness: Current status and future directions. *New Directions for Child and Adolescent Development, 2011,* 43–57.

Watts, R. J., & Flanagan, C. (2007). Pushing the envelope on youth civic engagement: A developmental and liberation psychology perspective. *Journal of Community Psychology, 35,* 779–792.

Wilson, N., Dasho, S., Martin, A., Wallerstein, N., Wang, C., & Minkler, M. (2007). Engaging young adolescents in social action through photovoice: The youth empowerment strategies (Yes!) project. *Journal of Early Adolescence, 27,* 241–261.

Yoshikawa, H., Weisner, T. S., Kalil, A., & Way, N. (2008). Mixing qualitative and quantitative research in developmental science: Uses and methodological choices. *Developmental Psychology, 44,* 344–354.

Youth Impact. (2001). *Youth impact report.* San Francisco, CA: Youth in Focus.

Zimmerman, M. A. (2000). Empowerment theory: Psychological, organizational, and community levels of analysis. In J. Rappaport & E. Seidman (Eds.), *Handbook of community psychology* (pp. 43–63). New York, NY: Kluwer Academic/Plenum Press.

27

Participatory Mixed Methods Research Across Cultures

REBECCA VOLINO ROBINSON, E. J. R. DAVID, AND MARA HILL

Understanding diverse human experiences is important in an increasingly globalized world. Research with culturally diverse populations has historically adopted either qualitative or quantitative methods, resulting in a body of literature that is either limited by generalizability or cultural relativity, respectively. Researchers are increasingly interested in mixing qualitative and quantitative research methodology to understand more completely the experiences of diverse populations. Mixed methodology is particularly useful when researching across cultures, as it allows for both cross-cultural (or etic) and cultural (or emic) investigations of phenomena. Incorporating community participation into mixed methods research designs increases the usefulness and potential benefits of the research process and its findings when working across cultures, especially with historically and contemporarily marginalized cultural groups.

In this chapter, we begin by acknowledging philosophical assumptions and research paradigms as a framework for discussing cross-cultural and cultural approaches to research. Next, we present participatory methods that are particularly salient to research across cultures (i.e., developing community partnerships, engaging cultural advisory boards, and creating knowledge mobilization plans), followed by an overview of mixed methodology and data integration strategies. Finally, we describe a participatory mixed methods study of resilience in the context of Somali culture and forced displacement. This study demonstrates the use of participatory mixed methods across cultures and shows how data can be integrated into a culturally and contextually grounded model of resilience.

INTRODUCTION TO CROSS-CULTURAL AND CULTURAL RESEARCH PARADIGMS

Underlying all scientific inquiry are assumptions about the nature and form of reality (ontology), the nature of knowing (epistemology), and the role of values and power in the production and ownership of knowledge (axiology). Research paradigms (or "worldviews") reflect these assumptions (Guba & Lincoln, 2005). Most community-based research can be categorized into three research paradigms: postpositivist, constructivist, and transformative.

Nelson and Prilleltensky (2010) explained how the ontological, epistemological, and axiological assumptions underlying each research paradigm align with a particular class of research methodology. The postpositivist research paradigm, for example, assumes the existence of a single, external reality that can be explained, predicted, and controlled. Quantitative research methods are primarily used, with the goal of producing universal, generalizable knowledge. On the other hand, the constructivist research paradigm assumes multiple realities, relative to the constructions of multiple stakeholders of the research, including the researcher. Qualitative methods are primarily used, with the goal of understanding and interpreting multiple realities. Finally, the transformative research paradigm assumes the existence of an external reality that has evolved throughout history and is situated within social and institutional structures. Qualitative, quantitative, and mixed methods are used, with the ultimate goals of raising critical consciousness and encouraging social change. The distinguishing methodological feature of the transformative research paradigm is the use of participatory methodology (Nelson & Prilleltensky, 2010).

Positioning research within particular research paradigms helps explain methodological choices and contextualizes the validity of research findings. Research with culturally diverse populations has historically aligned with either the postpositivist or constructivist research paradigms, resulting in two common methodological approaches to this area of research: the cross-cultural (or etic) approach and the cultural (or emic) approach (Berry, 1999; Kağitçibaşi & Poortinga, 2000).

Cross-Cultural and Cultural Research

Although there are always exceptions to the rough categorizations of the various research areas (e.g., cross-cultural research, cultural research, ethnic minority research), cross-cultural research is most aligned with the postpositivist research paradigm. Assumptions of a measureable reality and objectivity are reflected in the common use of quantitative methods (Prince, 2014). Cross-cultural research examines culture from the outside to identify similarities and differences between cultures and categorizes cultures as either one way or the other, for example, either collectivistic or individualistic (Zhu & Bergiela-Chiappini, 2013).

The World Health Organization (WHO) International Pilot Study of Schizophrenia (IPSS) exemplifies a postpositivist, cross-cultural approach to research. This large-scale study administered standardized psychiatric interviews and measures to elicit signs and symptoms of schizophrenia and other mental disorders among a large community cohort (N = 1,202) of patients across nine countries (Colombia, Czechoslovakia, Denmark, India, Nigeria, China, Soviet Union, United Kingdom, United States). The researchers then used these data to diagnose the patients according to the International Classification of Disease. About 400 participants met diagnostic criteria for a schizophrenic disorder, with similar prevalence across the nine countries (Sartorius, Shapiro, Kimura, & Barrett, 1972); follow-up data revealed cross-cultural differences related to recovery (Sartorius, Jablensky, & Shapiro, 1977).

In this study, the use of standardized, quantifiable measures with predetermined items reflects the underlying postpositivist assumption of an objective, measureable, and universal reality. The goal of identifying similarities and differences in rates of schizophrenia across nine countries highlights the cross-cultural approach of classification and comparison. Although cross-cultural research has led to many important discoveries, the approach has also been criticized for its focus on comparative studies and the primary use of quantitative methodology (e.g., Ratner & Hui, 2003). Administering a measure with predetermined questions prevents the emergence of culturally specific responses. Furthermore, most quantitative measures were developed by Western researchers and validated with participants living in Western contexts. Inferences from cross-cultural research findings are limited by these methodological characteristics.

Cultural research, on the other hand, is most aligned with the constructivist research paradigm. Assumptions of multiple realities and subjectivity are reflected in the common use of qualitative methods (Kral, Burkhardt, & Kidd, 2002). Cultural research emphasizes understanding culture from the insider perspective. Also, instead of separating cultures into different classifications, cultural research focuses on the details, complexities, and intricacies of one culture (Zhu & Bergiela-Chiappini, 2013).

Suhail, Ikram, Jafri, Sadiq, and Singh (2011) conducted an ethnographic analysis of expressed emotion in Pakistani families of people with schizophrenia. Expressed emotion such as emotional overinvolvement, criticism, and hostility is widely understood to negatively impact recovery from schizophrenia. However, cross-cultural differences in the form and function of expressed emotion on recovery from schizophrenia are also well documented (Hashemi & Cochrane, 1999). Suhail et al. conducted in-depth interviews with 64 caregivers of people with schizophrenia living in Pakistan and content-analyzed the data, searching for elements of expressed emotion. All three elements of expressed emotion were found in the data; however, culturally distinctive patterns of expressed emotion were noted. For example, emotional overinvolvement was the most salient form of expressed emotion in this study, followed by criticism and hostility. Many of the emotionally overinvolved behaviors described in the study could be considered normative in Pakistan; however, the researchers did note some behaviors that were well above and beyond the cultural expectations. Criticism and hostility were also wrapped in Pakistani cultural norms, most often directed toward socially objectionable behavior.

In Suhail et al.'s study, the use of qualitative interviews and analysis reflected the underlying constructivist assumption of subjectivity and multiple realities. The goal of understanding the indigenous expression of expressed emotion within the Pakistani cultural context highlights the cultural approach of exploration and description. Although cultural research can lead to a more accurate and nuanced understanding of specific cultural experiences, the approach is time-consuming and the research findings lack generalizability.

In summary, most research with culturally diverse populations has historically taken either a cross-cultural or cultural approach, adopting either qualitative or quantitative methods. Using qualitative or quantitative research methods alone, though, inherently limits either the depth or breadth of research findings. Researchers are increasingly interested in mixing quantitative and qualitative research methods (mixed methods)—an approach that allows researchers to form a more comprehensive understanding of diverse human experiences—making the methodology especially suitable for research with culturally diverse populations (Bartholomew & Brown, 2012). Positioning mixed methods research in the transformative research paradigm ensures consideration of power (e.g., power differentials and dynamics) and inclusion of participant voice in the research process (Nelson & Prilleltensky, 2010).

PROMOTING PARTICIPANTS' INVOLVEMENT IN CROSS-CULTURAL AND CULTURAL RESEARCH

Participatory research occurs on a continuum from informal consultation with community representatives, at one end, to fully integrated, participatory methodology where community voice drives all stages of the study, at the other end (Jason, Keys, Suarez-Balcazar, Taylor, & Davis, 2004). Other chapters in this volume describe different forms of participatory research, including community-based participatory research, participatory action research, and photovoice. Here we focus specifically on participatory methods that are helpful for research across cultures. We describe the importance of developing strong community partnerships for facilitation of a participatory research program, the role of cultural advisory boards in participatory research across cultures, and the use of knowledge mobilization plans as a way of disseminating research findings back into the community in culturally and contextually relevant ways.

Community Partnerships

The importance of building strong community partnerships cannot be underestimated in the facilitation of participatory research programs across cultures. Community partnerships may take many forms and can involve formal community organizations or informal community networks. The most important features of the community partnership include trust, reciprocity, and a shared vision for research and action within the community (Christopher, Watts, McCormick, & Young, 2008).

The first author's research program is positioned in the transformative research paradigm. A primary goal of the research program is the promotion of resilience and community empowerment through community-based research and action. Robinson's 5-year partnership with the Refugee Assistance and Immigration Services (RAIS) in Alaska has facilitated this research program. A relationship of trust has built over the 5 years through a variety of research and action programs involving university students, refugee community members, and RAIS.

This community partnership is mutually beneficial to RAIS, the researcher's university, and refugees living in Alaska. RAIS provides a framework for training opportunities in community and clinical psychology (e.g., exposing students to different cultures, and different lived realities of people), and university students and academics provide services to refugees (and RAIS) through practicum placements (e.g., job application assistance, assessments, therapy) and a community-based research program (e.g., community needs assessment, resilience promotion). The partnership involves a shared vision of improving the health and well-being of refugees resettling in Alaska.

Each research project conducted through this partnership involves the development of cultural advisory boards. The cultural advisory boards are comprised of members of specific refugee communities within which the research will occur. These cultural advisory boards are supported by the same facets of trust, reciprocity, and shared vision for the research.

Cultural Advisory Boards

Cultural advisory boards are one way of integrating community voice into the research process (Liebenberg & Ungar, 2009). In our research, cultural advisory boards are explicitly organized at the onset of a study. The cultural advisory board is comprised of individuals from inside the cultural community. The purpose of the board is to provide direction in the design, implementation, interpretation, and dissemination of the research. The cultural advisory boards have decision-making power (along with the research team), helping to equalize power dynamics across the stakeholders.

It is important to consider cultural, linguistic, and power dynamics when engaging in research across cultures (Foster & Stanek, 2007). Navigating these dynamics requires careful consideration of cultural norms and values and the historical context of the interacting cultures. Cultural advisory boards can help researchers navigate this complexity in cross-cultural research, as well as ensure that the research is conducted appropriately within the specific cultural context.

Organizing cultural advisory boards can happen quite naturally within a previously established partnership, such as the partnership described earlier. At other times the development of a cultural advisory board requires building new relationships. It is always important to consider issues of power within cultural communities when selecting members of the advisory board, especially when a preexisting partnership is not yet in place.

In our research, a cultural advisory board is organized at the onset of each study. The board is usually composed of individuals within the cultural community with whom the research will be conducted. The cultural advisory board can serve a variety of roles in the study. For example, the board may help define the research questions, design the study, identify and access research participants, select study measures, adapt and translate (if needed) study measures, interpret findings, and disseminate findings back into the community. We may also bring feedback to the cultural advisory board from research participants, which can lead to changes in the study design or implementation. The degree to which the cultural advisory board participates in the research process varies from study to study, but the function of the board remains consistent. Cultural advisory boards bring the community voice into the research from the onset of the project across all stages of the research. They help ensure the cultural relevance of the research and find ways to disseminate findings back into the community in culturally and contextually relevant ways.

Knowledge Mobilization Plans

The goal of knowledge mobilization (KMb) is to make research useful to a community (Naidorf, 2014). The use of a cultural advisory board is a step in the right direction for KMb. However, we advocate for explicit development of a KMb plan at the outset of a study to enhance the two-way collaboration between researchers and partners and ensure dissemination of the research findings back into the community in culturally and contextually relevant ways. Engaging a cultural advisory board in the creation of a KMb plan is one way to help make the research accessible, understandable, and useful for community members, especially when disseminating the findings back into the community.

In summary, when researchers enter cultures different from their own, the use of participatory methods becomes particularly important to ensuring the research's cultural sensitivity and contextual relevance. Close community partnerships, community advisory boards, and KMb plans are frameworks through which to consider participatory action. With participatory research as our backdrop, we now turn the discussion toward mixed methods research across cultures. Mixing qualitative and quantitative methods can allow researchers to address both cross-cultural and cultural research objectives within the confines of a single study, contributing both breadth and depth of data to the study.

MIXED METHODS RESEARCH ACROSS CULTURES

Mixed methods research is characterized by the collection, analysis, and interpretation of both qualitative and quantitative data within the context of a single study, investigating a single underlying phenomenon (Leech & Onwuegbuzie, 2009). Approaches to mixing methods are vast and allow for innovative research methodologies. Because there are so many ways of mixing methods, researchers may feel overwhelmed about how to choose the best approach for a given research question. In this section, we describe a typology of mixed methods research designs and strategies for integrating qualitative and quantitative data across the various typologies.

Typologies of Mixed Methods Designs

Leech and Onwuegbuzie (2009) created a typology of mixed methods research designs. The typology describes methodological choices along the following three dimensions: a mixing dimension (partially mixed or fully mixed designs), a time dimension (concurrent or sequential collection of quantitative and qualitative data), and an emphasis dimension (equal status or dominant status of qualitative and quantitative data). Design choices along these three dimensions (mixing, time, and emphasis) result in one of eight typologies: (a) partially mixed concurrent equal status design, (b) partially mixed concurrent dominant status design, (c) partially mixed sequential equal status design, (d) partially mixed sequential dominant status design, (e) fully mixed concurrent equal status design, (f) fully mixed concurrent dominant status design, (g) fully mixed sequential equal status design, and (h) fully mixed sequential dominant status design (Leech & Onwuegbuzie, 2009).

Along the mixing dimension, a study is either monomethod (not mixed), partially mixed, or fully mixed. Fully mixed designs integrate qualitative and quantitative methods across or within multiple levels of the study (e.g., research objective, types of data collected, data analysis, interpretation). Partially mixed designs integrate qualitative and quantitative data only at the level of interpretation, after all the data have been collected. Along the time dimension, qualitative and quantitative data can be collected concurrently (e.g., a quantitative survey with a qualitative interview) or sequentially (e.g., qualitative data inform development of a quantitative measure). Along the status dimension, a study might emphasize qualitative or quantitative data or both, resulting in either a dominant or equal status research design (Leech & Onwuegbuzie, 2009).

Integration of Qualitative and Quantitative Data

An important part of mixed methods research is integrating qualitative and quantitative data, producing a sort of conversation between the methodologies. O'Cathain, Murphy, and Nicholl (2010) suggested three techniques for integration in mixed methods studies: triangulation, following a thread, and the mixed method matrix.

Triangulation is commonly used in partially mixed methods designs because it is accomplished at the end of a study. The approach involves examining qualitative and quantitative findings after both sets of data have been analyzed for convergence, complementariness, and contradictions. Exploring intermethod agreement and discrepancy through triangulation can increase understanding of the particular research question.

Following a thread and the mixed method matrix are more aligned with fully mixed methods designs because integration occurs at the level of data analysis (O'Cathain, Murphy, & Nicholl, 2010). Following a thread requires researchers to examine each component of the data for key themes and for questions that require more exploration. They select one question or theme from the data and follow it throughout other components of the study. The mixed method matrix is useful for studies that have qualitative and quantitative data on the same cases in a data set. This approach allows researchers to identify convergence and discrepancy in data within and between cases, increasing the overall understanding of the phenomena of interest (O'Cathain et al., 2010).

In Figure 27.1, we integrate the work of Leech and Onwuegbuzie (2009) and O'Cathain et al. (2010) into a mixed methods decision-making framework for researchers. The framework includes choice points along the mixing dimension, the timing dimension, and the status dimension, along with suggested data integration techniques for each decision point within the framework.

In summary, mixed methods research is well suited for research across cultures. Producing data that are both descriptive and comparable allows for breadth and depth of understanding of a research question. Participatory mixed methods are particularly well suited for research across cultures. In addition to the benefits of incorporating both qualitative and quantitative methods, participatory methods increase the cultural relevance of research findings and introduce opportunities for participant empowerment and advocacy.

In the next section, we present the Somali Resilience Project as an example of a participatory

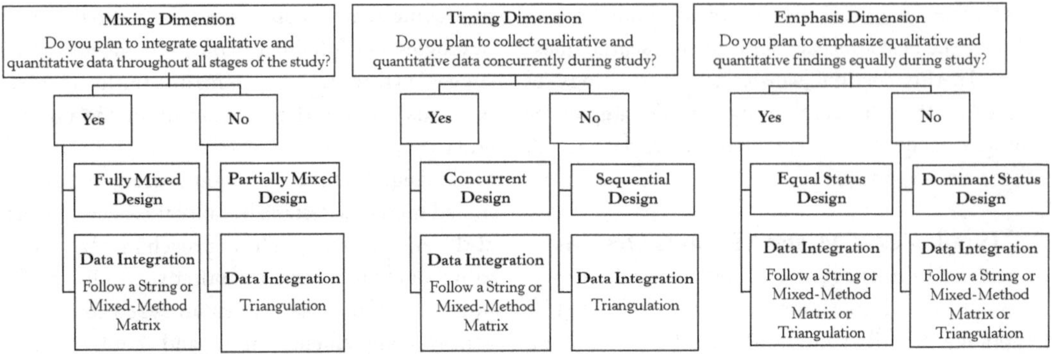

FIGURE 27.1: A mixed methods decision-making framework.

mixed methods study of resilience in the context of Somali culture and forced displacement. The study demonstrates how a close community partnership can lead to collaboratively developed research questions, initial study design, establishment of a cultural advisory board, and development of an explanatory model based on the findings.

CASE STUDY

The Somali Resilience Project used a participatory, sequential, partially mixed methods, equal status research design to examine pathways to resilience in the context of Somali culture and forced displacement. We wanted to understand what helped Somali refugees cope in the context of exposure to stress and adversity, and then work to promote resilience in the context of refugee resettlement.

Defining Resilience

The work of Ungar and Liebenberg (2009) at the Dalhousie Resilience Research Centre in Halifax, Nova Scotia, provided some groundwork for the study of resilience across cultures. The researchers completed the International Resilience Project (IRP), a participatory, mixed methods study on resilience among youth living in developing nations and in marginalized communities in Canada and the United States (Ungar & Liebenberg, 2009). They collected and analyzed life histories of youth living in these marginalized contexts, conducted community focus groups, and collaboratively developed and pilot tested the Child and Youth Resilience Measure (CYRM) across 14 research sites in 10 countries. From these data, Ungar (2008) posed the following contextual definition of resilience, which guided our inquiry into Somali resilience:

> In the context of exposure to significant adversity, whether psychological, environmental, or both, resilience is both the capacity of individuals to navigate their way to health-sustaining resources, including opportunities to experience feelings of well-being, and a condition of the individual's family, community and culture to provide these health resources and experiences in culturally meaningful ways. (p. 225)

This definition highlights the process of navigating and negotiating for health-sustaining resources, emphasizing the dynamic and contextually embedded nature of resilience. These navigation and negotiation processes help explain how more static resilience factors (e.g., individual, family, community) can work together to promote culturally meaningful and contextually embedded pathways toward resilience. Ungar and Liebenberg (2009) recommended using mixed methodology when researching resilience across cultures and advocated the use of cultural advisory committees during all phases of investigation.

Research Design

The Somali Resilience Project addressed both cultural and cross-cultural research objectives. We sought to understand the cultural intricacies of resilience among Somali refugees (cultural) in ways that were comparable across contexts (Somalia, refugee camps, and the United States) and cultures (cross-cultural). With a strong community partnership already in place (see previous discussion of Robinson and RAIS), we put together a cultural advisory board at the onset of the study. Cultural advisors were chosen based on their experiences with Somali culture, language, and community and their interest in the study. The cultural advisors helped design the research project; develop the qualitative interview protocol; conduct interviews; select, translate, and culturally adapt quantitative study measures; design the quantitative survey; and interpret and disseminate research findings.

Methodology and Results

The study was completed in three phases. During the first phase, we conducted in-depth qualitative interviews with 10 Somali refugees living in the United States about their experiences of adversity and coping across three distinct contexts (Somalia, refugee camps, and the United States). We sought to answer the following research questions: How do Somali refugees living in the United States conceptualize resilience? What resources contribute to resilience across contexts? How do context and culture shape experiences of resilience?

The research team and cultural advisors met regularly during qualitative data collection to listen to interviews, discuss narratives and emergent themes, and develop a codebook for qualitative data analysis. All of the interviews were transcribed and then uploaded into NVivo qualitative data analysis software. We subjected the data to thematic coding procedures in order to identify major themes in the data related to the aforementioned research questions. The following five main themes emerged from the data: (a) adversity across contexts, (b) health-sustaining resources, (c) individual characteristics, (d) family culture and relational networks, and (e) Islamic beliefs and meaning in life.

The most common forms of adversity noted by participants included exposure to physical and sexual violence, death of loved ones, harsh environmental conditions (e.g., semiarid environment, drought), lack of food and water, acculturation stress (e.g., communication difficulties, value conflicts), and discrimination. These experiences differed across contexts. Health-sustaining resources emerged in a hierarchy of needs, with physiological needs forming the base of the pyramid (e.g., access to clean water, food), followed by safety, shelter, and protection from violence. Opportunities for growth (e.g., employment, education) emerged as important health-sustaining resources, once basic needs were addressed. Individual characteristics included determination, future orientation, goal directedness, and assertiveness. Family and relational networks were described as essential factors in the navigation and negotiation process. All participants noted Islamic beliefs as the primary source of resilience across contexts. These beliefs produced a meaning-making system and provided direction for moving through extreme adversity.

During the study's second phase, the qualitative results were used for the selection of quantitative measures that we administered during Phase 3 data collection. We chose to administer the Personal Well-being Index, the Meaning in Life Questionnaire, the Postmigration Life Difficulties Questionnaire, and the Resilience Research Center–Adult Resilience Measure (the adult version of the CYRM; Ungar & Liebenberg, 2009). We hired a professional translation service and cultural advisors to engage in a process of translation and back-translation of study materials until the translators and cultural advisors deemed the materials culturally equivalent.

During Phase 3, a quantitative survey of resilience, life difficulties, well-being, and meaning in life, the Resilience Research Center-Adult Resilience Measure (RRC-ARM), was administered to 137 Somali people living in the United States. An exploratory factor analysis (EFA) of the RRC-ARM produced a three-factor (Individual, Relational, and Cultural) structure. The Somali RRC-ARM was positively associated with personal well-being and presence of meaning in life. The measure was negatively correlated with life difficulties. It also was found that resilience (as measured by the Somali RRC-ARM) was positively associated with the presence of meaning in life (MLQ-Presence) and that the presence of meaning in life predicted a good portion of the variance in personal well-being.

Integrated Research Findings

Through careful triangulation of qualitative and quantitative data, the research team and cultural advisors integrated the research findings into a Somali Multidimensional Multilevel Resilience (SMMR) model (see Fig. 27.2). The model brings together common qualitative and quantitative research findings into one cohesive whole. When placed in context, the SMMR model can be used to

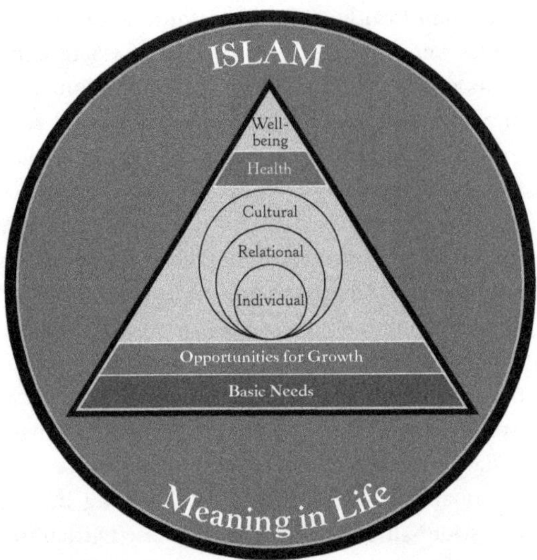

FIGURE 27.2: The Somali Multidimensional Multilevel Resilience model.

assess for individual, family, and cultural resources associated with resilience and to inform relevant interventions aimed at increasing resilience among Somali refugees.

Three levels of the SMMR model (individual, relational, and cultural) are consistent with the quantitative research findings; these are the three factors that emerged through the EFA of the RRC-ARM. The innermost circle of the SMMR model represents the individual. The resilient Somali individual was described in the qualitative data as determined, future-oriented, goal-directed, and assertive. Also, the factor analysis of the RRC-ARM revealed an individual-level factor, with items related to cooperation with others, social and behavioral intelligence, goal orientation, and interpersonal confidence.

The individual is embedded within the family system and other relational networks. Qualitative data clarified the definition of the Somali family and pointed to processes within the family that can promote resilience. For example, participants defined *family* beyond the Western confines of a nuclear family. They included aunts, uncles, cousins, and neighbors in their definitions. Additionally, the Somali family system serves as a conduit of social and emotional support across contexts. Family and relational networks also serve as facilitators toward health-sustaining resources by promoting resource sharing and mobility across contexts. Consistent with the qualitative findings, relational-level items that clustered together on the Somali RRC-ARM included those that captured emotional and social support, sense of security within the family, knowledge of supportive networks in the community, and opportunities to contribute to the broader community.

The qualitative findings suggested that cultural factors of resilience among Somali refugees include affiliation with a religious organization, having a life philosophy, and cultural and/or spiritual identification (e.g., feeling culturally grounded by knowing where one comes from and being part of a cultural tradition that is expressed through daily activities). Consistent with the qualitative results, the quantitative findings revealed that cultural-level items that clustered together on the Somali RRC-ARM included items related to ethnic pride, spiritual beliefs, family openness and communication, sense of belonging, purpose in life, and ability to contribute to the family system.

Based on both the qualitative and quantitative findings, we included a field of existential resilience around the entire model. This field demonstrates a culturally specific and very strong dimension to resilience in the context of Somali culture. The qualitative findings demonstrated how Islam and meaning in life are important and intertwined concepts among Somalis across contexts. The quantitative results supported this finding by statistically demonstrating how resilience and meaning in life are important contributors to personal well-being.

The qualitative results also demonstrated how resilience resides within broader geographic, political, and cultural contexts. Based on the qualitative findings, contextual factors that influence the experience of resilience among Somali refugees include geographic location, climate, and weather; historical context and political structure; safety and security in the environment; availability of sustainable resources; and accessibility of health-sustaining resources (e.g., food, water, safety, education, employment). These contextual factors placed boundaries around the experience of resilience and are essential elements of understanding resilience across cultures and contexts.

The Somali Resilience Project is an example of a participatory, mixed methods research project that addressed both cultural and cross-cultural research objectives within the same study. The project demonstrates how a close community partnership and a cultural advisory board can help ensure that the research methods and findings are culturally and contextually relevant. The cultural advisory board has continued to support this effort through the dissemination process. To date, the findings have been presented in a Somali newspaper in Minnesota, a local newspaper in Alaska, community presentations to Somali community organizations in the United States, and more formal academic outlets. As this study was the first study of refugee resilience conducted through this community partnership, we learned lessons that have informed our current work. For instance, one of these lessons was in the realm of KMb; we now create KMb plans at the outset of our studies to ensure that the dissemination of findings back to the community of study is at the forefront of our research objectives.

CONCLUSION

Participatory mixed methods research is particularly well suited for research across cultures. Mixed methodology allows researchers to address both cross-cultural and cultural research objectives within the context of a single study. Positioning mixed methods research in the transformative research paradigm introduces participatory methodology into the research design. Participatory strategies, such as developing strong community partnerships, utilizing cultural advisory boards, and developing KMb plans, can help break down power dynamics inherent in research across cultures, increase the cultural and contextual relevance of research findings, and ensure dissemination of findings back into the community. Although designing and implementing participatory mixed methods studies can be confusing due to the multitude of ways in which qualitative and quantitative data may be collected, analyzed, and integrated into a cohesive set of findings, we hope that this chapter can help researchers make design choices along the different mixing dimensions and choose data integration strategies in their efforts to conduct participatory mixed methods research projects across cultures.

REFERENCES

Bartholomew, T. T., & Brown, J. R. (2012). Mixed methods, culture, and psychology: A review of mixed methods in culture-specific psychological research. *International Perspectives in Psychology: Research, Practice, Consultation, 1*, 177–190.

Berry, J. W. (1999). Emics and etics: A symbiotic conception. *Culture and Psychology, 5*(2), 165–171.

Christopher, S., Watts, V., McCormick, A. G., & Young, S. (2008). Building and maintaining trust in a community-based participatory research partnership. *American Journal of Public Health, 98*, 1398–1406.

Foster, J., & Stanek, K. (2007). Cross-cultural considerations in the conduct of community-based participatory research. *Family and Community Health, 30*, 42–49.

Guba, E. G., & Lincoln, Y. S. (2005). Paradigmatic controversies, contradictions, and emerging confluences. In N. K. Denzin & Y. S. Lincoln (Eds.), *The Sage handbook of qualitative research* (3rd ed., pp. 191–215). Thousand Oaks, CA: Sage.

Hashemi, A. H., & Cochrane, R. (1999). Expressed emotion and schizophrenia: A review of studies across cultures. *International Review of Psychiatry, 11*, 219–224.

Jason, L. A., Keys, C. B., Suarez-Balcazar, Y., Taylor, R. R., & Davis, M. I. (2004). *Participatory community research: Theories and methods in action*. Washington, DC: American Psychological Association.

Kağitçibaşi, C., & Poortinga, Y. H. (2000). Cross-cultural psychology: Issues and overarching themes. *Journal of Cross-Cultural Psychology, 31*, 129–147.

Kral, M. J., Burkhardt, K. J., & Kidd, S. (2002). The new research agenda for cultural psychology. *Canadian Psychology/Psychologie Canadienne, 43*, 154–162.

Leech, N. L., & Onwuegbuzie, A. J. (2009). A typology of mixed methods research designs. *Quality and Quantity: International Journal of Methodology, 43*, 265–275.

Liebenberg, L., & Ungar, M. (2009). *Researching resilience*. Toronto, Canada: University of Toronto Press.

Lincoln, Y., & Guba, E. (1985). *Naturalistic inquiry*. Beverly Hills, CA: Sage.

Naidorf, J. J. (2014). Knowledge utility: From social relevance to knowledge mobilization. *Education Policy Analysis Archives, 22*, 1–31.

Nelson, G., & Prilleltensky, I. (Eds). (2010). *Community psychology: In pursuit of liberation and well-being*. New York, NY: Palgrave Macmillan.

O'Cathain, A., Murphy, E., & Nicholl, J. (2010). Three techniques for integrating data in mixed methods studies. *BMJ (Clinical Research Ed.), 341*, c4587.

Prince, M. J. (2014). Cross-cultural research methods and practice. In V. Patel, H. Minas, A. Cohen, & M. J. Prince (Eds.), *Global mental health: Principles and practice* (pp. 63–81). New York, NY: Oxford University Press.

Ratner, C., & Hui, L. (2003). Theoretical and methodological problems in cross-cultural psychology. *Journal for the Theory of Social Behaviour, 33*, 67–94.

Sartorius, N., Jablensky, A., & Shapiro, R. (1977). Two-year follow-up of the patients included in the WHO International Pilot Study of Schizophrenia. *Psychological Medicine, 7*, 529–541.

Sartorius, N., Shapiro, R., Kimura, M., & Barrett, K. (1972). WHO international pilot study of schizophrenia. *Psychological Medicine, 2*, 422–425.

Suhail, K., Ikram, A., Jafri, S. Z., Sadiq, S., & Singh, S. P. (2011). Ethnographic analysis of expressed emotions in Pakistani families of patients with schizophrenia. *International Journal of Mental Health, 40*, 86–103.

Ungar, M. (2008). Resilience across cultures. *British Journal of Social Work, 38*, 218–235.

Ungar, M., & Liebenberg, L. (2009). Cross-cultural consultation leading to the development of a valid measure of youth resilience: The International Resilience Project. *Studia Psychologica, 51*, 259–268.

Zhu, Y., & Bargiela-Chiappini, F. (2013). Balancing emic and etic: Situated learning and ethnography of communication in cross-cultural management education. *Academy of Management Learning and Education, 12*, 380–395.

28

Photoethnography in Community-Based Participatory Research

KATHERINE CLOUTIER

Photoethnography is a method well situated to pursue the goals of community-based research. It embraces the idea of learning from research participants' lived realities, allowing for such perspectives to be documented through photo or video (Schwartz, 1989). Although not inherently a community-based method, with slight alteration it becomes one of the strongest opportunities to demonstrate the impact of social issues on individuals and communities. Such alterations integrate the participatory nature of community-based research and the contextual richness of ethnographic approaches.

This chapter begins by providing an overview of photoethnography and describing its potential within a mixed methods research design. A case study will then be presented in which the author describes the implementation of a mixed methods research initiative in Barbados. This research initiative involved the use of photoethnography (specifically the photovoice methodology), quantitative survey methods, and performance ethnography.

INTRODUCTION TO PHOTOETHNOGRAPHY

Photoethnography is situated within the larger framework of visual ethnography and may sometimes be referred to as documentary photographic research, participatory photography, visual anthropology, or visual sociology (Schwartz, 1989; Wang & Burris, 1994). Photoethnography is strongly grounded in ethnographic principles but utilizes photos as data points, as well as opportunities to access further data points (Schwartz, 1989). There are several possibilities for photography to be incorporated into the research process (Schwartz, 1989). For instance, photography is an opportunity for social transaction, suggesting that the meaning behind the photo (from the photographer's perspective) may be just as significant as the interpretation of the photograph by the viewer. There is an interaction that takes place that cannot be overlooked and that remains an integral component of photoethnographic research material.

Schwartz (1989) considered "photographs [are] inherently ambiguous, their specifiable meanings emergent in the viewing process. This ambiguity is not a disadvantage or limitation; rather, the multiple meanings negotiated by viewers can be mined for the rich data they yield" (p. 122). In the research process, photos may be used to elicit data from participants, may be created by participants, may document aspects about communities, or may guide interviews with research participants. The use of photographs in the research process is dependent on several factors related to the research project, including the community, the issue being explored, the resources available, and the type of data being sought (Schwartz, 1989).

Some scholars classify photoethnography as "inevitably collaborative and to varying extents participatory" (Pink, 2008, p. 2). However, the strength in integrating photographs into the research process lies very much in the ability to understand and disseminate ideas from multiple viewpoints. As an approach, it allows for the understanding of both shared and distinct experiences within and across communities. It requires a strong engagement with and embracing of multiple ways of knowing social issues from multiple perspectives (Pink, 2008; Schwartz, 1989; Singhal & Rattine-Flaherty, 2006).

Embracing the Theoretical Foundation and Implementing Methods

Participatory photoethnography is built on feminist, empowerment, and social justice theories. Wang and Burris (1994) began using a method they referred to as *photo novella* to better understand health concerns among women in rural China. This method, later referred to as *photovoice*, promotes an expert role among participants and acknowledges community members as coinvestigators regarding research on the social issues that impact their everyday lives.

Photovoice utilizes a community-based participatory research (CBPR) framework, which has now become a widely used approach for conducting scientific inquiry. CBPR includes four major elements in the research process: participation, the coproduction of knowledge and control, praxis (a reflexive, iterative process in which theory and action validate each other; Prilleltensky, 2001), and equitable distribution of power (Wallerstein & Duran, 2003). Embracing these elements of CBPR, Wang and Burris (1997) began using documentary photography as an integral part of the research process. The method intends "to enable people to record and reflect their community's strengths and concerns, to promote critical dialogue and knowledge about important community issues through large and small group discussion of photographs, and to reach policymakers" (Wang & Burris, 1997, p. 370).

Wang (1999) outlined the following steps for the traditional photovoice method: (a) selecting and recruiting a target audience of policymakers or community leaders, (b) recruiting a group of photovoice participants, (c) introducing the photovoice methodology to participants and facilitating a group discussion, (d) obtaining informed consent, (e) posing an initial theme for taking pictures (in the form of framing questions), (f) distributing cameras to participants and reviewing how to use them, (g) providing time for participants to take pictures, (h) meeting to discuss the photographs, and (i) planning with participants a format to share photographs and stories with policymakers or community leaders.

Photovoice projects begin with the creation of research questions, which are broken down into more concise questions, referred to as framing questions. These framing questions are simple questions related to the larger research theme and are phrased in a way that participants are able to respond to them through photos and text. Once the participants complete the photovoice training and project orientation (which is covered in the first meeting for photovoice projects), the framing questions are presented (Wang, 1999).

Each participant takes a photograph and writes a personal narrative for each of the framing questions presented. The photos and narratives (written and later orally expanded on during the group meetings) serve as data for the research study. During the group meetings, minimal probing by the group facilitators takes place after each individual shares his or her photo and narrative to be sure that each story is understood clearly. This information is analyzed both to understand each unique story related to the project theme and to examine patterns across participants.

During each photovoice meeting a group discussion occurs as well. Facilitators have predeveloped probes that are used to guide the conversations and to gain deeper insight into the participants' experiences with the project theme. These run similarly to focus groups, and often the facilitation questions are constructed in a way that bridges the gap between the research questions and the framing questions to encourage a critical discourse around deeper meanings and themes. This group discourse also contributes to the research data, in that group conversations are recorded and included in the data analysis.

A final step in photovoice projects includes a public outreach component in order to disseminate and act on what was learned with community leaders or some targeted audience. By connecting the voices of individuals to the people who have decision-making power, researchers can help effect social change and facilitate the engagement of community members' voices in conversation regarding policies affecting their everyday lives (Wang, 1999).

The photovoice method is innovative for several reasons. Research participants are cocreating photos that are physical sites for learning and sharing information. It is from these creations that policy influence can happen; directly linking the photos and text to the realities of individuals, and using these photos and texts as a way to elicit change, establishes a clear path for community members to become actively engaged in influencing policy. Allowing participants to have control over the meaning that is ascribed to the realities of their lives also prevents the implementation of misinformed policies (Wang, 1999). Furthermore, cocreating the dissemination tool allows for a participatory analysis of the data, as the emergent themes are often shared through an exhibit or digital story at this point in the study. This step prevents researchers from ascribing misinformed meaning to participants' voices, ensuring that the same oppressive power dynamics that exist in society and lead to poorly informed policymaking are not replicated within the research process (Wang, 1999).

Strengths and Weaknesses of the Method

Photovoice and other photoethnographic methods have many strengths and weaknesses, with the strengths being well suited to fulfill the goals of community psychology. For instance, such methods provide insight into the unique experience of individuals nested within communities (Schwartz, 1989; Wang, 1999; Wang & Burris, 1994). This method creates space for community-based researchers to embrace an ecological systems theory and an intersectionality approach (i.e., one that takes into account the multiple and intersecting structural systems—gender, race, religion, and so on—that shape individuals' lives (Crenshaw, 1991; McCall, 2005)).

The way in which the photovoice method in particular unfolds allows for participants to voice their lived reality, specifically in relation to their social locations and the myriad of systems within which their lives exist (Wang, 1999; Wang & Burris, 1994). However, such methods may be limited in their ability to make larger generalizations about communities or populations, as they are often intended to gain rich insight into both the disparate and shared experiences of smaller, homogenous groups and their members.

Photoethnography and Mixed Methods Designs

Mixed methods designs are defined by Creswell, Klassen, Clark, and Smith (2011, p. 4) by the following criteria: "(a) focusing on research questions that call for real-life contextual understanding, multilevel perspectives, and cultural influences; (b) employing rigorous quantitative research assessing magnitude and frequency of constructs and rigorous qualitative research exploring the meaning and understanding of constructs; (c) utilizing multiple methods; (d) intentionally integrating or combining these methods to draw on the strengths of each; and (e) framing the investigation within philosophical and theoretical positions."

Photoethnography and photovoice provide the latter part of the second point written earlier, in that such methods provide insight into the "meaning and understanding of constructs" (Creswell et al., 2011, p. 4). However, they are lacking in their ability to demonstrate the enormity of social issues. Therefore, implementing photoethnography into a mixed methods design, specifically with survey or other quantitative methods, increases the potential significance or impact of the research.

CASE STUDY

The current project began in 2012, when the author was awarded an mtvU Fulbright scholarship to conduct fieldwork in Barbados. The original research project intended to explore issues solely related to youth sexual health. Unanticipated preliminary findings led to the research moving in a new direction, specifically toward the intersection of sexual health and gender-based violence. In using these preliminary findings, the initial project was further developed into a mixed methods, community-based participatory research initiative. Because it was not the project's original goal to explore gender-based violence, the next section will begin with a brief overview of sexual health, specifically in Barbados. Following this, the two major phases of the project, along with pertinent literature, will be provided. Figure 28.1 provides an overview of the methodological/implementation steps for each phase of the project. These

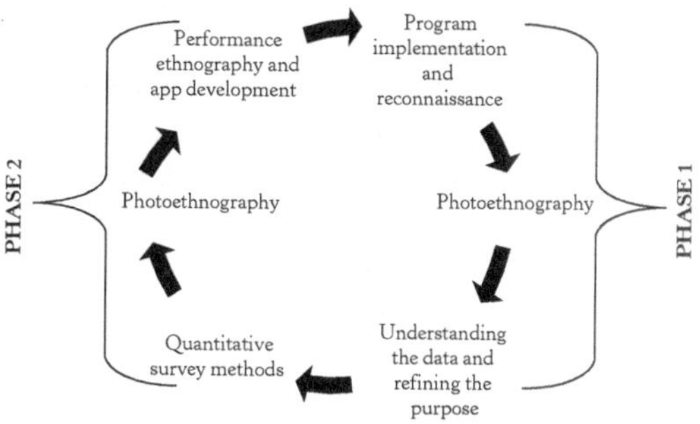

FIGURE 28.1: Overview of Phase 1 and Phase 2 of a photoethnographic community-based research project.

will be described in further detail throughout the remainder of the chapter.

Sexual Health

Sexual and reproductive health has taken many definitions throughout scholarly work but is best understood, through the World Health Organization (2006), as:

> . . . a state of physical, emotional, mental and social well-being in relation to sexuality; it is not merely the absence of disease or infirmity. Sexual health requires a positive and respectful approach to sexuality and sexual relationships, as well as the possibility of having pleasurable and safe sexual experiences, free of coercion, discrimination and violence. (p. 5)

The Joint United Nations Programme on HIV/AIDS (2013) estimated that 35.3 million people across the globe are living with HIV. "There were 2.3 (1.9–2.7) million new HIV infections globally, showing a 33% decline in the number of new infections from 3.4 (3.1–3.7) million in 2001" (UNAIDS, 2013, p. 4). With more than 1 million people acquiring a sexually transmitted infection (STI) every day (World Health Organization, 2013b), controlling STIs is now considered to be at the center of HIV prevention work (UNAIDS, 1999).

Barbados, West Indies

The island of Barbados is home to approximately 273,000 people (UNFPA, 2008a). The Joint United Nations Programme on HIV/AIDS has estimated that there are between 1,300 and 1,800 people living with HIV in Barbados, with an estimated HIV prevalence rate between 0.8% and 1.1% (of adults aged 15 to 49 years old). The percentage of individuals 15 to 24 years old living with HIV is estimated to be between 0.3% and 0.5% (UNAIDS, 2013). Research from the Joint United Nations Programme on HIV/AIDS (2010) has demonstrated that stigma and discrimination have had profound and direct effects on increased mortality rates in Barbados; many instances in which an HIV-positive individual has delayed his or her treatment are related to the experience of stigma and discrimination. Although heterosexual contact is the primary mode of transmission of HIV in the country, at-risk groups are consistently pushed out to the periphery of health care and outreach consideration. Among these groups are sex workers and men who have sex with men (UNGASS, 2008).

Phase 1: mtvU Fulbright Fieldwork

The first phase of the project involved approximately 1 year of fieldwork. There were various components of the fieldwork, including partnership building, program implementation, and community-based participatory research. Three main steps from this phase are highlighted next.

Phase 1, Step 1: Program Implementation and Reconnaissance

The primary community partner was an organization called dance4life. dance4life is an international program that is implemented in 28 countries worldwide. A core curriculum was developed by the original program in Amsterdam, and since its inception the curriculum has been adopted by each new country program and adapted to meet each community's particular cultural context. There are four core components to the dance4life program, including inspire, educate, activate, and celebrate. Each phase represents a different purpose of dance4life; however, the most significant aspects tend to be the educate and activate stages. During these stages the youth involved in the program are taught the entire dance4life curriculum (focused on youth issues, specifically sexual health and HIV) and are expected to turn what they have learned throughout the program into some form of community action (dance4life, n.d.).

dance4life Barbados is the primary program across the island that engages youth in comprehensive sex education, using music, dance, and peer education to inspire young people to make change among themselves and their communities. Partnering with the National HIV/AIDS Commission in Barbados, dance4life has developed its curriculum to provide HIV education and to meet the context of the communities with which it works. Recently, it has expanded into new settings in addition to the secondary schools with which it already partners (e.g., collaborating with a children's home and a specialized school for girls in the juvenile justice system) (dance4life Barbados, n.d.).

The author was fully involved in the implementation of the dance4life Barbados program in the secondary schools upon the start of the mtvU Fulbright scholarship. Participating in program delivery allowed the author to better understand the community partner's approach to sexual health education, to increase her knowledge regarding the contextual elements that impact sexual health and sexuality among young people in Barbados, and to gain access to secondary school students to recruit for the next step of the first phase of the project.

Phase 1, Step 2: Photoethnography

The photovoice methodology, as a photoethnographic approach, was decided upon as the primary opportunity for youth engagement and data collection during the project's first phase. As such, the mtvU Fulbright photovoice project was implemented in two schools with which the dance4life program was already in partnership. The author, along with the dance4life staff, adapted the photovoice method to incorporate the use of video; therefore, photovoice and videovoice were the primary methods of data collection to learn about youth issues throughout the early stages of this project. Aside from the incorporation of video, the photovoice method was implemented as described in earlier sections of the chapter. An overview is provided in Figure 28.2 to emphasize the main steps. Each of the steps involved a high level of engagement. The recruitment stage, for instance, required much time and effort in order to construct parental consent and youth assent forms that were culturally and contextually appropriate not only by community standards but also by the policies and practices of the secondary schools.

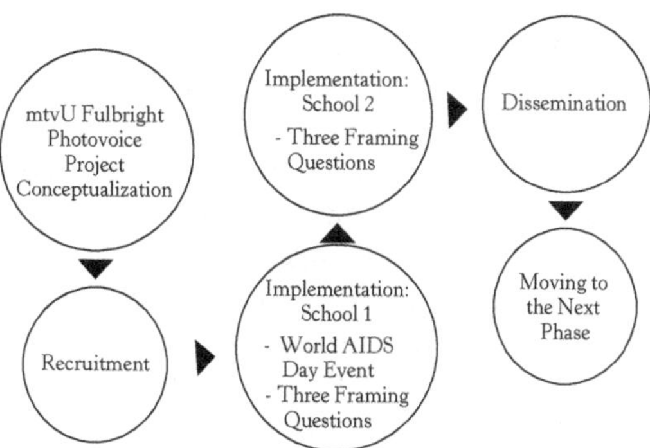

FIGURE 28.2: Overview of Phase 1, Step 2 of a photoethnographic community-based research project.

Phase 1, Step 3: Understanding the Data and Refining the Purpose

As the exploration of youth issues and sexual health in Barbados through photovoice and videovoice began, several themes emerged and were continuously discussed with dance4life staff. Given their urgency within and beyond the secondary school walls (i.e., in the general public) at the time, three were chosen as the primary focus for the remainder of the project. These three themes included general policy concerns (e.g., age of sexual consent versus age of majority), violence, and discrimination. The three photos in Figures 28.3, 28.4, and 28.5 (with the accompanying youth narratives) illustrate these three themes. Embedding the participant-generated videos was not possible for this handbook. However, the use of video creation provided an additional powerful and unique aspect to this research process. Future integration of video into the photovoice methodology should continue to be explored.

These three themes emerged consistently throughout the project but soon began contributing to the much larger issue of gender-based violence. The broader concern was that young people believed that their sexual health, to some extent, was not in their control, be it due to gender-based violence, policy issues that facilitated vulnerability, or the effect of discrimination on a person's ability to pursue positive sexual health. None of the photos or videos directly addressed gender-based violence; rather, the topic emerged naturally throughout the group dialogue process. This element of the photovoice method offers a unique insight into the shared experience among group members and, from the author's perspective, is where the power of this method lies. As participants began to speak about this issue, others in the group felt more comfortable in sharing their perspective as well. It was becoming clear that the issue of sexual health was very tightly connected to gender-based violence in Barbados.

Phase 2: Expanding the Methods

This qualitative, CBPR project laid the groundwork for the next phase of this multiphase study. Given the emergence of the themes of policy concerns, violence, and discrimination, and the emergence of gender-based violence in the data specifically, it became clear that in order to understand sexual health in Barbados, the issue of gender-based

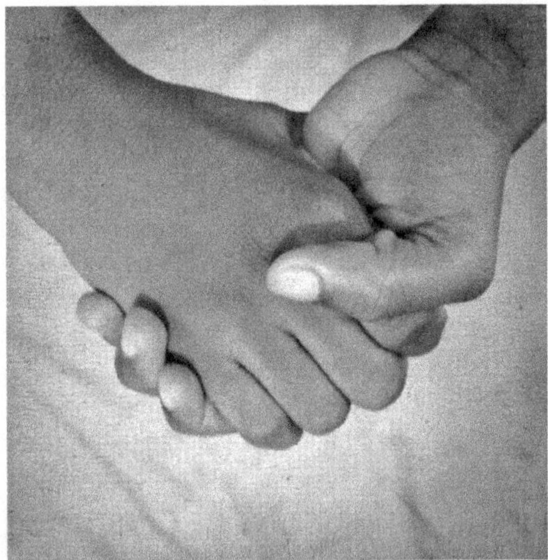

FIGURE 28.3: Photograph and narrative from participant:
"This photograph is meant to depict a holding of hands. In my opinion, an AIDS-free generation can be achieved by everyone simply being more united and careful with what they do. Also, unity amongst everyone (as the photo depicts) would help to achieve an AIDS-free generation because people would be more willing to cooperate. They would be more willing to be protected when engaging in sexual activity, and they would be more willing to get tested for HIV. One solution could be an amendment to the law in Barbados because sexual activity is legal for those of sixteen years of age or older, but one must be at least eighteen years of age to buy a condom. This probably promotes unprotected sex and increases the spread of STIs (including HIV) and should be fixed. I chose this photo because it is simple, yet it portrays exactly what I want it to. This photo symbolizes the strength, unity and trust that we all must have in order to achieve an AIDS-free generation. Also, when an AIDS-free generation is achieved, this sort of unity and trust will be present; this is what it will look like. This relates to my life because unity and an AIDS-free generation would benefit everyone, including me or my relatives."

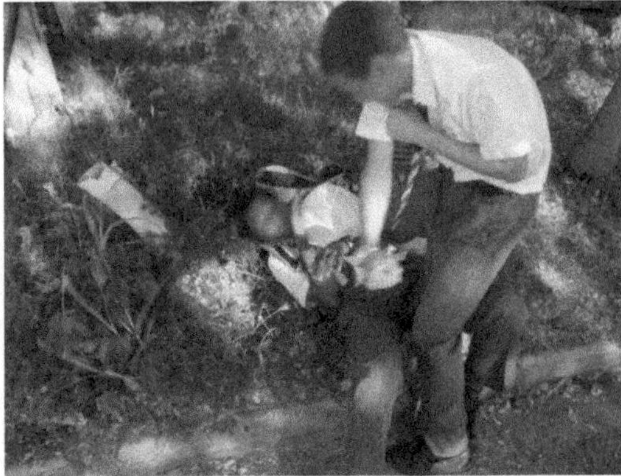

FIGURE 28.4: Photograph and narrative from participant:
"This picture depicts a conflict between two teenagers. This is an example of the lack of a loving environment. The lack of a loving environment is the issue that I have chosen to address in my picture. The lack of a loving environment, it being amongst your peers or your home and family life, can impact one's outlook and attitude towards life. Without love from others, we may act out in many ways such as violence, bullying and depression, just to mention a few. This relates to my life because I myself have found a loving environment amongst my peers and family. This has given me a positive outlook on life and everyday situations. A loving environment helps spread love and peace and prevent hatred and war."

violence needed to become a central component. A mixed methods design was explored to bring the project into the next stage. Before outlining the next phase, revisiting the literature and refining the research questions is necessary.

Revisiting the Literature

As the United Nations Population Fund (2008b, para. 1) noted, gender-based violence (GBV) "encompasses a wide range of human rights violations, including sexual abuse of children, rape, domestic violence, sexual assault and harassment, trafficking of women and girls and several harmful traditional practices." There is no one unified experience of GBV (Sokoloff & DuPont, 2005); as such, race, age, gender, sexual orientation, religion, and many other individual-level factors interact with the experience of GBV and translate into differing impacts of GBV as well (Sokoloff & DuPont, 2005).

Across the globe, "35% of women worldwide have experienced either physical and/or sexual intimate partner violence or non-partner sexual violence" (World Health Organization, 2013a, p.2). As the World Health Organization (2013a, p. 2) reported, among the consequences of such violence is that "in some regions, women are 1.5 times more likely to acquire HIV, as compared to women who have not experienced partner violence."

Women are disproportionately impacted by HIV/AIDS, as well as by GBV (Heise, Ellsberg,

FIGURE 28.5: Photograph and narrative from participant:
"HIV/AIDS has brought about a lot of discrimination from HIV-negative people towards HIV-positive people. Discrimination to the point that some HIV-positive people can't find partners or jobs. This obviously results in the HIV-positive person keeping their status a secret and living as though they didn't have the disease. In an HIV-free environment people won't have to hide behind secrets. Everyone would be HIV negative and would therefore not have to lie about their status. This photo that I took represents a young person, someone in the new generation, coming out of hiding because the discrimination towards people with HIV has passed and she can live freely."

& Gottmoeller, 2002; Maman, Campbell, Sweat, & Gielen, 2000; UNAIDS, 2012, 2013). GBV creates increased risk for an individual to be exposed to STIs (Maman et al., 2000; UNAIDS, 2012, 2013), and it tends to present as a recurring cycle in the lives of many individuals (Black et al., 2011; Wood, Maforah, & Jewkes, 1998). Living with an STI (specifically HIV) creates increased risk for an individual to be exposed to GBV (UNAIDS, 2013), and living with an STI makes an individual more susceptible to transmitting further STIs (UNAIDS, 2012, 2013).

Refining the Research Questions

This next phase sought to address the following questions: (a) To what extent are gender-based violence and sexual health connected in Barbados? (b) How are individuals nested or embedded within groups that make them more or less vulnerable to gender-based violence? (c) How are individuals nested or embedded within groups that make them more or less vulnerable to poor sexual health outcomes?

Phase 2, Step 1: Quantitative Survey Methods

Quantitative survey methods will be used in the first step for this research phase. Measures from the World Health Organization (2010) will be adapted to fit the cultural context of the sample and, in addition to demographic information, will explore participants' engagement in transactional sex, their identification with a sexual orientation group, self-report data related to STIs, and their experience of gender-based violence. To assess participants' composite score of sexual health, a section of the survey will include sexual health behaviors, practices, knowledge, and attitudes. As a large sample size is desired, this step will be administered across all the parishes in Barbados. This quantitative aspect of the study should offer insight into the issues of sexual health and gender-based violence that were inaccessible through the previous fieldwork and photovoice efforts. This method intends to understand the extent to which sexual health and gender-based violence are of concern across the island and whether these issues are uniquely affecting specific communities within Barbadian society. From a broader perspective, this data collection effort intends to illustrate the extent to which these issues are concerns in the larger population.

Therefore, a preliminary analysis of the data will be conducted once the final sample size is reached. If a particular group emerges as uniquely or significantly impacted by gender-based violence and poor sexual health outcomes, a second stage of data collection will occur. Such communities, for instance, may include the sex worker community or sexual minority communities. When a better understanding of the community impact of sexual health and gender-based violence is reached, the next step will begin.

Phase 2, Step 2: Photoethnography

To better understand the unique impacts that these issues have on communities, after the quantitative phase the author will return to another stage of photoethnography. Much in the same way as photovoice was implemented in the first phase, a second photovoice process will be pursued. Returning to this method, and guided by the preliminary

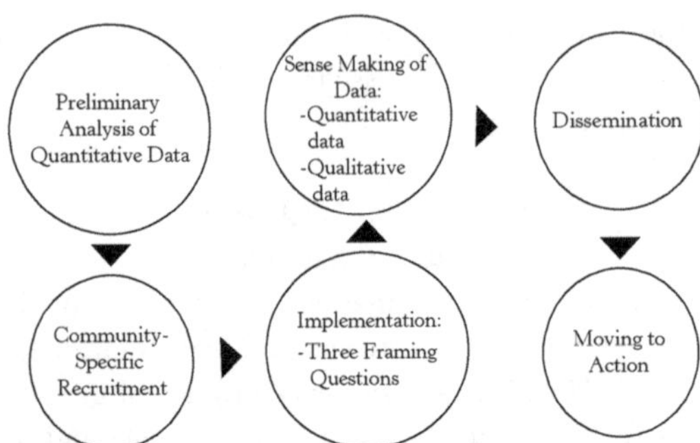

FIGURE 28.6: Overview of Phase 2, Step 2 of a photo-ethnographic community-based research project.

findings of the quantitative data, this step should yield a more refined understanding of the experience of gender-based violence and sexual health among subpopulations in Barbados. Figure 28.6 presents this phase.

Phase 2, Step 3: Performance Ethnography and App Development

With the significant amount of data produced from the early phases of the project, as well as the quantitative (survey) data and qualitative (photovoice) data, one of the final stages of the project will embrace a performance ethnographic approach. Through the partnership of the author/researcher, a screenwriter, members from the study samples, and representatives across the various partnership organizations, a screenplay will be produced that is thematically representative of the data collected since the onset of the mtvU Fulbright project in 2012 (Denzin, 2003). This step of the multiphase project intends to perform the data in a way that is culturally appropriate and accessible and allows for widespread dissemination of the project findings. Performance ethnography differs from traditional ethnography in that it "represents and performs rituals from everyday life, using performing as a method of representation and a method of understanding" (Denzin, 2003, p. 33). All pieces of data will be incorporated (photo, video, narrative, and survey data) and will embrace the truly mixed methods design of the current project.

In addition, a Web-based application is being developed to better meet the needs and capacities of the community members participating. This app will expand the opportunity for community members to participate in the data collection phases and may allow for a nuanced understanding of the social issues explored, as it offers a more familiar type of communicating for some community members and may even provide an increased sense of safety around sharing information related to such sensitive topics.

CONCLUSION

Community-based research would benefit from the further integration of multilevel theory and mixed methods designs into applications and interventions. Understanding group-level effects is particularly important given the salience of ecological systems theory in such research (Linney, 2000). Integrating empowerment-based and community-based participatory research approaches further strengthens the potential of multilevel theory, and, when coupled with multiphase research processes that allow for further exploration of group-level findings, a more rigorous, yet still context-rich, understanding and appreciation of intersectionality and human ecology may emerge.

Implementing a mixed methods design requires time and flexibility on the part of researchers, coinvestigators (e.g., partnering agencies/organizations, nongovernmental organizations), and participants. Specifically, when conducting research internationally or in a context/setting that is not considered to be the first home of the primary researcher, particular effort must be put forth in the design stages. A mixed methods design may offer researchers an opportunity to better understand the social issues of interest. Furthermore, a one-shot, single-method attempt to understand an issue as large as sexual health in a given community may even be considered unethical when the primary researcher is considered a foreigner. A more comprehensive, mixed methods approach appears warranted in such situations, with the outcome potentially offering significantly stronger implications for social change and ethical, international community psychology practice.

REFERENCES

Black, M. C., Basile, K. C., Breiding, M. J., Walters, M. L., Merrick, M. T., Chen, J., & Stevens, M. R. (2011). *The national intimate partner and sexual violence survey (NISVS): 2010 summary report.* Atlanta, GA: National Center for Injury Prevention and Control, Centers for Disease Control and Prevention.

Crenshaw, K. W. (1991). Mapping the margins: Intersectionality, identity politics, and violence against women of color. *Stanford Law Review, 43*, 1241–1299.

Creswell, J. W., Klassen, A. C., Plano Clark, V. L., & Clegg Smith, K. (2011). *Best practices for mixed methods research in the health sciences*. Bethesda, MD: Office of Behavioral Health and Social Sciences Research.

dance4life. (n.d.). *dance4life: Our work*. Retrieved June 2015, from http://www.dance4life.com/en/about-dance4life/

dance4life Barbados. (n.d.). *dance4life Barbados*. Retrieved June 2015, from http://www.dance4life-barbados.com/dance4lifebarbados/home.html

Denzin, N. K. (2003). *Performance ethnography: Critical pedagogy and the politics of culture*. Thousand Oaks, CA: Sage.

Heise, L., Ellsberg, M., & Gottmoeller, M., (2002). A global overview of gender-based violence. *International Journal of Gynecology and Obstetrics, 78*, S5–S14.

Linney, J. A. (2000). Assessing ecological constructs and community context. In J. Rappaport & E. Seidman (Eds.), *Handbook of community psychology* (pp. 647–668). New York, NY: Plenum Press.

Maman, S., Campbell, J., Sweat, M. D., & Gielen, A. C. (2000). The intersections of HIV and violence: Directions for future research and interventions. *Social Science and Medicine, 50*, 459–478.

McCall, L. (2005). The complexity of intersectionality. *Signs: Journal of Women in Culture and Society, 30*, 1771–1800.

Pink, S. (2008). Mobilising visual ethnography: Making routes, making place, and making images. *Forum: Qualitative Social Research, 9*, Art. 36.

Prilleltensky, I. (2001). Value-based praxis in community psychology: Moving toward social justice and social action. *American Journal of Community Psychology, 29*, 747–778.

Schwartz, D. (1989). Visual ethnography: Using photography in qualitative research. *Qualitative Sociology, 12*, 119–154.

Singhal, A., & Rattine-Flaherty, E. (2006). Pencils and photos as tools of communicative research and praxis: Analyzing Minga Perú's quest for social justice in the Amazon. *International Communication Gazette, 68*, 313–330.

Sokoloff, N. J., & Dupont, I. (2005). Domestic violence at the intersections of race, class, and gender: Challenges and contributions to understanding violence against marginalized women in diverse communities. *Violence Against Women, 11*, 38–64.

UNAIDS. (1999). *Sexually transmitted diseases: Policies and principles for prevention and care*. Geneva, Switzerland: The Joint United Nations Programme on HIV/AIDS.

UNAIDS. (2010). *The status of HIV in the Caribbean*. Geneva, Switzerland: The Joint United Nations Programme on HIV/AIDS.

UNAIDS. (2012). *Fact sheet: Adolescents, young people and HIV*. Geneva, Switzerland: The Joint United Nations Programme on HIV/AIDS.

UNAIDS. (2013). *Global report: UNAIDS report on the global AIDS epidemic 2013*. Geneva, Switzerland: The Joint United Nations Programme on HIV/AIDS.

UNFPA. (2008a). *Barbados*. Retrieved June 2015, from http://caribbean.unfpa.org/public/cache/offonce/Home/Countries/Barbados

UNFPA. (2008b). *Gender-based violence*. Retrieved June 2015, from http://www.unfpa.org/gender/violence.htm

UNGASS. (2008). *UNGASS country progress report Barbados*. Barbados: National AIDS Programme, The Government of Barbados.

Wallerstein, N., & Duran, B. (2003). The conceptual, historical, and practice roots of community based participatory research and related participatory traditions. In M. Minkler & N. Wallerstein (Eds.), Community-based participatory research for health (pp. 27–52). San Francisco, CA: Jossey-Bass.

Wang, C. C. (1999). Photovoice: A participatory action research strategy applied to women's health. *Journal of Women's Health, 8*, 185–192.

Wang, C. C., & Burris, M. A. (1994). Empowerment through photo novella: Portraits of participation. *Health Education and Behavior, 21*, 171–186.

Wang, C. C., & Burris, M. A. (1997). Photovoice: Concept, methodology, and use for participatory needs assessment. *Health Education and Behavior, 24*, 369–387.

Wood, K., Maforah, F., & Jewkes, R. (1998). "He forced me to love him": Putting violence on adolescent sexual health agendas. *Social Science and Medicine, 47*, 233–242.

World Health Organization. (2006). *Defining sexual health*. Geneva, Switzerland: World Health Organization.

World Health Organization. (2010). *Measuring sexual health: Conceptual and practical considerations and related indicators*. Geneva, Switzerland: World Health Organization.

World Health Organization. (2013a). *Global and regional estimates of violence against women: Prevalence and health effects of intimate partner violence and non-partner sexual violence*. Geneva, Switzerland: World Health Organization.

World Health Organization. (2013b). *Sexually transmitted infections (STIs)*. Retrieved June 2015, from http://www.who.int/mediacentre/factsheet

29

Data Visualization

GINA CARDAZONE AND RYAN TOLMAN

Data visualization is the visual representation of abstracted information, including quantitative and qualitative data (Friendly & Denis, 2001). Technological advances in data collection and analysis, coupled with the Internet-enabled instant accessibility of seemingly unlimited information, have fostered interest in finding the most efficient means of presenting huge quantities of data (Keim, Mansmann, Schneidewind, & Ziegler, 2006). Neuroscience has confirmed that the adage "a picture is worth a thousand words" is, if anything, an understatement. Visual processing occupies a large portion of our brains, and presenting information in visual formats can bring about improvements in processing speed, comprehension, and memorability (Tory & Moller, 2004; Ware, 2012).

At times, it may appear that data visualization is a new approach to addressing the relatively recent problem of information overload. In truth, data visualization has long played a role in social research and action. One of the most popular historical data visualization stories is that of Florence Nightingale, who created a novel graphical representation called the polar area chart, or "rose diagram," to present data demonstrating that soldiers were far more likely to die from infections than in direct combat (Friendly, 2008). This graphic was used to advocate successfully for improved sanitary conditions in the treatment of soldiers.

Although data visualization is theoretically and historically separable from modern information technology, in practice, they are deeply linked. The increasing availability of overwhelming amounts of data has been paralleled by innovations in data visualization. This includes newer static representations of quantitative data, such as sparklines, bubble charts, heat maps, and tree maps (Lysy, 2013), and qualitative data, such as phrase nets, graphic recording, and sentiment analysis (Henderson & Segal, 2013). It also encompasses dynamic and interactive representations of data that rely on technology. This chapter will focus primarily on innovations in data visualization that are particularly relevant to community research. First, we will explore the use of data visualization in exploratory data analysis, evaluation, and dissemination. Then we will present a brief step-by-step guide to data visualization. Finally, we will describe a case study of the use of free and low-cost data visualization tools to share pertinent data with members of a statewide coalition dedicated to preventing child abuse and neglect (CAN) in Hawaii.

INTRODUCTION TO DATA VISUALIZATION

Exploratory Data Analysis

Data visualization can facilitate hypothesis formation (Ware, 2012) and is often employed in exploratory data analysis. Scatter plots, histograms, and other graphical representations of data provide immediately comprehensible information and can help the viewer identify patterns and anomalies more readily than raw numeric data can. In community research, the ability of data visualization to allow users without statistical experience to identify patterns and develop research questions is particularly relevant in participatory research contexts. Participatory action research (PAR) and similar participatory research approaches focus on the inclusion of community members as participants in various stages of the research process themselves, rather than as only the subjects of research (Fisher & Ball, 2003; Nelson, Ochaka, Griffin, & Lord, 1998; Wallerstein & Duran, 2006).

Citizen science is another term that refers to instances where community members are involved in research (Bonney et al., 2009). It is a relatively new term that is used more commonly in the physical sciences and is exhibiting growing popularity. In fields such as ecology and ornithology, citizen science approaches have allowed community members to upload information about observations in their local environments. Technological advances, including advances in data visualization, have played a key role in the growth of citizen science, as they allow community members to then view data sets to which they contribute. Greg Newman, a citizen science expert who develops and evaluates online educational decision support systems utilized by citizen-based conservation organizations, noted the following:

> The role of data visualization is complex and involves science communication, making complex data more easy to understand, improving volunteer retention through engendering increased excitement among volunteers for their work, and ensuring that results are communicated back to volunteer data contributors. (personal communication, August 4, 2014)

Data analysis has long presented a challenge to participatory researchers because community participants do not always possess the specialized knowledge or technical resources necessary to participate in this crucial aspect of research (Wallerstein & Duran, 2006). As it makes complex data easier to understand, data visualization can improve the ability of lay researchers to participate in data analysis, particularly exploratory data analysis. By making raw data easily accessible, it can enable community members, who possess in-depth contextual knowledge about community history and conditions, to inform the development of research questions that researchers may never think of on their own. Researchers with knowledge in research design and advanced analytical techniques can then apply these skills in new studies based on data-driven community-informed research questions. They may then use data visualizations in their final products to communicate results back to community members.

Successful participatory or transdisciplinary action research requires collaboration over time between researchers and community members or leaders (Stokols, 2006). The integration of online communication platforms with data visualization technologies can facilitate open communication about data and remove some of the barriers to effective collaboration. Online communication in these platforms may benefit from disinhibition, by disrupting power dynamics or cultural barriers and opening communication (Chester & Gwynne, 1998). DeSouza and Smith (2014) suggested that the promotion of citizen science and the use of virtual experimentation platforms can help those studying social issues to take full advantage of the recent significant advancements that have been made in data collection and analysis.

Evaluation and Decision Making

Data visualizations that include a dynamic component provide opportunities for ongoing monitoring and data-driven decision making. The business sector has in some ways led the way in the use of these technologies to make strategic decisions, although its use is increasing in other fields, such as education (Dickson, 2005). It can be an invaluable tool in the evaluation of community programs, and in fact the American Evaluation Association released a two-part issue of *New Directions for Evaluation* dedicated entirely to data visualization (Azzam & Evergreen, 2013).

In their simplest forms, dynamic visualizations can be charts made in Excel that are connected to data in a spreadsheet so that they automatically update as data are modified or new data are added. In their most complex forms, data visualizations can be connected to multiple data sources and even XML or HTML data to pull in and display real-time data updated from the Web. Although dynamic visualizations include any chart or graph that is automatically updated as new data are added, their function is commonly applied to the use of information dashboards.

Information dashboards are customized visual displays of quantitative information that have been arranged to fit on a single computer screen for quick, real-time monitoring of program-specific objectives (Few, 2006). Dynamic dashboards were originally developed and used in business settings so that organizations could quickly assess and respond to changes. Given the need of many community organizations to demonstrate accountability, compliance, and programmatic results, dashboards could be an important tool when utilized by community researchers. Just like the dashboard in one's car, an information dashboard allows one to quickly glance and monitor the most important information about one's performance and progress toward objectives. If the fuel gauge in one's car is dipping below empty, then one is likely to take action toward locating a gas station to refuel. Similarly in community practice, the application of these real-time, information monitoring dashboards can help programs make evidence-based decisions to take corrective actions if they are not meeting their progress goals (Smith, 2013). This is compatible with an empowerment evaluation approach (Fetterman & Wandersman, 2005) because program leaders and staff may obtain ongoing information about their programs without an intermediary, once the dashboard is created and a refresh protocol is established.

Dynamic information dashboards are typically used with specific strategic, analytical, or operational purposes. Summary charts and data can provide management with information for strategic planning purposes. Dashboards with interactive capacities to drill down into the data can provide managers with analytical capabilities to evaluate and research programmatic data. Monitoring dashboards can provide dynamic feedback to programs in order to assess progress toward objectives, indicate if corrective action is needed, and provide operational functions including formative evaluation, program adherence, and quality assurance (Smith, 2013). When utilized to their full effect, dynamic visualizations and information dashboards can offer programs efficient displays of important program data, provide effective presentations of information, and empower programs with the capacity for real-time monitoring and data-based decisions for change and improvement.

For those with more modest visualization ambitions, there are ways to increase the ability to communicate visually even while sticking with that old reporting mainstay, Excel. Stephanie Evergreen and Ann Emery blog regularly about data visualization in program evaluation and have posted several tips for improving Excel charts. Together, they have created the Data Visualization Checklist (Emery & Evergreen, 2014) to help evaluators use basic design principles to transform cluttered generic graphs into streamlined intentional visual representations of data.

Dissemination

Data visualization is particularly important in communicating research results to a lay audience, including policymakers, organizational decision makers, and the general public. Visualizations can be shared via mainstream media or social media to promote public awareness. They can be used more strategically in communication with policymakers in order to promote evidence-based policies. The effective use of data visualization can transform research findings into persuasive messages that lead to individual or collective action.

One form of data visualization that has gained tremendous popularity is the infographic. Infographics present data in visual formats that are easy to understand and can be quickly consumed (Smiciklas, 2012). Editorial infographics are designed with the intention to tell a story, rather than to present unbiased information (Lankow, Ritchie, & Crooks, 2012). A well-designed infographic can provide a very compelling story; because of this, it can also be misused by media outlets to misinform the public. The ubiquity of infographics results from their efficiency in communicating data, their user friendliness, and the ease with which they can be used in multiple media formats: shared in social media, included in a newspaper or online article, or presented quickly on television in a news story.

The most common type of editorial infographic is a static and simplified image that combines a visual representation of quantitative data with limited text accompaniment. In contrast with data visualizations that are designed for a specific and invested audience (such as dashboards for businesses), infographics are often targeted toward a broad audience that may have no initial interest in the graphic's topic. Because an editorial infographic must entice a potentially unwilling viewer to look at it, as well as tell a story and possibly persuade the viewer to take action, there is an especially large burden for this type of visualization to be visually compelling. Graphic designers may play a larger role in the creation of infographics than other types of visualizations. However, there are tools that allow users without graphic design expertise to create infographics fairly easily.

Infographics are not limited to digital images. They can be shared in the form of animations, interactive Web graphics, or even public data displays. Claes and Moere (2013), contending that our visual landscape is cluttered with advertisements and other unwanted visual imagery, described an urban intervention they called Street Infographics in which they created simple infographics about resident characteristics and affixed them to four street signs. The graphics were strategically designed to match the street signs in color and size, so that they looked like an extension of the signs rather than a disruption. The graphics presented very simple information regarding the proportion of each street's residents in three categories: permanent resident, student, or international. They briefly interviewed 35 passersby who had stopped to look at the display and found that, although the passersby had different levels of recall in terms of detail, they all understood the infographics correctly. Many reflected on the meaning of the information, including one community member who reported modifying a previously held belief after reading the display.

Infographics represent only one method of using data visualization to disseminate information. There are more ways of using data visualization to disseminate information than could possibly be included in this chapter, including burgeoning methods such as the use of video games or mobile apps (Newman et al., 2012). In a sense, dissemination is always a goal of data visualization. In citizen science, ongoing or final results of research projects are disseminated to community researchers. In program evaluation, information is disseminated to program leaders or staff. The audience may be broad or narrow, and the amount of information included may be large or small, but in all instances, the strength of data visualizations is its ability to convey information in a way that is suited to the way the human brain operates.

CREATING A DATA VISUALIZATION: A STEP-BY-STEP GUIDE

The following steps were adapted from Smith's (2013) guide to creating dynamic dashboards. The order and the degree of time spent in each step may differ depending on the type and complexity of the visualization. However, the steps for creating an effective data visualization are ultimately the same, whether it is a complex interactive visualization, an artistic infographic, or a simple but well-designed Excel chart.

Step 1: Identify Your Purpose and Target Audience

This is necessarily your first step, because your purpose and target audience will determine which type of visualization you will create. It may be helpful to formulate a statement describing your specific purpose. For example, you may have the following goal: "To convince state policymakers that additional funding is necessary for women's health in my county."

Step 2: Determine the Specific Focus Area for the Visualization

In the earlier example, the general topic of the visualization has been identified: "women's health." However, this is a very broad topic, and any attempt to visualize it may result in something that is too generic to be effective. In this example, the visualization may focus specifically on a particular health problem that is more prevalent in your county.

Step 3: Locate, Vet, and Manipulate Data

This step may actually consist of many substeps, particularly if you are creating a sophisticated visualization that combines data from multiple sources. However, in the simplest case (as with a very simplified infographic), it may consist of finding a single reliable data point. In some cases, as with dynamic dashboards, the actual data may not be available when you are designing and building the visualization. In these cases, you still need to know what kind of information will be presented, and it is recommended that you obtain a dummy data set before you actually build the dashboard. In all cases, the source(s) of data used in the visualization should be included somewhere on the visualization itself or in accompanying documentation. Particularly for visualizations that are aimed at educating or persuading a broad audience, inclusion of this information is necessary to ensure that the visualization is viewed by audience members as trustworthy.

Step 4: Design

The next step is to begin designing the visualization. You may consider several different options for presenting the same information. This stage may consist of a quick pen-and-paper sketch or, in the case of more complex technical visualizations, a graphic mockup. When you are designing and building your visualization, you should be mindful of basic design principles. Upon creating a draft or prototype, it is recommended that you look explicitly for design problems or for opportunities to add or subtract an element.

There are many recommendations for best practices in data visualization. One of the most universal design rules is to simplify visualizations to the extent possible (Evergreen, 2013; Few, 2009; Tufte, 1983, 1990). This includes the removal of any visual clutter, such as extraneous gridlines and tick marks, unnecessary color gradations or three-dimensionality, and redundant information. It also means looking for opportunities to reduce the amount of work that people have to do in order to make sense of the data, such as directly labeling chart elements rather than having a legend, using line charts to describe change over time, and using bar charts rather than pie charts to compare quantities in recognition of the fact that, despite the loveliness of Florence Nightingale's rose diagram, people are generally not very good at visually determining the area of a circle.

Tufte (1983) was adamant about maximizing what he called the "data-ink ratio," and what Few (2006) renamed the "data-pixel ratio," such that visualizations consist only of what is necessary to make the data intelligible. However, there are some who disagree with this hard-line approach, saying that there are cases where what Tufte would call "visual noise" may actually facilitate cognitive processing. For example, the use of visual metaphor in infographics is extremely popular and often recommended (Lankow et al., 2012). Visual metaphors make connections between new information and existing knowledge. Computers are replete with visual metaphors in the form of icons, from the trash or recycling bin where you drag items that are no longer needed, to the folders where you store information, to the now quaint floppy disk you click on when you want to save a file. We take these images for granted, but they are actually visual metaphors that were crucial in helping early users of graphical interfaces understand how to interact with machines. Visual metaphors, when used appropriately, can improve comprehension and serve as mnemonic aids facilitating later recall (Eppler, 2006), although they also have the potential to be distracting or misleading. The use of visual imagery can also make information more emotionally impactful, which can facilitate later recall. The affective impact of visual imagery may be particularly important when the goal of the visualization is to persuade the viewer rather than to share unbiased information (Huddy & Gunnthorsdottir, 2000). The design strategy should be compatible with the goal of the visualization and tailored to the target audience. Even when the visualization incorporates what Tufte called "non-data ink," attention to simplicity can ensure that irrelevant visual features do not distract from the visualization's primary message or function.

Step 6: Build

Particularly in the case of complex interactive and/or dynamic visualizations, there may be a clear separation between the design and build stage. This latter stage may involve more complex technical linking of data sets or inclusion of interactive components. However, the boundary between designing and building, even in such instances, is fluid. Both may be subsumed under a step called "Experiment." During the build phase, problems with the initial design may be revealed. An ongoing process of reflection and refinement is necessary in order to create an effective visualization.

Step 7: If Possible, Get Feedback and Iterate

Ideally, before the visualization is finalized, you will have an opportunity to share it with other potential audience members and to gather direct feedback. This process may be formal and include structured questions, or it may be open ended and conversational. Regardless of the approach, having at least some direct feedback from people who have not been involved in the design process and who resemble your target audience can be extraordinarily helpful in ensuring that the visualization meets its main objectives.

Step 8: Finalize and Share

At some point, the refinement must end and the visualization must be finalized. When this occurs, it is important to have a plan for ensuring that it actually reaches your target audience. For simple static visualizations, this may consist of inclusion in a report or Web site, or a broader outreach effort that includes plans for sharing on social media or targeting specific news outlets. For more complex interactive visualizations, this may also include the creation of written or video instructions to ensure that people are able to use the visualization effectively.

When creating dynamic visualizations, such as dynamic dashboards, this must also consist of determining the refresh rate and creating a process to ensure that data are refreshed over time (Smith, 2013).The refresh rate indicates how often the dashboard will be updated with program data, and the protocol includes guidelines for data entry, steps for importing and managing the data, and procedures for reporting. Once the dashboard is constructed and populated with data, the dashboard can be published through interval reporting or by providing online access to key stakeholders. Once a dashboard is operational, some time and care should be taken to evaluate the utilization and effectiveness of the dashboard toward monitoring program objectives and meeting its intended utilization needs.

CASE STUDY

Background

This case study describes the use of data visualization with a coalition dedicated to preventing child abuse and neglect. Child abuse and neglect (CAN) is a pervasive problem that can have long-term consequences on mental and physical health (Norman et al., 2012; Shin & Miller, 2012). Programs and policies dedicated to preventing CAN and promoting child well-being are investments in the long-term health and well-being of adults. To achieve and sustain programmatic and policy changes that can support the prevention of child abuse and neglect, coordinated action at multiple levels is required (Daro & Dodge, 2009).

The Hawaii Children's Trust Fund (HCTF) Coalition is a statewide coalition of individuals and organizations dedicated to CAN prevention. The first author of this chapter began working with HCTF on a team evaluating the effectiveness of a public awareness campaign designed to promote knowledge of protective factors that have been linked to reductions in CAN rates (Cardazone, Sy, Chik, & Corlew, 2014). After completing this evaluation project, she collaborated with HCTF again in an effort to increase Coalition members' ability to use data. One element of this effort was the creation of several "data products," including a set of interactive data visualizations and an infographic.

The decision to create these products emerged after members were surveyed and the results indicated that most of the respondents believed in the importance of data-informed decision making, but that many perceived barriers to using data effectively. Based on the responses to open-ended questions regarding data usage and needs, the first author created a Knowledge Translation Survey. This survey included three sections: rankings of desired data product, rankings of desired data formats, and a checklist of data sources that were currently in use or that participants wished to use.

Coalition members indicated that they were most interested in obtaining data products that focused on effective CAN prevention programming and Hawaii CAN statistics and that they preferred to receive data in the form of data visualizations or infographics. Next, we describe the formation of two data products that were created to respond directly to this need. The first is an interactive data visualization of Hawaii CAN rates. The second is an infographic based on the results of a systematic review of home visiting programs, focusing particularly on their applicability to the field of CAN prevention.

Product 1: Interactive Data Visualizations of Hawaii CAN Rates

The participants indicated that they most often used data from the Hawaii State Department of Health (DOH) and Department of Human Services (DHS). However, some members noted a desire to have data from this source shared in a more easily accessible manner. The first interactive data visualizations were created with this in mind, as a way to introduce Coalition members to a new way to explore data from a familiar source.

Interactive data visualizations were created using Tableau Public 8.0 (www.tableausoftware.com/public), a free version of the proprietary Tableau data visualization software that is meant for use with public data. Data were transformed in order to conform to the Tableau guidelines, which require that each variable be represented only once per row and that all totals and subtotals be removed.

Although initially several different visualizations were created using various data sources, this approach changed after the first author collected initial feedback on early products. After this, efforts were focused on creating a single interactive dashboard based on a frequently used and relevant source of data, the substantiated CAN rates by region available from the DHS's annual Child Abuse and Neglect Reports. In the dashboard, several views were used in order to highlight different aspects (e.g., showing differences in average CAN rates by region vs. showing changes in CAN rates over time).

Because DHS data on CAN prevalence are presented in counts and not normed according to the population, demographic data were used in order to calculate the rates of CAN in different geographic regions. Additionally, because the regions used in these reports are judicial districts rather than census divisions, additional calculations had to be made using an equivalency guide for determining the relationship between judicial districts and census county subdivisions.

The data were presented in four formats: (a) bar graphs allowing easy at-a-glance comparisons of CAN rates in different regions; (b) line graphs depicting changes in CAN rates for each region over time; (c) a map of the Hawaiian islands with CAN rates by county; and (d) a tree map displaying nested rectangles representing each district, with the hue of each rectangle based on county, the shade based on CAN rate, and the size proportioned according to child population. The first three formats were also presented on a dashboard, which can be filtered by county or year.

For all products, efforts were made to adhere to principles of effective data visualization, such as the strategic use of color to convey meaningful information and the use of small multiples of similar graphics to allow for fast apprehension of large quantities of information (Tufte, 1983, 1990). Earlier versions of the visualizations in Figure 29.1 were improved in several ways based on reflection on design principles and feedback from stakeholders.

The map of Hawaii in the upper left corner of Figure 29.1 underwent the most substantial changes. Originally, it was a map with each of the four counties in different shades of the same color corresponding to their CAN rates. This shading

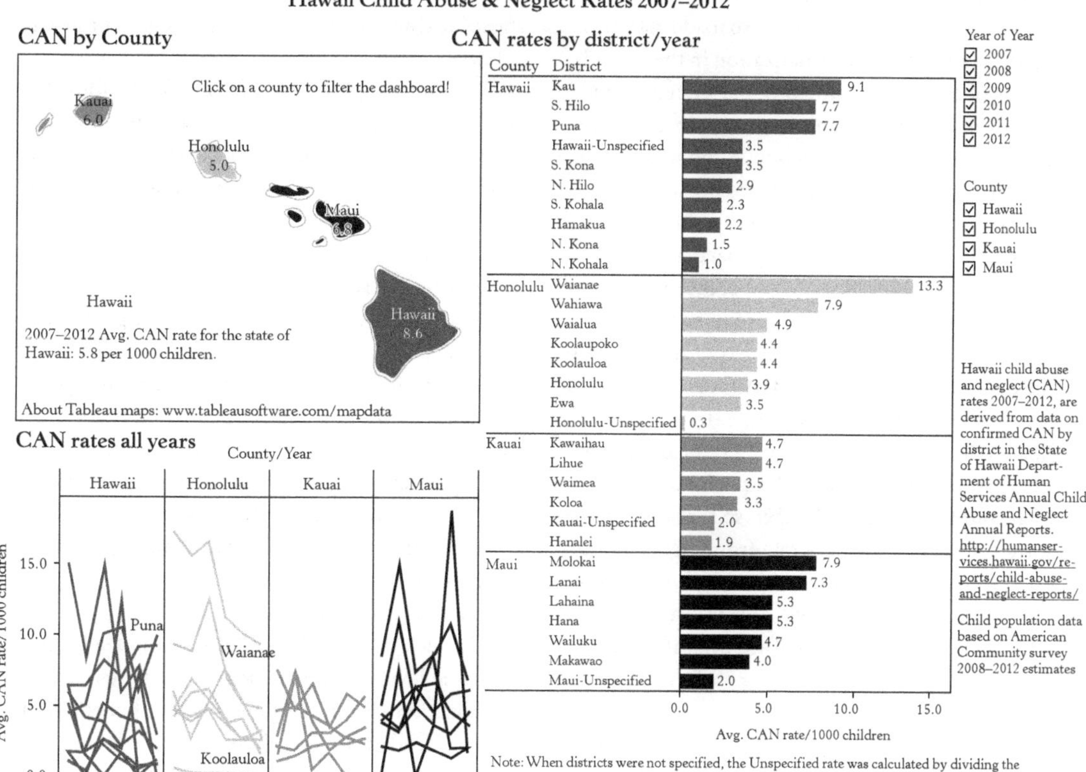

FIGURE 29.1: Hawaii child abuse and neglect rates for 2007–2012. Dashboard includes multiple charts, all of which can be filtered by year or county. Each chart is also visible in a full view via tabs.

did not provide a significant advantage in comprehensibility compared to a map without shading. Furthermore, the color scheme was not aligned with other visualizations in the dashboard. The map was therefore changed so that the color of each county followed the color scheme of the other visualizations. This provides a visual guide so that someone can quickly look at the map and contextualize the remaining images. This map was also made into an alternative interface for the interactive filter, so that, for example, one could click on the island of Kauai and the rest of the dashboard would be filtered so that only the results from Kauai are shown. The alternative interface for filtering by county through the use of checkboxes was kept, however, because it allows the user to more easily choose multiple counties to compare at once.

Perhaps most crucially, the overall Hawaii CAN rate, which had been entirely absent from the original design of this dashboard, was added in text in white space below the islands. This was in direct response to feedback from stakeholders, who thought it would help to contextualize the rates for each county and for individual districts.

Minor modifications were also made to the other visualizations. For the visualization in the lower left corner of Figure 29.1, the original design included data over time for all four counties in one image. This was extremely cacophonous and was changed to a small multiples format, where the same data for each county are presented side by side. Although the result is still visually busy, particularly in the dashboard view, it does allow some information to become instantly apparent, such as the fact that rates for Kauai districts are consistently low, while the district with the highest CAN rate in Honolulu has exhibited decreases over time. In the visualization on the right side of Figure 29.1, the original version had districts presented alphabetically within each county. This was changed so that districts are sorted according to CAN rate from highest to lowest. This is both visually cleaner and more immediately informative, as it will always list the district with the highest CAN rate first even if the results are filtered by year and the order changes.

Product 2: Infographic on Home Visiting

In response to the participants' stated desire for information regarding effective CAN prevention programs, an infographic was created based on information from the comprehensive Home Visiting Evidence of Effectiveness Review (HomVEE; Avellar, Paulsell, Sama-Miller, & Del Grosso, 2012). Although the HomVEE review included information about the effectiveness of select home visiting programs in a variety of outcomes, this infographic specifically highlighted programs with evidence of effectiveness in preventing child maltreatment. The infographic was designed for a lay reader, with a central theme guiding its development: Home visiting programs can be effective in helping to prevent child abuse and neglect. The goal of this infographic was to tell a story rather than to translate large quantities of data, and therefore much information was abbreviated or left out entirely in order to make an intelligible graphic.

The infographic was created using Piktochart (www.piktochart.com), a low-cost online tool that includes templates, icons, and other materials that facilitate infographic creation by people with limited graphic design expertise. There were some substantial limitations in the options for presenting information using this tool. However, this tool and similar Web-based tools can be extremely useful for those lacking access to a graphic designer or design software.

The infographic (see Fig. 29.2) has four sections. The first (top) section quickly describes home visiting programs for those who may be unfamiliar with them. The second section highlights the six programs that were identified by HomVEE as showing substantial evidence of effectiveness in preventing CAN. The third section describes the standards HomVEE used in determining effectiveness (e.g., rates of substantiated CAN, self-reports by parents using validated measures, emergency room visits and hospitalizations). The fourth section illustrates the other potential benefits of home visiting by showing the proportion of these six programs that also demonstrated positive outcomes in the following areas: child health, maternal health, child development and school readiness, and positive parenting practices.

The design of this infographic was not subject to the same level of refinement as the interactive data visualization (Product 1) and did not benefit from external feedback. Therefore, it probably contains more text and extraneous graphics than would be ideal. However, there was much refinement in conceptualizing the infographic. The author's original plan was to create an infographic that summarized a wide variety of literature on strategies to prevent child abuse. An early version of the infographic was completely different, and the author noted that it lacked the simplicity and narrative coherence that are necessary for infographics to be successful. There were also some inconsistencies in the literature regarding what CAN prevention strategies work under particular conditions. Accordingly, the subject of the infographic was altered to focus on one specific strategy (i.e., home visiting) that has repeatedly demonstrated success in CAN prevention. Instead of culling data from multiple sources, a single trustworthy source was used. The result is a more focused and, hopefully, more effective product.

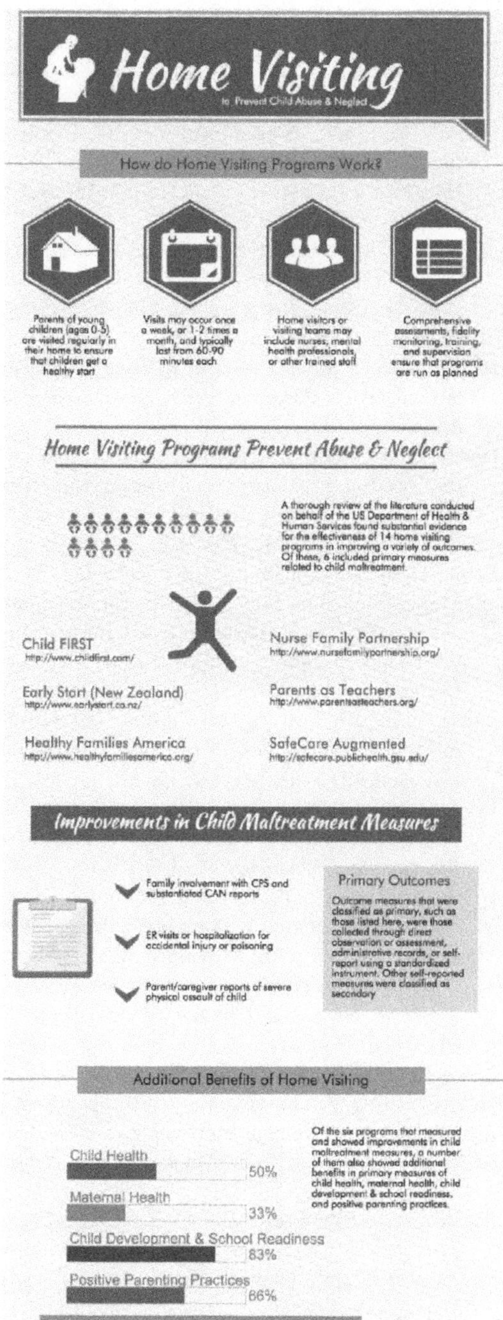

FIGURE 29.2: Infographic for home-visiting programs effective in preventing child maltreatment.

Data source: Avellar, S., Paulsell, D., Sama-Miller, E., & Del Grosso, P. (2013). Home Visiting Effectiveness Review: Executive Summary. Office of Planning, Research and Evaluation, Administration for Children and Families, US Department of Health and Human Services, Washington, DC.

CONCLUSION

Data visualization has become increasingly popular as people and organizations seek to cope with the astounding amount of information that is now available. For community researchers, data visualization has significant potential for bridging the divide between researchers and community members. Whether the goal is to facilitate participatory research, empower community-based organizations to monitor their program's progress, or share the results of research with a broad audience, thoughtful visualizations can make data more accessible and remove barriers to engagement. As technological advancements have increased the amount of information available, they have also spurred innovations in data visualization, such as the development of interactive visualizations and dynamic dashboards. However, even when developing simple graphics with rudimentary tools, attention to the principles of good design can improve the ability of researchers to make information intelligible to other researchers and to community members.

REFERENCES

Avellar, S., Paulsell, D., Sama-Miller, E., & Del Grosso, P. (2012). *Home visiting evidence of effectiveness review: Executive summary.* Washington, DC: Office of Planning, Research and Evaluation, Administration for Children and Families, US Department of Health and Human Services.

Azzam, T., & Evergreen, S. (Eds.). (2013). Data visualization[Special issue]. *New Directions for Evaluation, 139*(1 & 2).

Bonney, R., Cooper, C. B., Dickinson, J., Kelling, S., Phillips, T., Rosenberg, K. V., & Shirk, J. (2009). Citizen science: A developing tool for expanding science knowledge and scientific literacy. *BioScience, 59*, 977–984.

Cardazone, G., Sy, A. U., Chik, I., & Corlew, L. K. (2014). Mapping one strong 'Ohana: Using network analysis and GIS to enhance the effectiveness of a statewide coalition to prevent child abuse and neglect. *American Journal of Community Psychology, 53*, 346–356.

Chester, A., & Gwynne, G. (1998). Online teaching: Encouraging collaboration through anonymity. *Journal of Computer-Mediated Communication, 4*(2). Retrieved June 2015, from http://onlinelibrary.wiley.com/doi/10.1111/j.1083-6101.1998.tb00096.x/full

Claes, S., & Moere, V. A. (2013, June). *Street infographics: Raising awareness of local issues through a situated urban visualization.* Paper presented at the International Symposium on Pervasive Displays, Mountain View, CA.

Daro, D., & Dodge, K. A. (2009). Creating community responsibility for child protection: Possibilities and challenges. *The Future of Children, 19*, 67–93.

Desouza, K. C., & Smith, K. L. (2014). Big data for social innovation. *Stanford Social Innovation Review.* Retrieved June 2015, from http://www.ssireview.org/articles/entry/big_data_for_social_innovation

Dickson, W. P. (2005). *Toward a deeper understanding of student performance in virtual high school courses: Using quantitative analyses and data visualization to inform decision making.* Naperville, IL: Learning Point Associates

Emery, A. K., & Evergreen, S. (2014). *Data visualization checklist.* Available at: http://stephanieevergreen.com/wp-content/uploads/2014/05/DataVizChecklist_May2014.pdf

Eppler, M. J. (2006). A comparison between concept maps, mind maps, conceptual diagrams, and visual metaphors as complementary tools for knowledge construction and sharing. *Information Visualization, 5*, 202–210.

Evergreen, S. D. (2013). *Presenting data effectively: Communicating your findings for maximum impact.* Thousand Oaks, CA: Sage.

Fetterman, D. M., & Wandersman, A. (Eds.). (2005). *Empowerment evaluation principles in practice.* New York, NY: Guilford Press.

Few, S. (2006). *Information dashboard design.* San Francisco, CA: O'Reilly Media.

Few, S. (2009). *Now you see it: Simple visualization techniques for quantitative analysis.* Berkeley, CA: Analytics Press.

Fisher, P. A., & Ball, T. J. (2003). Tribal participatory research: Mechanisms of a collaborative model. *American Journal of Community Psychology, 32*, 207–216.

Friendly, M. (2008). A brief history of data visualization. In C. Chen, W. Hardle, & A. Unwin (Eds.). *Handbook of data visualization* (pp. 15–56). Berlin, Germany: Springer-Verlag.

Friendly, M., & Denis, D. J. (2001). *Milestones in the history of thematic cartography, statistical graphics, and data visualization.* Retrieved June 2015, from http://www.datavis.ca/milestones

Henderson, S., & Segal, E. H. (2013). Visualizing qualitative data in evaluation research. *New Directions for Evaluation, 139*, 53–71.

Huddy, L., & Gunnthorsdottir, A. H. (2000). The persuasive effects of emotive visual imagery: Superficial manipulation or the product of passionate reason? *Political Psychology, 21*, 745–778.

Keim, D. A., Mansmann, F., Schneidewind, J., & Ziegler, H. (2006, July). *Challenges in visual data analysis.* Paper presented at the Tenth International Conference on Information Visualization, London, England.

Lankow, J., Ritchie, J., & Crooks, R. (2012). *Infographics: The power of visual storytelling.* Hoboken, NJ: Wiley.

Lysy, C. (2013). Developments in quantitative data display and their implications for evaluation. *New Directions for Evaluation, 139*, 33–51.

Nelson, G., Ochocka, J., Griffin, K., & Lord, J. (1998). "Nothing about me, without me": Participatory action research with self-help/mutual aid organizations for psychiatric consumer/survivors. *American Journal of Community Psychology, 26*, 881–912.

Newman, G., Wiggins, A., Crall, A., Graham, E., Newman, S., & Crowston, K. (2012). The future of citizen science: Emerging technologies and shifting paradigms. *Frontiers in Ecology and the Environment, 10*, 298–304.

Norman, R. E., Byambaa, M., De, R., Butchart, A., Scott, J., & Vos, T. (2012). The long-term health consequences of child physical abuse, emotional abuse, and neglect: A systematic review and meta-analysis. *PLoS Medicine, 9*, e1001349.

Shin, S. H., & Miller, D. P. (2012). A longitudinal examination of childhood maltreatment and adolescent obesity: Results from the National Longitudinal Study of Adolescent Health (AddHealth) Study. *Child Abuse and Neglect, 36*, 84–94.

Smiciklas, M. (2012). *The power of infographics: Using pictures to communicate and connect with your audiences.* Indianapolis, IN: Que Publishing.

Smith, V. S. (2013). Data dashboard as evaluation and research communication tool. *New Directions for Evaluation, 140*, 21–45.

Stokols, D. (2006). Toward a science of transdisciplinary action research. *American Journal of Community Psychology, 38*, 63–77.

Tory, M., & Moller, T. (2004). Human factors in visualization research. *IEEE Transactions on Visualization and Computer Graphics, 10*, 72–84.

Tufte, E. R. (1983). *The visual display of quantitative information*. Cheshire, CT: Graphics Press.

Tufte, E. R. (1990). *Envisioning information*. Cheshire, CT: Graphics Press.

Wallerstein, N. B., & Duran, B. (2006). Using community-based participatory research to address health disparities. *Health Promotion Practice, 7*, 312–323.

Ware, C. (2012). *Information visualization: Perception for design* (3rd ed.). Waltham, MA: Elsevier.

30

Concept Mapping

LISA M. VAUGHN AND DANIEL MCLINDEN

Concept mapping (CM) is a mixed methods research approach that integrates qualitative and quantitative data collection methods of brainstorming, card sorting, and ratings with the multivariate statistical techniques of multidimensional scaling and cluster analysis to create a data-driven visual representation of thoughts or ideas of a group (Kane & Trochim, 2007; Trochim, 1989a). Several methods share the name "concept mapping." For example, Novak (1998) uses the term "concept mapping" to describe a qualitative method to graphically organize ideas and relationships between ideas. These other methods should not be confused with concept mapping of the type described here that relies on both qualitative and quantitative methods. CM methodology is uniquely suited to conducting research in a community within a participatory research framework (Burke et al., 2005; Rosas, 2012) for several reasons. First, the methodology enables researchers and community members to work collaboratively in the design of the study, the data collection, and the interpretation of results. Second, although CM involves members of a community, it is not a group process in the typical sense of attempting to build consensus. Rather, the unique perspectives of individuals emerge early in the data collection and remain present throughout the multiple steps of CM. Thus, the methodology is well suited for eliciting and including diverse perspectives of multiple constituencies within a community. Third, the results provide a basis for evidence-based action planning or policy development that can be cocreated with the community.

In prior work relevant to research in communities, CM methodology has been used to address issues in culturally competent intervention services (Shorkey, Windsor, & Spence, 2009), health disparities (Risisky et al., 2008), and other community-based research efforts to include cancer screening (Ahmad, Mahmood, Pietkiewicz, McDonald, & Ginsburg, 2012), strategies to increase physical activity (Kelly, Baker, Brownson, & Schootman, 2007), youth development programs (Urban, 2008), HIV/AIDS prevention (Abdul-Quader & Collins, 2011), school violence (Johnson, Burke, & Gielen, 2011), and immigrant experiences (Haque & Rosas, 2010). Methodological work has demonstrated the validity and utility of the CM approach (Jackson & Trochim, 2002; Rosas & Kane, 2012). CM addresses the challenges in community-based research of eliciting and including the multiple and diverse perspectives of all constituencies in the community throughout the research process, with the research design and resulting interventions and policies genuinely reflecting the perspectives of community members. In this chapter, we review the general CM methodology, including a summary of the typical steps, the benefits and challenges of the approach, and an application of CM focused on suicide prevention in youth.

INTRODUCTION TO CONCEPT MAPPING

Steps of Concept Mapping

CM methodology involves multiple steps and interaction with the target group or community at various points in time (see Fig. 30.1). Although the methodology is flexible and can be adapted to the unique circumstances of the issue and the community, there is a core set of common steps implemented in the following sequence: preparation, idea generation, structuring, representation, interpretation, and utilization (Kane & Trochim, 2007; Trochim, 1989a).

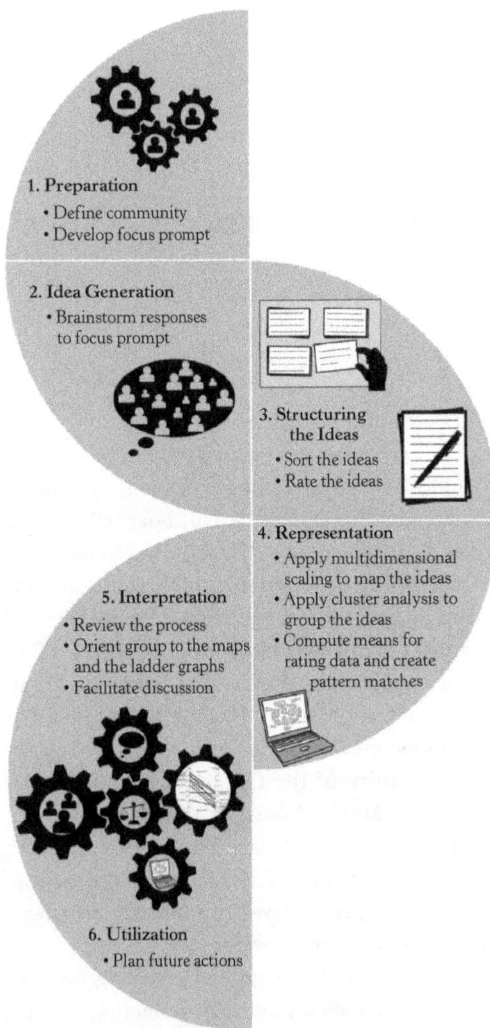

FIGURE 30.1: The steps in concept mapping.

The preparation step of CM involves defining the community, developing the research question, and determining who needs to be included. Representatives of the community work together to identify the multiple constituencies within the community and to ensure that the research process includes their participation. Representatives of the community also work together to develop a statement that enables the community to provide input to the research question. The statement is referred to as a focus prompt and is worded as an incomplete or fill-in-the-blank sentence. The intent of the focus prompt is to elicit multiple and diverse ideas from research participants who are asked to complete the statement. For example, in a study of bullying within an elementary school, teachers, parents, and students were invited to complete the following focus prompt: "In order to address bullying at our school, I believe we need to . . . ." (Vaughn, Jacquez, & McLinden, 2013). By defining the community to include multiple constituencies of school, the intent was to generate diverse ideas because individuals invited to participate had different experiences with and perspectives about the problem of bullying.

In the idea-generation step, research participants from the defined community complete the prompt and provide their individual perspectives. The key goal of data collection for this step is to obtain each participant's independent perspective about the focus prompt. Multiple participants provide several ideas each, and the result is many diverse ideas that represent the richness of thinking in the community. Although a list of thoughtful and innovative ideas is useful, more meaning can be obtained from the community. The next step, structuring, provides an opportunity to make clear the major themes among the ideas, as well as the value of these ideas and themes. Two tasks are involved during structuring: sorting and rating. In the sorting task, each participant is provided with all of the generated ideas on a set of cards, with one idea on each card. Participants are directed to work individually to sort the cards into groups of similar ideas and create a descriptive name that captures the meaning of the ideas in each group. In the rating task, participants are asked to work independently to value the ideas through ratings on one or more Likert-type scales (e.g., importance, feasibility). Data collection for idea generation, sorting, and rating can be accomplished in a number of ways using paper formats or online tools.

Representation also involves two tasks: computing the maps and computing the summary statistics for the ratings. Computing the maps involves applying multidimensional scaling (MDS) and hierarchical cluster analysis to the input provided by the community. MDS converts the sorting data into a visual representation, with each idea represented as a point on a map. MDS computes the location of each point based on the similarity of ideas. Points on the map will be located close together when the ideas represented by those points were often sorted into the same group by participants during the sorting task. Points on this map will be further apart when the ideas represented by the points were seen as different and seldom or never sorted together. Because there are often many points (i.e., ideas), it is useful to identify patterns among the ideas by examining how the ideas coalesce into a smaller number of key ideas or themes. Hierarchical cluster analysis uses the information from MDS to identify patterns or clusters of ideas based on the proximity of points on the map. Cluster analysis yields multiple solutions, and the number of clusters can range from 1 to *N*, where *N* is equal to the number of ideas. Choosing the appropriate number of clusters is an interpretive task that requires a decision about which cluster solution has a balance of sufficient yet manageable detail in order to have a clear understanding of the issue.

Simple descriptive statistics are used for rating data. Means of the ratings are calculated for each idea and for each cluster. This analysis illustrates the variation in value among ideas and clusters and also allows for the comparison of different dimensions of value (e.g., importance versus feasibility) and/or the analysis of the patterns of alignment and discrepancy among constituencies within a community. Pairwise comparisons (i.e., between value ratings or different constituencies) are often displayed as parallel number lines arranged vertically, with each cluster positioned on the respective number line according to the mean rating. Graphs of this type are typically referred to as *ladder graphs* and are so named because perfect alignment between the values on the left and right would resemble the parallel rungs of a ladder (Kane & Trochim, 2007). In practice, a ladder structure seldom occurs, and the graphic serves to illustrate to the community the alignment or the lack thereof among the multiple clusters on either the different value dimensions or among multiple constituencies. Referred to as *pattern matching*, the intent is to focus on the patterns of value across all of the concepts/clusters or among different constituencies as a basis for discussion and action planning rather than emphasizing individual data points (Trochim, 1989b).

The final steps of CM (interpretation and utilization) involve orienting the community to the maps, naming each cluster, and discussing how the concept map informs the original research question and project goals and how the maps can inform further action. Although individuals work independently to contribute their unique perspectives during data collection, the map and associated visuals are the result of integration of individual input to visualize a group's thinking. During the interpretation step, the researcher facilitates a session with the target group/community to qualitatively review the concept map by discussing the cluster domains and exploring the ideas within each cluster and to assess the alignment of viewpoints on the ladder graphs. Viewing the maps and ladder graphs provides the opportunity to see the meaning and values expressed as a group, discuss further insights, and determine what actions, if any, are necessary. Actions might be to simply understand an issue and promote dialogue among the community or may include forming action teams to develop strategies that address specific issues which emerged on the map. For example, O'Campo, Burke, Peak, McDonnell, and Gielen (2005) used CM as a means to understand the relationship of neighborhood characteristics to intimate partner violence. Although no interventions were developed, their CM research provided the basis for a deeper understanding of the complexities associated with intimate partner violence, increasing the likelihood that future research and the design of interventions would take into account such nuances. In a study about influences on physical activity within an urban African American community, Kelly et al. (2007) used the concept mapping results to engage the community and identify specific actions and strategies to increase physical activity. In a third alternative to developing actions, Szaflarski, Vaughn, McLinden, Wess, and Ruffner (in press) worked with multiple community stakeholders to develop a concept map to address HIV/AIDS in a Black faith community. The results were shared with the community and served as a basis for action planning. However, unlike the previous example, the researchers did not lead the action planning phase and were not part of subsequent decision making. In this case, the community took the responsibility for considering the results and then decided what actions needed to be taken.

Benefits of Concept Mapping

CM has numerous benefits as a community-based research methodology. Overall, CM methodology is "reflexive, flexible and iterative" (Cornwall & Jewkes, 1995, p. 1668) and can be used to answer a variety of research questions for different purposes (e.g., needs assessments, evaluation, knowledge generation). As a mixed method, CM is integrative because it combines multiple quantitative and qualitative techniques into a single integrated methodology. Although the structured data collection and the application of sophisticated analytical techniques provide rigor, the visual representation of the data through the maps means that the results are accessible to members of the community. Aside from the research/statistician supporting the statistical analysis, understanding the results does not require comprehension of the underlying mathematics. The visual results are, with some guidance, intuitive and easily understood by community members (Burke et al., 2005).

In addition to balancing rigor with accessibility by the community, a major strength of CM is that it can be used in a participatory, community-engaged manner. CM is uniquely suited to address the inclusion of multiple participants and communities in all aspects of research from data collection to developing meaning from results (Burke et al., 2005). Depending on the goals of the project and the participants, CM can vary in levels of involvement, decision making, and communication and can be considered to occur on a continuum, from academic researchers doing outreach to the community to shared leadership between academic and community partners (Centers for Disease Control and Prevention [CDC], 2011). The steps of CM methodology allow for the possibility of participants and researchers to engage with each other and collaborate in all stages of the research process. As a result, the likelihood increases that interventions, solutions, and decisions that result from the research are contextually relevant to those most affected (Ahmad et al., 2012; Vaughn et al., 2013). Indeed, "this integration of participants throughout the process is possible since concept mapping draws on methodologies that are part of the participatory learning and action tradition, which enable participants to share, analyze and enhance their knowledge of their own lives and prioritize and act on this knowledge" (Bayer, Cabrera, Gilman, Hindin, & Tsui, 2010, p. 2087).

Challenges of Concept Mapping

Like other research methods that have a qualitative component, CM has the same methodological limitations, such as a potentially small sample size, nonrandom sampling, and resource intensity (Burke et al., 2005). Possibly unique to CM is the response burden. The sorting task, which is central to CM methodology, can require a respondent to spend 30 or more minutes to complete the task, and this time can increase depending on the number of cards to be sorted and the diligence with which the individual approaches the task. The time spent by a respondent in the sorting task is in addition to time spent during other steps of the methodology. Also, the task of sorting is generally not familiar to most respondents and requires some additional explanation—more than is required with tasks that may be more familiar, such as completing a questionnaire. Despite these challenges, with sufficient explanation, most groups can easily participate in the process of CM. In fact, prior research has shown that neither language (Haque & Rosas, 2010) nor age (Borden et al., 2006; Chun & Springer, 2005; Davis, Saltzburg, & Locke, 2010; Ries, Voorhees, Gittlesonhn, Roche, & Astone, 2008; Vaughn et al., 2013) is a barrier to participation when involving the community in complex issues. Pertaining to researchers, CM requires that the researchers have the resources to create the maps, such as the capability to undertake the data management and analysis steps for the multivariate analysis and access to software for the analyses. The researchers also need a working knowledge of how these multivariate statistical techniques convert individual data into a map(s) of what the community thinks. The working knowledge is required in order to explain to community members the relationship of distance on the maps to similarity of ideas and the parsing of the many ideas into clusters. When CM is used in a participatory manner, skilled facilitation is required from someone who both understands the methodology and can manage group dynamics in order to help a group understand the maps and then interpret and use the maps toward future action. There are challenges to using CM, but they are not unique to CM because other sophisticated methodologies similarly require multiple capabilities on the part of the researcher.

CASE STUDY

In the United States, suicide is the third leading cause of death among youth (CDC, 2014; Miller & Eckert, 2009). Youth who have had personal experiences with suicide offer unique and invaluable perspectives that can greatly impact the development and successful implementation of suicide prevention efforts. In order to promote the direct inclusion of youth in teen suicide prevention research, we conducted a CM project focused on youth suicide prevention. Specifically, adolescents were asked to (a) identify and describe their perspectives about stopping teen suicide, (b) explore the relative importance and ease of implementation of different strategies to prevent suicide, and (c) use the concept map and the ladder graphs to guide future planning efforts.

Step 1. Preparation

We partnered with an established youth advisory council, the Youth Council for Suicide Prevention (YCSP) at Cincinnati Children's Hospital Medical Center, to develop the focus prompt and conduct the CM study. The 2014–2015 YCSP includes 32 high school teens from the Cincinnati area. Addressing the larger goal of youth suicide prevention in Cincinnati, the focus prompt for this study was "In order to stop teen suicide, we need to . . . ."

Step 2. Idea Generation

At various community events and meetings, a total of 237 Cincinnati youth completed the generation phase of concept mapping in response to the focus prompt, and this resulted in a large set of diverse responses that were relevant to stopping teen suicide. After editing the statements to eliminate redundant ideas and deleting ideas that did not respond to the focus prompt, 77 unique statements remained.

Step 3. Structuring the Ideas

Twenty-three of the 32 members of the YCSP worked independently via an online card-sorting program to complete an unstructured sorting of the 77 statements into groups of similar ideas that they created and named. Members of the YCSP Leadership Council (N = 10) and health professionals who work in the area of suicide prevention (N = 10) rated each of the 77 statements on a 1–5 Likert-type scale with respect to importance to youth suicide prevention (1 = *not important at all* and 5 = *extremely important*) and ease of implementation (1 = *very hard to do* and 5 = *very easy to do*). Respondents were informed that all ideas were important to some extent and could be accomplished; they were asked to consider the relative importance and relative difficulty of an idea among all of the other ideas and were encouraged to use all values on the rating scale.

Step 4. Representation

The sorting data from the respondents were analyzed using individual differences multidimensional scaling (de Leeuw & Mair, 2009). MDS created x,y coordinates and positioned the ideas as points in a two-dimensional map; hierarchical cluster analysis was applied to the x,y coordinates to compute clusters of points that identified themes or concepts among the 77 ideas. Analyses were conducted using R software (R Core Team, 2014). The multidimensional scaling results show how the 77 ideas are arranged in relation to each other (see Fig. 30.2). The eight-cluster solution was chosen and is represented by the boundaries around ideas in Figure 30.2. Mean ratings were computed for each cluster overall and then separately for youth and professionals. To visualize the values, ladder graphs were created to compare the pattern of importance and difficulty of implementation between youth and professionals (see Fig. 30.3).

Step 5. Interpretation

At one of their regular meetings, members of the YCSP leadership council reviewed the eight-cluster solution, including the ideas in each cluster and the names that were associated with each cluster during the sorting process. Using this information, the leadership council selected names for each cluster that represented the overall theme among the ideas in that cluster (see Fig. 30.1). Although a complete review of the map is beyond the scope of this chapter, a brief tour will illustrate the variety of ideas expressed by participants (see Table 30.1 for a list of representative ideas within each cluster). Beginning at the top of the map, Cluster 6, Connecting Teens to Help, expresses the need to encourage vulnerable teens to take action to speak up, reach out, tell someone, and so on. Because distance on this map is an expression of similarity, nearby clusters can be expected to have some overlap of ideas. Moving to the left, Cluster 2, Education and Communication About Mental Health, similarly expresses a need for action, but, unlike Cluster 6, which seems directed toward vulnerable teens, Cluster 2 expresses a need for action to change the environment around vulnerable teens. Moving to the right, Cluster 4, Encouragement and Suicide Prevention for Teens, emphasizes a more personal action of listening to ensure that someone feels he or she has been heard. Likewise, Cluster 7, Support and Reaching Out,

"In order to stop teen suicide, we need to...."

12. In groups, help ensure that people feel like they are being heard.
28. Help an at-risk teen find an outlet for feelings they might otherwise keep bottled up.
35. Connect teens that need it with the professional help they need.
41. Reduce the pressure teens feel to be perfect.
46. Encourage teens to tell someone about their problem(s).
65. Encourage teens to speak up and talk about problems.
70. Encourage teens to tell a teacher or counselor about their problem(s).
71. Use or create a network of people around an at-risk teen, find people who can tell them they are worthwhile.

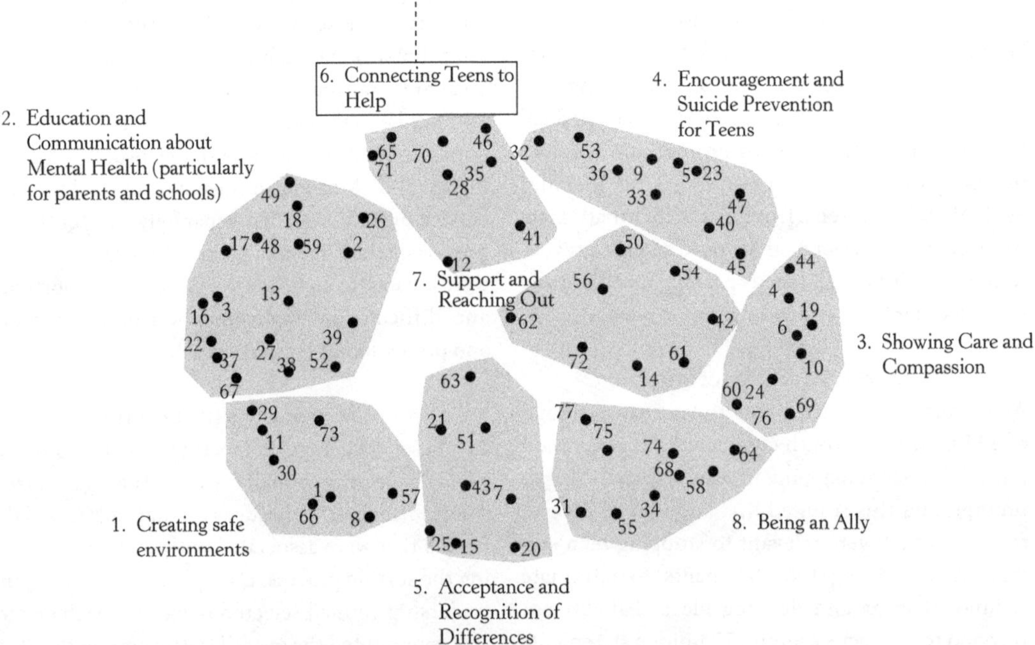

FIGURE 30.2: Clusters of points and the ideas that are represented on the map by the points. Typically, a session with the community would start with the point map and build to the cluster map with a review of the content within each of the clusters.

focuses on making sure that teens know that someone understands and is available to help. The sentiment of a personal concern is further expressed in Cluster 3, Showing Care and Compassion, and in Cluster 8, Being an Ally. Cluster 5, Acceptance and Recognition of Differences, continues the sentiment of care and concern but with the added nuance that other teens have a challenge and a responsibility to recognize and accept the uniqueness of others. Cluster 1, Creating Safe Environments, begins a transition back to Cluster 2 and is similarly about taking action on the environment but with a focus on personal actions.

To help inform priorities for the YCSP, the mean values of importance and difficulty were computed for all ideas within each cluster, first for all raters and then separately for the youth and the professionals (Table 30.1). To examine the pattern of results, multiple ladder graphs were constructed. Figure 30.2 shows a comparison of youth and professionals for each of the dimensions of value, importance of the idea to suicide prevention, and the difficulty of implementation. Although the table of data suggests minor differences in the mean values, a "pattern matching approach implies a different view of data . . . . [It] treats relevant data about programs, measures, participants, or outcomes as patterns or as a whole rather than just as a collection of individual measures or observations" (Trochim, 1989b, p. 358). The ladder graphs illustrate that, in general, the professionals and the youth agree on the importance and the difficulty of achieving the ideas in the eight clusters. However, the ladder graphs show that, compared to the youth, the professionals have

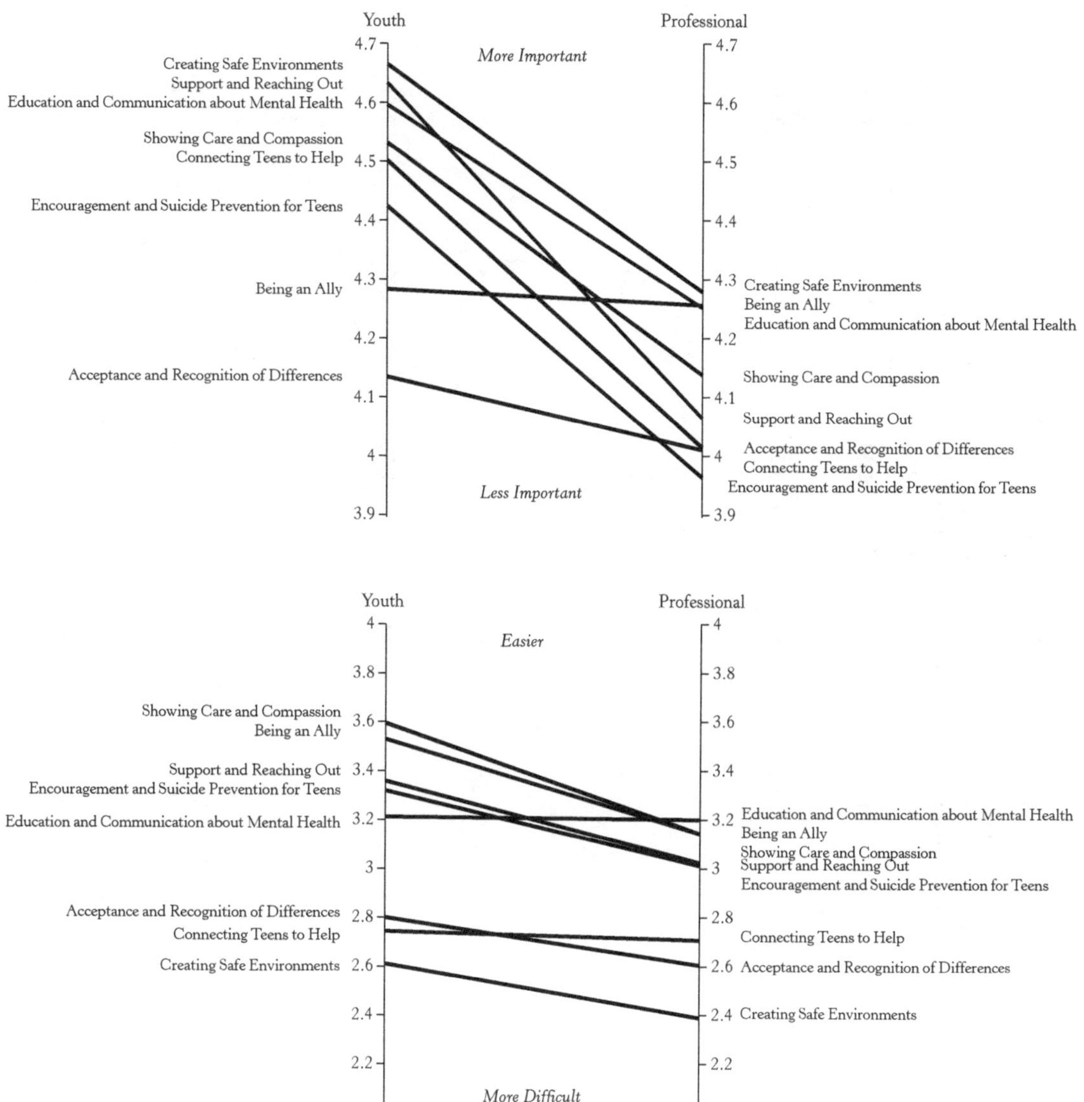

FIGURE 30.3: Ladder graphs of importance and easiness ratings that illustrate the patterns of youth perspective compared to professionals' perspective. This visual is open to interpretation by the community in a way that is often more robust than providing a table of data or more conventional graphics.

lower ratings on both graphs, indicating less importance and greater difficulty in implementing the clusters overall. This difference is interesting and a topic for further exploration with both groups. Furthermore, although both the youth and professionals are aligned on a number of clusters, there is also a noteworthy discrepancy on each of the ladder graphs. Cluster 8, Being an Ally, ranks near the bottom of importance by youth and near the top by professionals. When considering the difficulty of implementation, Cluster 2, Education and Communication About Mental Health, was seen as the least difficult by professionals and more difficult by youth. In both instances, the discrepancies indicate areas of further exploration and discussion with both youth and professionals.

Step 6. Utilization

The final concept map and results of the pattern matching were disseminated to all members of the YCSP to be used in future planning for the Leadership Council and each of the three working groups (i.e., Community Outreach, Social Media, and Youth Participatory Action Research).

TABLE 30.1: REPRESENTATIVE IDEAS AND MEAN RATINGS OF IMPORTANCE AND EASINESS FOR EACH CLUSTER

Clusters and Representative Ideas	Importance			Easiness		
	Overall Cluster Mean	Youth Cluster Mean	Professional Cluster Mean	Overall Cluster Mean	Youth Cluster Mean	Professional Cluster Mean
Cluster 1: Creating Safe Environments	4.47	4.66	4.28	2.50	2.61	2.39
1. Stop the gossiping and bullying						
57. Never tell someone that they are "sick" or "not normal"						
Cluster 2: Education and Communication about Mental Health (particularly for parents and schools)	4.43	4.60	4.25	3.21	3.22	3.20
3. Bring attention to suicide prevention, especially in schools						
13. Educate parents so they can help their teens, not reject them or not notice problems						
Cluster 3: Showing Care and Compassion	4.33	4.53	4.13	3.36	3.59	3.13
10. Help someone who is struggling realize that he or she is good enough and important						
44. Let people know that they are loved and they don't need to suffer alone						
Cluster 4: Encouragement and Suicide Prevention for Teens	4.20	4.43	3.96	3.17	3.32	3.01
33. Empower teens in their self-identity						
36. Listen to teens; let them be heard						
Cluster 5: Acceptance and Recognition of Differences	4.08	4.14	4.02	2.70	2.79	2.61
7. Have unique abilities accepted by more people						
20. Respect others for their personality and opinions						
Cluster 6: Connecting Teens to Help	4.26	4.50	4.01	2.73	2.75	2.70
35. Connect teens that need it with the professional help they need						
70. Encourage teens to tell a teacher or counselor about their problem(s)						
Cluster 7: Support and Reaching Out	4.34	4.63	4.06	3.18	3.34	3.01
56. Make sure people who are struggling know that someone cares/understands						
61. Let people know that there are people who can help						
Cluster 8: Being an Ally	4.27	4.28	4.26	3.34	3.53	3.14
74. Take time to listen and talk to people						
75. Let people know that it is OK to not be OK						

CONCLUSION

CM methodology is a mixed methods research approach that directly engages community members in a structured process of conceptualizing and visualizing thoughts about complex issues. The stepwise progression of CM contributes to an in-depth exploration of issues important to communities. The initial steps in CM involving data collection (i.e., idea generation and structuring steps) are completed independently and asynchronously. The independence of community member input helps ensure that each individual's perspective is not tempered by the perceived power of others, conformity biases, pressures to reach consensus, or any of the other challenges associated with group processes. The complexity of the research issue is not simplified; diverse and sometimes even conflicting ideas coexist throughout the steps of CM. Later steps of CM (i.e., interpretation and utilization) do involve group process as an important element of the methodology but are informed with the evidence that emerged from the community. The integration of quantitative and qualitative research methods produces visual representations in the form of maps and ladder graphs that allow community members to easily see and understand the relationship between ideas and the perspectives of various constituencies within a community. When CM is conducted in a participatory manner, all relevant constituents of the community can be actively engaged in the research process from beginning to end. This ensures that all voices are included, and that there is an increased likelihood that the CM results will have greater contextual relevance. Thus, rather than conducting research on or about communities, CM offers community-based researchers the opportunity to learn what the community thinks.

REFERENCES

Abdul-Quader, A. S., & Collins, C. (2011). Identification of structural interventions for HIV/AIDS prevention: The concept mapping exercise. *Public Health Reports, 126*, 777–788.

Ahmad, F., Mahmood, S., Pietkiewicz, I., McDonald, L., & Ginsburg, O. (2012). Concept mapping with South Asian immigrant women: Barriers to mammography and solutions. *Journal of Immigrant and Minority Health, 14*, 242–250.

Bayer, A. M., Cabrera, L. Z., Gilman, R. H., Hindin, M. J., & Tsui, A. O. (2010). Adolescents can know best: Using concept mapping to identify factors and pathways driving adolescent sexuality in Lima, Peru. *Social Science and Medicine, 70*, 2085–2095.

Borden, L., Perkins, D., Villarruel, F., Carleton-Hug, A., Stone, M., & Keith, J. (2006). Challenges and opportunities to Latino youth development: Increasing meaningful participation in youth development programs. *Hispanic Journal of Behavioral Sciences, 28*, 187–208.

Burke, J., O'Campo, P., Peak, G., Gielen, A., McDonnell, K., & Trochim, W. (2005). An introduction to concept mapping as a participatory public health research method. *Qualitative Health Research, 15*, 1392–1410.

Centers for Disease Control and Prevention. (2011). *Principles of community engagement*. NIH Publication No. 11-7782. Retrieved June 2015, from http://www.atsdr.cdc.gov/communityengagement/pdf/PCE_Report_508_FINAL.pdf

Centers for Disease Control and Prevention. (2014). *Suicide prevention: Youth suicide*. Retrieved June 2015, from http://www.cdc.gov/violenceprevention/pub/youth_suicide.html

Chun, J., & Springer, D. W. (2005). Stress and coping strategies in runaway youths: An application of concept mapping. *Brief Treatment and Crisis Intervention, 5*, 57–74.

Cornwall, A., & Jewkes, R. (1995). What is participatory research? *Social Science and Medicine, 41*, 1667–1676.

Davis, T. S., Saltzburg, S., & Locke, C. R. (2010). Assessing community needs of sexual minority youths: Modeling concept mapping for service planning. *Journal of Gay and Lesbian Social Services, 22*, 226–249.

de Leeuw, J., & Mair, P. (2009). Multidimensional scaling using majorization: SMACOF in R. *Journal of Statistical Software, 31*, 1–30.

Haque, N., & Rosas, S. (2010). Concept mapping of photovoices: Sequencing and integrating methods to understand immigrants' perceptions of neighborhood influences on health. *Family and Community Health, 33*, 193–206.

Jackson, K. M., & Trochim, W. M. K. (2002). Concept mapping as an alternative approach for the analysis of open-ended survey responses. *Organizational Research Methods, 5*, 307–336.

Johnson, S. L., Burke, J. G., & Gielen, A. C. (2011). Prioritizing the school environment in school violence prevention efforts. *Journal of School Health, 81*, 331–340.

Kane, M., & Trochim, W. M. K. (2007). *Concept mapping for planning and analysis*. Thousand Oaks, CA: Sage.

Kelly, C. M., Baker, E. A., Brownson, R. C., & Schootman, M. (2007). Translating research into practice: Using concept mapping to determine locally relevant intervention strategies to increase physical activity. *Evaluation and Program Planning, 30*, 282–293.

Miller, D. N., & Eckert, T. L. (2009). Youth suicidal behavior: An introduction and overview. *School Psychology Review, 38,* 153.

Novak, J. D. (1998). *Learning, creating and using knowledge: Concept maps as facilitative tools in schools and corporations.* Mahwah, NJ: Erlbaum.

O'Campo, P., Burke, J., Peak, G. L., McDonnell, K. A., & Gielen, A. C. (2005). Uncovering neighbourhood influences on intimate partner violence using concept mapping. *Journal of Epidemiology and Community Health, 59,* 603–608.

R Core Team. (2014). *R: A language and environment for statistical computing* (Version 3.0.3) [Computer software]. Vienna, Austria: R Foundation for Statistical Computing.

Ries, A. V., Voorhees, C. C., Gittlesonhn, J., Roche, K. M., & Astone, N. M. (2008). Adolescents' perceptions of environmental influences on physical activity. *American Journal of Health Behavior, 32,* 26–39.

Risisky, D., Hogan, V. K., Kane, M., Burt, B., Dove, C., & Payton, M. (2008). Concept mapping as a tool to engage a community in health disparity identification. *Ethnicity and Disease, 18,* 77–83.

Rosas, S. R. (2012). The utility of concept mapping for actualizing participatory research. *Cuadernos Hispanoamericanos De Psycologia, 12,* 7–24.

Rosas, S. R., & Kane, M. (2012). Quality and rigor of the concept mapping methodology: A pooled study analysis. *Evaluation and Program Planning, 35,* 236–245.

Shorkey, C., Windsor, L. C., & Spence, R. (2009). Assessing culturally competent chemical dependence treatment services for Mexican Americans. *Journal of Behavioral Health Services and Research, 36,* 61–74.

Szaflarski, M., Vaughn, L. M., McLinden, D., Wess, Y., & Ruffner, A. (2015). Using concept mapping to mobilize a Black faith community to address HIV. *International Journal of Public Health,* 7(1), 117–130.

Trochim, W. (1989a). An introduction to concept mapping for planning and evaluation. *Evaluation and Program Planning, 12,* 1–16.

Trochim, W. (1989b). Outcome pattern matching and program theory. *Evaluation and Program Planning, 12,* 355–366.

Urban, J. B. (2008). Components and characteristics of youth development programs: The voices of youth-serving policymakers, practitioners, researchers, and adolescents. *Applied Development Science, 12,* 128–139.

Vaughn, L. M., Jacquez, F., & McLinden, D. (2013). The use of concept mapping to identify community-driven intervention strategies for physical and mental health. *Health Promotion Practice, 14,* 675–685.

31

Functional Analysis of Community Concerns in Participatory Action Research

YOLANDA SUAREZ-BALCAZAR AND FABRICIO BALCAZAR

More than a half-century ago, Lewin (1946) coined the term *action research* based on the belief that research is relevant only if it is grounded in the realities of the poor and leads to action. This emphasis on action and its focus on the relevance of research to promote social change has led to the development of new approaches to working with community members. Following this line of inquiry, the Colombian sociologist Orlando Fals Borda (1959, 1968) proposed the term participatory research, which, in turn, influenced the work of Freire (1970) on promoting critical awareness among the poor in Brazil and Hall (1975) on working with indigenous communities in Tanzania. Later on, the term *community-based participatory research* (CBPR) took front stage, with large bodies of literature emerging (Israel, Eng, Schulz, & Parker, 2005; Jason et al., 2005; Minkler & Wallerstein, 2008).

CBPR has gained recognition in the health and behavioral social sciences fields as an effective research approach to promoting the active participation of community residents in the research process (Israel et al., 2005). CBPR in itself is not a methodology but rather an approach to research. It emphasizes the inclusion of and engagement with community residents and community stakeholders in the earliest stages of defining the research questions, setting research priorities, and designing intervention strategies (Israel et al., 2005). CBPR researchers posit that social issues are best understood, analyzed, and solved when the identification of issues and solutions comes from the participants themselves. In contrast to more traditional investigator-driven research methodologies, CBPR begins with the issues of greatest concern to individuals, communities, and relevant stakeholders (Minkler & Wallerstein, 2008). The present chapter provides an overview of a participatory action research community needs assessment methodology designed to facilitate a functional analysis of community concerns according to the views of the target population. We illustrate the methodology with an international case study.

INTRODUCTION TO FUNCTIONAL ANALYSIS OF COMMUNITY CONCERNS

Many CBPR approaches to community-needs assessment research have included a functional analysis of policy efforts to promote environmental health in partnership with communities and institutions of higher education (Minkler, Vasquez, & Shepard, 2006) and the use of community surveys to identify community assets and concerns (Hennessey-Lavery et al., 2005), among other approaches. The term *functional analysis* was used by Skinner (1953) to denote empirical demonstrations of "cause-and-effect relations" between environment and behavior. In the behavior analysis literature, Hanley, Iwata, and McCord (2003) explained that the term *function* has been used in two main ways. One use conveys the effect that a behavior has on the environment, or, as Hanley et al. (2003) put it, the purpose the behavior serves for an individual (e.g., the function of behavior is to terminate an ongoing event). The second use describes a relation between two variables (typically between some environmental event and a class of behavior) in which one varies given the presence or absence of the other (e.g., responding as a function of an event). Both uses of the term are relevant to a functional analysis of existing behavior, in that relations between behavior and environmental events are demonstrated in the context of learning about how the behavior operates in the environment (Hanley et al., 2003).

Based on their systematic review of 277 empirical studies that utilized functional analysis as an assessment tool, Hanley et al. (2003) found that most functional analysis studies had been conducted in hospital (inpatient) facilities (32.5%), schools (31.4%), or institutions (25.3%), with much less research (17.4%) having been conducted in other settings (e.g., homes and vocational programs). Although a substantial proportion of functional analysis studies (37.2%) included adults, the majority of studies included children, particularly those with some form of developmental disability, which reflects the current state of behavior analysis practice. Very few studies using a functional analysis behavioral approach have been conducted in community settings or with groups of community members. Such studies are described in Chapter 18 in this volume.

In this chapter, we posit that a functional analysis provides a general framework for understanding and analyzing relationships between community contexts, the behaviors of community members, and the general consequences of such behaviors in modifying—or not—relevant contextual features in the target community. Research methodologies that focus on a functional and contextual analysis of the community have included asset-based community development strategies (McKnight & Born, 2010), community mapping (Botello et al., 2013; Gelles & Ludeman, 2009), and mapping residents' perceptions of neighborhood boundaries (Coulton, Korbin, Chan, & Su, 2001).

Methodologies to conduct functional analysis of community needs are mostly framed under community needs assessments. One methodology developed by a team of researchers from the University of Kansas, including the first author of this chapter, and grounded in CBPR is called the Concerns Report Method (CRM). The CRM is a systematic CBPR approach for engaging participants in the research process, particularly for identifying concerns, conducting a functional analysis of community issues, and engaging in problem solving and actions to address identified concerns (Nary, White, Budde, & Vo, 2004; Suarez-Balcazar, Balcazar, Quiros, Chavez, & Quiros, 1995).

The Concerns Report Method

The CRM draws on a mixed methods approach to research, including focus groups, survey research, and analytic strategies that originate in discrepancy modeling (Ludwig-Beymer, Blankemeir, Casas-Byots, & Suarez-Balcazar, 1996). Furthermore, the CRM is grounded in theories of empowerment, self-help, and community development (Fawcett, Francisco, & Schultz, 2004; Suarez-Balcazar & Balcazar, 2007). The CRM has been used to identify and take action with diverse populations, including low-income families in Costa Rica (Suarez-Balcazar et al., 1995), people with physical disabilities (Suarez-Balcazar, Bradford, & Fawcett, 1988), Colombian immigrants (Balcazar, Garcia-Iriarte, & Suarez-Balcazar, 2009), residents of a rural Mexican community (Arellano, Balcazar, Alvarado, & Suarez, ,in press)), Hispanic immigrant families (Suarez-Balcazar, Martinez, & Casas-Byots, 2005), rural communities in the United States (Mayer & Seekins, 2013), and people with emerging disabilities (Nary et al., 2004), among other populations.

The CRM's social validity and reliability were established by Schriner and Fawcett (1988), who reported high ratings of the helpfulness, completeness, and representativeness for a concerns survey developed by low-income families. Mathews, Petty, and Fawcett (1990), calculating a Spearman rank correlation between the responses of 405 participants with disabilities to the same survey items on a survey developed by people with disabilities at 18-month intervals, found highly consistent scores ($rs = .94$).

The CRM goes beyond being a needs assessment CBPR methodology. It has been conceptualized as an agenda-setting, capacity-building, and empowering approach, as participants take control of decisions and actions that affect their lives. In this process, members of the target group take an active role in conducting a functional and contextual analysis of community issues that they care about. In that it involves the target group's active participation, this method calls for the utilization of focus groups and interviews with diverse stakeholders to develop a concerns survey and a town hall meeting to provide the target group with an opportunity to analyze the issues identified as concerns and community strengths through the survey. Focus groups and town hall meetings, essential components of the CRM, have been found to be effective and culturally appropriate with minority communities (Balcazar et al., 2009). Thus, the CRM can generate a set of priorities, including

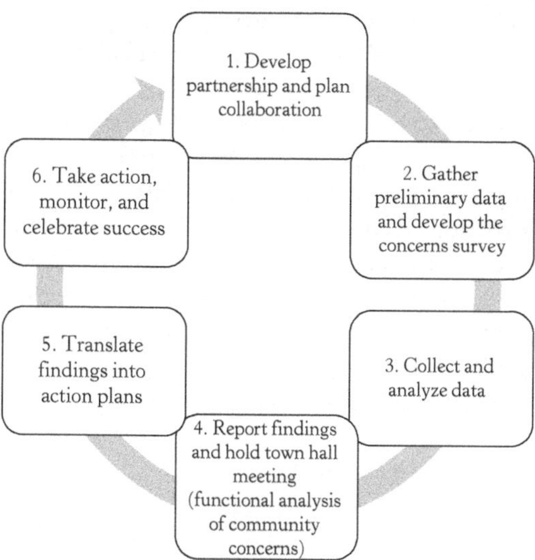

FIGURE 31.1: Concerns Report Method phases.

identifying community strengths and concerns from the perspective of participants that can be used in setting an agenda, conducting a functional and contextual analysis of community concerns, and informing services and policies regarding community issues. The survey results are analyzed, shared, and discussed with various stakeholders in town hall meetings and brainstorming sessions. During these meetings, participants discuss the dimensions of the issues identified and alternative solutions to address concerns.

The CRM includes the following six systematic phases (see Fig. 31.1): (a) developing partnership and planning collaboration; (b) gathering preliminary data and developing a concerns survey; (c) collecting and analyzing data; (d) reporting findings and holding town hall meetings to discuss data with community members and other stakeholders; (e) translating findings into recommendations and action plans through systematic stakeholder participation; and (f) taking action, monitoring, and celebrating success (see the Community Tool Box, 2014, for more details on the CRM). The following section discusses the six CRM phases within the context of a description of its application in a small rural community in Mexico.

CASE STUDY

Project Background

The focus of this case study was a small rural community in Mexico. The community has a population of 13,000 people, with approximately 57% of the residents younger than 29 years old (Consejo Estatal de Población de Jalisco, 2010). The rebirth of this community was an initiative that involved collaboration from multiple agencies seeking to work with community members to address the community's needs. Partner organizations included FEDEJAL, a federation of small business owners and regional clubs from the Mexican State of Jalisco in the United States; the Club Pro-Obras, a Chicago-based club of immigrants from the community in Mexico; the government of the State of Jalisco; the Necahual Foundation, a Chicago-based charity created to promote youth development activities in the Mexican community; and the municipality of the community itself, all of whom teamed up to create a transnational program focused on identifying community strengths and concerns and addressing the needs identified by community members. The second author introduced the CRM into the project as an action-oriented, participatory methodology to identify the community's needs and use the findings to promote social change. The following is a description of the various phases of the CRM as they were implemented in this community.

Stage 1: Develop Partnership and Plan Collaboration

During this initial stage, the partners should define the purpose of the CRM, identify relevant stakeholders and target community, and discuss plans for utilizing the data that might emerge. In the present project, leaders from FEDEJAL contacted the second author to ask for advice about how to proceed in helping the community in a meaningful way. The researcher proposed the use of the CRM in order to identify needs, determine priorities, and set an agenda for action. The proposal was well received, and a meeting was arranged with FEDEJAL's executive committee in order to make a formal presentation of the proposal. A month later, the researcher was invited to visit the town to meet with key community leaders to discuss the idea. Two town residents volunteered to coordinate the process and implement the methodology under the close supervision of, and training from, the researcher.

Several meetings were held during this early planning phase. During the first initial meeting with key stakeholders from the town—a political candidate, the parish priest, a long-time farmer from the township, the mayor at that time, and two community leaders—the researcher explained the process and method so that the group could identify potential participants, recruitment strategies, and the best strategy for administering the concerns survey once it was developed.

Stage 2: Gather Preliminary Data and Develop the Concerns Survey

For the gathering of foundational data, the CRM calls for using focus groups to identify the main values and issues that the target community cares about in order to narrow the focus. During this phase of the project, the researcher met with a group of stakeholders representing different community sectors (the town mayor, community business owners, farmer, leaders, and a local teacher) to reflect on values and gather preliminary data. A second meeting was conducted in the form of a focus group with a representative group of community leaders and members from the town to identify relevant community issues. This group of stakeholders, which reflected different interests, ages, and experiences, helped to generate the guiding framework for the development of the concerns survey and a preliminary list of survey items.

This qualitative-data collection phase was augmented with interviews and one-on-one meetings with key community stakeholders, including the former mayor of the town, a successful business owner, and two community leaders. Those who participated in the focus group or who were interviewed were asked to reflect on three general questions: What are the community issues that you value and that are important to you? What are the community issues that you worry about? What are the community strengths that you want to preserve?

Based on the preliminary data collected, the group developed a 53-item concerns survey. The survey's final draft was pilot tested with the help of five community volunteers. A 15-question demographic section at the beginning of the survey inquired about age, gender, marital status, education level, and types of disabilities in the household. The survey, created directly in Spanish, included two types of questions for each issue. The first question asked about the importance of a particular issue, such as affordable and decent housing ("How important is it for you that ...?"). The second question asked about the respondent's satisfaction with the issue ("How satisfied are you with ...?"). Both questions were rated on a 5-point scale, with 1 indicating *not important* or *not satisfied* and 5 indicating *very important* or *very satisfied*. Items that participants rate high in importance and high in satisfaction are considered *strengths*, while items that are rated high in importance and low in satisfaction are considered *needs/concerns* (see Nary et al., 2004).

Stage 3: Collect and Analyze Data

Concerns surveys can be administered in different ways, including door-to-door canvassing, community gatherings, small groups, and/or made available at different community public settings, including public libraries. Given the cultural and geographical characteristics of the community in the present project, the team decided that door-to-door canvassing was the most appropriate method. Once the survey was finalized, the state government printed the survey. The town's former mayor asked for support from a local high school and a local college to collect the data. Two local project coordinators who had been trained by the researcher trained a group of 30 volunteer students in conducting door-to-door canvasses and administering the survey. The students collected the data as part of their community service requirement for high school graduation. The mayor supported the initiative and facilitated the transportation of interviewers during the data collection phase, which was held on weekends for a month and a half. A total of 1,228 residents completed the survey; the average age of the respondents was 44 years. Participants were 60% female and 40% male. A total of 53% of the participants had family members living in the United States, residing mainly in California (64%) and Chicago (18%).

Table 31.1 summarizes the list of the top community strengths and concerns identified by residents. As is typical for such surveys, the main data reported were the mean percentage of importance and the mean percentage of satisfaction for each item (see the Community Tool Box, 2014, for specific examples of how to analyze concerns report data). These results were the topic of discussion

TABLE 31.1: MAIN STRENGTHS AND CONCERNS OF THE COMMUNITY

Issues	Percentage Level of Importance	Percentage Level of Satisfaction
Community Strenghts		
Having pride in being a citizen of this community	82.7%	85.6%
Preservation of the traditions and culture of the community	85.9%	80.9%
Conservation and protection of grassland areas	84.0%	80.8%
Being an active member of the community	89.9%	76.3%
Crime detection and prevention	89.4%	75.6%
Community Concerns		
Demand that the government penalize companies and individuals that pollute the river	89.8%	66%
Develop ideas for production and manufacture	88.2%	66.6%
Develop a project to produce local crafts	87.8%	64.6%
Create employment opportuniites in the community	84.2%	56.3%
Provide opportunities for affordable and decent housing	83.3%	60.5%
Create opportunities to attend the university	83%	58.6%
Improve access to public transportation in the community	83%	61%

Note: Percentages indicate the level of importance and satisfaction on a scale from 1 to 100.

during a subsequent town hall meeting and were targeted for action by community members.

Stage 4: Report Findings and Hold Town Hall Meetings

In reporting the data obtained from concerns surveys, the top strengths and problems are listed in a one-page brief report that serves as a concise statement of the issues identified by the individuals surveyed. Preparation of this report is then followed by town hall meetings to discuss the results. Town hall meetings, also referred to as public forums or community forums, are large open gatherings of individuals who share a common predicament or condition and who are interested in expressing their ideas and suggestions for improving their conditions. These forms of public participation have been cited as ways of exercising democracy and empowering individuals (Lukensmeyer & Brigham, 2003).

The town hall meeting also provides an opportunity for participants to conduct a functional analysis—an in-depth analysis of the contextual factors associated with the issue—of the community concerns and strengths. Stakeholders who attend the meeting brainstorm answers to the following questions to facilitate a functional analysis of each concern identified:

Functional and Contextual Analysis of Community Concerns

Discussion of Antecedents

1. Why is this a community concern?
2. What issues are contributing to this being a community concern?

Discussion of Behaviors

3. How are you and your family affected by the concern?
4. In what situations does this concern affect you the most?
5. What impact does the issue have on your family and significant others?

Discussion of Consequences

6. What are the consequences of keeping the community concern as it is?
7. What are the consequences of addressing the community concern?
8. What can you and your community do to address the community concern?
9. What are the priorities (ask if several ideas are discussed)?
10. For each priority discussed: (a) What actions are needed? (b) Who is responsible for taking actions? (c) By when should action be taken?

Functional and Contextual Analysis of Community Strengths

Discussion of Antecedents

1. What specific situations and conditions facilitate the promotion of this community strength?
2. Is there any current threat to the strengths that you worry about?

Discussion of Behaviors

3. How are you benefiting from the strength?
4. What do you need to do to sustain/maintain the strength?

Discussion of Consequences

5. What are the consequences that maintaining the strength has on you and your family?
6. What would happen if you and your community do not preserve the strength?

The report of the survey's results was shared during Sunday masses and at a community town hall meeting held in the downtown plaza on a Sunday after mass. The report was also posted in the mayoral office. During the town hall meeting, the mayor directed the discussion of the strengths and concerns identified by the community. A total of 100 attendees were asked to conduct a functional analysis of community issues using the questions provided earlier. The majority of community members had very strong feelings about the pollution of the river, and that became a priority concern. Promoting the culture of Jalisco through dance and music was of interest to many teachers and parents of children and youth.

Stage 5: Translate Findings Into Action Plans

During town hall meetings participants are invited to sign up to work on different issues identified as community concerns and/or strengths. This work can be done in small teams who meet to plan the actions needed to address top issues. Teams working on different concerns will need to identify what actions and resources are needed to address the concern, who is responsible for taking action, by when actions should be taken, and how the actions would be evaluated.

In the present project, community members were asked to join various committees that fit their personal interests (e.g., environmentalists joined the river pollution committee, while teachers and parents of school children joined a cultural committee). Community leaders used the survey results for planning and taking action. Some of the proposals involved increasing the promotion of social and cultural activities to enhance community traditions, such as celebrating Family Day to strengthen the town's families, providing field trips for children to visit museums in the nearby city, organizing soccer tournaments for children and youth, and conducting a traditional religious play on Christmas. The community leaders also proposed increasing community services and working with elementary school teachers to identify vulnerable children. Some of the ideas for new services included preventing violence against children, offering early-intervention workshops to improve early child development among low-income families, and instituting handicraft classes for youth. With respect to activities aimed at building community capacity, participants proposed to distribute environmental information on the status of the river in order to increase community awareness about the river's pollution and the health risks that it posed, and the group nominated a leader who would focus on improving the economic conditions in the agricultural fields near the town.

Stage 6: Take Action, Monitor, and Celebrate Success

Taking action to address issues is one of the joys of this methodology. It calls for the community researchers and local community partners to address the issues identified during the CRM process. During this phase a final report and a list of actions based on the recommendations from the results are developed and distributed widely in the community of interest. Copies of the report are sent to important decision makers who have a say in the concerns identified.

In the case of this community, one of the key project coordinators—a strong supporter of the project who was originally from that community and lived in Chicago—facilitated the community's addressing of its concerns by gathering funding from immigrants living in the Chicago area and the Mexican government and bringing together human resources to start the initiative. After the CRM results were analyzed and disseminated, community members came together to continue the discussion of ideas to enhance the strengths and address the main concerns that were identified.

Community Efforts to Enhance Strengths

Although the preservation of cultural traditions and family unity were identified as strengths, community members discussed threats, such as the lack of organizations for supporting families and addressing family violence. In order to increase community social services and promote activities that would enhance community traditions, community leaders decided to create a nonprofit association called Necahual Foundation. Necahual Foundation's mission was to help children and family members living in vulnerable environments in the community and to provide educational, cultural, and recreational activities to community members. Necahual Foundation operates with funds donated by immigrants living in the Chicago area. It created a social service delivery unit to offer support services and prevention to families affected by domestic violence. The unit provides free preventive, legal, and psychological services. In this vein, support from the university near the town enabled the university to conduct its clinical psychology internship program through the foundation. Currently, the university is collaborating with three clinical psychology interns to cover the growing demand for services. In addition, the Necahual Foundation offers the town's children a variety of social and cultural activities that enhance the community's traditions (e.g., Family Day and Children's Day celebrations and mini-Olympic games events).

Community Efforts to Address the Concerns

Club Pro-Obras members learned about a program called 3x1, created by the Mexican federal government to support efforts by Mexican immigrants living in the United States to improve the living conditions in their Mexican hometowns. The program involves the participation of Mexican federal, state, and local governments and hometown associations in the United States to facilitate community development. In the 3x1 program, for each dollar donated by an immigrant group in the United States, each level of the Mexican government donates a dollar, so a $1 donation can potentially become $4. The 3x1 program's objectives were to benefit communities with high levels of poverty by promoting employment and social development community projects, thereby reinforcing civil society and government partnerships, and to strengthen Mexican emigrants' relationships with their hometowns.

One of the most pressing community concerns identified by the concerns survey was the lack of opportunities for young adults to attend college. Club Pro-Obras donated seven scholarships in 2012 and three scholarship in 2013 to students who, for lack of economic resources, were at risk for abandoning their studies.

Another community concern that emerged from the needs assessment was that of the river's pollution. The river in this community had become increasingly polluted during the past 40 years. There is an industrial corridor located near the river, with the industrial waste dumped directly into the river without any type of treatment to filter out contaminants. The river had become one of the most serious health threats for community residents (Instituto Mexicano para el Desarrollo Comunitario, 2007). In an effort to address this concern, the governor of the state of the region inaugurated the first industrial waste-water filtration treatment plant near the river (Vargas, 2014).

In summary, the application of the CRM in this community was very successful in bringing the community together to identify concerns and take various actions to address pressing needs. The community has celebrated its many successes while at the same time continuing to galvanize to address its concerns and preserve its strengths.

Cultural Considerations

Communities are infused with cultural and contextual elements that inform how individuals define and conceptualize issues and needs, live their lives, and relate to social and health systems around them (Suarez-Balcazar et al., 2010). Several cultural and contextual factors were considered in this case study. All meetings about the project were held in Spanish. Concepts relevant to the CRM, such as concerns, needs, empowerment, and community action, were translated to reflect local beliefs, values, and customs. This is a community in which residents value personal, one-to-one contact. Therefore, door-to-door canvassing was utilized as the most culturally appropriate method of data collection. Other methods of data collection, such as mailing the surveys, would have resulted in a low return rate because mail service in this community is lacking. Community focus groups and town hall meetings were held at a local church and after mass, a common meeting place and time for this community. Finally, we note that, for the project to be successful, politicians such as the local mayor and the governor needed to be included, which is apparently typical of community projects in small Mexican towns.

CONCLUSION

In this chapter we have provided an overview of a participatory needs assessment methodology that utilizes a functional analysis of community issues. A needs assessment methodology such as the CRM should be utilized when there is interest in helping community members take action(s) on their identified needs. The CRM provides a systematic process for gathering the opinions of those most likely to be affected by programs and services (Mayer & Seekins, 2013). This mixed methods CBPR approach is a catalyst for community change by bringing community residents together in the process of pursuing social transformation.

Despite the successful application of the CRM, the process has some challenges. First, community members have to agree to participate, work together, and invest time and effort in the process. This may be challenging in some cases because many oppressed communities struggle to unite and seek common goals (Suarez-Balcazar et al., 2005). People have different priorities, and for the most oppressed community members, day-by-day survival takes away their energy to participate in communal endeavors. This is a paradox because those who could benefit the most from the process are less likely to get involved. We observed this in the case study. The most active members in the process were professionals, retirees, farmers, and community leaders. The poorest members of the community participated only as recipients of some of the services introduced by the process. Identifying effective strategies for involving the most marginalized community members continues to be a challenge that should be examined in future research.

Second, there are unanticipated political events that can either help or derail the community process. In this case we observed both. What was helpful was the personal relationship that the key community leader had with the governor of the state at the time. This relationship opened many doors and even led to significant investment of state resources in starting the process of cleaning the river. What was not helpful was the election of the next mayor of the town, who was from a different party and had a history of corruption.

Yet, overall, the CRM was an effective process for generating significant changes in the town. As noted earlier, this methodology has been replicated in different cultural contexts with equally successful outcomes. Engagement in the community transformation process is also likely to empower participants and increase their motivation to remain engaged. Future applications of the CRM should continue to document its strengths and challenges as we learn more about the effectiveness of this participatory methodology in effecting social transformation and justice in various community contexts.

REFERENCES

Arellano, R., Balcazar, F., Alvarado, F., & Suarez, S. . (in press)). *A participatory action research intervention in a rural community in Mexico.*Universitas Psychologica.

Balcazar, F., García-Iriarte, E., & Suarez-Balcazar, Y. (2009). Participatory action research with Colombian immigrants. *Hispanic Journal of Behavioral Sciences, 31,* 112–127.

Botello, B., Palacio, S., Garcia, M., Margolles, M., Fernandez, F., Hernan, M., Nieto, J., & Cofino, R. (2013). Methodology for health assets mapping in a community. *Gaceta Sanitaria, 27,* 180–183.

Community Tool Box. (2014). *Conducting concerns surveys.* Retrieved June 2015, from http://ctb.ku.edu/en/tablecontents/sub_section_main_1045.aspx

Consejo Estatal de Población de Jalisco. (2010). *Informacion sociodemográfica por colonias* [Sociodemographic information by suburbs]. Retrieved June 2015, from http://coepojalisco.blogspot.com/2012/11/informacion-sociodemografica- por.html

Coulton, C., Korbin, J., Chan T., & Su, M. (2001). Mapping residents' perceptions of neighborhood boundaries: A methodological note. *American Journal of Community Psychology, 29,* 371–383.

Fals Borda, O. (1959). *La teoría y la realidad del cambio sociocultural en Colombia* [The theory and reality of sociocultural change in Colombia] (2nd ed.). Bogotá, Colombia: Universidad Nacional.

Fals Borda, O. (1968). *Subversión y cambio social* [Subversion and social change]. Bogotá, Colombia: Ediciones Tercer Mundo.

Fawcett, S. B., Francisco, V. T., & Schultz, J. A. (2004). Understanding and improving the work of community health and development. In J. Burgos & E. Ribes (Eds.), *Theory, basic and applied research, and technological applications in behavioral science* (pp. 209–242). Guadalajara, Mexico: Universidad de Guadalajara.

Freire, P. (1970). *Pedagogy of the oppressed*. New York, NY: Herder and Herder.

Gelles, E., & Ludeman, R. (2009). Adapting question mapping as a methodology to help make sense of a community's collective wisdom and shared futures. *Nonprofit Management and Leadership, 19*, 367–385.

Hall, B. (1975). Participatory research: An approach for change. *Prospects, 8*, 24–31.

Hanley, G., Iwata, B., & McCord, B. (2003). Functional analysis of problem behavior: A review. *Journal of Applied Behavior Analysis, 36*, 147–185.

Hennessey-Lavery, S., Smith, M. L., Esparza, A. A., Hrushow, A., Moore, M., & Reed, D. F. (2005). The community action model: A community-driven model designed to address disparities in health. *American Journal of Public Health, 95*, 611–616.

Instituto Mexicano para el Desarrollo Comunitario. (2007). *Report on violations to the Right to Health and to a Safe Environment in Juanacatlán and El Salto, Jalisco, Mexico*. Retrieved June 2015, from http://www2.ohchr.org/english/issues/globalization/business/docs/ExecutiveSummarySantiagoRiver_en.pdf

Israel, B. A., Eng, E., Schulz, A. J., & Parker, E. A. (2005). *Methods for community-based participatory research for health* (2nd ed.). San Francisco, CA: Jossey-Bass.

Jason, L. A., Keys, C. B., Suarez-Balcazar, Y., Taylor, R. R., Davis, M., Durlak, J., & Isenberg, D. (2005). *Participatory community research: Theories and methods in action*. Washington, DC: American Psychological Association.

Lewin, K. (1946). Action research and minority problems, *Journal of Social Issues, 2*, 34–46.

Ludwig-Beymer, P., Blankemeir, J., Casas-Byotos, C., & Suarez-Balcazar Y. (1996). Community assessment in a suburban Hispanic community: A description of method. *Journal of Transcultural Nursing, 8*, 19–27.

Lukensmeyer, J. C., & Brigham, S. (2003). Taking democracy to scale: Creating a town hall meeting for the twenty-first century. *National Civic Review, 91*, 351–356.

Mathews, R. M., Petty, R., & Fawcett, S. B. (1990). Rating consistency on successive statewide assessments of disability concerns. *Journal of Disability Policy Studies, 1*, 81–88.

Mayer, M., & Seekins, T. (2013). *Effective rural outreach: Using the Concerns Report Method as a tool for change*. Retrieved June 2015, from http://www.ilru.net/html/training/webcasts/archive/2013/08-15-CIL-NET.html

McKnight, J., & Born, P. T. (2010). *The abundant community: Awakening the power of families and neighborhoods*. San Francisco, CA: Berret-Koehler.

Minkler, M., Vasquez, V. B., & Shepard, P. (2006). Promoting environmental health policy through community based participatory research: A case study from Harlem, New York. *Journal of Urban Health, 83*, 101–110.

Minkler, M., & Wallerstein, N. (2008). *Community-based participatory research for health: From process to outcomes* (2nd ed.). San Francisco, CA: Jossey-Bass.

Nary, D. E., White, G. W., Budde, J. F., & Vo, H.Y. (2004). Identifying employment and vocational rehabilitation concerns of people with traditional and emerging disabilities. *Journal of Vocational Rehabilitation, 20*, 71–77.

Schriner, K. F., & Fawcett, S. B. (1988). Development and validation of a community concerns report method. *Journal of Community Psychology, 16*, 306–313.

Skinner, B. F. (1953). *Science and human behavior*. New York, NY: Macmillan.

Suarez-Balcazar, Y., & Balcazar, F. (2007). Empowerment approaches to identifying and addressing health concerns among minorities with disabilities. In C. Dumont & G. Kielhofner (Eds.), *Positive approaches to health care* (pp. 153–168). Hauppauge, NY: Nova Science.

Suarez-Balcazar, Y., Balcazar, F., Quiros, M., Chavez, M., & Quiros, O. (1995). A case study of international cooperation for community development and primary prevention in Costa Rica. *Prevention in Human Services, 25*, 3–23.

Suarez-Balcazar, Y., Bradford, B., & Fawcett, S. B. (1988). Common concerns of disabled Americans: Issues and options. *Social Policy, 19*, 29–35.

Suarez-Balcazar, Y., Martinez, L., & Casas-Byots, C. (2005). A participatory action research approach for identifying health service needs of Hispanic immigrants: Implications for occupational therapy. *Occupational Therapy in Health Care, 19*, 145–163.

Suarez-Balcazar, Y., Taylor-Ritzler, T., Garcia-Iriarte, E., Keys, C. B., Kinney, L., Ruch-Ross, H., . . . Curtin, G. (2010). Evaluation capacity building: A cultural and contextual framework. In F. Balcazar, Y. Suarez-Balcazar, T. Taylor-Ritzler, & C. B. Keys (Eds.), *Race, culture and disability: Rehabilitation science and practice* (pp. 307–324). Sudbury, MA: Jones and Bartlett.

Vargas, R. E. (2014). Inaugura planta de tratamiento de aguas en Zapopan: Impulsar cambios de fondo, la ruta del gobierno-Peña Nieto. [Inauguration of a water treatment plant in Zapopan: Promoting deep changes is the path of the government of Pena Nieto]. *La Jornada*. Retrieved June 2015, from http://www.jornada.unam.mx/2014/07/23/politica/005n1pol

32

Network Analysis and Stakeholder Analysis in Mixed Methods Research

ISIDRO MAYA-JARIEGO, DAVID FLORIDO DEL CORRAL, DANIEL HOLGADO, AND JAVIER HERNÁNDEZ-RAMÍREZ

In recent years we have witnessed the spreading of the creative uses of network analysis that combine qualitative and quantitative data and analysis. Network methods are used concurrently with or sequentially to ethnography, psychometric techniques, focus groups, simulations, surveys, qualitative interviews, visualization, and data mining, among others (Domínguez & Hollstein, 2014). Such designs contribute to better data quality, increase the data's validity and reliability, improve the understanding of the phenomena studied, reduce the biases and limitations of data collection and data analysis, and make the results more generalizable (Hollstein, 2011, 2014).

The expansion of mixed methods—in social sciences in general and in the field of social network analysis in particular—has coincided in time with a moment in which network analysis is also more popular in the field of community-based research (see Chapter 22; Neal & Christens, 2014). Social network analysis is one of the methods that "capture context" (Luke, 2005, p. 185). Indeed, it is a way of describing the relational properties of the environment; it uses social interaction as a basis, and data are, by definition, contextualized. In this sense, research on sense of community and empowerment, to mention two central concepts in community-based research, can benefit from a relational approach (Maya-Jariego, 2004). Networks provide an integrated vision of the multiple levels that form a community, fit well with respect to researching multiple belongings, and consider, for example, neighborhoods and other clusters not in isolation but in their inmediate context. Another specific application with enormous potential is the evaluation of interorganizational networks as a way of operationally describing community coalitions, that is, as a proxy for community readiness.

In this chapter we will present a mixed methods approach combining network analysis with a community-based participatory research strategy, specifically, stakeholder analysis. In a case study, we shall demonstrate how utilization of this approach resulted in enhancing the involvement of fishing communities in the governance of natural resources.

COMBINING NETWORK ANALYSIS AND ETHNOGRAPHY

Networks can be integrated in mixed methods research designs of a sequential, parallel, or fully integrated nature (Hollstein, 2014). One frequent combination involves (a) surveys of personal networks, or whole network analysis of a section of a community, and (b) ethnographic research. This approach has been followed, for instance, in studies of acculturation of immigrants (Maya-Jariego & Domínguez, 2014), adaptation to new legal procedures in rural China (Avenarius & Johnson, 2014), and innovation networks in global organizations (Gluesing, Riopelle, & Danowsky, 2014).

It is very common for ethnographic fieldwork to be done in a second step, to validate and assist in the interpretation of structural patterns observed in networks. Less frequent is the exploratory use of ethnography, its combination in iterative designs, or the integration of approaches. However, the mix of networks and ethnography usually proves to be a robust combination of standardization and understanding, breadth and depth, which helps to elucidate the simultaneous dynamics of social structures and actors' cognition. In the next section we explore the combination of network analysis and ethnography in contexts of action research with participatory purposes.

Network Analysis and Stakeholder Analysis in the Governance of Natural Resources

The interest in promoting co-management of natural resources and the emergence of new forms of participatory governance has shifted attention toward community actors. For example, in the case of fisheries there is growing recognition of the value of knowledge and experience that both fishermen and traditional fishing guilds, among other actors, bring to the conservation of fishing stocks and the environment (Bodin & Crona, 2008; Crona & Bodin, 2006, Hogg, Noguera-Méndez, Semitiel-García, & Giménez-Casalduero, 2013). This has resulted in research that, either with an analytical-structural approach or a qualitative approach, has attempted to document the patterns of collaboration and conflict that occur in the exploitation of natural resources (Bodin & Prell, 2011; Sandström, Crona, & Bodin, 2013; Sandström & Rova, 2010a).

The predominant focus in network studies has been on the analysis of interorganizational networks in the management of natural resources (Bodin & Crona, 2009). In the case of fisheries, the network approach has been used to describe the relationship of traditional fishing guilds with fisheries authorities, trade organizations, and wider federations of the fishing industry (Marín & Berkes, 2010). In general, the involvement of the community in decision making seems to improve the management of fishery resources (Gutiérrez, Hilborn, & Defeo, 2011), although occasionally some dynamics of polarization and conflict between sport fishing associations and fishing managers have been observed (Sandström & Rova, 2010b). The sustainable management of natural resources benefits from effective community leadership (Bodin & Crona, 2008; Sandström et al., 2013), decentralization in decision making (Carlsson & Berkes, 2005), and co-responsibility of fishermen and their community settings (Grafton, 2005). From a structural point of view, these processes appear to be supported in network centralization, as well as in a certain level of heterogeneity in the composition of the network (Sandström & Rova, 2010a) and the development of weak ties between members of groups that use different fishing gears (Crona & Bodin, 2006, 2010).

Additionally, the personal networks of skippers, crews, and managers, among others, can provide information on industrial relations and knowledge management in fisheries enclaves or, more broadly, in the fisheries sector. Thus, there have been analyses at the individual level about friendship and kinship patterns, as well as exchanges of advice and social support, in small fishing ports in Kenya (Crona & Bodin, 2006). The most frequent approach has been to use egocentric (that is, pertaining to an individual, who is the "owner" of the network) networks information to create whole networks (Bodin & Crona, 2008; Crona & Bodin, 2010; Sandström et al., 2013).

However, with regard to participatory governance of natural resources, stakeholder analysis is probably the most widely used approach. Stakeholder analysis is a participatory process aimed at understanding socio-environmental systems. It typically involves identifying the key actors of a system, evaluating the corresponding interests of the groups involved, and establishing decision-making priorities (Grimble & Wellard, 1997). Descriptive, normative, and instrumental uses of stakeholder analysis have been distinguished; they are usually developed in a sequence of the three steps of identification, classification, and analysis of the relationships of key actors (Reed et al., 2009). In environmental policies, this strategy has been applied, among other uses, to identifying the most influential actors, facilitating participatory decision making, coordinating groups of organizations, and involving marginalized groups.

Recent experiences have demonstrated the utility of combining these research strategies of network analysis and stakeholder analysis. Prell, Hubacek, and Reed (2009) employed indicators of degree, betweenness, homophily, and tie strength in stakeholder selection for participation in management decisions in the Peak District National Park in the United Kingdom. They thereby avoided a type of selection based only on subjective evaluation, and the importance of communication relationships between actors was recognized. Also, Lienert, Schnetzer, and Ingold (2013) utilized the systematic analysis of stakeholders for delimiting

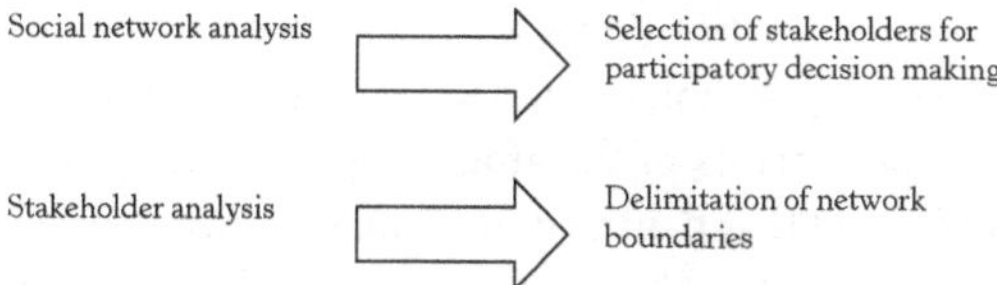

FIGURE 32.1: Two ways of mixing network analysis and stakeholder analysis.

network boundaries, one of the key issues in network analysis, in water infrastructure planning processes in Switzerland. Thus, the two studies differed in the order in which they used the two approaches (see Fig. 32.1). In both examples, each strategy generated complementary results for a better understanding of the socio-environmental system under study.

Communities play an important role in the conservation of natural resources. Therefore, environmental policies have given increasing importance in recent decades to community participation and social cohesion. Specifically, they seek to prevent marginalization of, and conflicts among, groups, as well as to ensure that a diversity of interests is adequately represented in decision making. In this regard, the role of the community is not only to contribute to informed decision making but also to be involved in the management of natural resources and, therefore, to be partners for conservation purposes.

The case of fishing is instructive in this regard. Fishing communities depend on the conservation of fisheries resources. Also, although it is less obvious, community dynamics may affect the viability of natural resources. Overexploitation of marine resources appears when fishermen operate independently, without communication between them, and when the rules of moderation and solidarity are eroded and the ability of collaboration and shared decision making is lost (Jentoft, 2000). For example, setting fishing quotas appears to have altered traditional, collaboration-based modes of relationship between fishermen. Regulations, such as fishing licenses, access limits, and catch quotas, introduce elements of social stratification that modify traditional patterns of organic solidarity (Symes, Steins, & Alegret, 2003). Similarly, the industrial restructuring of the sector changed patterns of relationship, interdependence, and mutual support that had developed over time and that were specific to each fishing community's environment and history.

Thus, the degree of community cohesion in fishing ports has a decisive impact on the conservation of marine natural resources. It is in this context that participatory processes, involving the stakeholder approach, were initiated. In the next section we present a case study where network analysis and stakeholder analysis were applied in parallel, producing insights regarding their joint use in mixed methods research.

CASE STUDY

Background and Aims

The Common Fisheries Policy (CFP) of the European Union establishes a set of regulations for conserving fish stocks. Both co-management of natural resources and participatory governance of fishing fleets seek to ensure that the fishing industry is sustainable and does not threaten the fish population size now and for the future (Regulation [Eu] N° 1380/2013 of the European Parliament and of the Council of 11 December 2013 on the Common Fisheries Policy). This has resulted in the establishment of fishing quotas, the reorganization of industry, and the promotion of artisanal fishing gears. Also, new initiatives to exploit the historic heritage and tourism value of fishing ports and sites have been launched.

In Andalusia, in southern Spain, the regional government is taking action to foster community participation in the fisheries sector in order to respond to the process of industrial restructuring occurring at the European level and to promote new economic and cultural usages with regard to fishing. The extractive activity in Andalusia is distributed among Atlantic and Mediterranean fishing grounds and is located in 35 fishery enclaves. In this context, a multidisciplinary team of researchers from psychology, anthropology, and economics conducted a study to determine the structure of the fisheries sector in Andalusia, as well as to facilitate new forms of organization and participation of fishing guilds, shipowners, crew members, and other industry players.

In this study we combined ethnographic fieldwork (i.e., stakeholder analysis) and social network analysis to describe the most relevant actors and organizations in the fisheries sector in Andalusia, as well as relations between them and the structuring of the sector. Specifically, an extensive inventory of stakeholders was developed, which involved conducting 322 qualitative interviews in 18 different fishing ports. At the same time, we surveyed the personal networks of a subset of 53 shipowners, crew members, and prominent individuals; finally, we analyzed the interorganizational network of 17 fishing guilds and 13 associations of shipowners in 21 ports. Thus, stakeholder analysis was applied parallel to the structural analysis of relationships at both the individual and organizational levels. Next, we describe the project's three research components.

Stakeholder Analysis

The widest part of the work was to document the relevant actors in the Andalusian fishing ports. For this, the stakeholder technique was developed in four phases. First, an inventory of organizations in each port, with the collaboration of a group of experts, was developed. Second, we classified this set of organizations based on their area of activity and their relative priority in the operation of the port. Third, 322 interviews were conducted with key informants, and the importance and influence of each organization in the process of community participation in the port were evaluated. The level of importance refers to the degree to which a participative governance project would be ineffective if the needs of that particular stakeholder were not taken into account, while influence refers to the relative power that the stakeholder has with respect to monitoring the plan of participation and the extent to which he or she can help or block the changes to be undertaken in the future. Fourth, using all of this information, we held forums in each port, in which stakeholders listed the main problems in each geographical area and made specific suggestions to improve participation in fisheries policy.

An essential feature of stakeholder analysis is that it is based on ethnographic exploration, by means of which we had an opportunity to meet the social actors and institutional agencies in each fishing enclave. Through fieldwork, we could know the relational dynamics between these actors, employing the procedure of selection of ethnographic informants defined by Johnson (1990) as data driven; that is, the experience in the field allowed us to access new significant informants in every social space. Thanks to this system, the relationship of entities initially selected to establish the interorganizational network was complemented with new stakeholders, with both the original and the new stakeholders participating later in forums.

The results of the aforementioned third phase indicated that fishing guilds and shipowner associations stand out in importance and influence above other organizations in the ports, namely, marina management entities, cooperatives of fishermen, aquaculture businesses, producer associations, restaurants, naval stores, canning companies, yacht clubs, sport fishing groups, and environmental organizations. Our findings also indicated that fishing guilds have more relevance and influence than do shipowner associations in the Mediterranean, while fishing guilds and shipowner associations have a more balanced weight in the Atlantic.

Personal Networks

The second component of the research consisted of a survey of personal networks, where a list of 45 alteri (that is, persons to whom a respondent relates) in the port for each of the respondents was obtained, generating a database of 2,385 alteri and 46,310 (out of 104,940 potential) relationships. The a priori establishment of a fixed number of alteri is a procedure originally proposed by McCarty (2002) to ensure a valid and reliable analysis of the structure of personal networks. The strategy of eliciting networks of the same size is an indirect form of standardization of data, which facilitates the comparison of indicators of centrality and other structural properties in samples of personal networks. From a practical standpoint, it facilitates the processing of data, reduces workload, and has proven to be a highly reliable sociometric nomination procedure. Furthermore, it has been empirically found that 30 or more alteri are sufficient to capture the diversity of personal network structures. In our case, in addition to information about who was related to whom (45 x 45 matrices) in each personal network, respondents were asked about the professional roles exercised in the port by each of the 45 alteri.

The next step was to summarize this information using a clustered graphs method, which is a strategy for visualizing personal networks through grouping the links into intra- and interclass relationships (Brandes, Lerner, Lubbers, McCarty, & Molina, 2008). In our study, for classification purposes we used the eight most relevant professional categories in the sample of alteri, namely crew members, skippers, shipowners, services,

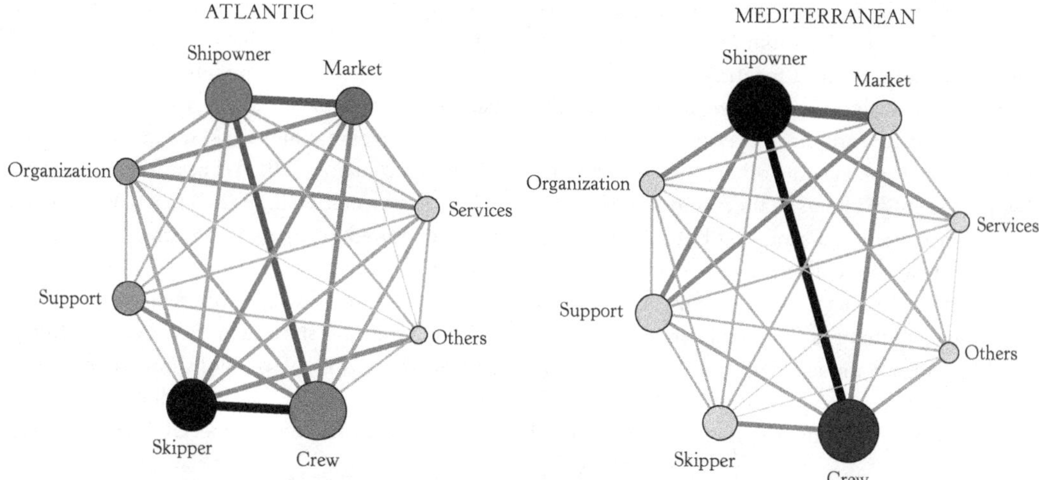

FIGURE 32.2: Clustered graphs of personal networks in the Atlantic and Mediterranean fishing sectors.

market, organization, support, and others. These are the most common activities in the harbor (Maya-Jariego, Holgado, & Florido, 2015). We generated two metarepresentations of the personal networks of respondents in the Atlantic ($n = 26$) and the Mediterranean ($n = 27$) fishing grounds (for methodological details, see Maya-Jariego, Holgado, & Florido, 2015). The results are shown in Figure 32.2. The weights of the intragroup relationships are represented by the color intensity of each node, while the weight of intergroup relationships is reflected in the size of each link. On the other hand, the size of each node, also on a weighted basis, shows the proportion of each professional category in the fishery concerned.

The results indicated a greater differentiation of professional roles in the Atlantic than in the Mediterranean fishing grounds. In the Atlantic, where industrial fishing predominates, relationships are more evenly distributed between the eight professional categories, and there is a clear differentiation between the roles of skipper and shipowner. The functions of management and direction of the boat are frequently performed by different people. On the other hand, in the Mediterranean, relationships are clearly focused on the link between shipowners and crew members. In this latter fishery zone, where artisanal fisheries clearly prevail, the owner of the boat usually goes fishing daily; that is to say, he works as a captain while also assuming management responsibilities. It is a less complex and smaller scale fishing ground, where fishing is organized around boats and informal relationships.

Therefore, the detailed analysis of relations demonstrates the existence of two patterns of sociability differentiated according to the fishing ground. This has consequences both in the way in which each fishery organizes labor relations and social participation and in the transformations required by the new fisheries policies and the restructuring of the sector. The small Mediterranean ports seem better prepared to adapt to a context in which the catches are limited and new tourism and heritage usages are promoted. In contrast, the organizational complexity of the Atlantic fishing ground will likely result, in practice, in a process of industrial restructuring, in which the greater polarization of relations will probably carry a higher incidence of labor unrest. Traditional fishing guilds are likely to continue to emerge as key players in this process both in the Atlantic and the Mediterranean.

Organizational Networks

We also analyzed the interorganizational network of 30 fishing guilds and associations of shipowners in Andalusia. We interviewed a representative of each organization. Respondents were selected based on their experience and position in the organization. In most cases, it was the skipper or the secretary in the fishing guilds, and the president or manager in shipowner associations. Specifically, four types of relationships were evaluated: acquaintanceship networks, interpersonal relationships, joint participation in meetings of the fishing sector, and co-management of fishing issues. The first three are informal relations that emerge in contexts of sociability in the ports, such as the cafeteria, nautical shops, or the rooms of the shipowners, which usually serve as a meeting point. However, co-management is a type of institutionalized relationship that depends more heavily on the initiative of govenment agencies and other regulatory bodies. Unlike the study of personal networks, in this case we did not conduct a sampling but rather a thorough fieldwork for collecting information, with all the guilds and associations of shipowners, to trace the complete interorganizational network.

The organizational network of fisheries in Andalusia forms a core-periphery structure, is clearly differentiated by fishing grounds, and is organized around a central core of guilds (see Fig. 32.3). Specifically, four guilds have the highest scores in prominence, centrality, and intermediation and are part of the core in the core-periphery structure of the four networks analyzed (Maya-Jariego, Holgado, Florido, & Martínez, 2015). These four guilds have a role of representation in the regional federations and are also located in ports with the greatest amount of fishing.

Two factors—the type of organization and the fishing ground—showed a significant influence on the formation of relationships. The analysis of the network, using the E-I Index and Constant Homophily procedure of the UCINET program,

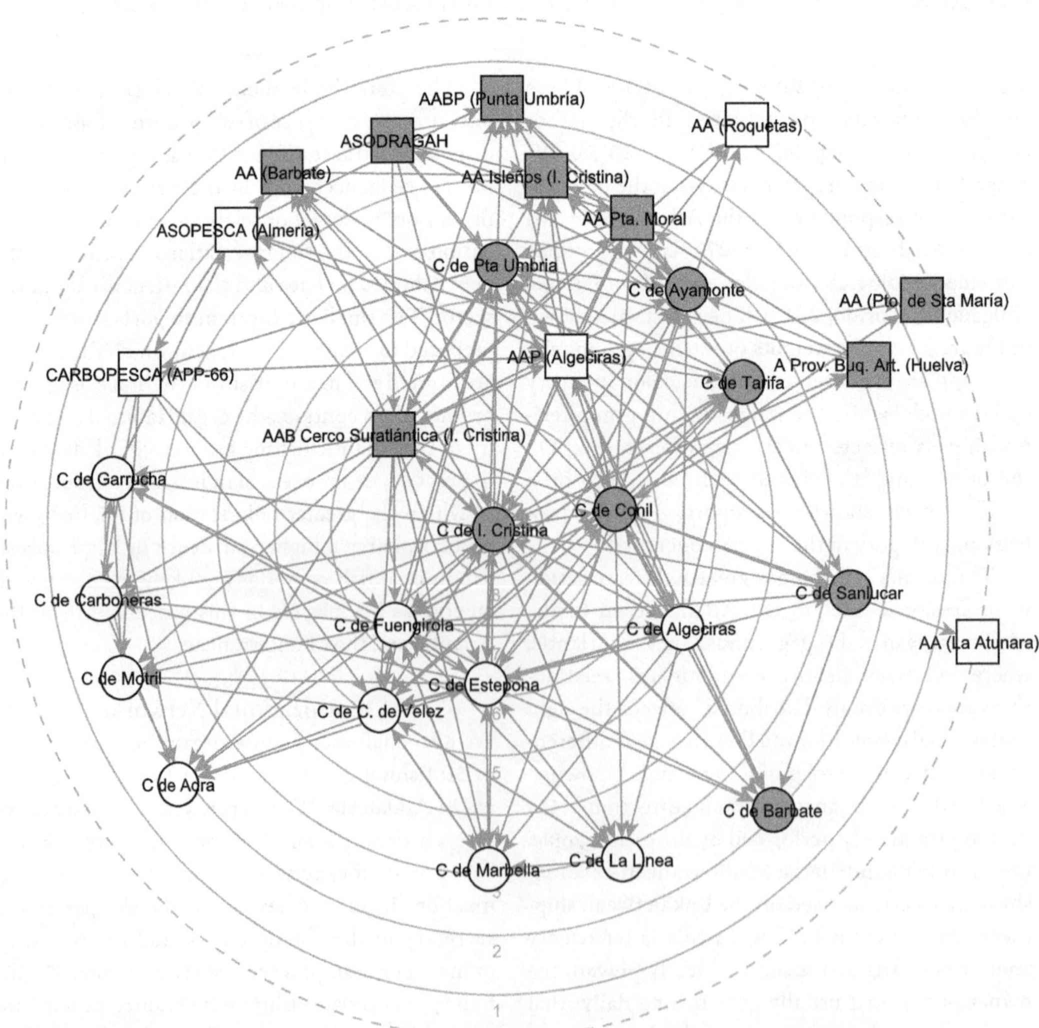

FIGURE 32.3: Interorganizational network of fishing in Andalusia. The position of the nodes is based on degree of centrality (concentric circles). White nodes represent Mediterranean organizations, and gray nodes represent Atlantic organizations. Circles represent guilds, and squares represent shipowners.

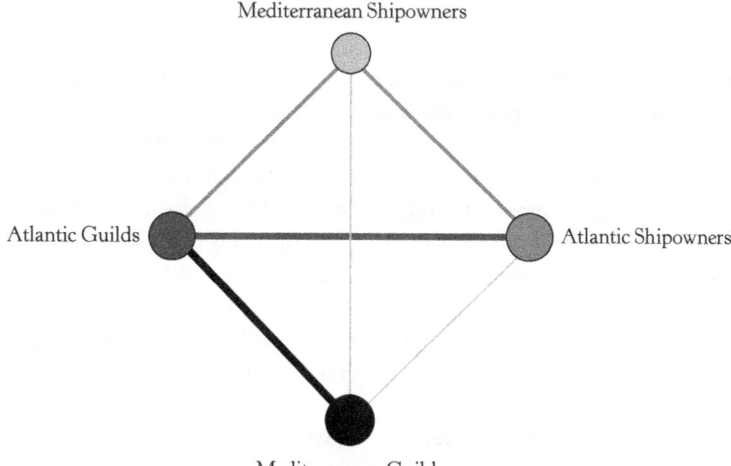

FIGURE 32.4: Clustered graph of the interorganizational network of the Andalusian fisheries.

demonstrated the existence of homophilic relations depending on the type of organization and, to a lesser extent, depending on the fishing ground. Employing the Joint-Count test, we found that the greater relative weight of intragroup relations is found in fishing guilds (if we refer to the type of organization) and in the Atlantic (if we refer to fishing grounds) (Maya-Jariego, Holgado, Florido, & Martínez, 2015).

We summarized this information with clustered graphs. Figure 32.4 shows the two joint axes of the Andalusian fisheries: the relationships between guilds and the projection of the Atlantic fishery. With respect to local harbor life, in the Mediterranean the fishing guilds are most relevant (that is, more central, better connected, and with more relative weight), with the shipowners having a secondary role. It is a context of artisanal fisheries, where the fishing enclaves organized around a guild are frequent. However, at the regional level, the guilds of the Atlantic have more prominence in the social network with respect to governance patterns. The Atlantic is characterized by the distribution of power between the guilds and shipowner associations. The industrial character, along with increased organizational complexity, is reflected in a greater differentiation of labor relations.

In summary, first, stakeholder analysis guided us to focus on fishing guilds and shipowner associations from among a variety of organizations in the ports. Second, interorganizational network analysis confirmed the observations from stakeholder analysis and the personal networks survey; namely, the Atlantic and Mediterranean fishing sectors have different structures in the relationships among key players, at both the individual and the organizational levels. Locally, fishing guilds are more central in the Mediterranean, while at the regional level Atlantic guilds have a key role in articulating the Andalusian fishing sector.

CONCLUSION

In this chapter we have attempted to demonstrate how stakeholder analysis and social network analysis can be used in parallel or as part of a sequential design, resulting in more, and more useful, information than either approach alone. For example, obtaining indicators of centrality, as well as the description of the properties of the network, *before* stakeholder analysis helps to identify key actors, providing systematic information and analytical accuracy. However, structural techniques can also be applied *after* ethnographic fieldwork has served to define, in a relevant and adapted-to-the-context manner, the network boundaries or has produced a census of actors useful for personal networks surveys.

Stakeholder analysis has considerable potential for identifying significant behaviors settings, through descriptive and exploratory study of the contexts of sociability, which improves the relevance of network analysis. Stakeholder analysis organizes the actors into categories, benefiting from previous substantive knowledge of the socio-environmental system under study. The classification and prioritization of the actors enable the researcher to study networks of subsets of actors or use the list of stakeholders for sampling. It is useful for defining the network pragmatically, and this detailed information on the population reduces the problem of accessing respondents and indirectly also reduces the percentage of missing data. Stakeholder analysis is very sensitive to institutional dynamics, making it complementary to the relational content on which network analysis usually focuses. Finally, it also appears to be quite sensitive to the determination of relevant actors in the function of the issues.

Social network analysis completes the description of the interests of the different actors, with consideration of structural, positional, and relational aspects. In an area where the indicators of prominence and functional differentiation of the actors have dominated, it introduces a fine-grained analysis of the roles that individuals and organizations deploy in the environmental policies scenario. Some of its contributions involve identification of leaders, mediators, and local interlocutors in different clusters of the network; operational description and classification of different patterns of collaboration; and detection of potential for innovations on the periphery of the network. The structural properties of the network may serve as the basis for an evidenced-based catégorization, supplementing the ratings derived from the subjective interpretation of stakeholders and experts (Boschetti, Richert, Walker, Price, & Dutra, 2012).

In addition, visualization of graphs is a catalyst for working with stakeholders. Besides communicating the properties of the network, it is in practice a form of intervention. Sometimes, when one provides feedback on the relationships of a set of actors through graphical representation, one can generate positive dynamics of engagement and participation, as well as efforts of actors to be nearer the core in a core-periphery structure (Molina, Maya-Jariego, & McCarty, 2014). In fact, the netmap technique, usually applied for identifying leaders and key players in a community during the implementation of cooperation for development projects, consists of a combination of qualitative interviews, maps of relationships, and group debates to interpret the sociograms (Schiffer, 2007). The visual display of networks helps participants to collaborate in resource mobilization and in consensus building. Thus, it is an appropriate way to reflect on a specific sector and implement community development initiatives.

We have attempted to demonstrate in this chapter that social network analysis contributes more than just centrality indicators and other measures. Beyond the enumeration of who are prominent actors, networks provide structural insight into the study and involvement of stakeholders. As we have seen with the case study, we can naturally deduce actions to improve network governance. Among others, we can launch operations to modify the network structure, arrange the context of relationships, and facilitate new forms of organization (Sandström et al., 2013). For example, in the case of fisheries in Andalusia, with the use of network information we could potentially form coalitions of fishing guilds and shipowners in the two fishing grounds, prepare the conditions for joint participation at the regional level, prevent exclusion of peripheral organizations of the Mediterranean fishing ground, mediate in cases of local conflict, and promote common agreements to address the restructuring of the sector.

The application of network analysis to the sustainable management of natural resources is an emerging field with considerable potential. Undoubtedly, in the coming years we will see new and exciting developments in the combination of structural analytics, such as network analysis, and community-based participatory research, such as stakeholder analysis, in this and other areas.

AUTHOR NOTE

Support for this research was provided by the Consejería de Fomento y Vivienda de la Junta de Andalucía (the equivalent of the Ministry of Public Works and Housing of the regional government of Andalusia, Spain). The study of networks and stakeholders is part of a wider project on fishing governance in Andalusia: "Dinamización de los Enclaves Pesqueros en el Sistema Portuario Andaluz: Usos Económicos, Gobernanza y Patrimonialización" [Revitalization of Fisheries Enclaves in the Andalusian Port System: Economic Uses, Governance and Patrimonialization] (2013–2015) (CP-2043/0073, GGI3001IDI0).

REFERENCES

Avenarius, C. B., & Johnson, J. C. (2014). Adaptation to new legal procedures in rural China: Integrating survey and ethnographic data. In S. Dominguez

& B. Hollstein (Eds.), *Mixed methods social networks research* (pp. 177–202). New York, NY: Cambridge University Press.

Bodin, Ö., & Crona, B. (2008). Management of natural resources at the community level: Exploring the role of social capital and leadership in a rural fishing community. *World Development, 36,* 2763–2779.

Bodin, Ö., & Crona, B. (2009). The role of social networks in natural resource governance: What relational patterns make a difference? *Global Environmental Change, 19,* 366–374.

Bodin, Ö., & Prell, C. (2011). *Social networks and natural resource management. Uncovering the social fabric of environmental governance.* New York, NY: Cambridge University Press.

Boschetti, F., Richert, C., Walker, I., Price, J., & Dutra, L. (2012). Assessing attitudes and cognitive styles of stakeholders in environmental projects involving computer modelling. *Ecological Modelling, 247,* 98–111.

Brandes, U., Lerner, J., Lubbers, M. J., McCarty, C., & Molina, J. L. (2008, March). *Visual statistics for collections of clustered graphs.* Paper presented at 2008 IEEE Pacific Visualization Symposium, Kyoto, Japan.

Carlsson, L., & Berkes, F. (2005). Co-management: Concepts and methodological implications. *Journal of Environmental Management, 75,* 65–76.

Crona, B., & Bodin, Ö. (2006). What you know is who you know? Communication patterns among resource users as a prerequisite for co-management. *Ecology and Society, 11,* 7.

Crona, B., & Bodin, Ö. (2010). Power asymmetries in small-scale fisheries: A barrier to governance transformability? *Ecology and Society, 15,* 32.

Domínguez, S., & Hollstein, B. (Eds.). (2014). *Mixed methods social network research: Design and applications.* New York, NY: Cambridge University Press.

Gluesing, J. C., Riopelle, K. R., & Danowski, J. A. (2014). Mixing ethnography and information technology data mining to visualize innovation networks in global networked organizations. In S. Dominguez & B. Hollstein (Eds.), *Mixed methods social networks research* (pp. 203–236). New York, NY: Cambridge University Press.

Grafton, R. Q. (2005). Social capital and fisheries governance. *Ocean and Coastal Management, 48,* 753–766.

Grimble, R., & Wellard, K. (1997). Stakeholder methodologies in natural resource management: A review of principles, contexts, experiences and opportunities. *Agricultural Systems, 55,* 173–193.

Gutiérrez, N. L., Hilborn, R., & Defeo, O. (2011). Leadership, social capital and incentives promote successful fisheries. *Nature, 470,* 386–389.

Hogg, K., Noguera-Méndez, P., Semitiel-García, M., & Giménez-Casalduero, M. F. (2013). Marine protected area governance: Prospects for co-management in the European Mediterranean. *Advances in Oceanography and Limnology, 4,* 241–259.

Hollstein, B. (2011). Qualitative approaches. In J. Scott & P. J. Carington. *Sage handbook of social network analysis* (pp. 404–416). London, England: Sage.

Hollstein, B. (2014). Mixed methods social network research: An introduction. In S. Dominguez & B. Hollstein (Eds.), *Mixed methods social networks research* (pp. 3–34). New York, NY: Cambridge University Press.

Jentoft, S. (2000). The community: A missing link of fisheries management. *Marine Policy, 24,* 53–59.

Johnson, J. C. (1990). *Selecting ethnographic informants.* Newbury Park, CA: Sage.

Lienert, J., Schnetzer, F., & Ingold, K. (2013). Stakeholder analysis combined with social network analysis provides fine-grained insights into water infrastructure planning processes. *Journal of Environmental Management, 125,* 134–148.

Luke, D. (2005). Getting the big picture in community science: Methods that capture context. *American Journal of Community Psychology, 35,* 185–200.

Maya-Jariego, I. (2004). Sentido de comunidad y potenciación comunitaria. *Apuntes de Psicología, 22,* 187–211.

Maya-Jariego, I., & Domínguez, S. (2014). Two sides of the same coin: The integration of personal network analysis with etnographic and psychometric strategies in the study of acculturation. In S. Dominguez & B. Hollstein (Eds.), *Mixed methods social networks research* (pp. 153–176). New York, NY: Cambridge University Press.

Maya-Jariego, I., Holgado, D., & Florido, D. (2015). *Clustered graphs of worker roles in Atlantic versus Mediterranean fishing enclaves: Ready for artisanalization in Andalusia?* Manuscript submitted for publication.

Maya-Jariego, I., Holgado, D., Florido, D., & Martínez, I. (2015). *Redes entre dos mares: Relaciones entre cofradías y asociaciones de armadores en los caladeros Atlántico y Mediterráneo de Andalucía* [Fishnets between two seas: Relationships between guilds and associations of shipowners in the Atlantic and Mediterranean fishing grounds of Andalusia]. Revista Española de Investigaciones Sociológicas (REIS).

Marín, A., & Berkes, F. (2010). Network approach for understanding small-scale fisheries governance: The case of the Chilean coastal co-management system. *Marine Policy, 34,* 851–858.

McCarty, C. (2002). Structure in personal networks. *Journal of Social Structure,* 3(1).

Molina, J. L., Maya-Jariego, I., & McCarty, C. (2014). Giving meaning to social networks: Methodology for conducting and analyzing interviews based on personal network visualizations. In S. Dominguez & B. Hollstein (Eds.), *Mixed methods social networks research* (pp. 305–335). New York, NY: Cambridge University Press.

Neal, J. W., & Christens, B. D. (2014). Linking the levels: Network and relational perspectives for community psychology. *American Journal of Community Psychology, 53*, 314–323.

Prell, C., Hubacek, K., & Reed, M. (2009). Stakeholder analysis and social network analysis in natural resource management. *Society and Natural Resources, 22*, 501–518.

Reed, M. S., Graves, A., Dandy, N., Posthumus, H., Hubacek, K., Morris, J., . . . Stringer, L. C. (2009). Who's in and why? A typology of stakeholder analysis methods for natural resource management. *Journal of Environmental Management, 90*, 1933–1949.

Sandström, A., Crona, B., & Bodin, Ö. (2013). Legitimacy in co-management: The impact of preexisting structures, social networks and governance strategies. *Environmental Policy and Governance, 24*, 60–76.

Sandström, A., & Rova, C. (2010a). Adaptive co-management networks: A comparative analysis of two fishery conservation areas in Sweden. *Ecology and Society, 15*, 14.

Sandström, A., & Rova, C. (2010b). The network structure of adaptive governance: A single case study of a fish management area. *International Journal of the Commons, 4*, 528–551.

Schiffer, E. (2007, May). *Net-map toolbox: Influence mapping on social networks.* Paper presented at the XVII Sunbelt Conference of the International Network of Social Network Analysis, Corfu, Greece.

Symes, D., Steins, N., & Alegret, J. L. (2003). Experiences with fisheries co-management in Europe. In D. C. Wilson, J. R., Nielsen, & P. Degnbol (Eds.), *The fisheries comanagement experience: Accomplishment, challenges, and prospects* (pp. 119–134). Dordrecht, The Netherlands: Kluwer Academic Press.

33

Mixed Methodology in Multilevel, Multisetting Inquiry

NICOLE E. ALLEN, ANGELA L. WALDEN, EMILY R. DWORKIN, AND SHABNAM JAVDANI

Community psychologists are frequently interested in phenomena that occur at multiple levels of analysis, including individuals, families, groups, neighborhoods, communities, and cultures. Taking an ecological view invites complex methodological questions regarding how to capture group- or setting-level influences on human behavior and community change. Given the centrality of understanding the interplay between individuals and their environments, the field frequently examines contextual effects and key sources of influence at the setting level (Todd, Allen, & Javdani, 2011). One way to do this is to engage in multilevel, multisetting research so that key patterns of setting-level variance can be observed across multiple sites. Yet "zooming out" in such multisetting research can result in a loss of the context-specific understandings offered by "zooming in" on a smaller number of settings. Indeed, consideration of cross-site and site-specific inquiry can even result in contradictory findings. Thus, a mixed methods approach affords the researcher an opportunity to engage in multifaceted exploration of multilevel, multisite phenomena. To illustrate this, the second part of this chapter will describe a study that aimed to capitalize on the strengths of mixed methodology in a multilevel, multisetting study of community collaboration in response to family violence.

Mixed methodology is particularly well suited to multilevel, multisetting inquiry, as it allows for the phenomenon of interest to drive methodological decision making. The employment of a mixed methods design encourages engagement with each level of analysis on its own terms and avoids sacrificing specificity at one level of analysis for another (Tashakkori & Teddlie, 2003). Applying mixed methodology to multilevel, multisetting inquiry is time and resource intensive, posing unique challenges related to site and participant selection and recruitment, study design, coordination of data collection efforts across sites that may be geographically distant, validity of data collected across sites, and data analysis and interpretation (e.g., Khorsan et al., 2013). However, mixed methods inquiry has the potential to yield an understanding that more richly presents the true complexity of the settings under study. A mixed methods approach to multilevel, multisetting inquiry invites us to engage such methods side by side and also to allow for their strategic interplay at multiple stages of the inquiry process from data collection to interpretation. Thus, it is not just the effective, independent use of quantitative and qualitative methods that is desired, but their interaction with one another, that produces a richer understanding than one would achieve by treating them independently.

INTRODUCTION TO MIXED METHODS INQUIRY

When designing a multisite study using mixed methodology, a critical consideration is the purpose of mixing methods. As with any research design, it is important that the methods be consistent with the study goals. Greene, Caracelli, and Graham (1989) articulated a set of five mixed methods purposes that have relevance to multisite work. We describe each and provide illustrative applications.

First, the mixed methods purpose of triangulation involves increasing the convergent validity of results by simultaneously collecting data on the same phenomenon using multiple, independent methods of data collection and analysis, with the goal of obtaining consistent results (Greene, Caracelli, & Graham, 1989; Greene & McClintock, 1985). Indeed, the perceived strength of triangulation derives from the intentional use of methods with counteracting biases in order to facilitate information corroboration (Greene, 2007). Although the beginnings of mixed methods research in social sciences can arguably be traced back to triangulation (Greene, 2007), the meaning and appropriate labeling of mixed methods research as triangulation remains an ongoing challenge; multiple variants of triangulation designs (e.g., Creswell & Plano-Clark, 2007) and applications of mixed methods mislabeled as triangulation are evident in mixed methods literature (Greene, 2007).

A number of common challenges in the effective utilization of a triangulation purpose have been noted. First, triangulation assumes the presence of a single, objective reality (Campbell, Gregory, Patterson, & Bybee, 2012), and this assumption may be complicated by the inclusion of qualitative methods, which are commonly associated with assumptions of co-created realities. Second, because triangulation seeks cross-validation of results, discrepancies invalidate results rather than serving as a source of further information. Third, it can be difficult to effectively maintain independence between methods and use them concurrently to describe the same phenomenon (Greene & McClintock, 1985). As an example of dealing with this challenge, Greene and McClintock (1985) described using two separate evaluation teams to maintain independence of methods in their multisite, multilevel study of an adult community education program. One team used questionnaires, and the second used interviews; both focused on the use of information in program development.

A second mixed methods purpose is development, or the use of the findings from one method to inform further methodological decisions (e.g., around sampling, measurement, or study implementation; Caracelli & Greene, 1993; Greene et al., 1989). Thus, methods are typically used sequentially rather than concurrently (Greene et al., 1989). As an example, researchers could conduct initial stages of qualitative data collection at selected sites to inform a broader multisite quantitative data collection effort. In this vein, Waysman and Savaya (1997) employed a three-stage development approach in their study of nonprofit organizations receiving assistance from an Israeli nonprofit called SHATIL. The first stage used qualitative methods (i.e., interviews with SHATIL staff and focus groups with staff from organizations receiving assistance) that were then utilized to inform the development of a questionnaire sent in the second stage to all organizations receiving assistance from SHATIL. In the third stage, the researchers selected organizations that reported being particularly satisfied or dissatisfied with SHATIL on the Stage 2 survey and conducted focus groups with staff members.

Third, the purpose of complementarity involves the use of different methods to complement, enhance, illustrate, clarify, or elaborate on each other (Greene et al., 1989). Mixed methods designs with a complementarity purpose measure similar (but not identical) aspects of the same phenomenon (Caracelli & Greene, 1993) and typically implement both methods concurrently (Greene et al., 1989). Researchers using mixed methods for the purpose of complementarity across sites could use one method to collect data about a phenomenon at the individual level (e.g., client perceptions of their own improvement, obtained from qualitative interviews) and a second method to collect data about a similar phenomenon at the setting level (e.g., percentage of clients graduating from the program, as recorded in archives). In a multisite study of learning outcomes in liberal arts institutions with a complementarity purpose, Seifert, Goodman, King, and Baxter Magolda (2010) quantitatively identified cross-institution aspects of the college experience that were associated with intercultural effectiveness among students while using qualitative interviews with students to elaborate on the specific experiences that led them to develop intercultural effectiveness.

Fourth, an initiation mixed methods purpose involves a search for contradiction or contrast between methods (Greene et al., 1989). This purpose can be contrasted with a triangulation purpose, which looks for corroboration across methods. Research questions using one method can be studied from a different perspective using a second method (Caracelli & Greene, 1993). In a multisite study, researchers could intentionally search for discrepancies between trends across all sampled sites and local manifestations of the same issues. Of particular relevance to community-based research, the exploration of contradictions can facilitate more effective action. The previously described SHATIL evaluation provides an example of an emergent initiation purpose in practice (Waysman & Savaya, 1997). While their qualitative focus group findings suggested that some clients felt patronized by SHATIL staff, their quantitative survey findings did not support that SHATIL staff were widely seen as patronizing. Thus, the researchers investigated which clients felt patronized and provided the results as feedback to SHATIL, increasing the organization's ability to promote culturally sensitive services.

Fifth, the purpose of expansion involves broadening the scope of inquiry through the use of different methods for different (nonoverlapping) phenomena (Greene et al., 1989). Although triangulation designs study identical phenomena and complementarity designs study similar phenomena, expansion designs study fully distinct phenomena (Caracelli & Greene, 1993). This purpose may be ideal for studies in which methods are pragmatically selected to study the phenomena to which they are best suited (e.g., quantitative archival methods can be used to identify program outcomes, while qualitative interviews can be used to understand how people at each program site understand the challenges of their work). When evaluations fail to demonstrate that a program has produced desired outcomes, expansion designs have been used as a strategy to illuminate other aspects of the program (Greene et al., 1989). As an example, the quantitative component of the Donmoyer, Yennie-Donmoyer, and Galloway study (2012) of principal preparation programs showed mixed results with regard to the programs' impact on student test scores; however, qualitative interviews with principals suggested a number of ways in which the program affected principal practices that might not be directly evidenced in student test scores.

CASE STUDY

Background and Aims

Sarason's broad conceptualization of settings include "any instance in which two or more people come together in new relationship over a sustained period of time in order to achieve certain goals" (Sarason, 1972, p. 1). This is a useful definition because it allows for settings to be conceptualized without the typical boundaries of formal organizations. Indeed, settings can take many forms, including, for example, classrooms in charter schools, councils and taskforces, grassroots organizations, and public housing advisory boards. The settings of interest in the current case study were Family Violence Councils (FVCs), a statewide (Illinois) network of coordinating councils that aim to improve systems' (i.e., criminal justice, human service, health care) responses to family violence, including child abuse, intimate partner violence, and elder abuse (Allen et al., 2009). These settings were formed over time by a state-level FVC affiliated with the administrative body of the state courts. FVCs were formed in each of the state's judicial circuits. These FVCs typically included a steering committee comprised of key local leaders (e.g., judges, domestic violence program executive directors, prosecutors, chiefs of police). They also included other committees that focused on particular geographic counties within judicial circuits and/or around particular substantive areas in the system's response to family violence (e.g., community/youth education, faith settings, law enforcement, child protection; see Allen et al., 2009, for a more extensive description).

FVCs provided a fascinating case for multisetting, multilevel research, given that each setting was embedded in a unique local community context with a different set of human and material resources. Yet they shared a mission and often aimed to achieve similar reforms locally (making desired outcomes common across sites), making cross-site comparisons meaningful. The study presented here aimed to answer multilevel, multisetting questions regarding council effectiveness and its correlates but also aimed to illuminate critical local processes by which these (relatively) new settings achieved local change.

In the study of FVCs, methods could be used in collaboration with each other to zoom in and zoom out in the pursuit of complex multilevel, multisetting research. In some cases, we were interested in an in-depth understanding of a single setting, for example, the specific forms that power negotiation and conflict resolution took in a council, with attention to those in different roles (e.g., advocates and judges). At other times, though, we were interested in drawing conclusions in multiple settings, for example, regarding the extent to which shared power in decision making and effective conflict resolution influenced councils' capacity to achieve institutionalized community change (e.g., Walden, 2011) and how perceived conflict, conflict resolution, and power interacted in council functioning (Walden, Javdani, & Allen, 2014). That is, when looking across multiple sites, we could ask questions regarding the extent to which these features of the council setting affected council effectiveness. When we considered conflict and power in a single setting, we could assume that this was an important facet of council work, given its salience to us as investigators and as students of group dynamics. Yet it is through the multisetting context that we could directly test that hypothesis. Did the degree to which power and conflict were effectively negotiated explain variance in effectiveness across sites? Given that FVCs had formed throughout a single state, we were interested in understanding the wholesale effect of these settings on improving the system's response to family violence and explaining differences in effectiveness across sites. To do the latter, we could capitalize on having multiple settings. Yet we wanted to retain sufficiently rich contextual information about the settings to shape cross-site data collection processes and make meaning of study findings.

Methodology

The study of FVCs included multiple types and sources of data. It had two major components: a statewide inquiry that included all FVCs in the state (with the exclusion of those differently structured in the context of a major city) and an in-depth examination of three exemplar sites. We mixed qualitative and quantitative methods within and across each of these components. The particular strength of the statewide inquiry was the ability to zoom out in order to examine variability across FVCs with regard to proximal and distal outcomes and to examine what accounts for such variability (e.g., council age, councils' collaborative capacity, community support). This study component involved cross-sectional analyses largely reliant on FVC members' perceptions of the council setting (i.e., interviews with FVC coordinators, surveys of FVC membership). However, the statewide inquiry also included analyses of archival criminal justice and service utilization statistics, as well as FVC annual reports, which provided a source of triangulation of member perceptions. Furthermore, the analysis of archival data (e.g., criminal justice system statistics recorded from 1996 to the present) provided an opportunity to conduct a longitudinal analysis of FVC effects on the system's response to intimate partner violence with regard to arrests and orders of protection.

Examining trends across FVCs was invaluable, but examining the effectiveness of FVCs could not be accomplished without considerable attention to the community context in which such collaborative efforts take place and the dynamic and developmental processes that characterize such efforts (Adler, 2002; Yin & Kaftarian, 1997). Thus, we zoomed in to focus on particular FVC councils via case studies. The case studies employed a series of key informant interviews, informal and formal observations of council meetings, and review of council archives. Three FVCs were chosen as exemplary efforts but also represented different organizational structures and geographic locations and configurations (e.g., councils varied with regard to the number of counties in their judicial circuit).

Mixed Methods Purposes Illustrated

The primary aims in employing mixed methods in the current study were initiation, complementarity, and expansion. However, each of the five aforementioned mixed methods purposes can be illustrated using examples from the study. Being explicit about the purpose of mixing methods in the planning process can aid in designing studies with intentionality. For example, by design our study was implemented in phases. This allowed us to make changes in real time as we pursued different purposes in our study process.

We often associate using multiple sources of data collection with the goal of triangulation. The assumption here is that there is some truth that we want to uncover and the convergence of findings from multiple data sources regarding a single phenomenon affirms our conclusion regarding this truth. On the one hand, our study was undeniably interested in summative judgments regarding whether or not FVCs were effective. However, we were not naïve in our inquiry and did not expect a simple yes or no answer given the complex nature of multisite work and the multiple levels of analysis at which outcomes could be measured. Triangulation was relevant to our study in that we could point to multiple data sources to support our conclusion that the FVCs had indeed resulted in observable community change. However, it is worth noting that triangulation was not the primary goal in mixing methods in our study. Indeed, triangulation was often coupled with a different purpose and was made possible because of the sequential nature of the overall study. For instance, we surveyed FVC conveners about how councils structured their efforts to address geographical challenges after this issue emerged as a clear theme in interviews with council coordinators, serving the purposes of both development (e.g., using interview data to develop items on the convener survey) and triangulation (e.g., multiple data sources corroborating an emerging hypothesis).

Our examination of council effectiveness highlights the benefits and challenges of pursing classic triangulation in multilevel, multisetting research. We did a survey of FVC members across the state and gathered information regarding perceived effectiveness of councils on key, common dimensions of change (e.g., improving policies and practices in the response to family violence). These data indicated that members across sites endorsed their councils to varying degrees as facilitators of desired change and provided a common metric that could be compared across all sites even though their specific local efforts and foci varied. Members' perceptions did not provide a source of objective data regarding council effectiveness (although we would argue that they are a critical subjective source of assessment and no less critical than other systems markers). One of the first sources of evidence for triangulation emerged with respect to studying the variability associated with whether and to what extent FVCs leveraged changes in policies and practices in the response to family violence. Across interviews with coordinators, key informants, and surveys with membership, we noted that FVCs were neither similarly positioned nor attuned to leveraging such changes, and, indeed, we found that this construct had among the highest setting-level variance in our hierarchical linear modeling of council member survey data.

We were further interested in identifying data sources that might support these conclusions (we will discuss contradictions in subsequent illustrations). Thus, we also analyzed 6 years of archival data regarding the specific activities of councils from their regular reports to the state FVC. We recorded all instances of changes in practice, protocol, and policy and found that the degree to which such specific changes were reported was significantly related to the overall ratings of councils by their membership. Members' assessments of their councils appeared to have some validity and supported the idea that some FVCs were indeed facilitating local change in the system's response to family violence. Notably, these data were still quite close to those produced by councils (i.e., based on their standard reports to the state).

We then explored other data sources that more directly reflected observed systems response to family violence, including arrest records and order of protection data. These data provided more objective indices of the specific ways in which the FVCs may have impacted institutionalized change. For example, we utilized existing data from all judicial circuits throughout the state over a 15-year period. Offering additional support for our conclusions regarding FVC capacity (although not uniform) to produce community change, we found that formation and development of the councils was associated with the accessibility of plenary orders of protection (Allen et al., 2013). However, our analysis of arrest data did not support our emerging conclusions but further enhanced them. We did not find support for the FVCs' impact on arrest rates but found that there was much variability within a given FVC's jurisdiction regarding law enforcement response (Javdani, Allen, Todd, & Anderson, 2011). This suggested that the councils may have been more effective at creating changes in the courts (centrally regulated within a judicial circuit) than with law enforcement (where no such central regulation is in place) (Allen et al., 2009). Looking at multiple data sources regarding the question of effectiveness allowed us to make a stronger case regarding the FVCs' potential to produce community change and to offer a more nuanced understanding of the types of outcomes that the councils may be best positioned to achieve.

As the previous example illustrates, full corroboration of findings across all methods, sites, and stakeholders is not a likely or generative goal with complex, multilevel phenomena. Discrepancies did emerge that would have undermined our findings had our sole purpose been triangulation. Our openness to initiation as an emergent mixed methods purpose thus allowed us to enhance our findings. In addition, it is important to note that the application of a triangulation purpose was accompanied by challenges compounded by the multisite and multilevel nature of our study. For instance, classic triangulation requires the assessment of a single phenomenon (rather than overlapping, similar phenomena, as in a complementarity mixed methods purpose), and whether one phenomenon is truly being assessed is sometimes a matter of debate. In our study, our qualitative methods assessed subjective member perceptions of effectiveness, and our quantitative methods assessed objective indices of system change. Although an argument could be made that both methods assessed system change, it could also be argued that the epistemological assumptions accompanying each method of data collection make the phenomena fundamentally different. An argument could also be made that the fact that these phenomena existed at different levels of analysis (member perceptions were at the individual level, and systems change was at the system level) also made them similar, rather than identical, phenomena. Thus, is it important to be clear about epistemology, particularly when adopting different stances depending on particular research questions (e.g., some qualitative data were collected with postpositivist goals, while others were not).

The purpose of development, or the use of the findings of one method to inform further methodological decisions, figured prominently in the current study. Importantly, development was not in place only at the start of the study; we used it throughout as each data collection approach was developed. This was possible because, by design, data collection was phased in over a multiyear period. A development purpose proved to be useful as we zoomed in and zoomed out across levels of analysis: findings from micro levels informed directions to take at macro levels, and vice versa. The study began with interviews with state FVC staff. This provided a foundation for the subsequent steps in the study, including decisions to seek permission to acquire and analyze order of protection and arrest data. These early interviews provided foundational knowledge regarding the structure of FVCs that informed the next phase of data collection with council conveners across the state. Those interviews then informed the development of a convener and member survey, which informed the development of an interview protocol with key informants in the three case study sites. This sequential design allowed for information gathered to guide next steps and to maximize the relevance of each step. Small findings regarding, for example, the ways that FVCs were structured in response to local geographic realities and considerable local variation in the focus of efforts (e.g., on child abuse, domestic violence, elder abuse) informed subsequent data-gathering efforts. Actively incorporating findings into subsequent data collection efforts became a reflexive process and involved all team members, including our community partners, in the study.

A driving purpose in the current study was complementarity, or the elaboration of findings about one phenomenon from one data source and analytic process with findings about a second, similar phenomenon from a second data source and analytic process. For example, in our quantitative analysis from member surveys, we found that our assessment of the intermediate outcomes that we termed "knowledge" and "relationship" development were highly correlated with one another (Javdani & Allen, 2011b). This could not be explained only by shared method variance, given these constructs' lack of shared variance with the other intermediate outcomes assessed in the same scale. Our qualitative data, including both key informant interviews and observations, helped us make meaning of this finding. Specifically, in the qualitative data, perhaps not surprisingly, discussions of relationships and knowledge went "hand in glove." We began to discuss this single construct internally as "intimacy" and later settled on the more conventional and often-studied construct of social capital to understand the inextricable relation between the constructs we had previously conceptualized as distinct (Allen, Javdani, Lehrner, & Walden, 2011). In the absence of the qualitative data and the ability to zoom in on the work of particular community contexts, we would have been inclined to interpret this largely in terms of a measurement failure (this may certainly still be part of the story). The juxtaposition of the quantitative data, gathered across multiple sites and more devoid of context, with the qualitative data, gathered with attention to local processes, gave it substantive meaning that resulted in our reworking of our understanding of our intermediate outcomes to reflect a single reinforcing process of relationship formation and knowledge generation.

Our complementarity efforts did not always bear fruit. Our data regarding the relationship between the formation and development of councils and the accessibility of orders of protection indicated that this was not a uniform finding across councils (our members' assessments offered similar cross-setting variability in effectiveness; Allen et al., 2013). Yet, despite our best efforts, our other data sources would not shed light on which settings were more likely to have increased access to orders of protection and which were not. This was likely due, at least in part, to the timing of the data gathered. The order of protection data gathered covered a multiyear period for which we did not have data—our data collection followed that period. Still, we "turned over every rock" we could think of regarding time-invariant factors, for example, geographic features (rural versus urban, circuit size) and council characteristics (e.g., year of formation) and were not able to elaborate on how or why councils varied in their capacity to increase access to orders of protection.

The purpose of initiation is to search actively for contradiction or contrast between methods. This was also a part of our process, particularly in the study's analytic phase, and sometimes as an emergent purpose when we were actually in the pursuit of complementarity, as discussed previously. In particular, we pushed in our qualitative case study inquiry to understand salient differences in the functioning of individual councils as compared to general cross-site patterns. For example, geographic constraints were discussed at great length in two case study sites. Yet, despite this being a shared concern at these two sites, when we zoomed out and looked across sites, we could find no evidence that geographic constraints were a source of variance in perceived effectiveness across sites. This is one example of contradiction, or at least a lack of convergence, depending on the perspective privileged. The lack of findings across sites could lead one to conclude that this was a not a key factor in explaining what constrained council efforts, but it was undeniably a salient factor from the perspective of single-site reports. This led us to further question how both of these seemingly contradictory findings were true and to take them up side by side in our inquiry with regard to other critical facets of council functioning, including, for example, member participation (Dworkin, Javdani, & Allen, in press).

The heart of this investigation is illustrated in the purpose of expansion, which involves broadening the scope of inquiry through the use of different methods for different phenomena. Different methods bring different strengths to the inquiry process. By casting a broad methodological net, we exploited the relative strengths of the methods. Quantitative approaches are particularly well suited to examining setting-level effects by exploring setting- and individual-level variance on key dimensions of interest (e.g., multilevel modeling). For example, by examining 15 years of archival data on orders of protection, we were able to examine how the introduction and development of councils were associated with access to orders across sites. The qualitative methods we employed in each case study site shed light on the local processes that made councils likely to achieve such outcomes. Qualitative approaches are particularly well suited to the rich understanding of the contextual realities that shape the way a setting functions and positions itself to influence (or not). For example, in our quantitative data we assessed leader effectiveness, a common factor implicated in the success of collaborative efforts. However, in our study, there was very little variability in our quantitative assessment. There was such a high degree of satisfaction with local council conveners that there was not appreciable cross-site variability. In the quantitative analysis, what does not vary does not covary. Yet it would be incorrect to assert that leadership was not a critical component of council success; indeed, it was uniformly important and often successful. Our qualitative interviews and observations offered a nuanced understanding of how leadership figured centrally in council functioning and also pushed beyond typical conceptualizations of leadership to explore the critical role that informal setting leaders (i.e., those not in the role of convener or chair) played in building council capacity to pursue institutionalized change efforts. These developing interpretations further led us to expand our conceptual models about, for instance, contextual factors that may promote member empowerment to pursue such changes across sites beyond formal council leadership (Javdani & Allen, 2011a).

In general, our multisite, quantitative analysis offered the opportunity to build models that work together to explain variation in effectiveness. However, by design, operating at the setting level of analysis across all sites required us to pursue more generic and universal aims. The findings from these facets of the study advanced generalizable knowledge of what is important in these settings, yet they left us wanting regarding the how and why of council effectiveness. The qualitative findings allowed for a more idiographic exploration of collaborative work, with attention to the critical processes involved in collaborative work and the realities of local sites.

Each of the five mixed methods purposes has clear application to multisite, multilevel research. Different methods may be better fits for phenomena at different levels of analysis, and in an expansion purpose, the phenomena of interest can drive methodological decision making in order to maximize coverage across levels. As we have emphasized, multisite work invites both zooming in and zooming out; in the present study we searched for both the nomothetic (generalizations across sites) and the idiographic (site-specific findings). We were able to obtain both and use information from one site or level to inform research at other sites or levels of analysis, as in a development purpose. We were also able to look for ways in which phenomena manifested at different levels of analysis (as in complementarity) and ways in which phenomena differed across levels (as in initiation). Finally, there are notable challenges in applying a triangulation purpose to multisite, multilevel research given its inherent complexity, but there may be cases in which it is possible to do so.

CONCLUSION

Mixed methodology in multisite, multilevel contexts allows community-based researchers to actively juxtapose the strengths of mixed methods in order to advance understanding. The research presented here illustrated how five purposes of mixed methods approaches—triangulation, development, complementarity, initiation, and expansion—can be operative in one study. Explicit attention to each purpose has implications at all phases of a study—development, implementation, data analysis, and interpretation—yielding rich rewards in the process.

REFERENCES

Adler, M. A. (2002). The utility of modeling in evaluation planning: The case of the coordination of domestic violence services in Maryland. *Evaluation in Program Planning, 25*, 203–213.

Allen, N. E., Javdani, S., Anderson, C. J., Rana, S., Newman, D., Todd, N., & Davis, S. (2009). *Coordinating the criminal justice response to intimate partner violence: The role of coordinating councils in systems change.* Report prepared for the National Institute of Justice.

Allen, N. E., Javdani, S., Lehrner, A., & Walden, A. L. (2011). Changing the text: Modeling council capacity to produce institutionalized change. *American Journal of Community Psychology, 48*, 208–221.

Allen, N. E., Larsen, S., Trotter, J., & Sullivan, C. (2013). Exploring the core components of an evidence-based community advocacy program for women with abusive partners. *Journal of Community Psychology, 41*, 1–18.

Allen, N. E., Todd, N., Anderson, C., Davis, S., Javdani, S., Bruehler, V., & Dorsey, H. (2013). Council-based approaches to intimate partner violence: Evidence for distal change in the systems response. *American Journal of Community Psychology, 52*, 1–12.

Campbell, R., Gregory, K., Patterson, D., & Bybee, D. (2012). Integrating qualitative and quantitative approaches: An example of mixed methods research. In L. Jason & D. Glenwick (Eds.), *Methodological approaches to community-based research* (pp. 51–68). Washington, DC: American Psychological Association.

Caracelli, V. J., & Greene, J. C. (1993). Data analysis strategies for mixed-method evaluation designs. *Educational Evaluation and Policy Analysis, 15*, 195–207.

Creswell, J. W., & Plano-Clark, V. L. (2007). *Designing and conducting mixed methods research.* Thousand Oaks, CA: Sage.

Donmoyer, R., Yennie-Donmoyer, J., & Galloway, F. (2012). The search for connections across principal preparation, principal performance, and student achievement in an exemplary principal preparation program. *Journal of Research on Leadership Education, 7*, 5–43.

Dworkin, E. R., Javdani, S., & Allen, N. E. (in press). If you build it, will they come? Explaining participation in family violence councils. *Journal of Community Psychology.*

Greene, J. C. (2007). *Mixed methods in social inquiry.* San Francisco, CA: Wiley.

Greene, J. C., Caracelli, V. J., & Graham, W. F. (1989). Toward a conceptual framework for mixed-method evaluation designs. *Educational Evaluation and Policy Analysis, 11*, 255–274.

Greene, J., & McClintock, C. (1985). Triangulation in evaluation: Design and analysis issues. *Evaluation Review, 9*, 523–545.

Javdani, S., & Allen, N.E. (2011a). Councils as empowering contexts: Mobilizing the front line to foster systems change in the response to intimate partner violence. *American Journal of Community Psychology, 48*, 208–221.

Javdani, S., & Allen, N. E. (2011b). Proximal outcomes matter: A multilevel examination of the processes by which coordinating councils produce change.

American Journal of Community Psychology, 47, 12–27.

Javdani, S., Allen, N. E., Todd, N., & Anderson, C. J. (2011). Examining systems change in the response to domestic violence: Innovative applications of multilevel modeling. *Violence Against Women, 17,* 359–375.

Khorsan, R., Cohen, A. B., Lisi, A. J., Smith, M. M., Delevan, D., Armstrong, C., & Mittman, B. S. (2013). Mixed-methods research in a complex multisite VA health services study: Variations in the implementation and characteristics of chiropractic services in VA. *Evidence-Based Complementary and Alternative Medicine, 2013,* 1–10.

Sarason, S. B. (1972). *The creation of settings and the future societies.* Brookline, MA: Brookline Books.

Seifert, T. A., Goodman, K., King, P. M., & Baxter Magolda, M. B. (2010). Using mixed methods to study first-year college impact on liberal arts learning outcomes. *Journal of Mixed Methods Research, 4,* 248–267.

Tashakkori, A., & Teddlie, C. (2003). *Handbook of mixed methods in social and behavioral research.* Thousand Oaks, CA: Sage.

Todd, N., Allen, N. E., & Javdani, S. (2011). Hierarchical linear modeling: Opportunities and challenges for community psychology. In L. Jason & D. Glenwick (Eds.) *Innovative methodological approaches to community-based research* (pp. 167–185). Washington, DC: American Psychological Association.

Walden, A. L., (2011). *Power and change: Examining individual and setting level characteristics in relation to perceived influence in council settings and collaborative outcomes.* Unpublished master's thesis. University of Illinois at Urbana-Champaign, Champaign, IL.

Walden, A. L., Javdani, S., & Allen, N. E. (2014). Engaging conflict: Supporting power-sharing through constructive conflict resolution. *Journal of Community Psychology, 42,* 854–868.

Waysman, M., & Savaya, R. (1997). Mixed method evaluation: A case study. *Evaluation Practice, 18,* 227–237.

Yin, R. K., & Kaftarian, S. J. (1997). Introduction: Challenges of community-based program outcome evaluations. *Evaluation and Program Planning, 20,* 293–297.

34

Mixed Methods and Dialectical Pluralism

TRES STEFURAK, R. BURKE JOHNSON, AND ERYNNE SHATTO

This chapter's focus is on applying dialectical pluralism (DP) and equal-status mixed methods research. We first provide an overview of (a) DP as a metaparadigm (that is, a paradigm that dialogues with multiple paradigms) and (b) equal-status mixed methods research, highlighting the central concepts and principles of both. This is followed by a case study illustrating the application of these concepts and principles to the evaluation of a community-based intervention program for juvenile offenders. We conclude with some reflections about the case study in particular and DP in general.

INTRODUCTION TO DIALECTICAL PLURALISM

DP is an approach to research that assumes there are many perspectives, paradigms, methods, theories, philosophies, and ethical systems in the world that deserve much respect. It provides a process philosophy and theory for engaging successfully with differences. At the level of ontology, it assumes that reality is plural (e.g., subjective, intersubjective, and objective realities all exist; different disciplines provide insights into different realities; and many additional sorts of reality can be identified). At the level of epistemology, DP states that dialectical and dialogical logics (including "epistemological listening") should be used so that we can engage with the many differences and produce new syntheses (socially agreed-upon wholes) that command respect. DP is a communication theory because it requires that one communicate dialectically/dialogically in a positive way to overcome the incommensurability of paradigms/theories/standpoints (Johnson, 2011, 2012; Kuhn, 1962); this is called "dialectical listening." In evaluations of interventions, DP provides a way to engage with differences among stakeholders.

Syntheses of differences are respected because of the process used in DP, specifically the use of deliberative democracy in teams. Background rules are set (e.g., equal power, listening to the other, setting superordinate goals), group process is facilitated by someone (e.g., the mixed methods researcher), and the democratic process is agreed upon as to be respected and followed. When this is the case, procedural justice is obtained because of the process. This results in findings and actions that are accepted as just, even when they do not fully follow one's personal perspective. DP uses social psychological principles to work toward win-win solutions or, at worst, compromise solutions in the face of conflict.

DP tells users to use a "both/and" logic when possible, rather than an either/or logic, because this is an effective route to overcoming conflicting differences. As a result, plural knowledge and outcomes are produced that include something for all key team members or stakeholders. DP allows one to agree on a set of values to be used in each evaluation or research study. Therefore, it can be "packed" with values to provide social justice in addition to its procedural justice. Any package of values can be incorporated; however, DP at its core always asks that John Rawls's (1999) two principles of justice be strongly considered and respected: (a) equality and (b) special consideration for the needs of the marginalized in society and micro situations.

DP is a metaparadigm because it provides a space beyond the paradigm wars, at a higher level, where one listens, respects, and learns from the other, including other paradigms. It also can be employed to listen to knowledge produced at local and at national levels (Johnson & Stefurak, 2013) to produce a better knowledge system or science. In short, DP is used to engage with difference at the level of method, methodology, paradigm, and any other difference we might encounter in evaluation and research.

Johnson, Onwuegbuzie, Tucker, and Icenogle (2014) recently identified social psychological strategies for obtaining agreement in situations of difference. First, to capitalize on the strengths of DP, one constructs a heterogeneous group. Second, one uses team processes, such as encouraging and reinforcing member open-mindedness, working for shared development and understanding of shared goals, obtaining agreement on process, ensuring process transparency, encouraging epistemological listening and constructive cognitive conflict, ensuring that all team members express their views and reasoning, encouraging generation and examination of alternatives, and ensuring that the group articulates clear rationales for positions and decisions. Groups must avoid tendencies for groupthink, unequal power, social loafing, and premature closure. A talented facilitator is required if DP is to be successful; we believe that, in evaluation and research, mixed methods researchers are in an important position to dialogue with differences. Some additional and important strategies for bringing diverse ideas together are collaborative logic modeling (Kaplan & Garrett, 2005), appreciative inquiry (Cooperrider & Srivastva, 1987), identification of preconditions and assumptions with ladder of inference (Lewicki, Weiss, & Lewin, 1992), reciprocity (Cialdini, 2008), third space (Gutierrez, Baquedano-Lopez, & Tejeda, 2009), the 4-C model of team development (Dyer, Dyer, & Dyer, 2007), debriefing interviews throughout the group process (Collins, Onwuegbuzie, Johnson, & Frels, 2013), future search (Weisbord & Janoff, 2000), open space (Owen, 1997), collaborative creativity (Sawyer, 2008), data retreats (Sargent, 2003), complexity-based sense making (Snowden, 2005), Delphi method (Rowe & Wright, 2001), ecological systems models (Onwuegbuzie, Collins, & Frels, 2013), and diffusion of innovation theory (Rogers, 2003). In short, DP is a philosophy, a metaparadigm, and a theory for dealing with difference, with many social psychological strategies that can be employed for its success.

DP is usually conducted in heterogeneous teams and requires that users do the following (from Johnson, 2012):

> (a) dialectically listen, carefully and thoughtfully, to different paradigms, disciplines, theories, and stakeholder and citizen perspectives; (b) combine important ideas from competing paradigms and values into a new workable whole for each research study or program evaluation; (c) explicitly state and "pack" the approach with stakeholders' and researchers' epistemological and social-political values to guide the research (including the valued ends one hopes for and the valued means for getting there); (d) conduct the research ethically; (e) facilitate dissemination and use of research findings (locally and more broadly); and (f) continually, formatively evaluate and improve the outcomes of the research-and-use process (e.g., Is the research having the desired societal impact?). In short, DP is a change theory, and it requires listening, understanding, learning, and acting. (p. 752)

DIALOGUE AND THE INTERPERSONAL ASPECTS OF DIALECTICAL PLURALISM

As already mentioned, DP requires that evaluators intentionally and deliberately engage divergent stakeholders. The heart of the paradigm is to cherish and learn from "the other" (Buber, 1923) and to intentionally seek out the perspectives of marginalized stakeholders and include them in the dialogue about the processes to be used, as well as the goals to be achieved, by the program evaluation. This process is fundamentally an interpersonal process. It is important to form teams that engage in dialogue across the spectrum of ideas, with the members taking care to engage and combine anomalous and different values and positions into new working wholes.

Second, evaluators and researchers encourage teams to view conflict as not a regrettable necessity, but rather as a valued catalyst for the evolution of the team's intellectual and values positions that will lead to useful methods of investigation and analysis of data. There can be no change without dissonance; therefore, constructive conflict is the engine of a team working within the DP paradigm. This requires that parties involved have equal power and a shared willingness to resolve conflict by gathering additional relevant information, learning from the other, and expanding and synthesizing positions (Johnson, Onwuegbuzie, Tucker, & Icenogle, 2014).

Third, the group is more than the sum of its parts when it comes to creativity arising from collaboration. Groups allow for the creation of an intellectual space qualitatively different than any one member's contributions. For each member of the group the intellectual space created becomes novel and a source of innovation and creativity.

Last, the vision of the DP metaparadigm is to foster efforts that spur conceptions of larger systemic changes beyond the particular changes found in any given research or evaluation project. Evaluation and research teams following the DP model would, over time, become more focused on the broader systemic sources of the problems they are studying and engage in increasingly broader and deeper dialogues, maintaining the same pluralistic, egalitarian, and procedural justice values as they do so (Johnson et al., 2014).

The conclusions reached in an evaluation conducted through the DP lens are not based upon any monistic or absolutist metric of truth. Rather, the goal is to draw conclusions that find broad agreement across diverse stakeholders. Judgments about reality and data are to be made on the basis of what Scriven (2012) called *probative inference*. This concept refers to conclusions made based upon the best available evidence, given agreed-upon shared epistemologies, ground rules, and values. Working from a DP perspective requires acknowledging that values and philosophical assumptions form the ground for our questions, methods, and conclusions, and we need to accept and acknowledge this explicitly rather than implicitly. Results are "thick," that is, embedded with social and scientific values. Practical and working truths, rather than absolute truths, are obtained. Theory and practice are combined into practical theories.

EQUAL-STATUS MIXED METHODS DESIGNS

DP can stand alone as a philosophy and theory in many settings. However, it works especially well in mixed methods research with equal-status designs. These are designs where the qualitative and quantitative components are treated equally. It is where high-quality qualitative and quantitative data are collected. It also is where the qualitative and quantitative research paradigms are given equal weight. Sometimes it is said that paradigms are incommensurable and cannot be mixed. However, they can be, using a dialectical and dialogical logic. That is why equal-status mixed methods designs are also called interactive mixed methods designs. In the following case study, the project team attempted to conduct an equal-status mixed methods evaluation.

CASE STUDY

The project presented here was an evaluation of a juvenile court program in which the investigators attempted to apply the principles of DP. The case study illustrates evaluation practice embedded in a multivalues system and conducted from a pluralistic epistemology using intentional collaborative dialogues. It demonstrates the importance of both scientific evidence and theory impacting practice. The evidence gleaned in practice should, as a general rule, according to DP, feed back into our science and scholarly viewpoint to produce a system of scientific knowledge that learns from practice and produces practical theory (Johnson & Stefurak, 2013).

Background of Juvenile Court–University Collaboration

This project was conducted as part of the Mobile Juvenile Court Collaborative (MJCC). The MJCC, formed in 2008, was a collaboration between the University of South Alabama and the local juvenile court and juvenile detention center. The project was founded upon a core value of mutual benefit to three distinct stakeholder groups: (a) youth and families served by the court, (b) court leaders and staff members, and (c) university faculty and trainees in the social service professions represented in the project. The project was also founded upon a shared value of sustainability. These common values helped produce some commonality across the stakeholders and could be resorted to when smaller values conflicted. Each stakeholder group still had its particular values of emphasis, many of which conflicted. The working toward shared and superordinate values in the conduct of evaluation research is at the crux of DP's paradigmatic vision.

As Johnson et al. (2014) noted, the creation of DP collaboration often requires effort far beyond what is required of an individual's job as an academic or professional working in the community. It requires continual dialoguing, listening, changing, and growing in order to produce a successful and sustainable whole.

The Transitions Program

Transitions was a new court intervention program established in 2012 that combined three tiers of intervention targeting youth whose offenses put them at risk of being sent to a state facility. The three intervention tiers included (a) increased monitoring, (b) intensive case management, and (c) in-home family therapy. Although not adopting a specific evidence-based practice (EBP) paradigm, such as multisystemic therapy (Henggeler, Schoenwald, Borduin, Rowland, & Cunningham, 1998), Transitions sought to embody as many EBP principles of intervention as possible and was created in close consultation with the university partners in the MJCC.

There were concerns on the part of court leadership regarding their organizational readiness and attitudes toward the changes represented by the Transitions program. The program required more intensive case management than had typically been practiced by probation officers or by previous intervention programs that the court had funded. Also, the program involved increasing the degree of collaboration and mutual holding of accountability across court probation officers, judges, and community-contracted program providers beyond what was previously the norm for these organizations. The professional workload would be higher than normal, and the program required an attitude shift away from the siloed and insulated culture of a court to a more open and accountability-oriented stance of a multiagency community intervention provider.

The MJCC faculty and graduate students were contracted to conduct a program evaluation of Transitions. The focus of this evaluation was not on program outcomes, as it was too nascent for these to be benchmarked effectively. Rather, the evaluation was to develop dialogical and effective procedures and processes for the Transitions program to be institutionalized. The court leadership team requested recommendations based on the conclusions of the evaluation as to how well actual practices in the program mirrored written procedural guidelines and how the administration of the program could be improved at the structural and interpersonal levels. All of this was in anticipation of the court having to show significant reductions in recidivism within 1 to 2 years of the program's onset.

Values-Based and Mixed Methods Program Evaluation

The conduct of this evaluation was complicated because the program did not involve merely the juvenile court but also the use of a local adolescent addictions agency to provide the tracker services and the local public mental health system to provide the in-home family therapy services. The program required that all three entities meet monthly to review the progress of each individual case. The evaluation's goals were constructed dialectically and dialogically through a series of discussions between the MJCC evaluators and juvenile court stakeholders. This process deliberately involved careful discussion of the values driving the goals of the court in general and the program in particular. Chief among these values were sustainability, mutual benefit, and accountability of all parties involved.

Following DP, through a series of meetings and dialogues an evaluation approach was agreed upon. The approach included evaluation targets that reflected the core values at work. It also included evaluation methods that focused on subjective/qualitative (e.g., stakeholders' perceptions of success in the program) and objective/quantitative (e.g., what predicted optimism and buy-in among court staff into the new procedures and philosophy inherent in the program) evaluation methods. The methodology selected emerged from the evaluators' valuing of equal-status mixed methods research, where neither quantitative nor qualitative methods are given a privileged status, as well as from an effort, in dialogues with stakeholders, to select methods best suited to answer the given evaluation questions. As noted earlier, DP perhaps fits best with the equal-status mixed methods research approach (i.e., better than with either qualitatively driven or quantitatively driven mixed methods research).

DP and equal-status mixed methods evaluation was a good fit for this project because the court stakeholders were concerned about both (a) the "brass tacks" of how Transitions members were behaving and what measured attitudes objectively predicted greater buy-in to the program and its new procedures and (b) the phenomenological issues of how each Transitions stakeholder constructed meaning around the issues that were most pertinent in his or her role/job and in the lives of the youth being served. The goals became to not sacrifice one dimension for the other and to allow data from both domains to inform each other dialectically and dialogically.

The dialectical process allowed the evaluators to listen to different Transitions team members, whose roles and places within the collaboration structure became associated with divergent subjective views of what their job was, what youth needed to be successful, and what the program itself needed to be successful and sustainable. Qualitative evaluation methods were instrumental in gathering these diverse perspectives among stakeholders. In balance to the subjective views of Transitions stakeholders, quantitative observational and survey methods were necessary to assess whether stakeholders were actually behaving in ways that mirrored their purported values and subjective opinions, as well as to determine which stakeholder factors were the most salient in promoting buy-in and openness to adoption of the new procedures inherent in the program. What follows, to give the reader a sense of the project's scope and end results, are brief overviews of each evaluation question, methods, and basic findings.

Evaluation of Service Provision

The evaluators sought to accurately catalog the roles and procedures of the service provision activities of the program. To accomplish this, they directly observed and coded interactions at four consecutive Transitions staff meetings and analyzed the content of official marketing materials created for the program. The results suggested that the view of the program held by its stakeholders greatly undervalued many of the actual services being provided. In particular, case managers were performing far more duties than were formally documented in program materials and/or in the perspective of upper-level leadership.

Profile of Youth Served

The evaluators systematically reviewed 29 juvenile court files on youth who were sampled at random from the youth enrolled in the program during its first year. The evaluators used the quantitative Youth Level of Services/Case Management Inventory-2nd Edition (YLS/CSM-2; Hoge & Andrews, 2011) to code each file and identify risk, need, and responsivity to treatment factors for each youth. The results revealed that a vast majority of the youth had major risk factors in the areas of delinquent peer bonding and poor recreational/leisure activity options which were not being targeted by the Transitions program. However, there were other areas of malleable risk factors (e.g., family functioning) that were clearly being targeted by facets of the program. In general, the program did not appear to focus systematically on targeting individualized malleable risk and protective factors, which is a common deficit of delinquency intervention programs and almost universally found in analyses of evidence-based practice in delinquency interventions (Borum, 2003; Underwood, Sandor von Dresner, & Phillips, 2006).

Evaluation of Perceived Program Goals

The evaluators created a mixed questionnaire (i.e., a questionnaire that included open- and closed-ended items) to assess the program's perceived goals. A mixed questionnaire is a type of *intramethod* mixing, that is, mixing within a single method of data collection (in contrast to *intermethod* mixing, the use of different methods of data collection, which was also employed in the present evaluation). The questionnaire inquired into staff members' perceptions of (a) what constituted successful completion of the program, (b) concrete factors that mitigated the program meeting its goals with each youth, and (c) questions regarding the length of time necessary to complete the program successfully. The results, based on the responses of 19 staff members, indicated that each contributing agency had slightly differing values and goals for the program, but all agencies, through some subsequent dialogue, agreed that improving educational outcomes was a common goal. Stakeholders also came to agreement that cooperation of the youth and family was the most critical element to successful completion. All stakeholders agreed that provision of support, as opposed to punitive measures, was called for when cooperation from a youth and family was not present. From this dialogue, the evaluators recommended developing concrete markers of success that were delineated in program materials and referred to at each staffing.

Collaboration Effectiveness

The MJCC evaluators used the Wilder Collaboration Factors Inventory (WCFI; Mattessich, Murray-Close, & Monsey, 2001) to assess collaboration effectiveness. The resulting quantitative scale scores were analyzed to identify places of relative collaborative strength versus weakness in the program. The evaluators also created a separate, nonverbal coding instrument based on the work of Kurien (2010) and Goman (2012). The researchers/observers coded qualitative data from this instrument for various nonverbal behaviors and quantitatively determined the frequency of contributions to staffing dialogue by specific team members. Thus, mixed methods were used.

The results from the WCFI suggested that stakeholders often perceived the collaboration as being successful, with half of the domain scores indicating perceived effectiveness. The strongest area of perceived effectiveness was in the domain of communication among collaborators, while areas of perceived collaboration weakness involved the domains of perceived disrespect and trust among members, inclusion of a representative cross-section of individuals, and willingness of members to compromise. This appears to mirror what is found in research on group process where groups, early in the process such as here, enter a "storming" phase in which norms and ways of relating are worked out. The results also suggested that the participants believed that the collaboration could improve its ability to adapt to changes in the community but were concerned as to whether the program could maintain an appropriate pace of development. The only factor that fell into the serious problem area was related to sufficiency of resources to implement the program.

The analysis of the behaviors during staffing indicated that there were more negative than positive disruptions observed. This was a strong and robust trend. Despite this, there was in the aggregate more positive than negative nonverbal behavior across meetings. This suggests that a civil tone was maintained and that the Transitions team was attempting to conflict productively. In its involvement in the project, the MJCC researchers had attempted to cultivate communication patterns endorsed by DP. Mostly, the Transitions team's early struggles were classified as positive conflict (i.e., group situations where conflict is viewed as normal and good for team growth), which is exactly what is called for in the ideal type of DP.

Organizational Readiness to Change

DP is a change theory, and it was used to gauge and facilitate organizational readiness to change. The evaluators put together a battery of quantitative instruments to gauge individual probation officers' perception of their job roles, perception of the needs of the youth and families that they served, perceived readiness for organizational change, and measures related to their own personality traits and values. The 36 probation staff participants were invited to complete the battery anonymously, with 21 completing it.

The quantitative results suggested that probation staff primarily viewed family factors, the youth's attitude, and substance abuse as the areas on which they focused the most in their work. They also reported a moderate degree of willingness to use a more formal, structured process to identify malleable needs of the youth and indicated a moderate degree of confidence in their individual ability to use the structured process. The staff members who were most willing and confident in themselves to utilize a structured approach with youth assessment were also those who reported the highest degree of perceived accomplishment in their work. Of the occupational burnout indicators of decreased personal accomplishment, depersonalization, and exhaustion, the last two factors were unrelated to willingness or confidence to use a structured evidence-based approach. Also, the results indicated that when probation staff perceived more support from supervisors and coworkers they were more likely to report less cynicism about organizational change and were more favorable to instituting new practices.

The evaluators also used qualitative methods to assess probation officers' perceptions. Individual semistructured interviews were conducted with nine individuals representing both front-line probation officers and probation officer supervisors. The questions focused on their perceptions of (a) the purpose and philosophy of probation services, (b) the methods by which the probation officers identified youth needs and made recommendations, and (c) contextual factors that affected how they went about their work. They also were asked what changes they recommended. The following broad themes emerged as desired organizational changes:

1. Adoption of more formal, but efficient, methods of assessing youth and family needs
2. Increased efficiencies in time management, paperwork, and referral practices
3. Increased options for diverting youth from probation, juvenile court, and state juvenile justice facilities.

Across these three themes, probation staff reported a consistent desire and readiness for change. Consensus was clearly present about the needed changes, but significant cynicism existed in perceived organizational self-efficacy to make the changes. Last, the results pointed to the need to reduce probation officers' duties in some areas in order to free up time to engage in the improved assessment and case management practices the court was implementing in the Transitions program.

The Transitions Program Evaluation in the Context of Dialectical Pluralism

This project was conducted soon after the initial formulation of DP as a metaparadigm in 2011 (Johnson, 2011). The idea of dialoging intentionally with broad stakeholders was on the minds of the MJCC evaluation team, as was the concept of identifying evaluation questions and methods that could find broad consensus among stakeholders and, in theory, yield results that would be reasonable and acceptable to all parties. Although many aspects of the evaluation are in line with the DP model, some aspects were not, and these also are discussed.

At the methods, methodology, and paradigm levels, the Transitions evaluation embodied the equal-status mixed methods position because both quantitative and qualitative data and approaches were treated equally. Equal-status mixed methods research approaches sit within a multidimensional continuum between rather dogmatic positions. On one pole of the continuum sits the position of Guba (1990) and Lincoln and Guba (2000), which posits that qualitative research is the best form of evaluation inquiry about humans and doubts that any objective reality exists. For these qualitative methodologists, all reality is mentally constructed, which yields the concept of validity, as typically conceived, impotent. On the other pole of the continuum is the positivist position that an objective reality does exist and that research methods should be evaluated based on the objective reliability and validity of the measurements used and on the replicability of findings.

In opposition to these polemic/dogmatic viewpoints is the position of Greene (2007), who searched for dialectical syntheses between the positivist and constructivist positions on a project-by-project basis. DP (a) directly builds on Greene's (2007) work in the philosophy of social science methodology, (b) provides a metaparadigm that enables paradigms and worldviews to dialogue, and (c) conceives reality as plural. The methods used in the case evaluation reflected (a) attempts to target "objective" realities (e.g., behaviors of staff in meetings) and (b) subjective or phenomenological realities (e.g., each team member's perceptions of his or her individual roles and responsibilities). At the most basic level, the program evaluation attempted to use an equal-status mixed methods approach to target the same question with both quantitative and qualitative methods and determine both how the results triangulated and how they were different.

As mentioned, the mission of the ongoing project, the MJCC, was in line with the concepts found in DP. The project that this evaluation emerged from was a product of consensus building and a deliberate dialogue between academic/researchers and juvenile justice officials over a period of time. The evaluation of the program was an organic outgrowth of a longstanding relationship between the two collaborative partners. Our evaluation emerged from collaboration and had a well-established baseline value of collaboration and dialectical consensus building as an end unto itself, as well as a means to such other ends as conducting research with at-risk youth and juvenile offenders and assisting in broad-based community change and social justice. According to DP, evaluators and researchers must be engaged in genuine, congruent, and transparent efforts to share power and decision making with other stakeholders.

Another feature of DP is an admonition for evaluators to deliberately seek out and listen in a deep and intentional way to all parties involved, particularly marginalized and less visible stakeholders. This goal is to garner all perspectives involved, include those perspectives in the construction and execution of the evaluation, and produce results that take into account a breadth of perspectives. Our evaluation partially met this DP aspiration. The Transitions evaluation included a deliberate attempt to seek out stakeholders *within* the network of providers collaborating to deliver the intervention program for juvenile offenders. The evaluators/moderators initially helped the various stakeholders (i.e., judges and court administrators, service providers, and trackers and case managers) identify consensus around goals of the evaluation and methods of data collection and analysis. With respect to the first goal, we believe that we achieved a strong degree of success. Stakeholders appeared to have a strong investment in and awareness of the goals of the evaluation. Achieving methods consensus proved more challenging. Many stakeholders had low levels of knowledge about the relative strengths of one evaluation method versus another. Although the stakeholders had an intuitive positive view of the mixed methods approach that ultimately comprised the final evaluation, the evaluators had to engage in much education about both the merits of different uses of data and which types of data stakeholders most valued. Many stakeholders brought methodological pluralism with them, but the stakeholders ultimately viewed choice of methods and data as a matter to be left to the expertise of the evaluators.

A key deficit, from the perspective of DP, was the failure to successfully include the voices and perspectives of the youth and families that were participating in the Transitions program. One paradigm in mixed methods research is *transformatism* (Mertens, 2007). This paradigm argues that the goal of research and evaluation is to achieve social liberation and empowerment for stakeholders, particularly stakeholders who are oppressed and disadvantaged. Our instantiation of DP emphasized this perspective. The goal of the evaluation was not just to obtain answers to evaluation questions but also to obtain answers that would lead to changes that improved the lives of those receiving the services of the Transitions program. Generally speaking, DP helps accomplish this social justice goal because it advocates genuine, ongoing dialogue with stakeholders in research and evaluation, including those with the least power. In the context of the evaluation, the evaluators needed to engage in real dialogue with the youth and families involved in the program. However, this did not occur—a glaring weakness, we believe, of the evaluation.

The goal of meaningful dialogue with the youth and families was a challenge throughout the evaluation. Challenging agencies to include the perspectives of the people they serve, who are often socially and politically marginalized, is a difficult task for a number of reasons. The task was made difficult in our case because of the presence of institutionalized racial, economic, and political privilege, as well as the current structure of the relevant organizations. The juvenile court sits at the tension point between empowering and developing youth and their families, on the one hand, and ensuring public safety, on the other. The court was largely staffed by members of the majority culture and middle-class stratum and they often struggled to take an empathic stance toward the individuals they served. A punitive stance was not uncommon. The presence of conservative political pressures that emphasized cost reduction and viewed criminal behavior as "chosen" rather than "caused" meant that the juvenile court often was unable to consider a pluralistic array of perspectives in making its decisions and structuring its programs. Although the formation of the Transitions program, the desire for more structure and evidence-based assessment methods, and the move toward interagency collaboration were progressive steps, much work in terms of building equitable social structures in this community was still left to be done.

We were able to build into the evaluation such methods as reviewing files and interviewing stakeholders regarding specific cases. These, however, hardly lifted up the voices of the youth and parents in the program. Our experience was that the stakeholders' objection to such data was partially due to perceived logistical difficulties of interviewing and tapping client perspectives. Therefore, evaluations like this should include data from transcripts of counseling sessions and other points of contact with the youth and family and through other naturalistic qualitative data collection methods.

The more insidious obstacles to collecting data were the political and cultural obstacles. Agencies providing social services need to measure and understand the authentic subjective experiences of recipients of their services. Too often, however, because of patriarchy, service providers ignore such perspectives. They may fear that these perspectives will cast doubt upon the legitimate authority of the court and its services. As a result, youth and parents experience both overt and subtle forms of racism and classism. Program recipients are viewed as corrupted or impaired, and their perspectives as having little practical value. Our use of DP in this project did not eliminate this lack of understanding and respect for the other, but we hope that mutual understanding will continue to grow over time.

CONCLUSION

DP requires that evaluators and researchers work toward the construction of a balanced synthesis of the values of all stakeholders and toward superordinate goals in a deliberative, democratic way. This requires open and equal participation and the giving up of some power. DP also advocates a participatory approach involving all stakeholders at all stages, including forming questions, collecting data, interpreting results, and constructing conclusions and recommendations. DP asks evaluators not to stand behind a veil of ignorance in which values do not exist or are seen as "threats" to the integrity of inquiry. The case study presented here illustrates the application of DP toward the promotion of community-based programs that are sustainable, beneficial to all parties, and delivered in ways that promote accountability. We encourage others to similarly apply the DP paradigm in their settings and to disseminate their research findings and experiences.

REFERENCES

Borum, R. (2003). Managing at-risk juvenile offenders in the community: Putting evidence-based principles into practice. *Journal of Contemporary Criminal Justice, 19*, 114–137.

Buber, M. (1923/2000). *I and thou*. New York, NY: Scribner.

Cialdini, R. B. (2008). *Influence: Science and practice* (5th ed.). Boston, MA: Pearson.

Collins, K. M. T., Onwuegbuzie, A. J., Johnson, R. B., & Frels, R. K. (2013). Practice note: Using debriefing interviews to promote authenticity and transparency in mixed research. *International Journal of Multiple research Approaches, 7*, 271–283.

Cooperrider, D. L., & Srivastva, S. (1987). Appreciative inquiry in organizational life. *Research in Organizational Change and Development, 1*, 129–169.

Dyer, W. G., Dyer, W. G., Jr., & Dyer, J. H. (2007). *Team building: Proven strategies for improving team performance*. San Francisco, CA: Wiley.

Goman, C. K. (2012). Body language. *Sales and Service Excellence, 12*, 3.

Greene, J. C. (2007). *Mixed methods in social inquiry*. San Francisco, CA: Jossey-Bass.

Guba, E. G. (1990). The alternative paradigm dialog. In E. G. Guba (Ed.). *The paradigm dialog* (pp. 17–27). Newbury Park, CA: Sage.

Gutierrez, K. D., Baquedano-Lopez, P., & Tejeda, C. (2009). Rethinking diversity: Hybridity and hybrid language practices in the third space. *Mind, Culture, and Activity, 6*, 286–303.

Henggeler, S. W., Schoenwald, S. K., Borduin, C. M., & Rowland, M. D., & Cunningham, P. B. (1998). *Multisystemic treatment for antisocial behavior in children and adolescents*. New York, NY: Guilford Press.

Hoge, R. D. & Andrews, D. A. (2011). *Youth level of services/case management inventory 2.0 (YLS/CMI 2.0)*. North Tonawanda, NY: Multi-Health Systems.

Johnson, R. B. (2011, May). *Dialectical pluralism: A metaparadigm to help us hear and "combine" our valued differences*. Paper presented at the Seventh International Congress of Qualitative Inquiry, Urbana, IL.

Johnson, R. B. (2012). Dialectical pluralism and mixed research. *American Behavioral Scientist, 56*, 751–754.

Johnson, R. B., Onwuegbuzie, T., Tucker, S., & Icenogle, M.L. (2014). Conducting mixed methods research using dialectical pluralism and social psychological strategies. In P. Leavy (Ed.). *The Oxford handbook of qualitative research* (pp. 557–578). New York, NY: Oxford University Press.

Johnson, R. B., & Stefurak, T. (2013). Considering the evidence-and-credibility discussion in evaluation through the lens of dialectical pluralism. *New Directions for Evaluation, 138*, 103–109.

Kaplan, S. A., & Garrett, K. E. (2005). The use of logic models by community-based initiatives. *Evaluation and Program Planning, 28*, 167–172.

Kuhn, T. S. (1962). *The structure of scientific revolutions*. Chicago, IL: University of Chicago Press.

Kurien, D. N. (2010). Body language: Silent communicator at the workplace. *IUP Journal of Soft Skills, 4*(1 & 2), 29–36.

Lewicki, R. J., Weiss, S. Ed., & Lewin, D. (1992). Models of conflict, negotiation and third party intervention: A review and synthesis. *Journal of Organizational Behavior, 13*, 209–252.

Lincoln, Y. S., & Guba, E. G. (2000). Paradigmatic controversies, contradictions, and emerging confluences. In N. K. Denzin & Y. S. Lincoln (Eds.), *Handbook of qualitative research* (pp. 163–188). Thousand Oaks, CA: Sage.

Mattessich, P., Murray-Close, M., & Monsey, B. (2001). *Wilder Collaboration Factors Inventory*. St. Paul, MN: Wilder Research.

Mertens, D. M. (2007). Transformative paradigm: Mixed methods and social justice. *Journal of Mixed Methods Research, 1*, 212–225.

Onwuegbuzie, A. J., Collins, K. M. T., & Frels, R. K. (2013). Foreword: Using Bronfenbrenner's ecological systems theory to frame quantitative, qualitative, and mixed research. *International Journal of Multiple Research Approaches, 7*, 2–8.

Owen, H. (1997). *Open space technology: A user's guide* (2nd ed.). San Francisco, CA: Berrett-Koehler.

Rawls, J. (1999). *The law of peoples.* Cambridge, MA: Harvard University Press.

Rogers, E. M. (2003). *Diffusion of innovations* (5th ed.). New York, NY: The Free Press.

Rowe, G., & Wright, G. (2001). Expert opinions in forecasting: Role of the Delphi technique. In J. S. Armstrong (Ed.), *Principles of forecasting: A handbook of researchers and practitioners* (pp. 125–144). Boston, MA: Kluwer Academic.

Sargent, J. (2003). *Data retreat participant's guide.* Naperville, IL: Learning Point Associates.

Sawyer, K. (2008). *Group genius: The creative power of collaboration.* Cambridge, MA: Perseus Books.

Scriven, M. (2012). The logic of valuing. *New Directions for Evaluation, 133*, 17–28.

Snowden, D. J. (2005). Multi-ontology sense making: A new simplicity in decision making. *Informatics in Primary Care, 13*, 45–54.

Underwood, L. A., Sandor von Dresner, K., & Phillips, A. L. (2006). Community treatment programs for juveniles: A best-evidence summary. *International Journal of Behavioral Consultation and Therapy, 2*, 286–304.

Weisbord, M., & Janoff, S. (2000). *Future search: An action guide to finding common ground in organizations and communities* (2nd ed.), San Francisco, CA: Berrett-Koehler.

35

Community Profiling in Participatory Action Research

CATERINA ARCIDIACONO, TERESA TUOZZI, AND FORTUNA PROCENTESE

The primary goal of social and health policies is to improve the well-being of local communities. Insofar as every plan of action requires knowledge of the research object—in this case the community—then getting to know the local context under study is the starting point of a successful intervention (Center for Urban Transportation Research, 2000; Forrest & Hill, 2013). Hawtin, Hughes, and Percy-Smith (1994) described the essence of the intervention through the following four steps: needs assessment, community consultations, social audits, and community profiling. Needs assessment is the preliminary goal for a researcher approaching a new social context. Knowing what local people are doing, how often, and with whom is a tool for auditing any dimension of community life at any given time. Within the framework of a community audit, Taylor and Burns (2000) focused specifically on local participation aided by such tools as baseline mapping, specific checklists, and measurement scales, in order to investigate and assess people's needs and their local participation. Moreover, Kirsten and Holt (2008) highlighted the benefit of involving the community in the decision-making process in assessing health priorities through community profiling.

Hawtin et al. (1994) described and discussed the procedure of community profiling as one approach to obtaining local participation. They highlighted its different aspects as follows: "A *comprehensive* description of the *needs* of a population that is defined, or defines itself, as a *community,* and the *resources* that exist within that community, carried out with the *active involvement of the community* itself, for the purpose of developing an *action plan* or other means of improving the quality of life of the community" (Hawtin, Hughes, & Percy-Smith, 2007, p. 5). In this chapter we shall first present the theory behind, and the steps involved in, community diagnosis and community profiling. We will then offer a case study illustrating the application of community profiling in an urban community.

INTRODUCTION TO COMMUNITY DIAGNOSIS AND COMMUNITY PROFILING

Community diagnosis based on community profiling constitutes a means for getting to know local communities (Arcidiacono, Sommantico, & Procentese, 2001). This is, indeed, a mindful and participatory way of reading people's needs. As such, it is a valuable aid for providing information related to the weaknesses and strengths of health, relational, and economic aspects of a community. At the same time it is a preliminary tool for community building and social change (Arcidiacono & Procentese, 2005).

Community diagnosis can be framed as a tool within the broader picture of participatory action research (PAR), a well-known methodology for identifying and solving common problems for individuals, groups, and organizations within a given community (Reason & Bradbury, 2008). This tool is designed to help people assess the quality of the place where they live, as well as to take action toward their betterment.

In PAR the understanding of social and psychological phenomena entails a thorough observation of the dynamics at stake in a given context.

Transformative theory and practice come together in a reciprocal process of mutual implementation in which hypotheses steer actions and the latter, in turn, stimulates and modifies theorizations. Cooperation between researcher and community member is crucial, and this can be built only on the mutual understanding of needs, competencies, and resources. PAR hinges on a process whereby local knowledge and professional expertise are merged to promote social change. Involving the very recipients of the intervention makes it possible to negotiate with the social actors to which the intervention is directed (Arcidiacono & Procentese, 2010). As a consequence, it helps to make important decisions more easily accepted by the members of the larger community. This technique plays an empowering role, in that its power to raise awareness and involve people in decision-making processes leads them to take action for social change.

Kagan, Burton, Duckett, Lawthom, and Siddiquee (2011) attempted to define the most relevant dimensions of community life that should be investigated in order to draw up a community profile, namely, characteristics of the population, local views and priorities, housing, education, environment, facilities and services, crime and safety, physical environment, transportation and communications, and health. They also drew up a list of different tools and methods to collect information for each dimension. Maps, data, and other forms of information from both local and national sources are considered, together with participant observations, community walks, focus group, interviews, diaries, video films, creative writing workshops, and services waiting lists. The aim is to investigate the characteristics of the community and, at the same time, to discover, together with the inhabitants, its cultural and symbolic representations, social structures, and eventually its own historical roots, "which still inform the contemporary understandings of what community means" (Kagan et al., 2011, p. 79). Cheong (2006) also highlighted the need to carefully recognize physical, psychological, sociocultural, economical, and technological domains. He specifically emphasized the importance of taking into account the relational features of the community, that is, the communication within and between different individuals and groups. Moreover, Kagan et al. (2011) introduced power as a further dimension to be considered. Related to this power dimension, the authors' experiences (Arcidiacono, 1996, 2004) in community profiling at the town level have made us aware of the importance of reflexivity among researchers and of trust between the latter and local bodies.

Community profiling informs knowledge about a certain territory, including its characteristics, people's needs, resources, and the shortcomings of institutions and services, as proposed by Martini and Sequi (1988, 1995) and further developed by Francescato and Ghirelli (1988). Francescato and Zani (2013, p. 3) defined it as "structured participatory action research, that can be used to find out what particular problems and strengths characterize a local community in the eyes of different groups of residents and what are their most desired changes." It is regarded (Francescato, Arcidiacono, Albanesi, & Mannarini, 2007; Francescato, Gelli, Mannarini, & Taurino, 2004) as a participatory tool usually solicited by local administrations interested in more than mere temporary, extemporary, and stopgap measures. In their guidelines for procedures and data collection for community profiling, these authors proposed the construction of an interdisciplinary research group (IRG) that is formed by those members of the community who display a high level of expertise with respect to the profile analysis to be carried out. The group then carries out a preliminary analysis through brainstorming, that is, a technique aimed at bringing out those strong points and critical aspects that the members of the discussion group regard as being the most important. This is one of the reasons why the IRG should be formed by stakeholders of the community who vary on such dimensions as age, social status and role, profession, and degree of knowledge of the local community. This preliminary analysis helps to plan the next steps more clearly by, for instance, highlighting which aspects will be further investigated, as well as identifying other local stakeholders who might best be contacted. The second step is to develop in more detail this preliminary and rough community diagnosis by collecting data, thereby providing a more complete community profile, that is, those aspects that characterize the community in this model (territorial profile, demographic profile, services profile, institutional profile, productive activities profile, psychological profile, anthropological profile, and profile of the future).

Tables 35.1 and 35.2 provide an example (Tuozzi, 2013) of community profiling in the town

TABLE 35.1: COMMUNITY STRENGTHS

	IRG (Interdisciplinary Research Group)	Focus Group	Interviews	Questionnaires
Territorial	Natural resources Geographic location Cultural and artistic heritage	Natural resources Geographic location Cultural and artistic heritage	Natural resources Geographic location Cultural and artistic heritage	Natural resources Geographic location Cultural and artistic heritage
Demographic	Medium-high educational level	Young population	Young population Demographic growth	Young population
Productive activities	Agriculture	Agriculture	Agriculture	Food Tertiary activities: bank
Services		School services Spa treatments Community-based projects Soccer field Catholic youth center		School services Soccer field Catholic youth center
Institutional		Administrative activities Police station Courthouse	Police station Courthouse	Administrative activities Police station Courthouse
Anthropological	Openness/solidarity/family	Openness/solidarity/family Traditions	Openness/solidarity/family Traditions Hard-working people	Openness/solidarity/family Traditions
Psychological		Social support	Cohesion	Sense of belonging Social support

Source: Adapted with permission from *Profilo di Comunità di Carinola: Risorse e Potenzialità* [Community Profiling of Carinola: Resources and Opportunities] by T. Tuozzi, 2013, pp. 29–31.

of Carinola based on the guidelines of Francescato and her colleagues. In this work, the preliminary brainstorming among the IRG regarding the strengths and weaknesses of the community was followed by a series of data collection activities, involving individual interviews, focus group interviews, and semistructured questionnaires. The IRG was composed of eight citizens: one majority politician and one opposition politician who were members of the city council, a representative of community associations, a teacher, an elderly retired person, an unemployed youth, one precariously employed young worker, and a craftsman. Following the IRG's brainstorming, 18 key informants—the mayor, four city councillors, a city councilwoman, one majority politician, one opposition politician, the chief of the municipal police, the chief of the police station, the director of the local prison, five parish priests, an elderly man, and an immigrant—were involved by means of individual interviews. Subsequently, there were 12 focus groups composed of local inhabitants (varying in neighborhood, age, and gender) involving a total of 87 people, including young students, workers, unemployed persons, and retired elderly.

The semistructured questionnaires were distributed to 89 citizens of Carinola. They included, in addition to questions about the strengths and weaknesses of the community, some specific items investigating respondents' satisfaction with respect to the services offered by the territory and the work of institutions. Some questions also inquired into the sense of belonging and social support perceived by citizens. Finally, there were questions on the perception of the

TABLE 35.2: COMMUNITY WEAKNESSES

	IRG (Interdisciplinary Research Group)	Focus Group	Interviews	Questionnaires
Territorial	Scarce promotion of the cultural and artistic heritage	Scarce promotion of the cultural and artistic heritage		Scarce promotion of the cultural and artistic heritage
	Scarce promotion of the local area	Scarce promotion of the local area		Scarce promotion of the local area
Demographic	Scarce homogeneity between groups of different factions			
		Demographic degrowth/population aging	Demographic degrowth/ population aging	Demographic degrowth/ population aging
Productive activities	Scarce promotion of tourism	Scarce promotion of tourism		Scarce promotion of tourism
	Scarce promotion of agriculture	Scarce promotion of agriculture	Scarce promotion of agriculture	Scarce promotion of agriculture
Services	Inadequate school structures	Inadequate school structures		Inadequate school structures
		Inefficient social and health services		Inefficient social and health services
	Lack of recreational structures	Lack of recreational structures		Lack of recreational structures
Institutional	Administrative shortcomings	Administrative shortcomings	Administrative shortcomings	Administrative shortcomings
		The local church not very involved in the community life		
Anthropological		Influence peddling		Influence peddling
	Citizen apathy/scarce participation	Citizen apathy/scarce participation	Citizen apathy/scarce participation	Citizen apathy/scarce participation
Psychological	Separatism	Separatism	Separatism	Separatism
		Neglect		Neglect

Source: Adapted with permission from *Profilo di Comunità di Carinola: Risorse e Potenzialità* [Community Profiling of Carinola: Resources and Opportunities] by T. Tuozzi, 2013, pp. 31–34.

future and the Scale of Italian Sense of Community (Prezza, Costantini, Chiarolanza, & Di Marco, 1999). The questionnaire data were supplemented with data obtained through the movie technique (see later), drawings, and participant observation, all of which were shared subsequently in community meetings with the IRG, local administrators, and research participants. These discussions allowed us to develop a more comprehensive psychological profile of Carinola. The detailed information collected through the individual interviews, focus groups, questionnaires, and supplemental data produced a fairly complete picture of the area, outlining all of the different profiles noted earlier.

Once this preliminary analysis of Carinola was completed, the next step consisted of the development of a shared idea of what that community was like and what changes were to be hoped for. The researchers used frequencies analysis to highlight those aspects most widely shared by Carinola's citizens. The results were then presented by the IRG in a final meeting in which citizens of Carinola proposed specific issues that they considered to be priorities for change.

There are numerous benefits in using profiles for community diagnosis. The technique depicts an accurate picture of the community; also, it does not restrict the analysis to mere data collection but also includes the feelings and thoughts of the members of the community collected through focus group and interviews. Indeed, the combination of objective (e.g., demographic and economic information) and subjective (provided by the stakeholders, informants, and questionnaire respondents) data allows for the identification of opportunities and deficiencies of the local community, as well as how these are perceived by the local people. However, along with the objective and subjective features, we should add a third one, the symbolic level, which emerges from involving local citizens in the use of free expressive tools, such as taking and discussing photographs (photovoice), making a drawing of the neighborhood (the "draw your neighborhood" technique), and developing a plot for a movie script about the community. The latter, called "the movie" technique, is a creative participatory tool that allows partcipants to "pick a genre of movie (e.g., historical, science fiction, comedy, or detective) and come up with a title, a plot, main characters, and dramatization, if they wish, for particular relevant scenes" (Francescato & Zani, 2013, p. 4).

The active participation of the local people in this type of research is crucial because, in addition to a mere diagnosis of the community's state of affairs, it enables an intervention of development and promotion of community life that hinges on confrontation, communication, and exchange of knowledge. In this light, community profiling allows for a self-sustained and self-determined process of social change (Martini & Sequi, 1995). Table 35.3 summarizes the data and the tools that were employed in the work done in Carinola.

The community profiling technique, however, does require a considerable amount of time and resources. This is especially important if the researcher aims at recruiting a representative sample by resorting to all of the instruments required for a complete community profile (Prezza & Santinello, 2002). With regard to this, a number of shorter community profiling versions are under development. In some of these, for instance, only some representative groups of local people are involved in the preliminary analysis and in the "movies." In some cases, it is advisable to carry out the research by focusing only on some key dimensions and issues that particularly concern the local community (Messer & Townsley, 2003). This is true for our case study, which we present next.

CASE STUDY

Background

Porta Capuana is one of the most ancient gates of the City of Naples and gives its name to the surrounding district. Its geographical location lies next to the central train station, the airport, and the port and, therefore, presents a high logistical potential together with a high tourism impact (enhanced by the presence of churches, as well as its architectural and monumental heritage). However, today Porta Capuana stands out as a pocket of urban degradation. For instance, it does not take advantage of its culinary heritage, the labor market is unregulated, and organized crime is widespread and deceptively concealed. This urban deprivation is also coupled with the presence of groups of migrants lacking in resources.

Psychology Loves Porta Capuana is a project developed by a research team of the University of Naples Federico II. The initiative is part of a broader endeavor championed by the I Love Porta Capuana project, which is a body of associations and institutions working together on participatory and sustainable urban regeneration. The organization has the goal of "developing a synergic network of local people, entrepreneurs, and social actors of the neighborhood of Porta Capuana in order to give value to the monuments as well as the local culinary and artisan heritage" (http://www.portacapuana.it). Invited by the I Love Capuana organizers, the authors were able to engage in community profiling of the area, with the aim of uncovering its needs and requests, both explicit and implicit. Given our awareness of the importance of reflexivity among researchers and trust between the latter and local bodies, we developed a research strategy enabling rich interaction and discussion among various stakeholders, associations, and researchers.

Research Procedures and Instruments

Small (i.e., two- to five-member) groups of undergraduate students from the University of Naples Federico II were invited by the researchers to

TABLE 35.3: COMMUNITY PROFILES: DESCRIPTION OF AIMS, THEMES, AND INSTRUMENTS

Profile	Description	Instruments
Territorial profile	This includes data regarding the characteristics of the local area, such as geographical extension, physical composition, climate, natural resources, infrastructures, environmental degradation, space allocation (e.g., housing, working environment, free time), and their usability.	Maps Town plan Tourism leaflets Photographs Observations "Community walk"
Demographic profile	This refers to the population size, distributed by age, sex, education, growth/degrowth rate, migration waves, and social mobility. Data on immigration/emigration are also included.	List of data provided by competent offices Data analysis
Productive activities profile	Productive activities are broken down into *primary, secondary, and tertiary*. Activities are to be sourced, taking into account the occupation of the people in all aspects (e.g., job security, unemployment, crisis in the labor market, illegal labor), as well as the rate of environmental pollution related to given productive activities.	Data collecting and analysis Semistructured interviews Questionnaires Observations
Services profile	Services include health services, socio-educational services, and cultural-recreational services. The data collected refer to the presence of these facilities, as well as their location, accessibility, user base, organization, and operation. Sometimes it is useful to draw a map of the connection between different structures and services.	Data collection and analysis Meetings Semistructured interviews Observations Focus groups
Institutional profile	This profile refers to the setup of the administrative and political organization of the local community, as well as the presence of its ideological landmarks and specific institutions, such as police stations, prisons, and churches, as well as the possible connection with social and community issues.	Data collection and analysis Interviews Analysis of institutional networks
Anthropological profile	This profile refers to the history of the community, its conception, value, traditions, individual and social responses to community issues, level of cohesion among its members, and their engagement in community life.	Books, booklets Statements Observations Interviews Photographs and videotapes Analysis of printed texts
Psychological profile	This profile indicates emotional dynamics, sense of belonging, and elements of collective identification. The data refer to the extent and density of social networks; the level of openness/closeness among various social subgroups within the community; and their level of participation, collaboration, and emotional safety.	Social support questionnaires and sense of community questionnaires Open and semistructured interviews Sociogram for small groups "Draw your neighborhood" technique
Profile of the future	This profile explores people's expectations with regard to the perceived future of their community. It can also identify the influence of the media on the perception of togetherness and community life.	Focus groups "Movie" technique

participate in an ethnographic observation of the area—the "community walk"—at different times of the day. These groups were also asked to take photographs of places of interest and post them on a Facebook group page that had been previously set up with the purpose of sharing experiences and research material. Each group was also asked to write a short report of its observations, describing what its members had observed and including their own comments and feelings. A total of 750 photographs were subsequently posted online and discussed in the classroom.

Next, a team of four researchers carried out the thematic categorization of all of the observational texts and conducted a SWOT analysis of these observations' reports by categorizing strengths, weaknesses, opportunities, and threats (i.e., SWOT) that the student-researchers had attributed to the area (Arcidiacono, Grimaldi, Procentese, & Di Martino, 2015; Braun & Clarke, 2006). This categorization constituted a good starting point for the local association representatives and the researchers to finalize the research objectives, locate key people and stakeholders (i.e., institutional and association representatives, migrants, retailers, craftsmen, hoteliers, restaurateurs, service providers, and school representatives) to interview, and develop interview guidelines. We also included tourists and casual visitors, as they are key informants able to reveal the impact that tourism has on the area and offer their own comments and suggestions.

Based on our preliminary work and the observations of the student-researchers, we outlined a quick and comprehensive image of the local area. This highlighted that, despite its architectural beauty as well as cultural heritage, the district of Porta Capuana was in a state of high deprivation, uncleanliness, and neglect. Thus, in formulating our interview guidelines, special attention was given to narratives concerning relational habits, meeting points, significant traditions, well-known songs and mottos, and knowledge of events of the area. Our goal was, in fact, not only to collect information but also feelings, memories, and emotions connected to the area.

We thus identified thematic areas for the interview grids and trained our student-researchers in how to carry out focused interviews (that is, narrative interviews that delve into specific research areas of interest) with the aforementioned stakeholders. In accordance with Arcidiacono (2015, in press), we constructed interview guidelines that would allow the interviewees to freely express their thoughts while at the same time focusing on the research questions. This method is a further development of the interactive structured interview proposed by Richards and Morse (2007), which is able to collect the "spontaneous voice" of respondents, thereby acquiring further knowledge on the topics of interest. Our aim was to collect data on the area's livability, as well as possible plans of action and projects for the future.

Results and Discussion

The transcribed interviews were then analyzed by means of Atlas ti.7. Four main themes emerged from the analysis of the content of the 359 interviews conducted: degradation (89%), garbage and uncleanliness (83%), lack of security (87%), and tourism as a possible resource (70%).

It is interesting to note how the interviews highlighted that, although some of the objective issues of the community, such as degradation, dirt, and lack of institutional intervention, were widely recognized, perceptions of their causes, as well as identification of resources, varied greatly among stakeholders and key informants. Love, Boxelaar, O'Donnell, and Francis (2007) underlined the potential of community profiling in facilitating the expression of the diverse voices of a community. In our case, for example, the local school staff, unlike retailers and restaurateurs, considered migrants to be a resource for the district, while the collective perception appeared to point to migrants as being the scapegoat for all problems in the district, being blamed for the widespread sense of insecurity, the lack of livability, and the garbage. At the same time, such a massive denouncement of degradation coming from all the stakeholders and key informants suggested the necessitiy of collective actions to tackle the issue.

Following the analysis of the interviews, feedback meetings, which were conducted through a series of *discussant cafés* (i.e., small discussion groups between researchers and members of the community), allowed for virtuous circles to take place, in which the community members proposed a number of interventions for the betterment of Porta Capuana, such as the following: security, road maintenance, antique market, street lighting, car parks, cleaning, video surveillance, interventions for the local deprived youth, meeting places, well-groomed playgrounds, and a research center. In these meetings, as well as in dicussions with local associations and government authorities, an important communication tool that we used to discuss the main issues uncovered by the research were short videos summarizing the most significant results.

What are the distinctive features of this intervention as a whole? We believe that its success rests on the synergy that we have built with the associations operating in the district. Because of this, the research team could access the considerable amount of information required to cover the various profilings suggested by Francescato and Zani (2013) without a costly deployment of resources in terms of time and money. Conversely, in return, the associations obtained a thorough feedback analysis of the district's livability, which allowed for the making of plans based on the priorities of the local area. In fact, the network of associations has turned into an institutional body that has started to draw actively on new resources and power coming from the district of Porta Capuana. For example, the mayor of Naples, after attending some of our meetings, started a proactive collaboration with some of his council members in order to tackle some of the issues that were already well known to the various associations but were more clearly highlighted by the interviews. Also, the area of Porta Capuana has become included among the goals of the USEACT project, a European Union-sponsored program, on which the Porta Capuana municipality and the I Love Porta Capuana committee have begun to collaborate.

Our next step for the project involves responding to the local needs that we have identified through this research. To this end, we are outlining some guidelines for the future urban plans of the city council and will work in synergy with the local organizations to apply for regional and European funds for urban regeneration. In the framework of participatory action research, the employment of community profiling has acted as the driving force for the outlining of shared objectives and plans of action.

CONCLUSION

This chapter has attempted to demonstrate how community profiling can provide a three-way interpretation of a local area, that is, through (a) practical facts and data (e.g., socioenvironmental and structural data), (b) perceptions and representations (e.g., the voices of residents, practitioners and providers of services, representatives of institutions, and tourists), and (c) symbolization (e.g., photos and videos). With respect to the specific aim of symbolization, for example, in Porta Capuana our students made short movies about the area with respect to impact, advantages, and threats, which were also useful in helping to understand the mood of the context. Throughout the chapter, we have emphasized the importance of interaction with local organizations and bodies as a tool to obtain information from stakeholders and key informants.

Community profiling can help us answer many questions arising from a local context by taking into account social, relational, and symbolic features of that context. The work that we have described in the case study took into consideration individual feelings and desires, the interests of stakeholders, and information from key informants. Public officers, employees, and health and social personnel dealing with people living in the area on a daily basis are, indeed, "raw experts" with respect to the local context, and their non refined data provide a ready indicator of what is occurring in a community, as well as the reasons for what is occurring. We encourage those seeking to conduct action research to consider seriously community profiling as a methodology for providing a quite comprehensive understanding of the coummunities in which they are working.

AUTHOR NOTE

The authors thank Franco Rendano, Fabio Landolfo, Anna M. C. Rossi, Annachiara Autiero, Ulderico Carraturo, Rosalba Impronta, Daniela Lepore and Fabrizio Mangoni, as well as the Psychology Loves Porta Capuana team formed by the 180 student-researchers and senior researchers (Linda Ascione, Giorgia Borrelli, Miriam Cozzolino, Alessandra Chiurazzi, Immacolata Di Napoli, Daria Grimaldi, Giuliana Miano, and Filomena Tuccillo) at the University of Naples Federico II. Thanks also goes to Salvatore Di Martino for his commitment to the translation and the revision of this text.

REFERENCES

Arcidiacono, C. (1996). *Diagnosi di comunità* [Diagnosis of community]. Napoli, Italy: Magma Edizioni.

Arcidiacono, C. (2004). *Il fascino del centro antico* [The charm of the ancient center]. Napoli, Italy: Magma Edizioni.

Arcidiacono, C. (2012). L'intervista focalizzata come strumento per superare chiusure e fraintendimenti nelle dinamiche interculturali [The focused interview as a tool to overcome closures and misunderstandings in intercultural dynamics]. In D. Giovannini & L. Vezzali (Eds.), *Immigrazione, processi interculturali e cittadinanza attiva* (pp. 373–384). Caserta, Italy: Melagrana.

Arcidiacono, C. (2015). *Rigenerazione urbana e ricerca azione partecipata: Psicologi a Porta Capuana* [Urban regeneration and participatory action research: Psychologists at Porta Capuana], Bergamo, Italy: Junior-Spaggiari Edizioni.

Arcidiacono, C., Grimaldi, D., Procentese, F., & Di Martino, S. (2015). *Participatory visual methods in the "Psychology loves Porta Capuana" project.* In press

Arcidiacono, C., & Procentese F. (2005). Distinctiveness and sense of community in the historical center of Naples: A piece of participatory action-research. *Journal of Community Psychology, 33*, 631–638.

Arcidiacono, C., & Procentese, F. (2010). Participatory research into community psychology within a local context. *Global Journal of Community Psychology Practice, 1*, 1–10.

Arcidiacono, C., Sommantico, M., & Procentese, F. (2001). Neapolitan youth's sense of community and the problem of unemployment. *Journal of Community and Applied Social Psychology, 11*, 465–473.

Braun, V., & Clarke, V. (2006). Using thematic analysis in psychology. *Qualitative Research in Psychology, 3*, 77–101.

Center for Urban Transportation Research. (2000). Developing a community profile. In *Community impact assessment: A handbook for transportation professionals.* Retrieved June 2015, from http://www.cutr.usf.edu/pubs/CIA/Chapter_4.pdf

Cheong, P. H. (2006). Communication context, social cohesion and social capital building among Hispanic immigrant families. *Community, Work and Family, 9*, 367–387.

Francescato, D., Arcidiacono, C. Albanesi C., & Mannarini T. (2007). Community psychology in Italy: Past developments and future perspectives. In S. Reich, M., Riemer, I. Prilleltensky, & M. Montero (Eds.), *International community psychology: History and theories* (pp. 263–281). New York, NY: Springer.

Francescato, D., Gelli, B., Mannarini, T., & Taurino, A. (2004). Community development: Action research through profiles analysis in a small town in Southern Italy. In A. Sanchez Vidal, A. Zambrano Constanzo, & M. Palacin Lois (Eds.). *Psìcologia Comunitaria Europa: Communidad, poder, ética y valores* (pp. 247–261). Barcelona, Spain: Publicacions Universitat de Barcelona.

Francescato, D., & Ghirelli, G. (1988). *Fondamenti di psicologia di comunità* [Fundamentals of community psychology]. Roma, Italy: Carocci.

Francescato, D., & Zani, B. (2013). Community psychology practice competencies in undergraduate and graduate programs in Italy. *Global Journal of Community Psychology Practice, 4*, 1–12.

Forrest, C. J., & Hill, R. (2013, July). *Enhancing community profile development: Identifying community characteristics and behavior templates.* Paper presented at the 13 Community Involvement Training Conference of the United States Environmental Protection Agency, Boston, MA. Retrieved June 2015, from http://www.epa.gov/ciconference/download/presentations/Thurs_StudioE_130PM_Forrest_EnhancingCommunityProfileDevelopment.pdf

Kagan, C., Burton, M., Duckett, P., Lawthom, R., & Siddiquee A. (2011). *Critical community psychology.* New York, NY: Wiley.

Kirsten, J., & Holt, M. (2008). Community profiling as part of a health needs assessment. *Nursing Standard, 22*, 51–56.

Hawtin, M., Hughes, G., & Percy-Smith, J. (1994). *Community profiling: Auditing social needs.* Buckingham, England: Open University Press.

Hawtin, M., Hughes, G., & Percy-Smith, J. (2007). *Community profiling. A practical guide.* Maidenhead, England: Open University Press.

Love, S., Boxelaar, L., O' Donnell, J., & Francis, J. (2007). Community profiling: From technique to reflective practice in community engagement for natural resource management. *Journal of Agricultural Education and Extension, 13*, 177–189.

Martini, E. R., & Sequi, R. (1988). *Il lavoro nella comunità* [Community work]. Rome, Italy: NIS.

Martini, E. R., & Sequi, R. (1995). *La comunità locale* [The local community]. Rome, Italy: Carocci.

Messer, N., & Townsley, P. (2003). *Local institutions and livelihoods: Guidelines for analysis.* Rural Development Division (FAO), Food and Agriculture Organization of the United Nations, Rome, Italy. Retrieved June 2015, from http://www.fao.org/docrep/006/Y5084E/y5084e00.HTM

Prezza, M., Costantini, S., Chiarolanza, V., & Di Marco, S. (1999). La Scala Italiana del Senso di Comunità [Scale of Italian Sense of Community]. *Psicologia della salute, 3*, 135–159.

Prezza, M., & Santinello, M. (2002). *Conoscere la comunità. L'analisi degli ambienti di vita quotidiana* [Knowing the community. The analysis of the environments of everyday life]. Bologna, Italy: Il Mulino.

Reason, P., & Bradbury, H. (2008). *Handbook of action research: Participative inquiry and practice* (2nd ed.). London, England: Sage.

Richards, L., & Morse, J. M. (2007). *Read me first for a user's guide to qualitative methods*. London, England: Sage.

Taylor, M., & Burns, D. (2000). *Auditing community participation: An assessment handbook*. Bristol, England: Policy Press.

Tuozzi, T. (2013). *Profilo di comunità di Carinola: risorse e potenzialità* [Community profile of Carinola: Resources and potentialities]. Caserta, Italy: Melagrana.

AFTERWORD

Over the past 30 years, the number of statistical methods has burgeoned. Whereas once it was sufficient to receive training in basic methods (e.g., probability theory, analysis of variance, factor analysis), this is no longer the case. Currently, graduate programs are pressed to teach classes where students learn more advanced methods, which are considered de rigueur for the doctoral degree and future research careers. Existing scholars and practitioners must also keep abreast of the latest trends. The current volume is a compendium of cutting-edge statistical techniques currently used in community science and community-based research. The utility of this book is that each chapter provides a thoughtful overview of a specific method so that the reader can understand its usefulness and, if necessary, pursue additional resources to build on this basic knowledge. In addition, the examples in each chapter demonstrate to the reader the application of the methods as well as how they advance community science and practice. Of course, the book is not an exhaustive compendium, and, yet, there are 11 qualitative approaches, 10 quantitative approaches, and 13 mixed methods approaches included. One feels humbled by all there is to learn.

But why should we care about newer methods? Why aren't the older methods good enough? One often encounters the notion that somehow newer methods are unnecessary, or, worse, that they can obfuscate and unnecessarily complicate the findings. In other words, many feel that older methods are sufficient for answering the crucial questions in a particular field. Therefore, it is important to ask: Do newer methods advance science? The methods described in this book indicate that the resounding answer to that question is "yes."

Greenwald (2012), in an incisive article, argued that one of the most important roles of methods is that they often lead us to good theory. He tracked the history of Nobel Prizes in the sciences between 1991 and 2011 and found that the overwhelming majority of the awards were for methods (82%). This same trend held for the field of psychology. Although only nine awards have been made to psychologists since World War II (in medicine and economics, given that there is no Nobel Prize for psychology), 78% were for methods. Clearly, research methods, as defined by Greenwald, cover a broad range of activities, not necessarily statistical. However, the significance of Greenwald's article is that methods are important, and this importance is documented and recognized by the organization that honors the "best" in a field of study. I believe the same case can be made for the importance of statistical methods.

Greenwald argued that there are two main reasons that the preponderance of Nobel Prizes focus on methods. The first is that "existing theories often provided the basis for design of awarded methods" (p. 106). The second is that "awarded methods had served to generate previously inconceivable research findings, which, in turn, led to previously inconceivable theories" (p. 106). If, in part, the latter is the case, to the extent that we privilege theory over methods, we run the risk of not discovering interesting and important theories. That is, the theories we cannot imagine now are waiting to be illuminated by the sophisticated methods we bring to bear as we engage in our research endeavors.

I would also argue that generating new theories in the field of community science (or any field of inquiry) is a rare event. Perhaps, then, it is also fair to say that methods often lead us to ask better research questions or develop more interesting models of the phenomenon under study. There is a synergy, as Greenwald suggested. Sophisticated statistical methods allow us to ask different research questions, and the research questions we ask cannot be answered without the sophisticated methods at our disposal. That is, methods can provide a framework for conceptualizing the research we conduct and the theory we generate.

In recent years, I have been thinking and writing about the issue of methods as it relates to a person-oriented approach to psychological research. Most published research is not only quantitative but also variable oriented—theoretical and/or statistical approaches that describe relationships between one or more variables (e.g., as income goes up, depression goes down). The variable-oriented approach focuses on finding differences (or sameness) on the specific dimension under measurement. It also focuses on finding universal laws that allow us to predict behavior, broadly defined. Most of the quantitative methods chapters in this book fall under this broad rubric. There is much to recommend this approach, as it has been the dominant paradigm in psychological research since the early part of the 20th century. However, there is another, complementary quantitative approach that does not focus on linear relationships or the search for generalizable, universal laws of behavior. Similar to qualitative research methods, person-oriented approaches can be more context specific. Person-oriented research focuses on finding patterns or profiles of individuals (or communities or organizations; see Bogat, 2009; Bogat, Zarrett, Peck, & von Eye, 2012) within a sample that take into account more than one variable. In other words, individuals, communities, organizations, and so on are complicated and multifaceted and cannot be described with one variable. It is the pattern of variables that, taken together, constitutes the individual, community, or organization. By taking such an approach, the researcher can discover subgroups within the larger group that are not necessarily the a priori subgroups the researcher might have expected to find. As Williams and Kibowski note in Chapter 15 in this volume, latent class analysis and latent profile analysis are two techniques that can be employed to find such subgroups. Statisticians are working on other approaches, including modifications of variable-oriented statistical techniques such as structural equation modeling and log-linear modeling (see, e.g., Bogat, von Eye, & Bergman, in press), to facilitate person-oriented research.

There are always difficulties incorporating new methods into mainstream science. For example, in her overview to the mixed methods section, Anderson in Chapter 23 notes the inherent difficulty in understanding when to use mixed methods and how to integrate them (she mentions at least 35 different types of mixed methods designs). She also notes that mixed methods have both benefits and challenges. This is true of all approaches and is something for professionals to keep in mind as they attempt to match theory/research questions with statistical methods.

One of the problems inhibiting the integration of new methods into the professional mainstream is the gap that exists between the scientists and practitioners using the new methods and the audience reading the research. The problem starts with reviewers who may or may not be familiar with various statistical techniques. Recently, my colleagues and I submitted an article to a biologically oriented journal. The analysis used was structural equation modeling—a fairly standard statistical approach used in many fields of psychology. However, the comments indicated how poorly the individual reviewers understood this statistical method—its purpose as well as what our particular findings were and their interpretation. Both reviewers repeatedly asked us to conduct several analyses of variance (ANOVAs), even though such analysis would not have thoroughly answered our research questions and doing so would have violated the basic assumptions of ANOVA. I am purposely using an example from a journal that was not in the field of community science, but I am sure that similar issues arise regularly in all journals. If the problems exist with reviewers not understanding structural equation modeling, then what happens when authors use one of the numerous newer techniques presented in the current book?

As professionals, we have a responsibility to be cognizant of the different methods available for data analysis, and this responsibility starts with those who review manuscripts for journals. As stated earlier, reviewers should understand the statistical techniques for the manuscripts they review. Otherwise, situations like the one described in the prior paragraph result. It should not be incumbent on the paper's authors to write a treatise on a specific statistical technique in order to educate reviewers or editors.

But there is also another, more positive, role that reviewers may play. The best reviewers understand that authors may have collected important and interesting data but that the data analyses have not fully realized the potential of that data to answer the stated research questions, especially if the methods do not match the questions. Reviewers can aid the entry of newer statistical techniques into the mainstream by making suggestions about alternative statistical methods the authors might use for data analysis. The current book provides a vast panoply of the newest statistical methods that authors can use, and reviewers can suggest, as we advance the field of community science.

G. Anne Bogat
Michigan State University
June 2015

REFERENCES

Bogat, G. A. (2009). Is the person orientation necessary in community psychology? *American Journal of Community Psychology*, 43, 22–34.

Bogat, G. A., von Eye, A., & Bergman, L. R. (in press). Person-oriented approaches. In D. Cicchetti (Ed.), *Developmental psychopathology* (3rd ed., Vol. 1). New York, NY: John Wiley.

Bogat, G. A., Zarrett, N., Peck, S., & von Eye, A. (2012). The person orientation and community psychology: New directions. In L. A. Jason & D. S. Glenwick (Eds.), *Innovative methodological approaches to community-based research: Theory and application* (pp. 89–109). Washington, DC: APA.

Greenwald, A. G. (2012). There is nothing so theoretical as good method. *Perspectives on Psychological Science*, 7, 99–108.

INDEX

Page numbers followed by *f* or *t* indicate figures or tables.

AA. *See* Alcoholics Anonymous
abductive reasoning, 107
ABM. *See* agent-based modeling
accretion, 16
action research, 8, 243–51. *See also* community-based participatory action research; participatory action research; youth-led participatory action research
  bridge research and action with, 246–47
  collaboration in, 244, 247
  interviews in, 245
  PAR and, 53–54
  pragmatism and, 244
  theory and, 247
activism, 69–70, 81
Actor-Partner Interaction Model, 225
Adams, A. E., 139–41
adjacency matrix, 209, 209*t*
administrative research, on neighborhoods, 94–95, 96
adolescent suicides, 172–74
Afghanistan, qualitative methods in, 19–21
agent-based modeling (ABM), 7, 129, 197–206
  case study for, 202–5, 204*f*
  heterogeneity in, 198
  methodological individualism of, 198
  modeling cycle of, 199–200
  simplicity of, 199
AI. *See* appreciative inquiry
AIC. *See* Akaike Information Criterion
AJCP. *See American Journal of Community Psychology*
Akaike Information Criterion (AIC), 144
Akinsulure-Smith, Adeyinka M., 3
Alaska Natives, 257–59
Alceste (software), 113
alcohol, 257–59
Alcoholics Anonymous (AA), 222
Allen, J., 259
Allen, James, 8
Allen, Nicole E., 9
Altman, I., 103
Alvarez, J., 18, 180
American Journal of Community Psychology (AJCP), 5–6, 126–27, 128*f*
American Psychological Association, 18
analysis of covariance (ANCOVA), 123–24, 127
analysis of variance (ANOVA), 122, 123, 125–26, 127
ANCOVA. *See* analysis of covariance
Andalusian fishing, 327–31, 329*f*, 330*f*, 331*f*
Anderson, Valerie R., 7
ANOVA. *See* analysis of variance
APA PsychNET, 33
appreciative inquiry (AI), 4, 53–59
  case study for, 55–58, 57*t*
  DP and, 346
  opportunity-based PAR and, 54–55
  problem-based PAR and, 53–54
  stakeholder analysis for, 58
Arcidiacono, Caterina, 10, 361
ARIMA. *See* autoregressive moving average
Arnstein, S. R., 253–54, 259
art
  photovoice and, 81
  for qualitative method data collection, 16
artificial intelligence. *See* data mining
arts, LCA for, 146–48, 146*t*, 147*t*
Ary, D., 178
Asparouhov, T., 149
Atkins, M. S., 208
ATLAS.ti software, 28
auditability, in grounded theory, 24
authenticity, 17–18
  ontological, 72
autonomy, 198, 265
autoregressive moving average (ARIMA), 179
axial coding, 25
Azelton, L. S., 258–59

Baker, C., 121
Balcazar, Fabricio, 9
Banyard, V. L., 35
Barbados sexual health, 285–90, 287*f*, 288*f*, 289*f*, 290*f*

Barile, John P., 6
Barker, R. G., 198–99
basis coefficients, in LGCs, 133
Baxter Magolda, M. B., 336
Bayesian Information Criterion (BIC), 144
Bazeley, P., 63
behavioral systems science, 178
Behavior and Social Issues, 178
behavior methods, 6, 177–84
  case study for, 182–83, 183*f*
  ecology and, 178–79
  external validity for, 179
  in GIS, 97–98
behavior setting theory, 198–99
Bentler, P. M., 159
Berg, M., 13–14
best-fitting solution, in LPA, 148
Best Practices Club, 268
biases. *See* worldview
BIC. *See* Bayesian Information Criterion
Biglan, A., 178
Bishop, Brian J., 5, 107
Blanco, Matte, 111, 112
Block, E., 256
BLRT. *See* Bootstrapped Likelihood Ratio Test
Blumer, Herbert, 69
Boessen, A., 97–98, 100
Boolean logic decision rules, 189
Bootstrapped Likelihood Ratio Test (BLRT), 144
both/and logic, in DP, 345
bounded empowerment, 264
Boxelaar, L., 361
Boyd, Neil, 4
Brackett, M. A., 124
Brady, Shane R., 4
Braun, V., 34–35, 38, 39
breakdown, 17
Breen, Lauren J., 5, 107
bridge research and action, 246–47
Brodsky, Anne E., 3
Bronfenbrenner, U., 29, 104–5
Bucci, Fiorella, 5
Buchanan, A. S., 220
Buckingham, Sara L., 3
Burke, J., 307
Burns, D., 355
Burris, M. A., 285
Burt, R. S., 211

CAIC. *See* Consistent AIC
Callahan, Sarah, 7
Campbell, D. T., 256
Campbell, R., 236–37
CAN. *See* child abuse and neglect
Canadian Clinical ME/CFS, 192
Caracelli, V. J., 335
Carbone, Agostino, 5
Cardazone, Gina, 8–9
Cardenas, Z., 267
Carli, Renzo, 5, 113
CART. *See* Classification and Regression Tree
case studies
  for ABM, 202–5, 204*f*
  for AI, 55–58, 57*t*
  for behavior methods, 182–83, 183*f*
  for CBPAR, 257–59
  for CLA, 106–9
  for CM, 308–11, 310*f*, 311*f*, 312*t*
  for community narratives, 46–50, 48*f*
  for community profiling, 359–62
  for critical ethnography, 73–76
  for cross-cultural and cultural research, 278–81, 280*f*
  for CRTs, 172–74
  for data mining, 191–95
  for data visualization, 298–301, 299*f*, 301*f*
  for Delphi method, 63–66
  for DP, 347–53
  for dynamic social networks, 222–25, 224*f*
  for ETA, 114–16
  for functional analysis, 317–22, 319*t*
  for GIS, 99–100
  of grounded theory, 27–31, 31*f*
  for house meetings, 87–89
  for LCA, 146–48, 146*t*, 147*t*
  for LGCs, 139–41, 141*f*
  for LPA, 149–50
  for mixed methods, 237–40, 337–42
  for MSEM, 158–62, 161*t*, 162*f*
  for multisetting research, 337–42
  for neighborhoods, 99–100
  for network analysis, 327–31, 331*f*
  for photoethnography, 285–90, 287*f*, 288*f*, 289*f*, 290*f*
  for photovoice, 87–89
  for qualitative methods, 3
  of qualitative methods, 19–21
  for SNA, 212–15, 213*t*, 214*f*
  for stakeholder analysis, 327–31, 331*f*
  for thematic analysis, 37–40
  for YPAR, 267–69
categorical coding, for LCA, 144
causal layered analysis (CLA), 5, 103–9
  case study for, 106–9
  coding for, 107, 108*t*, 109
  contextualism in, 103–4
  interviews for, 107
  layers in, 104–6, 104*t*, 109
  thematic analysis for, 105, 107
  themes in, 105, 108*t*
cause-and-effect relationships, 2, 121
CBPAR. *See* community-based participatory action research
CBPR. *See* community-based participatory research
CDC. *See* community development corporation
census units, 94, 95
centering, in MSEM, 158
CFA. *See* confirmatory factor analysis
CFI. *See* Comparative Fit index
CFP. *See* Common Fisheries Policy
CFS. *See* chronic fatigue syndrome
Chamberlain, P., 234
changing variable, in LGCs, 134

Charmaz, K., 17
Chertok, F., 255
Chicago School of Ethnography, 69
child abuse and neglect (CAN), 298–301, 299*f*, 301*f*
Child and Youth Resilience Measure (CYRM), 278–81, 280*f*
chi-squared difference test, 137
chi-square statistic, 156
  LRχ2, 144
Christens, Brian D., 7–8, 14, 249
chronic fatigue syndrome (CFS), 191–95
Chu, Tracy, 3
chunks, of coding, 25–26
citizen science, 294
CLA. *See* causal layered analysis
Claes, S., 295–96
Clark, Brian, 4
Clarke, V., 34–35
Classification and Regression Tree (CART), 189, 193
classification trees, 189
classifiers, for decision trees, 191
Clegg Smith, K., 285
Cloutier, Katherine, 8
cluster analysis, 122, 129, 307
cluster-randomized trials (CRTs), 6, 124, 165–74
  adaptive designs for, 168–69
  case study for, 172–74
  covariates for, 167–68
  data collection for, 165–66
  internal validity in, 166, 169
  matching for, 167–68
  MLM for, 169–71
  power in, 167–68
  pretest-posttest control group design for, 166
  for prevention, 171
  sampling for, 166–67
clusters, in ETA, 113–14
CM. *See* concept mapping
Cochran, S. D., 123
coding
  for constant comparative method, 25
  for CLA, 107, 108*t*, 109
  dichotomous, 144
  for LCA, 144
  for qualitative method data analysis, 16–17
  for thematic analysis, 34, 38
  theoretical, 26–27
cognitive social structures (CSS), 212
cohesion, in SNA, 211
Coleman, J. S., 211
collaboration
  in action research, 244, 247
  in behavioral methods, 178
  in community psychology, 1
  in critical ethnography, 70–71
  defined, 70
  in DP, 346, 350
  power and, 71
  in qualitative methods, 3, 16
  with photovoice, 81, 83
collusive dynamics, ETA and, 112, 113
Coman, E., 13–14
Common Fisheries Policy (CFP), 327–31, 329*f*, 330*f*, 331*f*
Communities Organized for relational Power and Action (COPA), 89
community-based participatory action research (CBPAR), 253–60, 283–90
  case study for, 257–59
  conscientization and, 255
  as paradigm shift, 256–57
  photoethnography in, 283–90
community-based participatory research (CBPR)
  functional analysis of, 315–22
  performance ethnography within, 8
  photovoice with, 284
  with PAR, 253–60
  as worldview, 253, 256, 259–60
community building, 1
community development corporation (CDC), 64–65
community narratives, 4, 43–51
  case study for, 46–50, 48*f*
  data analysis for, 45–46
  empowerment and, 44, 45
  interviews for, 45, 47–48
  logic model for, 45–48, 48*f*
  stakeholder analysis for, 45–46
  whole communities and, 43–46
community needs assessments, 316
community partnerships, cross-cultural and cultural research and, 275–76
community profiling, 10, 355–62, 356*t*, 360*t*
  case study for, 359–62
  "draw your neighborhood" technique in, 359
  interviews for, 361
  "the movie" technique for, 359
  PAR and, 355–56
  photographs in, 359
  stakeholder analysis in, 362
  transformative theory and, 356
community psychology, 1, 43
  behavioral methods and, 177–78
  CBPAR in, 256
  critical ethnography and, 70
  qualitative methods and, 3, 13
Comparative Fit index (CFI), 156, 159
compilation variables, 157
complementarity, 336, 340–41
composition variables, 157
concept mapping (CM), 9, 305–13
  case study for, 308–11, 310*f*, 311*f*, 312*t*
  cluster analysis in, 307
  ladder graphs in, 307
  MDS in, 306–7
  rigor for, 308
  steps in, 305–7, 306*f*
Concerns Report Method (CRM), 9, 316–17, 317*f*, 318, 320–22
confirmability, 18, 36–37, 40
confirmatory factor analysis (CFA), 143–44

conflict. *See also* dialectical pluralism
  Delphi method for, 62
Connell, Christian M., 5–6
Connexion, 112
conscientization, 255
consensus
  in Delphi method, 63, 65–66
  in grounded theory, 26, 28
  in qualitative methods, 17
  in YPAR, 268
Consistent AIC (CAIC), 144
constant comparative method, 24–25
constructivism, 33–34, 37, 233, 274
constructivism-interpretivism, 14
contextualism
  in CLA, 103–4
  data analysis and, 122
  functional analysis and, 320
  in MLM, 153–54
  in qualitative methods, 341
  in SNA, 211–12
contradictions, mixed methods and, 336–37
Cook, T. D., 167
Cooper, Daniel, 4
COPA. *See* Communities Organized for relational Power and Action
Copeland-Linder, N., 148
Corbin, J., 63
correlation, 122
covariance matrix, in SEM, 156
covariates
  for CRTs, 167–68
  time-invariant, 134
Crabtree, B., 13
Craven, R. G., 237
credibility, 18, 36, 39
Creswell, J. W., 63, 235, 256–57, 285
criterion-based sampling, in critical ethnography, 71–72
critical consciousness, 81, 84, 243, 265
critical discourse analysis, 72, 73
critical ethnography, 4, 69–77
  case study for, 73–76
  collaboration in, 70–71
  data analysis for, 71–72
  data collection for, 71–72, 73
  ethics in, 72
  PAR with, 73
  positionality in, 70, 73–74
  power and, 70, 71
  psychopolitical validity in, 72
  quality in, 72–73
  reflexivity in, 70, 73–74
  representation in, 72
  sampling in, 71–72
  social justice and, 69–70
  stakeholder analysis in, 71–72, 74
critical-ideologism (criticalism), 14–15
critical race theory, 70, 255
critical theory, 81, 255
CRM. *See* Concerns Report Method
cross-cultural and cultural research, 8, 273–81
  case study for, 278–81, 280*f*
  cultural advisory boards and, 276
  KMb and, 276
  power and, 276
  triangulation in, 279
cross-level interactions, in MLM, 155–56
CRTs. *See* cluster-randomized trials
CSS. *See* cognitive social structures
cultural advisory boards, 276
cultural analysis, for critical ethnography, 72
cultural research. *See* cross-cultural and cultural research
culture, LCA for, 146–48, 146*t*, 147*t*
curvilinear time-series analysis, 44
CYRM. *See* Child and Youth Resilience Measure

Darnell, A. J., 138
dashboards, 294–96, 298
data analysis. *See also* social network analysis
  coding for, 16–17
  for community narratives, 45–46
  contextualism and, 122
  for critical ethnography, 71–72
  for data visualization, 293–94
  for Delphi method, 65–66
  for ETA, 115
  for functional analysis, 318–19
  for grounded theory, 28–29
  for qualitative methods, 16–17
  for thematic analysis, 36, 38–39
data collection
  for critical ethnography, 71–72, 73
  for CRTs, 165–66
  for Delphi method, 62–63
  for ETA, 113
  for functional analysis, 318–19
  for grounded theory, 28
  photographs for, 81–85
  for qualitative methods, 15–16
  sequential design in, 9
  for SNA, 207–9
data mining, 6–7, 187–95, 188*f*
  case study for, 191–95
  decision trees for, 188–91
  machine learning for, 188–89
data visualization, 8–9, 293–301
  case study for, 298–301, 299*f*, 301*f*
  dashboards for, 294–96, 298
  data analysis with, 293–94
  for decision making, 294–95
  PAR and, 293
  with infographics, 295–96
David, E. J. R., 8
Davis, M. I., 18
DCP. *See* Developing Communities Project of Greater Roseland
decision making
  data visualization for, 294–95

Delphi method for, 62
mixed methods and, 278*f*
decision trees
for data mining, 7, 188–91
overfitting of, 189–90
degree centrality, 211
Delany-Brumsey, A., 123
Delphi method, 4, 61–66
case study for, 63–66
consensus in, 63, 65–66
data analysis for, 65–66
data collection for, 62–63
questionnaires for, 62
recruitment for, 64–65
thematic analysis for, 63
demarcation, in mixed methods, 235
dense words, in ETA, 111, 113–14, 115
dependability, 18, 36
dependent variable (DV), 123, 127
descriptive/interpretative approaches, to qualitative method data analysis, 16
design effect, with CRTs, 167
DeSouza, K. C., 294
Developing Communities Project of Greater Roseland (DCP), 258–59
Dewey, John, 61, 69, 244
dialectical pluralism (DP), 9–10, 345–52
AI and, 346
case study for, 347–53
collaboration in, 346, 350
empowerment and, 352
stakeholder analysis in, 349, 351–52
validity in, 351
dichotomous coding, for LCA, 144
discover, dream, design, and destiny (4-D cycle), 55, 56–58
The Discovery of Grounded Theory (Glaser and Strauss), 23
dog feces, behavior methods for, 182–83, 183*f*
Dolcetti, F., 115
domestic violence (DV), 37–40
Donmoyer, R., 337
doubly latent models, 157–58
DP. *See* dialectical pluralism
Draper, N. R., 199
"draw your neighborhood" technique, 359
drug abuse and addiction, 222–25, 224*f*
Dugard, P., 180
Dutta, Urmitapa, 4
DV. *See* dependent variable; domestic violence
Dworkin, Emily, 9
dyad-level measures, for SNA, 210*t*, 211
Dymnicki, A. B., 259
dynamic social networks, 7, 219–27
case study for, 222–25, 224*f*
friendship and, 221–22
mentoring and, 221–22
personal networks and, 219–20
whole networks and, 220–21
Dzidic, Peta L., 5, 107

EBP. *See* evidence-based practice
ECAs. *See* educational catchment areas
ecobehavioral, 178
ecological analysis, 2
ecological systems theory, 104–5
ecology
behavior methods and, 178–79
in community psychology, 1
LGCs and, 138
edges strategy, for NR, 49
educational catchment areas (ECAs), 94, 95
EFA. *See* exploratory factor analysis
egohoods, 99, 100
Elliott, R., 121
Ellis, L. A., 237
embedding data, in mixed methods, 257
emotional symbolization, 112
emotional textual analysis (ETA), 5, 111–16
case study for, 114–16
data analysis for, 115
data collection for, 113
dense words in, 111, 113–14, 115
empowerment
AI for, 58
bounded, 264
community narratives and, 44, 45
DP and, 352
house meetings for, 85–86
in PAR, 243
photoethnography and, 285
photovoice for, 81, 84
entropy value, in LCA, 144
epistemic validity, 72
Epstein, J. M., 198
equal-status mixed methods, 347, 351
erosion, 16
ESM. *See* experience sampling method
ETA. *See* emotional textual analysis
ethics, 18
in critical ethnography, 72
in CRTs, 166
in photovoice, 83
in SNA, 212
ethnography. *See also* critical ethnography; cross-cultural and cultural research; photoethnography
network analysis and, 325–27
evidence-based practice (EBP), 35, 348
expansion, mixed methods for, 337
Expectation Maximization algorithm, 144
experience sampling method (ESM), 98
exploratory factor analysis (EFA), 279–80
external validity, 179

Fabes, R. A., 208
Facebook, 208–9, 209*t*
Fals Borda, Orlando, 255, 315
Families and Schools Together (FAST), 237
Family Violence Councils (FVC), 337–42
Faris, R. W., 97–98

Farrell, A. D., 138
FAST. *See* Families and Schools Together
Faust, Victoria, 7–8
Fawcett, S. B., 178, 316
FCWA. *See* Food Chain Workers Alliance
FEDEJAL, 317–22, 319*t*
female juvenile offenders, mixed methods for, 237–40
feminist theory, 70, 255, 285
Ferdowsi, Z., 187
Fernández, Jesica Siham, 4–5
Ferrari, J. R., 18
Fidell, L. S., 122–23, 125
Fine, M., 71, 265–66
fishing, network and stakeholder analysis for, 327–31, 329*f*, 330*f*, 331*f*
Fiske, D. W., 256
fit indices, 156
Flanagan, C., 265
Flaspohler, P. D., 265
flat track roller derby, 106–9
Florido del Corral, David, 9
focus groups, 3, 14, 28
Food Chain Workers Alliance (FCWA), 245
formism, 103
Fornari, F., 112
for thematic analysis, 37–40
Foster-Fishman, P. G., 237
4-D cycle. *See* discover, dream, design, and destiny
Fowler, Patrick J., 6, 125
Francescato, D., 356, 362
Francis, J., 361
Frazier, S. L., 208
Freud, Sigmund, 111
friendship, dynamic social networks and, 221–22
Fukuda, K., 192
functional analysis
  case study for, 317–22, 319*t*
  of CBPR, 315–22
  contextualism and, 320
  CRM and, 316–17, 317*f*, 318, 320–22
  data analysis for, 318–19
  data collection for, 318–19
Furst, Jacob, 6–7
futurism, 103
fuzzy composition variables, 157
FVC. *See* Family Violence Councils

Gaddis, Jennifer, 7–8
GaFCP. *See* Georgia Family Connection Partnership
gains followed by maintenance, in LGCs, 135, 135*f*
Galea, S., 126
Galloway, F., 337
Garcia, A. P., 267
Garo Hills, India, 73–76
GBV. *See* gender-based violence
Geertz, Clifford, 69
Geiser, C., 149–50
gender-based violence (GBV), 288–89
generalizable findings
  in Delpi method, 61
  in quantitative methods, 2
  in YPAR, 266
generalized linear mixed models (GLMM), 127
generativist's question, 198
geographic information systems (GIS), 5, 93–101, 121–22, 129
  behavior methods in, 97–98
  case study for, 99–100
  ESM for, 98
  grid methods for, 98–99
  hierarchical linear modeling for, 93
  for neighborhoods, 93–101
  network analysis for, 97–98
  quantitative methods for, 93, 98
  for SOC, 99–100
Georgia Family Connection Partnership (GaFCP), 158–62, 161*t*, 162*f*
gestalt theory, 111
Ghirelli, G., 356
Gibson, J. E., 265
Gielen, A. C., 307
Giovagnoli, Fiammetta, 5, 115
Girls Moving On (GMO), 238
GIS. *See* geographic information systems
Glaser, Barney, 23, 24, 25, 26–27
Glenwick, David S., 2, 6, 153
Glesne, C., 18
GLMM. *See* generalized linear mixed models
global-local dichotomy, critical ethnography and, 71
GMO. *See* Girls Moving On
Goman, C. K., 350
Goodkind, J. R., 237
Goodman, K., 336
Gottman, J., 225–26
Graham, W. F., 335
grand tour question, 15
Grannis, R., 96
Grano, C., 149–50
Greene, J. C., 335, 351
Greeson, Megan R., 6, 139–41
Gregory, A., 124
grid methods, for GIS, 98–99
Grills, C., 267
groundedness, 23–24, 27
grounded theory, 3, 23–31
  case study of, 27–31, 31*f*
  constant comparative method for, 24–25
  consensus in, 26, 28
  data analysis for, 28–29
  data collection in, 28
  groundedness in, 23–24, 27
  iterative examinations in, 3
  memoing in, 26
  reflexivity in, 23–24
  rigor for, 27
  sampling in, 24
group level, in MLM, 154
Guba, E. G., 13, 36, 39, 351
Guerra, N. G., 237

Habitat for Humanity International (HFHI), 46–50
Hagelskamp, C., 124
Hall, B., 315
Hammersley, M., 72
Hänel, M., 219
Hanish, L. D., 208
Hanley, G., 315, 316
Hawaii Children's Trust-Fund (HCTF), 298–301, 299*f*, 301*f*
Hawtin, M., 355
HCTF. *See* Hawaii Children's Trust-Fund
health impact assessment (HIA), 248–49
Hegel, Georg Wilhelm Friedrich, 61
Heller, K., 2
Henry, D. B., 208, 259
Hernández-Ramírez, Javier, 9
heterogeneity
  in ABM, 198
  DP and, 346
  LGCs and, 137–38
HFHI. *See* Habitat for Humanity International
HIA. *See* health impact assessment
hierarchical linear modeling, for GIS, 93
high school participation, YPAR for, 267–69
Hill, Mara, 8
Hipp, J. R., 97–98, 100
HIV/AIDS
  CBM for, 200–202
  focus groups for, 14
  photoethnography for, 285–90, 287*f*, 288*f*, 289*f*, 290*f*
Hoeppner, B., 179–80
Hoffman, L., 124
Holgado, Daniel, 9
Holliday, J., 221
Holt, M., 355
Horner, P. S., 256
Horwitz, S. M., 234
house meetings
  case study for, 87–89
  for empowerment, 85–86
  in PAR, 85–87
Hox, J. J., 158
Hu, L., 159
Huang, F., 124
Hubacek, K., 326
Hurlburt, M. S., 234
hypothesis testing
  in evidence-based practice, 35
  for LGCs, 137
  in quantitative methods, 121

ICC. *See* intraclass correlation
Icenogle, M. I., 346
Ikram, A., 274
incubation, in LGCs, 135, 135*f*
independent variables (IVs), 123, 127
India, 73–76
indicator variables, 144–45
indigenous methods
  CBPAR and, 255
  critical ethnography and, 70
infographics, 295–96
informed consent, 166
Ingold, K., 326–27
injured workers' rights, 55–58, 57*t*
interdisciplinary research group (IRG), 356
intermethod mixing, 349
internal validity, 19, 166, 169
International Pilot Study of Schizophrenia (IPSS), 273
International Resilience Project (IRP), 278–81, 280*f*
interrater reliability analyses, 25–26
interrupted time-series designs, 2
interviews
  for action research, 245
  for CBPAR, 258–59
  for CLA, 107
  for community narratives, 45, 47–48
  for community profiling, 361
  for critical ethnography, 73
  for cross-cultural and cultural research, 275
  for ETA, 114–16
  for functional analysis, 318
  qualitative, 3
  for qualitative method data collection, 15–16
  for thematic analysis, 34, 38
intimate partner violence (IPV), 29, 139–41, 141*f*, 288–89
intraclass correlation (ICC), 155, 159, 167, 171
intramethod mixing, 349
Inzeo, Paula Tran, 7–8
IPSS. *See* International Pilot Study of Schizophrenia
IPV. *See* intimate partner violence
IRG. *See* interdisciplinary research group
IRP. *See* International Resilience Project
iterative examinations, 3, 83
IVs. *See* independent variables
Iwata, B., 315

Jaccard similarity coefficients, 212–15, 213*t*, 214*f*
Jafri, S. Z., 274
James, William, 244
Jason, Leonard A., 2, 6–7, 18, 153, 179–80, 182–83, 219, 255
Javdani, Shabnam, 9
Jiang, S., 187
Johnson, R. Burke, 9–10, 346, 348
Johnston, J. M., 179
Joint United Nations Programme on HIV/AIDS, 286
Journal of Applied Behavior Analysis, 178
juvenile offenders
  DP for, 247–353
  mixed methods for, 237–40

Kagan, C., 356
Kant, Immanuel, 61
Katz, E., 211
Kelly, C. M., 307
Kelly, J. G., 258–59
Kennedy, A. C., 139–41

Keys, C., 255
Kibowski, Fraenze, 6
King, P. M., 336
Kirsten, J., 355
Klassen, A. C., 256–57, 285
knowledge mobilization (KMb), 276
Knox, L., 237
Koenen, K. C., 126
Kohfeldt, D., 264
Kornbluh, Mariah, 7, 219
Kral, Michael J., 8
Kratochwill, T. R., 179
Kroeker, C. J., 14
Kurien, D. N., 350

ladder graphs, 307
Landsverk, J., 234
Langhout, Regina Day, 4–5
language-oriented approaches, to qualitative method data analysis, 16
latent basis model, 136
latent class analysis (LCA), 6, 124–25, 143–48, 145*f*
  case study for, 146–48, 146*t*, 147*t*
  coding for, 144
  posterior probabilities in, 144–46, 145*t*
  for time course of events questions, 126
latent class growth analysis (LCGA), 126
latent growth curves (LGCs), 6, 133–41
  advanced extensions of, 138–39
  case study for, 139–41, 141*f*
  delayed change in, 135, 135*f*
  gains followed by maintenance in, 135, 135*f*
  incubation in, 135, 135*f*
  linear change in, 135, 135*f*
  lost gains in, 135–36, 136*f*
  nonlinear change in, 135–39
  research question for, 139–40
  variation in rate of change in, 136, 136*f*
latent profile analysis (LPA), 6, 148–50, 149*f*
  best-fitting solution in, 148
  case study for, 149–50
latent transition analysis (LTA), 124–26
latent variables, 156
Latinos, 87–89
Latkin, C. A., 220
Lawlor, Jennifer, 7, 129
LCA. *See* latent class analysis
LCGA. *See* latent class growth analysis
Leech, N. L., 235, 277
Level-1 error term, for CRTs, 170
Level-2 error term, for CRTs, 170
Lewin, Kurt, 53, 243, 244, 255
Lewis, K., 208–9
LGCs. *See* latent growth curves
Liebenberg, L., 278
Lienert, J., 326–27
life story methodology, 4, 44
Light, John M., 7, 208, 219
Likelihood Ratio chi-square (LRχ2), 144
Lincoln, Y. S., 13, 36, 39, 351
Linked Difference Equation, 225–26
Litany, 104, 104*t*, 109
Live Oak Family Resource Center, 87–89
LMR-LRT. *See* Lo-Mendell-Rubin adjusted Likelihood Ratio Test
local culture, 111
Locke, John, 61
Lohmann, Andrew, 5, 97
Lo-Mendell-Rubin adjusted Likelihood Ratio Test (LMR-LRT), 144
lost gains, in LGCs, 135–36, 136*f*
Love, S., 361
Lowe, S. R., 126
LPA. *See* latent profile analysis
LRχ2. *See* Likelihood Ratio chi-square
LTA. *See* latent transition analysis
Lüdtke, O., 150
Luke, D. A., 122, 126, 129, 153, 211

Maas, C. J., 158
machine learning, 188–89
Madison, D. S., 69
Malterud, K., 14
MANCOVA. *See* multivariate analysis of covariance
manifest variables, 156
Mannarini, Terri, 3
MANOVA. *See* multivariate analysis of variance
Marsh, H. W., 150, 157, 237
Martín-Baró, I., 75
Martini, E. R., 356
Masyn, K. E., 148, 149
Mathews, R. M., 316
Mattaini, Mark, 6
Maya-Jariego, Isidro, 9
Mays, V. M., 123
McAdams, D. P., 44, 45
McCord, B., 315
McDonnell, K. A., 307
McIntyre, M., 266
McLinden, Daniel, 9, 307
McMurran, G., 97
MDES. *See* minimum detectable effect size
MDS. *See* multidimensional scaling
ME. *See* myalgic encephalomyelitis
measurement and structure questions, 125
measurement invariance, 156–57
memoing, 26
mentoring, 221–22
Menzel, H., 211
Mercken, L., 221
merging data, in mixed methods, 257
metaparadigm. *See* dialectical pluralism
methodological individualism, 198
methodological pluralism. *See* mixed methods
Mexican community, 317–22, 319*t*
Miller, K. E., 35
Miller, W., 13
minimum detectable effect size (MDES), 168

Minkler, M., 267
Mitchell, S. J., 145
mixed methods, 7–10
  action research in, 8, 243–51
  benefits of, 236–37
  case study for, 237–40, 337–42
  CBPAR in, 253–60, 283–90
  CBPR in, 8, 315–22
  challenges of, 236
  CM in, 9, 305–13
  community profiling in, 10, 355–62, 356*t*, 360*t*
  for complementarity, 336, 340–41
  connecting data in, 257
  contradictions and, 336–37
  CRM in, 9
  cross-cultural and cultural research in, 8, 273–81
  data visualization in, 8–9, 293–301
  decision-making framework for, 278*f*
  demarcation in, 235
  DP in, 9–10, 345–52
  embedding data in, 257
  equal-status, 347, 351
  for expansion, 337
  introduction to, 233–40
  merging data in, 257
  multisetting research in, 335–42
  network analysis in, 9, 325–32
  participatory, 8
  performance ethnography in, 8
  photoethnography in, 283–90
  pragmatism and, 121
  qualia in, 256
  quanta in, 256
  reclassification in, 235
  stakeholder analysis in, 9, 325–32
  transformatism in, 352
  triangulation in, 235, 236, 336, 338–39
  types of, 234–36
  YPAR in, 8, 263–70
mixture modeling, 144
MJCC. *See* Mobile Juvenile Court Collaborative
MLM. *See* multilevel modeling
MLQ-Presence. *See* presence of meaning in life
Mobile Juvenile Court Collaborative (MJCC), 347–53
modeling cycle, of ABM, 199–200
Moere, V. A., 295–96
Mohatt, N. V., 259
Monte Carlo simulation, 143
Moore, L., 221
Moos, R. H., 227
Morin, A. J., 150
Morse, J. M., 235, 361
"the movie" technique, for community profiling, 359
MSEM. *See* multi-level structural equation modeling
multicultural theory, 255
multidimensional scaling (MDS), 306–7
multigroup LGCs, 137
multilevel modeling (MLM), 6, 122, 124, 127, 129
  contextuality in, 153–54
  cross-level interactions in, 155–56
  for CRTs, 169–71
  LGCs with, 133
  for measurement and structure questions, 125
  MSEM and, 153–56
multi-level structural equation modeling (MSEM), 6, 153–62
  case study for, 158–62, 161*t*, 162*f*
  for measurement and structure questions, 125
  MLM and, 153–56
  sampling in, 158
  SEM and, 156–57
multisetting research, 335–42
  case study for, 337–42
multivariate analysis of covariance (MANCOVA), 124
multivariate analysis of variance (MANOVA), 124, 127
Murray, D. M., 166–67, 170
Murray, J., 225–26
Muthén, B. O., 149
myalgic encephalomyelitis (ME), 191–95
Myth Metaphor, 104, 104*t*, 109

Naivinit, W., 202
narratives. *See also* community narratives
  for critical ethnography, 72
  house meetings and, 86
  photovoice and, 81–82
naturalistic sampling, 15
natural resources, network analysis and stakeholder analysis for, 326–27
Neal, Jennifer Watling, 7, 129, 197, 203–4, 208, 212, 219
Neal, Zachary P., 7, 197, 203–4, 208
Neighborhood Revitalization Initiative (NR), 46–50, 48*f*
neighborhoods
  ABM for, 202–5, 204*f*
  administrative research on, 94–95, 96
  behavior-defined methods for, 97–98
  boundaries of, 94, 95*f*
  case study for, 99–100
  as census units, 94, 95
  defined, 94, 96
  existing data on, 95–96, 96*f*
  GIS for, 93–101
  meaning of, 95, 95*f*
  operationalization of, 94, 95*f*
  phenomenological research on, 94–95, 95*f*
  resident-defined mapping for, 96–97
  SOC for, 99–100
Nelson, G., 273
nesting units, in MLM, 154
NetLogo, 200
network analysis, 9, 325–32, 327*f*. *See also* dynamic social networks; social network analysis
  case study for, 327–31, 331*f*
  for GIS, 97–98
  for natural resources, 326–27
  organizational networks and, 329–31
  personal networks and, 328–29
network studies, 7
Newman, Greg, 294

Neyer, F. J., 219
n-fold cross-validation, 191
Nightingale, Florence, 293
non-data link, 297
nonequivalent comparison group designs, 2
nonlinear change, in LGCs, 135–39
nontangible development, 65
non-tribals, in critical ethnography, 74–75
normal abnormality, 75
Novak, J. D., 305
Nowell, B., 157
NR. *See* Neighborhood Revitalization Initiative
Nylund, K., 149

observed variables. *See* manifest variables
O'Campo, P., 307
O'Cathain, A., 277
ODC. *See* organizational development and change
O' Donnell, J., 361
OHs. *See* Oxford Houses
Okun, M. A., 149–50
Olazagasti, M. R., 14
OLS. *See* ordinal least squares
Olson, Bradley D., 4, 18
O'Neill, P. T., 18
ontological authenticity, 72
Onwuegbuzie, A. J., 235, 277
Onwuegbuzie, T., 346
open coding, 25
opportunity-based PAR, 54–55
optimal design, 168
Optimal Design Documentation, 168
ordinal least squares (OLS), 156
organicism, 103
organizational development and change (ODC), 53–54
organizational networks, 329–31
overfitting, of decision trees, 189–90
Oxford Houses (OHs), 222–25, 224*f*
Ozer, Emily J., 8, 264, 265, 266, 267

PABM. *See* participatory agent-based modeling
Pakistan, qualitative methods in, 19–21
Palinkas, L. A., 234, 236, 239
Paniccia, Rosa Maria, 5, 113, 115
PAR. *See* participatory action research
paradigm wars, 233
paradoxes, ETA and, 111
parameter sweep, 202
Park, Robert, 69
participatory action research (PAR), 4–5. *See also* community-based participatory action research; youth-led participatory action research
  AI and, 53–59
  CBPR with, 253–60
  community profiling and, 355–56
  critical consciousness in, 243
  critical theory and, 81
  data visualization and, 293
  Delphi method for, 62
  empowerment in, 243
  house meetings in, 85–87
  opportunity-based, 54–55
  photovoice in, 81–85
  problem-based, 53–54
  with critical ethnography, 73
participatory agent-based modeling (PABM), 202
participatory photo mapping (PPM), 98
PAS. *See* Promoting Academic Success Project
pattern of change, in LGCs, 133
Peak, G. L., 307
peer coding, 107
Peirce, C. S., 107
Pennypacker, H. S., 179
People Awakening, 257–59
Pepper, S. C., 103
performance ethnography, 8
Perkins, D. D., 155
personal networks, 219–20, 328–29
Petty, R., 316
photoethnography
  case study for, 285–90, 287*f*, 288*f*, 289*f*, 290*f*
  in CBPAR, 283–90
  research question for, 289
photographs
  in community profiling, 359
  PPM, 98
  for qualitative method data collection, 16, 81–85
photo novella, 284
photovoice
  case study for, 87–89
  for CBPR, 284–85
  collaboration with, 81, 83
  ethics in, 83
  iterative examinations for, 83
  narratives and, 81–82
  for PAR, 81–85
  power and, 85
  SHOWED method for, 83
  for social change, 84
  for YPAR, 266
piecewise models, for LGCs, 136
Pistrang, N., 121
Plano Clark, V. L., 235, 256–57, 285
Polkinghorne, D. E., 103, 107
Porta Capuana, 359–62
Porter C., 267
positionality, 70, 73–74
positivism, 14
  action research and, 244
  CLA and, 103
  GIS and, 95
  quantitative methods and, 121
posterior probabilities, in LCA, 144–46, 145*t*
postpositivism, 14, 121
posttest-only design, for CRTs, 170
power. *See also* empowerment
  collaboration and, 71
  critical ethnography and, 70, 71

cross-cultural and cultural research and, 276
in CRTs, 167–68
epistemic validity and, 72
photovoice and, 85
YPAR and, 264
PPM. *See* participatory photo mapping
pragmatism
action research and, 244
Delphi method and, 4, 61
GIS and, 95
mixed methods and, 121
prediction of group membership questions, 124–25
Prell, C., 326
presence of meaning in life (MLQ-Presence), 279
pretest-posttest control group design, 166
Prilleltensky, I., 72, 273
problem-based PAR, 53–54
Procentese, Fortuna, 10
Proeschold-Bell, R. J., 179–80
Promoting Academic Success Project (PAS), 212–15, 213*t*, 214*f*
propensity score methods (PSM), 129
psychoanalysis, 111
Psychology Loves Porta Capuana, 359–62
psychopolitical validity, 72
PsycINFO, 34
public policy, 62, 81–82
purposive sampling, 15, 71–72

qualia, 256
qualitative interviews, 3
qualitative methods, 2–5
AI in, 4, 53–59
authenticity in, 17–18
case study of, 19–21
challenges and benefits of, 19
CLA in, 5, 103–9
coding for, 16–17
communities of interest in, 15
community narratives in, 4, 43–51
community psychology and, 3, 13
confirmability in, 18
contextualism in, 341
credibility in, 18
critical ethnography in, 4, 69–77
data analysis in, 16–17
data collection in, 15–16
Delphi method in, 4, 61–66
dependability in, 18
ETA in, 5, 111–16
ethics in, 18
GIS in, 5, 93–101
grounded theory in, 3, 23–31
introduction to, 13–21
PAR in, 4–5, 53–59
participants in, 15
photographs for, 81–85
rigor of, 17–18
sampling in, 15
social justice and, 13
thematic analysis for, 3–4, 33–40
thick description in, 3, 69
transferability in, 18
trustworthiness in, 17–18
for women's rights, 19–21
worldview in, 14–15, 19
Qualitative Methods (journal), 34
quanta, 256
quantitative methods, 2, 5–7
ABM in, 7, 129, 197–206
agent-based simulations in, 7
behavior methods in, 6, 177–84
cause-and-effect relationships in, 2, 121
CRTs in, 6, 124, 165–74
current state of, 126–29, 128*f*
data mining in, 6–7, 187–95
degree of relationship questions for, 123
dynamic social network in, 7, 219–27
errors in, 13
for GIS, 93, 98
hypothesis testing in, 121
introduction to, 121–29
LCA in, 6, 143–48
LGCs in, 6, 133–41
LPA in, 6, 148–50
measurement and structure questions for, 125
MLM in, 6
MSEM in, 6, 153–62
prediction of group membership questions for, 124–25
research question for, 122–26
significance of group differences questions for, 123–24
SNA in, 7, 207–16
time course of events questions for, 125–26
time-series methods in, 177–84

Raicu, Daniela Stan, 6–7
RAIS. *See* Refugee Assistance and Immigration Services
randomized controlled methods, 35
randomized field experiments, 2
Rapkin, B. D., 153
Rappaport, J., 44, 48, 177–78
Rasmussen, Andrew, 3, 29
Raudenbush, S. W., 125, 167, 170
Rawls, John, 345
Real Food, Real Jobs, 246
Receiver Operator Characteristic (ROC), 189
reclassification, in mixed methods, 235
recruitment
for Delphi method, 64–65
for grounded theory, 27–28
Reed, M., 326
reflective understanding, for CLA, 107
reflexive journaling, 107
reflexivity
activism and, 70
in critical ethnography, 70, 73–74
in grounded theory, 23–24
in thematic analysis, 37, 40

refreezing, 53
Refugee Assistance and Immigration Services (RAIS), 275
regression, 122, 123
 CART, 189, 193
 trees, 189
reliability, of thematic analysis, 36, 39–40
repeated measures, 169
representation, in critical ethnography, 72
research question
 for LGCs, 139–40
 for photoethnography, 289
 for quantitative methods, 122–26
resilience, cross-cultural and cultural research for, 278–81, 280*f*
Resilience Research Center-Adult Resilience Measure (RRC-ARM), 279–80
Restaurant Opportunities Center United, 245–46
Revenson, T. A., 2
The Revolutionary Optimists (documentary), 270
Richards, L., 361
Riger, Stephanie, 3–4
rigor
 of CM, 308
 of grounded theory, 27
 of qualitative methods, 17–18
 of YPAR, 266–67
Ritterman, M., 264, 265, 266
Rivers, S. E., 124
RMSEA. *See* Root Mean Squared Error of Approximation
Robinson, Rebecca Volino, 8, 275–76
ROC. *See* Receiver Operator Characteristic
Roccato, M., 154
Rogoff, B., 103
roller derby, CLA for, 106–9
Ronzio, C. R., 145
Root Mean Squared Error of Approximation (RMSEA), 156, 159
Rovine, M. J., 124
RRC-ARM. *See* Resilience Research Center-Adult Resilience Measure
Ruffner, A., 307
rule for constant comparative methods, 25
Russo, S., 154

SACReD. *See* Santa Ana Collaborative for Responsible Development
Sadiq, S., 274
Salem, D. A., 237
Salovey, P., 124
Sample Size Adjusted BIC (SSABIC), 144
sampling
 in critical ethnography, 71–72
 in CRTs, 166–67
 ESM, 98
 in grounded theory, 24
 in MSEM, 158
 in qualitative methods, 15
 in thematic analysis, 38
Sampson, R. J., 125
Santa Ana Collaborative for Responsible Development (SACReD), 245, 247
Santinello, M., 155
Sarason, Seymour B., 14, 43, 44, 104, 264, 337
Sarmiento, Carolina S., 7–8
satisfaction surveys, 63
Savala, Jorge, 4–5
Savaya, R., 336
Scale of Italian Sense of Community, 357
Schaefer, D. R., 208
Scheibler, Jill E., 3
Schelling, T., 197–200
Schensul, J. J., 13–14
schizophrenia, 111, 273
Schnetzer, F., 326–27
Schwartz, D., 284
SCRA. *See* Society for Community Research and Action
Scriven, M., 347
Seidman, E., 2
Seifert, T. A., 336
SEM. *See* structural equation modeling
sense of community (SOC), 99–100
sensitizing concepts, in grounded theory, 23, 27
Sequi, R., 356
SES. *See* socioeconomic status
Sesto, C., 115
setting-level measures, for SNA, 209–10, 210*t*
sexual health, photoethnography for, 285–90, 287*f*, 288*f*, 289*f*, 290*f*
sexually transmitted infections (STIs), photoethnography for, 285–90, 287*f*, 288*f*, 289*f*, 290*f*
Shared Prosperity Campaign, 89
SHATIL, 336–37
Shatto, Erynne, 9–10
Sherif, M., 221
Shinn, M., 153
SHOWED method, 83
Shweder, R. A., 256
significance of group differences questions, 123–24
Sigurvinsdottir, Rannveig, 3–4
Sinclair, P., 221
Singh, S. P., 274
Skinner, B. F., 315
slope, in LGCs, 133–34
Sluzki, C. E., 31
Smith, K. C., 256–57
Smith, K. L., 294
Smith, L. T., 72
Smith, T. M., 155
Smith, V. S., 296
SMMR. *See* Somali Multidimensional Multilevel Resilience
SNA. *See* social network analysis
SNEM. *See* socio-spatial neighborhood estimation method
snowball sampling, 15
SOC. *See* sense of community
Social Causal, 104, 104*t*, 109

social change, 72, 84, 86
social exchange theory, 221–22
social justice
  CBPAR in, 256
  critical ethnography and, 69–70
  DP and, 345
  photoethnography and, 285
  qualitative methods and, 13
social network analysis (SNA), 7, 121, 122, 129, 207–16. *See also* dynamic social networks
  adjacency matrix for, 209, 209*t*
  case study for, 212–15, 213*t*, 214*f*
  cohesion in, 211
  contextualism in, 211–12
  data collection for, 207–9
  degree centrality for, 211
  dyad-level measures for, 210*t*, 211
  ethics in, 212
  for Facebook, 208–9, 209*t*
  individual-level measures for, 210–11, 210*t*
  setting-level measures for, 209–10, 210*t*
Society for Community Research and Action (SCRA), 126
socioeconomic status (SES), 155
socio-spatial neighborhood estimation method (SNEM), 99
Somali Multidimensional Multilevel Resilience (SMMR), 279–80, 281*f*
Somali Resilience Project, 278–81, 280*f*
Sparks, Shannon M., 7–8
Speer, P. W., 14, 249
SPSS Statistics software, 193
SSABIC. *See* Sample Size Adjusted BIC
stakeholder analysis, 9, 325–32, 327*f*
  for AI, 58
  case study for, 327–31, 331*f*
  for community narratives, 45–46
  in community profiling, 362
  in critical ethnography, 71–72, 74
  in DP, 349, 351–52
  for natural resources, 326–27
Staller, K. M., 256
Stamatakis, K. A., 129
standardized measures, in quantitative methods, 2
Stefurak, Tres, 9–10
Steglich, C., 221
Stevens, E., 219
STIs. *See* sexually transmitted infections
Stochastic Actor-Oriented Model, 220, 225, 226
Stone, A., 219
stories. *See also* community narratives
  house meetings and, 86
  photovoice and, 81, 85
Strauss, Anselm, 23, 24, 25, 26–27, 38, 39, 63
strengths, weaknesses, opportunities, and threats (SWOT), 361
Strickland, D., 258–59
structural equation modeling (SEM), 122
  fit indices in, 156
  LCA and, 143
  LGCs with, 133
  for measurement and structure questions, 125
  measurement invariance in, 156–57
  MSEM and, 156–57
Suarez-Balcazar, Yolanda, 9
substantive coding, 25
Suhail, K., 274, 275
suicide prevention, CM for, 308–11, 310*f*, 311*f*, 312*t*
Sullivan, T. N., 138
supervised data mining, 188
Swanson, C., 225–26
Sweetser, F. L., 94
SWOT. *See* strengths, weaknesses, opportunities, and threats
Symbol and Code (Fornari), 112
symmetrical logic, 111
system science methods, 197
Szaflarski, M., 307

Tabachnick, B. G., 122–23, 125
Tableau Public 8.0, 298
TAD. *See* Treatment Alternative and Diversion
Tandon, S. D., 258–59
tangible development, 65
Tashakkori, A., 235
Taylor, M., 355
Teddlie, C., 235
thematic analysis, 3–4, 33–40
  case study for, 37–40
  for CLA, 105, 107
  coding in, 34, 38
  confirmability in, 36–37, 40
  constructivism and, 33–34, 37
  credibility in, 36, 39
  data analysis for, 36
  data analysis in, 38–39
  for Delphi method, 63
  dependability, 36
  interviews for, 38
  interview transcription in, 34, 38
  limitations of, 40
  reflexivity in, 37, 40
  reliability of, 36, 39–40
  sampling in, 38
  stages in, 34–35
  themes in, 34–35
  transferability in, 39–40
  transparency in, 37
  trustworthiness in, 39–40
  validity of, 39–40
  value of, 35–36
  worldview in, 37
themes
  in CLA, 105, 108*t*
  in grounded theory, 3
  in thematic analysis, 3–4, 33, 34–35, 39
theoretical coding, 26–27
theoretical sampling, 24
theoretical saturation, 24

theory, 1–2
  action research and, 247
  DP and, 351
  in grounded theory, 3, 23
  LGCs and, 136
theory-building approaches, 16
thick description, 3, 69
time course of events questions, 125–26
time-invariant covariates, 134
time-series methods, 177–84
time-varying covariate, 134
T-LAB (software), 113
Todd, Nathan R., 6
Todman, J. B., 180
Tolan, P., 1, 255
Tolman, R. M., 139–41
Tolman, Ryan T., 8–9
Toro, R. T., 237
traditional action research, 53
transferability, 18, 39–40
transformatism, 352
transformative theory, 356
transformative validity, 72
transparency, 37, 84
Trautwein, U., 150
Treatment Alternative and Diversion (TAD), 248–49
triangulation
  in cross-cultural and cultural research, 279
  in grounded theory, 24
  in mixed methods, 235, 236, 336, 338–39
  in YPAR, 269
tribes, 74
Trickett, E. J., 259
trustworthiness, 17–18, 39–40, 265–66
t-test, 127
Tucker, S., 346
Tufte, E. R., 297
Tuozzi, Teresa, 10
Type 1 errors, 13, 123, 124, 144, 167
Type 2 errors, 13
Type 4 errors, 13
Type 5 errors, 13

Uddin, M., 126
unconscious, 111–12
"The Unconscious as Infinite Sets" (Blanco), 112
unfreezing, 53
Ungar, M., 278
United Nations Population Fund, 288
UNITE HERE, 246, 247
University of Wisconsin-Madison Center for Community and Nonprofit Studies, 247–50
unsupervised data mining, 188

Vaillant, G. E., 219, 227
validity
  in DP, 351
  epistemic, 72
  external, 179
  internal, 19, 166, 169
  psychopolitical, 72
  in thematic analysis, 36, 39–40
  transformative, 72
  in YPAR, 265–67
values. *See* worldview
variation in rate of change, in LGCs, 136, 136*f*
Vaughan, C., 266
Vaughn, Lisa M., 9, 307
verification, in grounded theory, 24
victim-victimizer binaries, 76
Vieno, A., 154, 155
Viola, Judah, 4
violence
  critical ethnography for, 73–76
  domestic, 37–40
  FVC, 337–42
  GBV, 288–89
  IPV, 29, 139–41, 141*f*, 288–89
visual metaphors, 297
visual noise, 297
Vive Live Oak!, 87–89
volunteering, 149–50

WAFP. *See* West African Families Project
Wagenaar, A. C., 178
Wagner, J., 219
Walden, Angela, 9
Wang, C. C., 285
Wang, J., 145
Wanis, M., 264, 265, 266, 267
Watts, V., 265
Waysman, M., 336
WCFI. *See* Wilder Collaboration Factors Inventory
Weerman, F. M., 221
Wess, Y., 307
West African Families Project (WAFP), 27–31, 31*f*
WFTDA. *See* Women's Flat Track Derby Association
WHO. *See* World Health Organization
whole communities, 43–46
whole networks, 220–21
Wiggins, B. J., 235
Wilder Collaboration Factors Inventory (WCFI), 350
Williams, Glenn, 6
Williams, K. R., 237
Wimmer, A., 208–9
WISDOM, 247–50
within-person change, 134
Women's Flat Track Derby Association (WFTDA), 106
women's rights, 19–21
women's sports, 105–9, 108*t*
working hypotheses, 17
working the hyphen, 71
World Health Organization (WHO), 273, 286, 289
worldview, 14–15, 19
  CBPR as, 253, 256, 259–60
  in thematic analysis, 37

Worldview Discourse, 104, 104*t*, 109
Wrzus, C., 219
Wyldbore, Denise, 4–5

YCSP. *See* Youth Council for Suicide Prevention
Yennie-Donmoyer, J., 337
YLS/CMI. *See* Youth Level of Service/Case Management Inventory
Yoshikawa, H., 14
Youth Council for Suicide Prevention (YCSP), 308–11, 310*f*, 311*f*, 312*t*
youth-led participatory action research (YPAR), 8, 263–70
 case study for, 267–69
 for critical consciousness, 265
 photovoice and, 266
 power and, 264
 rigor for, 266–67
 triangulation in, 269
 trustworthiness in, 265–66
 validity of, 265–67
Youth Level of Service/Case Management Inventory (YLS/CMI), 238, 349
YPAR. *See* youth-led participatory action research

Zani, B., 356, 362